EUROPE
IN THE
TWENTIETH CENTURY

Fourth Edition

EUROPE
IN THE
TWENTIETH CENTURY

ROLAND N. STROMBERG

University of Wisconsin-Milwaukee

Prentice Hall, Upper Saddle River, New Jersey 07458

Library of Congress Cataloging-in-Publication Data

Stromberg, Roland N., (date)
   Europe in the twentieth century / Roland N. Stromberg.—4th ed.
     p.   cm.
   Includes bibliographical references and index.
   ISBN 0-13-569344-6 (pbk.)
   1. Europe—History—20th century. I. Title.
D424.S77 1997   96-16291
940.5—dc20   CIP

Acquisitions Editor: *Sally Constable*
Editorial Assistant: *Justin Belinski*
Editorial/Production Supervision and Interior Design: *Barbara DeVries*
Prepress and Manufacturing Buyer: *Lynn Pearlman*
Cover Design: *Wendy Alling Judy*
Illustrator: *Accurate Art, Inc.*

This book was set 10/12 Baskerville by NK Graphics and was printed by
RR Donnelley & Sons Company. The cover was printed by Phoenix
Color Corp.

©1997, 1992, 1988, 1980 by Prentice-Hall, Inc.
Upper Saddle River, New Jersey 07458

Printed in the United States of America

10 9 8 7 6

ISBN 0-13-569344-6

Prentice-Hall International (UK) Limited, *London*
Prentice-Hall of Australia Pty. Limited, *Sydney*
Prentice-Hall Canada Inc., *Toronto*
Prentice-Hall Hispanoamericana, S.A., *Mexico*
Prentice-Hall of India Private Limited, *New Delhi*
Prentice-Hall of Japan, Inc., *Tokyo*
Pearson Education Asia Pte. Ltd., *Singapore*
Editora Prentice-Hall do Brasil, Ltda., *Rio de Janeiro*

Contents

Preface

For this fourth edition of a book originally published in 1980, I have tried not only to bring it up to date but also to incorporate a number of suggestions for improvement kindly offered by friendly critics. I want to thank all of these people. The third edition profited from comments and criticisms by Vincent Beach, University of Colorado; Geoffrey J. Ciles, University of Florida; Kim Munholland, University of Minnesota; William Roosen, Northern Arizona University; Taylor Stults, Muskingum College; E. Juliana Thomson, Mercy College of Detroit; and Ann Healy of the University of Wisconsin–Milwaukee. For the fourth edition, helpful readers include Mark Ciok, University of California, Santa Cruz. Naturally, I have made revisions in a number of places based on recent research, which is constantly at work providing us with new and better information; scores of industrious and skillful historians perform this service, as fresh sources become available and historical events are reevaluated accordingly. The Bibliography, located at the end of the book, has been updated.

The main changes relate to recent developments. We live in a fast-moving world, needless to say. The second edition ended with only the barest mention of Mikhail Gorbachev; virtually the whole amazing upheaval in which eastern Europe regurgitated its long Communist past lay ahead. The third edition took some account of this; but the Soviet Union's dissolution and struggles to adapt to a new order of things lay ahead. The dissolution of Yugoslavia amid civil war had barely begun in 1990. Mrs. Thatcher was still prime minister of Great Britain, something that now seems long ago.

But new material also appears that relates to earlier events. The opening up of Russian sources after 1990 is the leading instance of a flood of revelations about any number of important events in twentieth-century history.

The preface to the first edition noted Walter Ralegh's warning long ago that "Whosoever in writing modern history shall follow truth near the heels, it may haply strike out his teeth." Anyone rash enough to venture judgments on what is likely to come next in the affairs of humankind stands to suffer more than a few dental casualties. Yet the historian who must finish his or her narrative at an arbitrary moment, between which and publication there is always a certain lapse of time, has to take this risk. Students may want to keep their own notebooks and update events as they occur; by the time the last pages of this book reach their eyes, the whirligig of time will probably have blown them into the wastebasket of history. But that is part of what makes it all so interesting.

Introduction

People read history for enjoyment, instruction, orientation, stimulation, inspiration, even therapy; they study the record of past events to broaden their horizons, sharpen their critical sense, find their roots, strengthen their pride, criticize their society, discover other societies; they turn to history out of boredom, curiosity, discontent, piety. Some seek to discover the causes or the origins of success, progress, and power or failure, decay, and dissolution. The uses of the past are thus manifold and even contradictory. So is the past itself, encompassing as it does not only the record of public events but also the deeper, often silent processes of social change. It includes scientific, technological, and economic development; artistic and literary achievement; labor and leisure—all the varied activities of all kinds of people. "History is nothing but the activity of men in pursuit of their own ends," Karl Marx once wrote. Such a subject is obviously immense, there being many men and women.

The nitpicker will add that history is the sum of human activities that are both recorded in some way (the overwhelming majority are not) and significant enough to deserve being remembered and studied. The latter qualification is troublesome, for it must be somewhat subjective. A people with a high level of cultural unity, sharing the same traditions and experiences—a small, isolated society, say—might substantially agree on what is important and on the symbolic terms used to describe it. The more diverse, complex, and dynamic a society becomes, the less agreement there will be. We may be sure that the books of two historians on the same subject, if the subject is of any size, will differ markedly. All historians writing about the twentieth century will doubtless discuss some of the same things. It is hard to imagine any textbook leaving out the two world wars, the Great Depression, the Russian Revolution, Stalin, or Hitler. But one scholar will omit some matters found in another's book and include matters omitted in other histories. Each will vary in the space he or she devotes to issues, and each will interpret them differently, that is, will select particulars, assign causation, and judge the wisdom or virtue of decisions in varying terms.

This is no place to embark on a discussion of such issues; we wish only to warn the reader that there is no one history in the sense that there is one accepted electrical engineering. There are as many histories as there are historians, and the interests of historians change not only from person to person but from generation to generation. Thus the writing of history is an argument without end. The professional study of history, itself a chapter of the fairly recent past, has generated some common standards of research and a large body of valuable data, but it has provided little consensus on interpretation or even the methods of interpretation. If it did, this consensus would still be suspect on the grounds of a situational bias.

Selection is a special problem for anyone seeking to cover the entirety of the multitudinous twentieth century in a fairly short volume. Our century has certainly not been lacking either in action or in dynamic development in all phases of human activity. Change has become more rapid, and the total of human knowledge has increased explosively. We can easily argue that there has been more "history" in this century than in all previous ones combined, just as there have been more books published, more knowledge engendered, more wealth produced. More and more of humanity participates in social processes and is aware of an historical perspective. "The whole immense multitude of men enter finally into the light," that optimistic pre-1914 socialist Jean Jaurès declared. When at about the same time H. G. Wells announced that "'history will have to tell more about clerks and less about conquerors," he was noting the fact that clerks, peasants, and workers were ceasing to be merely the inert and passive materials of history and were beginning to play an active, conscious part in human affairs. Certainly a part of the ever accelerating dynamism of Western society is this movement of once almost silent populations into the "light" of consciousness and change—for better or for worse. Perhaps that was what James Joyce meant in the century's most amazing work of literature, *Finnegans Wake*, in which "history is a nightmare from which we are awakening"; awakening from a long dream of the human race comparable to the night's sleep of a single person.

The student will do well, then, to take this exercise in historical writing as only one man's opinion and to supplement it with others. Much historical research is being done today, shedding light on numerous neighborhoods in the huge city of modern humanity. To begin to read this rich literature is to enter an exciting world.

Nevertheless, I have sought not to be startlingly novel in selecting and interpreting material but rather to include those actions and processes that we should all understand because they have so deeply influenced our lives. In the last analysis, history's chief justification is its grasp of the cultural whole. We may, after all, learn about literature, economics, sociology, military science, and other subjects in the departments or schools dedicated to these special subjects. Only the historian looks at the movement of whole societies. He or she alone relates the particulars to the big picture. History discusses common experiences affecting the greatest number of people.

Awareness of these shared experiences binds us together in a society; knowledge of the continuity of historical change orients us to our cultural surroundings and makes us more human. Such is the historian's credo. "History is the only true way to attain a knowledge of our condition," Savigny declared. And, Lord Acton added, "Understanding the present is the prize of all history."

1

The Peoples and States
of Europe on the Eve of 1914

EUROPE IN THE WORLD

For the sake of an initial perspective, we might make a brief comparison between Europe as it stood at the beginning of the twentieth century and as it stands today. In terms of absolute wealth and power, the peoples and the states of Europe were then much less well off than they are today, for wealth and power have grown enormously through this century, even with all its troubles. The average citizen of England or France, Germany or Italy, Russia, or Hungary has many more material goods today than he or she did in 1900 or 1914; and, governments dispose of far greater resources. But in relative terms, Europe as a whole was then much more dominant in the world. Prior to 1914, no other region could compare with Europe in military power and political influence; only the United States was comparable in wealth and productivity. The United States had yet to enter the arena of world politics, and though she was rising rapidly, she was not yet the technological colossus she later became. The same holds true for that half-European or doubtfully European land that links Asia to Europe; Mother Russia was still a giant with feet of clay, extremely backward by European standards in her social structure and economic level of efficiency.

Europe's material superiority gave her cultural products great prestige, so that other peoples, looking at the power that had subdued them, were inclined to assume that the culture, the ideas, the lifestyle of these Europeans must be superior, too. For at this time, non-European peoples stood in considerable awe of a force that had recently reduced most of them to the position of subjects or satellites. In the 1880s and 1890s, nearly every part of Asia and Africa had been made subservient to the aggressive and competent Europeans. Some territories were annexed and governed directly; others were made into protectorates or spheres of interest that, though maintaining a nominal independence, had to grant various kinds of special economic and political privileges to the white foreigners.

This had not happened without resistance. The almost innumerable tribal revolts in Africa testify to this, as do uprisings on the frontier of India, the turn-of-the-century Boxer Rebellion in China, and the 1881 riots in Egypt, which brought British troops into the Suez Canal area, not to leave for seventy-three years. Wars with the Afghans, the Zulus, and the Dervishes of Sudan added a touch of glamour to English schoolboy reading. But the British always won, or, if they did not, they returned to gain the final victory, as General Gordon did at Khartoum in 1898. Native resistance was futile. Sabers could not defeat carbines:

> Whatever happens, we have got
> A gatling gun and you have not.

Great Britain led in this wave of imperialism, followed at no great distance by France and, later, by Germany and the United States. Meanwhile, Russia pushed her own borders into the Far Eastern periphery, as well as into the Caucasus, often by violent methods. (During the nineteenth century, the Russians waged massive and brutal campaigns to subdue Murids and Circassians in the Caucasian mountains.) With a big appetite but small teeth, Italy tried to take part. Of the greater powers of Europe, only Austria-Hungary forebore, from lack of naval power, to gain overseas possessions, but in compensation pushed her influence into the Balkans at the expense of the decaying Ottoman Empire. Little Belgium and the Netherlands acquired very considerable empires, Belgium in Africa and the Netherlands in Southeast Asia. Long ensconced as traders in the East Indies, today Indonesia, the Dutch pushed into the interior of the islands at this time.

Sometimes the European powers stumbled over each other in their haste to seize, exploit, destroy, develop, or civilize the "lesser breeds," and they became involved in conflict or the threat of it. This happened in 1885 between Russia and Britain, in 1898 between France and Britain, in 1905 between France and Germany, and on other occasions as well; but these encounters seldom led to war. It was easy enough to divide up someone else's property. The one great exception occurred in 1904 between Russia and the Westernizing Asian country of Japan, a major, straight-out imperialist war for domination of Manchuria and Korea. It was, however, not between two European powers. And, it gave notice, among other things, that the European monopoly of military power might soon end as non-Europeans learned to master the arts and sciences of the West. The effect of Japan's defeat of Russia both on land and sea in 1904–1905 was in fact enormous, leading to movements of anti-European nationalism in India, China, Iran, and Turkey destined to transform the world beyond all recognition. But this came later.

Europe's monopoly was not yet under serious threat prior to 1914. As the century turned, the British were engaged in a colonial war that badly shook the country; "we have had no end of a lesson," Rudyard Kipling observed. But this was a fight with another people of European origin, the Dutch settlers on the frontier of British South Africa, who had been aroused to resistance by the aggressive extension of British rule outward from the Cape. French and German opinion, and in fact world opinion generally, cheered for the Boers and chided the British bully in this David-and-Goliath encounter, which the British won only after early setbacks. When newly crowned King Edward VII visited Paris in 1903, he met boos and cries of "Vive les Boers!"; only later did he win the hearts of the French.

But this antipathy did not stop the French and Germans from joining with the British and Russians in organizing an expedition to punish the Chinese for having the insolence to dispute European control of the Celestial Empire. In revenge for antiforeign riots mounted against the White Devils by the "Boxer" societies, much of Peking was burned and looted in a disgraceful orgy that scarred a proud people too deeply for Europe's future comfort. At the time, it seemed a mere incident in the relentless march toward world hegemony of Europeans, who, their reigning scientific doctrines assured them, had a right to take over from the yellow and brown and black peoples because Europeans were indeed the "fittest." Although some European liberals and socialists protested against inhumane methods of imperial rule, not even they questioned the mission of Europe, by virtue of its higher civilization, to impose its economic and social system on the more "backward" peoples.

For all that, imperialism was not an essential component of Europe's strength. The theory developed by a few socialists, and later exploited by Lenin, that colonies were vital to the capitalistic economy, supplying essential outlets for capital investment at high rates of profit, cannot stand criticism. In general, markets and investments in their colonies or protectorates were neither very extensive nor very profitable to European countries. Empire flattered the pride of Europe more than it sustained her economy. It was more often pushed by politicians than by businessmen, by military or naval leaders than by capitalists. The French acquired a huge area of African land that looked impressive on the map but was largely worthless desert. The Russians were building the longest railroad in the world across Siberia in 1900, but it was a government prestige and military project, not an investor's dream.

Finding African natives uninterested in the work ethic, Belgians practiced such inhumane treatment that the Congo became an international scandal (it was exposed by British journalists in 1906), but forced labor did not make for great profits except in a few areas. Exposure of the seamy side of imperialism underscored the need to supply more services to the "natives." Ill-conceived though her plans might have been, Europe spent more money on the colonies than she received in profits, favorable prices on raw materials, or other benefits.

Making acquaintance with alien cultures more thoroughly than at any time in the past, some European artists, poets, and philosophers responded to them. In the 1900s, both Japanese and African styles in sculpture and painting influenced avant-garde art in such centers as Paris and Munich. Oriental philosophy, vaguely influential since the middle of the nineteenth century, continued to find a few disciples; the Pacific islands, to which French painter Paul Gauguin had fled, functioned as a symbol of some unspoiled spiritual realm to which one might turn for relief from a disgustingly materialistic, philistine, and bourgeois Europe. India in Herman Hesse's 1914 novel *Rosshalde* and the exotic settings in Joseph Conrad's pre-1914 tales *Heart of Darkness, Lord Jim,* and *Nostromo* were fascinating to their readers. "Europe bores me," André Gide declared; boredom with a commercialized culture affected a talented minority of alienated artists and intellectuals in these restlessly innovative *fin de siècle* years. Annie Besant, one-time English rationalist, socialist, feminist—friend of George Bernard Shaw and Karl Marx's daughter Eleanor—had now gone to India to launch another of her numerous lives, this time as theosophist and founder of the Indian Nationalist movement. The Bengalese sage Rabindranath Tagore was about to make a triumphal European tour; the leading European one, Leo Tolstoy, in his last years was deeply influenced by Indian mysticism.

But the vast majority of Europeans, complacent about their great success, had no interest in cultures other than their own except an occasional amused curiosity. French ex-president Jules Grévy, an enthusiastic imperialist, grumbled, as he watched certain exotic creatures at the 1889 Paris international fair, that belly dancers were all the people knew of imperialism—except, of course, the adventure stories of exploration, intrigue, warfare in the Dark Continent or Rudolf Kipling's India, which supplied exciting reading for the urban masses.

Non-Europeans, by contrast, had to take seriously these Europeans who impinged so forcefully on them. They might react with hatred, anger, and what resistance they could manage; but they might also decide that so formidable a power was worth imitating. "Resistance to the flood-tide of Western civilization is vain," Kemal Atatürk of Turkey decided; marveling at these people who "pierce the mountains, soar in the skies, see and illuminate all things from the invisible atoms to the stars," he determined to turn his country completely around and Westernize it, a strategy Japan had already practiced with much success. India's Jawaharlal Nehru, who thought that "the very thing India lacked, the modern West possessed and possessed to excess," hoped to inject some but not too much of this dynamic outlook into the somnolent body of Mother India. What historian Arnold J. Toynbee characterized as the "zealot" and the "herodian" reactions to foreign rule (resistance and adaptation), as well as all shadings in between, thus could be found in the attitudes of Asian, African, and Latin American victims of imperialism.

Even the proud Chinese admitted they had much to learn about ships and guns from those they considered barbarians. At the very least, Western technology had to be acquired. But political ideas of democracy, liberalism, socialism, and nationalism seeped into non-Western places too, often carried by those of their own people educated in the West. In the early years of the century, a young Indian named Mohandas Gandhi was studying law in London; a Chinese, Hu Shih, imbibed American political and philosophical ideas at Cornell and Columbia Universities; and Nguyen That Thanh, better known later as Ho Chi Minh, left his native Indochina for France, there to encounter Marxian socialism. All would return to lead movements that rebelled against Western rule in the name of Western ideas. Gandhi's famous philosophy of the simple life, handicraft industries, and militant pacifism absorbed elements of the Hindu tradition, but it also owed a great deal to such nineteenth-century Europeans as John Ruskin of England and Leo Tolstoy of Russia.

In 1900, there were some 400 million people in Europe, about double the number there had been in 1800; counting Russia east as far as the Urals, there would be 700 million in 1990. But Europe's percentage of the world total was higher in 1900, amounting to about one-fourth of the world total then, compared to not much more than one-eighth today (and falling). This despite the fact that over thirty million people emigrated from Europe between 1880 and 1914, the great majority of them to the Western Hemisphere. In 1890, a list of the most populous twenty cities in the world contained ten European ones, eleven if Constantinople is counted, including the first, third, fourth, and sixth largest. By 1983, only three European cities were in the top twenty, and the eight largest cities of the world were outside Europe. London, which had been first in the world in 1900, is evidently no longer in the top ten. (It is hard to determine the exact population of cities because of uncertainty about what constitutes a metropolitan area.) Vienna and Berlin, the great German capitals, have both fallen far from the top rank in population they once occupied.

This proportion was true also of wealth. In 1900, Europe as a whole produced some 60 percent of the world's manufactured goods. The three leading industrial countries, Great Britain, Germany, and France, alone accounted for a little over 40 percent of the world total. Since these three countries had less than 10 percent of the world's population, they were more than four times as economically productive as the average. Never again would Europe exercise such ascendancy. Powerful competitors would emerge, especially the United States and Japan. The "Great War" of 1914–1918 would set Europe back. Her technological skills did not end, but they never again shone quite so brightly as at the century's turn.

THE DIVISIONS OF EUROPE

One could speak of "Western civilization," of "European society," of "Europe"; but Europe, Otto Bismarck once declared (and Charles de Gaulle later repeated) does not exist. Politically, this was obviously true, in that no one government ruled over the Continent; rather, there were a number of sovereign states, which had in fact often waged war with one another in the past and were soon to do so again. In 1910, however, there had been no European war since 1871, and hope was growing that there never would be one again. Nevertheless, the sovereign states showed no inclination to relinquish their powers to any superstate. A United States of Europe movement can hardly be said to have existed before 1914, despite some internationalisms, among which the socialist International Workingmen's Association, the so-called Second International, was the most important.

Nationalism was everywhere in the ascendancy. It was found among intellectuals, common folk, and even among the socialists, many of whom said that the *Sonderleben,* the special life or culture of each nation, would continue even after the Social Revolution, which the international working class was supposed to make. Nationalism could be found on the right, on the left, and in the center; in the pub, the pulpit, and the palaces of the rich. The French truth, novelist-politician Maurice Barrès declared, is not the same as the English or the German truth. Philosophers affirmed that the thrust of history, which was the Absolute Spirit or God in motion, used the nation as its tool or vessel. Statues were built of Germania; Joan of Arc became a sacred symbol; and many less august peoples, discovering for the first time that they were national peoples, revived ancient languages and sagas. Such was the case, for example, in Ireland and in Scandinavia.

Popular nationalism could be regarded as an instinctual attachment to the group, transferred now from the tribe or region to the national community. It rested in part on the success these national communities seemed to have. In such countries as England, France, and Germany, the nineteenth century had brought a steady integration of the masses into the nation, by both action and propaganda. Other peoples, lacking their national independence, dreamed that all would be well if the foreign oppressor was overthrown. From Ireland to Poland, Catalonia to Finland, such unredeemed national groups, real or imaginary, found a beacon of hope in their ethnic solidarity.

Nation making had been going on slowly for centuries; in many ways, the period from about 1880 to 1914 marked its peak. One reason for this was technology's knitting together larger areas in a transportation and communication network, encouraging the breakup of regional isolation. Urbanization uprooted people from the localities they had long occupied. Greater geographical and social mobility disrupted ancient regional or local loyalties. By 1900, technology, in the form of railways, telegraphs, and telephones, had made possible a larger locale of loyalty, rendering obsolete Voltaire's eighteenth-century judgment that it is not possible to love anything bigger than one's home, village, city, or province. Millions loved, or thought they loved, Marianne or John Bull or Uncle Sam; they sang hymns to *Deutschland über alles* or called on God to save the King.

Democratization had assisted mightily in this process of nation making. By 1900, most of western Europe had evolved systems of government through parliaments or assemblies elected by universal manhood suffrage or something approaching it. The other countries were thought to be headed in the same direction. There were serious imperfections in these "democratic" systems, but at their best they provided a link between government and people that helped integrate the masses into the national community. Even more effective, perhaps, was the economic upgrading of the lower classes, which gave the majority of them some stake in the community, however modest it might be. At about the same time that British Prime Minister Benjamin Disraeli was writing on the two nations within his country, the rich and the poor, Karl Marx and Friedrich Engels were identifying class struggle as the key to modern history. But class conflict played much less a part in real life than it did in the ideas of discontented intellectuals.

A vital component of nationalism, of course, was language and the literature that had grown up in that language. Perhaps the real architects of national cultures were Schiller and Goethe, Dickens and Tennyson, Musset and Hugo, Pushkin and Lermontov, the beloved nineteenth-century poets and tale tellers. As a definer of nationalism, however, language, no more than any other one component, sufficed; the Swiss managed to be something of a nation with three languages, Belgium with two, though these were anomalous cases. A basically similar language did not unite Portugal and Spain, though they shared the same well-defined geographic area; nor did it prevent severe north-south strains in Italy or the separation of Austria from Germany.

In many places, the boundaries of European states did not coincide with ethnic divisions. Both nationalism itself, at times degenerating into a narrowly intolerant jingoism or xenophobia, and this failure of ethnic and political units to coincide were dangerous forces in Europe, threatening conflict and war. After Germany annexed Alsace and Lorraine in 1871, some French zealots kept alive the sense of grievance and the demand for redemption of the lost provinces; a whole literature of "suffering Alsace" existed around 1900 (it was largely false; German rule did not inflict persecution on the inhabitants of Alsace and Lorraine). Italians dreamed of recapturing some Italians who lived under the flag of Austria-Hungary. The most flagrant of many offenses against national independence was that of Poland, which had been divided among Russia, Germany, and Austria since 1795 except for a brief interval during the Napoleonic years. In 1830, the Poles had rebelled against Russia in a major uprising; a lesser but significant movement in 1863 also failed, and Russian Poland was subject to official Russification after that, forced to use the Russian language in its schools and government. Yet Polish ethnic identity and pride remained defiantly alive.

The sovereign states of Europe had been shaped in the centuries before the rise of nationalism. They had not been formed by consulting the wishes of the people or ascertaining their languages and cultures. They had grown up at a time when the decisive political principle was the quasi-feudal and antinational one of monarchism, or loyalty to a person. Boundaries had been determined by war and diplomacy, not plebiscites. As late as 1815, following the wars of the French Revolution era, the peacemakers had at least partly employed the traditional principle of ruling-house legitimacy (ancestral right) in drawing up countries' borders. They had deliberately placed Italians under Austrian rule and Poles under Russian. They had kept Germany divided and put French- and German-speaking people under one government in the Low Countries.

During the nineteenth century, the rise of democratic nationalism had impelled changes in these arrangements, and it was responsible for the chief impediments to peace. The revolutions of 1848 were in good part nationalistic. Italians rebelled against Austrian rule and searched for national unity, as did Hungary, while the Germans awkwardly sought to unify as a federal republic. Under the guidance of Otto Bismarck, Prussia then succeeded in uniting many small German states to make a larger German Reich, at the cost of brief wars with Austria (1867) and France (1870–1871). Nationalistic discontent among subjects of the Ottoman Empire, or the Austro-Hungarian Dual Monarchy (as it was after 1867), produced intermittent crises from 1878 until the beginning of World War I in 1914.

The states of Europe differed greatly in political constitution, social structure, and economic level. One common cultural element contributing to a tenuous basic unity was nominal adherence to the Christian religion, although Russia subscribed to the Greek rather than the Latin branch of the Church; there were numerous Jews, as well as a few Muslims, especially in eastern Europe; and Western Christianity itself had long been divided among Catholics and various Protestants. The most nationalistic of European powers, Germany, consisted of Roman Catholics and Protestants both. All European elites had inherited something from the rich Greek and Latin civilization of classical antiquity. More basically, except for the Finns, the Hungarians, and the Basques, nearly all Europeans shared an Indo-European language structure. This did not prevent their languages from being too different to be comprehensible to each other, however. Among numerous complexities of European cultural relations was the bond of unity possessed by the Latin countries (Italy, France, Spain, Portugal, and Romania), as against a Germanic group (England, the Scandinavian peoples, Germany, and the Netherlands), and the Slavs of eastern Europe. Yet this linguistic-cultural bond by no means ensured that the various states within the group would be on friendly terms. Shaw said that England and the United States were divided by a common tongue; Italy and France, Russia and the Poles might quarrel furiously. Even the Scandinavian countries, Sweden, Norway, and Denmark, separated after experiments in unity.

The principal basis of distinction among the score or so of European states was undoubtedly power. The five important powers were Russia, Germany, Austria-Hungary, France, and Great Britain, which at this time included all of Ireland as well as England, Wales, and Scotland. The smaller countries included Spain and Portugal on the Iberian peninsula; the Low Countries of Netherlands, Belgium, and tiny Luxemburg; and the Scandinavian states of Denmark, Sweden, and Norway (a union between the latter two was peacefully dissolved in 1905). In eastern Europe, there were fewer independent nations than there are today, chiefly because of the multinational Dual Monarchy. Bulgaria, Romania, Greece, and Serbia, together with her small sister Montenegro, did then exist, along with what remained of the Ottoman Empire in Europe; but Czechoslovakia was then part of the Dual Monarchy, and Finland belonged to Russia. Italy was a kind of intermediate or almost-great power; Switzerland was the classic neutral. For the rest, there were only the tiny states of Lichtenstein, Monaco, and Andorra, interesting primarily to gamblers and collectors of postage stamps.

Of the great powers, only France managed without a crowned head, and almost all the minor states had kings, too. If we think of Europe on the eve of 1914 as poised between past and future, the persistence of the 500-year-old Hapsburg dynasty in the form of the emperor of Austria and Hungary was a living link with the Middle Ages and even with the Roman Empire. The Romanovs had sat on the throne of Russia since 1613; the Hohenzollerns had ruled Prussia since the sixteenth century, though they added the throne of Imperial Germany only in 1871. No monarch was more popular than Britain's Queen Victoria, symbol of an age until her death in 1901; her son and successor, Edward VII, also became popular. But few of these royal personages any longer disposed of awesome power. The king of England was virtually a ceremonial symbol. Only the tsar of Russia claimed to be omnipotent.

Represented at each other's capitals by ambassadors, the governments of Europe conducted relations by making treaties or other formal agreements, worth only as much as their honor and interest allowed. It had long been considered essential to prevent any one power from becoming overmighty, thus threatening the independence of others, and so the chief formal goal of the art of diplomacy was a balance of power. Evidence that power prevailed over linguistic or cultural similarity, religion, or any other ideological affinity could be found abundantly in the history of European relations. The most recent surprise had come in 1894 when democratic France and autocratic Russia, poles apart in political outlook but drawn together by a common mistrust of powerful Germany, had formed a military alliance. The rather shaky Franco-Russian combination faced a Middle European bloc of Germany and Austria-Hungary. In a game of five, European diplomats sometimes said, the object was to line up three; but Great Britain preferred to stand clear, watch the balance, and practice "splendid isolation" except in severe emergency. As the 1900s were to show, the balance was precarious; imperialist rivalries, dissatisfied nationalism among the smaller countries, and internal insecurity within the Great Powers were destabilizers.

Despite jealously nationalistic sovereign states, Europe was in some ways a single society, more so then than later. Not only its goods but its ideas freely crossed national boundaries. In this pre-1914 era, the predominant economic ideology stressed free trade and an exchange of currencies in terms of gold, which provided in effect a single international money. International patents and copyrights, mail delivery among countries, canals and railroads, along with bigger and faster ocean-going ships and improved harbors, were knitting the countries of Europe together and bringing Europe closer to the rest of the world. It was common to hear talk of a global economy. War was thought to be obsolete because the economy was so interdependent that no country could possibly profit by war, which would disrupt commerce and wipe out investments. Barriers to trade among nations and to people traveling across frontiers were far weaker than they were to be later in the century. For example, except for a few backward and tyrannical lands in the East, there were no passport requirements for travel among countries.

One index of the rising European economy was the growth of international trade. Between 1880 and 1914, this commerce more than doubled, and Europe had the lion's share. Of Europe's trade, much the largest percentage was between the various countries of Europe, rather than with the other continents. Despite a certain trend toward protectionism in the later nineteenth century, tariffs were relatively low in 1900.

ECONOMIC PROGRESS AND PROBLEMS

The story of Europe at the end of the nineteenth century was in important ways a fabulous success story. Europe had refuted the long-held belief that population must always approach the limit of available resources, thus preventing any appreciable rise in the standard of living; for though population had greatly increased during the nineteenth century, wealth had grown even more rapidly. This was true, at least, of the more advanced industrial societies. Thus, between 1750 and 1900, the population of Great Britain increased sixfold, but national income rose at least fifteen times. In the last quarter of the nineteenth century, real wages rose 40 percent in Great Britain and nearly 25 percent in Germany.

This period was one of classic technological achievement; to it belongs the foundation of the modern industrial society. It was the age of steel, of railroads, of electricity, and of chemicals. The basic railroad grid of Europe took shape between 1870 and 1900. Steel output in Germany climbed from 1.5 million tons annually in 1880 to nearly 7.5 million in 1900. The recital of further technological advances is almost endless. The first practical automobile dates from the late 1880s. Hertz discovered radio waves in 1885, by which time the age of electricity was arriving in the form of electric lights, electric trolleys, and motion pictures (1889). Mass production of electricity had begun and so had the petroleum age, signaled by the first oil wells in 1869. Edison's first electric lamp

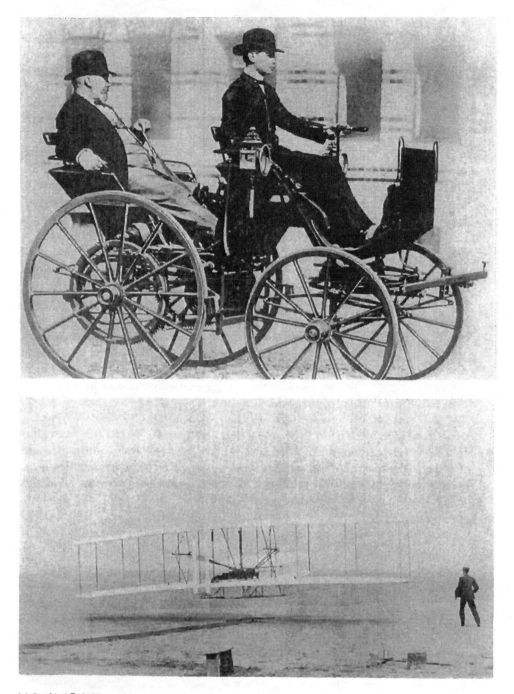

(a) Gottfried Daimler and his son in the first "horseless carriage," 1885. (*Courtesy Free Library of Philadelphia.*) (b) The Wright brothers with the first airplane, 1903. (*Smithsonian Institution.*)

twinkled in 1879. Berlin had an elevated electric railway by 1900. The French doctor Louis Pasteur's discovery of immunization in 1881 was followed shortly by the Koch-Pasteur germ theory of disease. The American Wright brothers, whose epochal Kitty Hawk flight took place in 1903, were inspired to undertake it by reading of German attempts earlier. German industrial chemistry brought forth a succession of minor miracles in dyestuffs; Roentgen perfected X rays. The Polish-French chemist Marie Curie discovered radioactivity, together with her husband Pierre winning the first Nobel prize in 1903.

Radio was already a reality by 1901; December 12, 1901, was the date of the first long-distance radio signal, sent from England to Newfoundland by Guglielmo Marconi. By 1912, radio was far enough advanced to have created a scandal in the British government over the awarding of contracts. Even such later marvels as television, atomic energy, and space travel were theoretical possibilities familiar to science fiction writers by that time. Of more current interest was the nearing of completion of the Trans-Siberian railway linking Europe and Asia. The Suez Canal had been finished in 1869; the United States was building the Panama Canal in 1903. Among many other maritime improvements were the Kiel Canal linking the Baltic and the Atlantic, the Manchester ship canals, and the improvement of the great Rotterdam waterway and port.

Such items only begin to tell the story of the burgeoning technological society of Europe and her offshoots. It was greeted on the whole with delight and was, more than anything else, responsible for the optimism that marked European thought in the nineteenth century. With this revolution in production came drastic dislocations and social problems, always tempering that optimism. Yet the comment of the American, E. L. Godkin, in 1888 is typical: "There is not a poor man in England," the celebrated editor wrote, "who is not conscious that he is vastly better off . . . than his grandfather was." Hymns of praise and wonder to the marvels of technology came as often from scholars and writers as from average citizens. Walt Whitman, sufficiently aware of grave imperfections and monstrous injustices, nevertheless hailed the

> Beautiful World of new, superber Birth, that rises to my eyes,
> Like a limitless golden cloud . . .

Europe was the source of that enormous revolution that altered the face of the earth more drastically than anything had ever done in all history.

As the twentieth century began, however, there was a strong feeling that the nineteenth century's impressive increase in power over nature, which some estimated in the neighborhood of a hundredfold and in which, clearly, it had far surpassed all preceding centuries, had not carried with it a comparable increase in human happiness. British critic Alfred R. Wallace asserted that "huge masses of people suffer untold misery and want in our great cities, and in country villages." Crime was increasing and so apparently was insanity; poverty, as Henry George put it, was paradoxically growing along with

Pre-motorized days in a metropolis: London's Regent Street about 1880. (*Courtesy B. T. Batsford Ltd.*)

progress. This was the state of affairs in the most industrialized part of the Western world. Certainly discontent was growing. This is not surprising, upon reflection: When people were unaware of the possibility of change, they were content with extreme privation; but, once they began to see the possibility of improvement, they quickly developed wants that far outstripped their ability to satisfy them.

Widespread impatience with traditional economic arrangements and answers was evident around 1900. Socialists asserted that "production is not carried on for the purpose of supplying the wants of the producers (workers), but solely with the object of creating wealth for a capitalist employer." They also asserted that governments, which had been content to resign the workings of the economic order to the natural process of individual competition, must now take intelligent action to guide the course of production and distribution. From Great Britain, where the Labour party was born in the year 1900, to Russia, where student strikes and demonstrations in the leading Russian cities in 1899–1900 foreshadowed agrarian uprisings in 1902 and then the revolution of 1905, social protest seethed in one form or another–legally in the more democratic West, violently in the autocratic East. Strikes in the Ruhr coal mines and on the London docks in the late 1880s had begun this epoch of unrest.

Whatever the definition of poverty, it was beyond dispute that great inequalities of wealth existed. In 1909, the British author Arnold Bennett thought that "the prosperous crowd," who stood out from the rest, numbered about one million out of the forty. Only 375,000 earners paid the new income tax (under protest!) in that year. In the country with the largest middle class, that class was smaller than 25 percent by any sort of reckoning: A contemporary British investigator estimated it at 23 percent, counting everything above the blue collar level, which obviously included many clerical employees of modest income. Statistics showed that in 1913, 10 percent of the population owned 92 percent of personal wealth in Britain; such social investigators as Seebohm Rowntree (in a famous study of poverty published in 1901) calculated that almost 30 percent lived below a tolerable standard of existence. Extremes of wealth and poverty, with corresponding attributions of cultural prestige and the lack of it, marked all the countries of Europe, even those most democratic in political form.

In the less modernized parts of Europe, the social gulf was greater. A vast, ignorant, and impoverished populace confronted a rich, proud ruling elite not only in eastern Europe but also in southern Italy and in the Iberian peninsula. In 1908, in a typical case of extreme polarization, assassination of Portugal's King Carlos was followed by fighting between an aristocracy backed by church and army and various types of revolutionary socialists and anarchists. Of greater importance was the 1905 revolution in Russia, where industrialism was just beginning and the greatest threat to the status quo came from a dissatisfied peasantry. This revolution, sporadic and uncoordinated, followed Russia's defeat in war at the hands of Japan. It petered out, leaving no major changes in the land of the tsar but the memory of "days of liberty" to be recalled in the future. The revolutionary urban workers had formed soviets, or committees, a term destined for much future importance. But the only tangible result of the 1905 disorder was a national assembly with extremely limited powers—the first Russia had had.

The protest was often against the economic and social order, which Karl Marx and others had called "capitalism," Henry Maine had described as based on "contract" rather than "status," and the liberal economists of the nineteenth century had discussed in terms of the "free market" or "free enterprise." Those who admired it pointed out that the free exchange of goods and services in the marketplace is both just and efficient. It rewards efficiency and penalizes ineptitude, awarding the prizes to those persons who produce the best products at the cheapest price and attracting capital investment to those areas where it is needed. It does all this by a natural process; the alternative is some monstrous bureaucracy making arbitrary decisions. The market economy, they held, was justified by its results, for it had presided over that vast increase in wealth that had set the nineteenth century apart from all others.

Those who condemned it sometimes lodged an esthetic objection against this regime of scrambled chance, which put a price on everything and joined people together only by the callous ties of what Thomas Carlyle had called the "cash nexus." More often they cried out against its injustice. The poor and the rich did not meet as equals in the marketplace. The competitive order was not really competitive, for monopoly still existed. Above all, it was cruel to dismiss all those who lost in the competitive rat race as deserving of poverty, humiliation, or even extinction. The system was not justified by its results, for it had enriched only a few and had left the many in dire want. Moreover, periodic depressions or panics had marred the growth of the economy. International in scope, somewhat mysterious in origin, such severe downswings in the business cycle had occurred in the mid-1870s, the mid-1880s, and from 1893 to 1896. No major one marred the years just prior to 1914. But fear of unemployment or bankruptcy haunted people. A structural crisis in agriculture in Great Britain, Germany, and the United States contributed to the severity of such depressions.

In the economic debate, several kinds of socialists or anarchists argued against either liberal or conservative defenders of a free-enterprise society. The debate had been going on since fairly early in the century. The pioneer socialists appeared at about the same time as the liberal ideology, not long after the French Revolution. An old and complex argument, sometimes hardening into bitter ideological passions, reached a climax at about the turn of the century. Socialists agreed with capitalists about the huge potentialities of wealth unleashed by technological discovery; they simply disagreed on the best means of tapping this reservoir. The growth of technology, bringing with it skills to flood great cities with light and power, make machinery to produce goods far faster than unaided human labor, and transport goods quickly and cheaply across vast distances, engendered a feeling that, for the first time in history, people might master their environment and shape for themselves a good life. But it also brought a bewildering complexity of problems far more difficult than those faced in the past.

Despite the socialist rhetoric, which emanated largely from the intellectual elite rather than the workers, most of Europe was not revolutionary in the 1900s. On the one hand, the discontents of modernization had not yet penetrated far into a society still largely dominated by traditional values. In a typical German town, men were content to stay in one's Stand, or appointed social station, except in unusual circumstances, and to follow one's father's craft with all the security that it brought. The excess of population, younger sons perhaps, was likely to migrate to the United States or Brazil if not to German cities. Social mobility, in brief, was deplorably low; but not many missed it. On the other hand, the urban working class in western Europe had retreated from the revolutionary militancy it had felt in the time of Karl Marx and the British Chartists back in the hungry 1840s. It was both materially better off and more cautious in its claims.

Trade Unionism were the words of the day, a practical movement not questioning the existing institutional structure of capitalism but seeking a bigger share of the proceeds for labor. From 1900 to 1913, membership in unions grew from two million to four million in Great Britain, from one million to three million in Germany, and from one-half million to one million in France, where huge industrial plants were less common. Ninety-five percent of all manufacturing units in Germany and 98 percent in France employed fewer than ten persons in 1907. In Great Britain, a distinctive working-class culture was emerging in the industrial cities; it was marked less by red flags and revolutionary cries than by the pub, the music hall, and the soccer game. The rise of professional football as a mass spectator sport dates from the 1880s; in 1910, 100,000 people watched a cup match. If this was the opium of the proletariat, it seemed to work. But in fact the working class was increasingly better off in terms of real wages.

EUROPEAN SOCIETY IN AN AGE OF URBANIZATION

In 1889, a British student of urbanization declared that "the concentration of population in cities" had been "the most remarkable social phenomenon" of the century just ending. The twentieth century has continued and extended this trend, but as in so many other matters, the nineteenth century pioneered the changes that the twentieth carried on. Between 1801 and 1891, the percentage of Britain's population living in cities of over 20,000 grew from 17 percent to 54 percent. Since the total population had more than tripled, this meant that the absolute number of city dwellers multiplied tenfold. The percentage of those living in cities of over 100,000 during the same period had increased from about 10 percent to 32 percent, as the number of cities in this category climbed from one (London) to sixteen. For Europe as a whole, the figure was close to 20 percent.

Overall, Great Britain was the most heavily urbanized of any major European country; certain regions in Germany were even more so. In 1871, less than 5 percent of the population had lived in German cities of over 100,000. The rapid surge of German industrialization after 1871 brought this figure up to 21 percent, a trend particularly marked in the heavily industrialized Rhine provinces and Saxony, areas that increased greatly in both total and urban population. The thrust of urbanization is suggested by the fact that in 1830, Germany had only two cities with more than 100,000 inhabitants; by 1910, there were no fewer than forty-eight such cities, two of them with over a million; Berlin had grown to four million. Total population increased from thirty-five million in 1850 to over sixty-five million in 1914, and two-thirds of this increase was in cities of over 100,000 by 1914. Thus, a number of people larger than Germany's total population in 1800 settled in unprecedentedly large cities over the course of about two generations.

Lagging behind in heavy industry, France nevertheless had fifteen cities of over 100,000 population by 1914; as in Germany, about one in five French citizens lived in such cities. The urban wave had still not struck with full force in southern and eastern Europe. Although there were such great capital cities as Rome, St. Petersburg, Warsaw, and Budapest, the largish secondary cities, usually a by-product of industrialization, had yet to increase in numbers. As late as 1920, 56 percent of Spaniards, 82 percent of Bulgarians, and 85 percent of Russians lived in rural areas, compared to less than 10 percent in England.

The nineteenth century had tackled massive problems accompanying urbanization. At its peak in the 1840s and 1850s, disease, in the form of typhus, cholera, and typhoid, had threatened the very existence of cities. Accustomed as we may be to thinking of the "crisis of the cities" as a recent phenomenon, we should realize that for the Edwardians the crisis had come earlier, and by the end of the century it had been surmounted, particularly in the areas of public health and sanitation. Death rates from contagious disease were down; streets and transportation facilities had improved (London had already built its underground rail system); and the worst conditions of dirt, squalor, overcrowding, crime, drunkenness, and general human degradation were no longer so common, even if much remained to be done. London had devised a new form of local government, the London County Council, to deal with the whole urban area. Beginning in the 1860s, Paris had submitted to a massive face-lifting process, which beautified the grand old city with boulevards and plazas at the cost of removing some of her narrow old streets. Berlin was the pride of Germany, and Vienna could claim to be the most civilized city in the world. In 1900, Budapest was the fastest-growing city in Europe, a fact often forgotten in the light of events that soon blighted Hungarian progress. The first electric underground railway in Europe opened there in 1896. This was in some ways the great age of the large European cities, which were past their initial crisis and not yet fully into a new one. Another great city that experienced dramatic growth in the later nineteenth and early twentieth centuries was Kiev, where Ukrainians, Russians, Jews, and Poles mingled to foment occasional anti-Semitic violence and revolution.

A good deal of the significant literature and thought of Europe around the turn of the century reacted in one way or another to the presence of the large city. Novels were more likely to have an urban than a rural or small-town setting. Of course, there are exceptions to this generalization, for there was already a literary and intellectual rejection of the city—as illustrated in the years from 1901–1910 by the Georgian poets, who sought out the simplicities of an older England, and an "arts and craft" movement, which sought a return to preindustrial workmanship. The influential French novelist Maurice Barrès dwelt on the "deracination" of man—his uprooting from the soil. The pioneer German sociologist Georg Simmel noted that city dwellers had different mental processes, different values, a different lifestyle from rural people.

Indeed, it might be argued that sociology's status rose at this time primarily because of the impact of drastic social change, at the core of which lay urbanization. Émile Durkheim, the French sociologist, used the term *anomie* to describe the condition of people who have lost contact with a firm social structure and who therefore feel confused and in need of values. The city released people from the control of traditional tightly knit communities, enabling them to be free. But sometimes this freedom was dangerous. Ferdinand Tönnies dis-

London, Bank of England, 1910. (*Courtesy Library of Congress.*)

tinguished between the *Gemeinschaft* ("community") found in the traditional rural society—tightly knit, face-to-face, strongly authoritarian—and the *Gesellschaft* ("society") characteristic of the city—vast, impersonal, governing by bureaucratic rules. To plunge from one milieu to the other, as many in this generation did—especially in rapidly industrializing Germany—was to experience cultural shock. "The deepest problems of modern life," Simmel observed, "derive from the claim of the individual to preserve the autonomy and individuality of his existence in the face of overwhelming social forces."

Human nature itself seemed to change in the new environment of the city, the factory, the mass society. Culture further altered under the impact of new techniques in communication. The radio was not yet a cultural factor in 1900, but the motion picture was beginning to be. The invention of motion pictures may be dated as of 1889; it was disputed among Edison, the French brothers Lumière, and a Frenchman named Le Prince who worked with British collaborators in Leeds, and who mysteriously disappeared, probably murdered, on a train from Dijon to Paris in September, 1890—the first movie mystery?[1] But

[1]See Christopher Rawlence, *The Missing Reel: The Untold Story of the Lost Inventor of Moving Pictures* (1990).

motion pictures were not commercially practicable until six or seven years later. Within a few years after that, Bijous and Apollos appeared on urban streets. There are good movies of Queen Victoria's funeral, the great public event of 1901. Cheap newspapers had been around for some years; there were more of them from which to choose in 1900 than there are today. Sensitive people complained of the vulgar fare offered in some of them, then as now. And, the automobile, of course, had not only begun its career but by 1910 was already eliciting complaints for polluting the environment, endangering life, and making an intolerable racket.

The arrival of professional spectator sports marked a transformation from bear-baiting, cock-fighting, and public executions, the last of which had occurred in England in 1865, as public entertainments. Life had become less raw and brutal. John Stuart Mill attributed this to "a perfection of mechanical arrangements impracticable in any but a high state of civilization," keeping pain and death out of sight. Livestock as well as criminals were now dispatched efficiently out of public view; the surgeon, the butcher, and the executioner plied their specialized trades behind closed doors. Nevertheless, the conditions of life of the lowest urban class, which Charles Booth described in 1895 as "almost savage" and which were still marked by riotous violence, belied this claim.

The city air accelerated processes of change and bred a restless spirit. In St. Petersburg on January 9, 1905, a huge crowd, intoxicated by the rhetoric of a labor organizer priest, assembled before the Winter Palace to petition the tsar. The troops' firing upon them touched off the 1905 revolution, which spread to factory workers and students in the cities and later spilled over into the villages. The same year, on November 29, an estimated 250,000 workers paraded through the streets of Vienna in an appeal for universal suffrage. The city was the scene of dramatic action and excitement. "From the village street into the railway station is a leap across five centuries from the brutalizing torpor of Nature's tyranny over Man into the order and alertness of Man's organized dominion over Nature," wrote George Bernard Shaw, echoing Marx's slap at "rural idiocy." Nostalgia for the countryside was rarer than it would later become, perhaps because people were too close to its realities. Shaw knew it as savage, malodorous, back-breaking, and unsanitary. The Futurists, leading artistic revolutionaries of the 1900s, exulted in the spectacle of "great crowds excited by work, by pleasure, and by riot . . . the multicolored, polyphonic tides of revolution in the modern capitals." (From their 1909 *Manifesto*.) The city was where, if one was fortunate, one could attend the theater or opera, watch a Russian ballet, or visit the cinema. It was also where, at this time, one might attend a socialist rally, a political meeting, or a trade union picnic.

Possibly an even more exciting urban modernism was the feminist revolt. At their peak around 1910, mass rallies attracted 250,000 women in London. Over 100 were arrested at one demonstration in front of Parliament. Women refused to pay taxes, broke windows, slashed pictures, tied themselves to railroad tracks, threw themselves under horses, went on hunger strikes in prison. The militant phase of the British suffragettes started in 1905. Hunger strikes began in 1908. The government's Home Secretary justified force-feeding by the "fanaticism" of women who "no more fear death in fighting for what they believe to be the cause of women than the natives of the Soudan feared death when fighting the battle of the Mahdi." These fierce martyrs were primarily women from the middle and upper classes. The "Cat and Mouse Act" permitted the authorities to release them when they went on hunger strikes in jail and reimprison them when they had recovered.

The embattled women were not only demanding the right to vote but also discussing everything from trial marriage to payment for housework, as they combated deeply ingrained Victorian prejudices. The feminist movement was much weaker in France; as the *Frauenfrage,* it had some currency in Germany; but it was stormiest in England. All over Europe just before World War I, emancipated women were announcing their claim to be the equals of men in the honored professions. They could already boast of a Nobel Prize winner in science, joining a handful of men in the vanguard of an exciting revolution in physics and chemistry: the Polish-born Frenchwoman Marie Curie, *née* Maria Sklodowska.

The astute American historian Henry Adams thought that at about 1900, humanity moved into a new phase of history in a change comparable to the scientific revolution that had occurred between 1400 and 1700. "Human character changed in 1910," Virginia Woolf remarked. All of consciousness seemed to be changing, as a new art, a new literature, and a new philosophy arose, and revolutions were under way in fundamental human relationships. This was not entirely because Western society had accustomed itself to city lights and sounds, but that was part of it. The pace of change had been quickening all through the nineteenth century, and it now reached so rapid a rate that the sense of continuity was being lost. The new art, announced in scores of manifestos during the 1900s, labeled itself futurist, expressionist, abstractionist, cubist, vorticist, suprematist, and a dozen other names; the new schools rejected traditional ways of painting, sculpture, music, and poetry in favor of startling novelty.

Traditionalists struggled to adjust to this modernizing world. In 1891, the new Roman Catholic pope, Leo XIII, attacked capitalistic greed and materialism in a famous encyclical, *De rerum novarum,* which called for a fundamental reorganization of economic life to correspond to Christian principles. This much-discussed call for a new social ethic inspired a renewal of Christian socialism. Christian social parties appeared in Austria and Germany in the 1890s. In France, Germany, and Italy, Catholic trade unions came into existence, and there were individual examples of capitalists (like Leon Hormel) moved to experiment with "the Christian factory."

So important an avant-garde writer as Charles Péguy in France might be called a Christian socialist, insofar as one could classify his social thought. There was a significant revival of Christian socialism in Britain at the end of the century, too. The prominent Edwardian *litterateur* G. K. Chesterton, along with his friend the popular poet Hilaire Belloc, formed an energetic party of their own; both Roman Catholics among a people traditionally suspicious of papists, they preached a kind of Christian socialism or anarchism, and their wit and wisdom gained them an audience.

There was a Catholic Revival among French men of letters and even some British ones. George Santayana's attraction to the "splendid error" of the Roman Catholic faith indicated the special sophistication of these conversions. So the religious spirit was abroad, but the winds of doctrine were various and confusing. The British scholar J. N. Figgis, writing just before 1914 of *Civilization at the Crossroads,* expressed dismay at the babel of voices–Nietzsche, Bergson, James, Tolstoy, Russell–preaching atheism, skepticism, intuitionism, the life force, the "will to believe," the will-to-power. The need for a faith, the bankruptcy of the old churches, the psychological roots of religious belief were all represented here. An embattled Roman Church had been split by the issue of "modernism" for some decades. Should it accept the so-called higher criticism of the Bible? Pope Leo XIII's successor thought not, returning to the conservatism of Pius IX.

THE POLITICS OF EUROPEAN DEMOCRACIES

From about 1880 on, certain sophisticated currents of European political thought revealed signs of a severe disenchantment with democracy in the form of representative government with a mass electorate. Many argued that it only transferred power from one elite to another, perhaps less desirable, ruling class. Some socialists thought it a bourgeois fraud. Nevertheless, the feeling that democratization was an irresistible tendency of the times prevailed, and most people thought that the tide of progress would gradually remove the imperfections. Those who worried about a cheapening of thought and culture often placed their faith in the expansion of education, a process that had equipped most European countries with free, compulsory public educational systems by 1914 and reduced illiteracy in western Europe to almost zero. It was still a major problem not only in eastern Europe, but in southern Europe as well; in 1910, illiteracy in Italy was still 38 percent.

Democracy was relatively successful under conditions of a high standard of living, cultural homogeneity, and social equality or at least mobility. Where substantial numbers of impoverished peasants were dependent on rich landowners, or where deep ethnic hostilities divided the land, as in Hungary, it could hardly flourish. Great extremes of wealth and poverty provided a barren soil for democracy. Urbanization and a highly mobile social order seemed to favor it. Some of the smaller states of northern and western Europe did better with it than the larger countries. Switzerland, Sweden, Denmark, and the Low Countries provided object lessons in the successful functioning of democracy, even direct democracy: Switzerland held frequent popular referenda on significant issues.

With all its uneven application and flawed performance, democracy (in the sense of universal manhood suffrage and government by elected representative bodies) was in more or less effective operation throughout most of Europe of 1913 and was expected to continue making progress. Although there was an undercurrent of grave concern about a political regime being dependent on the fickle mood of the masses, the great majority paid tribute to democracy as an ideal. Even the Marxian Social Democrats, or Socialists, substantially converted after 1890 to the view that the great change from capitalism to socialism or communism would come via the ballot rather than violent revolution. To a degree, their political parties took part in the democratic process. The end, Socialism; the means, the Republic.

Writing in 1908, the astute British political scientist Graham Wallas, in *Human Nature and Politics,* noted that representative democracy was in operation everywhere in Europe. "Forty years ago it could still be argued that to base the sovereignty of a great modern nation upon a widely extended popular vote was, in Europe at least, an experiment which had never been successfully tried." But Wallas, who noted a certain puzzled disenchantment with the results of democracy, thought that it was now an ongoing institution, even in Austria and Russia.

It was obvious that some if not all of these arrangements fell far short of a democratic ideal. The German Reichstag had no power to compel the German emperor to change his ministers; the Russian Duma turned out to have no power at all. Although government by popularly elected representatives worked best of all in Great Britain, even there, the hereditary House of Lords held some power until 1911, and the reins of government remained by and large in the hands of a small aristocratic group. France, the most democratic of the European nations, having no monarch and with a cabinet responsible to the democratically elected legislature, was often politically turbulent. Some said that France was governed by the permanent civil service, not the cabinet. There were other countries of Europe where democracy was a farce, but even in these places, its outward forms were likely to exist as a concession to the spirit of the age. Spain, Italy, and Bulgaria, for example, were all supposed to be governed by elected parliaments; Spain supposedly had universal suffrage after 1890, whereas in Italy suffrage was restricted by a literacy requirement until 1912. In all three cases, elections were rigged, and voters were subject to manipulation or compulsion. Thus formal democracy was as fraudulent as it was in certain American cities where political bosses ruled behind a facade of election.

The issues that had to be decided via this machinery of government in the years just before 1914 were important ones. Standing out among them was the question of whether the state should assume some responsibility for the welfare of the workers in an urban, industrialized society in which the old, personal, and often informal means of looking out for human needs had seemingly become obsolete. In 1881, Germany's Bismarck announced that the state must either assume such responsibility for the well-being of its citizens or watch them join revolutionary movements to overthrow it. He threw his heavy weight behind a plan of social welfare that would provide health, old age, and unemployment insurance for industrial workers out of a fund to which employers, government, and workers all contributed. Little Denmark pioneered in a similar system at about the same time. These plans became models for other countries; on the eve of their war with Germany, ironically, the British were engaged in setting up a national insurance system inspired by the German example. The passing of this National Insurance Act in 1911 signaled "the greatest scheme of social reconstruction ever attempted," a prominent British newspaper declared. The 1911 act provided for the government to contribute two-ninths of the sum set aside for unemployment insurance, the employer to pay three-ninths, and the employee, four-ninths. Modest enough by later standards, the government-administered welfare payments plan constituted a break with tradition and encountered strenuous opposition. The nineteenth-century legacy included a powerful strain of antistatist social and economic policy. British industry had flourished by allowing competition in the free market and by keeping taxes low and private businesses immune from state regulation and control.

The great Liberal party, even more than its perennial rival, the Conservatives, stood for maximum individual liberty in all respects against the state. In the words of the brilliant Fabian Socialist, Beatrice Webb, British liberalism "thought in individuals" and saw government as the foe of liberty. Not without great difficulty could it come around to a positive conception of government, the neoliberalism of the welfare state movement. But in their minority report to the massive investigations of the Poor Law Commission of 1905–1909, the Fabian socialists Beatrice and Sidney Webb argued that prevention of poverty, not its relief, should be the goal of government and that privation is a social problem, not a matter of individual effort.

The Liberal government elected in 1906 and in office until after World War I was a talented one, including among its young members Winston Churchill and David Lloyd George, who was chancellor of the exchequer in Prime Minister Herbert Asquith's cabinet after 1908. Confronted with expenses for the new welfare program and with rising defense costs in a naval race with Germany, the Lloyd George budget of 1909 proposed new taxes, including an income tax. Among the nicer things opponents said about it was that such a tax was inquisitorial, unfair, and socialistic. Sent to the House of Lords after being passed by the House of Commons, the budget was rejected by the peers in a breathtaking act of defiance, this being the first time in nearly 200 years that the hereditary house had refused to endorse an important bill passed by Commons. Dramatic scenes ensued. In 1911, when Asquith conveyed the news that the king had agreed to create enough new peers to assure a majority for the reform bills in the House of Lords, the normally sedate British Parliament became a screaming mob.

A Parliament bill deprived the upper house of the power to prevent legislation passed by Commons from becoming law, though it could still delay a nonrevenue bill. The country seemed mostly to agree with Churchill's assertion that the House of Lords, a voice from England's past, had become "an institution absolutely foreign to the spirit of the age." This act also authorized salaries for members of Parliament for the first time, a measure helpful in prying political power from the hands of the aristocratic elite that still largely controlled it. A landmark in the development of both democracy and the social state, this 1909–1911 imbroglio about the welfare state, taxation, and the power of the upper legislative house stood out in British politics in the prewar years, but it was not the only great issue nationally debated. Its chief rival was the issue of Ireland, a problem that came to a fever point just before the outbreak of World War I. On July 27, 1914, the *Times* of London announced that "the country is now confronted with one of the greatest crises in the history of the British race." The editorial did not refer to the international crisis then looming in Europe, which would erupt in major war just a week later. It was talking about a rebellion in the British army in Ireland and the creation of a volunteer army in northern Ireland to resist the granting of "home rule" to all of that country. Conservative political leaders in the British Parliament had encouraged this resistance. Civil war in Ireland between Green and Orange, Catholic and Protestant, seemed likely to spread to England.

Postponed by World War I, armed conflict did indeed break out in Ireland in 1920–1922. The issue was the refusal of Ulster, the Protestant part of the Emerald Isle, to join an autonomous Ireland, fearful of oppression at the hand of the Catholic majority, and the refusal of Irish Catholics to accept a partition of Ireland. Behind it lay seven centuries of English rule over the Irish, a long and mostly sorry record of cruelty and absentee domination, the repercussions of which still go on down to the present. Dependent on Irish votes after receiving a diminished majority in the election of 1910, the Liberal party pushed a home rule bill only to encounter this bitter opposition verging on mutiny in the army. Small wonder the *Times* called the crisis grave.

These and other questions made the prewar decade an exciting if turbulent period in British politics. Author Herbert Read later recalled that in his Edwardian youth "the great issues of Free Trade and Protection, Home Rule for Ireland, the Disestablishment of the Church, and the Reform of the House of Lords, were being debated with fervour and energy in every newspaper and at every street corner." Adding to the turbulence were the militant suffragettes, who were joined by crusaders for birth control, advocates of greater sexual knowledge, and believers in "free love" or release from Victorian moral conventions. The continuing thrust of trade unionism raised such issues as were dealt with in the Trade Disputes Act of 1906, which among other provisions largely exempted unions from damage liability resulting from strikes.

POLITICS: FRANCE AND GERMANY

Issues in other European countries were not greatly dissimilar from those in the oldest industrial society, Great Britain. In some ways, French politics differed from those of the British quite markedly. There were numerous small political parties rather than two large ones; no monarch; a past colored by passions reaching back to the great 1789 revolution and its sequels in 1848 and 1871; an underlying social structure of small farms, small businesses, small factories. France had several million landowners, whereas in England 1,500 great families held half the land. There was no real French equivalent to the industrial Midlands of England or the Ruhr Valley of Germany. The combination of a freehold peasantry and numerous small traders and producers endowed French politics with a decidedly "petty bourgeois" flavor. Trade unionism grew more slowly in France than it did in Britain and Germany—only one in six French industrial workers belonged to a union in 1914—but it was often extremely militant.

Fragmented until 1905, the French Socialists (SFIO) succeeded in electing about a sixth of the delegates to the Chamber of Deputies in 1914; the party was stronger among intellectuals and professional people than among workers. This contrasted with the much larger German Social Democratic party, which gained more than a third of the votes in 1912; and with the almost total lack of a socialist party in Britain. The British Labour Party, born in 1900, did not adopt a socialist platform until 1918 and was in any case very small prior to the war. A more radical offshoot, the Independent Labour Party, was even smaller. The Fabian socialists were influential but deliberately refrained from any effort to create a mass party, preferring to feed ideas to the established political parties.

As the century turned, France had just been torn apart by the Dreyfus case, which polarized left and right over the issue of national security versus individual rights, a kind of Gallic Watergate and Alger Hiss case rolled into one. The result of this protracted controversy—during which Captain Alfred Dreyfus submitted to two trials for treason, was sent to prison, touched off anti-Jewish riots, and was finally exonerated—was a qualified victory for the left. Consequently, between 1899 and 1905 a coalition of Radicals (a democratic party of the petit bourgeoisie) and moderates governed with Socialist support. But in 1904, after a long argument, the Socialists decided against participation in "bourgeois" governments, regarding this as a collaboration with the class enemy that could only prolong capitalism—a position they held until 1936, except during the 1914–1918 war. Nevertheless, under the leadership of the brilliant writer and orator Jean Jaurès, the SFIO was far from addicted to revolutionary violence.

The French Left was fragmented; but so was the French Right. This division into numerous small parties forced the Third Republic into numerous changes of government. Dependent on coalitions of parties to command a majority in the Chamber of Deputies, governments could be overthrown on small issues. It was a system that prevented major political decisions, but this suited petty-bourgeois France, which was suspicious of the state. Born of political defeat in 1871, long hated by the socialist Left as much as the monarchist Right, the Third Republic survived because no one could suggest or implement anything better; it was, as Georges Clemenceau said, the least intolerable of the many frightful evils.

France lagged behind in industrialization and in social policy, a backwardness historians tend to think of as a scandal: the stalemated society. But most of the French liked it that way, and can we blame them for not wanting to move into the age of big business, big industry, big government? With all their often bitter family quarrels, the French were basically a happy people. Certainly in this era France's intellectual and artistic brilliance continued. Paris was the cultural capital of the world. The most interesting movements in literature and art—symbolism, cubism, art nouveau—originated or centered in the French capital. The French also did more in the 1890s to develop the automobile than anyone else, as names like carburetor and chassis still remind us; they had given the world photography, X rays, pasteurization. Paris claims credit for the first cinema. As Charles de Gaulle later remarked, France was a greater land than her politics.

On the eve of 1914, a "national revival" mood swept over France, affecting prestigious writers and thinkers with the theme of a return to order, discipline, national tradition, the grandeur of *la belle France*. The rising menace of war with Germany deeply colored French politics. At the same time, there was working-class unrest and a wave of militant strikes. Labor strikes, often violent, also shook Italy in the 1900s, along with active socialist and anarchist agitation. But Italy was not doing badly. Under Prime Minister Giolitti, just before 1914, she "had attained a level of economic and political power unknown to Italians for centuries." The deep division between north and south remained, but some headway seemed to have been made on the post-Risorgimento project to "make Italians." ("We have made Italy, now we must make Italians.")

Basking in the highest growth rate in this period, Germany was less agitated; but there were massive strikes in 1905, and it was in Germany that the Marxist Social Democratic party (SPD) became the strongest such group in the world, winning more seats in the Reichstag in 1912 than any other party. It dominated the world socialist organization, the Second International, founded in 1889 by friends and disciples of Karl Marx and Friedrich Engels. In its own highly developed newspapers and magazines, the SPD radiated confidence that the coming victory of world socialism would begin in Germany. The party also entered into generally good relations with the powerful trade unions. Yet, it faced the frustration of having little influence on the authoritarian government of the kaiser, who could appoint the chancellor and cabinet without the approval of the Reichstag. Wilhelm II strove to be a friend to the workingman in his way, flattering himself that he was well abreast of the new age and its social issues. The German system of social insurance against sickness, old age, and unemployment, among the first to be established in Europe, was also the most advanced.

The paradox of Germany was that, although she was the greatest of industrial countries, her political structure was dangerously weak because it was lacking in liberalism and democracy. By 1900, she had passed Great Britain in both population and most of the indices of economic power, including production of coal, steel, chemicals, and electrical power. This economic strength allied to the potent military tradition of Prussia made the Wilhelmine Reich the leading power in Europe. This success not unnaturally induced a spirit many observers thought to be arrogant, or at least complacent. For centuries, a divided Germany had been victimized because she was weak. The miracle of the 1860s brought her unity and strength beyond her wildest dreams, and it is small wonder that Germans became overly proud of themselves. Unfortunately, their national political institutions had failed to advance as rapidly.

Underneath the formal unity, Germany was still a deeply divided country. Regional differences, especially those between the Catholic South and the Protestant North, were more marked than in France. The Rhineland and Alsace were almost French; Bavaria was pulled toward Austria. The states that made up the German Empire had substantial powers (Bavaria even had its own army), though the famous social security system was national, and the Berlin government also owned most of the railroads. By far the largest of these widely differing states, Prussia, with two-thirds of the population and the chief industrial areas, usually dominated the Reich. Despite its industrial might, Prussia was dominated politically by the agricultural barons, the Junkers. Whether this landed aristocracy was scandal or glory, aristocracy at its best or its worst, was a much debated question. Hard-working, honorable, loyal, they were also narrow-minded, greedy, and authoritarian.

Extremely rapid industrialization and urbanization after 1870 resulted in some social shock effects. If the political development of Germany was an oddity by the standards of France and Britain, probably the main reason was that the German national state had not grown up slowly over a long period of time but had been achieved suddenly in the 1860s. For the next two decades, the more or less benevolent despotism of the great Bismarck impeded the growth of parliamentary government.

Germany was far from an illiberal country. Civil rights under the law were fairly well protected; there were a constitution, a reasonably free press, elections. But there was no strong parliamentary system, no vigorous political life. Parliaments traditionally had a lower prestige in German culture than they did in English. In place of parliamentary government stood the bureaucracy, an honest and able body committed to high standards of administration but not democratically controlled. Most people, someone has said, want not to govern themselves but to be well governed. The Germans were not badly governed, but they did not govern themselves.

The stubbornly individualistic English and the passionately democratic French accused the Germans of bending their knees too readily to authority. In compensation, the Germans had pioneered in welfare legislation. Bismarck had handed it down from above, allowing Germany to avoid the bitter political battles waged over this question in France and Britain. The German industrial middle class had been politically too weak to resist. Although a greater social principle informed the German society, it was at the cost, it seemed, of individualism. Yet the liberal theologian Ernst Troeltsch pointed out in an essay on

"The German Idea of Freedom" that German undervaluing of voting and politicking accompanied a greater concern for inner spiritual and intellectual freedom, influenced heavily by Lutheranism as well as the philosophical tradition of Kant and Hegel.

The weakness of liberalism may be seen in the election results. In the 1912 election to the Reichstag, when the Social Democrats won their victory with about 35 percent of the total vote, the National Liberals and Progressives *(Fortschrittpartei)* together won only 26 percent. The rest went either to the conservative parties or to those representing local or particular interests. Of these, the Center party *(Zentrum)* was by far the most important, with about a sixth of the electorate; traditionally dedicated to the interests of the Catholic church, the Center tended to ally with the conservatives. The National Liberal party could not collaborate with the Social Democrats because of profound disagreement on questions of national defense and military policy. If liberalism meant refusing strong support to army, navy, and colonies, nationalism came before liberalism to this party, which represented the German middle class. The support the National Liberals had given to Bismarck and the whole authoritarian structure of politics in the German Empire precluded this group from developing much of a reform impulse.

Reform of this political structure seemed to be needed for Germany to evolve in a democratic direction. Changes in the constitution were blocked, as in France and Britain, by the upper house of the legislature. Unlike the French and British second chambers, the German upper house was based on the various states of the national union. Prussia, far larger and more powerful than the others, with some of the tiny states of the North that were her satellites, could block an amendment to the constitution. And within Prussia the voting system, harking back to 1851, was profoundly archaic. Frankly weighted in the direction of property, her "three class system" gave the wealthiest the most representation, the poorest the least. Reform tended, then, to focus on the Prussian voting system. The key to Germany was Prussia; so long as Prussia remained dominated by a conservative minority, no fundamental change was possible in Germany. In 1910, there were again extensive public demonstrations against the Prussian electoral system, but nothing came of it. Only a revolution, some said, could break the vicious circle of oligarchy.

But the great majority of the Social Democrats were far from revolutionary. They remained committed to peaceful and legal acquisition of power. Marxism itself had the effect of supporting this position. Marx had taught that there are inexorable laws of historical change that make the victory of socialism inevitable. Revolutionary agitation could be dismissed as left-wing infantilism or romantic adventurism. The wheels of fate rolled steadily toward the future, which would come in due time, Marxists believed; it could not be rushed, but it was certain. The working class was bound to increase in numbers and in proletarian consciousness. Capitalism destroyed itself by its own operation; it did not have to be shot down from outside.

At the beginning of the decade, the German Social Democratic party debated revisionism. Eduard Bernstein, one of the party's most talented writers, suggested giving up dogmatic Marxism altogether. Marx's prophecies had not proved correct. Capitalism was not steadily digging its own grave, the working class was not growing more miserable each day, society was not being polarized into two classes. The day of revolution was not inevitable, regardless of Marx's alleged laws of history and capitalist development. Socialists ought to work toward a more just society little by little and with a pragmatic attitude, like the English Fabians. After a rousing debate, the party rejected Bernstein's revisions and remained in principle committed to the Marxist dogmas. Like the French Socialists, they declared their unwillingness to accept power in any but a completely socialist government. Yet only a small left wing of the party took Marx to mean revolutionary activism. As Marx's collaborator, Friedrich Engels, had said before his death in the 1890s, the hour of revolutionary conspiracies led by elites had passed; the masses themselves, by democratic means, would bring about the great transformation to socialism.

For all its success, the Social Democratic party remained curiously impotent and isolated. With a million members and scores of publications, which were read by several million Germans, this huge organization had already developed its own hierarchy of bureaucrats and mandarins. It attracted highly educated bourgeois intellectuals as well as workers. In large German cities, it won almost half the vote in 1912, doing much worse (less than 20 percent) among the farms and villages. But its influence was at best intellectual and moral. A glowingly idealistic faith informed its adherents, but it was faith in tomorrow, after the revolution. Meanwhile, its critics on the left thought, it tended silently to support the status quo.

It was widely believed that the Germans had made the best of all adjustments to the machine age. More so than the British and French, they ranked as an up-to-date, go-ahead people in technology, commerce, education, social services, and industrial relations. As a leading authority remarks, "Of all the major countries in the world in 1914, Germany was the best run." Its civil service, its educational system no less than its famous army were the envy of other peoples. If the prestige of German science was high, German writers and artists such as novelist Thomas Mann and poets Stefan George and Rainer Maria Rilke won international acclaim, too. In Berlin, scientists Albert Einstein and Max Planck were at work revolutionizing humanity's conception of the cosmos. Science, to be sure, was an international enterprise: For example, the leading Viennese physicist Ludwig von Boltzmann took part in an international debate about molecular behavior and entropy (1900–1906) that had begun with the Scottish genius James Clerk Maxwell and the French engineer Sadi Carnot, and involved the German Wilhelm Ostwald, the American Willard Gibbs, the Frenchman Henri Poincaré, as well as young Albert Einstein. But the Berlin to which Einstein came just before 1914 to join Max Planck might well claim preeminence.

In Munich just before the war, a remarkable group of painters, including Paul Klee and the Russian-born Wassily Kandinsky, joined to create one of the leading movements of contemporary art. In philosophy, such figures as Edmund Husserl and Max Scheler continued the German dominance of pure thought, challenged in this generation only by Henri Bergson of France and Bertrand Russell of England. Sigmund Freud, who worked in Vienna, and Carl Jung of Switzerland belonged to the German-speaking culture. The preeminence of Germans in the new science of sociology—Georg Simmel, Ferdinand Tonnies, Max Weber, and others—has been mentioned. The German educational system, from kindergarten to graduate seminar, remained a model for the world, and in 1914 more Germans attended universities than was the case in any other country.

All in all, Germany was doing splendidly, except for the curious lag in political institutions. But the widely shared gospel of progress persuaded most people that her institutions would soon catch up. Germany was thought to be in the process of evolving toward parliamentary government. The autocracy of the kaiser and his bureaucracy would be democratized in one way or another. Indeed, perhaps this would have happened peacefully were it not for the Great War. Yet the impossibility of a breakthrough to parliamentary supremacy by any normal means was increasingly felt on the eve of the war, too, and thus the revolution that came to Germany at the war's end may have been a necessity under any conditions.

THE EASTERN POWERS

In 1910, Austria-Hungary was a land of fifty million people. It was the third most populous of the European powers, after Russia (165 million) and Germany (sixty-five million). Economically, it was by no means undeveloped, although overall it ranked well behind the highly industrialized countries. Certain areas of the Dual Monarchy, including the great cities of Prague, Vienna, and Budapest and the industrial region of the Sudetenland, were as advanced in all respects as any in Europe. "The Austrian half of the Empire," a leading student writes, "enjoyed a very high level of freedom for the individual and a much higher level of social welfare than for example, England." Vienna, with its great musical traditions, its gaiety and waltzes, its lovely baroque architecture, also possessed a distinguished scientific community; among the doctors it gave to the world in this period was Sigmund Freud. It was probably the most civilized city in Europe. Ambassadors and other foreign service employees thought so; they preferred Vienna to any other post.

Budapest, the glamorous capital of the Hungarian part of the Dual Monarchy, was almost Vienna's equal. A brilliant prewar cultural generation included Bela Bartok and Georg Lukacs. In Bohemia, as the Czechs' land had long been known, Prague boasted a great university where Kepler had once started the whole age of modern science, and a lively intellectual culture that just before the war produced Franz Kafka, one of the three or four greatest figures of Modernist literature.

The empire itself, of course, traced its ancestry back to the Holy Roman Empire, which had been at the center of the world in medieval times. The Hapsburg dynasty was the oldest and most distinguished ruling house in Europe, if not the world, and it formed Europe's most obvious link with its medieval past. The Hapsburgs could recall such past emperors as Charles V, who came close to uniting all Europe in a single state as late as the sixteenth century. Hapsburgs had once striven with France for the mastery of Europe; after the Napoleonic Wars, the great peace settlement of 1815 took place at Vienna, and for many years thereafter Austria's leading statesman, Count Metternich, served as a kind of prime minister of all Europe. As late as 1851, Austria outranked Prussia as a central European power.

Then came Bismarck and the Prussian coup of 1867–1871. Prussia smashed Austria in the short war of 1866 and went on to create the powerful new German state, attracting to it the smaller principalities that had once made up the Holy Roman Empire (after 1815, the German Confederation). In 1867, the Hapsburg empire signaled its expulsion from the German world by granting the Hungarians (Magyars) a large measure of autonomy and renaming the country Austria-Hungary, or the Dual Monarchy. With a single monarch in Vienna shaping a common military and foreign policy, Budapest got a free hand in domestic matters in its portion of the empire. The Magyars were a proud people, neither Germanic nor Slavic but derived from an oriental people out of the plains of central Asia who had invaded Europe as conquerors in the ninth and tenth centuries. They had long been restive under Vienna's domination, and they now hoped to build a new state.

But the two master peoples were not the only inhabitants of the Dual Monarchy. Its twelve million Germans and ten million Magyars shared the multinational house with twenty-four million Slavs of various sorts, including Poles, Czechs, Slovaks, Croats, Slovenes, and a few "Ruthenians" (Ukrainians). In addition, there were some four million Latins, mostly Romanians but also some Italians in the Trentino area, and a considerable Jewish population. Many of these groups had old and proud national traditions. In an age of rising nationalism, they increasingly demanded recognition of their rights to cultural or even political autonomy, to a role in the state equal to that of the Germans and Hungarians. By 1900, this had become the critical problem for Europe. The problem burgeoned in proportion as the "Sick Man" of Europe, the Ottoman Empire, weakened, for the waning of this threat made the small Balkan peoples less dependent on Austria. It also increased when after 1905 Russian policy retreated from its Asian mission and played up its role as protector of the Slavs.

As usual, scholars disagree about how badly treated the minorities were and whether it was possible to grant them all autonomy. To those who lodged complaints of intolerable arrogance against both German and Magyar—especially the latter, in whose zone of control lived numerous Croats, Slovenes, and Romanians whom the Hungarians tended to regard as an inferior class—the reply was that the subject peoples were not badly treated and that it would be impossible to give them territorial autonomy. Since they were so numerous and so widely distributed, any such plan would amount to chaos. Suggestions were made for a triple monarchy. But the Slavs were not in a geographically contiguous area. Czechs and Slovaks lived in the north, Croats and Slovenes in the south. The Poles, occupying the northeast, were not anxious to blend with Slovaks or Croats. The Poles in Austria were, in fact, treated well, and they regarded their own lot as much better than that of their fellows who were ruled from St. Petersburg or Berlin.

To satisfy everyone, it would have had to be not a triple but a quintuple monarchy. The sequel to World War I and the dissolution of the Dual Monarchy showed this clearly; it dissolved into four or five small pieces, not all of which were stable. Statesmen feared to open up this Pandora's box lest the state die in the ensuing pandemonium, and so the status quo basically continued. Some concessions short of self-government were granted to Czechs as well as Poles. The result was what has been described as "an intricate hieratic system." In the hierarchy of subject peoples, the Poles and Czechs stood highest, the Slovaks and Romanians lowest; the Croats had gained a small measure of autonomy. The Austrian part of the empire was not very repressive, the Hungarian part more so. Whether, in a nationalistic age, there was any possibility of evolving politically in a way that would satisfy all or most of the twenty-eight million majority made up of minorities is doubtful. Adding to the complexities, in Vienna the Social Democratic party, akin to the German socialists and hostile to the monarchy, was growing stronger.

The troubles of the Dual Monarchy were not confined to its discontented minorities. The two "master races" also quarreled. The Magyars, regarding the Compromise of 1867 as virtually an alliance between sovereign states, insisted on complete independence in their part of the dual state and often refused to cooperate on matters of joint policy. Count Tisza's refusal in July 1914 to go along with the war policy of Vienna against Serbia (see p.58) was typical. Franz Ferdinand, the heir to the throne, was violent in his dislike of the Magyars, a rather typical Austrian feeling; in private, among his kindest adjectives for them were "vile, perfidious, and unreliable." That the crown prince played with ideas of a triple monarchy, having a third capital at either Prague or Zagreb, probably reflected more his dislike of the Hungarians than his love for the Slavs.

Under such circumstances, parliamentary government naturally could not work. There was a national parliament, elected by something near universal manhood suffrage after 1906, but it was normally a scene of wild disorder featuring obstructive practices and occasionally erupting into violence, as each of the ethnic groups used the Diet as a forum for the agitation of its own demands. These were sham battles, as the body had no real power. As in Germany, the real work of government was carried on by a fairly honest and efficient bureaucracy, which took its orders from the emperor. The aged Franz Josef (he was eighty-four in 1914 but still quite vigorous) was one of the most beloved figures in Europe. He had reigned ever since 1848. Many wondered if his death would not prove to be the signal for a breakup of the ancient empire.

On the other hand, the perpetual political crisis did not destroy this state, which was needed geographically and economically. In Vienna, the light-hearted city, people said in jest, "The situation is desperate but not serious." So matters stood when after 1905 the rise of the small but ambitious neighboring state of Serbia intensified the difficulties, as we describe in the next chapter, and led to a frightful world war as the price of the dissolution of the Dual Monarchy. When this work of dissolution was done, many wished that the old empire would come back again.

For Russia, the huge land that led Europe into Asia (from St. Petersburg to Vladivostok, where the trans-Siberian railroad terminated, was 7,000 miles), the nineteenth century had not on the whole been a happy one. At the end of the Napoleonic Wars, playing a major part in the peace settlement as the most important of those that had finally inflicted defeat on Napoleon, the state built by the great tsars, Ivan and Peter, and by Catherine the Great, ranked high among the powers. Its problem in the nineteenth century was an inability to keep up with the West technologically. It suffered, too, from the weakness of the rulers in a uniquely autocratic system: The tsars claimed total governing power in a way never known in the rest of Europe. The four despots who followed Alexander I (1801–1825) were not an impressive lot, to say the least, and may be said to have gotten progressively worse.

At the end of the reign of Alexander's successor, Nicholas I, the Crimean War into which he had blundered resulted in a humiliating defeat and exposed Russian technical backwardness. This shock led to perhaps the most momentous decision of the century, the emancipation of the serfs by decree of Alexander II in 1861. It affected 75 percent of the people of Russia. Serfdom, established by both Peter and Catherine to control agricultural production in the vast empty spaces of the Russian plains, seemed to be the albatross dragging down the clumsy Russian giant; hopelessly inefficient agriculture was tied to an archaic land system, akin to that which western Europe had known in the Middle Ages. But emancipation turned out to be no remedy, at least not an immediate one, for most of the peasants were forced to pay for their freedom, and in order to do so had to borrow money from the state, to be repaid over a period of forty-nine years. Until the redemption payments were completed, most of them remained in the traditional peasant communal village, farming in scattered strips and without individual initiative, much as always. Russian industry developed slowly, and capital had to be raised primarily through foreign loans (German and French, chiefly, especially French after the 1894 alliance), making Russia—one of the Great Powers by virtue of her sheer bulk—something like a colonial dependency! Despite heroic efforts to industrialize, especially under

Alexander III (1881–1894), she fell further behind; at the time of Emancipation her average per capita production was about half that of western Europe, while in 1913 it was only one-third.

To the problems of a backward economy and inept rulers, the Russians added that of a discontented and rebellious educated class or "intelligentsia." Adorning Russia with perhaps the most brilliant literature in the world (who could surpass Tolstoy, Dostoyevsky, and Chekhov?) along with a good deal of overall intellectual quality, the educated elite contained a revolutionary element frustrated by Russia's problems, ashamed of its backwardness, and unable to make contact with the vast mass of illiterate peasants whom they yearned to save. Disillusioned with the results of Alexander II's reforms, they eventually turned terrorist and climaxed a wave of assassinations by killing the tsar himself in 1881. All this proved futile, of course. The new tsar proved more reactionary than his father and drove the revolutionaries underground. In her history of revolutionary terrorism in Russia between 1894 and 1917, Anna Geifman counts over 17,000 victims, killed or wounded.

We have mentioned the second humiliation in war, that at the hands of Japan in 1904, and the revolution that followed. With the return of the troops, who proved loyal, this petered out; Nicholas II, last and most unfortunate of the Romanovs, in a moment of weakness and fright had promised a constitution and a legislature, but he reneged on this promise. Though the Duma remained in existence, it was so deprived of all power and representative quality that most Russian liberals thought it illegitimate. The autocracy remained; Nicholas II was as sure as his great-grandfather had been that he and he alone was the government of Russia. So did the revolutionary intelligentsia, destined to make another revolution in 1917; Lenin's was the fourth generation of Russian revolutionaries, reaching back to 1825. And, needless to say, the socioeconomic problems of Russia also remained. In the aftermath of 1905, a vigorous and enlightened statesman, Peter Stolypin, tried to reform the agricultural system by encouraging the more industrious peasants to become individual entrepreneurs. He was assassinated in a Kiev theater in 1911.

The Bolshevik faction of the Russian Social Democratic party, breaking away from the passivity of the majority Marxists, created a revolutionary underground. Too weak to contemplate war after her stunning defeat by the Japanese, Russia submitted to several diplomatic humiliations in the Balkan arena between 1908 and 1914. Despite such imposing problems, some optimists thought Russia was on the way to ultimate success and would eventually catch up with the rest of Europe. Her economic growth rate was among the highest in the world; she was building industrial plants and an infrastructure of railroads; the Duma, although nearly powerless, was learning the ways of parliamentary government. Russia had set her feet on the path of progress, they thought, and would continue onward and upward. Historians argue about whether the great 1917 revolution would have come had there been no war. The best answer seems to be that it was chiefly the terrible war that caused the downfall of the Russian state in 1917. But, for this too it had the ineptitude of the tsars to thank; for Russia found herself after 1890 deprived of her traditional friendship with the other eastern European monarchies and allied with faraway France against both Germany and Austria-Hungary.

The greater glories of the land of the tsars were undoubtedly cultural and intellectual. Until Leo Tolstoy's death in 1910, his home had been a shrine visited by people from all over the world; he was the nearest thing to a globally famous prophet, sage, and genius that this era afforded. A silver age of literature, art, and music arose in Russia just after the time of Tolstoy and Dostoyevsky; destined to be blighted by the Revolution, this generation of the

EUROPE BEFORE THE WAR, 1914

1900s testified to the vitality of Russian artistic genius. In 1911, London lost its customary aplomb in a rage for the intoxicating Russian ballet, nothing like which it had ever seen. In the international mixture of ideas and styles that Europe enjoyed, from Yeats's Ireland to Rachmaninoff's Russia, the Russians made not the least contribution.

It was—or it was not?—*la belle époque* of carefree happiness before the roof caved in, suddenly and unexpectedly, in late July of 1914.

2

The Coming of the Great War

SOME GENERAL CAUSES OF THE WAR

> I see the time approaching when the nations of the world, laying aside their political animosities, will be knitted together in the peaceful rivalry of trade; when the barriers of nationality which belong to the infancy of the race will melt and dissolve in the sunshine of science and art; when the roar of the cannon will yield to the soft murmur of the loom, and the apron of the artisan, the blouse of the peasant be more honorable than the scarlet of the soldier; when the cosmopolitan armies of trade will replace the militia of death; when that which God has joined together will no longer be sundered by the ignorance, the folly, the wickedness of man; when the labour and the invention of one will become the heritage of all; and the peoples of the earth meet no longer on the field of battle, but by their chosen delegates, as in the vision of our greatest poet, in "the Parliament of Man, the Federation of the World."

This effulgent prophecy appeared in a book written by an English socialist, G. Lowes Dickinson, in 1905. It is quoted not because it was unusual but because the sentiment was so commonplace that only the adornments of rhetoric could give it any distinction. (Dickinson meant it ironically.) The nineteenth-century ideologies of liberalism and socialism alike prophesied that war would become obsolete as the feudal warrior gave way to the industrial producer. Among popular statements on war in the 1900s, Norman Angell's *The Great Illusion* stood out, its title self-explanatory. There could no longer be any glory or profit in war. The international economy was too complexly interdependent to stand for such archaic interruptions. As the American radical Randolph Bourne put it (in 1914!), "Our modern civilization with its international bonds of financial and economic dependence is a civilization organized for peace and for peace alone." In his article in *International Conciliation,* June 1914, Bourne declared that war is "definitely and for all time relegated to the dusty limbo of the past" and "almost unimaginable" today.

Only a few cantankerous outsiders thought otherwise. The widely read H. G. Wells, among whose range of writings were science fiction novels, had imagined a "war for the world," predicting atomic weapons and aerial bombardments, eventualities reserved for World War II (*War in the Air,* 1908, and *The World Set Free,* 1914). But Wells later wrote that he didn't really believe his fantasies; "I will confess I was taken by surprise by the Great War." Almost everyone was. The learned international team of scholars who had just completed the impressive multivolumed *Cambridge Modern History* saw a rosy future in general for Europe; its treatment of the current international scene argued that the rather high level of armaments was a force for peace, making it too risky for any nation to think of war. They also stated that Germany was stabilizing central Europe and Russia had turned toward peaceful domestic development after 1905. These opinions were those of the overwhelming majority, educated and uneducated, radicals and conservatives.

So much for the art of prophecy. Domestic issues much overshadowed foreign ones in every country. Newspapers, journals of opinion, and parliamentary debates found little room for foreign affairs, compared to those questions of social welfare and political democratization that seemed so vital. Overseas crises, first the Boer War and then the Irish question, neither of which had anything at all to do with the outbreak of war in 1914, alone had bulked large in British opinion. An exception might be made for the naval race with Germany, which had inflated the government budget and helped cause a tax crisis. At the other end of Europe, Russia also paid far more attention to such issues as Peter Stolypin's land reforms than to any matter of foreign policy, and after the embarrassing performance of 1905 against Japan, most Russians regarded few things less favorably than the prospects of another war. Experiencing an economic boom, the tsar's empire was in the process of modernizing its economy and its army with the aid of French capital, but the process was far from complete. In July 1914, public attention centered on a series of industrial strikes.

No wonder the sudden outbreak of a major international war at the beginning of August caught everyone by surprise. The sobering lesson was that war could happen without anybody seeming to want it or to will it. All kinds of myths grew up later, as bewildered people attempted to explain the collapse of peace. As usual, conspiracy theories flourished. Allied propaganda alleged that the Germans plotted war; Wilhelm II, the unhappy German monarch, was depicted in the French and British press as a monster with tentacles reaching out to ensnare small countries. That "Prussian militarism" was the canker in the olive branch became an article of faith in France and England and later, after she had joined the war, in the United States. For their part, the Germans believed that jealous neighbors plotted to encircle and destroy a country whose only crime was her economic success.

Then, too, the theory arose that the capitalistic economic system, far from being a force for peace, had engineered the war because war was profitable or because there was competition for markets and raw materials. Although they may contain germs of truth, all such simple-minded "devil theories" must be dismissed as inadequate to the serious study of events, more interesting as folklore than as history.

Though it is tempting to look for it, no single all-embracing cause can successfully explain the war or any other major historical event. We can, of course, say that the basic cause was something like the "system of sovereign states"; this diagnosis led to the many schemes that proliferated from 1914 on for a League of Nations or an association of nations or even a world state. However, people must be politically organized in one way or another; one might almost as well say that the "people system" caused the war. One could cite human nature, or more specifically humanity's relentless pursuit of power. Such explanations are too general to take us far; human nature is the necessary condition for any human activity, but it does not explain why this particular war happened at this particular time. Were the sovereign states more sovereign, human nature more aggressive, power more sought after in 1914 than in 1890 or 1880?

We may get an idea of the differences of opinion among those who sought to account for the war by noting how contradictory the explanations were. Some blamed it on lack of democratic control over foreign policy; but others said that an erratic and frequently bellicose public opinion had taken over the reins of power from the professionals. The military was a favorite scapegoat; but in fact, one may argue, the generals were far from eager to go to war, and were both astonished and dismayed when it came. More realistically, scholars have frequently alleged that nationalism was more pervasive and intense than at any previous time and that the balance of power had been upset. These two key factors, one subjective and one objective, are worth keeping in mind amid the vast concatenation of possible causes of the outbreak of war in 1914.

On anybody's analysis, the situation was a complex one. The five major powers—Great Britain, France, Germany, Austria-Hungary, and Russia—dominated the scene. Of the other states of Europe, neither the Scandinavian nor the Iberian countries (Spain and Portugal) played any significant part in the coming of the war. Neither did the neutrals, Switzerland and the Netherlands, although Belgium was to be dramatically if unwillingly involved. Italy ranked as almost a great power and was a part of the alliance system. The role played by Serbia and less directly by the other states of the turbulent Balkans (Bulgaria, Greece, Romania, and what was left of Turkey in Europe) was crucial. The United States of America was a powerful factor in the background. The European powers were engaged in colonial rivalries all over the globe, sometimes involving quasi-independent native governments. And, each of the powers had a highly developed, extremely complex machinery of government and richly diverse societies, consisting of many different interests, ideologies, occupations, and organizations.

The states of Europe were like individuals living in a primeval state of nature marked by incessant strife between one and another. They acknowledged no higher authority that might have forced them to keep the peace. What was called "international law" was not in fact binding on them, being backed by no more than a moral or customary sanction. In the optimistic climate of the pre-1914 years, nearly everyone assumed that international law was making steady if slow progress. Attempts were made to secure agreement on laws of war providing for humane treatment of prisoners, sparing of civilians, and rights of neutral and belligerent ships to trade in nonmilitary materials. In the 1914–1918 war, as also in the 1939–1945 one, the worthlessness of such rules became evident in the very first days of the war, as each side ignored them if there was an advantage in doing so.

Two international conferences on world peace held at The Hague, Netherlands, in 1899 and 1907 tried to establish a world court for the settlement of disputes among states. But this court was no more than a panel of jurists available for the conciliation or the arbitration of a dispute if the quarreling states wished to use it; it had no power to compel them to use it or to hale them into court if they broke the peace. Nothing in the nature of a world state or a European state existed. Among themselves, the states had various agreements, which they could always find a reason for dishonoring were a vital interest involved.

Of course, states exchanged diplomatic representatives and negotiated treaties and other agreements with one other. The traditions surrounding this activity, reaching back to ancient times and particularly to the fifteenth century, were numerous and complex. But underneath the velvet glove of diplomacy one could see clearly enough the iron fist of national self-interest backed by armed force. Within this tradition, war, the ultimate court of appeals, had its recognized place. It was itself the formalization of violence. No one doubted the right of nations to declare war under certain circumstances. Not until after 1918 did people seriously think of "outlawing" war. War had always been thought to be justifiable in self-defense; so was coming to the aid of an ally under attack. But even an aggressive war, it was generally conceded, might properly be undertaken under certain conditions: to forestall later disaster by "checking the overgrown power of some ambitious neighbor" (Jonathan Swift), to avenge an injury, or to pursue some other just cause. Rebels and radicals had stressed that fighting a war for liberty from a tyrant or for the freeing of an oppressed people was noble. They had also said it was a nation's duty to aid others fighting in such meritorious causes. Some anarchists preached the holiness of revolutionary violence. Hegel, Marx, and Nietzsche, leading nineteenth-century philosophers, all approved of war, which the first two saw as a "locomotive of history" and the latter as a means of redeeming the souls of men.

More and more people had acquired a larger stake in defending the state. This was the natural result of democratization and increase in wealth. All over Europe, 1914 was to prove that the masses as well as the classes were militantly patriotic when they thought their country was being attacked.

In a situation of sovereign states unlimited by a higher law and backed by nationalistic public opinion, balance of power was one means of keeping peace. Power does check power; a state is less likely to attack another if it fears retaliation, and it is more likely to do so if it has no fear of encountering resistance. This principle had long operated in European affairs, often drawing many states together to check an overmighty power that constituted a threat to all. They had united against France, for example, both in the later seventeenth century and during Napoleon I's rampaging years at the beginning of the nineteenth century. The great 1815 peace settlement at Vienna that followed Bonaparte's defeat labored hard to secure a balance of power; it did so at the expense of nationalism, not apparently anticipating that nationalism would grow during the nineteenth century. And, in the 1860s–that decade in which so many crucial decisions were taken, from America to Russia–the unification movements in Italy and especially Germany dangerously threatened the balance. The new German Empire, uniting most of the German world under Prussian leadership, became the strongest power in Europe.

The genius of Otto von Bismarck, as Prussian chancellor, had forged the intricate policies that overcame all obstacles to German unification in three short and carefully planned wars between 1863 and 1871. Bismarck remained in power for nineteen more years and dedicated his skill to keeping the peace by preventing an alliance of Germany's foes. The arrival of a new emperor, the neurotic and theatrical Wilhelm II, who promptly dismissed Bismarck, upset the precarious equilibrium after 1890. A crucial decision was Germany's refusal to renew the so-called Reinsurance Treaty with Russia, regarding this as inconsistent with her primary friendship toward Austria-Hungary. And, in fact, Russia and the Dual Monarchy were on a collision course in southeastern Europe.

Russia's estrangement from the other two monarchies of eastern Europe was something new for Europe. The close cooperation of Hohenzollern, Hapsburg, and Romanov, often at the expense of Poland, had been a feature of European politics in the eighteenth and early nineteenth centuries. Now, as Russia and Austria-Hungary increasingly clashed over the possessions of the crumbling Ottoman Empire in southeastern Europe, and Germany backed Austria, Russia was left dangerously isolated. (The beginnings of this alienation may be traced back to the Crimean War of the 1850s when, at war with France and Britain over issues connected with the Ottoman Empire and the Straits, Russia expected help from Austria and didn't get it.) From this situation emerged the leading diplomatic bombshell of the 1890s: a treaty of alliance between Imperial Russia and Republican France that took shape between 1890 and 1894. Each promised to come to the other's aid in case of an attack by Germany.

This alliance alarmed Germany with fear of encirclement and encouraged her to think of ways to prevent being caught in a squeeze. The famous Schlieffen plan, which formed the basis of German strategy in 1914, assumed the necessity of knocking out France with a massive and speedy attack before the slow-moving Russians could mount an offensive on Germany's eastern front. The balance of power between the Franco-Russian bloc and the Austro-German one was also dangerous because Germany was rendered dependent on Austria-Hungary, an unstable state, while France was dependent on an equally unstable Russia. Russian and Austrian interests clashed in the turbulent region of southeastern Europe. They dragged their allies into their quarrel, thus maximizing what might have remained a local conflict. The danger of alliances in a precarious balance of power is that any small war can escalate into a major one.

The only other country with a significant stake in the alliances was Italy, whose role as a semi-great power was anomalous. Italy was a nominal member of the Triple Alliance with Germany and the Dual Monarchy, but this connection, dating from 1882, no longer coincided with Italian interests, and no one expected Italy to be an active partner. Italy's territorial claims were chiefly against Austria-Hungary. Her quarrel with France, which had led her into the German camp, was no longer a factor after 1904.

THE DIPLOMACY OF THE 1900s

Against this background, significant events in the early years of the twentieth century threatened to upset the delicate balance. A key to the unstable equilibrium was the role of the only uncommitted great power, Great Britain, which had refrained from alliances and sought to keep the scales even. Her movement in this decade was clearly toward commitment to the Franco-Russian side. This marked a considerable change, for in 1900 Great Britain clearly regarded Russia as her first enemy and France as the second. Favorably disposed toward the Central Powers, she had a considerable tradition of friendship with Austria-Hungary. Though the German naval law of 1900, which provided for an accelerated battleship building program, had just introduced a sobering note, Great Britain had no real quarrel with Germany. (The anti-British implications of the German naval expansion do not seem to have dawned on the British cabinet until late 1902.) One sensational book of 1895 predicted a war to the death for world markets between the two industrial powers, but it was an irresponsible potboiler. Queen Victoria, of German extraction and the grandmother of German Emperor Wilhelm II, had been notably pro-German and anti-Russian. In 1899, prominent British politician Joseph Chamberlain, a leading figure in the government, declared that "the most natural alliance is that between us and the German Empire." In 1900–1901, Britain almost concluded a formal treaty with Germany. The negotiations miscarried, leaving some mistrust on both sides.

Later, second-guessers blaming the mercurial kaiser decided that the Germans played too hard-to-get and overplayed their hand.

The British animosity toward Russia led to a treaty with Japan in 1902. This was the first breach of a long-standing British refusal to enter into alliances. Because of the tsar's supposed designs upon India as well as a general detestation of his despotic government, British opinion had long looked upon Russia as the chief enemy, and the Japanese alliance was clearly made with Russia in mind.

A further diplomatic revolution lay just ahead. Traditional foes from Louis XIV's time, if not all the way back to the Hundred Years War, France and England had fought for supremacy between 1778 and 1815, but they had enjoyed moments of friendship in the nineteenth century. They astonished the world by fighting on the same side (against Russia) in the Crimean War of the 1850s. But this outbreak of congeniality scarcely lasted, and the British resumed acute colonial rivalries with their old foe during the late nineteenth-century outbreak of imperialism. The French believed the British squeezed them out of Egypt and wrested control of the Suez Canal from its builders in 1882. Then in the summer of 1898, the British under Kitchener and the French under Marchand arrived almost simultaneously at the upper Nile village of Fashoda and hoisted rival flags. This was a kind of grand climax to the scramble for African territory, which resulted in the annexation of almost all of that continent in the last two decades of the nineteenth century, mostly by Britain and France. But war was avoided.

It often happens in diplomacy that after a grave crisis has been surmounted, the momentum of détente carries on to much better relations between the erstwhile protagonists. The reverse is also true: A missed chance for agreement can lead to a long slide downhill. It seemed to work this way with relations between Britain, France, and Germany between 1900 and 1905. They reversed themselves dramatically. Between Westminster and the Wilhelmstrasse mistrust grew, while between Westminster and the Quai D'Orsay it lessened. Among forces affecting this development was the long ascendancy in the French foreign office of an able minister, Theophile Delcassé, whose steadfast goal was reconciliation with Britain in order to confront Germany. Delcassé pursued the politics of *revanche* dear to embittered French patriots who vowed never to forget the loss of the provinces of Alsace and Lorraine to Germany in 1871.

On the English side, the new monarch, Edward VII, was pro-French. The king took one of the earliest initiatives of reconciliation when in 1903 he invited the president of the French republic over for a visit. The popularity of Edward and the changed mood of Edwardian times induced one of those switches in the mercurial public's mood, and a wave of Francophilia swept over the normally "frog"-hating English. As for the French, although they jeered Edward in the beginning, he quickly captured their hearts. At home in Paris, the jaunty British monarch like to holiday at Biarritz.

The issue of Morocco happened to come up at this time. One way to pursue an anti-German diplomacy was to tug at the loose ropes binding Italy to the Triple Alliance, and Delcassé was not one to overlook this. Italy and France had been parted by Italy's hurt pride at seeing France monopolize North African colonial acquisitions. The descendants of the Caesars had been humiliated in Ethiopia in one of the few defeats an African people pinned on Europeans in this era, and they watched the French take Tunisia, which lay just across from Italy. But in 1900 a treaty between France and Italy promised Tripoli (today Libya) to Italy; in return, Italy recognized that the kingdom of Morocco lay within the French sphere of influence. This naturally led to discussions with both Spain and Great Britain, whose interest in Morocco centered on Gibraltar and control of the Mediterranean straits.

The French asked for British recognition of their Moroccan supremacy (as a protectorate), provided British and Spanish interests were protected and freedom of trade guaranteed. In return, France agreed to give up her old objections to Britain's protectorate over Egypt, a sore point ever since 1882. Long negotiations went on in 1903–1904 on these points and a few minor ones, culminating in an agreement signed on April 8, 1904. It is a significant date in diplomatic history, to be placed alongside the 1894 Franco-Russian treaty of alliance. This agreement was not an alliance; but it settled outstanding differences between France and England and was greeted with enthusiasm in both countries as ushering in a new era of friendship. We might be inclined to say today that the exchange, in effect, of Morocco for Egypt was in the worst tradition of imperialist diplomacy, bartering non-European peoples like pawns. Then, however, it was hardly viewed in such a light. Almost everyone accepted as inevitable and right that the more advanced European countries should lead the African countries down the path of progress. In 1903, even Jean Jaurès, the French socialist leader, agreed that the French had a civilizing mission in North Africa. Few Frenchmen doubted it. Jaurès later attacked the Entente on the grounds that it caused a quarrel with Germany, not that it oppressed Morocco.

The *Entente Cordiale* between France and Britain was a severe setback for German diplomacy. Everyone, it seemed, had been consulted about the fate of that kingdom except the Germans and, of course, the Moroccans. Italy and Spain, second-class powers, had been involved, but not Germany. The answer, that Germany was not a Mediterranean power and had no particular interest in Morocco, did not impress Berlin. The German chancellor, Bernhard von Bülow, later wrote that Britain and France had "disposed arrogantly of a great and most important field of colonial interests, without even deigning to take the German Empire into consideration." The snub rankled.

While Kaiser Wilhelm and Bülow meditated responses, the Russo-Japanese War erupted. It tended to confuse the issues. Wilhelm, who was fond of expatiating on the "yellow peril," pulled for the Russians. On the other hand, in a bizarre episode, some Russian battleships fired on English fishing boats off the coast of England, mistaking them for Japanese torpedo boats, which set off an anti-Russian uproar in Britain. The Russian Baltic fleet, dispatched to the Far East after the Japanese had mauled the Russian fleet there, had to take the in-

Wilhelm II, Emperor of Germany.
(*Library of Congress.*)

credibly long route all the way around Africa; the trip took eight months and the fleet finally arrived to be promptly wiped out by the Japanese. The Germans helped the Russian fleet en route with supplies. The Dogger Bank episode between Britain and Russia was smoothed over with the aid of the French, while the Kaiser wrote to his cousin Nicholas, the tsar of Russia, suggesting an alliance of Russia and Germany against England.

As the Russian cause worsened in Manchuria and revolution broke out at home, the Germans were strongly tempted to take advantage of the grave weakening of the rival alliance. Morocco lay at hand as a seemingly worthy case, and the Germans chose to make this their ground by openly challenging the Moroccan arrangements and refusing to accept them as binding on Germany. In a dramatic gesture, the German emperor himself landed on Moroccan soil on March 31, 1905, posing as the defender of Morocco against the Anglo-French vultures about to swoop down upon it.

Delcassé, facing an angry Germany without an ally, had indeed overplayed his hand. While the realistic Clemenceau accused the foreign minister of maneuvering France into dangerous waters, the idealistic Jaurès attacked him for favoring reactionary Russia and not believing in Franco-German reconciliation. Even on the far right, which mistrusted "perfidious England," Delcassé found little support. He resigned on June 6. The Germans demanded a conference to take up the Morocco question, and this was granted.

This moment of German victory coincided with the depths of Russia's misfortunes. Germany did not threaten Russia but sought to cajole her. Wilhelm went off to meet the tsar at Bjorkoe, on the coast of Finland, where the two emperors emotionally agreed to a friendship pact. "A turning point in world history," Wilhelm called it; but the rather simpleminded Russian monarch had acted totally on his own without consulting his ministers, who managed to persuade him to withdraw the pact as inconsistent with the French alliance. And, Bülow also threatened to resign over the issue of the kaiser's personal diplomacy. This experiment in monarchical summitry misfired badly.

Moreover, the Morocco conference held in 1906 at Algeciras in southern Spain proved disappointing to the Germans. Among the powers invited to the conference, including the United States and Italy as well as France, Great Britain, Russia, and the Dual Monarchy, only the latter proved a loyal supporter of Germany. England and France tended to draw closer together. The new Liberal government of England did not prove more pro-German than its predecessor, as Germany had hoped it would. On the key issue of placing the Moroccan police power in the hands of the French and Spanish, only Austria-Hungary—and Morocco—voted with Germany in opposition. The French case was strengthened by the proximity of France and Spain to Morocco, France having long had control of neighboring Algeria, where many French lived. Morocco was believed to be in a state of near anarchy. Police power is best exercised by a single state rather than a condominium.

Bülow collapsed on the floor of the Reichstag and had to be given a long rest. Almost everyone thought that German diplomacy had failed. It had managed to alarm the world with a war scare without achieving anything, except to solidify the other side and leave Germany almost isolated. Forcing the fall of Delcassé might be counted a minor victory, but neither England nor Russia had been pried loose from the French connection, and England was even closer to France than before.

In France and especially in Great Britain the Germans were seen, perhaps wrongly, as making a bid for world sea power. Already alarmed by Germany's building of a strong war fleet, the British noted that if Germany got control of Morocco she would have ports on the Atlantic, thus breaking out of her confinement in the Baltic and North Sea. The powerful French right-wing publicist, Charles Maurras, wrote a widely read book, *Kiel and Tangiers,* coupling the Morocco bid with the widening of the ship canal linking the great naval base at Kiel on the Baltic with the North Sea. From 1905 dates the firm belief of many in France and at least a few in England that the kaiser and his circle meditated ambitious plans of world conquest. This was undoubtedly 90 percent fantasy. But its acceptance indicates a clumsiness on the part of German policy, whose game of pressure by threat had backfired.

In 1908, the main problems of Europe shifted to the southeast. It was in this area that the war of 1914 really began. Postponing consideration of this powder keg for the moment, let us pursue the relations of France, Britain, and Germany. Between the latter two, the naval question, the *Flottenlproblem,* became an increasingly painful one. The new British foreign secretary, Edward Grey, was by no means averse to improvement of relations with Germany. Unfortunately, there appeared at this time (1906) a new and superior type of battleship, the Dreadnought. This larger and stronger ship made all previous ones obsolete. This change in the mechanics of warfare tended to favor the Germans, in that more of the larger British fleet was outmoded. The previous British superiority no longer existed or was considerably reduced. The situation touched off a naval building race, as the Germans quickly mastered techniques that had originated in Britain.

The Germans could hardly be blamed for seeing a magnificent opportunity to steal a march on the proud monarch of the seas. For their part, the English regarded supremacy on the seas as their very life's blood, and the entire nation instinctively reacted to any threat to this supremacy. The high cost of this naval competition certainly stimulated adverse British reactions to Germany. There were some converts to the idea of an inevitable showdown with the kaiser. In 1909, spurred by stories of an accelerated German production of Dreadnoughts, the English were chanting, "We want eight and we won't wait." Prime Minister Asquith pledged that Britain would build two ships for every one the Germans laid down, which in fact Britain could do and did.

When, partly as a result of domestic battles, Bülow resigned the German chancellorship in 1909, opportunities for fresh attempts to diminish this unfortunate rivalry emerged. The new German chancellor, Theobald von Bethmann-Hollweg, who was to remain in that office until 1917, inspired more trust than his predecessor. There were reasonably sincere efforts on both sides to find a formula for naval peace. Though the experts in the British foreign office tended to mistrust Germany, self-interest dictated a limitation of the costly building race. On the German side, even the personification of the big navy program, Admiral Alfred von Tirpitz, friend of the emperor and a powerful influence on German policy, was prepared to go along with an agreement. Germans thought the death of King Edward VII in May 1910 removed a powerful enemy, but British policy clearly did not depend on the will of the king.

Despite occasional hopes, agreement proved impossible. The British insisted on keeping their naval supremacy at a ratio of two to one over the German fleet. The Germans would accept this only in return for political concessions amounting to a British renunciation of the entente with France, including a guarantee of British neutrality in the event of war involving Germany. This Britain would not give. Lengthy negotiations failed to find any middle ground. The Germans thought Britain owed them a concession for permitting her to maintain her naval supremacy, but the British considered this supremacy non-negotiable and wanted an agreement only on numbers of ships to keep down costs. The Germans thought the British more vulnerable than Germany to the financial pressure of such a race. In Berlin, the kaiser and Admiral Tirpitz were not willing to sell cheaply their fond dream of Germania, the queen of the ocean.

Evaluation of this important failure contributing to the collapse of peace in 1914 must take two factors into account. First, it was not unreasonable for the British to insist on naval supremacy and to refuse to regard it as negotiable, when one remembers that the navy was their essential defense. England had no large standing army, manned by conscripted soldiers, as did the Continental powers; her navy was also her army. It had to defend not only the homeland but the far-flung overseas empire. The whole history of England was built around sea power, and she depended on imports of food and primary materials for her livelihood. The navy was not so essential to Germany for either national defense or economic welfare. It is a luxury to you, a necessity for us, Churchill told the Germans.

Second, to ask for English neutrality in the event of war, which could plausibly be a Franco-German war, was to ask too much of a country dependent on a Continental balance of power. Could England stand by and watch France be defeated? Could she pledge her neutrality in such an encounter? On the other hand, the Germans had a legitimate interest in trying to break up or defuse what must have appeared to them as a dangerous and hostile coalition. Sea power seemed a trump card to play against England, and there was no sense in throwing it away. Thus it is hard to blame either side, though historical partisans have blamed both for arrogance and vainglory. And, some of Germany's own best political brains thought it a grave mistake to alienate England in this way for no sufficient reason.

THE BALKANS

A second Morocco crisis was to further muddy the waters of Anglo-French-German relations in 1911. Meanwhile, the center of attention shifted to the region that was to prove the cockpit of war in 1914. Not many in the Western capitals attached high importance to what occurred in the (to them) remote and rather miserable southeastern part of Europe, as infamous for its tangled blood feuds as for its unpronounceable names. Bismarck had once made the notable statement that the Balkan region was not worth the life of a single German soldier. Bosnia, Novibazar, and Macedonia were hardly household names in London or Paris. But in such places fate was preparing the outbreak of the Great War in 1914. (A British humorist once remarked that the Balkans produced more history than they could consume locally.)

In 1908, the ambitious minister of foreign affairs in Vienna, Lexa von Aehrenthal, believed the time had come for a bold initiative in foreign policy as

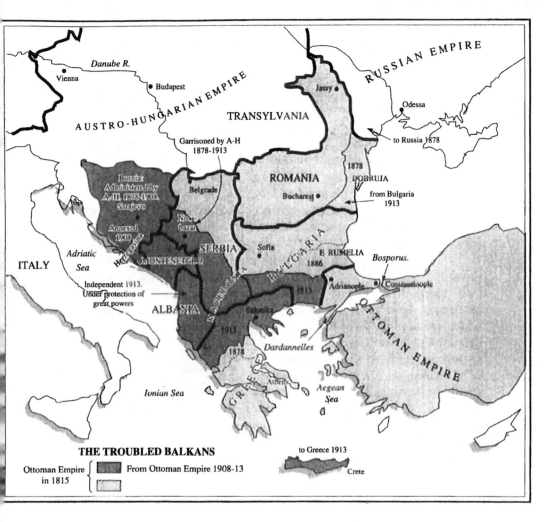

Vienna
Danube R.
Budapest
AUSTRO-HUNGARIAN EMPIRE
Jassy
RUSSIAN EMPIRE
Odessa
TRANSYLVANIA
to Russia 1878
Garrisoned by A-H
1878-1913
1878
Belgrade
ROMANIA
DOBRUJA
Bucharest
from Bulgaria
1913
Bosnia
Administered by
A-H 1878-1913
Sarajevo
Novi
Bazar
Annexed
1908
SERBIA
Sofia
Adriatic
Sea
MONTENEGRO
BULGARIA
E RUMELIA
1886
Bosporus.
ITALY
Independent 1913.
Under protection of
great powers
ALBANIA
MACEDONIA
1913
Adrianople
Constantinople
1913
OTTOMAN EMPIRE
1878
Dardanelles
Ionian Sea
GREECE
Athens
Aegean
Sea

THE TROUBLED BALKANS

to Greece 1913

Ottoman Empire
in 1815
From Ottoman Empire 1908-13
Crete

one way to solve the domestic difficulties of his deeply divided multinational
state. Traditionally, Austria-Hungary was content to follow Berlin's lead, since
she was the weaker partner. But Aehrenthal thought the time had come to
change this passive tradition. Helping him to this decision was the fact that the
little South Slav state of Serbia was being actively wooed by Russian diplomacy,
and Serbia was a source of propaganda aimed at stirring up discontent among
the South Slav (chiefly Croatian) subjects of Emperor Franz Joseph. The mounting conflict in the Balkans must be attributed in good part to three factors: first,
the reorientation of Russian policy toward Europe after the crushing rebuff in
the Far East in 1905; second, a palace revolution in Belgrade in 1903 that
brought to the throne of Serbia a pro-Russian dynasty; and third, the continuing

decay of the Ottoman Empire, culminating in the "Young Turk" revolution of 1908. All might be tied to the larger general force of nationalism.

Russian nationalists stressed Russia's Slavic mission. Speaking the Slavic tongue and sharing, to some extent, a Slavic culture with the Great Russians were the Poles; the Czechs and Slovaks; and the South Slav (Yugoslav) Serbs, Croats, and Slovenians. This common Slavdom by no means always meant brotherly affection; the Poles, for example, partitioned since 1795 among the three states of Russia, Germany, and Austria-Hungary, hated the Russian oppressor more than they did the Austrian. The Serbs had not always been pro-Russian, but the new ruling house, more popular and nationalistic, tended to look to Moscow as the big brother protector. Serbia's goal now was to escape from her vassalage to Austria, attain economic independence, and gain access to the sea. A small economic war went on between Serbia and the Dual Monarchy from 1906 to 1908.

Aehrenthal proposed to break up the Serbo-Russian threat. In 1878, a previous outbreak of the "Eastern question" had plunged Europe into a crisis from which Bismarck and Disraeli had rescued it at the Congress of Berlin. Since then, Austria had been permitted to administer Bosnia and Herzegovina, which adjoined the Dual Monarchy. These areas still formally belonged to the decrepit Ottoman Empire, whose decay was an underlying cause of the entire Eastern question. Austria could also keep some troops in the adjoining Sanjak of Novibazar, separating Serbia and Montenegro. These areas were populated chiefly by Serbs and Croats. Aehrenthal proposed to build a railroad through the Sanjak. The Russians challenged this as illegal. They felt that the move represented an attempt to extend Austrian influence further into the Balkans in order to forestall Russia and her client, Serbia. In this way, Austria could take steps against dangerous South Slav nationalist discontent within the Dual Monarchy.

The situation was soon complicated by the Young Turk revolution, which overthrew the despotic regime of old Sultan Abdul Hamid. The government of "Abdul the Damned," as Europe called him, had continued the low standards characteristic of the fading Ottoman Empire: cruelty, corruption, and almost every other possible mode of misgovernment. This government had scandalized the world for half a century and created most of the problems of the Balkans. In 1878, it had not been thrown out of Europe "bag and baggage," as British Prime Minister Gladstone demanded, but it had been considerably diminished. The sultanate still held some territory in Europe, including Thrace, which was coveted by Greece, and Macedonia, notorious for its anarchy. And, as we have noted, certain areas that still technically belonged to the Ottoman Empire were actually administered by others.

In Constantinople on July 24, 1908, young army officers engineered a palace revolution, which deposed the sultan. This revolution grew out of fears that the great powers would again intervene to put a stop to dreadful conditions in Macedonia, since all efforts to reform the sultan's government appeared to have failed. The immediate effects of the Young Turk revolution, however, were to sow more confusion and to cause European statesmen to think that now was the time to strike, while the Balkan iron was still hot and malleable. Aehrenthal struck again: On October 5, Emperor Franz Joseph proclaimed the outright annexation of Bosnia and Herzegovina.

This was a bombshell. Intrinsically, there was some merit in the proposal. The anomalous status of the provinces impeded their own progress, and they would probably be better off under Austrian rule, which was fairly progressive. But both Serbia and Russia were sure to object to the annexation. Aehrenthal was ready to offer Russia compensation in the form of opening the straits of the Dardanelles to Russian warships. He had discussed this with the Russians. But other powers had to agree to this change in the status of the strategically important straits, which involved treaties dating back to the Crimean War's settlement in 1856. While Russian Foreign Minister Isvolsky went off to Paris and London seeking to secure their agreement (vainly, as it turned out, in the case of England), Aehrenthal went ahead and announced the Bosnian annexation! At the same time, King Ferdinand of Bulgaria declared that his country was now completely independent rather than formally a part of the Ottoman Empire. Germany had not even been informed in advance of this startling move by her ally. Berlin at this time was in fact trying to woo Turkey.

The rage of Isvolsky, who felt he had been tricked, knew no bounds. Equally angry were the Serbs, whose country was to play a key role in the coming of the Great War. Inhabited by two and a half million people, mostly peasants, Serbia looked across the border to see some six million Serbs and Croats living under the rule of the Hapsburgs. It is true that between the Roman Catholic Croats and the Greek Orthodox Serbs some differences existed, which later hampered their efforts to live together (and still do). But at this time members of both communities declared they were a single people who should live together in an independent state. Serbia aspired to play the role that Prussia had played in the unification of Germany and Piedmont in the unification of Italy. She, together with her tiny sister, Montenegro, had been the first of the Balkan peoples to win independence from Turkey, and she had developed a strong sense of mission to liberate all the South Slavs, from Austria as well as Turkey, and to create a South Slav independent nation. This kind of mission was a noble one by all the standards of nineteenth-century ideology, summoning up the shades of Washington, Bolivar, Mazzini, and Garibaldi. Serbs believed in it with passion and courage. No account of the Balkan backgrounds of World War I could leave out this moral fervor. It must also be said that the terroristic methods employed by some Serbs—the assassination of June 28, 1914, was not the first—cost their cause much sympathy.

Obviously, the annexation of Bosnia struck a blow at Serbia's hopes. In fact, the major goal of Austrian policy here was to "root out the Serbian nest of revolutionaries." The new Turkish republican regime also naturally opposed the loss of the provinces, and it had more claim on sympathy than the contemptible tyranny it had just overthrown. Aehrenthal clearly was in trouble. His German ally was prepared to give but lukewarm backing. Yet in the face of the Austrian *fait accompli,* Russia and Serbia proved powerless. France and England, while arguing in behalf of Russia, were not prepared to go to war for her in this cause. British Foreign Secretary Edward Grey was not even willing to give Russia her "compensation" in the form of a revision of the Straits convention. Still suffering from the military trauma of 1905, Russia was not prepared to go to war alone. Turkey was bought off with a payment of money. The angry Serbs then had no choice but to back down, though for a time in 1909 an Austro-Serb war threatened.

German opinion was thrown into an uproar when on October 28, 1908, the London *Daily Telegraph,* one of England's largest newspapers, published an interview with the kaiser. Contrary to popular belief, Wilhelm declared, he was a true friend of England, offering as proof of this that he had even offered to give them a plan for winning the Boer War! He also assured his English friends that the German navy was aimed not at them but at Japan. The interview struck almost everyone as fatuous and caused a confrontation between Wilhelm and Chancellor Bülow, who eventually resigned. During the resulting storm in Germany, the kaiser was openly criticized from all directions. Though well-intended, the *Daily Telegraph* interview was a typical blunder on the part of the impetuous German monarch.

Despite this distraction, Germany stood loyally by Austria-Hungary during the Bosnian crisis, grumbling only in private. It was largely through German diplomacy that the crisis was wound down. The Bosnian crisis ended with Austria-Hungary annexing Bosnia, but at the price of having inflamed the Balkans, alienated Russia, and enraged Serbia. Omens were not good for the future; and the Balkans continued to simmer, down to the fateful moment of June 28, 1914. Indeed, they did more than simmer; they erupted into war in 1912–1913. France had failed to help her ally, Russia, in 1908, and thus felt impelled to stand by Russia the next time. Russia now had to back Serbia, and she embarked on a diplomacy of revenge in the Balkans.

Although it is difficult to moralize about the complex affairs of nations, and although Aehrenthal had excellent reasons for doing as he did, posterity has on the whole judged his 1908 initiative harshly. It stands out as a key moment in the drift toward war from 1904 to 1914.

FROM 1911 TO 1913

Morocco popped up again in 1911 as a touchstone of international rivalries. The outcome of the first Morocco crisis in 1905 had, of course, rankled in German hearts. As an aftermath of the Algeciras conference, Germany and France reached an agreement in 1909 by which, in return for French pledges to grant German economic interests equal rights with others in Morocco, Germany recognized the special French political position there, that is, her role as keeper of law and order. This did not work particularly well. In 1911, serious uprisings broke out in Morocco, making it necessary, for a time, for French troops to march into the capital city of Fez itself. The new German foreign secretary, Alfred von Kiderlen-Wächter, declared that this action violated the Algeciras agreement. To punctuate this point, a German gunboat, the *Panther,* landed at the Moroccan port of Agadir, on the excuse that the existing French-protected sultanate manifestly could not keep order and each state must defend its own citizens.

What the jovial, hard-boiled Kiderlen-Wächter wanted was compensation. If the French wanted to drop the pretense and assume sovereign power in Morocco, they might do so—but only if they gave Germany something in return. In the end, Germany got a slice of the French Congo as her reward for recognizing French supremacy in Morocco. The territory itself was not worth much. Kiderlen-Wächter evidently became a little frightened at the storm he had aroused and backed down, content with a formal victory. If a victory, it was hardly worth the price, for again the British reacted with strong indications of support for France. The spectacle of a German warship in an Atlantic port galvanized all the old British suspicions of a Teutonic menace.

The second Morocco crisis was most notable for the public excitement it engendered, evidence of an inflamed nationalism. The more popular sections of the press in Germany hailed the "Panther's spring" with glee and rejoiced at the thought of Germany at last wresting Morocco from the greedy hands of France. The French press cried for German blood. German opinion was disappointed when not Morocco but only a piece of the Congo passed into German hands. French opinion denounced the cession as surrender to blackmail. British opinion was aroused too, as Lloyd George, once a staunch peace man, took the podium to issue solemn warnings that England would never submit to international blackmail. It was at this time that word of secret Anglo-French military cooperation, begun in 1906, was allowed to leak out. These discussions, some later alleged, constituted a de facto British alliance with France, committing Britain to France's side in any Franco-German war. The two governments had secretly agreed to remove most of the British fleet from the Mediterranean, which the French took over, leaving the Royal Navy free to guard the North Sea against Germany's growing sea power.

The diplomatists themselves kept cool; Kiderlen-Wächter and the veteran French ambassador, Jules Cambon, actually seemed to have enjoyed the game. Yet the general public was not playing the game at all in this spirit. That this somewhat petty, if not sordid, squabble over colonial spoils, mixed with the politics of vindictiveness, could shake the structure of peace was not reassuring. Perhaps by this time nerves were raw from other rubbings. For the Balkans had entered the picture, first with the protracted Bosnian crisis of 1908, next with an Italian attack on Turkey, then by preparations for the two Balkan Wars of 1912–1913. Out of these grew the last fateful crisis of 1914.

The Italian attempt to seize Tripoli from the weakening hands of

Turkey (as the Ottoman Empire was called after 1908) is a kind of link between the two zones of conflict, the French-British-German competition centering on Morocco and on sea power, and the Balkan rivalries of Russia, Austria, and Serbia. For in order to buy Italy's support for the *Entente Cordiale* and win her away from the Triple Alliance, France had promised to support Italian claims to Tripoli at an appropriate time. The Italians thought that time had come and, inflamed by nationalism, sought to make amends for former humiliations and garner a share of imperial glory.

Wounded though he was, the Turk proved a stubborn foe. This involvement of their enemy in turn prompted the Balkan League, a union of Serbia, Bulgaria, and Greece, which had been formed in 1912 with the encouragement of Russia, to attack Turkey and drive her entirely out of Europe, seizing Thrace and Macedonia as well as the Sanjak of Novibazar. The Turks hastily made peace with Italy on the latter's terms, thereby losing Tripoli. Rather surprisingly, however, they still could not cope with the Balkan states in the First Balkan War of 1912. The Bulgarians overran eastern Macedonia and most of Thrace; the Serbs liberated part of Macedonia and the Sanjak; the Montenegrins seized the port of Scutari; and the Greeks were successful in southern Macedonia and Epirus. Serbs and Bulgars joined forces to take the important Thracian city of Adrianople. The Turk was now out of Europe "bag and baggage," except for a very small segment of Thrace. The island of Crete also passed to Greece.

The results of the First Balkan War were a disaster for Austria-Hungary and even alarmed Russia somewhat, the tsar's government having no desire to see the Bulgarians take Constantinople. Trying to regain control of the bad children in the Balkans, the Great Powers held a conference at the end of 1912 to deal with the problems. The London meeting forced Serbia away from the sea by creating an independent Albania. At one point in November 1912, the powers seemed to stand on the brink of war, Germany backing Austria and Russia committed to Serbia. The Russians again backed down, feeling unprepared for war, and accepted a defeat for Serbia. What was ominous about this was that Russia could not afford time and again to be humiliated and might next time desperately refuse to retreat.

The Balkan pot continued to boil. The victorious allies of the Balkan League proceeded to quarrel over the spoils. In July 1913, Bulgaria attacked Serbia and Greece, but she was soon defeated when Romania, previously not involved, fell on Bulgaria from the north. In August, Bulgaria was forced to make peace, granting the lion's share of Macedonia to Serbia, surrendering the important Aegean port of Salonika to Greece, and ceding territory on her northeast border (the Dobruja) to Romania. The Turks also regained some of Thrace. Again, Austria-Hungary reacted with alarm, forcing Serbia to remove troops from Albania; but the outcome nevertheless was a considerably enlarged Serbia, almost double her former size.

In hindsight, one can see the two Balkan wars of 1912–1913 setting the

A 1912 cartoon depicts the plight of the five Great Powers in the Balkans. (*Courtesy* Punch.)

THE BOILING POINT.

stage for the explosion of 1914. They heightened the tension between Serbia and Austria and applied mounting pressure on Serbia's and Austria's allies to support them. A final showdown between ambitious, rising Serbia and powerful but vulnerable Austria-Hungary, fearful of her many minorities, was clearly indicated. The question was whether this conflict could be kept localized. From the vantage point of London or Paris, these events seemed remote and somewhat bizarre; few there could believe they threatened a general European war. But what if a desperate Austria tried a double dose of Aehrenthalism—the destruction of Serbia as a solution for domestic problems? Would not Russia back Serbia, leading to a shootout between Hapsburg and Romanov for the entire southeastern theater? Could Russia let Serbia down again, and could France leave Russia in the lurch as she had in 1908? Did Germany have any other choice than to support her sole ally, Austria-Hungary? In 1914, statesmen found themselves prisoners of the past.

Acute observers in 1913 were already reading the future gloomily. In an article written for the *Vienna Neue Freie Presse* on March 23, 1913, the distinguished German scholar Gustav Schmoller asked, "Will the Balkan flame leap over to the Great Powers?" He answered that while he believed this time the European diplomats would overcome the crisis, "the storm will sooner or later return." Later the same year, French diplomatist Paul Cambon wrote privately, "Despite my usual optimism . . . I begin to find the atmosphere a bit charged. A great deal of calm and discretion will be needed to reestablish the equilibrium which is now disquietingly unstable."

In March 1913, the Reichstag voted to increase the German Army by more than 130,000 men, added to its existing size of some 800,000. Simultaneously, the French government proposed to lengthen from two to three years the term of military service which every able-bodied Frenchman was required to give. Fiercely debated, the measure was finally approved. Russia and Austria-Hungary took similar steps, increasing international tension. Late in 1913, in Alsace, at Zabern, an incident that was trivial in itself took on international significance in the light of Franco-German abrasiveness. Conversations between Germany and England led to settlement of minor colonial matters but failed again to reach agreement on the big problem of naval limitations. Russia and Germany bickered over the presence of a German general as adviser to the Turkish army, which was being reorganized. No one would have remembered these affairs except that they later seemed like straws in the wind before the gale.

THE IMMEDIATE ORIGINS OF THE WAR

The war was evidently brought on by a conjunction of three basic clashes: the rivalry of Austria-Hungary and Russia in southeast Europe, the Franco-German hostility reaching back to 1871, and the naval competition between Germany and Great Britain. On the other hand, not all issues ranged Germany and Austria against the French-British-Russian combine. The British retained a considerable measure of mistrust of Russia. If it came to a simple choice between Russia and Austria in the Balkans, British opinion would have voted overwhelmingly for Austria, with whom traditionally Britain had no quarrel. There was little enthusiasm in London for seeing the Great Bear on the Straits, as 1908 had proved. Not long before 1914, the French tried to draw Russia into the joint military planning of the Entente, but after an initial expression of interest Grey turned away from this. As an experiment in cooperation with Russia, Persia, which was divided between Great Britain and Russia in 1907, turned out to leave something to be desired. Definitely committed to France against Germany, the British were by no means committed to Russia against Austria or anybody else. Their ambivalence in 1914, which may have been dangerous, reflected this fact.

Everything was ready for the spark that set off the explosion. Serbia, more powerful and more ambitious as a result of the Balkan wars, redoubled her propaganda and her intrigues against the Dual Monarchy. In the latter's councils of state, there were powerful voices raised in favor of settling with Serbia once and for all. The assassination of Franz Ferdinand, nephew of the old emperor and heir to the throne, on a visit to Bosnia, the storm center of Serb-Austrian rivalry, was so obviously provocative an event that all kinds of suspicions about it have naturally existed. Conspiracy theories flourished. Did the Serbian government or at least prominent Serbian circles contrive the murder? Or did Franz Josef's high ministers deliberately sacrifice the crown prince to provide a good excuse for wiping out the troublesome Serbs? Or was it simply the action of one man who unknowingly pulled the trigger on the greatest war yet in human history? The assassination of June 28, 1914, gave rise to as many controversies and versions as did the assassination of John F. Kennedy in 1963. Charges were made that prominent persons in Austria-Hungary and even Germany plotted it, if not to provide the excuse for a premeditated attack on Serbia, then to get rid of the archduke because of his views on reform within Austria-Hungary: Franz Ferdinand was thought to favor a devolution to grant the Slavs more autonomy. Many wondered why the archduke went to so dangerous a place on the very day the Serbs commemorated the loss of their independence to the Turks in 1389. Why were police precautions so lax? And, on the other hand, Austria-Hungary labored to show that the terrorists who struck down the crown prince were helped by or encouraged by the Serbian government.

The murderer was a restless, idealistic, and alienated youth of a type all too familiar in the modern world. He had failed in school. His head was filled with an intoxicating cloud of the ideas available at the end of the nineteenth century—socialist, anarchist, Nietzschean. Though a resident of Bosnia and technically a citizen of the Dual Monarchy, Gavrilo Princip was a passionate Serb patriot. He and his two nineteen-year-old fellow conspirators were members of the Union of Death, or Black Hand, a secret Serbian terrorist society that received aid from the Russian government. The Serbian government knew of its activities but feared to destroy it because of public opinion. The Serbian prime minister even received intimations of the plan to assassinate Franz Ferdinand and tried obliquely to tip off the Vienna government, but he failed to get the message across. The youths were smuggled to Belgrade, where they received training and weapons, then smuggled back across the border with the aid of Serb customs officials. The top man of the Black Hand was the chief of intelligence of the Serbian General Staff, but the Serbian government as such did not support him and did not want war with Austria at this time, the Serb army having yet to recover from the Balkan Wars of 1912–1913. The assassin was thus not acting as an agent of the Serbian government; yet the government failed to take steps against the Black Hand and against inflammatory anti-Austrian propaganda, which streamed from the Belgrade press. Under international law, the Serbian government could be held responsible for acts of violence emanating from its borders against a foreign country.

Such were some of the details eventually disclosed about the assassination, surely history's most fateful one. The emperor's government in Vienna scarcely needed most of these details to reach the decision that the time had come to settle with Serbia once and for all. The foreign minister, now Count Leopold Berchtold, believed it necessary "to make Serbia forever powerless to injure the Dual Monarchy." The influential army chief of staff and practically everyone else in the Austrian government agreed that "the very existence of Austria-Hungary was at stake" and that the assassination, which turned world opinion against the Serbs, was too good an opportunity to pass up. But the reluctance of the old emperor and especially of the Hungarian prime minister, Count Stefan Tisza, who did not want Serbia annexed to Austria-Hungary, delayed an immediate ultimatum to Serbia. Berlin was consulted, too, and on July 5 Germany sent assurances of support, the so-called blank check, to Vienna to deal with the Serbs as she saw fit. The delay may have been costly.

It is possible, even probable, that a quick strike at Serbia within a few days after the assassination, while world opinion was still strongly against the Serbs, would have been allowed to pass. The effect of the German approval was to doom all resistance to the Serbian war in Vienna, but Tisza managed to delay matters a few days. Then for various reasons there was a delay of several more days. One reason appeared to be a desire to wait until French President Poincaré, who left for a visit to Russia with his foreign minister on July 16, was on his way home again. For obvious reasons Vienna did not want the message received while the two allies were meeting together. Also, the Austrians waited for completion of the investigation providing evidence for Serbian complicity in the assassination plot. Not until July 23 did the ultimatum find its way from Vienna to Belgrade.

By that time, the psychological moment had passed. Most people believed the crisis was over. Lloyd George in England made a speech declaring that conditions for peace were steadily improving in Europe! On July 9, British undersecretary Arthur Nicolson "expected the storm to blow over." When it blew up again, people were inclined to blame Austria. The ultimatum dispatched to Serbia was, Grey claimed, the most formidable document ever sent by one state to another. It demanded not only rooting out all the terrorists in Serbia but also ending anti-Austrian propaganda in Serbia, thus implying the suppression of newspapers engaging in this activity. To this end, it demanded that Austrian officials be allowed into Serbia to oversee the work and to keep an eye on educational practices. The note was a severe ultimatum in that it demanded either a total acceptance by the Serbs within forty-eight hours or else war. It was not expected or even desired in Vienna that the Serbs would accept these terms; they were the preliminary to a war against Serbia. But in deference to Hungarian wishes, Serbia was not to be destroyed, only forced into the role of accepting Austrian tutelage, much as minor Latin American countries had to allow the United States to police them.

If this crushing communication made a bad impression in Europe, the reply of the Serbs was a triumph. Within the stringent time limit, they produced what a prominent Austrian diplomat himself called "the most brilliant specimen of diplomatic skill" he had ever known. It accepted almost all the Austrian demands, rejected some on clear constitutional grounds, and suggested arbitration of these by the Hague court or a conference of the great powers. The note breathed a spirit of sweet reasonableness and seemed to remove all cause for war, despite its technical failure to meet all the sweeping Austrian demands. Even Wilhelm, the German emperor, believed that "every reason for war disappears," while explaining that the Austrian note had been composed without Berlin's knowledge.

But Austria had already set its war machinery in motion and was of no mind to stop it. The order to mobilize went out as soon as the forty-eight hours were up, on July 25. Eight army corps were ordered up; the other states did not know that they would not be ready until August 12. Mobilization was a process that played a critical part in the unfolding tragedy. Although the order to mobilize was thought to mean war, it took up to twenty days to bring the troops to a war footing. Germany could do it fastest; Austria Hungary was relatively slow; and the Russians were slowest of all because of their great distances and relatively poor transportation facilities. When Austria mobilized eight corps, Russia felt impelled to begin mobilizing, too.

On July 28, Austria-Hungary declared war on Serbia. A few bombs were dropped on Belgrade the next day. Russia decreed a partial mobilization of four districts, including Kiev and Odessa near the Balkan front. She had evidently received assurance of French support from the hawkish French ambassador in St. Petersburg. By this move, St. Petersburg intended to show that it was prepared for a possible war only against Austria, in defense of Serbia. This in turn stimulated the Austrians to escalate their mobilization to a total one. They were urged to this course by a telegram from the chief of the German General Staff, Helmuth von Moltke, leading to Berchtold's famous reaction: "Who then is giving the orders in Berlin?" Chancellor Bethmann-Hollweg was going the opposite route, trying to restrain the Austrians. And then Russia, on the thirty-first, changed its partial mobilization to a total one. Thus began the day that plunged Europe into the worst of wars.

Volumes have been written about the Russian mobilization order, which was all-important in that it frightened Germany into taking measures designed to defend the Reich against a Russo-French squeeze. In a sense, however, the issue was a meaningless one. If Russia went to war with Austria, Germany would have to help Austria by waging war on Russia. There was no escape from the balance of power logic via partial mobilization. Almost everyone thought the tsar's government did not want war, certainly not war with Germany. Russia felt compelled to back up the Serbs and was gradually forced to the conclusion that a war with Austria-Hungary could not be avoided if Vienna insisted on assaulting the "little brother" in which Russia had invested so much political capital. But Russia had every reason to try to keep this war localized. The decision for total mobilization lay at the door of her military men, who were aware of Russia's backwardness and terrified of being caught napping. If it did come to general war, of which there undeniably was grave danger, Germany could attack Russia within a matter of a few days because of her much more efficient railway network and shorter distances to the frontier. The Russian regiments, summoned from all over the vast country so inadequately served by railways, would take weeks to assemble in military preparedness on the western borders.

The generals managed to convince the tsar and his foreign minister, Sergei Sazonov, that immediate total mobilization was essential. Nicholas took this decision with every indication of sadness and even a sense of doom. He did not want war with Germany, toward which he felt almost an affection (he had always gotten on well with his cousin the German emperor). Yet he saw no alternative.

The Russians sought to explain that their general mobilization did not necessarily mean war, that it was an essential precaution related to the peculiar circumstances of their country. But now there was no restraining the German generals from mobilization. Military imperatives were taking over. There is certainly a sense in which the Germans, too, did not want war. They (Bethmann-Hollweg and the kaiser) had come to regret the impulsively given blank check of July 5; they remembered Bismarck's advice not to be dragged into a war by Austria for Austrian purposes. Did Germany really have that much at stake in the Balkans?

Plans for some compromise solution, by which Austria would get satisfaction and security from Serbia without war, emanated from the Wilhelmstrasse in the July 25–30 period. But Russian mobilization aroused the terror of encirclement. On July 31, a German ultimatum demanded that Russia cease mobilization; another addressed to France asked what course France intended to follow in the event of war between Russia and Germany. The ultimata had twelve- and eighteen-hour time limits, respectively, and the threat was of German mobilization. If the French did agree to neutrality, they were to be asked to pledge the frontier fortress cities Toul and Verdun as bond!

The Russians answered with a curt "Impossible!"; the French did not deign to answer at all. On August 1, Germany declared war against Russia, and France issued mobilization orders. At the same time, the French urged the British to announce that they would fight to defend France in the event of a German attack. Westminster, with a divided cabinet, would not do so. Some have thought they should have, and that this might have been the last hope for peace. Although this seems unlikely, the irresolution of the British government was hardly helpful. The Germans waited two days, until August 3, to declare war on France, out of a lingering hope that Britain might stay neutral if France could be induced to declare war first. A Russian-German war would certainly not draw her in; no Englishman would have fought for Russia in a war limited to the east of Europe. But in a German-French war, the likelihood of British intervention had to be rated high, whatever London might say—especially if the Germans took the initiative.

Unfortunately, as we know, the German war plans hinged on an early attack in the west, through Belgium into France, as the strategy to break the two-front nutcracker. France could thus be knocked out before the Russian army was ready. In 1870, Prussia had smashed France within a matter of weeks; in 1914, Germany was even stronger compared to France than she had been then. The strategy could hardly fail, German officers believed, but it depended on speed of execution. Furthermore, the plan as modified since 1871 required an attack through neutral Belgium, the French having heavily fortified the Franco-German border. For the English, this was certain to prove decisive. It would also put Germany generally in a bad light throughout the world, as a violator of a neutral state pledged by international agreements. Germany would begin the war and begin it as a treaty breaker. Such were the plan's grave political defects, which did not overcome its military advantages in the eyes of Germany's policy makers.

SOME FINAL CONSIDERATIONS

Thus the war began, to the incredulity of most of the world, when the Germans marched into Belgium on August 4. All bluffs had been called. On the eve of the war, a German diplomat (Ruedorffer) wrote a book in which he declared that diplomacy had become a game of bluff entirely, since no one wished to make war. Everyone bluffed with increasing recklessness, arguably because each was sure the bluffs would never be called. Thus the widespread feeling that in the end no one would really go to war may have contributed to the coming of war. One gambles for high stakes if one is pretty sure one will never have to pay. But there had been too many uncalled bluffs for the game to continue this way. The moment of reckoning finally came.

Controversy about the origins of the war both during the war and after it, when more data became available, became a major scholarly industry, as well as a continuing popular polemic; it is perhaps the classic historical debate. Such debates are in the end not entirely resolvable, since unprovable value judgments as well as factual evidence are involved. However, a good many things were eventually decided beyond reasonable doubt.

Only the least critical can believe in a deliberate plot of aggression. The nations were prisoners of their fears, and all acted as they thought they had to in self-defense. Austria-Hungary certainly willed the destruction of Serbia and was ready to go to war to achieve it; in this sense Vienna was guilty, and her policy from 1908 on was both aggressive and reckless. But public opinion throughout the Dual Monarchy was convinced that the very existence of the state was at stake. Not a German nor an Austrian but a British commentator, the fair-minded G. L. Dickinson, conceded that no state in existence "would not under similar circumstances have determined, as Austria did, to finish the menace, once for all, by war." Serbia had attacked her with words and deeds, with propaganda and murder when she was already mortally menaced by internal crisis. The old emperor, Franz Josef, was not a warmonger but the most respected gentleman in Europe; yet in the end he saw no other solution (it is not correct to say that Berchtold and Conrad von Hotzendorf tricked him).

The whole conduct of the Austrians during the final crisis speaks against any preconceived plan to wage war. As we know, their long delay may even have been one cause of the war. Had they been prepared to swoop down on Serbia within hours or even days of the murder, they probably could have carried it off without reaction from the other powers. But they delayed, argued, and finally after nearly four weeks produced not an attack but an ultimatum—and they began mobilizing their troops, which took three more weeks, only after Serbia's reply to the ultimatum. This was the response of both a cumbersome bureaucracy and a divided council, reflecting less an iron will to war than a floundering about from which war was a kind of last resort.

It is equally hard to blame the Serbs, who were in the grip of nationalism, for wanting to unite the South Slavs. It is futile, too, to blame nationalism itself. A deeply human emotion, nationalism was backed by the force of powerful nineteenth-century ideologies, and it appealed especially to peoples who had lived in the shadows of history, backward and ill-treated, and who wanted to assert their dignity and worth. We would have to condemn Washington and Lincoln, Bolivar and San Martin, Joan of Arc, Martin Luther, and Martin Luther King—indeed, condemn virtually the whole of modern history—if we were to reject nationalism.

One school tried hard to shift the blame from the Central Powers to Russia, noting how deviously the Russians intrigued in the Balkans after 1908. They helped organize the Balkan League and poured money into Serbian terrorism. By backing Serbia in 1914, they converted a local conflict into a general war. They were greedy for the Straits. But Russia could plead legitimate interest in the fate of fellow Slavs and in the need for access to the sea. The humiliation of 1908 damaged the tsar's prestige and made future diplomatic defeats unacceptable. Many sins can be laid at the door of the tsar's government, no doubt, but it did not want war in 1914. It simply saw no honorable alternative to backing a client and ally against the threat of extermination that would ruin Russia's status forever throughout southeastern Europe. The prestige of great powers may strike us as unworthy, but it exists as a brute fact of political life and human nature. Russia's severe internal problems made the tsar's throne itself shaky, as 1905 had shown; he felt unable to afford another international humiliation.

During the war and for a long time afterward, most people in England and France assumed that Imperial Germany had plotted war and that the kaiser was a great criminal. But in fact, Berlin did not call the shots in the Balkan crisis; she was as unconsulted by Count Berchtold in 1914 as she had been by Lexa von Aehrenthal in 1908. On the eve of the war she was trying to restrain Austria as best she could. Erratic, impulsive, on the whole a misfortune for his people and for Europe, Wilhelm did not want war in 1914 in any deliberate sense.[1] The Germans suffered severely from the fear of encirclement for understandable reasons. They were surrounded by the hostile Franco-Russian team, believed they had been deliberately snubbed in 1904, thought the English arrogantly denied them great-power status on the seas. When the German emperor told the American emissary Colonel E. M. House just before the war that "every nation in Europe has its bayonets pointed at Germany," he was doubtless sincere. Germany in 1914 simply could not afford to abandon her last ally, Austria-Hungary, in her hour of need. The plans that dictated Germany's aggression against Belgium, right or wrong, were the fruits of long consideration on how to avert disaster in a two-front war.

French diplomacy pulled off the most brilliant but most dangerous coups of the preceding decade by winning first Russia and then Britain as allies, breaking out from the isolation that Bismarck had imposed on France. (She was helped in this feat, of course, by German ineptness.) French desires for a return to a position of preeminence in Europe were understandable in view of the shock and humiliation of 1871, feelings that were kept alive by the German annexation of Alsace-Lorraine. Equally natural was her fear of her much more powerful neighbor to the east, which possessed a mighty army, a greater population by far (some sixty-five million, compared to forty million people), and an increasing industrial superiority. France needed allies to feel secure against the threat of Germany. France certainly did not want war in 1914, but she felt, like Germany, that she could not abandon an ally, the more so because she had previously let Russia down. If Germany could not see Austria crushed by Russia, France could not stand by while Germany and Austria smashed Russia.

British diplomacy has been blamed for irresolution, not only by others but by the English themselves; Lord Derby expressed a common view when he remarked in 1920, "I have always believed that if Germany had known we were going to range ourselves along side of France, she would never have unleashed the offensive." But this irresolution was inherent in the British position. Moreover, Derby's proposition is questionable, if only because the Germans counted on a quick victory over France, a victory that the British, who kept no large standing army, would be able to affect very little. The British cabinet was divided on going to war even after the German invasion of Belgium. Two cabinet members resigned over the issue. Most British citizens saw no advantage in supporting Russia. Britain was not committed to the defense of France by any formal alliance. In reality, it was impossible for Britain to allow Germany to overrun France, but British reluctance to be drawn into the maelstrom of the Continent's alliances was old and deep-rooted. Lord Morley, in his memorandum on resignation from the cabinet, said, "If Germany is beaten and Austria is beaten, it is not England and France who will emerge preeminent in Europe. It will be Russia. Will that be good for Western Civilization?"

---

[1]German historian Fritz Fischer claimed that the kaiser and his war chiefs decided on war in a December 1912 meeting, but this has not stood up.

A great majority finally disagreed; but since British opinion rested on such nebulous calculations about the balance of power, rather than on direct and obvious interests, it was necessarily uncertain. Eyre Crowe's key memorandum of July 24 asked, what if Germany crushed France and stood on the Channel, with her sea power as well as her military might? But Crowe, notably anti-German, also raised the question, what if France and Russia won by themselves? Or were defeated and then joined Germany in an attack on Britain? The only conclusion was that to defend her interests Britain had to enter the war, one way or another! It may be noted that Germany offered the British assurances that she would annex no French, Belgian, or Dutch territory as a result of the war if Britain would remain neutral.[2]

If it is difficult to make any one state the villain, it is equally hard to blame any one class or economic interest group. It is an illusion to suppose that great capitalists or financiers had much direct influence; few of them were anywhere near the corridors of power. A fairly small body of professional diplomatists made policy. In the last analysis, a handful of men committed Europe to the flames in 1914. Of all types represented in this ruling political elite, men of business were the least prominent. In Russia and very largely in Austria and Germany, the diplomatic corps was a last preserve of the aristocracy; it was filled with people who abhorred businessmen as vulgar. The Liberal government of Asquith and Grey in England, devoted to social reform in its domestic policies, was not known for its closeness to capitalistic economic interests. The news of the war caused stock markets to plunge all over Europe, and Lloyd George reported finding no man of finance or industry in the country who was not appalled by the war, which they thought would bring socialist revolution.

The prime minister and the foreign minister of France were both (independent) socialists, and the socialists as well as the trade unionists rallied enthusiastically in support of their countries, forgetting whatever vows they had made to internationalism. This was also true of the intellectuals—the vast majority of writers, artists, historians, scientists, clergymen, all hailed, blessed, and delighted in the war at its beginning. The later attempt to find scapegoats for what was at its start "the most popular war in history" cannot conceal this fact. A war into which professional politicians had blundered could not have been waged for more than four years without the nearly total commitment of popular opinion.

The argument occasionally presented that Europe's leaders deliberately sought war as a way out of severe domestic difficulties is also preposterous. A superficial case for it, based on circumstantial evidence, can be made. There were serious problems at home. Asquith, just after the assassination and before

---

[2]Psychohistorians have suggested that German and English diplomats disliked each other because of differing customs of childhood and upbringing. However that may be—and it is not clear why they should have liked each other before 1900 and disliked each other after that if persisting family patterns were involved—there are certainly some examples of a peculiar cultural antipathy, of which Crowe is among the most notable. During the war, the German-English animosity was greater than that between any other two peoples, on a personal basis.

the magnitude of the Serbian crisis became apparent, remarked to a friend that he welcomed it because it would take people's minds off Ireland! But it would be grotesque to argue that Britain helped rig up a war to escape from the Irish question. As we know, it is correct to say that Austria-Hungary regarded the elimination of Serbia as a solution for the minorities problem at home. But she did not want, and hoped somehow to avoid, general European war. There were serious strikes in Russia, serious constitutional issues in Germany on the eve of 1914. But these had existed many times before without bringing war. Social conditions generally in 1914 were not worse but better than they had been in 1878 or 1885 or 1898, and war had been averted in each of those years. Anyway, it was no answer to leap from internal fire into external frying pan. Nicholas of Russia was sadly aware that a war would bring down his regime. Regimes weakened by threat of revolution can seldom afford the risk of war. A threat of internal dissolution did exist in Austria-Hungary and possibly in Russia, but not elsewhere in 1914. The workers who had struck with frequency during the 1905–1914 period sought not social revolution but tangible economic benefits within the capitalistic system.

Imperialism was not a main cause of the war, either. Colonies or protectorates sometimes served as pawns in the game of power, but they were not an essential component. Morocco had no great economic value to either the French or the Germans; they quarreled over it because of prestige. France and Britain had been the chief colonial rivals from 1880 to 1904, but their rivalry did not lead them to war, and they used colonial concessions to cement their alliance. Great Britain and Germany were able to resolve such colonial issues as the Baghdad Railway in 1913–1914; they went to war for other reasons. Southeastern Europe was the chief arena of conflict leading to World War I. The rival interests of Russia and Austria were indeed deployed there, in a matter, however, of power and strategy more than economics, for this was the poorest part of Europe.

Military men, far more influential in decision making than were businessmen, did play too great a role. Historians have noted, probably correctly, the relative weakness of the civilian leadership. Bethmann-Hollweg, the kaiser, Grey, Viviani, Sazanov, Nicholas II, and Berchtold were not an impressive lot, to say the least. They "glided, or rather staggered and stumbled" into a war they did not want, was the verdict of Lloyd George. Rather irresponsible militarists, such as the kaiser's friend Tirpitz, or Conrad von Hotzendorf, the Austrian chief of staff, or the mad Russian Sukhomlinov, found their judgments too readily accepted. It is hardly correct to argue that "the enormous growth of armaments," in Grey's words, led to war. By today's standards, military budgets were not large. More to the point, nations arm because they are afraid; thus the real cause is to be sought in the reasons for their insecurity. The naval race between Germany and England clearly takes rank as one of the several primary and unresolved antagonisms that lie in the background of the war; by itself; however, it would not have led to war. It had been going on for some years by 1914, was not any worse than it had been, and in fact seemed to be improving. Winston

Churchill has described how just hours before the outbreak of war, German and British sailors fraternized during ceremonies at Kiel.

Few had expected war; it came with dramatic suddenness. When it did come, the typical reaction was not that of Edward Grey. Standing at his office window on the night of August 4 and watching the lamps flicker off as the British ultimatum to Germany to withdraw from Belgium expired, Grey said, "The lights are going out all over Europe, and no one now living will ever see them come back again." The historian must regretfully record that a sense of joy rather than of gloom prevailed. Huge cheering crowds surrounded the kaiser, stood outside Buckingham Palace, saluted departing French troops at the railroad stations, made love publicly in St. Petersburg. A Parisian observer on August 2 described a "human torrent, swelling at every corner" screaming, shouting, and singing the "Marseillaise." In Berlin, crowds passed through the streets incessantly for two days singing "Deutschland über Alles" and "Wacht am Rhein." A mob attacked the German embassy in St. Petersburg. An "indescribable crowd" blocked the streets around government offices in London a few minutes after midnight August 4–5 and continued to fill the streets for days. It was with exultation, not sorrow, that the peoples of Europe greeted the war, a fact that in the last analysis may go further to explain its coming than all the details of diplomacy.

3

The Great War of 1914–1918

THE FIRST YEAR

In his memorable description of the battle of Borodino in *War and Peace,* Tolstoy argued that on the battlefield all is confusion, plans go awry, orders are not carried out, and in this "fog of war" chance determines the outcome. The German general staff thought it had reduced war to an exact science, but the outcome of history's most famous gamble, the attack through Belgium that began on August 4, 1914, perhaps vindicated the Russian author. In the end, the German offensive failed by a margin small enough to have depended on accidents. Certainly some plans did go astray; some orders were disobeyed. One celebrated story attributes the German defeat to a disobeyed British command. At the battle of Le Cateau, Sir Horace Smith-Dorrien in declining to follow his order to retreat probably thereby saved the little British expeditionary force from annihilation and may have saved the entire Allied cause. His stand checked the Germans and allowed time for Allied consolidation prior to the critical counterattack along the Marne River. This counterattack frustrated the German drive, which up to then, after four weeks of steady advance, was ahead of schedule in its plan to turn the left flank of the French armies in one mighty thrust. (For his pains, the British officer was implacably persecuted by the incompetent British Commander-in-Chief, Sir John French.)

Moltke, the German commander, was so sure of victory at that point that he took troops away from the western front to send to meet the Russians, who were advancing in the east more rapidly than most had thought possible. French Commander-in-Chief Joffre's improvised counterthrust between two German armies took advantage of this window of opportunity and halted the German offensive. The German armies had outrun their supplies, stretched their endurance too far, and lost their communications on the very threshold of victory. The "miracle of the Marne" resuscitated French morale.

The biggest mistake about the war was the almost unanimous prediction that it would be a short one, lasting six months or, at the outside, a year. Previous experience as well as general principles argued for this. Since 1867, all European wars had been brief; the destructive force of modern armies seemed too great to be sustained very long. The entire German strategy was based on the premise that one great battle would settle it. In England, the brilliant young economist John Maynard Keynes explained to his friends that the war could not last much more than a year, because convertible capital would be exhausted. What happened confounded generals and economists alike. The defensive suddenly triumphed over the offensive, technology dictated long stalemates on the western front, and the people found ways to supply and endure the war for more than four agonizing years.

Once the massive German thrust had collapsed just short of its objective, with the guns of battle audible in Paris, the two armies tried to outflank each other. Reaching the English Channel to the northwest and the mountains to the southeast, they dug in for the winter and thereafter found they could not move each other at whatever cost of lives. Armies did not have tanks, as they would have in 1940. Each side built deep fortifications of trenches, barbed wire, and concrete pillboxes—low, enclosed gun emplacements that defied enemy attack. (No one had anticipated this essentially improvised defense.) When attacks were tried, they resulted in appalling losses for paltry gains of territory. The sweeping fire of machine guns mowed down the advancing foot soldiers even after hours or days of cannonading had prepared their way.

Though deep in French territory, the Germans had not destroyed the French armies. With a million troops tied down on the western front, they faced war in the east against Russia. As a million volunteers joined the British army, the Allied position strengthened, even though the Germans had a slight advantage of interior lines. Having failed in their great gamble and facing the dreaded encirclement, the Germans were in a grave situation. However, they succeeded brilliantly in the east.

At the beginning of the war, the total population and potential resources of the Entente or Allied powers—France, Russia, and Great Britain—considerably exceeded those of the Central Powers—Germany and Austria-Hungary. One must add Serbia to the Allied side, of course; and within a year Italy and Romania joined the Allies, while Turkey and Bulgaria threw in their lot with the Germans. The population of the three main Allied countries outnumbered Germany and Austria-Hungary by better than two to one, about 245 million against

115 million. The British, controlling the international sea lanes, could draw additional strength from their dominions and colonies. But two-thirds of the Allied population was in ill-equipped Russia, which soon revealed its inadequacy for modern warfare. On the other hand, Germany's ally, Austria-Hungary, was severely handicapped by its many doubtfully loyal minorities. The acquisition of Italy was supposed to be a coup for the Allies; but Turkey aided the German cause even more by making it difficult to ship badly needed supplies to Russia through the Straits.

The German army was probably the best in the world, but the French army was excellent, too. Germany held about a tenth of France, including the most industrialized part, which contained four-fifths of French coal and nine-tenths of her iron resources, plus an excellent rail network around Lille; the Germans also occupied almost all of Belgium, including the port of Ostend, which proved valuable as a submarine base.

In terms of military strength, then, one can find many reasons for the

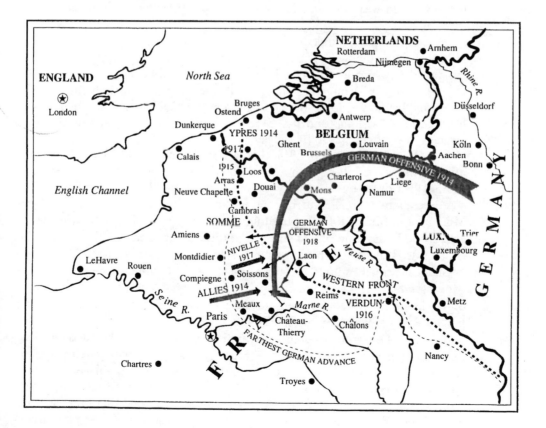

long stalemate that ensued, in which each side was to suffer cruel frustration. In the end, the New World tilted the balance.

The Russians advanced quickly against eastern Germany, loyally carrying out their commitment to France, and perhaps they forced withdrawal of German troops from the west. At any rate, whether from overconfidence or anxiety, Moltke shifted a substantial number of men on August 25. The results were dismaying to the tsar's forces. Russia's technical backwardness and insufficient network of strategic railroads severely handicapped her. The Russian troops were magnificently brave and capable, at times, of great élan as well as incredible feats of endurance, but they lacked equipment, supplies, transport, medical care, and adequate military organization. They sent messages uncoded on the new radio equipment of which they had too little, and they forgot to tell each other where they were taking their armies. The Germans dealt them shattering and demoralizing blows in the early battles on the eastern front. Surrounded at Tannenberg at about the same time as the climax of the war in the west in late August, a Russian army lost 120,000 prisoners, and its commander committed suicide. The defeat was soon repeated at the Masurian Lakes. Here, there was no trench-warfare stalemate, for the terrain was not suitable, and the Russians lacked the equipment and supplies.

On the other hand, the Russians fared well against the armies of Austria-Hungary. (Even the Serbs were able to do that in early December; it took Bulgarian aid to overrun Serbia in 1915.) At the Carpathian frontier in southern Poland, the Austro-Hungarians lost 350,000 men. But the Russians were unable to exploit the victory, for as they plunged into the Dual Monarchy their supply lines became too long, and the Germans sent troops to stiffen the Austrian armies. This pattern was to be repeated.

By the beginning of 1915, Russia was already in bad shape. Of her six million soldiers, no more than a third could even be supplied with rifles. Accepting their disastrous inferiority to the Germans, the Russians confined offensive operations thereafter to the south, where they again attacked the Dual Monarchy in March 1915, forcing their way through the Carpathian passes at great cost. At this time, Italy was moving toward entrance into the war on the Allied side. The goal of knocking out Austria seemed feasible, a feat that might persuade the small neutrals, Romania and Greece, to "come to the rescue of the winning side." But the Germans rescued Austria again, and the Russians were drawn in too far. A counteroffensive caused them to flee in a near rout, losing practically all of Poland in the summer of 1915.

But the Germans could not win the war by mauling the Russians. Unlike Napoleon, and later Hitler, the German generals refused to be tempted into an invasion of Russia. There was a great debate about this. Paul von Hindenburg, German commander of the eastern front, wanted to invade Russia, but he was overruled. Chief of Staff Erich von Falkenhayn argued that there was no way of annihilating a country with such immense reserves of space and manpower, whose transport problem would improve as her armies returned homeward. It would be preferable to hold the front with relatively small forces. But the Russians would not make a separate peace, although forces around the tsar, including Rasputin, wished to do so. With quixotic gallantry the tsar stayed in the war, even assuming personal command of the armies in September 1915–a step often seen as crucial on the road to revolution, for it laid Nicholas's personal prestige on the line.

Both Germany and the Western Allies, it appeared, were "fettered to a corpse." The most promising or at least imaginative idea on the Allied side in 1915 was to revive their corpse by injecting the lifeblood of supplies. Substantially cut off from the West, Russia could hope to receive such badly needed equipment only through the Straits of Constantinople, but Turkey blocked this route. To knock Turkey out of the war by a combined naval and land assault, thus opening communications between the Western Allies and Russia, was an obvious strategic idea. Credit for it is usually awarded to the dynamic Winston Churchill, who was serving as first lord of the admiralty in the British cabinet. But both the British naval mission commander in Turkey and the Greek general staff had thought of this earlier than Churchill, who did push it as early as September 1914 and continued to do so. Unfortunately, a divided Greece refused to enter the war on the Allied side, King Constantine, a brother-in-law of the kaiser, being pro-German. Had Greece followed the wishes of Prime Minister Venizelos, who later rebelled against the king to set up a separate, pro-Allied government at Salonika (1916), the Dardanelles campaign might have turned out differently.

As it happened, however, the failure of the Dardanelles campaign cost Churchill his job and almost his career. Aided by German advisers and two German warships that had slipped through the Mediterranean, the Turks possessed formidable defenses. At Whitehall there was much debate and many delays in mounting the campaign. Unfortunately, any plan to divert extensive forces, either naval or land, to the eastern theater (Lloyd George backed another plan to send troops through the Aegean to Serbia) ran into opposition from those who argued that it was dangerous to denude the western front or the North Sea, where the British navy stood guard against a possible eruption of the German fleet from its Heligoland lair.

An Anglo-French fleet bombarded the Straits in February 1915, stopped, resumed in March, and brought in an expeditionary force only in late April, by which time the Turks had had time to bolster defenses. Surprise was lost, and the initial expeditionary force was too small. The Gallipoli peninsula, which extends like an upper jaw over the narrow passageway that links Europe and Asia, proved a trap for the mainly British and Australian and New Zealander troops who fought there all through the long, hot summer of 1915. Reinforcements had to be sent, which intensified the dispute within the British government about priorities. To no avail, over 200,000 men were lost (dead or wounded), along with some naval vessels, victims of German submarines.

Though Turkish losses were at least equally heavy, the expedition was finally withdrawn. This episode damaged not only Churchill but also the Asquith government itself and became a prize example of faulty planning in this war in which nothing seemed to go right. It was all appropriate end to the first frustrating year of war.

1916: THE YEAR OF SLAUGHTER

The Central Powers might take comfort from Gallipoli and from the brilliant German performance against Russia, which was achieved with much smaller numbers of troops. The eastern front lay almost quiet from October 1915 to March 1916, as the Russian bear licked his deep wounds. During this period, Bulgaria entered the war on the German side. Striking at Serbia from the southeast while Austro-German forces invaded her from the northwest, Bulgaria brought about Serbia's defeat. What remained of the gallant Serb army escaped in a wild flight into Albania, whence it was conveyed by British and Italian ships to the island of Corfu (technically a Greek possession). After this, Venizelos set up his pro-Allied Greek splinter regime in Salonika, which was occupied by Allied troops departing from Gallipoli.

All this, however, was not decisive. The Allies were mildly heartened by Italy's adhesion to their cause in May 1915, by a growing war trade with the United States, and by Japan's entry on the Allied side in August. But 1916 was to be the year of the western front: the year of Verdun and the Somme. During 1915, the western front had lain relatively quiet as the rival forces perfected their defenses by digging, stringing barbed wire, and cementing pillboxes. What action there was gave ominous warning of the difficulties of an offensive. The Allies were tempted to try one anyway to help Russia; the Germans felt a sense of urgency because, landlocked and blockaded, they were more vulnerable to a war of attrition. And, both sides were pushed toward an offensive by an impatient public that saw little sense in a war that lasted forever. Armies were expected to win wars, not sit dejectedly in trenches. With the collapse of the Dardanelles campaign, Allied attention returned to the main theater; meanwhile, the Germans absorbed the fact that they could not win the war by mauling the Russians, no matter how badly. So 1916 was fated to be a year of sickening losses in France and Belgium.

Analyzing the situation, the German General Staff chief, Erich von Falkenhayn, convinced himself of the necessity for a German offensive in the west. The impregnable fortress of Verdun was a symbol of France's will to resist. Falkenhayn seems to have reasoned like the football coach who says, "Attack them at their strongest point"–though the defenses of the Verdun trench line had been left relatively thin by Joffre. The great battle of Verdun, the largest of the war, began in February and was not broken off until December, thus stretching over most of the year; it is estimated to have cost the almost unimaginable total of 700,000 casualties, of whom slightly more were French than German. Falkenhayn believed that the French would be bled white at Verdun and that they could afford the losses less than more populous Germany. If, as has been claimed, Verdun was the most terrible battle in all history, Falkenhayn's decision must surely stand as one of history's greatest follies, if not its greatest crime.

The German offensive began with a titanic artillery barrage from 850 big guns, including 420 of the huge "big Berthas." Advised to withdraw to the more easily defended west bank of the Meuse River, French Premier Briand refused on the grounds of morale; he had taken the German bait in prizing Verdun as a symbol. In the swaying and bloody battles of the next months, the defense of Verdun did indeed raise French morale. It became a national expression of the will to resist: "They shall not pass." Verdun sealed the fate of General Falkenhayn, who became one of many high military leaders to fall in disgrace during the war. Among the French, however, a reputation was made, that of General Philippe Pétain.

Falkenhayn's example did not keep the Allies from a similar folly. The hell of Verdun was followed by the slaughter on the Somme. The Somme offensive was waged partly to get the British involved; the French having paid

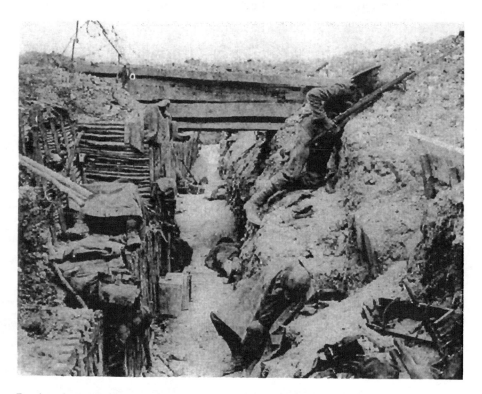

Trench warfare on the Western Front, July 1916. (*Courtesy Imperial War Museum.*)

their sacrifice of life at Verdun, it seemed monstrous that the British should not bleed too. This chiefly British-held sector lay some 150 miles northwest of Verdun in the north of France (Flanders), within fifty miles of the English channel. Here were to fall hundreds of thousands of British soldiers, nearly all of them volunteers. Seven days of continuous bombardment preceded the attack, creating an unearthly noise that seemed to some like a strange music. The assault began on July 1, with 100,000 men advancing across "no man's land"; more than half of them were killed or wounded, which set the pattern for all that followed. The immense bombardment had not destroyed the deeply implanted German machine gunners. For weeks, the grisly battle went on. Although Douglas Haig, the British commander, had hoped for a breakthrough, it turned into a battle of attrition like Verdun. The Germans suffered terribly, but the British could gain only slight ground, and any gain was likely to be wiped out by a well-timed counterattack before engineering could consolidate it. The total losses in the vast Somme battle seem to have exceeded even those at Verdun.

At least two million men died in battle in Europe in 1916. In addition to the titanic struggles on the western front, the Austrians and Italians were busy fighting in the east. To take pressure off both the French at Verdun and the Italians in the Trentino, the Russians gallantly if inexplicably renewed the war on the eastern front in June. They had raised new armies and accumulated supplies

Shelling to prepare for an attack, eight-inch howitzers at the Battle of the Somme. (*Courtesy Imperial War Museum.*)

since the 1915 disaster. After an ineffective tangle with the Germans in March, the Russians reverted to their favorite target, Austria, under fresh leadership from General Alexei Brusilov. Seeking this time the advantage of surprise, something that days of preliminary bombardment at Verdun and the Somme obviously failed to attain, Brusilov launched attacks on a broad front from eastern Poland south to the Romanian border. These began successfully; an Austrian army was routed, gains up to fifty miles made, many prisoners taken. But the Russians could not exploit their gains. They ran out of supplies, and Germans were sent to stiffen the Austrian forces. To the north, Russian commanders feared, with good reason, to attack German armies. At the cost of much acrimony between the two Central Powers, substantially a single command under German management was now established over the whole eastern front.

"Brusilov is the only commander of the First World War after whom a great victory has been named," war historian Cyril Falls noted. The Brusilov offensive was a stellar one-man performance, but it was not enough. Curiously, so great an effort had the effect of sinking both sides. For the Dual Monarchy, it was a staggering blow, and Vienna lost independent control of its forces to Berlin. The death of the old Emperor Franz Josef shortly thereafter sealed the fate of the polyglot empire, and it began to dissolve. Its threatened dissolution had begun the war, and the war completed that dissolution.

For Russia, the Brusilov campaign was also the last straw. From here, the road led steadily toward the 1917 revolutions and the breakup of her suffering armies. Another country also suffered: At the height of Brusilov's success, Romania was finally persuaded to enter the war on the side of the Allies, having been promised both Transylvania and some Bulgarian territory. The Romanian army proceeded to attack in both directions, only to encounter double trouble. One of its opponents was the recently deposed German commander-in-chief, Erich von Falkenhayn, who proved himself a capable field commander in a brilliant campaign in the Transylvanian Alps. As a Bulgarian-Turkish-German army invaded from the south while Falkenhayn crashed through from the north, most of Romania was overrun, and its capital, Bucharest, was taken. Aided by rain and the onset of winter, the Romanians were able to hang on to a piece of their country in the north, establishing an emergency capital at Jassy.

The bloody year of 1916, during which the storms of battle swirled from the English Channel to the plains of Romania and the mountains of Italy, tested men's courage and endurance to the limit. Yet in the end, victory again eluded both sides, and stalemate was the word at the year's end as much as at its beginning. In one further arena, the result was a draw. War at sea broke out for just about the only time in a major battle between the rival war fleets. The celebrated Battle of Jutland was fought May 31–June 1, 1916.

The bulk of the British navy stood guard in the North Sea, maintaining the blockade of Germany but not willing to risk destruction by venturing into the Baltic. Had the British navy destroyed the German Fleet, it would have opened a lifeline to Russia. For its part, the German fleet did not dare to take on the larger Royal Navy, although it did conduct night raids on British ports. The Germans had a powerful naval fortress at Heligoland in the North Sea, from which the ships could slip back into the Baltic through the Kiel Canal should the British try sailing through the Skagerrak. The bulk of the British Dreadnought fleet stayed at Scapa Flow, off the north coast of Scotland.

The one great naval battle of the war was not exactly planned; it resulted from German Admiral Scheer's tactic of attempting to divide the British fleet by luring part of it out to pursue raiders and then hitting that part with the German main fleet. During this engagement, to speak of the "fog of war" is an understatement; it would require a volume to describe the confusion of ships all over the North Sea in an intricate naval chess game of which both commands lost track. The fog was more than a metaphor. At one point, Scheer's trick seemed to have backfired and the British had him trapped. The German ships escaped by sailing north, while Jellicoe, the British admiral, guessed south; the Germans made their way home down the coast of Denmark, though in the mists of night the fleets brushed each other. When it was all over, after a furious afternoon and night, both sides bore scars, and their mutual respect was intensified. The British lost slightly more than the Germans in terms of tonnage sunk and casualties; but the British Dreadnought fleet remained powerful, and the Germans had had a close call. (The ships lost were entirely battle cruisers, light cruisers, and pre-Dreadnought battleships; no Dreadnought was sunk.)

Neither side cared to repeat the performance. For the British, the risk was too great, since to lose their fleet would bring down the whole blockade and the assurance of their world supply routes, including the growing trade with the United States. The Germans turned increasingly to submarine warfare; the High Seas fleet's idleness in port was a cause of the mutiny that later broke out at Kiel. Historian Arthur Marder, a leading student of the Royal Navy in this war, claimed that it actually won a great victory at Jutland, though this was not everywhere appreciated, especially by the French. The British fleet contained and rendered impotent the kaiser's proud navy. But by denying the Baltic (and the Straits) to Allied sea power, the German fleet guaranteed the collapse of Russia.

THE CRISES OF 1917

In desperate straits, leaders searched for a way out of the terrible impasse. Tanks were used for the first time by the British late in the Somme campaign, but they were yet too few and too primitive to have much influence. It was not until 1918, in the last months of the war, that tanks made any significant contribution. Airplanes were, of course, available in World War I; the "dog fights" of individual aviators in one-seaters provided about the only glamorous dimension of the war. But these tiny craft were used mainly for reconnaissance, in which capacity they were helpful to ground forces but did not play an independent tactical role. Zeppelin raids, before these unwieldy monsters were abandoned in 1917 after many were shot down or blew away, killed or wounded about 1,800 in London, a few less than airplane raids; Paris suffered more from long-range cannons in 1918 than from air attack. The day of the bomber lay far ahead. Tanks and military aircraft, the two chief innovations that emerged from the war, were developed afterwards. Although they dominated World War II, they had nothing like that capacity yet in the first war. Near the end of the war, American airmen devised a plan for landing troops behind enemy lines from the air, but it did not have a chance to get tested.

More widely used was poison gas. It was also widely discussed as one of the more hideous ideas of World War I. Allied propaganda made much of the German inauguration of chlorine gas in 1915 on the western front. The Germans used chlorine gas first near Ypres; both sides subsequently experimented with several types of poison gas. Chemical warfare killed some 90,000 and injured more than a million during the war. Eminent scientists lent their talents to research on the subject. The trouble was that winds were too prone to shift, and gas masks could be used as counteragents.

As the carnage continued into 1917, military leaders' careers were ruined, the penalty for their failure to find a way to victory and to avoid the frightful casualties. It was a veritable slaughter of the top brass and some civilians, too. After Joffre had removed over a hundred French generals in the first few months, he himself had to go in 1916. Moltke, the first German commander-in-chief, gave way to Falkenhayn, who in turn left after Verdun. Douglas Haig succeeded John French as chief military commander on the British side, only to be tagged as the butcher of the Somme. Winston Churchill was the victim of Gallipoli, and in 1916 Lord Kitchener, the British war secretary, was lost at sea when, starting on a visit to Russia, his ship hit a mine left over from the recent Battle of Jutland. He had been under strong attack, and the Russian visit was partly to get him out of the way. The Russian war minister, Sukhomlinov, was tried for high treason but convicted only of gross incompetence.

These are only some examples of the premature retirements that were forced by this war. They reached a scale hardly matched in history. Nor were the heads of government immune. France switched premiers twice before choosing the old Tiger, Georges Clemenceau, in 1917. After one cabinet shakeup in May 1915, Herbert Asquith was deposed as British prime minister in late 1916, a major upheaval bringing in a coalition headed by David Lloyd George. The maneuver left permanent scars on the Liberal party. "War always destroys the government that waged it," John Bright had claimed. This proved true in 1914–1918, for no government in power at the beginning was there at the end, and in three cases the fall encompassed the entire regime. German Chancellor Bethmann-Hollweg lost his office in 1917, preceding his emperor by only a little more than a year.

The vast demand for war materiel was one problem for ministers. The habit of prefacing any attack by up to seventeen days of steady bombardment, with hundreds of heavy guns and thousands of smaller ones virtually wheel-to-wheel for miles, naturally required quite a bit of ammunition. It is estimated that at the 1917 battle of Messines alone, three and a half million shells were fired. Millions of tons of high explosives were set off underground, planted by miners under the Messines ridge near Ypres, the Belgian town around which four mighty battles were fought during the war. Such war requirements forced a kind of "war socialism," in which the government had to ration goods, set priorities, impose price and wage controls, and requisition factories. In Britain, War Secretary Kitchener and Commander in Chief John French, both of whom were accused of mishandling their demanding jobs, bickered constantly, French claiming he got insufficient supplies of ammunition and Kitchener implying that supplies were wasted.

Asquith, the British prime minister, shrank from measures of compulsion, even from conscription of manpower; until mid-1916 the British armies were filled by volunteers. Lloyd George came to think him weak.[1] In 1917, Great Britain and France found leaders who were able, popular, and ruthlessly dedicated to victory at any price. Revolution came to Russia, and Austria-Hungary began to fall apart. In Germany, a political crisis forced the replacement of Bethmann-Hoilweg; the actual rulers of Germany were the ablest generals, Hindenburg and Ludendorff. In compensation for the almost total collapse of Russia, the Allies won the biggest prize of all: the United States of America.

A year that began with the accession of a new British government and ended with the Bolshevik Revolution in Russia, a year that included a mutiny in the French armies, Clemenceau's assumption of office, a political crisis in Germany, Italian disaster at Caporetto, and the entry of the United States into the war, was not lacking in action and indeed might well be called the critical year of this century.

The Russian Revolution is discussed later in this chapter. It is enough to note here that the first Russian revolution of 1917, the February Revolution (actually early March, on the calendar used in the West), brought to power a government pledged to democratize Russia and to continue the war with a more effective system. Perceptive observers were skeptical, but not until the next November did a group that was pledged to take Russia out of the war at any price manage to seize power. During the summer of 1917, the Russian armies were rapidly breaking up as attention turned to domestic revolution and a struggle for power following the abdication of the tsar. But an illusion existed in the West that the new Russian government, having thrown off the shackles of tsardom and proclaimed democratic principles, would actually strengthen the Allied cause. A delegation of European socialists brought words of encouragement to the Russian provisional government in the spring.

At just that moment, however, socialist support of the war was beginning to waver in the West. A small fraction of the German Social Democrats, led by Rosa Luxemburg and Karl Liebknecht, son of a founding father of the party,

---

[1]Asquith's despondency was connected to his having been jilted by Venetia Stanley, his long-time lady friend.

opposed the war at its outset. Liebknecht's was the only vote cast against war credits in the Reichstag late in 1914. A year later, nineteen others joined him. But socialist support for the war in all countries remained remarkably firm, with only slight signs of wavering. Called at the initiative of Italian socialists, the Zimmerwald Conference held in Switzerland in September 1915 witnessed the debut of Lenin's drive to turn the international war into a class war within each country. But few socialists from the warring countries even attended, and the Zimmerwald socialists did not entirely accept Lenin's platform. Three obscure French socialists voted against the war credits in May 1916 after attending another conference at Kienthal.

In frustration, Friedrich Adler, also the son of a famous socialist, assassinated the Austrian prime minister, Count Karl von Stürgkh, at his midday meal in a Vienna restaurant on October 21, 1916. The following year in Berlin, a large and distinguished minority of the German socialists founded the Independent Social Democratic party. The Independents were not Leninists; they did not oppose the war as such, but they did oppose annexationist war aims, considering only a defensive war to be justifiable and alarmed at openly proclaimed goals of acquiring additional territory if the kaiser's government won the war. The collapse of Russia was beginning to raise this issue sharply. The socialists were joined by others, including the great sociologist Max Weber, in demanding democratization of Germany so that a truly popular basis for the war might be found. This was a position resembling that adopted in England by the Union of Democratic Control, a group of intellectuals and socialists who, without denying the need to wage a war of self-defense, campaigned for a compromise peace and asked for democratic control of foreign policy. They accused British policy of having helped cause the war by its secret commitments to France.

The German crisis of July 1917, however, was mostly the result of disappointed submarine hopes. In May 1916, the Germans called their submarines off of commercial vessels after the sinking of the *Sussex* brought a sharp American warning. The previous year's sinking of the British ocean liner *Lusitania*, with considerable loss of American life, had blighted German-American relations, already strained by the American tendency to grant loans to the Allies for purchasing war supplies. But desperation nourished renewed hopes that using her large submarine force might win the war for Germany. Beginning the war with a fairly large submarine force, the Germans energetically added to it until they had more than 400 of these relatively new weapons. The blockade was beginning to tell on the Central Powers; actual hunger faced them. In January 1917, Berlin took the momentous decision to resort to unrestricted warfare around the British Isles, sinking everything in an effort to starve out the British. High naval leaders assured the kaiser that this strategy could win the war within five months.

In March, the Germans made some withdrawals on the western front to a more heavily fortified line, the "Hindenburg line"—tacit admission that there no longer was any hope of winning the war in this area. Germany could afford no more Verduns.

The submarine campaign resulted in a declaration of war by the United

States against Germany on April 6. German defiance of previous American warnings against submarine warfare would inevitably mean the loss of American lives and property. After April, however, it became evident that the sub war could not deliver its promised results. U-boat victims were numerous, over 100 boats a month; but after rising between February and April, the toll of tonnage began to subside. Countermeasures in the form of destroyer-protected convoys were effective enough to assure the survival of Britain, now aided by her powerful American ally.

On July 6 in the Reichstag, Matthias Erzberger exposed the failure of the submarine war. Two weeks later, the Reichstag passed a resolution supported by Centrists as well as Socialists, calling for a peace without annexations. This followed by five days the resignation of Bethmann-Hollweg. He was replaced by the obscure George Michaelis, who in fact was subordinate to General Ludendorff's influence. The German government allowed delegates to attend the Stockholm Socialist meeting then going on, which was more than the British and French governments did. And, a little earlier, the emperor had announced an end to the notorious Prussian three-class voting system in favor of a democratic suffrage. All this was a curious mixture of reform and reaction, indicative of faltering German will to carry on the terrible war. The summer of 1917 also brought the first revolt at the Kiel naval base, the harbinger of a much greater one in November of the next year.

The Germans would have felt better had they known about the mutiny that swept through the French army at this same time. This crisis of morale followed a disastrous offensive that bears the name of French general Nivelle, who had replaced Joffre as commander-in-chief. Radiating confidence, Nivelle concocted an ambitious plan of attack over a broad front. At Arras and in Champagne, British and French attacks in April failed so badly, again with ghastly casualties, that soldiers finally lost all confidence in the high command. They refused en masse to obey orders to attack. The extent of this mutiny is indicated by the official figures: 23,385 court martials and 432 death sentences. As many as 50,000 soldiers were actively involved. Nothing like that had occurred before; the war had been marked by high morale and an infinitesimally small desertion rate. The mutiny affected almost all the five French armies (fifty-four divisions) that had taken part in the offensive, perhaps a third of the total French forces. With the aid of General Pétain, the hero of Verdun, control was regained at the cost of a promise of no more offensives. The French joined the Germans in wishing no more part in the long game of mass slaughter. It is remarkable that the Germans learned so little about the mutiny.

Nerves were stretched taut. A former premier of the French Republic advocated a negotiated peace and was imprisoned for it. The British sent Union of Democratic Control leader L. D. Morel to jail for the same heresy; and when Lord Lansdowne, a distinguished elder statesman, made a similar suggestion it was received with a shower of abuse. The grimness of the situation persuaded some that it was time to end the madness, but others reacted by asking for ever greater dedication and showing a savage intolerance of defeatism. After shedding so much blood, could one settle for less than victory?

MORALE AND PROPAGANDA

The war began with wild celebrations in an ecstasy of general rejoicing. Such a mood later seemed incredible, was therefore almost forgotten, and, in many accounts of the war, ignored. It should not be, for the "August ideas" constituted an essential basis for the widespread support that held public morale high through several years of what one would have thought unendurable agony.

The war spirit embraced the articulate classes as well as the masses. Indeed, one of its principal ingredients was a joyous rediscovery of solidarity in the community of battle. Alienated European intellectuals—a term that had come into general usage only in the preceding generation—happily returned home to the bosom of the people. "Our petty social divisions and barriers have all been swept away," Kipling exulted. In every belligerent nation, an exultation at being "again one people," feeling the "sacred union" of national brotherhood, afflicted the educated elite, it seems, even more than the average person.

At any rate, a quite irrational, mystic sentiment of this sort found expression in many outbursts. "I discovered to my amazement," Bertrand Russell wrote—he was one of a small minority not sharing the mystique, but appalled by it—"that average men and women were delighted at the prospect of war." A flood of manifestoes and declarations that blessed the war, damned the foe, and strove to put their side in the right before God and history testified to an equal delight among leading philosophers, poets, scientists, historians, sociologists. University youth were among the most eager to volunteer; there was a strong feeling that the war was a youth movement, and such young poets as Rupert Brooke and Alain-Fournier who marched off to die became heroes.

A desire for adventure after the tameness of a bourgeois society marked by mediocrity—*Wust und Tand* ("trash and triviality"), German poet Stefan George called it—was one obvious motive for young men to march off to a war that they initially expected to offer glorious excitement and a chance for heroism. It was a poet's war, although between 1914 and 1918 the poetry changed from celebration of honor and bravery to grim commentary on useless bloodshed. In the beginning, as Robert Graves recalled,

> Never was such antiqueness of romance
> Such tasty honey oozing from the heart.

But the war was more than adventure; serious thinkers hailed it as a chance for "moral regeneration," a cleansing fire burning away the corruptions of a decadent society or "washing away the ruins of a shattered world" (wrote Ernst Lotz, a young German poet, the Rupert Brooke of his land). People who later had trouble understanding how they could have behaved so foolishly were swept

The Western Front: the mud and blood. (*Courtesy Imperial War Museum.*)

into the war craze in a rage of excitement. "When war is declared we all go mad," Shaw commented. The madness that accompanied the outbreak of this war was exaggerated by boredom with the long peace; the restless discontents with a shabby commercial culture; and the Nietzschean mood, which taught that through struggle and battle the spirit might redeem itself and the world.

Few indeed were the voices raised against the hysteria, and they were reduced to despair. "Among the elite of each country," Romain Rolland lamented, "there is not one who does not proclaim and is not convinced that the cause of his country is the cause of God, the cause of liberty and of human progress." Rolland's plea to the intellectuals to stand *au-dessus de la melée* ("above the battle") went largely unheeded and scorned for at least two years.

Though the feverish idealism of the first days naturally proved ephemeral, its results tended to last. The intelligentsia in each country manned the ministries of "information" if they did not actually fight, as many of them did even at quite advanced ages. There were numerous examples of enlistments by men of middle age, and old Anatole France–socialist and radical–even tried to shoulder a rifle at seventy. The "decadent" Italian novelist and poet Gabriele D'Annunzio, associated earlier with eroticism, compiled a heroic war record although he was in his fifties. Popular writers and entertainers visited the front to raise morale. Women proved as warlike as men; anxious to assert their equality, most suffragettes supported the war with deeds as well as words. Reversing the lesson of Lysistrata, girls cold-shouldered sweethearts who wouldn't sign up, chanting "We don't want to lose you but we think you ought to go" at every able-bodied young male they sighted.

With few exceptions, socialists and trade unionists were patriotic. In England, veteran independent socialist Keir Hardie found himself hissed at by workers when he questioned the duty to subordinate everything else to winning the war. If nationalism proved far stronger than Marxist ideology, it also pulled harder than religion. French and German Jews rallied loyally behind their respective governments, in order to fire at each other as enemies. And, "French Protestants," writes Charles Bailey, "showed themselves ardent patriots, whose commitment to *la patrie* was far stronger than any sense of loyalty to the European community of Protestantism" including their numerous fellow Protestants in Germany.

This excess of belligerent ardor led to propaganda that extended even to the more or less deliberate manufacture of stories about the enemy. Allied propaganda soon developed a view of the Germans as barbarians, "Huns" who descended without warning on small nations, determined to extinguish their independence. Led by "Prussian militarists" to whom they were blindly obedient, encouraged to be ruthless by Nietzsche (actually a hater of German nationalism), they had not only deliberately contrived the war to impose their German culture on everybody, but they delighted in cruel treatment of their victims. Teutonic love of despotism, of course, was contrasted with the democracy of the Allies, a line to which Russia was something of an obstacle until March 1917 (though an English scholar declared the Russians to be at heart really democratic[2]).

Less successfully, German propaganda accused the British of sordid materialism, the French of decadence, the Russians of menacing Europe with a savage barbarism, all of jealousy of German cultural and economic superiority. Governments organized and subsidized the publication of such bizarre distortions, freely offered by the leading brains of each country. The extensive literature of this sort has to be seen to be believed.

The home front was more affected by propaganda than were the soldiers, who soon found themselves distanced from it. On the whole, soldiers in the trenches showed greater respect for a brave foe. Still, the famous "Christmas truce" of December 1914, when rival forces suspended hostilities to celebrate the holiday season with gifts and parties, was not repeated. Disenchanted with their leaders, the "scarlet Majors at the Base" who in Siegfried Sassoon's poem "speed glum heroes up the line to death" and toddle home to die in bed, as well as with those at home who could not grasp how it really was at the front, the men in battle developed a remarkable camaraderie based on their mutual dependence. They learned to hate the war but love each other and often found the frightful experience humanly valuable.

Each side accused the other of atrocities. Most of these stories were made up. Ironically, these falsehoods contributed to a failure to believe in the

---

[2]See J. Dover Wilson, in R. W. Seton-Watson et al., *The War and Democracy* (London: Macmillan, 1914).

very real atrocities of World War II; so much skepticism had been engendered by learning of the deliberate lies of 1914–1918 that at first few would accept stories of mass murder in Nazi concentration camps. In any war terrible things happen, of which both sides are guilty–shooting prisoners, for example. There was vast Allied indignation at the German execution of a nurse named Edith Cavell, but the French also executed female spies as well as male spies in considerable numbers. In 1917, the *Times* of London claimed that the Germans were converting human corpses into fertilizer and even food, a story later found to have been based on a mistranslation (horses, not people). Other mistakes were not so innocent, and after the war there was a wave of rueful confessions by people who had manufactured tales of enemy inhumanity. The Germans were most vulnerable, since they were the occupiers of Belgian, French, Serbian, Romanian, and Russian territory, whereas no foreign soldier stood on German soil throughout the war–this was largely true, too, of the Dual Monarchy. (It is a curiosity of this war that the defeated were never invaded.) They also bore the onus of submarine warfare with its inevitable loss of civilian life. And one of the few authenticated cases of something like the genocides practiced during World War II implicated Germany's ally, Turkey, whose attempt to exterminate the Armenians was unfortunately not a new practice. The Germans made what capital they could of alleged bestialities inflicted by French African soldiers on their victims. In actuality, whenever conditions of battle made it possible, the soldiers on both sides seem to have behaved honorably, and German administration of the occupied zones was far from barbarous.

The atrocity stories and the war propaganda did neither side credit. The war was atrocious enough in itself. It was mechanized slaughter, impersonal and unheroic. As Shaw put it, the soldier

> has no sight or knowledge of what he is doing; he only hands on a shell or pulls a string. And a Beethoven or a baby dies six miles off . . . The notion that these heavily bored men were being heroic, or cruel, or anything in the least romantic or sensational, was laughable.[3]

World War II, with its tank battles and vast movements, was more interesting than World War I. Typically, men sat in idleness behind the front or in the trenches, waiting for those occasions when they went "over the top" into "no man's land" protected by nothing but a helmet and loaded down with equipment, probably to be mowed down by gunners who never came near them.

On the other hand, Shaw was wrong in supposing the guns would hit a baby; unlike the next war, civilians were reasonably safe in this one. The western front battle zone itself became what Edmund Blunden called "the most ter-

---

[3] *The Wit and Wisdom of Bernard Shaw,* ed. Stephen Winsten (New York: Collier Books, 1962), pp. 311–312. Cf. the Viennese Shaw, Karl Kraus, "Mit der Uhr in der Hand," *Die Fackel,* May 1917, pp. 457–461. Shaw's account of his visit to the front first appeared in the *London Daily Chronicle,* March 5–8, 1917.

"Over the top" to almost certain death in World War I, Western Front. (*Imperial War Museum.*)

rifying devastated area perhaps ever yet seen on our planet," but it was a narrow zone. In such savagely contested regions, as in the country around Verdun or Ypres, all life was wiped out; villages disappeared forever; shells and even bodies could be found for years afterwards. But towns just a few miles behind the lines were never shelled. There, in rest and recreation centers, soldiers might write or relax between spells of duty at the front. It is erroneous to suppose that they spent all their time being eaten by rats and lice in the trenches. A considerable number contracted venereal disease. Improvement in the treatment of such diseases was one form of medical progress that resulted from addressing war-related problems with the resources of governments—one of the uses of adversity.

In the end, the war was a test of the wills of whole peoples. The elder Moltke, genius of the German Army, was one of the few who had predicted the nature of this war long before. "It will become a war between peoples which will not be concluded with a single battle but which will be a long, weary struggle with a country that will not acknowledge defeat until the whole strength of its people is broken."

In such a contest, ideology and propaganda were all-important; and it is fair to say that the Germans lost this battle. Persuaded that their cause was just, the Germans had trouble explaining it, and they had less access to the outer world. Much of the neutral world, though not all of it, thought that democracy, progress, and freedom were on the side of the Allies. In the greatest neutral arena of all, the Allies won the moral struggle by persuading the United States of America to join them. Though critics alleged then and later that the American motive was a material one (profitable war trade and saving those who owed them money), one cannot realistically leave out the ideological factor. Most Americans had become convinced that the kaiser and the Prussian war lords were waging a "warfare against mankind," in President Woodrow Wilson's words, and that "the principles of peace and justice in the life of the world as against selfish and autocratic power" would be upheld by opposing the Central Powers.

WAR AIMS AND WAR DIPLOMACY

Except for Austria's desire to eliminate Serbia, no warring power had any clearly formulated goals beyond self-preservation when the war started. Whatever propagandists alleged, neither side went to war in 1914 in conscious search of territorial or other aggrandizement. But the very fact that war had occurred caused demands to be raised. Each thought it had been attacked or forced to forestall attack because its security had been insufficient, and victory would have to bring changes. Besides, the large casualties cried out for compensation. Were such immense sacrifices to be made in vain? No government could survive that did not press for future gains and the reward of victory, so that the foe would be prevented from striking again and one's own necessary security would be provided.

Complicating the formulation of such war aims were more immediate and pressing goals: keeping allies happy, avoiding costly quarrels within the team of fighting powers; winning new allies by persuading or bribing neutrals to enter on one's own side; and stirring up trouble within the enemy camp if possible. These goals could clash painfully, forcing hard choices. If the British and French kept Russia happy by agreeing to her goal of acquiring the Straits of Constantinople, they could not expect to gain Turkey as an ally. They alienated an ally, Serbia, and sacrificed an opportunity to weaken the shaky allegiance of Austria-Hungary's Slavic subjects, if, to lure Italy into becoming an ally, they offered to give Slavic territory to Rome. The possibility of getting the Dual Monarchy to make a separate peace—a real coup, which the Allies in fact thought existed—contradicted a policy of weakening her by appealing to her minorities to rebel and set up separate governments.

All these dilemmas were actual ones, and there were others. The Germans had to make the memorable decision whether submarine warfare was worth the enmity of the United States; and they had to decide whether to woo Russia into a separate peace or assail her by offering aid to her discontented subjects.

There was the further possibility, if unhappily a rather remote one at most times, that terms between the enemy powers short of absolute victory could end the dismal slaughter by some sort of compromise. The friendly offices of neutrals might perhaps facilitate this process. In January 1915, President

Wilson sent Colonel E. M. House, his trusted aide, to visit London, Paris, and Berlin and sound out prospects for a settlement; House was forced to judge the situation hopeless. Each side had a shopping list. The Allies demanded, at the least, German withdrawal from all invaded territories with indemnification for damages, the return of Alsace and Lorraine to France and the Straits to Russia (Britain and France had already promised this to Russia by secret agreement, an issue growing out of the Dardanelles campaign). But German opinion would tolerate no drawing back from territory gained and demanded at a minimum keeping strategic areas in Belgium and France.

Nearly two years later, another American initiative failed. At this time, in response to a Wilson request for a statement of aims, the German government declared that in general it was ready to make peace, but it irritated the Allies by implying that it was, if not victorious, at least not defeated. It has been debated whether the Germans at this time were ready for a peace without annexations; the Allies did not think so. German efforts to make a separate peace with Britain in 1917 and 1918 also came to nothing. An initiative from Pope Benedict in 1917 made no more headway than American industrialist Henry Ford's Peace Ship.

From one point of view, the huge human and material losses, the disruption of the whole fabric of international life, and the hateful propaganda seemed to be destroying Western civilization; surely peace was in everyone's interest. From another point of view, however, the more blood and treasure spent, the less easy it was to accept an end to the war without commensurate gains. Could one confess that the whole thing had been a mistake and go back to where one had begun after losing a million lives? A grisly logic decreed that terms for peace rose and positions stiffened in proportion to the length and cost of the war. At any given moment in a war, if one is doing relatively well, why compromise? We may win tomorrow. Or if one is doing badly, why not wait until tomorrow to bargain? Today we are in too weak a position. The time is never ripe for peace until one side totally collapses.

Of such ingredients was wartime diplomacy made. The "secret treaties" in which territories were pledged to Italy, to Russia, and to Romania in order to gain their adherence to the Allies and their entry into the war later became a notorious issue. Russia and Romania subsequently left the war and wiped out the agreements, but the Bolsheviks exposed the secret agreement of 1915 about the Straits soon after they seized power in late 1917. The (not so) secret Treaty of London with Italy (April 1915) caused trouble at the peace conference. In fact, it caused trouble earlier than that, for the Serbs and other South Slavs resented it. Italy was promised part of Dalmatia, across the Gulf of Venice; the Istrian peninsula, inhabited mostly by Slovenes; territory from Austria-Hungary south of the Brenner Pass; and miscellaneous islands. This was largely inconsistent with the national self-determination principle sometimes proclaimed as an Allied war aim.

In 1917, secret negotiations went on between Austria-Hungary and the

Allies. The new emperor was eager to get out of the war and perhaps save his throne. One obstacle was a strong South Slav lobby in London, where a Czech government in exile, headed by Thomas Masaryk, set up headquarters in 1916. The goal of liberating the various Slavic minorities–Czech, Slovak, South Slav, Polish–made effective propaganda: freedom for small peoples, national self-determination. Breaking up the Dual Monarchy would also unlock the back door to Germany and allow the Allied force based on Salonika to enter. Making terms with the emperor on the basis of Austro-Hungarian territorial integrity precluded such a strategy. On the other side, since late 1916 the Germans had been increasingly in effective military control of Austria-Hungary. Negotiations for a separate peace nevertheless went on between Vienna and London or Paris all through 1917. The gloomy prognosis for victory that many Allied leaders shared in 1917, after the Russian Revolution and the French mutinies, encouraged these talks. But the Italians complained, the South Slavs complained, and Vienna would not agree to the dismemberment of the empire. These talks dragged on into 1918, and in the end events overtook the diplomats.

The other theoretical possibility would seem to have been a separate peace between the Central Powers and war-weary Russia, but though there were sporadic contacts through Sweden and even through Japan, they never came to anything. The tsar's loyalty to the Allies is less astonishing when we reflect that the Germans were prevented by their alliances from offering anything the Russians wanted. Russia had gotten the Allies to pledge her the Straits, a long-coveted prize; Germany, of course, as an ally of the present owner, Turkey, could not match this offer. Perhaps the Russians would have liked more of Poland, but Germany and Austria possessed this themselves. The Russians stood to gain much from Allied victory, nothing tangible by a peace with the Central Powers. Defeat and dismemberment of the Dual Monarchy would presumably favor Russian policy in southeast Europe, which had, of course, been the initial source of the war.

Realizing this impasse, German policy sought to sow dissension in Russia by subsidizing and encouraging revolutionary movements among such dissident nationalities as Georgians and Ukrainians as well as among the antiwar socialists. Quite early in the war, Germany began to make use of the talents of the remarkable Alexander Helphand ("Parvus"), a former Russian revolutionary socialist and one-time friend of Trotsky and Lenin, who now worked for the Germans. He used his knowledge of the Russian revolutionary underground to funnel financial aid to any group that would sabotage the Russian war effort. This policy culminated in the famous "sealed train" that brought Lenin back to Russia, through German territory, in April 1917. Obviously this strategy played with fire, but the immediate goal of winning the war took precedence over all other motives.

Allied propaganda aimed at Austria-Hungary's discontented minorities was inhibited, as we have mentioned, by the hope of a separate peace with Vienna; but in the last year of the war Allied policy tended to look more and more in the direction of disrupting rather than seducing the Hapsburg state. Growing American participation in the war strengthened this trend because Wilson, an enthusiast for "rights of small nations" and "self-determination," was much more inclined than the Europeans to stress broad, idealistic slogans as war aims. He was about to give to the world his Fourteen Points. The good Lord himself had only ten, Wilson must have fourteen commandments, grumbled the blunt old tiger, Clemenceau. But European "cynicism," expressed in secret deals and old-fashioned diplomacy, had seemingly failed. The Americans came preaching "open diplomacy," principles of justice, and morality in politics.

Winning the United States as a powerful ally, which was destined to tilt the balance for victory in the end, was less a triumph for Allied diplomacy than an exposure of German ineptness. Miffed because the Americans sold goods to the Allies, the Germans early tried sabotage, to the great annoyance of Americans, and used their U-boats to sink merchant ships. This cost innocent lives, including American ones.

But American opinion was initially neutralist, and neither the president nor the public had any desire to enter an affray whose causes they only dimly understood. An important German community in the United States naturally pulled for its own land of origin. The Poles were at best divided, Russia being the most hated of the oppressors, and Jews were also inclined, if anything, to be pro-German because the worst persecutor of Jews in the pre-1914 era had been Russia. Most Irish-Americans were more anti-English than anti-German. The

German submarines at Kiel, 1918. (*National Archives.*)

broad hinterland of the American states simply believed that European wars were irrelevant to American life and interests. Sale of goods to the Allies did not reflect lack of neutrality but the opposite, since American policy traditionally stood for maximum rights of trade with both sides in a foreign war; it was only by accident that the British, controlling the high seas, could take advantage of this and the Central Powers could not.

A series of blunders extending to the famous Zimmermann note, which solicited Mexico as an ally in a German-American war, marked a suicidal German policy of losing friends in the United States. The decision to renew all-out submarine warfare, taken early in 1917, was a military-based blunder that exposed the basic weakness of German political leadership–so thought so great a German as Max Weber.

Finally entering the war in 1917, in part because of the failure of efforts to arrange a negotiated peace, the United States did not formally join the Allies but was an "associated power," pursuing something of an independent course. Unprepared for war, the United States was not able to make much of an impact until 1918; she then exerted a decisive influence in the final months of the war.

REVOLUTION IN RUSSIA

Strikes and bread riots in early March 1917 signaled the last gasp of battered Russia's discredited government; it simply crumbled. The staggering losses suffered in battle during the war in which Russia could not cope with the better equipped Germans was less a factor in this spontaneous revolution than the collapse of her infrastructure of transportation and administrative services. The meager railroad system broke down under the strain; engines wore out and could not be replaced. It must be remembered that her Allies could supply Russia with little, since the Straits as well as the Baltic lay in the Central Powers' hands. Hunger in the cities in the bitterly cold weather led to riots in which soldiers shot down the desperate protesters, including women and children; finally, they simply refused to do it, and mutiny, once begun–perhaps one may think of a single soldier who first had the courage to disobey–spread rapidly in Petrograd on the "remarkable day" of March 12 (February 28 by the old calendar then in use in Russia). Deserted by everyone, Tsar Nicholas abdicated three days later, seeking vainly to hand the throne to his brother. The crown went begging; nobody at this stage declared its abolition.

This almost bloodless revolution deposited power in the hands of a Provisional Government, pending elections to a constitutional assembly that was destined never to meet. Based partly on the largely powerless and unrepresentative national assembly (Duma) in existence since 1905, the Provisional Government was initially headed by moderate liberals: a prince, Georgy Lvov, and a history professor, Paul Miliukov. The Petrograd Soviet was its co-sponsor. Soviets or revolutionary committees of workers or soldiers were the spontaneous creation of the Revolution; they had initially appeared in 1905.

Bolshevik demonstrations in Moscow in the summer of 1917. (*Library of Congress.*)

Moral authority seemed to lie more with the concept of the soviets than anywhere else; but these innumerable small bodies somehow had to become organized. The soviets took on many of the real functions of government. There was a gulf between those who had organized the revolution and those who held the nominal political authority. This "duality of power" has characterized other revolutions.

Meanwhile, as the machinery for electing a constituent assembly went on slowly, so did the war and the problems of wounded Russia. The initial leadership of the Provisional Government reflected the views of those who thought that Russia would now establish a liberal and democratic form of government like that of her Western allies, France and Britain. Some of those who believed this were socialists, for the Menshevik faction of the Marxian Social Democrats—actually a majority of the party—had long held that Russia must pass through bourgeois democracy and capitalism before she could advance to the higher stages of socialism and communism.

As we noted, the new leadership did not contemplate taking Russia out of the war but even thought in terms of a more effective prosecution of it and closer relations with the now ideologically compatible Western Allies. London, Paris, and Washington were equally optimistic; the latter, trembling on the brink of entrance into the war, saw Russia's conversion to democracy as an additional reason for taking the plunge. Many thought that the revolution would unleash new military strength, much as the French Revolution of 1789–1793 had done.

Unfortunately, there was to be a second revolution in 1917. In institutional terms, there are three keys to what happened between the February and October revolutions: (1) the Provisional Government steadily lost what little prestige it had and failed to win respect as the legitimate authority; (2) the soviets exercised more and more real power through their central elected body and their central executive committee, which began to speak for them; and (3) the Bolshevik party (later called the Communist party), which was the radical, antiwar wing of the Social Democrats, gained control of the soviets. After April, the Bolshevik party was dominated by Lenin.

Why did these things happen? Certainly the most damaging thing the Provisional Government did was to try to carry on the war. Authority in the army was breaking down; the famous Order No. 1 issued at the start of the revolution transferred substantial powers to the soldiers' committees. The Provisional Government postponed land reform and other basic issues while awaiting both the end of the war and the new Constitution; but peasant restiveness increased, and the peasants in some places took the law into their own hands. Soldiers began to desert in order to return to their villages for the expected land redistribution.

The attempt to keep Russia's mind on the war rather than on domestic reform brought forward a talented leader. The only socialist in the first Provisional Government ministry, Alexander Kerensky was a Petrograd lawyer (born, interestingly enough, in the same Volga town that produced his rival Lenin) and a persuasive orator. He emerged as the strongest figure in the government, moving to the War ministry and then becoming Prime Minister in July, succeeding Lvov. Kerensky tried to galvanize the troops by passionate appeals to their patriotism. But a summer offensive soon collapsed, just as it had before, with costly reverses. As the army began to break up in disorder, the commander-in-chief whom Kerensky himself had appointed, General L. G. Kornilov, decided to use his troops to march on Petrograd and overthrow the Kerensky government, which he blamed for the breakdown of military discipline. Kerensky turned to the Bolsheviks for support against this counterrevolutionary movement. Like the émigré nobles in the French Revolution or the Presbyterians in the Puritan Revolution, Kerensky might have deserted the revolution and returned to the arms of the old regime, but he did not do so; he was to be devoured by the revolution anyway, from the left rather than the right.

Why was the Bolshevik party able to eat up Kerensky and emerge as the ruler of Russia by the end of the year? That outcome was unprecedented in the history of major revolutions, for the extreme left had gained and kept power in none of the classic modern revolutions, including the English Puritan revolution of the 1640s, the French Revolution of 1789–1794, the American Revolution, and the 1848 revolutions. Historians are nearly unanimous in attributing this success primarily to the genius of Lenin. Surely, if ever one man swayed the course of history it was he, beginning with his dramatic return to Russia in April.

When the 1914 war broke out, the forty-four-year-old Lenin was living rather obscurely in Zurich, having been exiled from Russia for most of the time since 1900. The son of a relatively prosperous Volga-area bureaucrat, young Ulyanov was expelled from Kazan University in 1887. He was allowed, however, to study for the examination leading to a law degree and passed it easily at Moscow University in 1891. In 1887, his brother Alexander had been involved in a plot to assassinate the emperor, Alexander III, and was put to death for this along with several others. Perhaps it was this that turned Vladimir Ulyanov into a revolutionary; but he had from the beginning a violent, powerful nature and a vigorous, polemical mind.

He was a revolutionary before he became a Marxist. The district school supervisor's son read Nikolai Chernyshevsky's *What Is to Be Done?* at the age of sixteen or seventeen, and this oddly influential book, written in prison in 1863 by one of the revolutionary nihilists, converted him to the life of a professional revolutionary, prepared to sacrifice everything to the cause. From Chernyshevsky and others of this generation, he got the idea of a revolutionary elite, totally dedicated and fanatical, the "salt of the salt," which would seize power and hold it in the name of the people—a very un-Marxian idea, for Marx and Engels had almost invariably opposed such romantic conceptions of revolution.

Marxism was becoming popular in Russia in the 1890s, and Lenin adopted it in 1891 or 1892. Until 1900, he was on the whole an orthodox Marxist engaged in the scientific study of social development rather than spontaneous acts of heroic will; he authored a legally published scholarly work, *The Development of Capitalism in Russia,* in 1899. This did not prevent him from being arrested in 1895, exiled to Siberia in 1897, and expelled from the country in 1900. He returned to Russia late in the 1905 revolution and stayed until 1907, when he was again threatened with arrest. Abroad, mostly in Switzerland and France, Lenin participated in the politics and publications of the Russian Social Democratic party. His imperious will and potent personality soon pushed him to break with its leadership and mark out for himself a new position.

The trouble with orthodox Marxism as applied to Russia, from Lenin's point of view, was that it counseled waiting a long time for the socialist revolution. To Plekhanov, the founding father of Russian Marxism, this seemed to follow from the rather mechanical sort of Marxian determinism then current. Society has to pass through the capitalist phase, drawing from it all that it has to offer, before the time is ripe for the more advanced stage of socialism. One must crawl before one can walk. Russia had barely begun the capitalist crawl. A Marxist should work with the existing currents of history to push Russia through bourgeois ascendancy, political democracy, and private capitalism.

As a Marxist, Lenin (the revolutionary name he adopted) accepted some of this, but his subtle mind searched for ways to accommodate his impatient spirit. He split the party in 1903 on the issue of the party: Should it be a mass, democratic one or, as Lenin argued, a small, tightly organized, highly disciplined vanguard, boldly guiding a working class unable to lead itself? "Independently and by its own intellect," Lenin argued, the working class can never develop a "socialist consciousness"; it can rise no higher than a "trade union consciousness."

This frank elitism shocked the majority of pre-1914 Marxists, who were committed to the slow development of democratic socialism. Lenin was regarded as an inveterate troublemaker, and his Bolshevik faction remained small, a minority of a very small group to begin with. In early 1917, there were no more than 25,000 or 30,000 Bolsheviks in Russia. He studied, wrote, and dominated a small number of doting disciples. (Lenin was not even the unquestioned Bolshevik leader; there were other Bolshevists who disagreed with him.) To his idea of an elite, vanguard party, he added theories to justify in Marxist terms a revolutionary seizure of power. Russia was only a part of world capitalism, in fact its "weakest link." So the Russian Communist party might seize power, touching off revolution throughout the world. Or, it might guide the country through the capitalist phase, greatly speeding up this unpleasant growth period if not by-passing it. The latter theory of "permanent revolution" Lenin shared with his brilliant colleague, Leon Trotsky. He did not, however, adhere altogether consistently to such views.

Fairly early in the war Lenin began to preach that it should be transformed somehow into a civil war, a class war within each country, leading to an international proletarian revolution. But a majority of the Russian leftists were "defensist," thinking like the socialists of other countries that their country had to be defended; would it, or they, be better off under the heel of German imperialism? At the Zimmerwald international socialist conference of September 1915, Lenin and Trotsky (whose real name was Lev Bronstein) got some of their antiwar ideas adopted, but few socialists from the main warring countries attended. Busying himself with philosophical studies, Lenin seemed destined to remain a lonely rebel until the first Russian revolution of 1917, and the German decision to ship him back to Russia, changed the course of history.

Arriving at the Finland station in Petrograd on April 16 after an eight-day journey from Zurich across Germany and Sweden, the famous iron horse carried Lenin and other leading Bolsheviks, including Karl Radek and Grigory

Zinoviev, as well as Lenin's wife and his sometime mistress, Inessa Armand. But the one that counted was Lenin himself. He immediately changed Bolshevik policy from support of the Provisional Government to denunciation of its continuing the war. Peace should be made immediately, and there should be social revolution and liberation of oppressed peoples in Russia. International revolution would then begin in Germany: "the German proletariat is the most loyal and reliable ally of the Russian and international proletarian revolution." The magnetism of Lenin's personality and the power of his oratory gained supporters, but many were angered and astonished at such a plan, which involved apparent surrender to the Germans, whose agent they thought Lenin to be. Kerensky defeated Lenin by a five-to-one margin during the first All-Russian Congress of Soviets on June 17.

Events were on Lenin's side. The July offensive crumpled and the Kerensky government faltered. In three years of war, the Russians had mobilized an astonishing total of some fifteen million men and had lost half of them as prisoners and casualties. The troops not fighting, those on garrison duty behind the front, were the most susceptible to subversion (this was true also in the French mutinies of 1917 and later in the German revolution). The Petrograd and Moscow garrisons, the Kronstadt fortress near Petrograd, the Baltic fleet—these were the sources of insurrection. The Bolsheviks also drew support from the Red Guards, a civilian armed militia that sprang up spontaneously as governmental authority began to break down. Like the soviets, this popular military force was organized and absorbed by the disciplined Bolsheviks—an amorphous revolutionary energy that the genius of Lenin and Trotsky managed to focus under their control.

The new Russian government had of course declared freedom of speech and released political prisoners. But Lenin made no secret of his desire to overthrow the Provisional Government in the name of the soviets, increasingly dominated by Bolsheviks. Lenin's party undoubtedly was gaining in popularity as it denounced the war and demanded immediate land reform. "All power to the soviets!" and "Peace, bread, and land!" were attractive slogans. When the Bolsheviks instigated riotous protests against the government in June and July, Kerensky decided to crack down on them. At this time, he released evidence of Lenin's financial connections with Germany. Lenin was forced to flee in disguise across the border to Finland, as other Bolshevik leaders went underground or were arrested.

But the Kornilov revolt, as we noted, forced Kerensky to seek support from the Bolsheviks. The Petrograd soviet brought about the collapse of the General's coup, as his soldiers deserted him and railroad workers refused to transport his troops. Lenin began to call for a revolutionary coup, but other high Bolshevik leaders, including Kamenev and Zinoviev, opposed him. Was this Marxism? More practically, what could one do with the power? The prospect of inheriting a ruined country, defenseless against the Germans and probably faced with civil war, dismayed all but Lenin. He continued to demand a coup

Lenin. (*Library of Congress.*)

and with Trotsky's aid finally was able to convince his colleagues. It was, however, a last-minute attempt by Kerensky to arrest the Bolshevik leaders that precipitated the latter's seizure of power.

The so-called October Revolution (November 6–7, new style), like the February one, was achieved rather easily. With Lenin issuing orders from Bolshevik headquarters at a former seminary for aristocratic ladies, soldiers and workers of the Petrograd soviets seized communications, transportation, and utilities. No one rallied to defend Kerensky, who fled after vainly trying to raise loyal troops. In Moscow, there was only a little resistance. Government ministers were arrested; a soviet congress voted power to a Council of People's Commissars, with Lenin as its president. It remained to be seen whether the peasant masses of Russia would obey this regime and whether amid defeat and disorder the Lenin regime could last. Most observers thought it would not.

The Bolsheviks had won partly because they had a leader of genius and partly because they were both disciplined and ruthless. "The dictatorship of the proletariat is power based on force and not constrained by any laws," Lenin had written. Mostly, though, they won because no one else in Russia was able and willing to govern in a hopeless situation. Amid suffering, starvation, economic chaos, the dissolution of the army, and outbursts of long-suppressed popular desires for drastic social change, the established order had simply ceased to exist.

Kerensky was unlucky. A year after his flight from the victorious Bolsheviks in November 1917, the war he had vainly tried to win finally came to a victorious close for his side. In April 1917, just as Lenin was returning to Petrograd, the United States of America had entered the war against Germany, in what was bound to prove a decisive intervention. Unfortunately, the Americans were totally unprepared for war and took about a year to tool up. Not until the summer of 1918, rather than the summer of 1917, were they able to turn the tide and force peace on the exhausted Central Powers. Had they done so sooner, Kerensky would have been able to deliver peace with victory and might have looked like a hero. Russia would have received the Dardanelles, had an honored place at the Peace Conference, and been assured a major role in the affairs of postwar Europe. Lenin's pack of desperate men would have easily been brushed aside. But, as it happened, Russia was not able to survive another year of war; the Americans came too late.

RUSSIA LEAVES THE WAR

Lenin's appeal for an international revolution was not heeded, at least not for more than a year after the October Revolution. Meanwhile, the Germans were at the gate. The battle line ran from Riga on the Baltic southeast to not far west of Minsk; in the south, troops of the Central Powers, holding most of Romania, stood close to the Ukraine. With its Army virtually extinct, Russia was at the mercy of the Germans. In early December, the Bolshevik government began negotiations for an armistice with the German military command at the latter's headquarters in the Polish town of Brest-Litovsk; the armistice announced on December 16 was followed by peace negotiations that opened in the same place on December 22.

Lenin's government had already published and denounced the secret treaties made with the Allies. Since practically all the diplomatists of the foreign ministry had walked out or been arrested, it was a rather unkempt bunch of erstwhile revolutionary conspirators who met with clean-skulled and monocled German aristocrats at Brest—one of the strangest peace conferences in history. The Germans had no interest in doing more to Russia than would enable them to withdraw troops to the western front, where they had long since known the war must be decided. The Bolsheviks hoped to use the conference as a sounding board for world revolutionary propaganda. They demanded that Paris, London, and Washington join the talks, threatening these governments with working-class revolution. They also tried to appeal over the heads of the Central Powers representatives, directly to the people. Trotsky irritated the Germans by behaving much less like the representative of a defeated power than that of a victorious one. His illusions soon vanished. The Allies were not going to make peace, the workers were not going to rise up, and the Germans were in a hurry.

Further complicating the situation was a decree issued by Lenin's government in the first flush of revolutionary enthusiasm, granting any nationality within the Russian empire the right to withdraw from it if they chose. The Ukrainians took advantage of this to proclaim autonomy and then independence, as Finland had already done. A veritable orgy of self-determination broke out, stimulated by the Bolsheviks' publication of the secret treaties. Lloyd George and Wilson, who at this time (January 8, 1918) unfurled his Fourteen Points, competed with the new Russian regime in maintaining a right of peoples to independence on the basis of nationality. If applied to Russia, such a principle meant wholesale disruptions. Thinking in terms of a future world socialist state, Lenin was initially prepared to accept the breakup of the Russian empire.

Faced with the demands of the military-dominated German emissaries that Russia surrender huge amounts of territory, Trotsky played for time, suggested not signing any treaty—"neither peace nor war"—and opposed Lenin in the Central Committee of the party. Lenin's amazing flexibility manifested itself here as a determination to sign the humiliating treaty immediately. With the German Army set to march into Russia, any other policy was sheer illusion. A majority of the Bolshevik leaders finally came around to Lenin's view, and the treaty of Brest-Litovsk was signed on March 3. The territory under Soviet control shrank by some 26 percent of the population, 27 percent of cultivated soil, and 75 percent of iron and steel production. Poland, the Baltic provinces, the Ukraine, and some Caucasian areas ceded to the Turks were either annexed by the Central Powers or became independent, which meant that they were in actuality subject to German domination. Wiped out later by German defeat in the west, the Brest peace was truly draconian; but Russia was powerless to resist it. It further divided Russia and weakened Lenin's popularity. Cries of "Traitor!" rang from the Congress of Soviets' executive committee as this body approved the treaty by a narrow margin. The great revolutionary had seemingly presided over the total liquidation of the Russian state, gambling for the stakes of world power via social revolution and losing.

THE LAST MONTHS OF THE WAR

Both sides approached despair at the end of 1917, a year that witnessed Russia's agony and ultimate departure from the war, mutinies in the French armies, signs of war weariness even in England after another bloody failure around Ypres, and, as a final disaster, the Italian rout at Caporetto. Here in the mountain war, the Italian troops, demoralized and confused in a battle fought in a snowstorm, simply threw away their guns and ran. The Italian losses included 10,000 killed, 300,000 prisoners, 400,000 deserters! This was the only Austrian victory of the war and a near catastrophe for Italy. With Allied help, the Italians finally stabilized the front along the Piave River. Italian morale was low; in August the Vatican had called for an end to "this useless slaughter," and workers had gone on strike in Turin.

But while the Allies were buoyed by American troops just beginning to arrive, the Central Powers had their own share of gloom, not least from hunger and declining morale. Everybody was near exhaustion. There were food riots in Vienna in January, and a strike in Berlin had to be crushed by the military. In 1916, eighteen socialist Reichstag members had been expelled from the party for voting against the war credits. Only a tiny minority, the Spartacists who followed Rosa Luxemburg and Karl Liebknecht directly resisted the war; but a larger minority, including distinguished elder statesmen Karl Kautsky and Eduard Bernstein, founded the Independent Social Democratic party in 1917 to oppose annexationist war aims. The peace of Brest-Litovsk severely disillusioned them. In January 1918, a half-million German workers went on strike in Berlin, defying their trade union leaders; the strike was broken, ironically, by troops released from the eastern front after the Bolshevik Revolution. Under the virtual military dictatorship of Ludendorff, there was little overt unrest in the ensuing months, which were dominated by the final German offensive.

Brest-Litovsk supplied the Germans one final ray of hope. This annexationist peace further alienated the German socialists at home, but it freed some divisions for use in the west. There was a chance to finish off the Allies in France before American troops came in large numbers. One last titanic effort might do it. It was widely understood that this was the last bid for victory.

The team of Ludendorff and Hindenburg was now firmly in command. The former was probably the most talented military leader the war produced, the latter a respected symbol. Ludendorff showed immense skill in planning the "last act" German offensive of 1918, taking incredible pains to conceal troop movement (wagon wheels wrapped in feathers!) and inventing a new type of warfare. This was based not on mass frontal assault, the recipe for lethal failure all through the western war, but on initial infiltration by elite "storm troop" units. To preserve the element of surprise, the artillery barrage, though very intense, was short. The Germans hit the British in the north on March 21 with some success, gaining 40 miles at one point and capturing nearly 100,000 prisoners. But the attack fell short of real breakthrough, as did another offensive in the Ypres-Armentières area in April.

On April 12, with the war trembling in the balance, the Germans stood close to a major victory. For the first time, the Allies achieved a united command, as French General Foch was placed in command of all the Allied armies. These German offensives won more territory than any previous offensive by either side. But they failed to gain victory. The Allied armies remained capable of counterattacks. April 24 was notable for the first significant tank battle, in which metal mastadons capable of the immense speed of 7 miles per hour fell into holes or scorched the men inside of them—a forecast of the warfare of the future but hardly an auspicious debut.

The Germans tried again in May, choosing an area further to the south, and on May 27 they advanced a record 12 miles in a day. Shells were heard again in Paris. The front was at last becoming more fluid. But the gaunt German soldiers stopped to loot, feast, and drink the wines of Champagne (perhaps their famous national beverage saved the French). At this time, American troops, green at first but young and eager, received their baptism by fire.[4] German morale began to collapse with the failure of this final offensive to force a decision. Within two months, the Allies launched a counteroffensive with increasing numbers of tanks as well as Americans, and they began slowly but steadily to push the Germans back. August 8 would be the black day of the German Army. The final gamble, like the first, had failed.

On September 14, Austria-Hungary unilaterally published a peace statement, in effect announcing its departure from the war. Bulgaria asked out of the war on September 29. Romania, which had been forced to accept harsh terms from the Central Powers after the collapse of Russia, managed to come out on the winning side by declaring war again a few hours before the Armistice! Greece also belatedly leaped in the direction of the victors. As the Germans desperately sought for terms short of total surrender, mutiny and revolution broke out at home.

The German war leaders were ready in September to negotiate an armistice, which they hoped would lead to a compromise peace. In October, a change of government in Berlin, engineered from above, was designed to clear the way for peace. Prince Max of Baden, who had long favored a compromise settlement, was appointed chancellor. Facing the news that victory was not possible, German morale suddenly fell apart. On November 3, a naval mutiny broke out at Kiel and became the signal for a series of uprisings all over Germany. The discredited Wilhelm, whose presence had become an obstacle to an armistice, was forced to abdicate, and socialist leaders proclaimed a republic.

Subsequent investigations of the Kiel mutiny—a German parliamentary committee conducted elaborate inquiries in 1925—determined that socialist propaganda had not been a significant factor. Much more important was deterioration of morale from long inactivity, poor food, the arrogance of officers, and excessively strict discipline.

Facing defeat, the Germans sought to make peace on the most favorable terms possible. They appealed to the principles Wilson had expounded as his idea of a just and lasting peace, the Fourteen Points. It appeared that under the Fourteen Points, Germany would have to return the provinces Alsace and Lorraine to France and would probably lose some territory on her eastern border to a restored Poland, but she would incur no further penalties. The Allies

---

[4]An Allied deception convinced the Germans there were far more Americans in France than there actually were.

were scarcely prepared to be so forgiving, and Wilson himself was by no means committed to lenient armistice terms. The American commander, General Pershing, opposed anything short of an unconditional surrender. Handling of the armistice was left to the Allied commander-in-chief, the French Marshal Foch. When the Germans tried to appeal directly to Wilson, he refused to deal with the kaiser's government at all. This pushed Germany toward the revolution which broke out early in November. A war-weary people, now without faith in their government, overthrew authority in the navy and in city after city; the kaiser was forced to abdicate and flee to Holland.

Although the Germans who faced Marshal Foch in the forest of Compiègne on the morning of November 11 represented the new socialist-led government, the armistice terms were severe. They were not quite as severe, however, as some Allied leaders had wished. Later it seemed an incredible blunder, the climax of a bungled war, that the onus of signing the surrender and later the humiliating peace treaty fell upon the new government rather than the old, on liberal rather than reactionary Germany. Hitler was to declare with superficial plausibility that the socialists and republicans had betrayed Germany. The Germans had to agree to withdraw their army behind the Rhine; surrender all their submarines and heavy artillery and the major part of their navy; and allow the establishment of Allied garrisons east of the Rhine at Mainz, Coblenz, and Cologne. With their country in chaos, the German delegates could do nothing else. The war was over, and Germany lay helpless.

But Allied armies did not invade and occupy Germany, as they did after World War II. There seemed no need for it, and the Allies themselves were heartily weary of the war. The German Army retired into Germany in good array, clearly beaten but not really shattered in the field. In World War II, Hitler defiantly refused all terms, and the Allies refused to grant him any, so that the only possible outcome was the invasion of Germany. Things did not proceed so far in 1918. The armistice terms, the chaos in Germany and also Austria-Hungary, the abdication of the kaiser, and the naval blockade, which continued until the signing of the peace treaty, gave the victor powers sufficient security that the Central Powers could not hope to renew the war. It remains a curious fact that the armies of the defeated power were still on enemy soil at the war's end.

The remarkable bitterness of this frenetic crusade was exemplified in the continuation of the blockade for half a year after the signing of the armistice, condemning much of central Europe to hunger and resulting disease. In revenge, the severe influenza epidemic of 1918–1919 spread to all parts of the world, not sparing the victor countries. "No plague ever killed so many people in so short a time," writes the historian of this "pandemic" in the United States.[5]

Austria-Hungary had collapsed, never to be reconstructed; the Czechs, Slovaks, Croats, and Poles were busy making arrangements to create several

---

[5]Alfred W. Crosby, *America's Forgotten Pandemic: The Influenza of 1918* (New York: Cambridge University Press, 1989).

new states where the Hapsburg Empire had lain for half a millennium. The war had destroyed the three great dynastic empires of eastern Europe. The democracies had proven stronger, it was said. But Germany had put up a magnificent resistance against heavy odds. In his history of the Great War, Winston Churchill, with that gallantry toward a brave foe that was one of his attributes, graciously acknowledged the magnitude of the German achievement; though succumbing in the end to insurmountable odds, they had held out longer than anyone could have thought possible. The Germans felt they had earned the right to honorable terms. But the fact remained that their inadequate political structure had collapsed, they were helpless, and public opinion in the democracies, aroused by war propaganda, did not follow Churchill's lines but was almost hysterically vindictive, calling for appropriate punishment to be inflicted on the guilty aggressor. *Vae victis.*

4

Europe Transformed:
The Aftermath of War
in the 1920s

THE PARIS PEACE CONFERENCE

The sense of a world in crisis lent urgency to the convening of a peace conference at Paris soon after the end of the war in November 1918. It began with almost unseemly haste, within a few weeks of the armistice, and produced a peace
treaty with Germany by June 1919. Lenin, someone said, was the invisible partner at the Paris conclaves. One of the many postmortem criticisms of this peace
was that it would have been better to wait until passions cooled; but at the time,
the very turbulence of these passions seemed reason for cooling them by the
clear mandate of an authoritative settlement. Boundaries lay in obscurity; three
great empires had collapsed; revolution was rife; and the world demanded a de-
finitive end to the war so that it might begin the process of reconstruction.

To Paris, then, in January of 1919, came President Woodrow Wilson,
the first American president ever to leave his native shores while in office and a
symbol of hope to many in the Old World. David Lloyd George represented
Britain, with France's Georges Clemenceau and Italy's Vittorio Orlando round-
ing out the Big Four; hosts of their ministers and advisers of course accompanied the leaders. Subsequently, a great array of "suitors and suppliants" came
from all over the world, each seeking something from the supposedly all-powerful statesmen who had assembled to end the terrible war with a peace of justice. The notable absentees were Russia and the defeated power, Germany.

Unfortunately, the statesmen proved neither omnipotent nor omniscient. The world was not altogether consoled, and many of the suppliants went away empty-handed. The Paris peace conference of 1919 remains one of history's most dramatic scenarios, around which a furious controversy raged. Some thought the victors had imposed harsh and vindictive terms on Germany, guaranteeing that feelings of revenge would furnish the ground for another war. But others thought Germany was too leniently handled, getting off with slight loss of territory and indemnities that never were actually paid.

Although one rationale of the settlement was national self-determination, unsatisfied nationalisms remained to plague the future. Strategically, the peace was glaringly weak: Too few had a stake in maintaining it, too many in overthrowing it. Judged by its results, the settlement obviously left something to be desired, for another world war broke out within twenty years. This peace turned out to be nothing but a long armistice. Whether this can be blamed on the participants in the Paris conference is another question. Many forces were beyond their control. They could hardly put the Dual Monarchy back together again, even if they wanted to. Neither could they cause Lenin's Bolsheviks to cooperate with the capitalists. Nor could the bitter hatred aroused by a war that had cost so many millions of casualties be eliminated.

The victorious Allies were far from united in their approach to the peace settlement. Though two of Wilson's Fourteen Points were specifically withdrawn at the time of the armistice, they constituted a quasi-official basis for the peace. Wilson was the man of the hour; millions of cheering people crowded to greet him as he made a brief triumphal tour of the Continent prior to the convening of the conference on January 18, 1919. The Fourteen Points were often vague, but they indicated disarmament on all sides; "a free, open-minded, and absolutely impartial adjustment of all colonial claims"; return of Alsace-Lorraine to France; "a readjustment of the frontier of Italy . . . along clearly recognizable lines of nationality"; "autonomous development" for the peoples of Austria-Hungary; and an independent Poland with access to the sea. They spoke of "historically established lines of allegiance and nationality" as guides to a Balkan settlement. The Fourteen Points were against secret diplomacy and for "open covenants openly arrived at." They recommended "a general association of nations . . . under specific covenants," [*covenant* was one of Wilson's favorite words] "for the purpose of affording mutual guarantees of political independence and territorial integrity to great and small States alike"–the famous League of Nations so extensively discussed during the war.

From these and other Wilsonian pronouncements, people perhaps inaccurately associated the American president with a nonpunitive peace, one that would not leave too many scars on the defeated powers or breed a spirit of revenge. But in discussions with the Allies about what the Fourteen Points meant, Wilson withdrew point 2, relating to "freedom of the seas," on British protest, and inserted a statement that Germany must pay compensation "for all damage done to the civilian population of the Allies and their property by the forces of Germany." It became evident at this time, just before the armistice, that the French and the Italians objected to nearly all the points. The United States threatened to withdraw from the war if they were repudiated, however.

Against the Wilson peace outlook, with which they almost entirely disagreed, the French had drawn up a shopping list. It included (1) French military control of the Rhine, (2) a crushing indemnity levied against Germany, (3) German disarmament, (4) German territorial reduction, (5) "crippling the German political organization," and (6) depriving her of economic resources. Marshal Foch and his military advisers cared little about anything except the destruction of German power and her territorial dismemberment. To the French, determined to prevent a repetition of 1914, some such program was almost a sine qua non; and Clemenceau fought hard for it, although he did not personally believe in the partition of Germany. A League of Nations appealed to the French less as an idealistic new way in diplomacy than as an alliance to stand guard against Germany.

The British government stood somewhere in the middle, but Lloyd George had tied his hands by promising the British people that Germany would be made to pay for the war. Britain's best interests might dictate keeping Germany intact. Whereas the French believed that their security depended on destruction of German power per se, the British were much more inclined to settle for a payment to ease the British taxpayer's burden.

Also limiting the peacemakers' freedom were the secret treaties–particularly, now that Russia and Romania had cancelled out, the one with Italy, which promised German and Slavic territory to the Italians. Others dealt with Asia. There was a series of evidently contradictory dispositions about the Middle East: Palestine, someone quipped, was the much-promised land. In the famous Balfour Declaration, which was designed partly to win Jewish support for the war, it had been promised to the Jews as a homeland. But it had also been promised to King Hussein of the Arabs as a reward for joining in the fight against Turkey. Meanwhile, the Sykes-Picot agreement of 1916 seemed to have partitioned the region between France and Britain. The Americans cared little about the Middle East, but they turned out to care a great deal about China. Japan's acquisition of Shantung, formerly in the German zone of influence, struck American opinion as a sordid "imperialist" deal.

Of such jarring counsels was the hectic peace conference made. The Allies (France, Britain, Italy, and the United States) did not argue with the defeated powers; they argued with one another. They excluded Russia, boycotting the communist regime completely and at one moment coming close to recognizing the Siberian warlord, Admiral Kolchak, as the legal Russian government. Lloyd George initially wanted to invite the Bolsheviks, but he stood alone in this position and, criticized even within his own government, soon gave in. It is doubtful that Lenin's government would have come anyway, or come in any spirit of cooperation. Allied policy was rapidly retreating from giving any great amount of aid to the Whites, though Winston Churchill advocated it. The compromise solution was to neither recognize nor intervene against the Russian

Reds, which added up to total negativism. Such positive policy as there was took the form of hoping for a zone of new states to serve as a buffer against bolshevism and to be potential allies for France.

The loss of Russia as a powerful ally was a key to French policy at Paris. France felt it was necessary to weaken Germany and to build up a strong Poland as a potential substitute alliance partner. Thus many of the features of the settlement with Germany may be traced to the silent factor of Russia's defection.

The adjustment of Big Four disagreements was accomplished at the cost of much friction. At one point, Wilson summoned his ship to take him home. Italy's Orlando did walk out, after furious exchanges with the American president, although he subsequently returned. Clemenceau regarded the moralistic Wilson as a self-righteous and narrow-minded hypocrite; Wilson considered all the Europeans to be touched with evil. Lloyd George, aided by the more supple Wilsonian chief adviser, Colonel House, worked to secure compromises. Wilson's relative ignorance of complex European questions hampered his attempts to teach virtue to the soiled Europeans. Sigmund Freud, who joined with American diplomat William Bullitt in attempting a psychoanalysis of Wilson, thought the American President suffered from neurotic indecisiveness traceable to his ambivalent feelings about his father, but one may question whether it was indecision so much as inadequate experience of world politics that handicapped Wilson.

Furthermore, the United States, powerful though her role had been, had not expended nearly as much blood and treasure in the war as had France and Britain. Wilson was a disappointment to those European liberals who had expected much from his leadership; he was "unable to clothe with the flesh of life the commandments which he had thundered from the White House," John Maynard Keynes wrote. Yet Wilson withstood terrific pressure for a truly "Carthaginian" peace, including the partition of Germany.

The most acute clash of wills at Paris occurred when the British and the Americans joined in refusing the French demand for territorial dismemberment of Germany. The French wanted the western, Rhineland portion of Germany to be made a separate state. Wilson stood firm on the principle of self-determination; the British had more in mind the balance of power, fearing that any drastic weakening of Germany might open the dikes to bolshevism. Germany did lose some territory. She had to return Alsace and Lorraine to France and a small portion of land to Belgium. The Saarland was given over to French economic use, under international administration, for fifteen years, after which there would be a plebiscite. Most galling to the Germans were significant cessions to the restored Poland in the east. The German city of Danzig was internationalized, Memel given to Lithuania. The "Polish Corridor" now awkwardly separated part of Prussia from the rest of Germany. But Germany was neither partitioned nor deprived of the great bulk of her population, resources, and territory.

In few cases were the territorial cessions really unjust; not even the Germans complained about returning Alsace-Lorraine to France, and the popula-

The Big Four at the Paris Peace Conference: Orlando, Lloyd George, Clemenceau, and Wilson. (*National Archives.*)

tion in the east was ethnically mixed, so that a minority of one group or another was inescapable. Since Poland had to be given an outlet to the sea she was ceded Danzig and the Corridor. Poland received less territory than she and the French had wanted. East Prussia remained German at the insistence of Wilson. All told, Germany lost about 10 percent of her 1914 population, mostly from Prussia's provinces of Posen, Silesia, Brandenburg, and West Prussia. Within a few years, natural population increase made up her losses, so that Germany's 1933 population exceeded that of 1910. Her most serious resource losses were the iron ore of Lorraine and coal from the Saar. Yet, after the war French iron had to come to the German steel mills in the Ruhr.

By way of compensation to the French for a sacrifice they regarded as tremendous, Germany was subjected to immense reparations claims. Here the British supported France, and Wilson had to give in. Some British economic advisers were skeptical about the reparations bill, fearing that it would disrupt the world economy. Some French hoped to use it as a basis for future German dismemberment. The total figure was left open, to be finally calculated by May 1921. But the inclusion of indirect damages (for example, payment for pensions to widows and orphans of dead soldiers) as well as direct damages meant that the bill would be astronomical by current standards; many billions of dollars.

Additionally, Germany lost all her colonies, which Germans thought a clear violation of one of the Fourteen Points. Although German colonies were put under League of Nations "mandate," the Allies did not surrender their own colonies to supposed international control. Germany was unilaterally disarmed; she had to reduce her army to 100,000 men without a General Staff and give up large guns, submarines, military aircraft, and all but six warships. The Heligoland fortifications were to be demolished. Any army so deprived of the tools of modern war would be impotent. The Allies were to occupy strategic points on the Rhine for at least fifteen years, and Germany was forbidden to keep troops in a demilitarized zone extending 30 miles east of that river. This gave France strategic security so long as the ban was maintained, but the area remained German.

While severe, the terms were hardly savage. Perhaps, as some argued, they were either too harsh or too lenient. Machiavelli had long ago pointed out that you can either crush a foe or make friends with him; what is most dangerous is to insult him and let him go free. The compromise of Versailles treated Germany as if she were guilty and hurt her in small ways, but it by no means destroyed her as a potentially powerful state. It offended her pride without greatly impairing her strength. Could one enforce the disarmament provisions or collect the indemnities against a Germany determined to resist them? Much depended on the shape of events to come.

Given a chance to make a statement before signing the Versailles treaty, the Germans protested that it was "a peace of violence and not of justice." The reply of the Allies was that justice was being done for Germany's "crime against humanity." Germany won a few minor concessions as the result of her appeal. This has led to speculation about what Germany might have achieved had she been able to worm her way into the conference as Talleyrand had done in 1815. No such diplomatic talent emerged from the German side on this occasion.

Both sides thus accepted the view that this was a punitive peace, the Allies alleging German war guilt (which was specifically affirmed in article 231 of the treaty), the Germans denying it. This led to an intellectual battle of historical interpretation in the ensuing years, leading on the whole to a qualified German victory: In the 1920s, most scholars who studied the records with care concluded that either everybody was guilty or nobody was. Versailles left an uneasy sense of guilt in the West, and the whole peace conference was said to have been poisoned by irrational hatreds. "Paris was a nightmare, and everyone there was morbid," Keynes thought. "The Treaty is a crime born of blind revenge and insatiable greed," U.S. Senator William Borah declared as he prepared to lead a senatorial rejection of the Versailles treaty, chiefly because of the League of Nations. Colonel House himself, one of the treaty's leading architects, wrote gloomily in his diary just after the treaty's signature on June 28 that

To those who are saying that the Treaty is bad and should never have been made and that it will involve Europe in infinite difficulties in its enforcement, I feel like admitting it.

But, House added, "I would also say in reply that empires cannot be shattered and new states raised upon their ruins without disturbance." "Sad peace! Laughable interlude between the massacres of peoples!" exclaimed Romain Rolland, thus ending his long wartime journal on June 23, 1919. Rolland was one of the very few European writers who had opposed the war from the start. To him, the peace was as bad as the war.

The treaty with Germany, which also contained the Covenant of the League of Nations, was only one of several made in various parts of Paris in 1919 and 1920. Some of the negotiations dragged on long after the signing of the Treaty of Versailles, which took place with a great flourish in the Hall of Mirrors on June 28, 1919. Wilson sailed home to encounter a hostile Senate and suffer a stroke later in the year. Europe continued in disorder as the Russian civil war went on, bolshevism appeared in Hungary,[1] and near anarchy reigned in both Germany and Italy. The signing of the Versailles treaty permitted an end to the Allied blockade of Germany. Soviet Russia was also subject to the blockade, which was a factor in the terrible Russian famine of 1921.

The treaties of St. Germain and Trianon treated Austria and Hungary, the two remnants of the new dismembered Dual Monarchy, as defeated powers, limiting the size of their armies, compelling them to pay reparations, depriving them of territory, and forbidding Austria to unite with Germany, even though this was undoubtedly the wish of an overwhelming majority of the Austrian people. They were required to recognize the independence of Poland, Yugoslavia, and Czechoslovakia, the other successor states. Austria ceded territory to Poland, Italy, and Yugoslavia. Italy's demand for what had been promised in the secret Treaty of London had occasioned one of the sharpest clashes at Paris when Wilson refused to be bound by the treaty. The Italians declared that having lost his virtue to France and Great Britain, the American president sought to regain it at their expense. They demanded even more than had been promised them, adding the city of Fiume to the list. In the end, a compromise only partially appeased the angry Italians.

Hungary was handled even more savagely than Austria. Having sacrificed any lingering claim on Allied sympathy by going communist in the middle of the Paris conference, the Magyars after being invaded and pillaged by the

[1]Hungary was ruled for four months in the spring and summer of 1919 by a Hungarian Communist, Bela Kun, who had been a prisoner of war in Russia and knew Lenin personally. In alliance with the Hungarian Social Democrats, he tried to carry out an ambitious program of agricultural and industrial nationalization. But Romania, encouraged by the Allies, intervened to overthrow his government and counterrevolutionary terror followed.

Romanians were forced to sign a treaty that gave away most of the old Hungary to Czechoslovakia, Romania, Yugoslavia, and even to Austria—and were required to pay reparations on top of this. Of all the victims of the war, Hungary could perhaps claim the most injustice, for although it was Vienna, not Budapest, that had wanted war in the first place, Budapest's losses were the greatest of all the countries. But Slovaks, Croatians, and Romanians who had suffered second-class citizenship under Hungarian rule in the past could muster little sympathy for their former oppressors, and they were on the winning side.

The boundaries of these more fortunate successor states were not determined without a struggle. Yugoslavia and Italy quarreled over territory along the northeastern shores of the Adriatic, previously a part of the Dual Monarchy. The two countries set the boundary late in 1920 by a treaty at Rapallo, although there was still more trouble until Fiume was given to Italy in 1924. Yugoslavia, the new kingdom of the Serbs, Croats, and Slovenes, also had to settle its boundaries with Romania and Austria. Two of the other new states, Poland and Czechoslovakia, clashed over Teschen, which Lloyd George confessed he had never heard of before coming to Paris. The battling Poles also fought Russia for two years, as we know, to settle their eastern borders, and they struggled with Lithuanians for possession of the city of Vilna, an issue at length decided by a plebiscite in favor of Poland. The restored state of Poland, by winning rather generous settlements from all her neighbors, thereby incurred their ill will, which haunted the Poles down to 1939.

The device of a plebiscite did not always persuade the losing party that justice had been done, for much depended on how the voting unit was defined. For example, while Fiume and Trieste, both Adriatic cities, were themselves mainly Italian, the surrounding rural regions were Slavic. In the important industrial region of Silesia, inhabited by both Poles and Germans, voting results depended on the size of the district polled, and the Germans complained of gerrymandering.

Bulgaria's fate was settled in the Treaty of Neuilly in November 1919; she also lost territory, agreed to pay damages, and had to reduce her army to a handful. But in attempting to treat Turkey as a defeated power, the Allied peacemakers caught a tartar. A nationalist revival under Mustapha Kemal, hero of the Dardanelles victory, brought the former Ottoman Empire out of the war with high morale. The 1920 treaty of Sèvres dismembered the Turkish empire, depriving it of its Arab provinces, delivering territory in Thrace to the Greeks, and declaring the Straits (once promised to Russia) an international zone. But Kemal's nationalist movement repudiated the government of the sultan that signed this treaty; then he turned on the Greeks, who had marched in to enforce the treaty, and eventually defeated them. This war dragged on until 1922, by which time the Allies had almost ceased to exist. In 1923, a new treaty, signed at Lausanne, secured more favorable terms for Turkey, where Kemal now headed a new government. Turkey recovered some territory from Greece and regained control of the Straits, which she agreed to demilitarize and open to ships of all nations. Turkey was the only defeated country, or even victorious one, that came out of the war with better morale than it started with.

All of this confused even the experts at Paris in 1919, and if the student finds it confusing, small wonder. Empires had been shattered and new states raised. Let us try to summarize. The three great empires of the Hapsburgs, the Romanovs, and the Hohenzollerns had fallen. No fewer than nine new states appeared in Europe (and several others in the Middle East). Finland, Estonia, Latvia, and Lithuania, formerly subject to Russia, were now lined up along the east shore of the Baltic Sea, a kind of *cordon sanitaire,* as the French said, between Bolshevik Russia and the West. Poland, a large country, was restored to national existence for the first time since 1795, receiving land from each of her former partitioners, Russia, Austria-Hungary, and Germany. Czechoslovakia and Yugoslavia came from the now-defunct Dual Monarchy, Czechoslovakia entirely and Yugoslavia partially. Yugoslavia, of course, contained prewar Serbia as its nucleus but added large chunks of pre-1914 Hungary and Austria and a little of Bulgaria. The other two new states (new as such) were Austria and Hungary. Disjointed relics of the old empire, each was left derelict by the detachment of its former possessions. Romania emerged as a much larger state—luckiest of all, considering her war record.

But these new countries in the east and center of Europe were untested. Those who looked into the future with trepidation stressed the instability of boundaries and the strategic weakness of a "Balkanized" continent. The losers of the war, especially Germany and Russia, would surely try to regain what they had lost. The winners, including Poland, Yugoslavia, Czechoslovakia, and Romania, were not only new and weak but divided among themselves. Several of them had never existed in all previous history.

It was frequently remarked that to create new boundaries is to create new problems. The attempt to organize Europe along principles of nationality resulted in political instability, not only because it created many small and unstable countries but because it had proved impossible both to honor the principle of nationality and to divide up Europe in a way that gave each linguistic or cultural unit its own independent government. Ethnic minorities were left over even in the new Europe. Czechoslovakia was an amalgamation of Czechs and Slovaks, with some Germans thrown in; and the two Slavic peoples did not always perfectly harmonize. The Croats, Slovenes, and Serbs who were to try living together might all be Yugoslavs, but they had very different traditions and characteristics; they were divided by culture and religion.

Poland contained German, White Russian, and Lithuanian minorities. Romania had absorbed many Magyars. There were disputes between Yugoslavia and Italy, Poland and Czechoslovakia, and Greece and Turkey in areas where peoples were hopelessly intermixed. There was no way to satisfy every ethnic claim and still retain states large enough to be prosperous and to have defensible borders. The new Europe was a kind of desperate compromise among the conflicting and incompatible demands of cultures, economics, and defense.

THE LEAGUE OF NATIONS

Its creators knew better than anyone else the serious defects of the peace settlement. We have not named all these defects. In general, the non-European peoples, victims of colonialism who had expected that the war and the new Wilsonian diplomacy would bring them relief, went away disappointed. It scarcely lay within the province of the peace conference to tell the British to grant independence to India and Ireland, or Japan to free Korea, or France to surrender Indochina. Among the disappointed suppliants at Paris in 1919 was one later known as Ho Chi Minh, who thereafter turned to communism. The war had led to demands from these and others for their freedom. All over the colonial world, the war deflated the white man's image and encouraged movements of liberation from Western domination.

The Arabs, who had fought alongside the British against their Turkish overlords, now bitterly reproached the Allies for not giving them their liberty; and in the Far East both China and Japan, for different reasons, lacked confidence in their wartime partners. Japan had entered the war with a promise that she would receive Germany's former island possessions in the Pacific and the German leasehold in the Chinese province of Shantung. China had entered the war in its later stages chiefly to be able to make an appeal against imperialism at the peace conference. At Paris, Japan got her rewards, imperialism received no rebuke, and the Chinese were bitter. In the United States especially, a strong reaction against this seemingly cynical "deal" caused angry denunciations of both Japan and the Paris peace. Shantung as much as anything was the reason many Americans decided to repudiate the Treaty of Versailles, to refuse to enter the League of Nations, and to write off the European world as morally lost.

At Paris, the Japanese requested and were refused a statement affirming the equality of races; also rejected was a Chinese demand for an end of the "unequal treaties" by which the Europeans in China obtained a privileged position.

The months following the "peace" of 1919 witnessed violence in Ireland, India, Egypt, and Korea, as well as in Russia, Turkey, Hungary, and Dalmatia; there seemed to be less peace than there had been even during the war. In 1920, Lord James Bryce, one of the leading architects of the League of Nations, saw "lunacy everywhere. . . . We all say to one another that the war was bad, but this sort of peace is worse." "No one believes that the inequalities temporarily established by the Treaty of Versailles can be made the basis of a real peace," added Swiss professor William E. Rappard. Faced with a world in such volcanic eruption after the mighty upheaval of 1914–1918, Wilson and others hoped that new machinery of international relations could work as a stabilizer. The League of Nations might serve as adjudicator of disputes, administrator of world justice, and, in the last resort, maintainer of the peace. As the world cooled down, this agency of world government, replacing the old "international anarchy," should preside over its readjustments.

At Paris, President Wilson devoted a great deal of his personal attention

EUROPE AFTER THE WAR, 1919

to the drafting of the "Covenant" of the League—his own word, one intending to convey the solemnity of a biblical rite. The League was indeed the object of an almost religious faith. It was widely believed that the "old regime" in foreign affairs was now as obsolete as the pre-1789 internal political order; it was to be swept aside by a revolution in the conduct of international relations. This discredited old way employed such dubious means as secret treaties, rival alliances, and devious diplomacy; it represented national selfishness dependent on armed might, and it tried to keep the peace only through the balance of power. Had it not failed so badly in 1914 that an entirely new way must be found? The world must replace power blocs and national militarism with international cooperation.

In a general way, almost everybody approved the popular idea of a League of Nations during the war. And, a number of groups had attempted to work out the specific plans of such a league. When one got down to details, though, agreement often broke down in the face of practical difficulties. Would the greater nations really relinquish control of their armed forces to an international institution—which would then be a world government or superstate? Would they agree in advance to abide by the decision of such an international body in any dispute? If not, could the League be anything more than a place to exchange views? On the one hand, utopian expectations surrounded the notion of a League of Nations—it was expected somehow to abolish war and usher in the international millennium. On the other hand, when the moment of truth arrived nations simply were not prepared to hand over to the League any real power, for this would mean surrendering the jealously guarded sovereign power to choose war or peace, to defend the nation, to provide for national security.

Wrestling with such contradictions at Paris, Wilson and the other Allied statesmen hammered out the Covenant and wrote it into the Treaty of Versailles. Some people thought it a mistake to tie it so closely to the peace settlement. Some thought it too weak; others feared it might be too strong. It was attacked as a "Holy Alliance" of the big powers rather than true international democracy, because it gave somewhat more power to the larger nations, who were to hold permanent seats on the council, or upper chamber. Briefly, the member nations who joined the League (initially, it excluded Germany and the other Central Powers, a feature often criticized) agreed to submit their disputes to conciliation or adjudication before going to war; that is, they had to first try to settle conflicts by peaceful means through the machinery of international organization. If after trying this procedure they still could not agree, presumably they might go to war with the League's blessing—another point that was criticized by those who hoped to do away with war altogether. If member nations went to war before going through this procedure, they were liable to such punishment as the breaking off of normal relations, economic boycotts, or even war.

Another article of the Covenant, one put in at the insistence of President Wilson, declared that all members guaranteed the political independence and territorial integrity of each member state. In case of a violation, however, the League might only recommend action; it could not demand it. The meaning of this article 10 was somewhat obscure, not by accident. It represented an ambiguous compromise between those who, like the French, wanted a strong League and others who wished to avoid ironclad commitments. Article 10 was destined to cause the most controversy when the United States Senate debated the League and finally refused to approve it, after proposing a number of "reservations" that Wilson refused to accept. Its foes claimed that Article 10 violated the U.S. Constitution and endangered the nation by constituting an obligation to go to war automatically at the behest of a foreign body. In fact it obviously did not mean that; yet its lack of clarity helped discredit the League.

While all members sat in the League's assembly, only twelve held seats on the council, where the important decisions, such as whether a violation of the Covenant had occurred, were made. The major powers held permanent seats on the council, and the unanimous vote of this body was required on important matters. But the parties to a dispute could not vote when it came up for decision.

There were other important features of the League. To deal with the thorny issue of imperialism, the League provided for a mandate system; countries held colonies as trustees of the League and were supposed to report to the League on their progress. Also established were various agencies for international cooperation in such fields as health, conditions of labor, and collection of information. A permanent secretariat was to administer the League's activities from headquarters in Geneva, Switzerland. An affiliated World Court was expected to develop into a real instrument of international law.

What did all this mean? Those who had dreamed of a world state were obviously disappointed, for the League had no real power except as the separate member nations chose to grant it on any particular occasion. The League did not possess its own armed force, for example; it would have to request forces from the various member states in case of an emergency. That the Covenant ventured as far as it did in Article 10 was sufficient to frighten off the United States, which dealt the young institution a serious blow when it refused to join. The system of sovereign national states was far from dead. The war, in fact, had everywhere strengthened nationalism. No major power would accept in advance an obligation to uphold the status quo; boundaries were too insecure, their moral value too unclear.

What the League might amount to only time would tell. Those who were skeptical about its ability to install a whole new peace system hoped that it might at least serve a useful purpose in bringing nations together on a regular basis, teaching them habits of cooperation, and providing a forum for the solution of disputes. But with the refusal of the United States to take part in the League, the French felt that a blow was dealt to their hope for security in Europe. Her allies politely declined to take any appreciable part in upholding a peace settlement they had helped to write. In addition to the ambiguous pledges of the League, France had obtained from Wilson and Lloyd George promises of a guaranty treaty pledging the United States and Great Britain to defend the Versailles treaty frontiers. This, too, the United States refused to approve; in fact, it was never even brought to a Senate vote, the situation being hopeless.

Thus the Allies were breaking up, another ominous sign for the future. In his memoirs of the war, one of many literary masterpieces the war produced (its only saving grace), British poet Robert Graves remarked that just after the war "Anti-French feeling among most ex-soldiers amounted almost to an obsession. . . . Pro-German feeling was increasing." His buddies said they would never fight another war, unless it was against the French! American-French relations cooled rapidly, too, after an initial euphoria. And, American opinion turned sharply on England because of the rebellion in Ireland. The Americans retreated to their isolation from foreign entanglements as suddenly as any great people has ever changed. Britain and its Dominions (Canada, Australia, South Africa, New Zealand), which had played such a stalwart part in the war, were only a step behind. The great era of disenchantment with the war and with the peace was about to begin. In such soil, the League of Nations could hardly take root and grow.

Shorn of its American sponsor, the League struggled in the 1920s. Its location bred a controversy, until the Swiss city of Geneva, city of Calvin and Rousseau, received the honor. Then the design of its buildings caused another, when the Swiss architectural modernist Le Corbusier had his proposal rejected in favor of a stately neo-classical edifice. The League survived, but not as a system of "collective security" guaranteeing the status quo. In 1925, the defeat of the so-called Geneva Protocol made it clear that most member states wanted no part of a commitment to go to war against an "aggressor" upon word from the League. But the "Geneva spirit," as it became known in the later 1920s, counted for something. In the Swiss city, statesmen might meet and discuss problems in a peaceful atmosphere. The League developed an institutional momentum. It continued to exist as a small beacon of hope in a turbulent world.

CIVIL WAR IN RUSSIA

Bolshevik ideology suggested the dissolution of the state. Lenin's essay, "The State and Revolution," written during the very year 1917, affirmed the utopian element in Marx's thought: After the proletarian revolution inaugurating a classless society, the last turn of history's wheel, the state would (in Engels's phrase) wither away, at least as a coercive authority. Affairs would be administered by plain men in their everyday activities; workers and peasants would replace ministers and judges. Everything would be handled spontaneously and informally by those freed from exploitation and oppression. Neither law nor government in their objectified forms would be needed. Workers would manage the factories; comrades gathered together in friendly conclave would deal with what antisocial behavior lingered on as a vestige of the past. Of course, crime and corruption could be expected to vanish, along with the poverty and injustice that bred these social evils. The economy was supposed to work somehow without money or market, those "alienating" forces associated with capitalism.

Of such dreams is utopia made; the realities of postrevolutionary Russia were far different. It was a nightmare world of brutalized masses driven mad by the sufferings of war and now released from social controls. Having seized power by insurrection, using a fairly small number of urban workers and soldiers, the Bolsheviks did not have the support of a majority of Russians; or if they did at one moment have it, that moment did not last long. Even among the revolutionaries, the Bolsheviks were a minority. In the elections to the constitutional assembly, the Bolsheviks won only about one-fourth of the delegates. The largest party was that to which the peasants were most loyal, the Social Revolutionary party. But the Red Guards were loyal to Lenin, and on his orders they dispersed the Constituent Assembly (left over, as it were, from the first 1917 revolution) when it attempted to meet early in 1918.

The process of making Russia a constitutional democracy was rudely shattered by brute force; as historian Richard Pipes observes, "The boundless brutality with which they [the Bolsheviks] thenceforth ruled Russia stemmed from the knowledge, gained on January 5, that they could do so with impunity." All other parties, except a few left-wing SRs who lasted until the summer of 1918, left the government. The liberal Constitutional Democrats were suppressed first, along with the "bourgeois" press: "We cannot give the bourgeoisie the opportunity to slander us," Lenin declared. The SRs and the Mensheviks continued in existence for some time, but their publications were censored and they were subject to harassment. All non-Bolshevik parties were outlawed in July 1918. "The Terror and the Cheka [Bolshevik political police] are indispensable," Lenin said. He was quite prepared to "carry out merciless mass terror." Only sentimentalists believed you could create a new society without smashing the old ruling class; you seized state power and used it ruthlessly. Later, the utopia; now, the final great battle of the class war. And, in war, whoever is not with us is against us; a Menshevik who shrinks from revolutionary terror is "objectively" an imperialist reactionary.

"White" rebellions against Lenin's government began in May 1918. White Guards and Red Guards had begun fighting in Finland in January, the Germans supporting General Mannerheim's White (antisocialist) forces. With Russia rapidly falling toward anarchy, local regimes sprang up, usually under the leadership of some military commander who rallied former tsarist army elements and capitalized on growing disenchantment with the Bolshevik regime.

Although Lenin had tried to win their favor, the peasants mistrusted the Bolsheviks. The immediate need was food for the primary source of Bolshevik power, the urban workers. The government fixed prices at a low level, and when the peasants refused to sell at these prices it sent troops to seize farm produce. Thus, they alienated the peasants, who were engaged in seizing the land formerly owned by landed nobility and the state. The peasants seem to have hated both sides in the civil war. (Involved in the fighting in some areas, the Cossacks were a third force, neither reactionary nor Bolshevik.)

Of course, until November the war was still going on in Europe, and

White regimes could pose as friends of the Allies against the Bolshevik defectors, whose separate peace with Germany made them highly unpopular in France, Britain, and the United States. To compound the confusion, 30,000 Czech prisoners of war got loose in Russia and fought the Bolsheviks all the way to Siberia; the minorities in the Dual Monarchy were making their own nationalist revolutions, which depended upon Allied victory. Chiefly to protect military supplies in such areas as Archangel, the Crimea, and the Baltic states, the Allies adopted a policy of limited intervention and sent some aid to the White leaders. The Japanese entered Siberia by way of Vladivostok. They were followed by the Americans, who were as concerned to watch the Japanese as to combat communism. At one time, various White regimes held a good part of Russia, receiving some aid from the Allies. But the White groups could not cooperate with each other, and some of them were viciously reactionary. Finns, Poles, and Balts, fighting for their national independence, were not compatible with such Russian chauvinists as Generals Wrangel and Denikin, White warlords of the South.

It is false to assert, as the Russian Communists did, that the Western capitalist powers intervened to try to overthrow Lenin's government primarily because their reactionary capitalist hearts hated socialism. The Allies had no clear understanding of what was going on in Russia for some time and no desire to get involved in the massive and hopeless task of governing Russia or reshaping its society. They did dislike the Bolsheviks intensely, less because they were Communists than because they were helping Germany. Lenin was regarded, for understandable if erroneous reasons, as simply a German agent. The British feared that a German-Russian combine might threaten India and the Middle East. There was a widespread belief, some of it justified, that the Bolsheviks were cruelly persecuting people who had befriended the Allies during the war. There were military supplies in Russia, which the White generals promised either to keep away from or to use against the Germans. German troops were being transferred to the west in 1918 to mount the last great offensive, and anything that promised to delay this was attractive. Had Lenin been willing to fight the Germans, the Allies would have clasped him to their bosom no matter what his politics, just as they embraced Stalin in 1941. Lenin incurred their displeasure by leaving the war, not by being a Bolshevik. It is true that the new regime's repudiation of all Russia's foreign financial obligations went down hard, particularly with the French, who held large amounts of Russian debt.

The amount of Allied support given the Whites was not very great. President Wilson in particular insisted on limiting intervention to a few thousand troops; he was interested only in protecting military supplies and helping the Czech legion get out of Russia. After the war ended, the Allies lost most of their enthusiasm for aiding the Whites, and by early 1920 the last of them had surrendered or been evacuated. The French took General Wrangel and some

135,000 of his followers from the Crimea. At the Washington Conference of 1921–1922, the Western statesmen persuaded Japan to abandon her intervention in Siberia.

Though the Russian Reds failed to win back Finland, the Baltic states, and Poland, by 1921 they had the rest of the former Russian empire under control. The Poles, aided by France, finally defeated the Red Army after a wildly fluctuating war. In August 1920, the Poles led by Marshal Josef Pilsudski inflicted a decisive defeat on the Red Army at the gates of Warsaw, and thereafter the tide of battle turned against the Russians. In the 1921 Treaty of Riga, the Poles gained favorable eastern boundaries that took in some territory ethnically more nearly Russian than Polish. But within Russia the Red Army, forged chiefly by Leon Trotsky, was generally victorious over the White forces. Against a disunited foe on the peripheries, the Red government held the solid center of Russia, moving the capital to Moscow. Forcing former Imperial officers to serve by holding their families hostage, instituting a compulsory draft, and enforcing strict discipline, the Bolsheviks forged a tyrannical state even more stringent than the one they had overthrown. The chief founder of the Soviet state, perhaps, was the Polish aristocrat Felix Dzerzhinski, who created Lenin's secret police system, and later by throwing his support to Josef Stalin probably ensured the latter's victory in the struggle to be Lenin's successor.

It was a grim and nasty war, as all civil wars tend to be. This one was charged with the authoritarian fanaticism of the Bolsheviks, class hatred of them by their old-regime enemies, and the hopeless rage of much of the peasantry against both. Unspeakable cruelties were committed by both sides. The civil war left Russia prey to famine in 1921. Lenin's regime had proved that his iron will and the stern discipline of his elite Communist party could hold on to Russia, but it looked like they had won a lifeless body.

The crowning event of this ghastly interlude was a futile revolt in 1921 by the soldiers and sailors of Kronstadt, the island base in the Gulf of Finland. Originators of the revolution, in the name of freedom and of the soviets they now accused Lenin's government of betraying the revolution. Their ideology of left-wing communism tinged with anarchism, they claimed, spoke for the real revolution—the one the soviets had envisioned as a free, decentralized, democratic, nonauthoritarian society. The bloody suppression of the Kronstadt revolt, in which the army of the workers' revolution shot down the workers, symbolized the first great moral crisis of the Soviet Communist state.

"The Revolution which had promised peace, bread and land thus produced instead civil war, famine and (after a few years) the serfdom of collectivization," Robert Conquest remarked. He adds that Russia might well have lost far fewer lives had she elected to fight on for another year in the world war. Having lost two million dead, she might have lost another million; but the death toll of civil war, terror, famines, and epidemics that resulted from Lenin's policies is estimated at not less than fourteen million by 1922.

FROM LENIN TO STALIN

If Germany was a republic without republicans and Italy a great-man state without real leadership, the Union of Soviet Socialist Republics[2] might perhaps be said to have been a proletarian Communist regime without proletarians or Communists. (It is hard to estimate how many "industrial workers," Marx's classical proletariat, there were in Russia in 1917; some authorities doubt if there were any at all.) Certainly the most startling paradox was that the 75 percent of Russia that was peasant did not want socialism or communism at all. The peasants were for the Bolsheviks when they threw out the landlords and redistributed the land, but they were against the Bolsheviks when they nationalized the land. The peasants wanted individual land holdings. They had not created soviets, and they did not like communism. During the revolution, they had reverted to their traditional peasant village, the *mir,* even more strongly than before. The *mir* was an institution with profoundly cooperative features, but it presented a united front against the urban-oriented and urban-based Communist regime. Leninist attempts to stress a class division within the peasantry between rich capitalists and poor proletarians did not have much basis in peasants' mentality.

This was but one facet of the main bolshevist dilemma. Lenin's party contemplated the failure of world revolution, leaving its lone Communist regime holding a backward, almost precapitalist country, if a vast and potentially powerful one. In many of his pre-1914 writings, Lenin had conceded that a revolution in Russia alone would make no sense. Seizure of power by a small vanguard elite in a land of backward peasants with very little industry could by itself mean only a reversion to "Asiatic despotism." One cannot, on Marxist principles, escape the need for revolution to be a part of an entire social process. As we know, Lenin believed that the Russian Revolution would touch off revolution in the West. Russia was a part of world capitalism, not a separate society. As the weakest link of world capitalism, it would crack first, and the whole world capitalist order would follow. The vanguard party was justified only insofar as it could perform this initial function in the global class struggle, capturing, as it were, one vulnerable salient on the long capitalist front, enabling other forces then to move in for the main battle.

When the revolution did not occur elsewhere, Lenin's party was left with a problem, and it is no wonder it engaged in strenuous debates. Should one continue to expect world revolution? Meanwhile, what should be done with Russia? How could the Bolsheviks avoid betraying the basic values of Marxism if they ruled in Russia alone? Would not the dictatorship, based on a primitive social structure, revert to a traditional despotism? On the other hand, the in-

---

[2]This name was not formally adopted until 1924, when previously independent Ukrainian, White Russian, and Transcaucasian SSRs were merged with the Russian, and others created to form a "union" of what were supposed to be "culturally autonomous" republics, but were in fact increasingly under centralized control from Moscow through the Communist Party.

dustrialization of Russia must entail either intensifying the dictatorship or allowing capitalism to return, perhaps under the general control of the party, in accordance with the theory of "permanent revolution." This latter was in fact what Lenin decided to do in 1921.

"War communism," which between 1918 and 1920 had nationalized all industry and seized food from the peasants by force, was justifiable only as long as the emergency lasted, Lenin thought. In deciding that it would never do as the basis of Russia's peacetime society, Lenin again startled most of his Communist colleagues. Lenin thought that like the Brest peace, another drastic if temporary concession to reality would be necessary. One could not, in Russia, proceed immediately to a communistic economy. Such an economy did not exist and could not exist for some time in the social conditions of Russia. It was "necessary for a time to live within the bosom of capitalism"! Lenin's capacity for daring paradox seemed revealed in this proposal that the Communists preside over capitalism, but it was in fact a reasonably obvious conclusion from Marxian theory applied to Russian conditions. Early on, Leon Trotsky as well as Lenin had suggested something of the sort. Continuing to hold political power via the machinery of the state, the disciplined vanguard party would permit a kind of controlled capitalism to function. Unless and until the revolution spread to other countries—and hope for this could not entirely vanish—the party must engage in a holding action in Russia.

In his late years, Lenin seemed sometimes, like some of the Western Marxists, to believe that a democratic cultural revolution had to accompany or precede socialism. If so, he was not well understood by most of the Bolsheviks. In May 1922, the unquestioned leader of the party suffered a paralytic stroke. (This may have stemmed from the wound Lenin received in August 1918 from a bullet fired by a Socialist Revolutionary woman, Fanny Kaplan. This shooting was a signal for an outburst of bolshevist terror aimed indiscriminately at "bourgeois" elements.) He partly recovered from the stroke, but clearly his political career had ended. Though the secret was guarded, from that time on Lenin was a dying king around whom the possible heirs gathered to watch both him and each other.

The Communist party was already hardening into an arrogant power elite. Although the party adopted the New Economic Policy, permitting private trade by small businessmen and farmers, it kept the reins of political power firmly in its hands. Its hierarchical structure was growing. A small group of men on the Politburo, a steering committee of the Central Committee, determined policy; "democratic centralism," more centralist than democratic, meant that once a decision had been taken by the party—i.e., its small ruling cadre—all members must accept and obey the decision unquestioningly. The party's legitimacy came not from any personal charisma but from its alleged mastery of the secrets of scientific Marxism. The party's infallibility was openly proclaimed, but this was because, rather like the medieval Catholic church, it collectively held the keys to the Marxian kingdom.

So, if Lenin in his last year had doubts about what had become of the Revolution, he was powerless to change his own creation. There can be no myth of a gentle or humane Lenin; he had consistently called for ruthless terror, and in 1922 was still calling for it. In that year, the trial and condemnation to death of twelve Socialist Revolutionary leaders marked an extension of the repression to fellow revolutionaries of a different hue, who could by no means be called reactionaries or bourgeoisie. (The trial caused a bad reaction among socialists abroad, and the death sentences were commuted to life imprisonment—a mere stay of execution, as it turned out.) What can be alleged is that Lenin did not intend to perpetuate the terror, and he became dismayed when it looked as if a harsh despotism was settling in for good. To him, the terror was a brief interlude between the old order and the new, not a permanent way of life. He grumbled about illegality, a low level of culture, "bureaucratic misrule and wilfullness," abuse of authority, and "lack of civilization." But his comrades probably thought him a victim of brain softening. He had another stroke on March 9, 1923, just short of his fifty-third birthday, and was pathetic after that. He died on January 21, 1924.

Had he lived as long as Mao Tse-tung, Tito, or even Stalin, who knows how drastically the history of the world might have been changed? Careful students of Lenin think he may have intended the New Economic Policy (NEP) to be quasi-permanent. Russia would have to go through a prolonged bourgeois phase before it developed sufficient civilization for socialism. But most of the Bolshevik leadership thought of NEP as only a breathing space. It would buy a few years of time while they regrouped, considered the situation, and hammered out a policy. The stage was set for a momentous and memorable debate, along with a struggle for power, in the three years after Lenin's death. Meanwhile NEP semicapitalism brought a modest degree of recovery; by 1926 the economy was almost back to its 1913 level![3]

"Comrade Stalin, having become General Secretary, has accumulated enormous power in his hands, and I am not quite sure whether he will always be able to use that power carefully enough." Thus wrote Lenin in December 1922 when, increasingly ill, he penned his "last testament." A year later, when Lenin was a hopeless invalid nearing the end of his life, a group of prominent party members complained that "free discussion in the party has all but disappeared," and the Central Committee is no longer elected by the general party membership but determined by "the secretarial hierarchy."

Thus Stalin's famous seizure of power began while Lenin was still alive, and indeed Lenin's later strokes may have resulted from his agitated anti-Stalin campaign in late 1922 and early 1923. The doctors had prohibited all but the

---

[3]This was achieved with capitalist help. Responding to an appeal from the great writer Maxim Gorki during the terrible 1921 famine, an American Relief Administration headed by Herbert Hoover provided much food to Russia between 1921 and 1923. A confirmed anti-Bolshevist, Hoover ironically helped Lenin's regime to surmount the crisis.

smallest amount of work, but Lenin ignored the orders. Yet the Georgian, born Josef Dzhugashvili, with his rude manners and his Caucasian accent, was still not considered to be at the top of the party heap, though a city (the old Tsaritsyn) was named after him in 1922. After Lenin, the usual ceremonial hierarchy was Lev Kamenev, Gregory Zinoviev, and Trotsky. Intellectually more distinguished than Stalin, certainly more cultured, these men were unfortunately no match for the practical general secretary, whose talents were both administrative and political.

The story of how Stalin outmaneuvered his rivals and became the all-powerful boss of an increasingly dictatorial Communist party has stimulated many attempts at explanation. The least mysterious is Stalin's obvious ability, which, of course, is not the same thing as virtue. Many people, not least the Trotskys, Kamenevs, and Zinovievs, whom he defeated and eventually murdered (along with literally millions of others), have thought that Stalin betrayed the Revolution, and indeed that he was a moral monster without equal in all the bloody annals of history. And, among Stalin's qualities a certain gangster-like cruelty and amorality is evident. He owed his initial rise in the party to his success as a train robber. He did not lack knowledge of a crude Marxism, nor the ability to write and think cogently, though his theoretical manner was simplistic. He added to these abilities an immense capacity for work, a vast talent for intrigue, and an utter ruthlessness that frightened even Lenin.

Stalin stood for absolute authority at the top, because, he declared, "we are surrounded by enemies" and must be able to move quickly, maneuver rapidly, and "strike a sudden blow." It was his mission to eliminate whatever remnants of grassroots influence remained in the party, converting it into an instrument of power completely under the control of its single-minded master. Rather short, not very handsome (the later portraits were touched up), and for long an indifferent public speaker, Stalin did not gain power through his charismatic appeal, like Hitler and Mussolini, but by his skill at manipulating the machinery of power. He found that machinery already in existence, waiting to be set in motion toward a goal. Lenin's elite party of dedicated, disciplined, revolutionaries had already been forged and tempered, and brutalized, in the fires of long revolutionary activity before, during, and after the October Revolution. It had eliminated all its organized enemies, who had been killed or imprisoned or had fled Russia during the civil war. Gone was a high percentage of the old ruling and educated class. Lenin and Trotsky had established instruments of terror, including the secret police (Cheka, GPU, NKVD). This power structure had laid hold of the state.

In theory, power belonged to the soviets, or people's councils, but the All-Russian Congress of Soviets delegated its power to an executive committee, which in turn delegated it to a council of commissars made up solely of Communists. The Congress under Stalin was to turn into a farce. It met for a few days each year to approve, by unanimous vote, everything that had been done. The Communist party, the only political party allowed, had a parallel hierarchy, culminating in the Central Committee and its various bureaus, especially the Politburo. A small group of fifteen or twenty men, sitting on both the Politburo and the Sovnarkom, ruled Russia.

Trotsky, before he became a Leninist, once made the acute remark that when you have substituted the party for the proletariat, it follows inevitably that you will substitute the Central Committee for the party and finally one man's will for the Central Committee. This was an accurate prophecy of what happened, the irony being that Trotsky allowed himself to accept the first two steps and became the victim of the last. Yet, under Lenin the Bolshevik oligarchy functioned as a team. If they followed Lenin's leadership, it was because they willingly deferred to his superior intellectual powers. There was much debate within the Politburo, and Lenin did not always have his way. Trotsky, Bukharin, and others did not hesitate to argue with him. "Democratic centralism" decreed iron discipline once a decision was reached, but it allowed open debate within the party in reaching that decision.

Stalin was to end all this and rule by a combination of manipulation and terror. But he did not much change the basic pattern developed in the first years of bolshevist rule; he only extended it in directions already begun. The wily Georgian used his seemingly secondary post as general secretary of the Central Committee to influence selection of members to the Central Committee, to the "purge" machinery, and to administrative and executive positions at all levels of the growing political apparatus. Thousands upon thousands of local Communist party leaders, the *apparatchiks,* owed their careers to Stalin's sponsorship and watchful eye, and they were as attached to him as any feudal knight to his lord. Trotsky and the other high Communists, Kamenev, Bukharin, and Zinoviev, woke up too late and found that while they had been making the speeches, Stalin had been working quietly behind the scenes to put his men in key party positions.

He also exploited jealousies among them. A personal feud between Trotsky and Stalin reached back much earlier; it was based on a natural antipathy between the intellectual, esthetic, essentially aristocratic Trotsky, whose favorite sport was hunting, and the plain, boorish, tough-minded Stalin. But real issues confronted the Communists–major questions of what path to take, assuming one could not long remain in the NEP stage of lapsing into capitalism. One of the issues was the relative stress on world revolution and the possibility of building socialism in Russia alone. Should the USSR continue to work toward world revolution, or should it resign itself for the time being to the necessity of going it alone? Hopes for the spread of revolution to Germany, to Italy, or to China faded between 1921 and 1927. There was a Communist disaster in Bulgaria in 1923, too. Using Russia as the headquarters for an international revolutionary movement dictated different policies than did placing primary stress on Russian development. The most obvious difference was that under the latter policy, Communists would have to cultivate good relations with foreign capitalist states, a goal inconsistent with attempts to stir up revolutions inside them.

Other difficult decisions had to be made about domestic policy. Marx had said remarkably little about how to organize socialism, and even Lenin had seemed confused. Should the peasants be conciliated by allowing them to hold farms and sell produce to the cities? Should industrialization and urbanization be pushed forward rapidly or slowly? Should there be a totally centralized economic system, with everything nationalized and the state planning the whole economy, or was this too drastic and too un-Marxian, given the Marxist and occasional Leninist stress on the state's disappearance under socialism?

This discussion within the party was reasonably open. Many who were later arrested and shot still spoke freely in the debate of the mid-1920s, and a variety of views were expressed. In the great economic debate of the 1920s, some economists recommended squeezing the agricultural sector through manipulating prices in order to raise capital for a massive industrialization program; forcing the peasants into collective farms had not yet occurred to them. Others favored building up agriculture by favoring the peasant; the surplus that would be produced could be exported to pay for industrial goods. In 1928, the peasants held back produce, waiting for better prices.

Stalinism was later to stand for (1) rapid, forced industrialization; (2) open war against the peasants, forcing them into collective farms; (3) "socialism in one country," making international revolution subordinate to this goal; and (4) centralized planning, with total control of economic activities by the central bureaucracy. To carry out this draconian program, Stalin imposed absolute dictatorship, the use of terror on a gigantic scale, and repression of all freedom to criticize. But these were not what Stalin had always advocated. Earlier, he doubted that rapid industrialization was possible. In 1925, he warned against pushing the peasants too hard. In 1927, he tried (and failed) to mastermind the Chinese Communist revolution. He first supported the right's opposition against Trotsky, isolating that moody personality whom many envied and disliked.

Stalin later sought to conceal much of his earlier association with the right in the party's divisions. It was agreed in the 1920s that no one leader could replace Lenin. In the collective leadership, the five most important personalities were Trotsky, Zinoviev, Kamenev, Bukharin, and Stalin. By the mid-1920s, the first three, overcoming some initial conflicts, had joined together as a left opposition (to the prevalent NEP policy); but Stalin joined with Bukharin, the party's leading intellectual and a genuine moderate, in controlling a majority on the Politburo. Decisive was Stalin's control of the Central Committee and eventually the Politburo, which he packed with three additional members in 1925. Trotsky, and then Zinoviev and Kamenev, could not win. They sent in Lenin's widow, Krupskaya, at the crucial Fourteenth Party Congress in 1925, but even she failed to impress the pro-Stalin majority.

Stalin profited by being underestimated. He was considered a good clerk but, in Trotsky's contemptuous words, "a third-rate, provincial mind." It was Trotsky who was vulnerable and who made mistakes. Stalin kept reminding the party cohorts that Trotsky was not an Old Bolshevik but had joined the party only in 1917. In failing to attend Lenin's funeral, though he had the excuse of being a long distance away and ill, Trotsky put a trump into his enemies' hands.

In any case, by 1926 Stalin was strong enough to get Zinoviev, Kamenev, and Trotsky removed from the Politburo and other high posts, making their opposition to him seem like disloyalty to the party. In 1927, Trotsky's group was expelled from the party congress, and Trotsky himself was shipped out of the capital. When the former hero continued to try to oppose Stalin, he was finally forced to leave the country. Trotsky subsequently lived in Turkey, Norway, and Mexico, always hounded by Stalin's agents and finally murdered in Mexico. Zinoviev and Kamenev were tried and convicted, along with thousands of lesser officials, in the sensational political trials of 1936–1938; by that time, those Old Bolsheviks like Bukharin and Radek who had cast their lot with Stalin in 1925–1926 were in the dock with them, headed for the same firing squad.

The beginnings of Stalin's reign may be dated from 1927 when he horrified his erstwhile partner Bukharin by taking direct action against the peasants, confiscating produce without authority from the party or its Politburo. This marked an abrupt end of the NEP era. Bukharin, who had just helped Stalin destroy Trotsky, now accused the Georgian of being a "Genghis Khan" in return for which he was attacked as a "right-wing deviationist." There ensued the launching of the first five-year economic plan and the violent campaign to force the peasants into collective farms, accompanied by moves to bring all branches of thought under strict party discipline.

This set the stage for the great struggle to build "socialism in one country," a slogan Stalin used in the ideological battle with Trotsky. Trotsky felt that attempting such a campaign in backward Russia was bound to fail or to lead to drastic distortions of the socialist ideal. As we have noted, that was probably Lenin's view, too. It seemed like irreproachable Marxism. But it suffered from the practical disadvantage of negativism. Given the realities of no world revolution, was one to sit and do nothing in Russia while capitalism crept back? The economy was in any case in serious trouble. The powerful machinery of the party stood ready to act. Such machinery cannot remain idle, or it will destroy itself. "With the party as his army and the Secretariat as his general staff, Stalin launched his war in 1929," writes historian Adam Ulam. The aim of the war was to develop Russia into an industrial state surpassing even the largest capitalist ones, but in some ways it turned out to be a war against the Russian people.

ABORTIVE REVOLUTIONS IN CENTRAL EUROPE

Lenin had expected the spread of revolution throughout Europe, placing most hope in Germany. But there was no German "revolution" like the Russian one. Many on the left believed the Spartacist revolt of January 1919 was about to succeed when it was betrayed by the treachery of the majority Socialists, who allied with the right to crush it. It is true that a cleavage existed between the majority socialists, who had supported the war, and a minority that was partly revolutionary and partly pacifist. But even the latter were rarely revolutionary in Lenin's sense. Rosa Luxemburg did not approve of the Bolshevik philosophy. She repudiated a minority revolution; the socialist revolution must "secure victory for and through the great majority of the workers themselves." The Spartacists were not Bolsheviks; they would not take power without a mandate from a majority of the workers. This they never came close to having. They never seriously contemplated a coup like Lenin's. Rosa agreed with the Lenin of "State and Revolution," who dreamed of a republic of soviets, or workers' councils, abolishing the military-bureaucratic state. The Spartacus Union, she said, "is no party wanting to climb into power on the shoulders of the mass of workers" but rather "the conscious party of the proletariat." She severely criticized the Bolshevik dictatorship, though somewhat moderating her rebukes near the end of her life. At the same time, the Spartacists denounced the majority Socialists, who headed the new German government, as "lackeys of the capitalist class" and called for a true socialist revolution to come from "the great mass of the socialist working class." But the great mass of the German people, confused by the trauma of defeat and suffering from severe food shortages and disease (the terrible flu epidemic raged at this time), did not want a socialist revolution.

The alleged Spartacist putsch attempt of January 1919 emerged from a situation in which some radical trade unionists, the "revolutionary shop stewards," joined the new German Communist party, which was made up mostly of Spartacists, for a mass demonstration. Together they called for the overthrow of the government. This demonstration was a chaotic and rather leaderless outburst, which the German Communist Party (KPD) leadership supported only hesitantly, Rosa Luxemburg being decidedly ambivalent. The government suppressed the disorders; and on January 15, Rosa Luxemburg and Karl Liebknecht were arrested, released, and then murdered by Berlin soldiers in what amounted to a lynching. Although the crime further embittered the radical left, the whole episode revealed the weakness and the indecisiveness of the German Communists. They had produced no Lenin. Even if they had, Germany was simply not Russia, and a revolutionary dictatorship was scarcely conceivable.

Disorders spread throughout Germany as the new government, saddled with the onus of defeat, struggled with the returning army and a host of economic problems. It lacked legitimacy in the eyes of many Germans. Bands of ex-soldiers (the Free Corps) often took the law into their own hands. In Bavaria, an unlikely place for a revolution, dislike of Prussia combined with particularist sentiment for the local Wittelsbach dynasty, which still survived from the 1871 amalgamation of German states. These emotions helped trigger a revolution that temporarily deposited a socialist government in power. Munich seemed on the brink of becoming a communist city. On January 12, an aristocratic monarchist assassinated left-wing socialist Kurt Eisner. Further turmoil ensued, and on April 7 a group of writers and intellectuals proclaimed a Soviet

Republic in Munich. No more interesting group ever appeared than these poets, playwrights, and philosophers—Ernst Toller, Gustav Landauer, and Karl Korsch among them—but the Communist party denounced them as romantic amateurs, a "coffee-house clique." Free Corps troops commanded by a Prussian general soon invaded the city and began a White terror.

Although there were somewhat similar episodes in other German cities, what may have seemed to Moscow like the beginning of the world socialist revolution was in reality more nearly the reverse. Amid the confusion, a strong right-wing reaction was evident. Bewildered by Germany's loss of the war after so much heroic dedication, returning soldiers more often than not blamed the Socialists and Communists—not much distinguishing between them—for betraying the nation at a critical moment. Socialists and communists were accused of delivering a *Dolchstoss,* a stab in the back, to the valiant troops who, they alleged, had not been defeated in the field. The soldiers resented the upstart regime that had replaced the kaiser. In Russia, a completely demoralized army came home to help a revolution of the left; but although it had been forced to end the war, the German Army was not completely demoralized. Regrouping as the Free Corps, the more brutalized and adventurous elements of the army terrorized the left and once even attempted to seize power (the Kapp putsch, 1920).

Partly to control them, the republic made terms with the Free Corps, diverting some of them to fight Poles and Lithuanians in the East. They were not brought under control until 1922, by which time they had been absorbed into the reorganized army or had joined nationalist political clubs such as the one Adolf Hitler led. Specializing in assassination, these terrorists of the right out-Lenined Germany's would-be Lenins. A new political phenomenon, to be known as Fascism, was arising. Fascism was popular but antisocialist, counter-revolutionary, nationalist. Fascists hated Jews, intellectuals, and socialists as well as the old aristocracy and plutocracy. They wanted to restore order and protect the little man's property, if he were a good German.

Other postwar revolutions of the left outside Russia proved equally ephemeral. Russian-inspired revolutionary regimes like the one in Budapest and a similar one in Munich filled a temporary vacuum of power left by the collapse of the old order, but they had no sufficient social basis to last.

"The spectre of unrest haunts the whole world from the Western United States [where I.W.W. revolution flared up at this time] to China," the *Times* of London commented on July 19, 1919. "The symptoms are everywhere present that the elementary bonds of society are torn and decayed as a result of the long exertion." Karl Marx had understood that war is the midwife of history. The exigencies of war had uprooted peoples and flung them into new and trying circumstances, not only on the battlefield but on the home front. For the first time, millions of women left the home to take over jobs left vacant by men departing for military service. "Soldiers from the war returning" found it hard to take up the threads of life as before. The cake of custom had been broken.

PROBLEMS OF RECOVERY IN THE WEST

Census statistics dramatically revealed the loss of life in the countries that had borne the major brunt of the war. In France, the 1921 count disclosed a shortage of about two million males, more than a million of them from twenty to forty years old. What French statesman Edouard Herriot called "the sinister balance sheet of slaughter" also showed two million Germans lost, and a half-million Italians; how many Russians, no one knew. One scholar who recently investigated the British military casualties, J. M. Winter, could discover no reliable figures; his estimates based on indirect evidence find considerably more deaths than usually stated, 722,875 versus the official total of 548,749.

Herriot's estimate of eight and a half million total battle deaths for Europe was surely conservative; other guesses ran from ten million to thirteen million. The war itself slid into the postwar revolutions, anarchies, civil wars, famines, epidemics. To battle deaths were added the tolls from influenza and other diseases, which struck most severely at the aged and infirm. Overlooked in some of the citations of statistics, little Serbia, the original crux of the conflict, had suffered most of all in terms of percentage of population lost—some 12 percent. Authorities put the Russian toll altogether, counting the civil war and the famine, at twenty million.

For every battlefield death there were probably two soldiers permanently wounded, so that the Frenchman who could not show his wooden leg or at least his lost ear was almost an oddity. Such grievous casualties, hitting at the youngest and most robust, "a loss even more serious in quality than in quantity," was, needless to say, a fantastic disaster; it silently weakened Europe for many years and may have accounted for her slippage in economic strength after the war. It might be noted that this war took a higher toll on the upper classes than the lower classes: The higher up in the social scale, J. M. Winter finds for England, the better the chances of death.

On the other hand, the physical disaster can be exaggerated. The resiliency of populations is amazing; the cynicism of Napoleon, who remarked after a military defeat that "Paris can make it up in one night," seems justified. Germany, despite war casualties and ceded territories, had by 1933 regained her 1914 population of some sixty-five million. Even the French losses amounted to no more than 4 percent of total population. In none of the Western countries save perhaps Italy was there a real breakdown of the social fabric and the administrative order. Even the situation in postwar Germany did not at most times and in most places amount to anarchy. As for war damages, they were confined to a fairly narrow zone. Although everything along the western front was totally destroyed, outside this battle region losses were slight by World War II standards, when whole cities were destroyed from the air. Nothing like that happened in the 1914 war.

Familiar with the spectacular economic boom that followed the much more destructive World War II, we may wonder why Europe did not recover rapidly after 1920. In fact, she did not, on the whole. Though in Great Britain the immediate postwar economic adjustment was heartening, within two years unemployment soared, and it remained high all through the 1920s—about 16 or 17 percent on the average. It fell to 9 percent in the "prosperous" year of 1929, but after that the Great Depression shot it up to 20 to 23 percent. The effects were somewhat mitigated by an extension of unemployment insurance in 1916 and 1920 and by a general reduction of the hours of work. A normal fifty-four-hour work week changed to between forty-six and forty-eight hours right after the war. But strikes, leading up to the great general strike of 1926, reflected the restless disappointment of workers, as did the rising strength of the British Labour party.

Unemployment was most severe in traditional export industries, including coal, textiles, and shipbuilding. The war had caused Britain to lose markets, which passed primarily to the United States and Japan during the years in which the British had turned their resources to war production. Britain had also lost income because she had liquidated overseas investments to raise war funds. She still owed billions in war debts to the United States.

"Europe has lost its role as banker to the world. The financial power of the United States is increasing. The power of Japan is growing. Our North American friends have seized domination of the great routes which lead from the Atlantic to the Pacific." This complaint came from a Frenchman, Edouard Herriot. Great Britain was more dependent on overseas markets than was France, having built the structure of her economy during the nineteenth century when she was "workshop of the world." But all of Europe felt this migration of basic economic power to other continents.

In France and Germany, the question of war reparations payments clouded the economic scene for several years. As you may recall, the Versailles treaty fixed no exact sum for Germany to pay; the amount was to be calculated by a reparations commission. The French figured the liability as high as $200 billion; the Germans thought it unfair that they should pay anything. Unenthusiastically, they offered about $7 billion. More detached analysts thought Germany could not afford to pay anything like the total potential bill without ruining her economy and disrupting the international monetary system. But the French government floated large reconstruction loans based on the expectation that the Germans would pay for them. In the immediate postwar years, Germany was expected to deliver large amounts of coal as payments on her reparations bill. Although they sent some, the Germans partly could not and mostly would not fulfill the Allied quotas. A conference at Spa in July 1920 resulted in agreements that led only to new arguments. The Germans, who were allowed to deliver less than previously required, demanded further reductions. The French bitterly charged betrayal and, with the British, wondered whether they should send troops into the Ruhr. Germans and some British argued that Germany could not recover until she was free of the burden of reparations and that German recovery was essential to general European recovery. In their opinion, the sum Germany owed ought to be clearly established and much pared down.

Muddle was the word for the reparations question; it was complicated even further by the American attitude toward Allied debts, which was almost as unfeeling as the French view of what Germany owed. American insistence on repayment of war loans forced France and Britain to maintain their hard line on German reparations payments. But the two Allies had trouble keeping a united front, the British being more prone to compromise than the French. In 1921 and 1922, opinion in both France and Germany hardened, the Germans unwilling to continue shipping their surplus off to the West, the French determined to make the "Boches" pay for French reconstruction. The 1921 economic slump intensified this standoff and put the two countries on another collision course. For advocating "fulfillment," the brilliant Walther Rathenau, who had steered the German economy through the war and was now in charge of reconstruction, suffered death at the hands of right-wing terrorists.

Suffering from inflation, strikes, and economic stagnation, the German government in 1922 adopted the slogan, "First bread, then reparations." The Germans offered to settle the reparations bill for fifteen billion marks, a figure insulting to the French. Though the British refused to go along, French Premier Poincaré resolved to employ sanctions by sending troops and engineers into the Ruhr early in 1923. This was virtually a renewal of war, and the episode did not end until it had caused grave damage to the European economy. Germany resorted to passive resistance; workers struck in the Ruhr; and German inflation shot up to fantastic heights, as the economy ground to a virtual halt while money continued to be printed in massive quantities. The 1923 crisis threatened to finish what World War I had begun, the ruin of Europe.

The year 1924 was a turning point. The death of Lenin may be set alongside the settlement of the Ruhr-reparations crisis, after its devastating eruption in 1923. In 1923, Hitler attempted a putsch in Bavaria; 1924 saw the Nazi leader in jail and his party almost destroyed. For the Soviets, this period meant the collapse of the last hopes for world Communist revolution. Such hopes had remained alive, particularly in Germany in 1923, and while they were, Soviet leaders could live with the NEP, their eyes still fixed on the impending world revolution. The last failure was to come in China in 1927, when the slaughter of the Moscow-directed Communists by Chiang Kai-shek's Nationalists led to acrimonious disputes in Russia about where to fix the blame.

French and Belgian troops marched into the Ruhr in January 1923, following the breakdown of the last of many reparations conferences. The German managers of the Ruhr coal syndicate left, the local people adopted passive resistance, and the German government declared that it would subsidize the striking Ruhr workmen out of public funds and suspend all reparations deliveries to France. By seizing the Ruhr industries, French Premier Poincaré hoped to force the Germans to make good on reparations payments. The Ruhr basin contained

80 percent of Germany's coal and 80 percent of her iron and steel production. It could well claim to be the industrial heart of the Continent.

German defiance and British opposition did much to frustrate Poincaré's plans. British diplomacy sought to bring the United States back into the picture and, with American aid, to negotiate a reasonable reparations settlement. And, world opinion tended to side with the Germans against the French. The most extraordinary consequence of this virtual renewal of war was the collapse of the mark. This was history's most stupendous inflation. Incredible as it may seem, by the end of 1923 the German lucky enough to have 10,000 marks in the bank found that that sum, which had once been worth $2,500, now equaled about a millionth of a penny. In January, the value of 10,000 marks had already fallen to about half a dollar, but during the spring and summer of 1923 it grew more and more valueless each day and each hour. Life savings were wiped out, and money lost all value. A 100-billion-mark note, which would have bought the whole Rhineland a few years before, would now hardly be enough for a loaf of bread.

One historian characterized the French action as the cause of Hitler's triumph and therefore the cause of World War II. The loss of faith in all values prepared the German mind for Hitler's nihilism. But in fact some German industrialists profited from the inflation.

Desperate, the Germans finally capitulated; but some of the French tried to go further and separate the Rhineland from Germany, thus achieving the old 1919 goal of French policy. They proclaimed a "Rhineland Republic" in October and enlisted a few Germans to head it. A British report condemned the "revolver republic" forced upon the local population against its will by French military force. Poincaré then gave up, the separatist movement evaporated, and a number of the quislings were assassinated. The franc showed signs of following the mark into oblivion. Poincaré's government fell. A leftist bloc won the elections in the spring of 1924 and brought a different attitude to the French government.

Meanwhile, the old mark having gone on its flight into the stratosphere, the Germans created a new currency, the *rentenmark*. A trillion old marks for one new mark was the exchange rate. The new currency was based on a mortgage taken against the national wealth held by bankers, merchants, industrialists, and farmers. Stabilization succeeded but at the cost of massive temporary dislocations resulting in huge unemployment. Nevertheless, Germany came through this grave crisis without a revolution. The German Communist party (KPD) increased its percentage of the popular vote to 12.6 percent in the May 1924 elections, but it sank to 9 percent in another election held in December. The leading right-wing party, the nationalist DNVP, gained 20 percent, and a right radical National Socialist Freedom party got some support. The extreme right outgained the left. An attempted Red uprising in Hamburg failed.

Small wonder, though, that Lenin, brooding over the troubles of the

Soviet socialist state in his last months, took heart from the fact that, after all, the capitalists were even more stupid: "Because of greed they hate each other." Capitalist France seemed bent on ruining capitalist Germany and wrecking the very heart of European industry in order to meet short-range obligations. Great Britain and France were at odds. But the capitalists rallied to save the situation, finally. American bankers, headed by the formidable J. P. Morgan, were persuaded by the British that they had a stake in international stabilization. Was not repayment of Allied war debts dependent on a reasonable reparations settlement? Furthermore, the whole circuit of international trade was at stake. The United States was slowly recovering from the shock of revulsion it had felt against Europe in 1919 and 1920, when the Senate had rejected membership in the League of Nations amid a wave of isolationism. Though it refused to muddy itself with European politics, the American colossus was prepared to make a modest economic contribution. An American, the distinguished banker and government financier Charles G. Dawes, chaired the committee of economic experts who worked on a solution to the reparations muddle in 1923 and 1924. The time was ripe for a settlement, for the Franco-German silent war was about a standoff. If Germany was in utter economic chaos, France had advanced little if at all toward her objective of extracting wealth from Germany, her Rhineland policy had failed, and much of world opinion criticized her for recklessly fomenting trouble.

The Dawes Plan, agreed upon by all parties in 1924, considerably scaled down reparations obligations, established a manageable annual schedule of payments, and created a plan to finance the payments in Germany by various bonds and special taxes. Sweetening the package for Germany was a $200 million foreign loan. French troops were to be withdrawn from the Ruhr, and in the future no creditor nation could unilaterally apply sanctions, as France and Belgium had done in 1923. Though extreme German nationalists denounced it for retaining reparations payments, most Germans greeted the plan with relief. It represented a fairly major French defeat. But for the French, too, Morgan money made the bitter dose go down more easily.

France suffered a period of cabinet instability while grappling with the financial issue. So did the Weimar Republic. For both parliamentary systems, there was little relief from the problem of juggling a half dozen political minorities to create a workable coalition. In 1926, German unemployment stood at 18 percent, and her industrial production was about 92 percent of 1913 production. In the next two years, it rose to 118 percent of 1913 production. In France in 1923, industrial production was 87 percent of the 1913 rate; by 1927, it had risen to 126 percent. The prosperity of the later twenties, spectacular in the United States prior to the great collapse of 1929, was never as great for Europe as a whole.

POSTWAR POLITICS IN THE WEST

Behind this mismanagement lay the muddled politics of the postwar years in all the belligerent countries. The new, precarious German Republic, struggling to establish its credibility against Spartacists and Communists on the left and disgruntled nationalists and monarchists on the right, had to unite moderate socialists with liberal, Catholic, and moderate conservative parties. Such a coalition was necessarily vacillating and vulnerable.

The German "revolution" of 1919 had not led to a Bolshevik-style dictatorship but to a parliamentary democracy. The majority Social Democrats had not forged a Red Army to destroy the old regime. They had not dismissed the constituent assembly but had summoned it to write a liberal constitution, and they leaned on the old army to put down a mildly threatening revolt from the left. Moderate conservatives applauded this relative defense of order, but they retained a suspicion of the potential for socialism lurking in a republic whose first president was a socialist, Friedrich Ebert.

A new Democratic party arose to rally nonsocialist liberals to support the republic and collaborate with the Social Democrats. Somewhat to its right but still willing to accept democracy was the People's party, led by a man destined to become the leading German politician of the 1920s, Gustave Stresemann. Both DDP and DVP *(Deutsche Demokratische Partei, Deutsche Volkspartei)* were remnants of the prewar Liberals, who had been destroyed by the war (as, in effect, had been the British Liberal party). These successor parties never succeeded in getting a mass following. The Social Democrats, themselves split, could not command a majority in parliament without seeking allies among the bourgeois democrats. The Weimar majority consisted of a rather incongruous amalgamation of industrialists, trade unionists, army officers, and Roman Catholics, all struggling for stability against the forces of disintegration.

The Weimar Republic of 1919–1933 was so called because its constitution was framed in this Thuringian town famous for its associations with German culture (Cranach, Bach, Liszt, and especially Goethe). This happened to be the place of the Republic's origin less because of any conscious desire to invoke "the other Germany" than because in early 1919 Berlin was too disorderly. The seat of government soon returned to Berlin, the traditional capital.

The first "Weimar coalition" of Social Democrats, Democrats, and Catholic Centrists resigned in June 1919 over the peace terms. In the troubled year 1920, a labor strike helped defeat the Kapp Putsch attempted by Free Corps elements. But in the elections of June 1920, the Weimar parties' strength fell from over 75 percent of the popular vote to less than half, beginning Weimar's strange career as a "republic without republicans." The right-wing Nationalist party (DNVP) gained, as did the dissident left wing of the SPD, the Independents (USPD), and the Communists (KPD), though the latter was a small minority. This made finding a ruling coalition all the more difficult. A precarious government was finally assembled under a Centrist premier, the SPD not in it but agreeing to support it in the parliament. In 1921, this ministry stumbled over reparations troubles, and another Centrist, Joseph Wirth, formed another shaky government, which was fated to watch the mark sink to one-fiftieth of its 1914 value by the end of the year. Wirth resigned in October 1921, when the League of Nations ruled against Germany in plebiscite disputes involving Upper Silesia, much of which passed to Poland. But he came back again with a shuffled cabinet when no alternative emerged.

Quarrels between wage earners and employers simmered during the reparations and economic crisis; who should bear the burden? Employers said that lengthened workweeks and suspension of strikes were essential to stabilization; the socialists and trade unionists naturally found these prospects less than persuasive. In 1922–1923, the director of the Hamburg-America ship line, Wilhelm Cuno, replaced Wirth and proceeded to precipitate the reparations crisis. This capitalist was thus destined to preside over the liquidation of middle-class savings and incomes.

In France, too, the elections of 1919 brought in a rightward-leaning *bloc national*. Dissatisfaction with the outcome of the peace settlement, which the French thought yielded too little security and too little recompense for the vast damages they had suffered, dominated the public mind. When Georges Clemenceau sought the presidency of France, an honor he coveted and seemed to have earned by his war leadership, he was defeated because of French anger over the peace settlement. The "battle of the Ruhr" in 1923–1924 hurt France almost as much as Germany and did not solve the reparations problem. This unhappy outcome caused a turn to the left in 1924, when a coalition of Socialists and Radicals took office. Their election set the stage for the politics of accommodation, which replaced the politics of resentment from 1924 to 1930.

The most significant development in postwar British politics was "the strange death of Liberal England"–the almost complete collapse of the once dominant Liberal party. It is ironic that the party of John Bright and William Gladstone and David Lloyd George, the party associated with peace, anti-imperialism, and domestic reform, had led England into the war and then through all of that dismal experience. In 1914, a few Liberals angrily resigned. Then when Lloyd George replaced Asquith as prime minister in 1916, a minority of Asquith Liberals never forgave him. More significant, perhaps, was the fact that the war and the postwar depression pushed the working class and others toward the Labour party, which had adopted a socialist platform in 1918 and whose leader, Ramsay MacDonald, was one of the few who had opposed the decision for war in 1914. In a basically two-party system, Labour moved up rapidly as the alternative to the Conservatives. It won more parliamentary seats in the elections of 1922, 1923, and 1924 than did the Liberals.

In 1922, the Conservatives won a comfortable majority after they had precipitated an election by leaving Lloyd George's wartime coalition government. The next year, Prime Minister Bonar Law retired because of illness, being replaced, to the infinite chagrin of the abler but incurably aristocratic Lord Curzon, by the rather obscure Stanley Baldwin. Baldwin decided to appeal to the country in late 1923 on the issue of protective tariffs versus free trade, a venerable British political battleground. He was defeated, and a Liberal-Labour partnership took office with Ramsay MacDonald as the first Labour prime minister. This coalition soon broke up, though MacDonald's year was a memorable one in foreign policy, coinciding with the French withdrawal from the Ruhr and the Dawes Plan dealing with reparations. In a most controversial action, MacDonald had extended diplomatic recognition to Soviet Russia. The doughty Scot, who had resigned leadership of Labour in 1914 rather than approve the war, was again to enter on a lonely course in 1931 during the second Labour government. This first one, dependent on Liberal votes, ended after nine months when MacDonald was censured for not prosecuting a case of sedition against a communist publication. The ensuing election, in which Red-baiting of Labour was a feature, again firmly installed the Conservatives in power; it was remarkable for nearly wiping out the Liberals, who have never since regained their status as a major force in Parliament.

So the dismal years immediately after the war were marked by an unmistakable drift to the right, which moderated a little as the decade of the 1920s wore on. This was true in the main countries of Europe except for Communist Russia, and even there a similar trend, in a sense, emerged during the "retreat to capitalism" that began in 1921. One of the reasons for this conservative trend in the West was the fact of the Communist regime's existence. Fear and hatred of bolshevism dominated the European middle classes and even some of the trade unionists. It is true that the French seemed to fear and hate the Germans even more, but their desperate search for security can be traced back to the loss of their Russian ally. In the 1924 British election, an alleged letter from a high Russian Communist (Zinoviev) advising the Labour party on how to seize dictatorial power cost Labour many votes. (MacDonald had negotiated a trade treaty with Russia.)

The election of a Conservative government had something to do with the general strike of 1926, Britain's closest approach to a social revolution. Though Winston Churchill drew up plans for the disposition of troops in the event of class war, the general strike turned out to be something less than that. It began where much of postwar British working-class discontent had been concentrated, in the Welsh coal mines. One of Britain's major industries before 1914, coal became a declining industry after the war, partly because oil was replacing coal as a source of power and partly because British mines suffered from technological obsolescence and fell behind foreign competitors. Ironically, by restoring a large source of coal to efficient production, settlement of the Franco-German struggle over reparations in the Ruhr war of 1923 hurt the British. The coal miners called for nationalization as a means of overcoming stagnation; the mine owners resisted this, needless to say, and a Conservative government sympathized with them. Their answer was cutting wages and increasing hours of work, which scarcely pleased the miners. A strike began in 1926, and the Trades

Union Congress, the British national labor organization, called for a general strike in sympathy with the miners.

The general strike was never intended to be the social revolution in the way anarchist theory postulated; it was merely an expression of solidarity with the miners. Treated almost "in a holiday spirit," as Winston Churchill recalled (he himself got out a government newspaper that had a circulation of three million copies), the general strike petered out. The genial disposition of Prime Minister Stanley Baldwin helped smooth the way to its early end. Nevertheless, the coal strike dragged on for months and ended in defeat for the miners, who were forced to accept a reduction in wages. The miners' defeat set the pattern for a period of trade union decline, with membership far down from wartime highs and strikes infrequent.

Other and subtler reasons for the rightward swing in the twenties have to do with the whole movement of thought and culture, which is discussed in the next chapter. Disenchantment with all political causes accompanied the reaction against the "great crusade" of 1914–1918, with its high-sounding phrases. The "best people" in the 1920s cultivated a cynical disdain for politics, along with a distaste for democratic culture. They sought relief in art and literature, laughed at mass culture and the common man, contemplated the wasteland of a dying civilization with sophisticated despair. There was a return to religion because of the loss of faith in worldly progress, secular utopias, and the benevolence of human nature. Science, too, was interesting though apparently baffling in the age of Einstein and Planck. The "lost generation" felt that all gods were dead and all causes exhausted. This attitude helped the right more than the left, which thrives on secular hope. The apolitical attitude is quasi-conservative.

The fiasco of the general strike typified the generally conservative mood of the times, underneath which lurked a pervasive fear of the Reds. It may be time to return to the affairs of the new Bolshevik or Communist regime in Russia, which, alarming many in the West as much as it heartened others, constituted a divisive issue without equal.

THE RISE OF ITALIAN FASCISM

Between 1919 and 1924, Italy gave birth to a new political phenomenon, *fascism,* an extremism of the right that arose in response to disorders on the left.

The year 1919 was as wild in Italy as in any country in Europe. Her citizens were never as firmly united in support of the war as the other belligerents', and the rout at Caporetto then shattered national confidence. Finally, at the peace conference Italians thought they were treated with contempt. Meanwhile, the Russian Revolution aroused great excitement in Italy. There were socialist riots and strikes, the latter stimulated by inflation and wartime shortages. Threats of a Lenin-type revolution brought a strong reaction, however. In March, the pro-war, ex-socialist Benito Mussolini organized *fasci di combattimento* ("combat groups") to fight the subversive elements. With Parliament deeply divided, Orlando's government fell on June 14, a victim of the "mutilated peace"; his successor, Francesco Nitti, also found himself attacked from both left and right. He called for new elections in September, soon after the celebrated author and war hero Gabriele D'Annunzio marched at the head of a small private army into Fiume, the city on the Adriatic that was a symbol of frustrated Italian war demands. The government did not dare dislodge D'Annunzio.

To confuse the political scene further, a new Popular Catholic party rose. Left, right, and center were all divided within themselves. The indecisive results of the November election led to more strikes and clashes between socialist and fascist followers. Inflation continued. Peasants in the south of Italy began to invade and confiscate state, church, and privately owned estates, while northern farm workers joined in a wave of often violent strikes. The disorders continued into 1920 with factory takeovers and a showdown between the socialist unions and the great Turin industrialists, Fiat and Olivetti. Postal, railroad, and other government employees joined in the strikes. Italy looked to be in the process of a socialist revolution, which a confused and divided government was powerless to stop. On June 9, Nitti was forced to resign the premiership, replaced by the old prewar political boss, Giolitti.

At about this time, the initiative swung away from the left. Constant strikes and disorders infuriated large sections of the populace and turned the Italian bourgeoisie toward the right. Workers controlled local factories in accordance with the syndicalist, or "soviet," philosophy of the Italian socialists. But this system was unable to cope with economic problems on a national scale. Never a majority in the parliament, the socialists did not try to seize the state. The divided government was too weak to institute effective reforms. In this vacuum arose the private armies of the fascist *squadristi,* who battled with the socialists in city and country. At the end of 1920, the brilliant Italian Communist, Antonio Gramsci, wrote that the bourgeois state was decomposing and splitting into two components: "The capitalists are forming their own private state just like the proletariat." The impotence of parliamentary democracy, others might say, was forcing Italy toward civil war.

Editor of the Socialist party newspaper, *Avanti,* Benito Mussolini had long been identified with the left wing of the much divided pre-1914 Italian socialists. In the debate about whether to enter the war that had animated Italy between September 1914 and May 1915, this son of an anarchist blacksmith, a man of much humbler birth than Lenin, had thrown his literary and oratorical talents on the side of intervention, whereas a majority of the traditional socialists held back. Money to support his pro-Allied activities evidently came from French socialists, some Italian industrialists, perhaps from the Italian foreign office. His erstwhile comrades accused him of betrayal, and he broke with them. He had indeed done a complete turnabout from his *"Abbasso la guerra!"* at the beginning, but Mussolini's switch resembled that of many Italians who had swung to the side of the democracies, the "fellow Latins" against "Prussian militarism." Syndicalists, anarchists, republicans, some socialists all found reasons for entering the war; many felt that the best reason was given by labor leader Corridoni: "Neutrality is for eunuchs!" Mussolini, disciple of Nietzsche as well as Marx, was neither a eunuch nor perhaps one to resist the tide of popular opinion.

A man with some intellectual interests, Mussolini helped provide fascism with an ideology, constructing this from various fashionable pre-1914 ideas borrowed from Friedrich Nietzsche, Georges Sorel, Henri Bergson, and others. Mussolini's credo stressed action, elite leadership, and a new set of values to organize the masses. Fascism was a quasi-religion, frankly accepting the need for symbol, ritual, and myth. D'Annunzio had already pioneered in organizing the private uniformed army with parades and mass meetings, the leader addressing crowds of massed followers from a balcony and they roaring slogans back at him. Adolf Hitler was to embroider on this pattern, but in 1921 Hitler was a most obscure person, an odd little ex-private addressing a handful of disciples in Munich beer halls. In 1921, Mussolini and his Black Shirts rose like a comet. Pope Pius XI called him "a man sent by God," and the king of Italy was temporarily converted to fascism.

Eloquently proclaimed by Mussolini, fascism asked for national revival and blamed the parliamentary system and "the lie of universal suffrage" for Italy's weakness. It was thus antidemocratic as well as anti-Marxist. It was also antimodernist, preaching the natural inequality of man and exuding a Nietschean neobarbarism seeking to purge corruption and decadence from society. Not many Italians could be found to defend the corrupt and ineffective parliamentary system, though after it was gone they regretted not having done so. Although it found support from industrialists and landowners anxious to destroy socialism and communism, fascism could scarcely have triumphed had it been a conspiracy of only the rich. It possessed a mass appeal. Peasants, shopkeepers, some white- and even some blue-collar workers accepted at face value this great man who promised to solve Italy's problems. They were tired of chaos and thought socialism had missed its chance.

The fascist program was vague, but it suggested that the state should be an instrument of bringing the "corporations" of capital and labor together in fruitful cooperation rather than in class strife. This idea came to it from rightwing Catholic social thought; but on its left wing, Italian fascists gathered in Syndicalists who believed in a decentralized working class collectivism. Fascism was in fact a fusion of discontents held together uneasily, and in the end unsuccessfully, by Mussolini's leadership. Its principle of national unification had special appeal to a land that had long struggled with a basic cultural disunity between North and South; Fascism was strong in the agrarian, largely premodern South.

Those who regarded fascism as the morbid excrescence of a dying world may have been more nearly right than those who hailed it as a new principle of social reconstruction. What mattered most in 1921 and 1922 was that chaos reigned, parliament was impotent, and Mussolini alone seemed a forceful personality. Between May 1921, when the Fascists won only a handful of seats in the elections, and the march on Rome in October 1922, fascism rapidly gained converts. Philosophers, as well as the king, responded to its dynamism. The old system of government, never very successful since the *risorgimento* (unification) of Italy in 1860–1870, had broken down under the strain of the war and the postwar crisis.

Named prime minister after the march, Mussolini moved to strengthen the executive power and weaken parliament while building the Fascist party into a great national political organization. Not until 1925 did he begin to crush opposition, arrest and imprison enemies, bring the press and education under fascist control, and create a one-party state. Prior to this reversion to simple tyranny, Mussolini received much praise from all over the world for restoring order in Italy and creating a new sense of national purpose.

He turned out to have no plan capable of transforming the Italian society and economy, but at least he managed for a time to restore national morale. Puzzled by fascism, Marxists were inclined to tag it as petty bourgeois. But its appeal lay in a claim to abolish class warfare and regain that sense of all pulling together, that organic unity people had felt at the beginning of World War I. And, its heroic, pseudo-aristocratic mystique was anything but bourgeois; indeed, it affected to despise the merely calculating and commercial spirit. Fascism borrowed Lenin's idea of a dynamic elite and turned it toward a different goal, that of national solidarity and greatness. Unlike German nazism, Italian fascism did not place much stress on race (it was not anti-Semitic); rather, it talked of Italy's ancient glories reaching back to the Roman Empire, which it dreamed of restoring. War, Mussolini announced, "brings all human energies to their highest state of tension, and stamps with the seal of nobility the nations that dare to face it."

While indulging in such chest-thumping rhetoric, *il duce* in practice struggled with deep divisions within his Fascist party, some elements of which soon predictably denounced him for betraying its goals. In 1923, Mussolini discharged his belligerence on the relatively safe target of Greece. Following the assassination of an Italian member of the commission to establish the frontier between Albania and Greece, Italy sent an ultimatum to the Greek government and bombarded the Greek island of Corfu. Greece appealed to the League of Nations, whose failure to take any significant action against an act of aggression was an early demonstration of its impotence.

OTHER DEMOCRATIC FAILURES

As the supposed "victory of the democracies" in World War I slipped away into a swamp of disillusionment, other dictatorships arose in postwar Europe. Most were not as novel as those of communism and fascism. In Romania, Yugoslavia, and Bulgaria, unsatisfactory experiences with parliamentary government gave way to old-fashioned personal monarchical rule. King Carol of Romania and King Alexander of Yugoslavia were exercising royal dictatorships by the end of the decade. In Yugoslavia, the union of the Serbs, Croats, and Slovenes born of World War I failed to work, and in 1928 a breakdown of parliamentary government followed the assassination of the Croatian peasant leader, Radich, on the floor of the Assembly. The Croats quickly came to resent Serb domination of the multi-ethnic state, which was made up almost entirely of Slavs, true, but Slavs with varying traditions and experiences. Belgrade treated Croatian nationalism harshly; the assassination of the king in 1934, in Marseille, France, was a later and most significant outcome of this ferment in South Slavdom.

Political murder was an old Balkan custom, and in 1923 Macedonians and army conservatives brutally killed the Bulgarian peasant leader, Stambolisky, who was an ardent advocate of a union of the Balkan peoples on the basis of a common peasanthood (the "Green International"). Peasant strength, along with land reform, made southeastern Europe remarkably resistant to bolshevism. The Green International was the best antidote to the Red; as in Russia, where they did not get their way, Balkan peasants wanted land of their own, not socialized agriculture. But political democracy could not survive the turbulence of this area, where too many peoples were mixed and where experience in democratic practices was lacking. In Poland, which had no king, the popular military leader Pilsudski exercised nearly absolute power.

In Spain, a power emerged from behind the throne. Miguel Primo de Rivera, a general who became dictator from 1923 to 1930, was a picturesque personality somewhat resembling Mussolini but scorning anything so lowbrow as an ideology. An enemy of the corrupt old regime, Primo made some attempt to modernize Spain economically and spent money on public works, but he lost the support of the liberals and the intellectuals. (His son later founded the Falange, the organization of Spanish fascism, and was executed by the Loyalists at the beginning of the Spanish Civil War in 1936.) Primo de Rivera the elder's resignation and exile in 1930, followed soon by the abdication of the king, inaugurated the Spanish Republic. After five turbulent years, civil war broke out, and Spain was the unhappy fulcrum of European politics from 1936 to 1939. The great gulf between the classes, bitter class hatreds, and Catalan separatism doomed Spanish democracy as did much the same kind of combination in other countries of the south and east of Europe. Premodernized societies do not generally accommodate patterns of democracy, in the sense of a pluralism of interests and outlooks adjusted by compromise. Compromise depends on a relativism and skepticism about absolute values that has to be acquired gradually.

Several kinds of socialism and anarchism had more appeal to Spanish workers than did either democracy or communism. Peasant-based "populist" ideologies, rather like the old Social Revolutionary party in Russia, sought the breakup of big estates, land redistribution, and aid to the small independent landowner. Such ideologies flourished in the southeastern part of Europe, the real home, as Stambolisky claimed, of the peasant interest.

The remnants of the Hapsburg Empire had special problems because of their newness, their smallness, their disruption from old patterns. Austria and Hungary were left stranded, the great cities of Vienna and Budapest deprived of their hinterlands by new boundaries and barriers to trade. Austria was destined to endure a cruel civil war as well as national bankruptcy. Vienna itself was dominated by the Social Democrats, but the countryside was Catholic and conservative. Until they were all swallowed by Hitler in 1938, the Austrians fought among themselves, occasionally in open civil war. The little republic had wanted to join Germany, but the Paris peace prohibited this; again in 1931, a close and controversial decision of the World Court vetoed the *Anschluss* (annexation) of Austria to Germany.

The Austrian socialists were too civilized to attempt a ruthless dictatorship. In opposition to them, an Austrian version of fascism, the *Heimwehr,* formed a secret militia and plotted against the republic. There was street fighting in Vienna in 1927 between left and right; Austrian students, in these days, were generally on the latter side. The able Jesuit priest Ignaz Seipel was chancellor through much of the 1920s and served Austria well, arranging for international loans to keep her afloat, but he was strongly antisocialist and, his foes charged, secretly sympathetic to the *Heimwehr.* He feuded with the Viennese socialists. Mussolini's intrigues and, later, those of the Nazis complicated the harried life of the little country that had been created by a process of elimination.

In the aftermath of the White Terror that followed the overthrow of Bela Kun's short-lived Communist dictatorship, Hungary fell under the rule of a strongly conservative, aristocratic regime that frustrated the peasant smallholders. The batterings Hungary took from the peace settlement, leaving her shorn of territory to everybody else's gain, made foreign policy dominant in Hungary; every effort had to be bent toward revising the treaties. But for Hungary this was a forlorn quest. Elections were rigged, and there was no real democracy; a fascist element looked to Italy and later to Nazi Germany for leadership.

Among the new states, only Czechoslovakia adapted reasonably well to a liberal and democratic order. The republic fathered by Thomas Masaryk produced other able leaders committed to a free society. The new Czech republic abolished the old semifeudal system of land ownership and created small holdings. The Agrarian party consistently dominated Czech governments. This process was made easier by the fact that the large estate-owners had mostly been German, while the Slovaks and Czechs were peasants. Yet not only did three and a half million Germans remain, constituting a more or less disaffected minority within the Czechoslovak state, but the Slovaks and the Czechs were only slightly less incompatible than Serbs and Croats. Culturally more backward because of conditions within the old empire, in which the Czechs had received favored treatment, the Slovaks were Roman Catholics (like the Croats), whereas the Czechs had a significant Protestant (Hussite) tradition. Slovak separatism, fed by resentment of Prague's domination and to some extent by a

Czech habit of looking down on these country cousins, was not a serious threat, but it did lurk in the background. The German minority, inhabiting the more highly industrialized part of the country, considered itself mistreated by those it regarded as its cultural inferiors.

Despite these problems, Czechoslovakia seemed to be both an economic and a political success, a keystone of relative stability in disturbed central Europe. Wiser leadership and greater prosperity softened the impact of the frictions. Unfortunately, Czechoslovakia quarreled with Poland over boundaries. The two chief partisans of the Paris peace, enemies of territorial revisionism and allies of France in upholding the existing boundaries of Europe, Czechoslovakia and Poland were themselves not on the best of terms.

Political instability was not a monopoly of backward southern and eastern Europe. Civil war broke out in Ireland after the war. The war had interrupted a dangerous situation. The Protestants of the North, with the British Tories backing them, violently objected to home rule for Ireland. During the war, most of the Irish loyally supported the Allied side, and their members sitting in the British Parliament backed the war. Conscription, however, which was introduced in 1916, was far less popular. The Easter Week rebellion in Dublin in 1916, though the action of a tiny minority, left behind a romantic legend: "a terrible beauty was born." The British blundered by court-martialing and shooting fifteen of the little group of nationalists who had, in typically Irish fashion, launched an impossible uprising. But widespread Irish anger awaited the end of the war, when the Irish expected home rule if not full independence. Fighting broke out in 1920 between the Irish independence party (the Sinn Fein) and the British "black and tans," or constabulary police. Savagely fought by both sides, the civil war aroused world opinion against the British, who were cast in the role of oppressors; Irish-Americans helped defeat the League of Nations on the grounds that it underwrote British imperialism.

The British offered home rule (Dominion status) within the empire to the southern and northern parts of Ireland separately. A narrow majority of the Sinn Fein accepted this solution, but the Irish Republican Army continued the insurrection. Its members were not content with partition of the Emerald Isle, and they demanded full independence. The Irish problem did not entirely quiet down until 1927, when an assassination caused a reaction against the extremist Republicans. The Irish Free State, as it was known, accepted the oath of allegiance to the Crown, but it had a large measure of self-government. In 1926, the Ottawa Declaration announced the Dominions to be "autonomous communities within the British Empire, equal in status, in no way subordinate one to another in any respect of their domestic or external affairs." Thus to all intents and purposes, the Irish Free State was really free of British rule at long last, though the moral bond of Commonwealth unity remained until after World War II. The most galling thing was partition. The Irish Republican Army carried on a tradition of illegal violence that had begun in the civil war of 1920–1921.

Thus, with the Catholic three-quarters of Ireland almost but not quite independent, and the rest of the Emerald Isle fiercely Protestant and still attached to Great Britain, the troubles of Ireland were far from over, as events in the future were to show. Yet in that cycle of violence and accommodation that has long seemed to mark the Irish-English relationship, the latter phase replaced the former about 1927.

The self-governing dominions of the British Commonwealth were Canada, Australia, New Zealand, South Africa, and the Irish Free State. This was spelled out in the 1931 Statute of Westminster. Northern Ireland preferred to become a division of the United Kingdom of Great Britain and Northern Ireland, sending members to the British Parliament though also having its own government. Other portions of the empire were still crown colonies with a British governor advised by native consultative bodies that he appointed. In India, there were major riots, strikes, and campaigns of "civil disobedience" led by the great Indian nationalist leader Mohandas Gandhi in 1920–1921 and through the 1920s.

Such was the rather mixed record of the European countries in the 1920s. Looking at the scene in 1927 or 1928, one might have felt justified in concluding that Europe was gradually recovering from the tremendous shock of a war that had destroyed empires, caused revolutions, formed wholly new states, and stirred up further claims for freedom. That such a trauma produced enormous problems of reconstruction was hardly surprising. In time, these might have been solved. Unfortunately, time was not to be allowed.

THE LOCARNO SPIRIT

The nightmare experiences of the first five postwar years gave way to a much more stable period between 1924 and 1930 through most of Europe. The stabilization of the mark, the Dawes Plan, and loans from abroad cleared the way for a considerable economic recovery. In Germany, responsible conservatives gave support to the republic, the extreme right faded, and though its political life was never easy, the parliamentary regime seemed to be making progress in these years. The election of old Field Marshal von Hindenburg as president in 1925 strengthened the republic.

In France, Premier Edouard Herriot and after him Aristide Briand, who remained foreign minister through a series of French governments, were willing to move cautiously toward reconciliation with Germany as an alternative to the failed policy of disruption and dismemberment. On the German side, the able Gustav Stresemann, an architect of the 1924 stabilization, had a long tenure as foreign minister under Chancellors Hans Luther, Wilhelm Marx, and, after the elections of 1928, Hermann Mueller. Stresemann and Briand worked well together. They caught the imagination of a world barren of political heroes in the 1920s. They were a symbol of Franco-German reconciliation and a new era of peace.

While extremists of both left and right denounced him for surrendering to the enemies of World War I and to the Allied capitalists, Stresemann preached that cooperation with Germany's former foes was her only possible route back to national strength. An ardent nationalist, Stresemann protected the Reichswehr, which was engaged in some practices that would hardly bear inspection, from the eyes of the Allied Control Commission. He did not accept a weakened Germany. He simply thought that a Western orientation offered the best chances for recovery. There were Germans who thought otherwise, and in 1922 they had secured a treaty with Soviet Russia (the Treaty of Rapallo). Secret and mutually profitable military arrangements between the two countries began in 1921.[4] But Stresemann wooed the West with much success.

In 1926, Germany entered the League of Nations, from which she had previously been excluded, and after some controversy received a Great Power position on the League Council. A year before, the Locarno treaties had signaled the new orientation, and the "spirit of Locarno" symbolized a new era. In these agreements Germany, France, Italy, and Britain joined in guaranteeing the existing frontier between Germany and France-Belgium. This meant that Germany accepted as final the cession of Alsace and Lorraine to France and Malmédy to Belgium. She also repeated her acceptance of the Rhineland demilitarization provisions. In these ways, Locarno was a curious reiteration of the Treaty of Versailles and the League of Nations, as if the powers were saying, "We really mean it this time." The powers also agreed to submit their disputes to arbitration.

Although representatives from Czechoslovakia and Poland also came to Locarno, Germany gave no such German guarantees in the east. Nevertheless, arbitration treaties were signed, and France pledged help to Czechoslovakia and Poland if they were attacked by Germany. In later years, people spoke of the *équivoque*, the ambiguity, of the Locarno pacts: Each side understood them in a different way. To the Western powers, the agreements that were concluded in October 1925 in the little Swiss town of Locarno meant that Germany totally accepted the post–World War I peace settlement. To the Germans, Locarno meant that they accepted the settlement in the west but hoped for a future revision in the east. We are familiar enough, from many later examples, of pseudo-agreements constructed of ambiguous words that each side interprets in its own way. (Compare Yalta, 1945, or Geneva, 1967.)

The reward held out to Germany for renouncing any attempt to revise

[4]Bolshevik foreign policy initially was based on the view that all the capitalist states would unite against the USSR and its only hope lay in worldwide revolution. With the waning of this hope yet the survival of their regime in Russia, some of the Bolshevik theoreticians postulated both the need and the possibility of a period of "peaceful coexistence" with all the capitalist world, which might provide Russia with economic aid. But the commissar for foreign affairs in the early 1920s, Chicherin, held that Great Britain was the Soviet Union's primary foe, the Versailles system the leading capitalist front, and friendship with Weimar Germany the best bet for Soviet policy.

Versailles boundaries included early withdrawal of the Allied troops that had been occupying the Rhineland since 1919. Originally, this occupation had been set for fifteen years, with the possibility of renewal, but after a series of reductions all forces were removed by 1930. The Military Control Commission, appointed to see that Germany complied with the disarmament provisions of the treaty, went home in 1927. Germany continued to ignore some of these provisions; in particular, she reorganized the equivalent of a General Staff, and she used Russia as a place of military training. The Allies certainly knew about and chose to ignore these noncompliances. So the effective pledges that France held against German renewal of the war were gone. The Germans pledged themselves to respect the demilitarized zone, and Locarno provided for Franco-British-Italian cooperation in the event they breached this commitment, but there was no longer any concrete obstacle to their sending troops into the region.

Finally, a disarmament conference that began in 1927 at Geneva, Switzerland, site of the League of Nations, was based on a kind of commitment to equalize armaments by disarming the Allies to Germany's level. All in all, the Locarno agreements and their sequels constituted a considerable German victory. Later, the French thought that "the seeds of Munich were in Locarno"; that is, the policy of appeasement of Germany had begun. But of course from 1925 to 1933 Germany was not ruled by Hitler. Extremist movements of both right and left had subsided. In the election of 1928, the Communists received 10 percent of the popular vote, while Adolf Hitler's NSDAP got only 2.6 percent. The "Weimar parties" now had a sizeable majority in the Reichstag, and even the German Nationalist party (DNVP), with 73 seats, was no longer a completely implacable foe of the system. The republic seemed to have succeeded. The peaceful Social Democrats and Catholic Centrists were the strongest political parties.

Weimar suggested a brilliant renewal of German culture, symbolized in the Bauhaus school of art and architecture founded there. Great German writers like Thomas Mann renounced their World War I attitudes and changed into advocates of peace and internationalism. Berlin, Frankfurt, and Munich resumed their positions as international centers of the arts. Berlin was wickedly decadent, but this suited the mood of the hour. The Wilhelmine Germany of pointed helmets and goose-stepping soldiers belonged to a now remote past, given the fast pace of change in the postwar world. No one foresaw the Germany of brown-uniformed storm troopers and screaming mass political rallies that lay just a few years ahead.

The Locarno spirit merged with the Geneva spirit, for the League of Nations, damaged at its birth by American refusal to enter and soon confronted with the hopelessness of its ambitious plans for a new sort of "collective security," began to take on some prestige as an international meeting place. Attempts in 1924–1925 to clarify and strengthen the commitments of members to the security provisions of the Covenant, that is, to participate actively in putting down any "aggression," revealed that Great Britain and the Dominions were as opposed to this as the United States had been. No longer dreaming of becoming a world government, the League was content to be a vehicle of communication and an instrument of social service. Its specialized agencies encouraged international cooperation in dealing with problems of working conditions, health, transportation, and crime. Statesmen came to Geneva to consult and hold conferences.

The great disarmament conference began there in 1927 with high hopes. An organization began to take shape. A somewhat tattered symbol of "the peace that passed understanding," the League looked a little brighter in the late 1920s than it had at the end of the war. And so did nearly everything else in that short moment of hope before the economic roof caved in, crushing the frail plant of international understanding.

A further emblem of the times was the Kellogg-Briand Peace Pact, which was named after an American secretary of state and a French statesman. It was signed amid great fanfare in 1928 by nearly all the governments of the world (sixty-three of sixty-seven) after it was ceremonially initialed in Paris. The fact that the United States co-sponsored it was significant. A vague encomium to peace entailing no concrete commitments, the pact had only a moral value; but world opinion thought it highly important that war had been outlawed by this solemn declaration. Its signers "condemned recourse to war" and "renounced war as an instrument of national policy." Future events, unhappily, revealed how little this might mean. A clash between China and Russia managed to coincide with the final promulgation of the pact in 1929! But that its creation was something of an international sensation in 1928 testifies to the hopefulness of that year, if also to its pathetic illusions.

5

The Dissolution of the Ancestral Order: Culture and Thought in the Postwar Era

POSTWAR PESSIMISM

Einstein, Freud, Picasso, Le Corbusier, Virginia Woolf, James Joyce, and many another spokesperson of the mind or spirit brilliantly lit up the 1920s, contrasting with the rather depressing spectacle of public affairs. There were also exciting political ideas, but these were revolutionary and iconoclastic, and politics in general was not in favor; it was subject to one of those spells of profound disillusionment with the whole process that periodically afflict democracies. In the postwar decade, there was a strong reaction against the overheated political idealism of the Great Crusade. "No intelligent man can afford to be caught holding the illusion that any public event matters very much," American political commentator Walter Lippmann complained, and internationally renowned American novelist Ernest Hemingway put these words into the mouth of the hero of his great war novel, *A Farewell to Arms:*

> I was always embarrassed by the words sacred, glorious and sacrifice and the expression in vain. . . . There were many words that you could not stand to hear and finally only the names of places had dignity.

"The holy war to save humanity," as the *Manchester Guardian* put it, preached by the politicians in exalted rhetoric, had not only bloodied the soil of Europe but had left the world weary of politics.

Virginia Woolf. (*Courtesy National Portrait Gallery, London.*)

Few of the politicians of the postwar decade, the age of Baldwin and Coolidge, could rally political hopes. "I do not remember whether I voted in those years, certainly not for whom," German writer Ludwig Marcuse recalled. The Russian Revolution had supplied a ray of hope, but it seemed to fade. Although the liberal intelligentsia might defend Russia against its foes and march in sympathy with those alleged martyrs of intolerant antiradicalism, Sacco and Vanzetti (the Massachusetts case was an international *cause célèbre*), their heart was hardly in it. Intellectuals had bad experiences with the Communist party in the 1920s. Ironically, it was not until the full Stalinization of the Soviet Union in the 1930s that a major movement of Western intellectuals toward communism took place. Alienated and disenchanted, the 1920s avant-garde could not get interested in any political crusade.

One of the most widely read books of the decade, written by the French critic and essayist Julien Benda, called *The Treason of the Intellectuals (La trahison des clercs)*, rebuked the intellectuals en masse for having rushed after various political causes and advised them to return to the eternal verities. The term intellectual itself was of fairly recent origin. It first became current during the Dreyfus case in France around the turn of the century, when a "manifesto of the intellectuals" appeared. The word came to mean not merely someone who, as writer or artist, makes his living and lives his life as a "toiler of the brain" and who, being neither businessperson, farmer, nor factory worker, seems peculiarly without a class, but also one whose exceptional sensitivity sets him apart from the "kindly race of men." As we know, the war in some ways represented an attempt by the intellectuals to join the national community in a worthy cause. The vast majority of them rallied enthusiastically to the war in 1914, characteristically viewing it as a chance for solidarity as well as splendid adventure. But for most of them the experience failed. They spat out their distaste in a host of war novels that adorned the 1920s. The war was certainly a literary success, but its literature deflated it. In many of the war books, there is a strong feeling for the war as a memorable experience and for the comradeship of the trenches. But the ultimate verdict was one of powerful disillusionment. The bravery of the soldiers had been betrayed by homefront hypocrisy or profiteering or blundering. And, the heroes who returned, leaving many a comrade under the soil, found it hard to adjust. The war was over, but their spiritual hunger remained. One could never again believe in the romance of the battlefield. The war literature was poignant with memories of those

> . . . who went
> Ungrudgingly, and spent
> Their all for us. (Wilfrid Gibson, "A Lament.")

It told of the restlessness of the ex-heroes who tried to return to humdrum postwar life. Gradually, the most popular theme became that of simple disgust, feeding the *nie wieder krieg* (no more war) sentiment that waxed in the thirties.

A list of books written about the war, either as novels, plays, poetry, or as straight autobiography or personal narrative, would be a long one; among the best known were Henri Barbusse's *Le Feu,* by one who became an uncritical Communist; Erich Maria Remarque's *All Quiet on the Western Front (Im Westen Nichts Neues),* which was made into a memorable movie; Hemingway's *A Farewell to Arms;* poet Robert Graves's classic personal narrative *Goodbye to All That;* the tetralogy of Ford Madox Ford. This list is no more than a sampling. The war made the literary reputation of dead poet Wilfred Owen and enhanced that of novelist Romain Rolland, who had been its leading opponent from the start. *Heartbreak House* was Shaw's play about the war, and such it was–a breaking of hearts over heroism wasted, great deeds come to naught. A play by an English insurance agent, R. C. Sheriff, called *Journey's End* (1929), set in the trenches, became an international hit. Such bitterly negative writings about the war appeared most frequently around the end of the 1920s and the early 1930s.

The war now seemed not a means of salvation but a seal of the ultimate damnation of the West. Postwar thought lamented the defeat of Western civilization. A retired German schoolteacher named Oswald Spengler had started work on his *Der Untergang des Abendlandes* before the war and had it finished in time to catch the crest of postwar gloom; as *The Decline of the West,* the book had an international success. So deeply implanted in the popular mind was the theme of slow but certain progress, from the benighted Middle Ages onward through the age of kings to the era of science and democracy (and/or socialism) that to be told that Western civilization peaked in the later Middle Ages and had been falling apart ever since was startling, as much so to the left as to the right. A need for total reexamination of the past impelled another amateur excursion into world history to fabulous sales: Famed British writer H. G. Wells' *Outline of History,* by no means as pessimistic as Spengler's, catered to this anxious reassessment of Europe's traditions. The shock of war started Arnold J. Toynbee on an even vaster chronicle of comparative civilization, seeking to discover why civilizations fail; the first volumes of his monumental *A Study of History* came off the press in 1934. A Russian émigré historian who had settled in the United States, M. I. Rostovtzeff, addressed himself to the question of Rome's fall, with many signs of intruding contemporary perspectives; Rome fell from an excess of democracy, a decline of public spirit. "Things fall apart, the center cannot hold," as Yeats memorably put it.

Decline and Fall was the title of Evelyn Waugh's first novel (1928), a brilliant satire by the English writer who converted to Roman Catholicism as a sign of his rejection of the whole modern age. A similar kind of wittiness with a sting in its tail came from Aldous Huxley, in a series of 1920s novels that held the Victorian idols up to ridicule, as did Lytton Strachey of London's Bloomsbury Circle in *Eminent Victorians*. And, a similar if more serious gesture of rejection arose on the Continent, especially in the German-speaking world. Soon recognized as the greatest of modern theologians, Karl Barth began a sharp attack on liberal theology, which had adopted the idea that human progress is the realization of God's purposes. Influenced by Hegel, pre-1914 German theology had visualized history mediating between God and man; it is the Holy Spirit working to realize God's purposes by translating His goodness into tangible things.

Now the Lutheran Barth, the Swiss Calvinist Emil Brunner, and others reminded a generation of optimistic vipers that Christ's kingdom is not of this world. There is a barrier between man and God, a dialectical gap, and that barrier condemns earthly existence to tragic imperfection. The old Lutheran and Calvinist message of original Sin, the depravity of man's fallen nature, never received stronger stress than it did at this time. The obvious motivation of these works was a refusal to accept the idea that present-day human society is in any way a realization of God's purposes. Much more is it the Devil's work.

Karl Barth's 1919 *Epistle to the Romans* was a theological bombshell. At the same time, the works of the nineteenth-century Danish seer Søren Kierkegaard were revived; Russian Orthodox refugee from communism Nicolai Berdyayev and Jewish theologian Martin Buber brought much the same message. "The belief in Progress," said England's Dean William Inge, "has been the working faith of the West for about a hundred and fifty years." But "if we turn to history . . . we find . . . that civilization is a disease which is almost invariably fatal, unless its course is checked in time." Berdyayev thought that "Man's historical experience has been one of steady failure, and there are no grounds for supposing it will ever be anything else." All the idols of the nineteenth century, associated as they were with this crumbled idea of progress, came under attack. The scientist's dream of perfecting knowledge and leading humanity to a glorious conquest of nature had turned sour; scientists had spent the war making poison gas, and in any case their formulae offer nothing for the real human needs, those of the spirit. Lord Tantamount, in Huxley's *Point Counter Point,* eyes glued to the microscope, does not understand human relations at all. The Einsteinian revolution attracted wide attention precisely because it seemed to explode all the assumptions of nineteenth-century materialistic science.

Sigmund Freud, a hero of the intellectuals, turned increasingly in the 1920s to moral and philosophical speculation, represented by one of his most popular books, *Civilization and Its Discontents.* The aging founder of psycho-analysis, shocked by the war into believing in a death wish as well as a life force, presented the pessimistic view that humanity can never solve its problems; people will always be torn asunder between the conflicting demands of psychic in-dividuality and of society, the id and the superego–the more civilized we become, the more society must repress the individual. "The price of civilization is neurosis." It was a vision strangely congenial to that of the neo-orthodox the-ologians; the tough-minded scientific atheism of Freud was in the same camp with the return to religion. The human subconscious is a snakepit filled with the demonic forces Christians had always called sin.

The Viennese doctor's remarkable influence was most notable in liter-ature and the arts. Not only had Freud pointed the way to articulating previ-ously unmentionable sexual urges, including the incestuous and homosexual, but he suggested a tragic framework, the clash of individual desire and social in-hibition, id and superego. From the great American dramatist Eugene O'Neill to the remarkable novels of D. H. Lawrence, James Joyce, Marcel Proust, and Franz Kafka in Europe, the shocking thoughts of the secret self provided allur-ing new material, while the drama came from conflict between unconscious de-terminants and rationalized motives. Freud had stripped the last illusions of reason and dignity from the human race.

Democracy was another fallen idol. Not likely to go all the way with ei-ther Lenin or Mussolini, intellectuals of the 1920s were inclined, like George Bernard Shaw and Georges Sorel, to admire both. This was simply because they abhorred what they considered to be a flaccid bourgeois democracy, the tyranny of the hopelessly philistine average person. Many Italian intellectuals were half implicated in fascism, since they believed in elite rule, not democ-racy–in those qualitatively a majority if quantitatively a minority, as Benedetto Croce put it. Repelled by the vulgar mass civilization abundantly visible in the 1920s, the intellectuals typically sneered at the common man, hoped for some sort of guardian or "clerisy" class to rule, lamented with Yeats that

> Base drove out the better blood
> And mind and body shrank.

In Spengler's scheme of decline, democracy is a product of the decay of natural, organic culture and of positive values, a kind of detritus left by skepticism, nihilism, and social disintegration. Weimar Germany produced whole schools of neoconservatives who lamented "The Rule of the Inferiors" (the title of a 1927 book by the Lutheran romantic reactionary Edgar Jung) and dreamed of a mandarin elite. Although they helped prepare the way for Hitler's Brown Shirts, most of them saw the Nazis as upstarts from the vulgar masses. Later they were Nazi victims.

Antidemocratic strains were by no means confined to Germany. The Spaniard José Ortega y Gasset's widely read essay *The Revolt of the Masses* articulated the sense of dismay at the collapse of civilized traditions. In the United States, Henry L. Mencken's sophisticated set laughed at the "gaping primates" of rural and small-town America.

Marxists could agree that bourgeois culture was dying in the West while having faith that a new and better one, based on the proletariat, was coming to rough birth in the East. Most Western intellectuals in the 1920s were skeptical of this innocent faith. Beatrice and Sidney Webb, the deans of British socialism, wrote in 1923 about *The Decay of Capitalist Civilization,* but they were not yet prepared, as they would be a decade later, to find a worthy successor in Soviet civilization. John Maynard Keynes lectured in 1926 on *The End of Laissez Faire,* but what would take the place of old-fashioned competitive capitalism? The great economist was not yet sure.

In the main, the writers of the 1920s found their consolation in making brilliant art of their vision of social decay. T. S. Eliot's celebrated poem *The Waste Land* begins with a quotation from Petronius: we yearn to die. "April is the cruellest month" because it can no longer bring forth new life; the world has lost its creativity. Filled with all the subtle devices of modernist technique, Eliot found images to express the futility of religion, love, everything once productive of life:

> Here is no water but only rock.

The energizing springs of culture that fertilized Western society in the past had dried up, leaving people fearful and timid. The great tradition ends not with a bang but a whimper.

THE LITERARY AND ARTISTIC RENAISSANCE

Such visions of ruin stand in strange opposition to an actual revival of the arts that marked one of the most esthetically exciting of Western decades. There was a feast for the eye, the ear, and the mind during the postwar years. As even Yeats admitted,

> Though the great sung return no more
> There's keen delight in what we have:
> The rattle of pebbles on the shore
> Under the receding wave.

The literature, architecture, and art of the 1920s were more than the rattle of pebbles. The modernist movement that had begun before the war now burst on the world with full force, charged with the special tone of revolutionary defiance that the war had induced. "Before and after 1914 differed absolutely, only nominally on the same earth," Franz Kafka's friend Max Brod declared, and we should not forget this complete change in mood even when we observe continuities between pre-1914 and post-1914 techniques in the arts. Form might be carried over, but content was new.

Writers Kafka, Joyce, Yeats, Eliot, D. H. Lawrence, Marcel Proust, and Thomas Mann; painters Klee, Picasso, and Kandinsky; architects Walter Gropius and Le Corbusier; and many other ornaments of literature and the arts had begun their careers before the war. But it was after the war that they attained their greatest fame and, in most cases, their fullest development. By breaking the authority of tradition, the war prepared the public mind for the startlingly novel qualities of the new art. This art still shocked people, but it did make an impact. James Joyce's *Ulysses,* which began its life in one of the numerous "little magazines" devoted to experimental literature and art, was first banned, then published in Paris. The first, limited edition of 1921 quickly escalated to $300 a copy. It immediately became controversial. Called "morbid and sickening," "an immense mass of clotted nonsense," and "the foulest book that ever found its way into print," it was also hailed as a work of supreme genius. T. S. Eliot, the angular American from St. Louis who was working as a bank clerk in London while readying his *Waste Land* and other poems, was among those who acclaimed it. On one level, a vivid, realistic, comic, often hilariously ribald story of one day in the life of present-day Dubliners, *Ulysses* was also an allegory of the human situation and evidently a commentary on the decay of man since Homeric times. It quickly gained and kept its place as the century's greatest work of literature.

Technically, Joyce made breathtaking use of "stream of consciousness" to show us the unedited thoughts of people in all their illogical complexity. This intense subjectivism, along with the eroticism that sometimes accompanied it (people's secret thoughts presumably not excluding sexual fantasies) suggested Freudianism, but may also be viewed as the consequence of a flight from public themes and from the whole social order. Virginia Woolf's Mrs. Dalloway, the heroine of another novel exploring one day in the inner life of a person, cannot get interested in the life of her politician husband and retreats to an inner world of fantasy; it is this world that Mrs. Woolf tried to recreate.

"I will not serve that in which I no longer believe, whether it call itself my home, my fatherland, or my church," Joyce had declared (through Stephen Dedalus in *Portrait of the Artist*). It was a time of exiles. Americans Ernest Hemingway, Gertrude Stein, T. S. Eliot, and Ezra Pound fled to Europe; Europeans fled sometimes to America (D. H. Lawrence to New Mexico, Malcolm Lowry to Mexico and British Columbia) or elsewhere. "In Europe he had made up his mind that everything was done for, played out, finished, he must go to a new country," someone says in a Lawrence novel. Writers sought out primitive peoples or exotic cultures; Lorca, the Spanish poet, turned to the gypsies, Lawrence to the Indians. Herman Hesse was among the first to discover Buddhism. One's own society was a wasteland; anywhere else was better.

To express one's own esthetic consciousness and make art out of an inner chaos were the achievements of the modernist painters and sculptors. Whether they called themselves expressionists, abstractionists, cubists, surrealists, or something else, they agreed in the program "Away from the Thing, away from Matter"; "abolish the sovereignty of appearances." In brief, they chose not to represent the everyday world realistically (something that anyone with a camera could now do anyway), but to depict something else, perhaps an inner vision such as might appear in dreams or perhaps a purely formal design, the imagination working in mathematical dimensions. Surrealism sought to tap the unconscious mind; symbolism looked for something deeper than the external phenomena of nature. The new "depth" psychology of Sigmund Freud and Carl Jung fertilized this strain of modern art, Jung in particular suggesting the importance of archetypal images manufactured in the collective unconscious of the human mind—images of religious as well as esthetic significance, as old as humanity, redolent of primeval myth and symbol.

Joyce's invention of virtually a new language (more notable in his second great interwar novel, *Finnegans Wake,* finished in 1939) was an aspect of this search for a new country of the mind. Here was the literary equivalent of

James Joyce. (*National Portrait Gallery.*)

Einstein's physics or Kandinsky's painting–strange, wonderful, incomprehensible. His novels draw heavily on myth and, in the case of *Finnegans Wake,* a kind of dream language in which appear the perennial archetypes of human experience. The object is to find in dreams a realm of art and magic that modern rationalized humanity has, to its detriment, lost.

Clearly this nonrepresentational art flowed from the desire to evade existing reality; the escape was to an inner world of the pure imagination, an abstract world of geometrical patterns, an ideal world or a metaphysical one. Klee, Kandinsky, Mondrian, Picasso–a Swiss, a Russian, a Dutchman, a Spaniard, working chiefly in Germany or Paris–were among dozens of great artists creating a fresh vision of life. Strange as their work seemed to eyes unaccustomed to it, they now received a degree of acceptance, no longer the targets of vegetable throwers or the police as had been the case just before 1914.

Futurist acceptance of the machine age continued somewhat into the twenties, spurred by the new inventions of technology and by interest in Einsteinian science. The *Neue Sachlichkeit* reacted against expressionist subjectivism in the direction of a severely mathematical esthetic.

Architecture, too, experienced a revolutionary transformation. In revulsion against the old forms–classical, gothic, and baroque–designers tried to create a completely different building style, breaking altogether with tradition. Sometimes they tried to relate architecture to the machine age, but elements of a new esthetic were also present. Among the greater names in the architectural revolution were the Swiss-French who called himself Le Corbusier and in Germany the master of the Bauhaus, Walter Gropius. The Bauhaus was the leading expression of the "Weimar renaissance," which gave Germany a few brief years of renown before Hitler moved in to repress modernism as Jewish-internationalist decadence. The painters Klee and Kandinsky joined Gropius in this institution, which was at once a community, a school, and a place for creative work design of all sorts. The goal was a style uniquely suited to twentieth-century civilization–urban, industrial, technologically modern, yet beautiful. It would owe little or nothing to the ancient modes.

Le Corbusier's defeat in the League of Nations competition clearly indicated the resistance that still remained to such startling novelties. But Le Corbusier, Gropius, and the American master Frank Lloyd Wright began to be known. The Bauhaus settled in Dessau in 1925 in buildings designed by Gropius. The advent of Hitler forced Gropius out of Germany; he joined numerous other German luminaries in Britain, France, the United States, and elsewhere. Gropius was later to work at Harvard and design many American structures, as Mies van der Rohe did in Chicago. An authentic twentieth-century style in architecture made its public debut in the 1920s after being born just prior to the war.

Other manifestations of the creative German spirit appeared in the new art of cinema, where German expressionist films *(The Cabinet of Dr. Caligari, Blue Angel)* came as close as any to giving this popular genre significant esthetic expression. Bertolt Brecht's strikingly innovative theater also flourished in this period, when Berlin was wicked, decadent, exciting, its cabarets where every adventurous spirit wanted to be. In this post-Kaiser and pre-Hitler interlude, Germany seethed with new ideas. The philosopher Martin Heidegger was writing his *Sein und Zeit*. Critical Marxists of the Frankfurt school began to try to rescue Marx from Stalin.

One of the decade's literary masterpieces was Thomas Mann's *Magic Mountain* (*Zauberberg*, 1924). Like Ulysses and like Marcel Proust's mammoth chronicle of the decay of French society, *Magic Mountain* sought a total revaluation of the tradition. Set in a Swiss sanitarium among the sick and dying—a symbol comparable to Eliot's wasteland—the novel contains figures representative of the modern mind: a scientific rationalist, a Dostoyevskyan irrationalist, a pagan sensualist, a soldier, and others. The device resembles Huxley's gallery of types, including communist, fascist, nihilist, scientist, esthete, in *Point Counter Point*. There is an exotic Russian girl with whom the protagonist, Castorp, has a brief but intense affair—perhaps a sign for the ephemeral appeal of communism. The quest is for some value Western civilization can seize hold of to rescue itself. In Mann's masterpiece, Hans Castorp (whose name may suggest catastrophe, castration, chaos, Castor and Pollux, caste, or casting about) nearly dies in a snowstorm but rouses himself by sheer effort of will.

The ultimate reliance on an elemental will to live, accepting life in all its terrible irrationality, and building values by human affirmation, is Nietzschean, existentialist, and Lorenzian. It was the creed of D. H. Lawrence, the most creative writer England produced in this era, whose *Sons and Lovers, Women in Love, The Rainbow,* and *Lady Chatterley's Lover* from 1913 to 1928 proposed salvation via the miracle of physical love. Lawrence's great talent was for taking us into real human situations and making us feel intensely the actual anguish of the living searcher.

Proust died in 1922; the concluding volumes of the series that comprised *A la recherche du temps perdu*, begun in 1909, were published after his death. Translated as *Remembrance of Things Past,* their impact was scarcely less than Joyce's. Franz Kafka, dying of tuberculosis in 1924 while barely forty years old, as Lawrence was to do a few years later, with his great novels still unfinished and unpublished, had to wait several years before being recognized as one of the modern masters; the Prague Jewish writer's vivid visions of a nightmare world made their impact in the 1930s.

The attempt at total revaluation was a feature of the new art and philosophy, along with formal experimentalism and revolutionary novelty. Sometimes, in reaction against the modern world, the quest led back to old religions, as happened with the neo-Lutherans, the neo-Catholics, the primitivists, and the Western disciples of the Buddha. Lawrence found solace in the ancient Etruscans, who represented a path not taken by Graeco-Christian culture. Eliot, most daring of poetic experimenters, soon announced himself an Anglo-Catholic, a royalist, and a classicist! "Revolutionary traditionalists," someone tagged these people. By and large, they were reactionaries, for they found in older societies, more ordered and more esthetic, an antidote to the whole ugly face of modern industrial, mass-democratic civilization.

Yet the restless quest went on. The French surrealists flirted with left-wing politics in the 1920s, only to reject the Communist party's inhuman discipline and especially its turn toward "socialist realism" under Stalin, which made the party of political revolution artistically reactionary.

WRITERS UNDER DICTATORSHIP

A special and tragic chapter in the saga of the postwar writers unfolded in the Soviet Union as it passed from revolutionary euphoria to the grim stage of totalitarian organization. In one way or another, the process took its toll of poets and intellectuals. Alexander Blok, poet of the October Revolution *(The Twelve)* died during the 1921 famine. In the same year, Nikolai Gumilyov was shot (without trial) as a counterrevolutionary. Yessenin, after the breakup of his stormy marriage with the fabulous American dancer Isadora Duncan, committed suicide in 1925. Five years later, so did the great Vladimir Mayakovsky, who like all these poets had greeted the Revolution with enthusiasm, only to find he could not adjust to its demands for conformity and propaganda. Mayakovsky killed himself a few days after getting into a furious row with an audience who heckled him and called his poems incomprehensible. Art and revolution were in hopeless conflict.

The Silver Age of Russian art and literature–some think it should be called the Golden Age–blossomed just before the war, producing genius seldom matched anywhere. The composer Alexander Scriabin died during the war; Rachmaninoff left Russia to spend the rest of his life abroad, as many other Russians did, in a massive migration of the White Russians especially to Paris and Berlin. In exile, many were condemned to waste their talents. In exile, they might yearn to come back. One of the saddest cases was that of Marina Tsvetayeva, a brilliant poet who returned in time to be a victim of Stalin's purge, committing suicide in 1940. Of those who stayed, unable to leave their beloved country, the greatest ones could not make their peace with an increasingly tyrannical regime. Doubtless they would have hated any established order. Lenin called them "hooligan Communists" because of their highly irregular artists' lives, and thus began a long warfare between the Soviet state and independent minds.

Of the great Silver Age writers, Boris Pasternak survived but largely ceased to write, except privately; many years later, he would publish *Dr. Zhivago* and become a belated martyr. Anna Akhmatova also lived on, though subject to some mistreatment, writing insincere poems in praise of Stalin and, in World War II, sincere ones in behalf of Russian patriotism.

There was a kind of philistinism about the Communists, expressed in

Lenin's often quoted remark that he could not let himself be seduced by the beauty of Beethoven's music while there was revolutionary work to be done. One cannot readily combine the business of extinguishing the ruling class with tender nights watching the ballet or opera. Moreover, Marxian dogma readily lent itself to the view that the old bourgeois culture was tainted all the way through. "Bourgeois decadence" was the epithet applied to those artists too subtle, too individualized, too preoccupied with formal novelties. Art should serve the "people," which meant the Communist party; in other words, it must be propaganda, filled with simple ideas attuned to the mass consciousness.

As the Revolution passed into its Stalinist phase, the philistines and the bureaucrats more and more forced writers and artists either to join the party and serve its interests or to perish. Rewards were held out for those who joined and served, but the nonconformist increasingly found life difficult. The state monopoly of publication, the censorship, and the punishment visited on "enemies of the Revolution" crushed individuality. The situation worsened in the 1930s, when the party adopted the esthetic principle of "socialist realism" and the dictatorship tightened. Writers who had managed to survive the 1920s perished a decade later. For writing a poem against Stalin that was never published but read only to a small group, Osip Mandelstam died in a prison camp. Vsevolod Meyerhold, the famous theatrical producer, also died in a camp, although the movie director Sergei Eisenstein, whose films about the Revolution were among the most prestigious productions of Soviet art, lasted until 1948. Stalin himself seemed to have longed for great Soviet artists, realizing that most of those who served him were hacks; an Eisenstein was a rarity. But Stalin demanded total obedience, and his own taste in the arts was appalling.

"A negative depiction of contemporary life" was the worst fault; the writer mustn't speak critically of Soviet realities, for this was to serve the class enemy. And the Stalinized party was soon condemning, as "formalism," practically all of what writers and artists regarded as progressive, exciting, and interesting, all that had been happening since about the turn of the century. They were supposed to go back to the realistic or naturalistic style of the nineteenth century, but they were not even allowed to use it critically. They were asked to be Balzacs, Dickenses, and Tolstoys without exposing corruption and hypocrisy.

Those who refused to bend the knee to Mussolini faced a similar predicament. It is true that by the standards that Stalin and Hitler set, Italian fascism was a mild thing. In her classic study of twentieth-century totalitarianism (the century's one original contribution to the art of government, someone has disquietingly remarked), Hannah Arendt refused to classify Mussolini's regime as truly totalitarian, though it invented the idea. Hitler and his German Nazi comrades agreed with this, acknowledging an intellectual debt to Mussolini but holding that he had failed to carry the thing through. "Fascism has nothing in common with National Socialism," Joseph Goebbels noted in his journal. "The latter goes to the roots, the former is only superficial." The Nazis thought that Soviet communism was totalitarian, the true rival and enemy of their own, and they accorded it a certain respect for its total fanaticism and ruthlessness. Whereas the Nazi and Communist dictatorships were to slay millions, Italian Fascist terrorism, by comparison, took scarcely any life at all. Special tribunals to deal with political "crimes" were indeed set up, but not only did they condemn relatively few, they adhered to a certain semblance of legality. This was enough to brand fascism as utterly flabby in the eyes of true totalitarians. Arendt counted only seven condemnations to death between 1926 and 1932, which were the most active years; there were about 1,600 prison sentences and many more exiles, but no fewer than 12,000 were acquitted, "a procedure inconceivable under the Nazi or Bolshevik terror." The great Italian Communist leader Antonio Gramsci was jailed, but while in prison he wrote essays and books that were subsequently published and became landmarks of Marxian theory. The same thing happening in a Soviet prison camp or a Nazi concentration camp is hard to imagine. Nor was Italian fascism disfigured by the anti-Semitism that German National Socialism featured.

Nevertheless, one should not overlook the illiberal and dictatorial features of Fascist rule. Mussolini's rhetoric had proclaimed not only "the lie of universal suffrage" but, in 1923, fascism's willingness "to trample on the more or less decomposed body of the Goddess Liberty." The Fascists turned the elections of April 1924 into a farce, as their "squadrists" terrorized opponents, though Mussolini's undeniable success in restoring order probably earned him an honest majority at the polls. There soon followed the famous episode of Giacomo Matteotti's murder by Fascist thugs. This action shocked the entire country, and the martyred Socialist member of Parliament seemed destined to bring down Mussolini's government. "Supported by king and pope, by Senate and industry," Ernst Nolte puts it, he did not fall, but turned to the right, breaking his last ties with the socialists among whom he had spent so many years. There were several attempts on *il duce*'s life in the next few years. Some of these may have stemmed from extremists in his own party, who alleged betrayal of fascism's true goals in Mussolini's tendencies to come to terms with the old established order. Not without some evident regret, in 1927 Mussolini turned to such illiberal measures as suppressing hostile newspapers, arresting political foes, banning opposition parties, and constituting the "corporative state," which deprived Parliament of power and deposited it in a fascist Grand Council dominated by Mussolini.

If this power was used less ruthlessly by Mussolini than by Hitler or Stalin, it nevertheless laid claim to totality: Every Italian was supposed to serve the state, making it a "monolith" of one national will expressed through the leader. There was no place for opposition or dissent. Yet, somewhat inconsistently, Mussolini proceeded to negotiate a treaty with the papacy in 1929, leaving the "care of souls" to the church.

The most distinctive element in the somewhat erratic Fascist "ideology" was the idea of a "corporative" economy, which was held to be the natural successor to capitalism. In opposition to capitalism, Marxism had proclaimed the sterile program of class conflict, Mussolini explained; fascism proposed the constructive plan of collaboration between capital and labor through the mediation of the State. Italy, a poor country struggling to catch up with more industrialized ones, could not afford strikes and lockouts. The state, representing the public interest, would bring big capital and big labor together, as equals, but with itself as the third and presumably strongest party. Agreements on wages and working conditions would then be reached in a manner equitable to all parties. Opponents claimed that in practice, by undermining independent trade union leadership, Mussolini's corporative state played into the hands of the capitalists, who were almost ecstatically happy to find themselves in a world without strikes. There is, however, little reason to doubt Mussolini's sincerity in proposing a new and more progressive way toward industrial peace and growth. The idea was reasonable enough to appeal to the American reformist President Franklin D. Roosevelt early in his New Deal regime (the National Recovery Act, 1934).

Mussolini had a fairly good press in Western countries; many Italian-Americans were exuberantly enthusiastic about his supposed restoration of Italian strength. Yet a number of courageous Italians opposed his illiberal regime. Some were his own early followers, like Cesare Rossi, who broke with Mussolini at the time of the Mattcotti affair, dared to write a hostile exposé, and was sentenced to imprisonment. (He survived to write post-1945 books, unlike Trotsky and Ernst Röhm.)

Gaetano Salvemini, one-time socialist colleague of Mussolini, joined the distinguished G. A. Borgese among those in exile who wrote eloquently from the United States against the Fascist regime. The Italian emigration was indeed extensive, including leaders of anti-Fascist political parties, such as Francesco Nitti, Filippo Turati, and Don Luigi Sturzo. The Communist Togliatti found his way to Moscow, while the engaging writer Ignazio Silone at length left Italy to publish his widely read political novels of the 1930s, the best known of which was *Bread and Wine*. Inside Italy, there was some underground resistance; but the major impact came from Italians of the emigration like Salvemini, Borgese, and Silone, whose books became favorites of the anti-Fascist, anti-Nazi, usually pro-Communist intelligentsia of the 1930s. Silone first joined, then left the Communist party, a story he told in the series of essays later published by disillusioned ex-Communists, *The God That Failed*. The experience of being driven underground helped the Italian Communist party to develop habits of cooperating with non-Communist anti-Fascists. In later times, this distinguished it from other Communist parties. Writing his notebooks in an Italian prison, Antonio Gramsci searchingly reevaluated Marxist theory.

FRONTIERS OF SCIENTIFIC THOUGHT

If intellectual life in the 1920s generally turned away from politics, this was because of not only the dismal quality of political leadership but also the attraction of other areas. In addition to the exciting experiments in art and literature, there were general ideas, philosophical in nature, that provided rich fare for inquisitive minds.

Though the school of psychoanalysis had emerged before the war, it now became more widely known. Sigmund Freud, having developed the germs of his system as early as 1892, wrote his main masterwork, *Dream Interpretation,* as the century turned and then founded with Carl Jung the International Psychoanalytical Association in 1910, when the two psychoanalysts, one Austrian and one Swiss, carried news of their revolutionary ideas as far as the United States. The psychoanalytical movement was mature enough to produce its first major schism in 1913, when Jung and Freud parted company. Yet it is safe to say that only the intellectually precocious were more than dimly aware of psychoanalysis before the war. Now the Freudian doctrines burgeoned in the atmosphere of the 1920s, when the founding father was aging and ill but still creative. Freud lived and worked in his native Vienna until Hitler took Austria in 1938, at which time he fled to London, where he died the following year.

Freud was a universally acclaimed master of the interwar generation, and there were attempts, usually unsuccessful, to synthesize Freudianism with Marxism, with Christianity or Judaism, and with nearly everything else. Stream-of-consciousness novelists as well as surrealist poets and painters acknowledged his influence. Freud coincided with many cultural trends in the 1920s, some of them contradictory. To many, his bold emphasis on physical sexuality as the prime mover of human behavior stamped him as leader of the revolution against Victorian morality and prudery that marked the postwar years. This association rather overlooked the fact that Freud, who was apparently one of the few major intellectual figures of his generation who stayed faithful to his wife, thought that the wild urges of the primal unconscious had to be kept under tight social control or they would destroy civilization. Again, attempts to marry him to Marxism or other left-wing social ideologies ran aground on Freud's views about human nature, which, he thought, contains ineradicable traits that no social engineering can alter. We have already mentioned the modish pessimism of *Civilization and Its Discontents.* While this pessimism agreed with the neo-orthodox stress on man's imperfect nature, Freud was a determined atheist.

His genius conformed to no other mold, and its unique vision of man imposed itself ineluctably on an age eager for new formulations of human nature and destiny. To some it was utterly subversive, for it completed that relentless unmasking of human ideals begun by Darwin and Marx. Those ideals, including all religion and art and philosophy, might be traced back to the wolf lair of some secret sexual encounter, some traumatic event of childhood, some anal or oral fantasy. People are not the masters of their own motives, which are the product of unconscious forces. On the other hand, Freud held out the hope that by scientific understanding such heretofore undiscovered forces could be brought under control. Professional psychoanalysts supplied, for a goodly fee, the modern equivalent of the confessional. Although Freud's own fascinating case histories suggest that the curing of neurosis is scarcely an exact science, it was now purveyed as such. Beset by the stresses of modern life, people went to the psychiatrist in lieu of the priest.

The Viennese doctor's influence extended not only to the psychiatric profession, and to literature and art, but also to education. In general, the Freudian vocabulary grew to be part of the language of knowledgeable people, a tool of understanding and of interpretation; *id* and *superego, dream analysis as wish fulfillment, oedipus complex, libido, transference,* and other Freudian terms became almost household words. Not far behind him in this role was his erstwhile colleague, Carl Jung of Zurich, popularizing *introvert, extrovert,* and *archetypes of the collective unconscious.* With such terms did harried twentieth-century people arm themselves against their troubles.

Freud's disciples, most of whom, like Jung, eventually broke with him (reenacting the Oedipal drama of son rebelling against father that the doctrine taught), carried his teaching all over Europe and the United States: Ferenczi in Budapest, Abraham in Berlin, Melanie Klein in London set up influential branches of the IPA marked by exciting battles of rival schools, much like the early Christian Church. Many saw psychoanalysis as more a religion than a science. But Freud, suspicious of all strayings toward metaphysics, certainly saw it as a science.

The other great name of the twenties was Albert Einstein. Here again, the roots of the "revolution in physics" go back well before 1919, but only then did they become literally front-page news. A startling introduction to the mad

Albert Einstein. (*Courtesy Yerkes Observatory.*)

1920s was the worldwide fascination on May 29, 1919–just as the Versailles treaty was being readied for signature–with observations designed to confirm or refute Einstein's recently announced General Theory of Relativity. The world for a moment dropped its interest in the proceedings at Paris to watch another and, it seemed, far greater change, in "the very fabric of the universe." A rare total eclipse of the sun occurred on that day, a thing awesome enough in its own right; now scientists all over the globe were watching to see if rays of light coming from the other side of the sun would bend as they approached it–as Einstein's theory predicted, challenging the very foundations of physical science as revealed 230 years earlier by Isaac Newton. The next day's headlines trumpeted "SPACE CAUGHT BENDING." Einstein, it seemed, had won. His earlier relativity theory (1905), raising paradoxes about time, space, and motion, understood by few, now came in for further examination. The observations of May 29 made Einstein almost overnight the celebrity of the century.

Conscientious intellects, anxious to keep up and aware that the Jewish genius was on to something immensely important, struggled to understand him, a task far from easy; many books appeared attempting to explain relativity and other elements of the new physics to lay persons–for example, Bertrand Russell's *ABC of Relativity*. It seemed clear in a general way that the foundations of the physical sciences, which had been thought certain since the seventeenth century, had been severely shaken, if not overthrown–proof, to some, of ultimate skepticism or intellectual anarchy. "The last certitude," science, had fallen. Newton's laws of motion and gravitation no longer stood as universally valid. Space and time were no longer separate, nor mass and velocity. Absolute space and time did not exist. Light was not wave but particles. The unity of physics was broken, for the behavior of subatomic particles followed radically different rules. Determinacy no longer reigned at the level of the smallest particles, which indeed might be only ideas; or if they existed, they exhibited qualities impossible to comprehend.

The nineteenth-century picture of the world was rapidly disappearing with the discoveries of Einstein, Max Planck, Niels Bohr, Werner Heisenberg, and other brilliant students of a "mysterious universe." The return to religion or metaphysics as well as the pessimism of the twenties often took sustenance from this apparent revelation of chaos where there had been Newtonian order. The world of Dr. Einstein was as curious as was Dr. Freud's dream world, the prose of James Joyce or the visions of Picasso. Bertrand Russell, thinking of the odd unpredictability of individual electrons, called it an anarchist universe. Perhaps also an idealist one: "Matter" seemed to vanish in a cloud of mathematical equations.

The paradoxes resulting from Einstein's exposition of the necessary absence of any absolute measurement of time and space (the ether having been exposed as a nonentity) defied common sense: Time is longer to the observer of a moving body than to one on it, so that if you were able to go off on a trip around the cosmos at high speeds, on your return you would be younger than you were in comparison to those who stayed behind. One would also become squatter and heavier at extreme speeds, reaching a stage of virtually no mass but extreme weight as one approached the speed of light.

Public interest in an incomprehensible scientific elite who seemed to be disclosing fantastic secrets of a mysterious universe continued through the 1920s with the focus shifting to the subatomic arena. In days past, the atom had by definition been the least possible unit of matter; but since 1900 it had turned out to be a mostly hollow shell, within which swarms of electrical charges somehow swirled. (This led to suspicions that the concept was an artificial construct, a pure "as if" hypothesis not to be confused with material reality.) Atoms can disintegrate. "The discovery of radioactivity," Mme. Curie said, "marks an epoch in the history of science." No one had ever before thought that atoms had an internal structure. Now this unsuspected dimension became the new frontier of scientific research, destined to dominate science for the rest of the century and radically influence all human thought.

In the 1920s, brilliant young physicists and mathematicians, the offspring of Einstein who now functioned as a revered father figure (somewhat appalled at what he had started!) explored the paradoxes of "quantum mechanics." In the end, the electron could not be pinned down; it was indeterminate in that its location and velocity could not both be known precisely, and it behaved, impossibly, like both a particle and a wave. One could not observe electrons objectively because the act of observation, forced itself to use electrons, interfered with them.

Another incredible feature of Einstein's world became all too true with the atomic bomb: Energy and mass are interchangeable, $E = mc^2$, c being the speed of light. By another curious coincidence, the work on neutrons and the fission of heavy nuclei ripened in 1939, just as World War II began. In 1919, Rutherford had split the atom. "If I have disintegrated the nucleus of the atom," Rutherford wrote in June of 1919, "this is of greater significance than the war." In 1914, he had pointed out in a popular lecture that the potential energy stored inside atoms was now, after Einstein, known to be incredibly great: "many million times greater than for an equal weight of the most powerful explosive." The possibility of tapping this source by "causing a substance like uranium or thorium to give out its energy in the course of a few hours or days, instead of over a period of many thousands or millions of years"–in other words, to greatly speed up radioactivity–was not then practical. But in 1932, Rutherford's younger colleague, James Chadwick, discovered neutrons. From there, the path to atomic energy was reasonably clear.

Heisenberg said that in the summer of 1939, this knowledge was known to only about twelve people in the world, who by coming to an agreement might have prevented the construction of atom bombs. This indicates how extremely difficult these frontiers of thought were. Other scientists made various important contributions to the new field of nuclear physics. Science was an organized international field of collaboration. Even Einstein, in 1905, emerged from a pack of scientists to just win the race to $E = mc^2$.

All this added up to a radically different vision of the universe. Television, X rays, radiation, and other electronic miracles joined nuclear energy as the practical by-products of this theoretical speculation. Real as these powers were, their foundations were mysterious. Max Planck's quantum theory found a constant number relating energy to frequency of radiation, and the number bobbed up again in subatomic "wave mechanics." Like the speed of light, it provided a clue to the workings of physical nature. But what it meant could not be discerned. "The world as seen by science is not the world as it really is," Joseph Needham noted. One could no longer visualize a common-sense universe. Nineteenth-century scientists had the goal of making science clear enough to be understood by everyone. It now became evident that science could not get to the bottom of reality. This conclusion would not have surprised Immanuel Kant, but it upset the whole mechanical-materialistic model that had dominated progressive European minds for a century.

One result was that scientists became comparatively humble. "We are no longer taught that the scientific method is the only valid method of acquiring knowledge about reality," J.W.N. Sullivan observed in a 1933 book titled *The Limitations of Science*. Scientists themselves talked of "the mysterious universe" and speculated on the possible truth of philosophical idealism: Mind determines what we know about the world; what is "out there" is in itself formless and meaningless. Reality is, in brief, a set of mental constructs. Niels Bohr, the Danish genius, suggested that the world might be inherently ambivalent or dialectical.

Mathematics itself experienced a comparable crisis of certainty and objectivity at this time. Alternate geometries, using different basic postulates than Euclid's, were shown to be both consistent and, in Einstein's universe, applicable: The geodesic curvatures of space-time were based on Riemann's elliptical geometry. Mathematics, then, is not a picture of the world but a game based on arbitrary rules, with many different games possible. It was argued, saving the dignity of math, that the different mathematical systems are at least complete and self-consistent (Hilbert's formalism). But in 1931, at about the same time that Chadwick found the neutron and Hubble (working at the Mt. Wilson observatory in California) confirmed the expanding universe, Gödel convincingly attacked mathematical formalism by showing that all systems contain unprovable propositions and none are complete. This seemed to leave "the language of nature" in a perilous state, evidently something arbitrary and subject to the limitations of human linguistic conventions. This was a position analogous to that adopted by perhaps the century's greatest philosopher, Ludwig Wittgenstein, in the 1920s and 1930s: We can never know how our language relates to the world, because we would have to discuss that in language itself! This may be compared to the interference principle of the atomic physicists.

It was at this time, too, that the universe grew, in our understanding, to even vaster dimensions. There are countless other galaxies like that of which our own solar system is an infinitesimally small part. Ancient and medieval thinkers had in effect supposed that our own planetary system, of which the earth is the solid center, comprised the whole cosmos. Galileo's proof that the sun is the center and that the other planets are qualitatively like earth began the demotion of human beings from central figures in the cosmic drama to insignificant specks of dust; but now layer on layer of immensity was piled on, until the size of the universe became unimaginable. (Perhaps 10 billion galaxies each with billions of stars.) It is evidently expanding constantly and with extreme rapidity. The theory that it will eventually contract back into a body as small as the original atom, to explode again in 80-billion-year cycles, bore a startling resemblance to ancient Indian metaphysics or to Nietzsche's vision of eternal recurrence. The scientists produced ideas more bizarre than those of poets or prophets.

The brilliant Russian physicist Alexander A. Friedmann in 1922 was the first to draw from Einsteinian relativity the conclusion that the universe is expanding. (Friedmann died in 1925; under Stalin, Soviet science rejected Einstein and Friedmann's disciples were liquidated.) After Hubble's observations confirmed the expanding universe, the Abbé Lemaitre used the mathematics of Friedmann to develop his primal-egg theory.

POPULAR CULTURE

Though Einstein and Freud did become familiar names, it is doubtful that most ordinary people in the 1920s concerned themselves much with such dazzling perspectives. They would not have read more than fragments of *Ulysses*–perhaps those with the groundbreaking four-letter words–or of Lawrence, Proust, Mann, or Kafka. But the "common" man or woman took an extraordinary interest in the ancient Egyptian monarch King Tut, whose tomb British archaeologists opened in 1922; and in the American aviator Charles Lindbergh, who flew alone from New York to Paris in 1927, though his was far from the first transatlantic flight. Returning in 1921 from a trip to the United States to receive honors and a gift of radium, Marie Curie was surprised to find the boxing match between American Dempsey and French Carpentier crowding her out of the headlines.

If popular culture seemed silly and stupid to the intellectuals of the 1920s, its "shop-girl mentality" a leading feature of the *Waste Land* landscape, its popular music inane and its reading material beneath contempt, this was perhaps mainly because of the many new toys technology had provided, which were more interesting than books or paintings. The automobile, the airplane, the cinema (movies), and radio were of course the foremost of these. Though developed in rudimentary form before 1914, mass consumption of them awaited the postwar years and was in some ways a product of the war; large-scale production of motorized vehicles and radios for military use led to the need to find other markets when the war ended.

The three inventions (along with radio's electronic spinoff, television) that have most affected social and cultural life in this century followed a rather similar time schedule of development. The first practical automobile dates from the late 1880s. Hertz discovered radio waves in 1885, and Marconi made radio transmission and reception a reality by 1901. (All these electronic wonders stemmed ultimately from James Clerk Maxwell's formulation of the laws of electromagnetism in the 1860s.) The first motion pictures jerked dimly across the screen in 1889. They all underwent significant development in the 1890s, became commercially feasible by the 1900s, and then took off into the growth stratosphere after the war. Autos were only for the rich before 1914, and roads were still inadequate. In Great Britain in 1913, a total of 34,000 motor vehicles were built; they came in 198 different models. After the war, annual output rose to 95,000 in 1923 and to 511,000 in 1937. Meanwhile, the price fell from an average of about £300 ($1,500) to £130 ($650), and the market was dominated by six manufacturers. The first "mass car" builders, analogous to Henry Ford in the United States, were Austin and Morris, who dominated the market in the 1920s but ran into competition from more luxurious models in the 1930s.

"Wireless" broadcasting, as distinct from telegraph-like communications, was entirely a postwar development. Use of radio for public entertainment and information is said to have arisen as the unexpected outcome of an advertising campaign by the Westinghouse Company in Pittsburgh, where the first radio station was established. In Britain, unlike the United States, where private broadcasters soon covered the country, broadcasting became a public monopoly under the British Broadcasting Company (later, Corporation). Before long, receiving sets, much less expensive than automobiles, multiplied until there were more than two million of them in 1926, a number that had increased to nine million by 1939. Prior to World War II, by no means all British households possessed a motor car—the ratio was more like one in four—but almost every home was equipped with a radio receiver of some sort. The first practicable TV transmission was in 1936, and by 1939 there were about 20,000 TV receivers in the British Isles. In *Finnegans Wake,* completed in 1939, Joyce included a television skit, "verbivocovisual." The BBC operated more than a score of radio stations and broadcast several kinds of programs, both regional and national. (The Third Programme was serious and intellectual, the First, light and frivolous.)

The economic and social effect of these new contrivances was enormous. The manufacture of automobiles not only became a great industry in itself, employing tens of thousands of people, but it also created or expanded many related industries: rubber, oil refining, metals, glass, road building, service and repair. Living habits—all the way from how one spent one's holidays and weekends to where one lived—were profoundly changed. All things considered, the automobile clearly has claims to priority as the leading technological influence on the life of mankind in this century. But if we think of things more specifically cultural, relating to interests, ideas, taste, and leisure activities, then the movies and radio or television can challenge for the first spot. Transportation affects people physically, because it helps determine both their work and their leisure in geographic terms; and what one is physically able to do impinges on the quality of one's activities. Changing habits of courtship, of visiting friends, of travel to distant areas for cultural purposes entailed psychic alterations of all sorts. Some detected a relationship between changes in sexual morality and the culture of parking in dark places. But to provide new objects of consciousness, visual and auditory, for millions of people in most of their nonworking hours was the destiny of the new media of entertainment and communication.

The major development of airplanes as a transportation industry lay ahead, but a passion for flight, stimulated by the war, continued after the war as public attention focused on the romantic excursions of transoceanic pioneers like Lindbergh and Amelia Earhart. Lindy, the Lone Eagle, was a hero for the age. But it was the new media that made him so. Such phenomena stemmed primarily from the new case of mass communications. Not only radio, but newspapers and magazines, old media but now distributed more widely and more quickly via automobile and airplane, spread the "news" to an insatiable audience. The need to supply this immense demand impelled the exploitation if not the manufacture of sensational items. It cannot be claimed that the sort of newspaper that specialized in scandal, crime, and sex was new, for such organs were familiar in Victorian times and even earlier. But they now had infinitely larger circulations. Radio enabled a vastly enlarged audience to sit in on athletic events, thus swelling the craze for sports. And, popular movie actors and actresses became the best-known of personalities, much more famous than mere politicians or writers.

Little that happened in this decade was unaffected by the new media. Critics of popular culture noted, among other manifestations, a tendency toward crazes, fads, sensations, novelties, a nine days' wonder each fortnight destined probably to quick oblivion. Popular songs flitted in and out, one being heard incessantly for a few weeks, after which some equally inane ditty replaced the former "hit," now happily sunk without trace. Sports heroes were glamorized; records were broken every month or so to ecstatic applause: first woman to fly the Atlantic, fastest flight over Atlantic, first person to swim the English Channel, first woman to swim the Channel, and so on.

Discussed since the 1880s (or earlier[1]), the New Woman appeared in the 1920s as a new sexual ideal: the "flapper," marked by "a serpentine slimness" (Aldous Huxley). As the heroine of Huxley or Hemingway or Scott

---

[1] In a much-discussed essay of 1868 (in the middle of the Victorian era) titled "The Girl of the Period," Eliza Lynn Linton described with some alarm a "new kind of woman" who flirted, painted her face, dyed her hair red, disobeyed her parents, and, it was implied, might do far worse things in her self-indulgent pursuit of pleasure. This suggests that we may have here a perpetual, generic term.

Fitzgerald novels, she was wild, promiscuous, boyish, sophisticated. Although, according to some, the Great War had contributed to the liberation of women, this does not seem to have been altogether true. The end of the war found the women who had taken factory jobs or even served in the military returning to more traditional roles. The movies and the fashionable "smart set" featured in novels and newspaper stories offered them a vision of glamour, based on their sexuality. The ambivalence of this emerged in the rather androgynous style of beauty. At the end of the war, women were given the vote in Great Britain (not in France), and some of the old taboos and restraints about personal behavior weakened. No strong feminist movement flourished, despite Virginia Woolf's impassioned appeal for female independence *(A Room of One's Own)*. The Bolshevik Revolution was virtually an all-male show; an occasional woman activist like Alexandra Kollontai was made to feel out of place, and Marxists generally discouraged and disparaged feminism as a movement, arguing that women should support their men in the more important work of liberating both sexes from capitalism. There was no rush of women to public offices in the postwar decade. Britain had to wait until 1980 for a woman prime minister.

But some women now found more career opportunities outside of household drudgery. The war destroyed the venerable institution of domestic service: Upstairs/downstairs, the community of masters and servants living together as unequals in a microcosm of organic hierarchy, so beloved of the ancestral order in England, no longer existed. The new freedom, or what Dora Black, Bertrand Russell's second wife, called "the right to be happy," was taken up especially by the New Woman, who on the model of H. G. Wells's *Ann Veronica* (Dora's original inspiration) dared to have her romance and even her children outside the bonds of matrimony. The oldest of patriarchal institutions had begun to crack.

Regarding the revolution in manners and morals just after the war, the American writer and world traveler Vincent Sheean wrote in his autobiographical *Personal History* that

> It was very swift, this decay. When I left the University [Chicago] in 1920 it had scarcely begun. Five years later it was, so far as I could determine, common among people of my age in the bourgeoisie. . . . The gulf between generations had suddenly become immense. . . . To our grandparents the ordinary manners, conversation, conduct and morals of educated and "respectable" people would have seemed suitable to the underworld.

Evelyn Waugh thought this was the first significant estrangement between old and young in all English history. There are countless similar statements. Some kind of a cultural fracture had occurred, whether because of the war, the profound postwar disenchantment, the new literature, the Russian Revolution, the mass media, technological change, the Freudian and Einsteinian revolutions, or all of these together.

Popular culture tended to be international. American movies went everywhere. Long disparaged as culturally backward, if mechanically progressive, compared with Europeans, the Americans now showed their genius for democracy by excelling in low culture. But "American" is a bit misleading. The Hollywood producers who pioneered in film production—Samuel Goldwyn, Louis Mayer, Adolf Zukor, and others—were almost all born in eastern Europe, or of parents who had just come through Ellis Island. So were the popular song writers like Irving Berlin and Jerome Kern. The former's personal drama was a marriage to a fashionable and wealthy New York woman whose father indignantly refused to accept a Lower East Side Jew into his family, only to find him becoming wealthier and more famous by far. This curious dominance of popular culture by east European Jewish migrants to the United States helps explain Adolf Hitler's aversion to "popular culture" and perhaps much of the Nazi ideology.

Movies were not art as it had been understood for centuries in Western and other civilizations, in the sense of being the inspired creation of individual genius. They were triumphs of organization. They manufactured an art-product with skills analogous to the factory assembly line, which was now becoming the chief method of commodity production. To make a movie was to synchronize a large team of builders, painters, actors, photographers, electricians, special effects experts, and, later, with the introduction of "talkies" in 1928, sound technicians. The mass market for films enabled huge investments to be made in such elaborate organizations, creating on some "set" a whole world of fantasy. The key figures were producers. Gathered in Hollywood, California, these people manufactured dreams for the masses. For prestige, they might gather in authors as distinguished as Aldous Huxley or F. Scott Fitzgerald, but for the most part no such literary genius was needed or wanted. Plots could be made to formula, dialogue turned out in standardized format. Even people might be replaced by animated cartoon figures.

In the process of being manufactured on the assembly line, such cultural products were purged of all complexity, subtlety, sophistication, irony; they lacked any aura of "style." They became primitive statements of the least common denominators of mass consciousness, rendered palatable by dazzling techniques and the sheer giganticism of screen effects, simulating huge battles, or stampedes, or giant apes toppling city skyscrapers. Occasional works of art did make an exception to the rule, and from the early days of filmmaking emerged the genius of a Charlie Chaplin. But as they became organized and Hollywoodized, elements of personal artistic creation vanished from the great bulk of movies. In some ways, they were a kind of modern communal rite, celebrating the same simple myths of love, heroism, and adventure over and over. As such, they played an enormously important part in mass consciousness. And, they irritated the artist-intellectual beyond all measure, standing for everything he or she detested.

"Mass culture" thus seemed a new phenomenon. In the past, there had been elite cultures, shared by that relatively small number who had the leisure

Marlene Dietrich in *The Blue Angel*. (*AP/Wide World Photos.*)

and the wealth to absorb the complex inheritance of Western civilization stretching back to the ancient Greeks. The size of such elites may be suggested by the number who attended universities—only a few thousand before 1914, less than one person in a thousand in most countries. But social historians think that as late as about 1600, the culture of all classes was much the same: Shakespeare's plays were enjoyed by high and low alike. Printing, the Reformation, and the scientific revolution each contributed to a "great divorce" between high and low culture, the folk culture coming to seem ignorant and superstitious to the educated. The high culture then steadily fragmented as knowledge grew and became ever more specialized and professionalized.

Something midway between the literate culture of a civilized elite and the folklore of a traditional peasant society emerged fairly early in the career of modern nation-states. There were subcultures in urban underworlds, in the urban working class, in the Victorian lower middle class, but these were too fragmentary and tentative to provide more than footnotes to cultural history.[2] Research into the less lighted corridors of literary history has uncovered "trash literature" reaching back to the beginnings of book production–an abundance of it existed in the eighteenth as well as the nineteenth century. It is thus not possible to claim that "cheap" literature, printed in detective novels, movie magazines, household journals, *True Confessions,* or in pornography ("girlie" magazines, in the argot of the twenties) and the like, was something new, extruded from the unhappy twentieth-century mass consciousness. It only appeared in greater quantities and perhaps in even worse taste. There had long been a gulf between those who read Shakespeare or listened to Beethoven and those whose taste ran to the evening tabloid and the latest tune from Tin Pan Alley. But this gulf, far from diminishing with the passing of the years and the advance of public education, had even increased.

The British *Annual Register* for 1926 noted with some dismay that "Detective stories" came from the publishers in a positive torrent to meet an eager public demand. The vogue for whodunits, coinciding with one for crossword puzzles, bridge, and other games, suggests a need for something challenging but innocuous to occupy the mind and can thus be related to withdrawal of interest in public affairs as well as to the tedium of jobs in the assembly-line age, and to more leisure provided by shorter working hours and improved transportation. Many more people now had a secondary school education.

The inexorable advance of social democracy had been going on since the early nineteenth century, more frequently deplored than welcomed by European intellectuals. With the bourgeois revolution of the nineteenth century, aristocratic claims of social superiority on the basis of birth suffered fatal blows. Contractual relations between legally equal individuals replaced status as members of an "order" or corporate group as the basis of social relations, the source of rights and obligations. This dissolution of social community into an assemblage of atomistic individuals gradually penetrated into wider and wider circles. Largely an urban phenomenon, it spread with the triumph of city over country, the erosion of rural conservative communities.

From the vantage point of those who cherished Europe's civilized traditions, this could seem like a disaster. The artist, as French poet Stephane Mallarmé declared, has to be an aristocrat, inasmuch as he does not believe in the equality of values. The "plebification" of knowledge, thought, and culture degraded them. High art, along with all difficult, advanced thought, is for only the

---

[2]Vernon Lidtke, in *The Alternative Culture: Socialist Labor in Imperialist Germany* (1985), notes that German Social Democracy offered an alternative cultural environment of festivals, meetings, and so on. In Great Britain, Robert Blatchford's vaguely socialist-labor revival of "Merrie England" folk culture was something comparable just before 1914. The Austrian socialists invented the May Day labor parades and other rituals. But in the end, these efforts to tie the working-class economic movement to a living popular culture must be judged as failures, surviving only feebly.

few, and this precious commodity has to be protected. In Nietzsche, Ibsen, and other end-of-the-century haters of a society that seemed stupid, tasteless, and vulgar, the outcry against the mass-men, the noisy dwarves, the newspaper-reading "last men" who represent the dregs of a dying culture reached a stage of near hysteria. "What the majority of people think is stupid" became their motto. And, by and large, the disciples of the Nietzschean generation dominated European literature in the 1920s. Freud's "aristocratic distaste for the rabble" was matched by that of Yeats, Eliot, Lawrence, Gide, and many others. They feared that in this "tragedy of mediocrity," mankind would lose "everything of genius, beauty, grandeur" (Edmond Scherer).

The masses themselves certainly viewed the matter otherwise. Esthetically uncertain as their new culture might be, for most of them it was better than their parents' lives of poverty and unremitting toil. An expansion of consciousness was going on. Appalling degradation of taste as measured by a former aristocratic standard might look like a decided elevation if the comparison was made with the Victorian lower class, which had dwelt in foul slums often without manners or morals. A large gulf existed between the people of letters, art, and science on the one hand and the shopgirl or tabloid-newspaper reader on the other. But the shopgirl of the 1920s probably had more cultural awareness than her mother.

Despite the many complaints about a radical gulf between low and high culture—weeds and wildflowers, the American literary critic Van Wyck Brooks put it—examination of the literary market reveals a lively middlebrow segment. While Joyce and most of Virginia Woolf was too much for them, a middle-class reading public in England supported a vigorous literary industry, showing a taste for biography, autobiography, history, as well as fiction of a less formidable variety than *Ulysses* or *To the Lighthouse*. They made bestsellers of H. G. Wells' outlines of knowledge, Bertrand Russell's history of philosophy, Winston Churchill's history of the war, and other serious works. Their taste in novels ran to such now-forgotten amusements as Michael Arlen's *The Green Hat* (sophisticated adultery, a popular line) and Margaret Kennedy's *The Constant Nymph*. (Stalin blamed his wife's suicide in 1932 on *The Green Hat*, which she had been reading.) American writers were read in England as never before, especially Sinclair Lewis, perhaps because he showed his countrymen in such a bad light. More sentimentally, American hits including Thornton Wilder's *Bridge of San Luis Rey* and Edna Ferber's *The Show Boat* appealed to an earnest if not very critical British audience. As for American movies, of course, the complaint was that the British film industry was totally unable to compete with them and had trouble surviving.

This ingestion of Americana was true in somewhat smaller measure in France and Germany. To the high-culture intellectuals, of course, the United States symbolized all that they hated: a regimented ant-world, a "cosmic man" without culture, total dehumanization. The French writer Georges Duhamel's *Scenes of Life in the Future* (1930; *Scènes de la vie future*) was once printed with the subtitle *America, the Menace*. "Modern America has no national art and does not even feel the need of one," wrote the Frenchman André Siegfried in his 1927 appraisal, *America Comes of Age*. Similar dismissals came from Bertrand Russell, who made his living insulting the Americans on lecture tours, and innumerable others (cf., C.E.M. Joad, *The Babbitt Warren*), not least of whom were American intellectuals themselves, who fled in disgust to Europe in the twenties. Yet the American writers Ernest Hemingway and William Faulkner deeply influenced French literature in the 1930s.

In this connection, Adolf Hitler's tastes are revealing and not atypical. His political success was based in no small measure on a kind of intuitive understanding of the mind of the "little man." Devotee of Nietzsche and Wagner, Hitler felt and conveyed a Spenglerian sense of "cultural pessimism" associated with stinging verdicts on the corruption of modern mass-man by commercialism and democracy. Yet his favorite author was really Karl May, a German equivalent of Zane Grey or Sax Rohmer, who was the author of scores of trite adventure stories. He enjoyed Wagnerian opera but also movies and sentimental operettas. And, he despised twentieth-century modernist art, music, and architecture, branding it Jewish and decadent.

In general, it could be said (alas) that the Nazis mirrored in exaggerated form many of the prejudices and beliefs of the "average man," who was patriotic, didn't much like Jews, hated modern art and snobbish intellectuals, was cynical about politicians, the Church, and other Establishment leaders and institutions, had little patience with legality if it stood in the way of getting things done, believed criminals should be punished more severely, and so on. In a sense, Hitler could claim to speak for the masses against educated and entrenched elites.

The war had accelerated the democratic revolution in various ways. The democracy of the trenches had challenged class lines. Labor leaders entered into governments; politicians promised that soldiers on their return should be rewarded without regard to pedigree. The Socialist Friedrich Ebert, later president of the post-1918 German Republic, declared in the Reichstag, April 5, 1916, that "The masses returned from the trenches" will demand equality and will have earned it. This feeling was found in all countries. Those (if any) who came back from the trenches to England were promised "homes fit for heroes," in a catchphrase of the day. "No more rich or poor, proletarians or bourgeois, right wingers or leftist militants; there were only Frenchmen," declared Roland Dorgelès. The war did more for a classless society than Karl Marx. In his *Mein Kampf*, Adolf Hitler talked about the army as a great equalizer: "In the Army a corporation director was no more important than a dog barber."

As Lord Curzon discovered, aristocratic traits of dress and temperament were now fatal handicaps to high elective political office. After the war, "it was harder to tell what class someone belonged to by looking at their clothes," an Englishwoman observed. Arnold J. Toynbee recalled how as a child in end-of-the-century London he watched the people in the streets and sorted them out by their dress, the working-class women with their shawls contrasting with the bonneted ladies. That was no longer possible.

The era of Coolidge, Baldwin, Herriot, and Mussolini was in one of its various manifestations an era of the "common man." The new modes of transportation and communication broke down old provincialisms, opening visions of a richer world to the view of countless people. Mass taste was shocking to a refined few, and the whole mixture of values, accompanied by the intellectual revolution of the 1920s in so many different areas, gave rise to a feeling of acute crisis. At the end of the decade, American commentator Walter Lippmann summed it up as "the dissolution of the ancestral order."

6

Depression and Dictatorship
in the 1930s

THE ECONOMIC CRISIS

It was appropriate that the terrible economic slump of the 1930s started in the United States, to which Europe seemed to have surrendered economic leadership during the Great War and on which she had been dependent ever since. The stock market crash that began on a black Friday in October 1929 and deepened in the ensuing months had immediate repercussions in Europe. Indeed, even before this, the superheated boom in stock prices that marked the bull market of 1928 siphoned money from Europe. The pricing of the bubble sent shock waves throughout the world. Large exports of American capital had helped sustain Europe, besides providing an outlet for American surpluses of capital, during the 1920s. Investment in European bonds now contracted sharply and swiftly, as banks that were "caught short" with too many of their assets invested in securities desperately tried to raise money. By June 1930, the price of securities on Wall Street was about 20 percent, on average, of what it had been prior to the crash; between 1929 and 1932 the Dow-Jones average of industrial stock prices fell from a high of 381 to a low of 41!

The American market for European imports also dropped sharply as the entire American economy went into shock; and, to compound trouble, Congress insisted on passing a high tariff law in 1930, against the advice of almost all economists. Effective operation of the international economy required that the United States import goods to allow foreign governments to pay for American loans. Moreover, the raising of tariffs set off a chain reaction as every government tried to protect itself against an adverse trade balance leading to currency deterioration. The result was a drying up of world trade that further fueled the economic downturn. The Americans, additionally, continued to insist upon repayment of war debts, until finally in 1931 a general moratorium was declared. Well might Europeans complain of American blindness, but these events only exposed Europe's vulnerability.

Economic depressions were by no means a novelty. Severe and prolonged ones had afflicted the world in 1873–1878 and 1893–1897. Others had been shorter. They were usually preceded by a speculative and inflationary boom. A typical boom had immediately followed the war, in 1918–1919, giving way to a short and sharp slump in 1921–1922, which had in turn led to the general prosperity of the years up to late 1929. The exceptions to this we already know: Great Britain remained in a kind of chronic slump, which was the result of her loss of overseas markets and which her refusal to devalue the pound in the 1920s intensified. Germany had experienced the strange agony of the massive inflation, climaxing in 1923, because of the continuing struggle with France over war reparations. The Communist revolution had largely cut Russia off from the world economy, despite its limited toleration of capitalism from 1921 to 1928. Carving up the Hapsburg monarchy left Austria a charity case, and in 1931 a fresh wave of economic disasters started with the failure of the Austrian central bank.

These exceptions may seem more numerous than the rule, but the United States and most parts of Europe did enjoy relatively favorable economic conditions between 1924 and 1930. But it turned out that this prosperity rested on American loans and American markets, which now almost vanished. A European economy still recovering from the trauma of the war and its aftermath was too frail to weather this storm.

Table 6–1 The Great Depression

	INDICES OF INDUSTRIAL PRODUCTION, 1929–1938, IN MAJOR EUROPEAN COUNTRIES (1937 = 100)									
	1929	*1930*	*1931*	*1932*	*1933*	*1934*	*1935*	*1936*	*1937*	*1938*
France	123	123	105	91	94	92	88	95	100	92
Germany	79	69	56	48	54	67	79	90	100	92
Italy	90	85	77	77	82	80	86	86	100	100
Great Britain	77	74	69	69	73	80	82	94	100	101

	UNEMPLOYMENT (IN THOUSANDS)									
	1929	*1930*	*1931*	*1932*	*1933*	*1934*	*1935*	*1936*	*1937*	*1938*
France	neglig.	13	64	301	305	368	464	470	380	402
Germany	1,899	3,070	4,520	5,575	4,804	2,718	2,151	1,593	912	429
Italy	301	425	734	1,006	1,019	964	—	—	874	810
Great Britain	1,216	1,917	2,630	2,745	2,521	2,159	2,036	1,755	1,484	1,791

Policies of "autarchy" had developed after the war and were to be perpetuated during the Great Depression; that is, countries that were no longer prepared to trust the international order tried to insulate their economies by tariffs, import quotas, or a managed currency. During the 1920s, while sometimes readjusting the rate at which their currencies exchanged for gold, most nations clung to the gold standard, which facilitated international trade by permitting currencies to be freely exchanged in terms of gold. But beginning in 1931, when Great Britain was driven off the gold standard, country after country left it in order to protect themselves against a flight of gold leading to deflation and unemployment. The flight from gold was followed by all kinds of nationalist economic policies including exchange controls. International trade was thus further impaired.

According to the economic theory dominant throughout the nineteenth century and still uppermost in the minds of public leaders, these periods of depression represented a temporary disequilibrium that would soon right itself. The traditional wisdom did not see any role for government in an economic crisis further than to provide "financial stability," which meant balancing the budget and avoiding inflation. The idea of having the government borrow and spend in order to counterbalance deflation ran counter to orthodox economic theory. Unpleasant no doubt in the short run, the orthodox policies were supposed to restore economic health, like a nasty medicine needed to cure a disease. Thus, at the cost of unemployment, deflation would lower prices and lead to the recovery of markets. Interest rates would fall, again attracting capital investment. The needle of the business cycle meter was supposed to hover around full employment, and the natural operation of forces would soon draw the economy back upward, unless a ham-fisted government in its ignorance tampered with the delicate machinery. This machinery was supposed to function under conditions of a stable currency, political stability, international free trade, and a competitive economy.

This model was based on impressive theoretical work reaching back to the later eighteenth century; it had the imprimatur of most of the great economists of the "classical" nineteenth-century era, with only a few outcasts dissenting. In the light of later analysis, based on sad experience, this theory came to seem disastrously naive in assuming all kinds of ideal conditions that did not exist in the real world. Perfect competition was obviously lacking in an era increasingly prone to both corporate business monopolies or semimonopolies and trade union influence on wages. The model made no allowance for wars, revolutions, dictatorships, the dismemberment of countries, and all kinds of political factors. Of course, unconverted advocates of the traditional economics might argue that their remedy did not work because it was not tried; governments did not adhere long enough to the spartan measures necessary to make it work. But facing massive unemployment, bankruptcies, and bank failures, governments now could not resist demands to do something other than wait patiently for the storm to run its course. Not knowing quite what to do, they floundered, and their flounderings probably made the situation worse. The de-

Panic! A huge crowd in Berlin waits to withdraw savings from a bank, July, 1931, as
Americans were to do a year and a half later. (*AP/Wide World Photos.*)

pression of the 1930s found the old economic world dying and the new one still
struggling to be born. The result seemed to be the worst of both worlds.

Whatever the causes, panic soon spread through Europe. In 1931, after
the World Court refused to allow Austria to enter a customs union with Germany, that economically distressed country collapsed. Its central bank failed,
touching off a panic that threatened Great Britain next. President Herbert Hoover
of the United States proposed a moratorium on all war debts and reparations,
but French opposition delayed its acceptance.

In Britain, a Labour government faced a flight of gold, which threatened the pound. Winning 289 seats to 260 for the Conservatives in the 1929
general election, Labour depended on the 58 Liberals in parliament for a majority. The 1929 swing away from the Conservative victory of 1924 reflected already a concern about high unemployment. As unemployment now soared
even higher, payments to the jobless under the national insurance program
strained the budget. A special committee recommended cutting unemployment
benefits, and bankers in New York and Paris refused to lend money to the beleaguered British unless this was done. The Labour cabinet split over this issue.
On August 24, 1931, Prime Minister Ramsay MacDonald, Chancellor of the Ex-

chequer Philip Snowden, and some other Labour ministers joined Conservative and Liberal politicians to create a "national" government; elections in October gave this coalition an overwhelming victory. But the action divided the Labour party and left scars that were long in healing. The party expelled MacDonald and his friends as traitors.

Bowing to the edict of the international banks did not save Great Britain from being driven off gold, which happened on September 20. The whole episode reflected the confusions of policy. Labourites and, in Italy, Fascists were as uncertain what to do about the economic blizzard as anyone else. The only thing that was indisputable was the continuing catastrophic collapse. Unemployment rose to 22 percent in Britain, and industrial production sagged to 84 by 1932 (1929 = 100). This was much better than other countries did, but Britain started from a lower base. In 1932, French production stood at 72 percent of 1929, German and American at barely more than half (53 percent). In July 1932, world industrial production was 38 percent less than it had been in June 1929. Few parts of the globe escaped.

Historian Arnold Toynbee called 1931 the *annus terribilis,* the terrible year. This year of descent into the economic depths of mass unemployment, hunger, breakdown of international exchange, and failure of great financial institutions was also a year of floundering governments, the rise of the National Socialist party in Germany, and Japan's absorption of Manchuria. Japan's move, at least partly inspired by economic desperation, later looked like the beginning of the decay of international order, which led to World War II. From the vantage point of a despairing West, caught in what looked like the last capitalist crisis, Stalin's First Five-Year Plan appeared to many as a beacon of hope. In fact, however, Soviet Russia went through the awful experience of the Communist government's forcible extermination of peasant landed property, a veritable war that cost millions of lives.

In the ensuing years, things got a little better in some places. Apparently saved by what the experts regarded as a disaster, the British economy improved after departure from the gold standard resulted in a substantial devaluation. The recovery that took place between 1932 and 1937 reached a sort of boom in 1937, when unemployment fell to a mere 9 percent, low for the interwar years. But it rose to 13 percent in 1938–1939. Worldwide, by 1937, the indices of economic activity had returned to the 1929 level. France had not climbed back quite this far; Germany just about had.

One of the most punishing features of the depression had been the drastic fall in agricultural prices and those of other primary products. The years from 1925 to 1928 brought good harvests all over the world. The price of grain tumbled just as the industrial and financial slump hit, compounding the crisis. Loss of urban and international markets afflicted farmers already in trouble from overproduction and, frequently, from a burden of debt incurred in expanding production and buying agricultural machinery. With unemployed workers suffering from hunger, the sight of farmers refusing to harvest crops because the price was too low to make it worthwhile drove home the bitter lesson of poverty in the midst of plenty, the curse of Midas fallen on man. But, by 1936, agricultural prices had recovered somewhat.

DEPRESSION POLITICS

For understandable reasons, the economic disaster was usually fatal to the party or parties unlucky enough to be in office when it struck. The fall of the British Labour government has been mentioned. In the national coalition that succeeded it, the same prime minister, Ramsay MacDonald, presided over a mixture of renegade Labourites, Conservatives, and Liberals. It continued to govern England, with an even stronger Conservative complexion after 1935.

Around the 1931 change, legends clustered, especially on the left—MacDonald had conspired to betray the cause, he was the lost leader who had sold out to the upper classes ("Fame is the Spur," one novel based on these events alleged). Defenders of the Scotsman, who had been one of the Labour party's founding fathers and who had shown outstanding courage in World War I when he opposed the tide of martial spirit, claimed that he had the courage in 1931 to put country above party. It seems likely that MacDonald had gradually lost his early faith in socialism as he confronted the sobering responsibilities of power. In this sense he was a "traitor" to socialism. But the bankruptcy of the Labour party program as a means of dealing with the depression was underscored by its shattering defeat in the October election. Brandishing worthless German marks during that campaign, MacDonald indicated how strongly the shadow of 1923 lay over these years: To avoid inflation at almost any cost was the goal, and he accused his former Labour colleagues who had voted against reducing unemployment benefits of "fiscal irresponsibility."

The remaining four years of his prime ministership were not happy ones for MacDonald, a man without a party. He struggled with the reparations problem only to see that whole house of cards fall to the ground, as everybody simply reneged. Banking on partnership with the United States, he received a rebuff when, at the London economic conference of 1933, new American President Franklin D. Roosevelt rejected international monetary stabilization in favor of unilateral American devaluation of the dollar. Nor was this long-time advocate of disarmament any man to confront Adolf Hitler. MacDonald became increasingly an anomaly in a cabinet dominated by Conservatives; he resigned in 1935 in poor health. Stanley Baldwin took over the prime minister's post, and in the elections that followed, the national coalition won another overwhelming victory; but with Baldwin at its head and a Conservative also at the foreign office, it looked much less like a coalition than a Tory government spiced with a few mavericks from the other parties. The fading Liberals were in as much disarray as Labour, for in 1935 they split three ways, one of which became a kind of branch of the Conservative party.

Thus, in Britain a basically Conservative government faced the Depression, and it did comparatively well. Under provisions of the Housing Acts of 1936 and 1938, slums were cleared and new housing constructed. This was the most notable social program of a regime headed by a far-from-reactionary Tory. Housing was recognized as a public service, along with education and health; Baldwin's government added millions of people to health insurance coverage and built hundreds of thousands of public housing units. In the end, it was most condemned for its "appeasement" of Hitler's Germany, but in the mid-1930s British public opinion wanted nothing less than a bold program of rearmament and confrontation.

Britain's relative success in rising from the ashes of 1932 did not prevent depression-bred bitterness; the literature of the 1930s turned to social realism, describing poverty, unemployment, the humiliation of being on the "dole" (unemployment benefits), the class struggle. But the energetic leftism of the intellectuals (described further below) was scarcely reflected in popular opinion. Of the 615 members of the House of Commons elected in 1935, only one was a Communist. Nor was there a single Fascist, though one of Labour's most brilliant members, Oswald Mosley, deserted the party to organize the British Union of Fascists in 1932, in imitation of Mussolini and Hitler, and Fascists fought with Communists in the streets of London. The British adhered to their traditional moderation, their suspicion of intellectual novelties, even in hard times. Not Stalin nor Mussolini, those violent and flamboyant types, but Mr. Average Middleclass Englishman, Stanley Baldwin, presided over their Depression politics.

The Depression affected French political life by quickening the already rapid ebb and flow of governments. There were six of them between late 1932 and early 1934, barely over a year. The issues were similar to those of Great Britain in that attempts to balance the budget, under conditions of declining revenues and increased demands for government aids, caused strife. Strikes broke out as employers tried to cut wages. A deep sense of malaise culminated in the Stavisky scandal that surfaced late in 1933 and threatened to become another Dreyfus case or Panama scandal, joining earlier episodes of this sort that crystallized French national controversy around a single dramatic "affair." Serge Stavisky was a flamboyant and talented swindler, originally a small-time crook (he began by stealing gold from his dentist father) who worked his way up to an empire of high living and high finance based on manipulation of municipal lending institutions. Neither the first nor the last shady financial speculator to profit by political corruption, Stavisky was one of the most outlandish. He found friends in the Chamber of Deputies, and when, his crimes about to catch up with him, he was reported to have committed suicide under somewhat bizarre circumstances, there was suspicion that he had been done away with. Charges of extensive parliamentary corruption and a conspiracy to suppress the truth were wildly exaggerated. (In 1974, Alain Resnais made an excellent movie about this affair.)

The Stavisky affair on top of the dismal showing of the legislature set off an anti-government campaign organized by the French Fascist leagues. On February 6, 1934, some 200,000 demonstrators attempting to storm the Chamber of Deputies fought police in an all-night battle. A number of people were killed, and thousands of demonstrators and more than a thousand police were wounded. It was an affray to match any in the bloody annals of Paris uprisings, a ceremony performed at least once every generation (more violent if less prolonged than the student revolt of May 1968, of more recent memory). Hitler had just conquered Germany, and this demagogue still had the mystique of sudden and dramatic success. Fascism seemed to be spreading over Europe. Three-quarters of a million Frenchmen joined fascist organizations, the most notable of which was the *Croix de Feu*.

That fascism did not prevail in France, which might have proved a key to its international success, was owing in good part to a rallying of the nation around its elder statesmen, a French habit in time of self-induced internal crisis. There was no one *Führer* in France to play Hitler's part—the French Fascists predictably fought among themselves. The Daladier government, which had just replaced the Chautemps government, resigned on January 30, 1934, a year to the day after Hitler became the German chancellor; but a solution to the crisis was found in a government of national union, somewhat comparable to the British 1931 move. Elderly figures, including Marshal Pétain of World War I fame, rival party leaders Edouard Herriot (a Radical Socialist) and André Tardieu, the long-time spokesman of conservative nationalism, joined under the premiership of former President Gaston Doumergue. Tardieu had retired from politics in 1931 to pen some severe criticisms of the whole French parliamentary system, which he thought incapable of governing in the national interest. Had he lived long enough, he would have joined Charles de Gaulle. He was condemned to die watching his beloved France defeated and occupied by the Germans. He was no Fascist. Tardieu's rallying to the Republic in 1934 typifies a French dedication to liberty in the last ditch, which saved France from fascism.

The national union government of Doumergue, however, proved little more enduring than any other, lasting less than a year. French politics continued its turbulent course. By 1935, the left had succeeded in temporarily suppressing some of its violent divisions, chiefly that between Communists and Socialists, and a Popular Front government prevailed for a time, amid sit-in strikes and fears of socialism. Having bungled badly in helping Hitler destroy the German republic, only to find that he had used them rather than vice versa, the Communists, under orders as usual from Moscow, switched strategies and began to advocate a "popular front" of all anti-fascist groups. Previously, they had stood aloof, condemning the democratic Socialists as "social fascists" and refusing any cooperation with such bourgeois parties. More or less uneasily working with the other left-wing parties, they backed a government headed by the distinguished socialist intellectual and politician Leon Blum, which sponsored a French "new deal" including pro-labor legislation and the nationalization of a few industries, to the accompaniment of bitter criticism from business circles.

Unfortunately for the French New Deal, it had to deal with a deteriorating international situation and the threat of war; the Popular Front broke up at the time of the Munich Pact of 1938. Disunity over foreign policy was added to controversy about social policy. On the eve of World War II, France still presented a picture of internal disunity and weak government that did much to encourage Hitler on his path of aggression. It had surmounted the threat of fascism and achieved some economic recovery (slightly less than in England or Germany), probably from natural processes–the record suggests that governments did not make much difference to the process of recovery. To judge by the charts of economic activity from 1929 to 1939, a Conservative government in Britain, a New Deal progressive one in the United States, a Fascist one in Italy, and a Nazi regime in Germany achieved about the same results as the French anarchy. But the Third Republic's politics remained a scandal, and the Depression further envenomed the ideological divisions that fueled these political quarrels.

THE TRIUMPH OF NAZISM IN GERMANY

A messenger in the German army during World War I, Adolf Hitler was considered a rather ludicrous figure although a good soldier.

> He was neither popular nor the reverse with his fellows; they just smiled at him and his vague rambling speeches on everything in the world and out of it. . . . He interested himself particularly in the important question of seeing the officers' washing done or doing it himself. This secured for him the good graces of the colonel who removed him from the more constant dangers of the trenches and appointed him a runner between regimental headquarters and the front line.[1]

Hitler spent most of the war as a private because, his adjutant later said, "we could discover no leadership qualities in him"! But by most accounts, Hitler was a brave soldier; at the war's end he was in hospital recovering from a blinding gas attack incurred at Ypres.

The son of a middle-level Austrian government employee, young Adolf lost both his father and his mother before he was 18. The moody boy was an indifferent student. He hoped to study art in Vienna (he really wanted to be an architect), but after receiving the crushing news that his drawings, in the judgment of the Vienna Academy, were "unsatisfactory," he left his home town of Linz to live a marginal existence in Vienna. He worked at odd jobs and took to postcard painting, but most of the time he spent in museum visiting, reading, going to the opera (he was a Wagner addict). He tried many kinds of writing and drew up architectural plans. He raged against the world and developed para-

[1]From an account of Hitler as soldier published in the *New Statesman,* July 29, 1933.

Adolf Hitler. (*Library of Congress.*)

noid feelings. He tried again to get admitted to the Academy and again failed. He had few friends. In brief, he followed the course of many a reasonably bright, socially not very adroit, undisciplined, unguided young man trying to find his way in the confusion of the modern world in a great city.

The twenty-four-year-old Hitler moved to Munich in 1913; mainly, it seems, to escape military service in Austria. But the outbreak of war filled him with patriotic exuberance—"My heart, like that of a million others, overflowed with a proud joy"—and he enlisted in the Bavarian army. With the war's end, he experienced the bewilderment that many Germans felt at having lost the war, without ever experiencing defeat on the battlefield. After so much sacrifice, it had all been in vain. He blamed the kaiser and the old aristocratic leadership of Germany and for a time evidently accepted the Communist government that briefly ruled Munich in 1919. He entered into beer-hall politics and found himself as a public speaker, transformed from a private nonentity to a hypnotic orator possessed by certain simple ideas. His National Socialist German Workers party (NSDAP), however, was only one of a number of right-wing groups grumbling about the betrayal of the country by Jews, profiteers, politicians, or Communists and demanding a return to discipline and ancestral values.

The man who, along with Stalin, was most to dominate, fascinate, and horrify the world in the 1930s and 1940s seemed to have vanished from the pages of history after a brief and inglorious appearance in 1923. While inflation raged and Germany seemed to be breaking up, military hero Ludendorff and the ex-Army messenger Adolf Hitler, an incongruous pair of conspirators, tried to overthrow the Bavarian government, or to force it to march on Berlin. This "beer hall Putsch" failed ignominiously, and Hitler went to prison for a few months in 1924, taking advantage of the enforced leisure to write his autobiographical *Mein Kampf* (My Struggle). But this proved to be far from a bestseller, and for the next five years Hitler's National Socialist Workers' party was all but forgotten. The coming of better times after 1924 caused all extremist movements to decline. A reputable history of Germany published in England in 1930 mentioned Hitler only in a footnote, remarking that he fell into obscurity after 1923. In the elections of 1928, the National Socialist (Nazi) party got 2.8 percent of the vote, winning 2.5 percent of the Reichstag seats.

In that election, the Social Democrats won about 30 percent, the Communists received 10.5 percent, and, on the right, the respectable conservatism of the German Nationalist party got 14 percent, easily outdistancing Hitler's bunch of hardly reputable roughnecks. The Nazis were an unusual political phenomenon. Some theorists on the left made them out to be puppets of the great capitalists, but nothing could be further from the truth. They were very much "little men," restless misfits usually from a lower-middle-class or declassed background, with some intellectual pretensions. It is wrong to underestimate the extent to which Hitler, a brooding loner, read omnivorously if erratically in his dropout years between 1908 and 1914. He acquired a large store of general ideas from which he would build his *Weltanschauung*, his worldview.

It is true that Hitler fascinated (and exploited) some rich ladies of the bored *bon ton*, whose "radical chic" led them to lionize this charismatic political curiosity. Though a few mavericks from the upper classes supported the movement early, the great bulk of respectable wealth came to his rescue only after he was obviously a winner. A Hermann Goering of aristocratic connections or a Fritz Thyssen from the capitalist class were exceptions. It was difficult for the people of money to find much attraction in a party whose speechmakers exhorted their listeners to "Storm the commercial banks! Set the money on fire! String up the white and black Jews!" The finances of the NSDAP are shrouded in mystery because it kept few records, of which even fewer were preserved. At first, it was very short of funds, but by 1923 it clearly began to dispose of larger sums. Most of this probably came from the enthusiastic support of many small contributors, but there may well have been money from wealthier people who, in the desperate conditions of 1923, were willing to bet on any anti-Communist. Nevertheless, all evidence indicates that Hitler made no deals with big business.

Konrad Heiden called the Nazis "the armed intellectuals"; Thomas Mann dubbed them "truants from school." Among the would-be intellectuals in the early Nazi party were the civil engineer and amateur economist Gottfried Feder; the anti-Semitic Wagnerian folklorist and poet Dietrich Eckhart; the aspiring founder of a pagan Nordic religion, Alfred Rosenberg; frustrated artist and writer Joseph Goebbels; small pharmacist Gregor Strasser; and industrial chemist Robert Ley. There were, of course, the ex-soldiers who could not adjust to peace, among whom the airplane pilot ace Hermann Goering was one. Founder in early 1919 of the German Workers party, from which the NSDAP evolved, Anton Drexler was a machinist angry about trade-union tyranny as much as "price-gouging" profiteers.

Skilled workmen and small shopkeepers gave the Nazi faithful a decided petty-bourgeois character. But what really tied the Nazis together was their susceptibility to seizure by ideas–simple yet strong ones, ideas of a conspiracy by the rich and the Jews to ruin the German people, of criminal Marxists who had betrayed the country into defeat, of corrupt politicians and swindling businessmen, of "interest slavery" and "speculation" as the enemies. Nazism has been called a revolt of the losers, and many have found the leading psychological traits of the Nazi activists to be a rebellion against the norms of their particular group: emotional nonconformism. For this reason the movement made a considerable appeal to disturbed youth.

In his study of 581 early Nazis *(Political Violence under the Swastika),* Peter Merkl found "a childhood of poverty and frustrated upward mobility in the city" to be prominent in the social background of the most militant Nazi activists. "The life story of the Nazi leaders," Jean Baechler comments, reveals that "all without exception experienced a major setback that prevented them from realizing their life ambition." Hitler wanted to be an architect, Himmler a scholar, Goebbels a writer, Heydrich a naval officer. The major ideologists such as Houston Stewart Chamberlain and Alfred Rosenberg were people with a certain literary talent who lacked the qualities necessary to professional success. Modern society, of course, produces many such cases: people with intelligence and energy who find their careers frustrated, perhaps by their own orneriness, perhaps by circumstances.

A strong element in the Nazi ideology was a leveling, antiaristocratic, quasi-democratic spirit among the *Volksgenossen,* the racial comrades, who were all held to be equal. Hitler himself, the Army private first-class who rose to lord it over haughty Prussian generals, was a symbol of the little man climbing to the top. Many of his followers harbored a desire to climb with him, winning recognition and success by their participation in a revolt of the outsiders.

Ruined petty bourgeoisie, souls damaged by the war and postwar insecurity, the "fatherless generation" resulting from the war, those whose confidence in all government had been shattered by the loss of savings in the great inflation–such people were more numerous in Germany at this time than in most societies. Still, one must explain why a political party that amounted to little in 1928 suddenly, within four years, swelled to become the largest party in Germany, supported by a third of the electorate.

The obvious answer is the Depression, which brought fresh distress, mass unemployment, the ruin of farmers and small businessmen. As in France, government fell into impotence when the economic crisis shattered the coali-

tion on which a workable parliamentary majority depended. The German republic, of course, had shallower roots by far than did the British and French parliamentary democracies. Born of defeat and nurtured in civil strife, the Weimar
Republic had a claim on the loyalties of too few Germans.

One answer to the question of why so bizarre a concoction as National
Socialism triumphed in Germany is simply that there were no viable alternatives. Winston Churchill thought it had been a mistake to destroy the monarchy; but that had been done, and indeed by the German people themselves,
who clearly had enough of the kaiser. One option that was contemplated in the
crisis of parliamentary government that began in 1930 was a military dictatorship, but the Versailles army was not up to such a task and shrank from it. President Hindenburg, a father figure to the Germans, who was reelected in 1932 by
a resounding majority with Hitler running against him, was too old to do more
than help in some plan of political reconstruction. Communism, redolent of
Russian tyranny as well as war defeatism, chipped away somewhat at Social
Democratic strength among the working class but commanded the support of
only a small percentage of Germans, its share of the vote rising from about 10
percent to 15 percent between 1928 and 1932. There was no outstanding German Communist leader; the party had fallen into the hands of obedient clerks
carrying out orders from Moscow. The right was split between monarchists and
supporters of the republic, the left between Communists and Social Democrats,
the center between Catholics and liberals. The death of Gustav Stresemann in
1929 deprived the parliamentary republic of its one outstanding leader.

The Depression broke up the coalition between socialists and middle-
class parties and turned the wrath of the people on all the parties associated with
the government, thus pushing protest votes toward the extremists. A two-party
system enables the voters to vent their rage on the incumbents by voting for the
opposition party, as American voters did in 1932. More than six million American voters changed their minds between 1928 and 1932, not because they
knew much about Democratic presidential candidate Franklin D. Roosevelt,
but because they wished to register a resounding protest against the Republican
administration that had failed to cope with the economic disaster. In so doing,
they did not need to vote for a radical party. But when all the moderate parties,
as a coalition, are the "ins," popular frustration can express itself only by voting
for the extremes.

The Mueller government of 1928–1930 broke up on economic differences between Social Democrats and the bourgeois parties over the familiar issues of the government budget and wages. The government had no choice but
to pare government spending because of Germany's dependence on foreign
loans, imperiled by its low credit rating after 1929. In July 1930, Heinrich Brüning's government fell when the Social Democrats joined Communists and Nazis
in voting against it, deserting their former allies in the Weimar coalition. It was
a shortsighted decision that the SPD had cause to regret. Obviously the extreme
unpopularity of the retrenchment policies of the government among industrial

workers, including cuts in unemployment benefits, was a key factor. Yet Brüning (a Centrist) represented the last hope of responsible and democratic forces to deal with the terrible economic situation. After the 1930 election, when Brüning ruled by decree, the Social Democrats attacked him rhetorically but tolerated the government.

The elections of September 1930 registered a slight Communist rise, to 13 percent, and a large Nazi gain, all the way up to 18 percent. No combination could find a majority in the Reichstag. The Constitution through its article 48 provided for a way out; though hardly intended to apply to this situation, it did allow government by decree if a public emergency existed. President Hindenburg put the 1930 budget into effect by decree after the Reichstag rejected it, and thereafter for nearly two years the Brüning government governed by such decrees, as the Depression worsened. The chancellor pursued policies of the orthodox sort, keeping government expenditures down, hoping by deflation to regain export markets, and through low interest rates to stimulate reinvestment. Such were the policies followed by Herbert Hoover in the United States, by the MacDonald government in Britain, and by most other governments, adopting the prescriptions of traditional economic theory.

Government by presidential decree could not go on forever. Brüning resigned in May 1932 when Hindenburg refused to authorize a decree that would have broken up bankrupt East Prussian estates into holdings for small farmers. The president was himself a "Junker," a member of this East Prussian landholding aristocracy. Franz von Papen then formed a cabinet that included General Kurt von Schleicher as minister of defense. In July 1932, the path of a general election was tried again, with even more disastrous results (see Table 6–2). This time, over 37 percent of the Germans voted Nazi, the maximum that the party reached under free conditions. It fell to 33 percent in another election held in November. The Communist vote again rose slightly, reaching nearly 17 percent in November; with the SPD losing heavily and the People's party nearly wiped out, prospects for a workable coalition now totally vanished.

Historians have severely criticized the maneuvers that preceded Hitler's coming to power early in 1933, but unless the army established a military dictatorship, which it was unwilling to do, there seemed no answer other than an attempt to draw Hitler's party into the government. Perhaps the experience of holding office would tame the Nazis, or that as part of a coalition, they would have to compromise. General Schleicher also hoped to detach the more responsible wing of the Nazis, if such a thing existed, from Hitler. Gregor Strasser was his hope, but this plan did not work, and the party stayed loyal to Hitler. For their pains, Schleicher and Strasser were to be among Hitler's victims on the "night of the long knives," June 30, 1934.[2]

---

[2]Gregor's brother Otto Strasser survived; after fleeing Germany in 1933, he attempted to lead an anti-Hitler movement, working with the British, in World War II. This had little success and the British dropped him. He returned to Germany from Canada in 1955.

Table 6–2   Reichstag Election Results, 1928–1933

	MAY 20, 1928	SEPT. 14, 1930	JULY 31, 1932	NOV. 6, 1932	MARCH 5, 1933
			% of eligible voters voting		
	75.6%	82.0%	84.0%	80.6%	88.7%
Party					
Communist (KPD)	10.6%	13.1%	14.6%	16.8%	12.3%
Social Democratic (SPD)	29.8	24.5	21.6	20.4	18.3
German Democratic (DDP)	4.9	3.8	1.0	0.9	0.9
German People's (DVP)	8.7	4.5	1.2	1.8	1.1
Center (Catholic)	12.1	11.8	12.5	11.7	11.2
German National (DNP)	14.2	7.0	5.9	8.8	8.0
National Socialist (NSDAP)	2.6	18.3	37.4	33.1	43.9
Misc. others	17.1	17.0	5.8	6.5	4.3

Hitler was not about to settle for half a loaf after the electoral successes of 1932. The brown-shirted Nazi "storm troopers" stepped up their lawless violence, as street wars between Nazis and Communists became a nightly occurrence. When the November elections again failed to break the political deadlock, the Nazis' slight loss being balanced by a Communist gain, von Papen resigned. Hitler was offered the chancellorship under limiting conditions, which he rejected. Hindenburg, no friend of the Austrian guttersnipe, refused his demand for emergency powers. Schleicher formed a new cabinet but could not gain sufficient support in the Reichstag. His resignation paved the way for Hitler's assumption of the chancellorship on January 30, 1933, bringing Nazis Hermann Goering and Wilhelm Frick into the cabinet but also accepting other ministers who were not Nazis.

Franz von Papen thought he had caught Hitler and would now tame him. But the Nazi leader was able to work his way into complete control. He soon forced fresh elections, which took place under intimidation by the now uncontrolled storm troops. It was during this election campaign, on February 27, that the Reichstag fire took place; branding it a Communist plot, Hitler persuaded President Hindenburg to issue emergency decrees suspending basic liberties of free speech and press. Many thought the Nazis themselves had set the fire, and evidence strongly suggests that they did manipulate a demented Dutchman by the name of Van der Lubbe. When the elections gave the Nazis 44 percent of the vote, they found allies among the Nationalists and Centrists who agreed to outlaw the Communist party and pass an Enabling Act, which granted dictatorial powers to the government for four years. Only ninety-four votes, all by Social Democrats, were cast against the Enabling Act in the end. Germany had surrendered to Hitler.

The extent to which his was a legal accession to power may be debated; Nazi violence and intimidation, along with abuse of the emergency decree power, provided a decidedly illegal atmosphere. Nevertheless, all was done by technically legal actions, and it is evident that Hitler had a considerable mandate from the German people. It is often pointed out that at most 44 percent of the German people, and probably fewer, approved of the Austrian fanatic; but this was far and away the largest percentage to vote for a party in all the years of the republic. No other party in 1932 came within 13 percent of this total, and in the March 1933 election the nearest competitor was 25 percent behind. Given the circumstances, a party that could win 35 to 40 percent of the vote was a marvel and could hardly be excluded from power according to the normal rules of parliamentary democracy. Moreover, Hitler's party got out voters who normally stayed at home; the 1932 and 1933 elections attracted a significantly larger than usual number to the polls (more than 80 percent of those eligible), and most of these new voters seem to have voted Nazi. It was difficult to deny that Hitler was entitled to some share of office.

The Enabling Act that granted Hitler's chancellorship unusual powers was not entirely different from the United States Congress voting unprecedented emergency powers to newly elected President Franklin Roosevelt in 1933 to deal with the economic crisis. The Reichstag renewed the 1933 act in 1937 and 1941, and in 1937 Hitler had his authority confirmed by a plebiscite—in which, to his disappointment, he won a mere 84 percent of the vote. He wanted 100 percent. Meanwhile, he had also been elected President. In a whirlwind of propaganda and ideology, he used his powers to mesmerize the German people into believing in his vision of a single, united racial community—"one people, one state, one leader."

THE NAZI IDEOLOGY

Why did Hitler win? There was grave need to combat the terrible depression, of course, which hit Germany harder than any other major country. But Hitler's party offered no economic program worthy of the name. *Der Führer* had an aversion to economics, and it was not even clear whether his party stood for socialism or capitalism, since it fulminated against both Marxism and "international capitalism." The Nazis alleged that the Jews dominated both, as part of a secret conspiracy to conquer the world, apparently after thoroughly confusing it. Claiming to stand for a kind of socialism, the Nazis in rejecting the Strasser brothers seemed to turn away from any specific socialist doctrine. They exuded an anticapitalist spirit, often in association with archetypes of rural rootedness and folk culture. "Among his phobias," Joachim Fest writes of Hitler, "were American technology, the birth rate of the Slavs, big cities, 'industrialization as unrestricted as it is harmful,' the 'economization of the nation,' corporations, the 'morass of metropolitan amusement culture,' and modern art. . . ."

Like more recently alienated people, who would not want to be associated with fascism, Hitler disliked modern urban industrial society and harbored images of a pastoral utopia where nature reigned and people lived in premodern simplicity. Walther Darré, Hitler's agricultural expert, developed an ideology that pictured the German farmer as the quintessence of both racial Nordicism and the German national soul; Nazi propaganda consistently glorified the Bauer. Yet farmers made up only 3.6 percent of those who joined the party between 1925 and 1930. Hitler himself had an urban background, as did most of the Nazi faithful.

It is sometimes said that the Nazis won because they were superb propagandists, putting on a good show with their parades, uniforms, and songs and knowing how to appeal to the mass mind. But this does not explain why before 1930 most of Germany laughed at Hitler, with his rustic accent, and paid little attention to his antics. In 1926, a rally in Weimar at which Hitler wore his leather-belted raincoat and army boots, while saluting his uniformed followers in the manner of Mussolini, impressed most observers as a dreary affair. Did the propaganda suddenly become more effective? This seems unlikely.

One comes back to the point that Germans were not really voting for the Nazis so much as they were expressing their dislike of the reigning establishment in the only way possible. Of course, they could have voted for the

Nazi rally at Nuremberg (Nürnberg), 1936. (*AP/Wide World Photos.*)

Communists, who certainly expected to profit by the breakdown of capitalism and democracy. It is wrong, incidentally, to accuse Hitler of waving the flag of war and imperialism to distract the minds of the workers at this time (a frequent Marxist interpretation), for he said little or nothing about this during his climb to power. These themes were not popular in Germany, a country most of whose people are (contrary to legend) neither very nationalistic nor very militaristic. Hitler tried to mount a campaign in 1929 against the Young Plan, which further revised reparations payments downward while still retaining them. This was an extension of the Briand–Stresemann–Wall Street compromise by which the Germans were expected to "fulfill" their payments for war damages while having these considerably reduced and getting American loans. But this campaign fizzled, and the Social Democrats in 1928 won electoral victory on a "food, not armaments" platform. Thereafter, the Nazis played down talk of rearmament and defiance of treaties. In opposing "the fetters of Versailles" in principle, they joined nearly all other Germans; this was not a distinctive Nazi slogan.

We are left with the Hitler charisma, which undoubtedly existed. Many who came to laugh stayed to succumb to the hypnotic spell that emanated from this erstwhile clown. On paper his ideas seem a weird amalgamation of enthusiasms, but he could cast a spell when he addressed an audience. He had worked hard to make National Socialism mean Adolf Hitler's genius. He had demanded, as the price of his leadership, absolute and unquestioning obedience from all party members. He spoke of the party as an analogue to the Catholic church, with himself as the infallible pope. He refused to manufacture a party program because, he solemnly assured Germans, they should trust his genius to improvise the right policies at the right time. This strange image of a superman hero-leader was built up with the aid of parades and banners, searchlights playing on the swastika symbol, howling crowds shrieking "Heil!" to the uniformed figure with his right hand rigid in a raised salute. The spectacle reached deeply into the unconscious minds of simple people and touched chords of unreason. Familiarity with subsequent phenomena at rock-music concerts and festivals or the hysterical crowds which even in the 1920s wept at the funeral of movie star Rudolf Valentino takes us closer to the Hitler effect than does anything previously known in European politics. This was "pop" politics.

This demagoguery was not entirely a triumph of unlettered instinct. Hitler borrowed from many movements and ideologies, past and present. He learned from Lenin the value of the disciplined elite party and outdid the Russian in fanaticizing such a gathering of the militant faithful. He borrowed from Mussolini the idea of a totalitarian society, completely molded into one shape, but he went far beyond Mussolini in seeking to carry this out. Hitler read omnivorously in his earlier years, soaking up ideas to fit into his patchwork philosophy. The ideas on which Nazism drew—some of which it shared with Italian fascism—were substantially of three sorts (each of them subject to subdividing): (1) racism or extreme nationalism; (2) atavistic populism, that is, a revulsion against modern urban society, sometimes including capitalism; and (3) irrationalism, as a belief in the irrationality of the masses or the use of symbols, myths, and ritual.

Hitler, a person to whom, however confusedly, ideas were powerfully important, and who certainly knew how to use them effectively, picked them up from a number of pre-1914 sources. None of them were exclusively German, and indeed it is remarkable that the chief sources of the above three units included an Englishman and a Frenchman, while Italian fascism was a predecessor and a model (Hitler always revered Mussolini as a pioneer of the faith).

Though the roots of Fascist/Nazi doctrine are more complex than we can reveal here, the two people mentioned may be briefly identified. The Englishman who more than anyone else influenced Nazi racism was Houston Stewart Chamberlain, author of the widely read *Foundations of the Nineteenth Century,* originally written as a turn-of-the-century piece in 1901. Disciple and son-in-law of Richard Wagner, friend of Kaiser Wilhelm II, Chamberlain drew his racial ideas heavily from an earlier Frenchman, the Comte de Gobineau, called "the father of racist ideology," who wrote in the mid-nineteenth century. This was a sweeping interpretation of world history in terms of the superior creativity of the Aryan race and the degeneracy of the impure, mongrelized races. Alfred Rosenberg, leading ideologist among the Nazis, based his *Myth of the Twentieth Century* on Chamberlain. Myth it was indeed, resting on all manner of historical errors, yet like other such keys to the total past it attracted many. It flattered the Germans by assigning them the historic role of *Herrenvolk,* superior to all others and uniquely creative. It included anti-Semitism, which Chamberlain got from Wagner; but it also disparaged the Mediterranean peoples as mongrelized and decadent, which could hardly have pleased Mussolini. (Versions of this Anglo-Saxon Nordicism, deploring the "inferior" Latins as well as Slavs who were mongrelizing the old American stock in the "new immigration" of the 1880–1910 period, appeared in the United States at this time; an example is Madison Grant's *Passing of the Great Race.*)

Mussolini and Hitler both learned from Gustave Le Bon's perennially popular study of mob psychology, translated as *The Crowd.* (By 1929, thirty-six editions of this book originally published in 1895 had appeared, and it is still in print.) Like Chamberlain a talented amateur of ideas, Le Bon taught Mussolini and Hitler that men are not politically rational, they are in the mass easily dominated and indeed want to be dominated, and they can be powerfully swayed by the right emotional appeals. No one today is likely to deny this, but the idea was less familiar then and Le Bon gave it striking expression in his *Psychologie des foules,* a book that influenced Sigmund Freud. The political aspect of this right-wing French nationalist was his message that socialism is an affair of the intellectuals; the working class finds Marxism too abstract and abstruse, and in fact—so Le Bon argued in his *Psychology of Socialism*—is at heart in many ways both conservative and bourgeois.

Hitler's pathological hatred of the Jews was born in Vienna, capital of the pre-1914 multinational Hapsburg Empire, filled with Slavs and other minorities, where the Germans themselves were a rather small minority compared with the non-Germanic peoples. (Baltic Germans were also prominent in the Nazi party.) There, in the thought of such Pan-Germans as Hitler's youthful idol, Georg Ritter von Schoenerer, who used the swastika symbol, the myth of the "master race" threatened by inferior blood strains was born. There, stories circulated from the East of a great Jewish conspiracy, such as that contained in the fraudulent *Protocols of the Elders of Zion.*

It is a curious fact that in Germany itself, where the biggest anti-Semite of all times was to win power and attempt to exterminate the Jewish race, virtually no Jewish "problem" existed. A Jewish population of just over a half-million, less than 1 percent of the total population, had become assimilated into German culture; there were no ghettoes as there were in east Europe and perhaps even less social resentment of Jews than in France or England. It is especially curious that the Nazi vote in Germany was strongest in those regions where there were the fewest Jews: East Prussia, Pomerania, Schleswig-Holstein, Hannover, Lower Saxony—that is, the agricultural North. Dispersed all over Germany, the Jews were an insignificant minority everywhere, and they were growing less and less significant all the time. Hitler's anti-Semitism was entirely mythological, and it is therefore oddly logical that it should have been most effective where no real Jews existed.

One part of the myth was the allegation that Jewish capitalists owned everything and ruled Weimar Germany; in fact, Jewish influence was confined to a few cases, such as large department stores, some of the (better) big newspapers, and entertainment. The great industrial corporations were no more Jewish-dominated than were the professions, literature, or, despite significant Jewish contributions, intellectual life. Those Jews who did rise to intellectual prominence did not exhibit any peculiarly Jewish qualities. Zionism was weak. Though Hitler outrageously alleged the opposite, Einstein's physics was no more peculiarly Jewish than was Stefan Zweig's widely popular fiction. It is probably true that both Marxism and Freudianism attracted a higher than average Jewish component; but both rejected Judaic traditions. It is singular that these allegedly Jewish ideologies repudiated or ignored Jewish religion and Jewish nationalism. They were in fact a way station for Jews engaged in losing their Jewishness.

In brief, Hitler's anti-Semitism was a triumph of fantasy over reason; yet, as a scapegoat symbol the International Jew was effective, for the symbol brought together all those otherwise illogically linked things that Hitler hated and that millions joined him in hating. Exploitative capitalism, financial speculation, political corruption, disloyalty to and betrayal of the German state, Marxist subversion, the decay of traditional society, vulgar mass culture—all these could be blamed on a mythical Jew. This Jew ruined small businessmen, corrupted German women, organized revolutions, and spoiled German culture. He overcharged the worker, made bad movies, created an ugly commercialism, spied for Russia, and sold out Germany in diplomatic negotiations with Wall Street capitalists and conniving Frenchmen. He was indeed a versatile villain.

Only a people morbidly ill could believe such legends, it will be said; but indeed the German mind was shell-shocked from war, defeat, inflation, unemployment, and economic depression.

Such ideological and *massenpsychologie* uses of anti-Semitism seem more important than purely personal elements of Hitler. Psychobiography has not passed by Adolf Hitler. Did the roots of his scarcely rational anti-Semitism lie in a transferred self-hatred? Or, in his somewhat abnormal childhood, his relationship with his father, or the Jewish doctor whom he is said to have blamed for his mother's death (though this has been denied)? These and other theories may be found in several psychoanalytical studies of the Hitler personality. Jean-Paul Sartre wrote an existentialist analysis of the anti-Semite. All of this is extremely interesting and recommended for student reading. The sadder truth seems to be that since tribal days, humanity has characteristically been intolerant of cultural outsiders, prone to rally behind charismatic leaders in time of crisis, all too apt to respond to simple scapegoat symbols, and—as Hitler had read in Le Bon—irrational in the mass.

NATIONAL SOCIALISM IN POWER

People often complain that politicians do not keep their promises; in Hitler's case, the trouble was that he did. He had promised a complete change in the system, a "revolution comparable to the Russian Revolution," to "get rid of a world of opinions and install another in its place." The frightening thing about Hitler was that he really meant everything he had said in his campaign. In the end, this meant war against the Slavs for German living space, and it meant the slaughter of the Jews.

Initially, Hitler moved cautiously in foreign affairs. He did create a sensation by taking Germany out of the Geneva Disarmament Conference, where for many years Germany had pleaded for arms equality without much success. Now, in 1932, Germany won the concession of a statement favoring equality of armaments in principle. But faced with French stalling in implementing this principle, Hitler suddenly withdrew from the conference, and also from the League of Nations, in October 1933. It was a bold defiance of the Versailles system, which in retrospect may be seen as the first crucial step on the road to World War II. There was talk of sanctions and war against Germany but, just as he did five years later, Hitler felt sure the Allies were bluffing; their peoples were in no mood for military adventures.

An immense propaganda campaign preceded a plebiscite in Germany on November 12, 1933, one day after the fifteenth anniversary of the armistice, to approve this action. A huge majority endorsed the withdrawal from the

League, relishing the nose-thumbing at the arrogant victors who had humiliated Germany for so long. But Hitler followed this bold action with a surprising nonaggression pact with Poland in 1934 and presented to the world an apparent picture of moderation and restraint. "Germans and Poles will have to learn to accept the fact of each other's existence," he said. In other speeches, he insisted that Germany asked only equal rights and desired peace.

Once in power, Hitler was able to expand and intensify his pageantry. The organization of parades, spectacles, and rituals dazzled Germany and astonished the entire world. It was a good show. "Germany now enjoyed a splendor of ceremonies such as it had never previously known," the French ambassador, François-Poncet, wrote in semiadmiration. Wagnerian opera came to politics in a massive way. These quasi-religious rites were tuned to the theme not only of Hitler as the supreme leader but of a new national unity. There was a surge of community feeling reminiscent of August 1914.

This honeymoon phase of the Nazi revolution brought almost everyone temporarily over to Hitler's side. With what later seemed to have been surprisingly little resistance, the intellectuals, the universities, the churches followed the masses in joining the all-German team that, according to *der Führer*, was to bring a renaissance of the German spirit as well as recovery from the Great Depression. Something of this lyrical optimism is caught in Leni Riefenstahl's extraordinary movie, *Triumph of the Will*, made in 1934.

The ugly side of Nazism quickly manifested itself also. A book-burning symbolically purged the country of writings not amenable to the "racial community" as National Socialism visualized it. Jewish businesses were boycotted, and government pressure forced newspapers to conform or be squeezed out of business. A distinguished body of intellectual leaders, not all of them Jewish, chose to migrate rather than face harassment. Abroad when Hitler came to power, Einstein renounced his German citizenship and did not return; the Nazis seized his property and denounced his "degenerate Jewish science." But the loss of hundreds of eminent writers, scholars, scientists, and artists was countered by the support given to the Nazi regime by a coterie of eminent figures, ranging from musicians Richard Strauss and Wilhelm Furtwangler to philosopher Max Scheler and Nobel Prize-winning scientist Johannes Stark. Most of the university faculty joined the Nazi party (64 percent at Hamburg, according to a recent study). Intellectual leaders as eminent as Martin Heidegger evidently felt sympathy for this outburst of the archaic collective unconscious. Einstein's old collaborator Max Planck remained silent, though he too later regretted this, and his son became a martyr in the cause of anti-Nazi resistance.

Triumph of the will: So Hitler conceived the goal. A single national will, organized by the "leadership principle," should direct the nation, which should be a "racial community," a *Volksgemeinschaft*. Such a focusing of national energy would make anything possible, he thought. The revolution that would bring this about had to keep the masses keyed up by constant propaganda, it had to destroy pitilessly anything that stood in the way of unanimity, and it had to get rid of all remnants of the selfish individualism of the past. This included such matters as political parties and freedom to criticize the government. The price paid for a *Volksgemeinschaft* was persecution and intolerance. Hitler set about the task of *Gleichschaltung* ("coordinating") German institutions, that is, bringing them into line with the Nazi spirit. The task was never completed, and in fact as an administrator Hitler turned out to be a good artist. But much was done to Nazify education, the press, the arts, the law, labor, and every other facet of the national life.

Under Hitler, Germany achieved a good deal of economic recovery, which of course might well have come anyway. Rather like American President Franklin D. Roosevelt, whose New Deal came into being about the same time as Hitler's New Reich and tried similarly, though by less illiberal means, to restore national confidence, Hitler put into effect large public works projects, of which the Autobahn superhighway network was the best known. He ignored the bankers' orthodoxy by loosening credit and spending government money; he organized a Labor Service, which may be compared with the New Deal's Civilian Conservation Corps, to put idle youth to work. Rearmament contributed to a dramatic reduction in unemployment. Hitler went much beyond Roosevelt in merging all trade unions into a single state-sponsored Labor Front. This action wiped out strikes, to the joy of employers, but it compensated somewhat by providing vacations, travel, and various cultural activities for workers. The Volkswagen, the "people's automobile," was an eventual product of this "Strength through Joy" workers' recreation program, lavishly subsidized by the government. It may have been fascism's only constructive idea (Mussolini's similar *dopolavoro* has been given good marks; see Victoria di Grazia's study of it.) Real wages fell, but workers were thankful they at least had jobs.

Hitler also employed the banking wizard Hjalmar Schacht to manage foreign trade successfully. Schacht's methods included exchange controls, which allowed currency rates to vary from country to country, and bilateral trading agreements, which were successful in winning markets in southeastern Europe. Agricultural prices were artificially raised, as they were in other countries. Until 1935 at least, Nazi economic policies by the standards of the day were far from unenlightened.

This achievement earned Hitler rather widespread respect. In 1935, Winston Churchill praised Hitler's "courage and vital strength" and as late as 1938 repeated that, "If we had been defeated in war, I would hope we might find a Hitler to lead us back to our rightful position among the nations." Regaining international prestige at the risk of war did not come until after 1937; until then, by and large, the German dictator concentrated on internal problems. His success came at a heavy cost. Constitutional safeguards of all sorts were swept away. The totalitarian state allowed no limitations on its authority. The seventeen German states, or "lands," lost their powers, at least on paper; the Reich became a unitary state, no longer a federal one. In principle, individuals had no rights and liberties, since the rights of the national community took precedence (and Hitler decided them). There was not supposed to be any separation of powers; an independent judiciary was subverted by the existence of a secret police system outside it—the dreaded Gestapo (*Geheime Staatspolizei,* Secret State Police, which later became a part of the Security Service)—as well as by Hitler's appointments to the judiciary. *Ein Reich, Ein Volk, Ein Führer*—as Stalin spoke for the "working class," so Hitler spoke for the German people.

The most ominous event of the Third Reich's early years was the massacre that took place on the night of June 30, 1934. In large part, this was Hitler's settlement with powerful rivals within his own party. A violent and lawless movement, the NSDAP had attracted violent and lawless men, especially those *condottiere* from the Free Corps who had joined the party. One of them, Captain Ernst Röhm, was commander of the SA, the storm troopers. The SA *(Sturmabteilung),* organized in 1921 chiefly from ex-soldiers, was the quasi-military arm of the Party. By 1934, the SA had become a huge private army, wanting to take over the old German army which it hated. It had always been quasi-independent. Röhm, a brawling soldier, had contempt for the "artist" and politician Hitler who he thought was selling out to the Establishment. Hitler was right in thinking they had become a danger to his rule. Mussolini faced the same problem with the "old fighters" of the Fascist party after his accession to power; and one may perhaps draw a comparison with Stalin's position vis-à-vis Trotsky. The revolution devours its own children. The SA began to talk of the need of a "second revolution," viewing Hitler as a Kerensky or a Mirabeau: one who had failed to carry the revolution to its completion.

Röhm burst into open and outspoken criticism of Hitler, thus violating the leadership principle: "Only one man can be the Leader." The SA captain evidently lacked the clarity of thought or the resolution to do more than bluster, and thus, by being "willing to wound and yet afraid to strike," he sealed his doom. Other high Nazis, including Goebbels and Goering, envied him. And, a rival source of armed power arose in the form of the SS *(Schutzstaffel),* an elite guard originally a subdivision of the SA, headed by Heinrich Himmler, who was soon to control the Gestapo also.

With President Hindenburg now on his death bed, Hitler felt released from what restraints the old chief had placed on him. On the night of June 30 and the following day, a series of raids arrested and summarily executed Röhm and some 200 other SA leaders, throwing in for good measure a number of Hitler's other foes of past and present. Former Chancellor Franz von Papen, close to Hindenburg, just barely escaped with his life and was shipped off to Turkey. It was not merely on the left, among Communists and modernists, that Hitler took his revenge; traditional conservatives were equally if not even more his victims. They had generally despised him as a barbarian.

In this lawless slaughter, which Hitler himself called "vigilante killing on a grand scale," the victims were arrested and shot, sometimes on the spot but sometimes after a brief court-martial trial. Carrying out this drumhead justice were units of the newly organized SS, the SD (Security Service), and the regular army. This massive purge could not be kept secret. Hitler waited two weeks before attempting to justify it in a rambling speech to the Reichstag, pleading the need to save the nation from those who had "lost sympathy with any ordered human society." If this was so, the menace had come from his own organization, and Germany seemed to be at the mercy of rival gangsters, one of whom had gotten the draw on the others. The terroristic basis of the Nazi state stood unmasked. But President Hindenburg thanked Hitler for "saving the German people from a grave peril," and the army sighed in relief. Their turn would come. With the death of Hindenburg, Hitler assumed the presidency as well as the chancellorship, getting this move ratified by a plebiscite on August 19, 1934, in which 84.6 percent voted "Ja."

Despite the lawlessness of the "night of the long knives," Hitler's first years in power were more constructive than his later ones, and indeed the slaughter of the Röhm gang could be viewed as an attempt to control the more violent and fanatical wing of the Nazis. A change began about 1937. In that year, relatively moderate influences within the government left. Hjalmar Schacht resigned in late 1937, his economic functions passing to Hermann Goering. Early in 1938, Joachim Ribbentrop, a Nazi, replaced traditional diplomatist Konstantin von Neurath at the foreign office. It was in this year that Hitler evidently made his decision for war. He moved to secure control over the army, a campaign climaxed in 1938 by the Fritsch affair, in which the leading general of the German Army was deposed after being accused (falsely) of homosexuality and general immorality. The proud German *Wehrmacht,* allowing this to happen, here yielded its honor and its independence. Also getting rid of Minister of Defense Werner von Blomberg, Hitler personally assumed command of the armed forces.

The campaign to enlarge Germany's frontiers by aggressive war, securing "living space" in the East at the expense of the Slavic "inferior men," dominated Hitler's mind. He talked of building a Reich so strong it would last a thousand years. Always the architect, he dreamed of a rebuilt Berlin able to hold ten million people—the capital of the world! As Hitler moved down the road to war, through the Austrian and Czechoslovakian crises of 1938, persecution of the Jews intensified. Pogroms, or violent attacks on Jews and destruction of their property by SA thugs, grew more numerous in 1938. They reached a dreadful climax on the night of November 9–10, the excuse being the assassination in Paris of a German diplomatic official by a young man whose parents had been mistreated in Germany. Egged on by Goebbels, who declared that all German Jews could be held accountable for the crime, Nazi storm troopers burned hundreds of synagogues, plundered Jewish shops, arrested and mistreated Jews. The clumsiness of this method of "solving the Jewish problem," involving damage to the economy and adverse publicity abroad, caused a reaction against Goebbels, who, though protected by Hitler, was generally despised in high Nazi circles. Goering, Himmler, and Heydrich, who became head of the SD, thought there were tidier ways of making Germany "free of

Jews." Wild rioting of this sort against Jews was not repeated, but the infinitely more sinister plan of a "final solution" by systematically exterminating all the Jews began to take shape.

While the outer world received through Nazi propaganda an image of a totalitarian society, in which everyone was forced into one mold by a master plan, the truth was that Hitler failed to accomplish his goal of restoring a pure "folk community." He did next to nothing for that *Mittelstand,* or petty bourgeois, sector that had been the main source of his strength, or for the farmers. The urbanization of Germany continued; big business, if willing to bow to Nazi desires, prospered at the expense of small. Agriculture diminished in importance. And, the National Socialist government, far from being perfectly organized, was a chaos of private administrative empires. Goering, Himmler, Goebbels, the SA, the SS, the local party officials, and others formed a mixture of factions struggling for power, held together only by the brooding Hitler's unquestioned command over them all. This was a structure for which feudalism seems the best model, rather than the totalitarian state. Hitler was better at grandiose visions than day-to-day administration.

His turn toward imperialism and war reflected the failures and contradictions of his regime. The economic problem, he came to feel, was solvable only by conquering new domains for Germany to exploit. So was the Jewish problem, for the great bulk of world Jewry dwelt outside the Reich, chiefly in eastern Europe. Above all, the Nazi movement had to be dynamic, a trait it shared with Stalin's Communist party. The restless forces Hitler controlled had to be given a goal capable of channeling their energies. War alone provided such a focus.

It should be added that in many ways Hitler's movement did accomplish a kind of democratic revolution in German society. The "little man," provided he was not contaminated by Jewish blood (and the number of Jews in Germany was, even by the most generous reckoning, hardly more than 1 percent of the population), could use the Nazi party as a ladder to climb up the social scale.[3] Nazi doctrine taught the equality of all the "racial comrades"; in brief, one German was as good as another. The spectacle of the erstwhile army private Hitler giving orders to aristocratic Prussian generals or to haughty barons of business delighted the hearts of all who had once kowtowed to these mighty people. Many new men made their way to positions of power, usually in the swelling bureaucracy, or perhaps in a state-owned enterprise like the Herman Goering Steel Works. (Born of a need to keep the old steel barons under

---

[3]The small number of unassimilated Jews in Germany was a reason for the lack of resistance to Hitler's outrages against them. Had there been a large and influential Jewish community its leaders would have raised an outcry; one can imagine how American Jewish organizations, for example, would have responded. Hitler was in fact picking on a hopelessly tiny minority.

control, this enterprise bore the name of the famed corpulent Nazi lover of the good life, who also stole a great art collection for himself.) Many others who aspired to similar success had to be given opportunities. It was a kind of socialism of greed. In the end, only by ever-new conquests of territory could National Socialism satisfy its built-in appetites for power. It was an old story, for the classic student of power politics, Machiavelli, had long ago pointed out that despots must look to war to keep their power.

STALIN'S REVOLUTION

In the 1930s, Western intellectuals typically found Stalin's regime to be more defensible than Hitler's, not only because Russia had the excuse of her "backwardness" (they often pointed out in apology for Stalinism that Russia had never known human rights and the rule of law as these existed in the West), but even more because they thought the goal at which Stalin aimed was a worthy one. Not just another industrialized country was being created, but a new kind of human being, freed from all the old corruptions. Soviet communism appropriated the symbols of the old European socialist faith, itself pretty obviously a secularized version of the Christian Gospels. The toilers of the world were on the march toward the promised land, these symbols proclaimed. In the atmosphere of the Great Depression when capitalism's failure seemed self-evident, the Soviet experiment, glimpsed from afar, looked like a beacon of hope.

Contemporary observers were not unaware of the cost of the Great Socialist Offensive, which began in 1928. An American engineer, John Scott, who had worked at the industrial center of Magnitogorsk that the Soviet planners tried to create beyond the Urals, wrote that "Men froze, hungered and suffered, but the construction work went on with a disregard for the individual and a mass heroism seldom paralleled in history." The Czech observer Maurice Hindus published in English a widely read account of The Great Offensive, describing Stalin's terrible war on the peasants with much awareness of its dimensions.

Stalin later told Winston Churchill that the drive to collectivize the peasants was a worse war than was World War II. It raged between 1929 and 1932 as the leading campaign of the First Five-Year Plan. By 1928, Stalin had completely triumphed over his rivals for leadership within the Communist party of the Soviet Union (CPSU). Unquestioned master of the powerful party apparatus, Stalin decided to use it in a great offensive to build socialism in Russia alone, which meant putting world revolution on the shelf for the time being. Good relations with the capitalist countries would be necessary to secure their aid so that technologically backward Russia could achieve the goal of "overtaking and leaving them behind." Collectivization of the peasants was the primary task. That individual peasant ownership of small plots of land was less efficient than large units, which could be run like factories, was probably a less compelling argument to the Communist leadership than a political one: Peasant Russia was the bastion of private property. The peasants had shown that, by holding out for higher prices, they could frustrate the government's efforts to compel them to accept a lower share of the national wealth. The answer was to deprive them of private property and market choices.

What was in fact a war against virtually the whole peasantry was disguised as a class war between poor and rich peasants. The enemy was declared to be the *kulak*, the rich capitalistic peasant. According to Communist propaganda, the mass of the peasantry was willing and eager to join the collective farms, where they would jointly own and jointly work the land. (State-owned farms, the *sovkhozes*, also existed but were much less numerous than the *kolkhozes* in which, theoretically, peasants cooperatively and jointly owned the land. In practice there was not much difference.) In fact, there was little class feeling in the countryside, where poorer and richer peasants generally stood together against the threat of losing their property. So the war against the kulaks was really a war against a majority of the peasants, waged by party enthusiasts who were backed by the Secret Police (GPU). "Accession to the collective farms must be voluntary," it was solemnly proclaimed; but in actuality party officials, prodded from the top, forced peasants into the collective farms by confiscation and, if there was resistance, by arrest and imprisonment. Peasants fought back as best they could with terror, with arson, sometimes with sabotage, killing farm animals rather than surrender them to collectivization. This terrible human tragedy in the end cost several million lives and dealt Russian agriculture, particularly livestock production, blows from which it took many years to recover. It also further brutalized the Party.

Yet at first, collectivization seemed to succeed. Figures showed rising numbers of collective farms together with an increase in grain production. In 1930, the drive was stepped up. The goal was nothing less than total extinction of peasant proprietorship, immediately. Being a kulak or a member of a kulak's family was like being a Jew in Nazi Germany: They were "vampires and bloodsuckers" who must be purged from society. And, Stalin decided who a kulak was, as Goering said he decided who was Jewish in Germany. The collectivization campaign swelled to a peak of hysterical extravagance, driven by the party's massive zeal. On March 2, 1930, Stalin signaled a retreat in a *Pravda* article titled "Dizzy with Success." It had come to his attention that some peasants were being forced to join the collectives! Comrades, let us not be too rash, the general secretary cautioned. The truth is that his own rashness and ruthlessness had brought Russia to the verge of national disaster. A new famine threatened.

Stalin, as he did on so many other occasions, put the blame on the "wreckers," who were trying to discredit collectivization by the excesses. Reasonable Stalinist policies had been unwisely distorted. A new set of scapegoats was found. Meanwhile the campaign momentarily subsided. Peasants were allowed to keep small plots of their own, on which they might raise vegetables and dairy products for the market in their spare time after their work days on the kolkhoz—a concession that remained thereafter in the USSR, fluctuating in amount but never entirely abandoned. The goal of collectivization was by no means given up, however. Slightly subtler means were used—crushing taxation levied on the individual proprietor, tax concessions to the collective farms. By 1937, almost all of agriculture was organized in collective farms. A virtual famine in 1932–1933, marked by a drop in meat consumption of almost two-thirds since 1929, had not deterred the regime from this dreadful progress. Indeed, it has been argued, famine was deliberately used in the Ukraine as a means of breaking peasant resistance.

The goal was to convert farms into factories, to wipe out the gulf between city and country, destroy the peasants' petty bourgeois mentality, and create a homogeneous totalitarian society. This conversion accompanied rapid industrialization. Surplus population driven from the country by consolidating small farms into large collective ones was forced into new industrial areas. To control this sudden influx of millions into cities where housing was deplorable, the government required them to carry identity papers and to move only with permission—a kind of compulsory labor system.

Russia did industrialize under Stalin. The cost was appalling, leading to charges that even the horrors of capitalism could not have been as bad. Communism, the ultimate goal, lay far in the future. The formula for the interim stage of preparation for communism was "from each according to his abilities, to each according to his work." There were wide differences in wages. A managerial class received special privileges and higher salaries than did common workers. Managers were given the power to discipline the workers, who were no longer protected by trade unions—for the unions, a relic of capitalism, were said to be no longer necessary in the "workers' state." Soviet communism resembled German National Socialism in serving as the vehicle for ambitious new men who rose to power over the bodies of the old ruling class. And, those workers who performed heroic feats of exceeding their quotas and working overtime—without pay—were rewarded with citations and decorations!

Stalin's principle was to build heavy industry's basic plant first and only later consumer industries. Thus the Russian citizen was forced to postpone the fruits of industrialization. Great steel works and hydroelectric plants arose. The totally planned economy, in which decisions were made at the center for the entire country, could successfully divert resources toward particular targets. The Five-Year Plans (first, 1928–1932; second, 1933–1937) set targets and tried to surpass them, sometimes successfully. The cost, critics alleged, was not only human freedom but gross inefficiency in the consumer and distribution sectors of the economy. But Soviet propaganda, enthusiastically disseminated by the party faithful all over the world and believed by sometimes naive "fellow travelers," declared that Stalin's was the only rational way for a backward and exploited people to raise itself to the level of the capitalist economies.

Some unusual features of the Soviet economy emerged early. It could provide full employment and a basic minimum for everybody; food and housing were very cheap, when available, and utilities often were free. It was estimated that one-third of Russian households suffered from overcrowded housing conditions at the end of the Soviet period. Cheap, fixed rents for state-owned housing went with scarcity, poor quality, and poor maintenance. Consumer products familiar in the West (if one could afford them) were either nonexistent or incredibly scarce in the USSR. No mass automobile industry developed there; even in 1975, only 12 of every 1,000 Soviet citizens owned cars, compared with 448 in the United States and 234 in the United Kingdom. Scarcity took the form not of high prices but of unavailability; long waiting periods for a meager apartment, or long queues whenever goods got to the stores were the rather dismal Russian experience—perhaps no more dismal in the 1930s than lack of money to buy plentiful goods in the capitalist countries. Poor quality and failure to innovate or update products also marred the Soviet economic performance, but it could generate massive special projects like the Moscow subway system or the giant power plants.

Moscow claimed extraordinary rates of economic growth in the 1930s. Students of Soviet economics suspected that statistics were falsified, or misleading. Still, most of the world grudgingly accepted that the centrally planned "command economy" could perform miracles of capital accumulation. Whole new industrial cities arose in the Ural region—not so surprising, in view of the fact that such urban centers are always an accompaniment of industrial revolutions, but presented by Soviet propaganda as a miracle of human energy. Such stir and bustle in the heretofore stagnant Russian society contrasted with unemployment and demoralization in the depression-ridden capitalist world.

The crash program of collectivization and industrialization demanded the sacrifice not only of personal freedom but of many of the revolution's original social goals and ideals. Free love, the emancipation of women, easy divorce and abortion, liquidation of the bourgeois family—such modernisms were eagerly proclaimed just after 1917 by Communist intelligentsia, but faded under Stalin, who reinstalled the values of motherhood and the family, as well as patriotism and other "bourgeois" standards. Yet the USSR made progress in reducing illiteracy and improving scientific education.

Stalin's "socialism" differed from the standard kind in several illiberal ways: It was a socialism (a) of poverty rather than plenty (b) of sharp social stratification rather than relative equality (c) of repression rather than emancipation (d) of Russian chauvinism rather than internationalism (e) of state power rather than decentralized autonomy. It also, however, differed from the usual kind in one other way: It was real. It actually held power in a great land. Socialists had filled volumes with their theories and dreams, they had formed organizations and movements, but they had never gained full power in any major country. Even the mildest of them might be prepared to overlook a few of Stalin's shortcomings for the sake of this one great advantage.

THE COST OF SOVIET SOCIALISM

"In the end, Stalin perfected and exploited the machine which he inherited from Lenin," Sovietologist Leonard Schapiro concluded. The Bolsheviks had always practiced ruthless terror against their class enemies, but until the 1930s, they had rarely terrorized members of their own party. Even the Mensheviks, erstwhile comrades in the Social Democratic party, were allowed to leave Russia in the 1920s if they wished. In 1931, Mensheviks who had chosen to stay in the USSR were placed on trial, scapegoats for the failure of forced collectivization. Both native and foreign engineers who were so unfortunate as to have worked on projects that did not progress speedily enough found themselves accused of sabotage. Shooting some of them to encourage the others was a favorite Stalin incentive system. But all this was a mere warm-up for what astonished the world in 1936 and 1937, the spectacle of well-known Old Bolsheviks, comrades of Lenin and Stalin in the Revolution, placed in the dock where they confessed to enormous crimes of treason, sabotage, spying.

In mid-1934, the OGPU was reorganized to become the NKVD. This change in the Secret Police accompanied creation of a central Purge Commission under Nikolai Yezhov, who succeeded Genrik Yagoda as NKVD chief in 1936. Yagoda was tried along with others in 1938 and executed, an example of Stalin's habit of getting rid of his own tools. Several thousand Yagoda men in the NKVD were killed, the terrorists themselves being terrorized. Yagoda was associated with the Bukharinite "opposition," destroyed in the last great trial of the 1930s. (In 1932, the last stand of the Old Bolsheviks against Stalin was led by Bukharin and Kirov, a Leningrad leader whose murder in 1934, arranged by Stalin, was then used as an excuse for the party purge!) The names of Yagoda, Yeshov, and of the head of the Central Committee's "special sector," Stalin's own private secretary, A. N. Poskrebyshev, were to become the most sinister ones in Russia.

This renovation of the security machinery signaled Stalin's drive to purge the party, which he did with both savagery and thoroughness during the next few years, until hardly more than a handful of the Old Bolsheviks remained alive. And, before being led away to the firing squad, they were made to abase themselves, confessing to crimes it is clear they never committed and abjectly apologizing for nonexistent errors and sins. In these public "trials," opened to foreign observers and much discussed throughout the world, it was evident that the guilt of the accused had already been settled; the purpose of the trials was to inflict public humiliation on them or to expose the depth of their degradation. As Stalin's loyal henchman Vyacheslav Molotov once put it, "The guilty will be brought to trial."

Meanwhile, hundreds of thousands of lesser party members, involved with these higher-ups, with Zinoviev and Kamenev, the old "opposition," or with Bukharin, Radek, Rykov, or high military men now accused of spying for the Germans, suffered the fate of their friends and employers, in a widening circle of victims that seemed to expand endlessly. Each arrested person, subject to NKVD torture, implicated others in order to end his ordeal. Torture was regularly used to extract confessions, also threats against the families of the accused. The memo of a private Stalin speech to insiders in December 1937 has been found, threatening to wipe out all the "clan" of any traitor.

A particular mystery surrounds the almost total wiping out of the high army brass, which cruelly damaged Soviet military power at a dangerous time in world affairs. Did Stalin really believe that his generals were planning a coup? Few historians think that they were. As for German-Russian military collaboration, that had come to an end in 1933 if not earlier. Forged documents, passed on from the German security service to Stalin by way of the obliging Czech president Benes, supplied evidence for treasonous contacts of this sort; perhaps this was a German plot to disrupt Russian military organization. But evidence indicates that Stalin himself was in on the forgeries! If in collaboration with German intelligence (hard to believe in 1937) he planted evidence against his own generals, he did not use it or need it, for the military victims got no show trial, they were just taken out and shot after a drumhead court martial, much like the way Hitler had handled the SA. (Maybe Stalin admired and wanted to imitate this famous massacre.)

Why did Stalin do this? Students of this strange and powerful man, no less fascinating than his counterpart, Adolf Hitler, find it difficult to agree. The diminutive Georgian was paranoid, vindictive, stubborn, and cruel. He fully shared the Bolshevik view of morality (Lenin had held it) that "whatever helps the Revolution [the party] is right," that individuals do not matter, that the drive toward utopia justifies any immediate sacrifice. Along with the other surviving Bolsheviks, he had been hardened in the fires of revolutionary violence and civil war. The fanaticism that goes with absolute faith marked Soviet Communism as well as German Nazism. The enemy was always felt to be at the gates, constant vigilance was necessary lest the enemy return—necessitating censorship, secret police, and concentration camps. This was part of the psychology of embattled religions.

Horrified by the collectivization campaign, Stalin's second wife, Nadezhda, committed suicide in 1932, and this loss (he seems genuinely to have cared for both his wives, the first of whom died in 1910 not long after their marriage) left Stalin more alone and stony-hearted.

More objectively, Nazism was abroad in these years, and German generals had in the past cooperated with their Russian counterparts. The exiled Trotsky, whom Stalin's agents finally succeeded in murdering in Mexico only in 1940, had a large world following who argued that Stalin was a false leader. Countless Russians had reason to hate Stalin, who could feel safe only by terrorizing the opposition. It is doubtful that Stalin himself knew the extent of the terror, which, as we noted, got out of hand and spread of its own momentum like a wildfire.

Victims of their own illusions, Stalin and his staff projected grandiose goals in the Five-Year Plans and then, when these goals were not met, assumed that the reason was sabotage. Georges Sorel had written of "the blood-thirsty frenzy of an optimist maddened by sudden resistance to his plans," and this phrase seems apt for Stalin. Their blind fury, Reinhold Niebuhr remarked of the Communists, was a result of "the frustration when pretended omnipotence and omniscience meet recalcitrant forces in history not obedient to their mind or will."

Of course, apologists for Stalinism frequently pointed out that Russia had never really known either democracy or liberalism. It was still overwhelmingly rural and largely illiterate. Life had long been cheap.

When all this has been said, and there is some truth in each of the explanations, one must feel that on the bottom line of the terror is written Lord Acton's edict, "absolute power corrupts absolutely." Stalin had obtained absolute command of the immensely powerful Communist party machinery and could use it as he wished. Not a single voice was raised in the Central Committee or its Politburo to protest any of this ghastly business. Not until three years after Stalin's death, twenty years later, did people dare to speak out.

How many people perished as victims of one sort or another of Stalin's police state? The best scholarly research puts the figure at some twenty million people between 1930 and 1953. First there were about seven million casualties of collectivization. Later, during the time of the great party purge of 1936–1938, between seven million and nine million people were arrested, of whom roughly a million were executed and the rest sent to labor camps in distant places where life expectancy was short (probably about a third of the prisoners died in their first year). A Russian expert using recently available Soviet sources (Dmitri Volkogonov) says 21.9 million were "repressed" between 1929 and 1953; of these, a third were shot, the rest sent to camps where many died. A Khrushchev commission reported 19.8 million repressed between 1935 and 1941. A recent Russian Security Ministry team says 18 million were arrested and 7 million shot between 1935 and 1945. No exact figures were ever kept. There are "revisionist" historians, somewhat comparable to those who deny that Hitler's Holocaust ever happened, who defend much lower figures. Yet it seems safe to say that in all the bloody annals of man's inhumanity to man, it is hard to match this record. "What happened in the Soviet Union was without precedent in peacetime in modern history," Walter Laqueur writes in his *Stalin: The Glasnost Revelations* (1990), noting that "even in Nazi Germany, up to the outbreak of war, the number of those sentenced to death and killed in the camps measured only in the thousands."

DEPRESSION LITERATURE AND THOUGHT

The terrible economic and political crisis of the early 1930s hit European writers and intellectuals just when they were ready for a change anyway. Withdrawal to the ivory tower of aristocratic estheticism is a pleasing gesture; one casts scornful glances at the disgraceful scenes below and meditates on the collapse of civilization. But it soon becomes tiresome, and one yearns to rejoin the human race. Ever since the earlier nineteenth century, the Western literati had vacillated between revolution and revulsion. The revolution of 1848, a "revolution of the intellectuals," failed so badly that the next generation found solace in science and "art for art's sake." Ecstatic participation in World War I was followed by the profound disillusionment of the 1920s. The mood changed again about 1930.

Events in the real world became exciting, a fact that helps explain the shift. Apart from the rise of Nazism and Stalin's Five-Year Plan in the Soviet Union, there were dramas closer to home for British and French writers. The Depression-bred growth of trade unions among the less skilled led to new excitement on the labor front. The CIO story in the United States was paralleled in France, where union membership grew from three-fourths of a million to four million between 1934 and 1937, climaxed by great "sit-in" strikes in 1936 when workers occupied factories. The London streets were filled with marches of the unemployed and with occasional physical conflict between fascists and communists. The American New Deal and the French Popular Front brought activists back to politics. The grand climax was the Spanish Civil War, which the intellectuals of the 1930s made into their Great Crusade. The whole amazing sequence of events in the 1930s suggested a final apocalyptic struggle between good and evil. Nazism and fascism were ranged against communism, with little left in between. Hitler's phantasmagoria of embattled anticommunism faced Stalin's cohorts in a last struggle for the world. Everyone must choose.

The Spanish Civil War was wrongly forced into such a framework. Prior to outside intervention, neither fascism nor communism had much strength in Spain. But the grim strife that began in Spain in 1936 with the rebellion against the republic (discussed in the next chapter) grew into a symbol of the war between Left and Right, socialism and fascism.

> And private stars fade in the blood-red dawn
> Where two worlds strive,

wrote C. Day Lewis, one of the young British poets who turned toward communism. Artists must descend into the arena, "drop those priggish ways forever," and join the struggle. Suddenly, refined esthetes and intellectual snobs were out; proletarian poets on the barricades were in. It is true that not many of the poets managed to make this conversion in actuality, but many tried, and at least in spirit they were all for commitment and participation. When we find Virginia Woolf writing for the *Daily Worker* and Harriet Weaver, the eccentric rich woman who had backed James Joyce in the 1920s, now selling copies of the Communist paper on street corners, we realize what a change there was. Romain Rolland, the hero of the antiwar movement, a resolute nonconformist who had almost alone held out against the tide in 1914, criticized the Communists in the twenties for repressing individual consciences; but now he became one of the "fellow travelers." He joined a band that included German novelist Lion Feuchtwanger, French writer Henri Barbusse, and the "Red Dean" of Canterbury, English churchman Hewlett Johnson, in glorifying Stalin and defending every action of the Soviet Union. Barbusse's 1935 biography of Stalin, an example of hagiography scarcely equalled since the Middle Ages, was hardly unique in this respect.[4] And, these writers were major figures, not hacks or time-servers.

Among the conversions, none was more startling or more famous than that of Sidney and Beatrice Webb, venerable intellectual leaders of British socialism, whose Fabian Society pedigree had heretofore guaranteed their respect for democratic, gradualist methods. But the Webbs lost their faith in gradualism during the Great Depression and, after visiting the USSR in the early thirties, published a massive treatise on *Soviet Civilization* that hailed the birth of a new humanity in Stalin's Russia. Hewlett Johnson's *Soviet Sixth of the World,* an even less critical paean of praise, sold millions of copies.

These Western intellectuals had totally lost faith in their own civilization, which they now saw on its deathbed–a dying culture that, being only one phase of human evolution, would give way in the era of revolutionary turmoil to a higher one. "I have seen the future and it works," American writer Lincoln Steffens declared upon his return from a visit to the USSR. Through a haze of preconceptions, he and others idealized what they imaged to be the brave new world of communist Russia. Their guided tours of the USSR were carefully managed by the Communists.

A spate of books announced the news that capitalism was now at last, as Marx had foreseen, strangling on its own insoluble problems of social relations. Only an end to private ownership of the means of production and the socialization of industry could realize the productive potential of modern technology, leading to plenty for all rather than poverty and unemployment amid idle plants and unused resources.

Well might Karl Radek (soon to be a victim of Stalin) boast in 1934 that, "In the heart of bourgeois England, in Oxford, where the sons of the bourgeoisie receive their final polish, we observe the crystallization of a group which sees salvation only with the proletariat." This was even more true at Cambridge, where a notorious group of future Soviet agents was being recruited in the early thirties from among the British elite (Kim Philby, Guy Burgess, Donald Maclean, Anthony Blunt), who would enter the Foreign Office and Intelligence

---

[4] A representative passage: "If Stalin has faith in the masses, this is reciprocated. The new Russia worships Stalin, but it is a worship created by confidence, which has risen wholly from the bottom. The man, whose silhouette on the gigantic posters appears superimposed on those of Karl Marx and of Lenin, is the man who looks after everything and everybody, who has done what has been done and who will do what is to be done. He has saved Russia in the past, and he will save it in the future." *Stalin, A New World Seen Through One Man,* trans. (New York: Macmillan, 1935), p. 281.

services to work as spies during and after World War II. The Left Book Club flourished; so did *Left News,* the *Left Review.* Left was right. And, Left meant, by and large, the most militant and confident of the radical groups, the Communists, radiant with the message that salvation was coming through Soviet Russia's great experiment in remaking humanity.

The new Marxists' crystal ball was occasionally clouded. A widely read 1932 book, John Strachey's *The Coming Struggle for Power,* foresaw a war between Great Britain and the United States, in which the desperate capitalists fought over receding markets. It predicted a Communist victory in Germany. Strachey also thought that John Maynard Keynes was about to become a Fascist. Keynes' *General Theory of Employment, Interest, and Money,* published in 1936, actually became the most important answer to Marxism published in this decade, offering a middle way between the apparently sterile formulae of the traditional economics, which counseled in effect doing nothing, and the doomsdayism of the extreme socialists.

In seeking to combat the Depression, the governments of Europe and the United States had followed the best advice they could get. They cut back government spending and allowed prices to fall; the conventional wisdom believed that this would encourage investment and lead to a natural correction of the deflation. This policy condemned the economy to stagnation, thus deepening the Depression. So much for science and intelligence! Why did this happen? Keynes believed that low interest rates failed to act as an automatic stimulant to investment and production, as they were supposed to do, because of a "liquidity preference": People preferred to save their money even at low interest rates, rather than invest it, because they wanted to have it ready for quick withdrawal. The reason for this might be fear of revolution or a general lack of confidence in business investments. The economic dissidents further argued that contrary to orthodox theory, "aggregate demand" is not normally high enough in a mature capitalism to produce full employment. In 1937, even so conservative an economist as A. C. Pigou, who had first rejected Keynes's arguments, in his *Socialism and Capitalism* came down somewhat on the side of the former. Capitalism was in trouble, deserted by even its friends if defined as competitive private enterprise without state regulation or intervention of any sort.

The Keynesians proposed to save capitalism by administering first aid rather than, as Marxians suggested, allowing the patient to die. Against the orthodox policy of balancing government budgets to lower costs, Keynes proposed that the government borrow and spend to counterbalance an alleged tendency to underinvest. A temporarily unbalanced government budget–*deficit spending*–would stimulate the private sector in crucial ways. Keynesianism departed from traditional dislike of government intervention without advocating total government control of the economy. Using its fiscal powers as a balance wheel, the government should expand or cut spending, lower or raise interest rates as the economic situation dictated. The economy would not "go of itself," as economic science had basically assumed ever since Adam Smith; but neither should one scrap private capitalism and the free market for an entirely different and probably unworkable system of state management.

The Keynesian model resembled that of some Swedish economists and was tried out in Sweden as well as, partially, in the American New Deal. It was to become the leading plan of theoretical macroeconomics for the next generation outside the Communist world. As Keynesianism mollified the harsh alternative of starvation or communism, the attractions of Russian-style communism weakened in the later 1930s. Ironically, the Western intellectuals discovered Soviet communism just as it was hardening into a grim tyranny. They sought to make an idol of a cruel dictator. The dynamism of the first Soviet Five-Year Plan, which many in the West contrasted with the passivity of their own governments, accompanied a war to collectivize the peasants that cost millions of lives. There was no unemployment in Russia, but there was virtual slavery.

The Moscow purge trials of the mid-1930s confronted Western intellectuals of the left with a painful dilemma. Just then at the peak of their enthusiasm for Soviet Russia, with Popular Front Communist-Socialist collaboration growing, they often tried to explain away the evidence of faked confessions extracted by torture, of the arrest and execution or imprisonment of huge numbers of obviously innocent people without trial or with a travesty of one. But the doubts grew. The immensity of Stalin's crimes could be more than guessed at in the 1930s: The American philosopher John Dewey headed a committee of investigation that exposed most of them, for which he was reviled as a "Trotskyist" by leftist pundits.

The Spanish Civil War itself brought doubts about the Communists to some of those who fought for or sympathized with the Spanish Republic, for the Communists under Russian domination used their power to terrorize other left-wing factions in the Republican coalition. Chief victim of Communist repression among the leftist parties in Spain was the POUM (Partido Obrero de Unificacion Marxista, that is, Workers' Party of Marxist Unification), which the Communists branded "Trotskyite," but which was in fact simply anti-Stalinist. George Orwell returned from Spain to record such indictments of the Communists in his book *Homage to Catalonia;* he had difficulty getting the book published and was abused for it by much of the left in 1938.

The Nazi-Soviet Pact of August 1939 was the real lesson in Soviet duplicity for most of the left-leaning writers of the 1930s. Whatever its sins or excesses, the Soviet Union, they thought, at least fought fascism at a time when the Western democracies were abjectly yielding to Hitler's demands. When Stalin, for whatever reason, made a deal with Hitler, who called him "a hell of a fellow" (and turned German Communists in Russia over to Hitler's vengeance), it was the signal for a mass exodus of those Western intellectuals remaining in the party; they later filled volumes with repentant explanations of "the god that failed."

In flight from "a hideous and decomposing world" in which they felt "an anguished sense of alienation," writers might join the Communist party seeking a faith to live by and write about, but once in they were far from happy and seldom stayed long. Writers who completely committed themselves to communism almost invariably found the experience creatively frustrating, because they had to conform to a formula. Those who did stay, like Bertolt Brecht, had to learn to suppress all individuality and obey the party blindly—difficult indeed for artists and intellectuals. Brecht's adherence to communism did not save his plays from being banned in Moscow as "formalist" and "decadent." For the Stalinist-Marxist as well as the Fascist-Nazi ideology rejected "modernisms" of whatever variety in the arts, or in science (Einsteinian). (Weirdly enough, these truly revolutionary twentieth-century creations were Communist to the Nazis and Nazi to the Communists. Stalin and company called them bourgeois decadence, the same tag they put on fascism; the Hitlerites saw both modernism and communism as stemming from the disintegration of a sound racial society under Jewish influence.)

Nevertheless, the decade produced an exciting literature. Some centered on Depression-bred themes: George Orwell's *Road to Wigan Pier* and his novels of down-and-outers, and John Steinbeck's *Grapes of Wrath* about American dustbowl migrants, for example. Others focused on the great political issues: Ernest Hemingway wrote now about the Spanish Civil War, and André Malraux also devoted one of his greatest works, *Man's Hope,* to the same struggle. Vast Balzacian chronicles of fictionalized social history appeared. Jules Romains produced no fewer than twenty-seven volumes in his *Les hommes de bonne volonté* cycle, carrying his "men of good will" through the twentieth century's memorable events from then to now. Other French novelists who specialized in the *roman fleuve* were Georges Duhamel and Roger Martin du Gard. Communist luminary Louis Aragon, once a surrealist, authored a political trilogy after his conversion to Communism. Such works generally focused on the congenial theme of social decay, chronicling the collapse of a civilization as revealed in the lives of sensitive individuals. Its decadents were more convincing than its socialist or proletarian heroes. George Orwell finally came to see that in fact all the socialists were bourgeois intellectuals: "The first thing that must strike any outside observer is that Socialism in its developed form is a theory entirely confined to the middle class."

Even as they attempted social realism, French writers could not escape the subjectivist influences of those subtle psychologists, Marcel Proust and André Gide. Gide himself flirted briefly with Stalin but was a notable defector at the time of the Moscow trials. Romains was a Socialist, not a Communist. Orwell, after being very close to the Communist party in the early 1930s, finally became its most persistent critic. Another was Arthur Koestler, a versatile German writer whose widely read novel *Darkness at Noon* explored the nightmare psychology of the purge trials and whose autobiographical writings, *Arrow in the Blue* and *The Invisible Writing,* give a matchless picture of life in the party.

A few conformed to the spirit of the 1930s in committing themselves to a cause but defied that spirit by going right rather than left. The neo-Christian revival started by Karl Barth and Jacques Maritain continued in the 1930s. T. S. Eliot, once the most thrilling of modernists, now announced himself a High Anglican, a royalist, and a classicist. As the editor of *Criterion,* he rallied religious humanists around a defense of traditional Western values against both fascism and communism. He saw both of them as rival religions, debased ones, that filled the vacuum in the Western soul left by its apostasy from the ancestral faith. A similar point may be found in Arnold J. Toynbee's inquiry into the decline of the West, *A Study of History* (Vols. 1–6, 1934–1939). Evelyn Waugh, C. S. Lewis, and others made their way back to traditional religion, "mere Christianity."[5] More startlingly, the leading British poet of the 1930s, W. H. Auden, originally a hero of the left, made his way through communism to emerge a Christian by the end of the decade. French novelist François Mauriac continued his long literary exploration of the roots of human nature's profound corruption. After having written in 1926 about *Notre Inquietude*–modern humanity's restless distress of spirit–Henri Daniel-Rops worked on a long multivolumed history of Christianity that was as popular as any work of historical scholarship these years produced, not only in France but elsewhere.

This very distinguished body of traditionalists sheds doubt on the generalization about the 1930s belonging entirely to the Marxists. But even traditionalists, in their apparent conservatism, reflected a radical alienation. In some ways their position embodied a more basic critique of all modern civilization than the Marxists'. Marxists accepted industrialism, science, democracy, and most other characteristics of modern Europe, claiming only to be able to manage them better than the bourgeoisie. But to actually believe in "mere Christianity"–what position could be more at odds with all the dominant forces of the twentieth century? "The world is trying the experiment of attempting to form a civilized but non-Christian mentality," wrote T. S. Eliot in 1930. "The experiment will fail."

A third group of writers of the thirties might be identified: those whose bitter despair found no solace either in Marxism or in Christianity or Judaism. One of these was Louis-Ferdinand Céline, author of *Le Voyage au bout de la nuit,* a book one critic described as "a terrible satire on the human race." Céline's voyage to the end of the night led him to become a Nazi collaborator with the German conquerors of his native France in World War II. In the same year that Céline's scatological masterpiece was published, 1932, Aldous Huxley turned to savage satire in his *Brave New World.* One of the first of the "dystopias," or reverse utopias, this novel showed what the triumph of technology and science and socialism and "progress" could bring. An earlier but then less well-known example of this genre was Yevgeny Zamyatin's *We,* by an early critic of Soviet

---

[5]C. S. Lewis's *The Screwtape Letters* was reprinted eight times within a year after it came out in 1941 and has since been read by millions; it may have converted more people to Christianity than Billy Graham. Those it converted were more likely to be, like the New York City Jewess Joy Davidman whom Lewis married, former atheists and communists.

Communism. *Animal Farm* and *1984* were George Orwell's well-known sequels, published just after the war.

A final case is Jean Paul Sartre's first novel published in 1938 and titled simply *Nausea*. This acclaimed work was the beginning of a quest that led the most famous of the existentialists to a courage beyond despair, but this first novel affirmed chiefly the terrible absurdity of existence.

Even Sartre was always a man of the left, dominated by his hatred for the class from which he sprang. The bourgeoisie had always lacked culture; now they could not even produce material goods. Their "system" of universal self-ishness stood convicted on not only moral but practical grounds. Capitalism was in deep trouble; fascism, the Marxists claimed, was its death agony; only so-cialism was sailing along toward a bright future under Stalin's benevolent guid-ance. So things seemed to an alienated intelligentsia in the era of the Great Depression. "In communism I see hope," said the British novelist E. M. Forster in 1936. "It does many things which I think evil, but I know that it intends good." Such faith—in a "working class" they did not understand and a dictator-ship they did not even know—was typical of mid-1930s intellectuals. They turned to it as solace from human suffering in their own land and the spectre of Hitlerism abroad, as the last remaining hope.

Although they were aware of some of the harsh features of Stalin's rule, which they accepted as "the necessary price of forging a new humanity"—no omelets without some broken eggs—most people in the West who were pro-Soviet had no notion of the magnitude of the suffering and killing, nor of Stalin's sadistic megalomania. Nor did most people in the USSR. Stalin's effective pub-lic relations team presented him as the kindly leader, stern only with traitors and wreckers, leading the USSR steadily upward toward a more humane and bountiful society. With such illusions did some Europeans and Americans steady themselves in the doleful Depression years.

7

The Background
of the Second World War

———————————————•————————•————————•——————————

The approach to World War II differed markedly from the beginnings of World War I. For one thing, World War I had come unexpectedly, a bolt from the blue, while the second war was all too predictable. As soon as they read the 1919 peace treaties, shrewd observers knew that another round was coming. The 1919–1939 period was a "long armistice" with only brief moments of stability. After Hitler solidified his control over Germany, it hardly required gifts of clairvoyance to perceive the dire threat to peace. And, from 1935 on, the world lived with almost constant international tension. Statesmen put off the inevitable with desperate expedients until they ran out of them in 1939.

There was far less enthusiasm for war this time. Not wildly cheering crowds but quiet, almost sullen ones greeted Hitler's announcement of war against Poland at the end of August 1939–quite a contrast with that other August a quarter of a century earlier. From a British perspective, T. S. Eliot noted the paradox in September 1939: "It is strange that in 1914 we did not expect a war and were not confused when it came. Now we have been expecting this for some time but are confused when it has come." What confused the approach to World War II, of course, was the deep revulsion against war, scarcely present at all in 1914 but very much so in the 1930s. Hitler was incomparably more evil than Wilhelm, Germany much more arrantly the aggressor in 1939 than in

217

1914—in this regard, the choice should have been easier for Germany's foes in 1939 than in 1914. But the feeling against war operated to inhibit preparations for war and thus inadvertently played into the Nazi dictator's hands. He profited from the weakness of the democracies.

"The distinguishing feature of the 1930s in England was that it was a time of resolute non-heroism," writes L.C.B. Seaman. While dictators in Italy, Russia, and Germany advertised dynamic ideologies, and even in the United States a charismatic president exhorted his people toward a "rendezvous with destiny," while Spain experienced a civil war and France had furious ideological battles, Great Britain celebrated the Silver Jubilee of King George V and re-elected Stanley Baldwin in 1935. The earnest entreaties of Britain's Left Book Club could not much disturb the complacency of a people who seemed able to enjoy even the Depression. George V himself, who warned in 1934 that "Germany is the peril of the world," could not persuade his people and ministers to take alarm. Later revealed as the scandal of the 1935 election was Baldwin's characteristically frank admission that he did not dare tell the truth about German rearmament to the British public, for raising such disturbing prospects would have guaranteed his defeat. Instead, there was a great "peace ballot," which demonstrated that the people would like the League of Nations to do something about the dictators, while Great Britain disarmed.

Franklin D. Roosevelt's rendezvous with destiny was, prior to 1940, conceived purely in American domestic terms (although FDR started out boldly in world affairs back in 1933, only to retreat when his projects badly miscarried). The United States was so profoundly isolationist that it enacted measures severely restricting trade with both sides in any future war. In 1934, also, the Congress passed a bill denying loans to European countries that had defaulted on their war debts. This bill was aimed primarily at France and Britain. The United States Army and Navy in the 1920s had devoted most of their planning to an anticipated war with the United Kingdom!

The "storm cellar" idea, which sought to insulate the United States from future wars by cutting off all contact with the belligerents, was a policy obviously based on the supposition that there could be no American interest in any war. It was based also on an interpretation that American entry into World War I had been totally and tragically mistaken. This wave of antiwar sentiment, marked by pacifist plays, novels, organizations, and demonstrations on college campuses, was at its peak about 1935. It was found most strongly among exactly those people who cheered for Roosevelt's programs of domestic reform—people on the left, the naturally anti-fascist. In this instance, they were objectively pro-fascist, in that their emotional hostility to war impeded any resistance to Hitler.

Young men in England took the "Oxford Oath," a popular vow among university students never again to march to war "for king and country." The motto of the French Socialists was "not a man, not a cent" for any military appropriation. Some even declared, "better servitude than war"—so deeply had the hatred of war penetrated: The eminent British philosopher Bertrand Russell wrote a pamphlet in 1936 arguing that it would be better to submit to Hitler than face another war (*Which Way to Peace?*). During the Popular Front of 1936–1938, as we noted, the Communists were unable to persuade the French left that there should be preparations for a war against Germany.

France, in fact, suffered from defeatism almost from the start. She simply was not prepared to face the prospect of another war with Germany, unless it was a war in which she could stay on the defensive and rely on her allies, Britain and the United States, to carry the brunt of battle. Again helplessly watching the rise of a powerful Germany, much more populous now than France—for French population was stationary at about forty million, while Germany's had risen to sixty-five million—the great majority of French people could not bring themselves to think about another conflict. World War I had drained them of the will.

Another factor preventing a firm front against Hitler was ideological conflict within the democracies. In conservative circles, the greater fear was of Stalin's state. "Better Hitler than Stalin!" (or even Blum!) was the motto of a part of the French right. While the left opposed fascism in principle but rendered this position useless by its pacifism, the right found fascism preferable to communism. The left, one English commentator remarked, wants to intervene everywhere and disarm; the right wants to rearm but intervene nowhere. In France, ideologists of the far right as well as the left fully accepted the drastic view that democracy was dead, and it only remained to choose between fascism and communism. Leaders of business and finance felt that fascism maintained order and upheld private property; bad as it was, one could live with it (Mussolini was admittedly a better model than Hitler). Communism was far worse, they thought. Faced with the unpleasant alternatives of war against Hitler, alliance with Stalin, or coming to terms with the German dictator, they much preferred the last.

The third sentiment that made it difficult for the victors of World War I to resist German resurgence was their sense of guilt about the Treaty of Versailles. This, too, was true on the left as well as the right. Historical investigations into the origins of World War I in the 1920s tended toward the "revisionist" view, that the Central Powers had not been solely guilty of bringing on the war. Perhaps the Allies had been equally to blame, or perhaps the culprit was that convenient abstraction, "the system"—political or economic. The peace settlement, it was widely believed, had been an act of unjustified hatred and revenge, in which the Allies had betrayed their own principles of democracy and self-determination of peoples.

Between 1935 and early 1939, Germany's aggressive actions could be interpreted as no more than her claim to rights that other countries held. In 1935, Germany demanded equality of armaments; in 1936, she asserted the right to send troops into her own territory. The Austrian *Anschluss* and the annexation of the Sudetenland, granted to Hitler in 1938, might be justified on the grounds that Germans lived in these regions. Neville Chamberlain, prime architect of the much-criticized policy of "appeasing" Germany, reflected such an outlook in March 1939 when he declared that, up until then, all of Germany's gains—the Rhineland, Austria, the Sudetenland—"however much we might take exception to the methods," might be defended, "whether on account of racial affinity or of just claims too long resisted." The British prime minister may have been looking for excuses, but Hitler had been able to make a case, attractive to large sections of British opinion, for righting the wrongs of an unjust peace and restoring equality of rights to Germany. The West's uneasy conscience assisted him.

The appeasers of Germany, as they were later called, at this time plausibly argued that in the long run a stable world required Germany's readmission to the comity of nations. One could not forever hope to exclude a great and powerful people from equal rights in the international community. Given these rights, Germans would perhaps lose their resentments, even reject Hitler, and resume a constructive role. Denied them, the Germans would support Hitler, brood on their wrongs, and plan a war of revenge.

The architects of appeasement later were called fools, though at the time few opposed them. (In 1937, a pacifist clergyman defeated Winston Churchill in an election to the rectorship of Glasgow University.) They were indeed poor leaders. But in truth, they were in an uncomfortable position as leaders of peoples who made no secret of their reluctance to countenance military measures. Preoccupation with the great economic depression mingled with ideological strife and, in France, the usual weakness of coalition governments to frustrate any strong foreign policy. But the most important factor was the hatred of war that World War I had left behind. "Never again!" "No more war!"

GERMANY REGAINS HER STRENGTH

Such views had been prevalent in Germany, too, prior to the Nazi revolution. One of the most famous of all antiwar novels, read all over the world and made into a poignant movie in 1931, was Erich Maria Remarque's *All Quiet on the Western Front*. Weimar wits made fun of Prussian militarists. Thomas Mann led a parade of repentant intellectuals and theologians (among them the future anti-Nazi Resistance hero, Dietrich Bonhoeffer) who embraced pacifism. But German opinion was always strongly colored by resentment at the unjust Treaty of Versailles and by feelings of revenge.

Even before 1933, Germany was not so helpless as she has often been depicted. The respectably democratic Weimar Republic secretly evaded some of the disarmament provisions of the Treaty of Versailles. The 1922 Treaty of Rapallo between Germany and the Soviet Union, a marriage of outcasts, accompanied significant military cooperation between the two governments. Germany provided Russia with war materials and established factories on Russian territory, and in return *Reichswehr* units were trained in the USSR.[1] If the Weimar Republic spent little on the military, the same was true of France and England, as public opinion turned against the fighting forces. While technically complying with the Versailles limit on the size of her army (100,000), Germany made it an "army of captains" capable of rapid expansion into a much larger force. After repudiation of the Versailles military clauses in 1935, the German military expanded rapidly to 800,000 by 1939 with a million more in reserve; during World War II, ten million Germans were to be mobilized.

It is also clear that the attempted breakup of the German General Staff did not succeed in ending German military planning. The Germans proved more inventive in the arts of war than did the World War I victors during this period. Colonel Charles de Gaulle tried in vain to interest the French in mobile tank warfare, which the Germans were to use with such devastating effect in 1940. The French thought in terms of the defensive, building great lines of fortification and, for the rest, playing with theories of victory by strategic air power. The Germans developed military aviation as a tactical arm that could cooperate closely with ground forces in offensive operations. They used Spain as a practice ground for these tactics (though to be sure they drew wrong conclusions about bomber design from experience in Spain, which contributed to their losing the Battle of Britain). Hitler restored two-year compulsory military service in 1935 and raised the morale of the previously neglected armed forces by praising the *Wehrmacht* as the incarnation of German character and will. Proud Prussian generals succumbed to the ex-enlisted man because of the favors he lavished on the fighting forces and his obvious interest in building them up.

The 1919 safeguards against German military revival broke down, one by one. Allied occupation of the Rhine bridgeheads came to an end in 1930. In 1935, as provided for in the Versailles treaty, a plebiscite was held in the coal-mining and industrial area of the Saar, on the Franco-German border, a region the French had been allowed to administer since 1920. The result was an overwhelming majority for reattachment to Germany. When later in this same year Hitler openly denounced the military provisions of the peace treaty, he met no resistance. The British, at least, had already conceded Germany's right to arms equality; and they proceeded to negotiate a naval treaty with Hitler that in effect acknowledged their own discarding of the Versailles disarmament terms. By this treaty, the Germans were to have a fleet no more than 35 percent of Britain's, thus maintaining Britain's historic two-to-one ratio.

Given the disarray of his foes, Hitler moved with considerable circumspection at first. His provocative actions included taking Germany out of the

[1]There is no evidence that military collaboration persisted between Germany and Russia to any significant extent after 1933. Indeed, it diminished after 1927 when withdrawal of Allied inspection removed much of the need for conducting military exercises outside of Germany. German-Soviet collaboration came to a halt with Hitler's arrival to power in 1933, though Stalin accused his generals of continuing to work with the Germans, as a pretext for his massive purge of the Red Army in 1937.

Geneva arms conference and out of the League of Nations, denouncing the Treaty of Versailles, and proceeding to rearm Germany. Having gotten away with these, in 1936 he sent German troops into the demilitarized zone of the Rhineland, defying not only Versailles but the Locarno Pact. It was a bold move, for such plans as the French had for security against Germany relied on keeping allies in the East–Poland and Czechoslovakia–by occupying a position of menace against Germany. They held such a position as long as the rich and populous Rhine regions of Germany lay undefended and thus open to attack. Once the Germans had reoccupied this region, they could and did build powerful fortifications, which rendered a French attack extremely difficult. So the 1936 move was crucial, and many historians have placed the decisive surrender at this point. For when Hitler turned next to the annexation of Austria and the Sudetenland, there was not much the French and the British could do about it.

Nevertheless, they did not react in 1936. The Germans were, after all, occupying only their own territory, something every other sovereign state had a right to do. We have already discussed the reasons for diplomatic passivity in the democracies. They were subsequently to regret their missed opportunity of 1936, when German rearmament had not yet proceeded very far. Neither, however, had British or French rearmament, both of which had been neglected for many years. France was undergoing a characteristic cabinet crisis. Moreover, both countries were distracted at this time by a quarrel with Italy. And again, what would be the result of marching into Germany? The French had memories of 1923. Chaos would result, perhaps Hitler would gain rather than lose German support, and the problem of restoring Germany to her normal status would remain. Out of weakness, the French tossed the ball to the British, who were in no doubt of their decision to postpone the fatal reckoning. After all, something might "turn up."

THE POPULAR FRONT

At this time, the Soviet Union had reversed its previous position, following the stunning Nazi success in 1933–1934, and decided on a new tactic of attempted cooperation with other socialist and even "bourgeois liberal" parties, in a common front against the menace of Hitlerite Germany.

The great purge trials were about to begin in Moscow. They were intended to strike terror into the hearts of all enemies of the Soviet state and thus strengthen that state. But from the evidence of the millions arrested, one had to assume either that the USSR was filled with treason from one end to the other, or else that a madman was at its helm. In particular, the vast army purge, wiping out the entire leadership of the Red Army including its most able and vigorous figures, such as Marshal Tukhachevsky, threatened incalculable damage to Soviet military capability. Thus the result of the purge, which subsided somewhat only in late 1938, was to increase distrust between the USSR and the outer, capitalist world. Paradoxically, though, at this same time Stalin was trying to woo the outside world. Though a rationale of the purge was the need to stand guard against assumed attempts by the agents of capitalism constantly to spy on, to wreck, to subvert the workers' state, yet Stalin had now decided, with another part of his mind, for détente with France and Great Britain.

From 1935 on, the strategy of the popular front dominated Russian foreign policy. By 1936, Stalin was granting interviews with foreign journalists and writers, for example. H. G. Wells and the American newspaper tycoon Roy Howard, in which he assured them that Russia did not seek to export Communist revolution. "Socialism in one country" required peaceful relations with the outer world, trade with capitalist nations, and normalization of diplomatic relations with their governments. This abrupt change in 1935 was the first of two about-faces in the 1930s that embarrassed those party members who had qualms about being intellectually inconsistent.

Hitler's triumph had caused a basic rethinking in Moscow. Underestimating and misunderstanding the Nazi movement, Communists had actually helped Hitler gain power. National Socialism's evident solidity and German rearmament forced the Kremlin to adopt an entirely different line, with stress now on the strategy of seeking allies against fascism among other parties of the left. Having spent much of their time since 1927 calling the socialists "social fascists" and hired agents of reaction, the Communists now suddenly began to hail them as comrades. The main object was to influence foreign policy, especially in France, a potential ally against Germany. To strengthen French military power, secure an alliance with the Soviet Union, and prepare to defend against Hitler's expected attack became the goal of the French Communist party—which, now that the German Communists had virtually disappeared, was the leading Communist party of Europe outside of the USSR.

The Socialists (SFIO) were the larger of the two French left-wing parties. In 1934, it was the second-largest French political party, with 131 of the 618 deputies. But the previously quite small Communist party increased its strength after 1931, and the two parties were bitter rivals for the leftist vote. The SFIO was itself split, with a left wing close to communism and a right wing closer to the bourgeois liberals. Bad feeling between the two parties stemmed from the war and the secession of minority Socialists to join the Third International just after the war. French Socialists resented Moscow's persecution of Menshevik Social Democrats, their comrades in the Second International, while Communists sneered at the Socialists as "traitors to the working class." Socialists replied that the French Communists were kept by Moscow gold, and insults were freely exchanged until the reconciliation of 1935–1939.

Communists who had yesterday jeered at "social chauvinism" now became ardent patriots, as well as proponents of class collaboration. This strategy persisted until September 1939, when another startling *volte face* accompanied the Nazi-Soviet pact. Stalin had by then decided, for all too evident reasons, that the Popular Front had failed to swing French foreign policy to resist Germany.

But between 1935 and 1938, until the Munich Pact, Communists in all countries outside the USSR were willing and eager to work with other parties to form coalitions. The other parties were understandably wary of this sudden change of heart, coming as it did from those who had long assailed them with bitter denunciations. That the new line was manufactured in Moscow was all too apparent.

On the other hand, the logic of a united front against fascism, both within the country and without, did appeal to Western socialists and liberals. Yet opinion on the left in France, Britain, and the United States was generally hostile to rearmament and to risks of war. The Communists faced a losing battle in their attempts to convert the left to war in the atmosphere of the Great Depression. In France, they supported Leon Blum's government in alliance with Socialists and Radical Socialists, then supported even the Radical Socialist Edouard Daladier. But when Daladier's government initialed the Munich settlement of October 1938, appeasing Hitler at the price of Czechoslovakia, the Communists tried to organize a general strike in protest against this policy. This met with no success.

If the Popular Front in France was a failure from the Communist point of view, it was equally a disappointment in Spain, the other main arena where it was tried out. With the outbreak of the Civil War in 1936, Spain became a main focus of European politics and provided one of the decade's most dramatic contests between communism and fascism/Nazism, as we have already noted.

THE SPANISH CIVIL WAR

Established in 1931, the Spanish Republic stumbled over the same obstacle that troubled other parliamentary democracies: the rivalry of numerous disagreeing parties, who were unable to form the basis for a stable government. One of Spain's leading philosophers and historians categorized her as "invertebrate," that is, lacking unifying elements. The dictator Primo de Rivera fell in 1930, followed soon by the monarchy itself. (Alfonso XIII did not abdicate but withdrew, expressing the hope that eventually he would regain the love of his people. The Cortes soon voted him guilty of high treason.) A wave of republican sentiment swept over Spain, and a peaceful revolution seemed to have the support of almost everybody. This proved to be an illusion. The republic's history was to be short and tragic.

The revolution aroused hopes of widely varying sorts, which the new regime was too weak to fulfill, and bitter hostilities reappeared. The Cortes elected in June 1931 contained a majority of Socialists and leftist liberals; with the right temporarily discredited and the Anarchists on the extreme left abstaining from politics, there appeared to be a comfortable parliamentary basis for a moderate coalition. But the more extreme Socialists, headed by Francisco

Largo Caballero, demanded proletarian revolution—seizure of power and property by soviets of workers and peasants. They were also violently anticlerical, in
a country where many associated the church with aristocracy and monarchy.
The first republican government alienated the army by drastically reducing
the number of officers and began to confiscate estates to give land to the rural
poor. Divided between moderates and revolutionaries, the republic thus earned
the bitter hatred of three powerful elements on the right: army, church, and
aristocracy.

A split between the president, Alcala Zamora, and the prime minister,
Manuel Azana, provoked the fall of Azana and new elections in 1933. The left
now suffered a reverse; the antisocialist Catholic Popular Action emerged as the
strongest party. Meanwhile the son of a former dictator, José Antonio Primo de
Rivera, created a Spanish Fascist movement, the Falange, distinct from the
more traditional, monarchist right. In 1934, the Asturian miners rebelled
against the government and were put down with the aid of Moorish troops, at
the cost of several thousand casualties. The socialists cried that the revolution
was being betrayed; the army conspired; the Catalans of the northeast insisted
on autonomy. A general strike was called. The events of October 1934 were a
rehearsal for the bloody civil war that began two years later. Governments became feebler and shorter in duration. Invertebrate Spain reverted to its disunity.
Elections held in early 1936 brought a lurch back to the left. Proclaiming a crusade against fascism, the new government now found itself confronted by an
open rebellion led by army elements under the command of General Francisco
Franco and General Emilio Mola.

World public opinion was to dramatize the Spanish Civil War as a
showdown conflict between communism and fascism. With the intervention of
Mussolini, and to a lesser degree Hitler, on the side of Franco's "Nationalists,"
and of Soviet Russia on the side of the Republican "Loyalists," it did take on
some such quality. But it should be noted that neither communism nor fascism
had much strength in Spain when the civil war began. A small Spanish Communist party existed, but communism of whatever sort usually made little appeal to the Spanish radicals, who gave their allegiance either to a democratic,
gradualist socialism or else to the Anarchists. In largely premodernized Spain,
the strength of the revolutionary movement lay in the country, not the city. Anarchism, with its romantic cult of direct action, its suspicion of the state and all
centralized power, its intense moral idealism and "cult of courage," appealed to
the Spanish temperament. Anarchist doctrine preached economic rather than
political action, total destruction of the state rather than seizure of it, and a decentralized society after the revolution. As anarcho-syndicalism, such ideas
found their way into the labor movement; the revolution would come via the
general strike, after which the unions would manage industry locally and democratically. French anarcho-syndicalist ideas, strong at the end of the nineteenth
century, made a powerful impression in Spain.

As for Spanish fascism, represented by the Falange, it was unimportant prior to the civil war, and, contrary to a persistent legend, never struck roots in Spain. Only military dependence on Italy and on Russia caused the Spanish Fascists and Communists to exercise influence out of all proportion to their numbers once the civil war began in earnest. The execution of Primo de Rivera early in the civil war gave the Falange a martyr, but Franco always distanced himself from this rather revolutionary Spanish fascism, which was anticlerical and populist and which never had a very large following. Hitler raged at the "priests and monarchists" who had seized power in Spain, rather than a true National Socialism. These were his "mortal enemies"! Communism attained some popularity in 1936–1937, aided by the charisma of Dolores Ibarruri, "La Pasionaria."

No military genius, Franco was forced to depend on German and Italian military advice as well as aid. The same thing happened to the Republican Loyalists in the later part of the civil war. Sustained by Soviet aid, the Loyalists had to allow the Spanish Communist party power as the price of this aid. The anti-Communist Socialist, Indalecio Prieto, resigned as minister of defense in April 1938, on the issue of Communist influence. Juan Negrin, the professor of physiology who became prime minister in May 1937, was not a Communist, but he worked closely with the Communists, feeling that this was the only way the war could be won.

If the failure of the republican regime was in part the fault of too many divisions among its supporters, so too was their defeat in the civil war of 1936–1939. Basically, the split was among these elements: (1) moderate Socialists, along with some Liberals or Republicans (Prieto and Azana were among this group); (2) the left-wing Socialists, aligned loosely with Anarchists and the anti-Moscow POUM Communists (often called "Trotskyists"); and (3) the official Communists and those who, for practical reasons, allied with them. But such a model scarcely does justice to the volatility of the Iberian temperament. Largo Caballero, most formidable of the Republican leaders, was an emotional revolutionary socialist whose rhetoric alarmed middle-class elements but who also resisted Communist police-state methods, which he said smacked of the fascism they were fighting.

The Western democracies failed to support the Loyalists. While until mid-1938 France permitted supplies from the Soviet Union to enter via the Spanish-French border, neither France nor Great Britain sent aid to the republic after the first few weeks. They organized a nonintervention committee among the powers, which Hitler and Mussolini joined even as they were openly aiding Franco's Nationalist side. Refusing to distinguish between the legitimate government and its rebel foes, France and Britain declared an arms embargo, and the United States followed suit in voting a ban on the sale of weapons to either side. Britain under Neville Chamberlain was well-launched on its policy of appeasing Hitler. From the beginning of the civil war, Spain became a pawn in the games of the great powers. Hitler sent the Condor Legion to practice modern warfare; Mussolini wished prestige; the Russians were playing for a Popular

Front alliance with the Western democracies against Nazi Germany. None really cared much about Spain, and that was a part of the tragedy. In November 1937, discussing plans for German expansion at a secret conference, Hitler argued that a complete Franco victory in Spain was not immediately desirable; to have the war continue would best serve German interests, by keeping alive tensions between Russia and the democracies and diverting attention from other areas.

The Spanish civil war became a symbol of the age chiefly because, in this ideology-intoxicated era, the intellectuals of the world adopted it as one. They sent volunteers to fight fascism in a crusade reminiscent of 1914, only this time it was seen as an international civil war ranging the sons of light against the sons of darkness. Forty thousand volunteers served in the International Brigade, where many anti-Hitler refugees from Germany joined British, French, and American idealists. The Abraham Lincoln battalion came from the United States. André Malraux volunteered and hired twenty pilots. "Spain was the first and the last crusade of the British leftwing intellectual," Neal Wood writes, with only a slight exaggeration. "Never again was such enthusiasm mobilized."

The war was a dramatic one, colored by the somber tones of the Spanish countryside and the Spanish temperament. It was bloody. Of some 2,500 British volunteers, nearly 550 were killed. The whole war, marked by massacres and cruel reprisals against civilians by both sides, cost at least half a million lives (popular lore said a million), in a land with a total population of twenty-five million. The victorious Franco regime perpetuated the memory of atrocities committed by the Loyalists, such as the execution in November and December 1936 of several thousand Nationalist military prisoners, but seldom mentioned their own crimes.

The visitor to Madrid today can still see the destruction of the wealthy homes that had adorned the city's stately avenues. The apparently pointless extinction of the defenseless Basque town of Guernica by German bombers inspired Pablo Picasso's immortal painting. The heroism of the armed workers was celebrated in liberal circles all over the world. But from the start, the rebel Nationalists, with most of the regular army, held the military advantage.

Germany supplied only a few thousand men but several hundred planes and military supplies. Mussolini kept about 30,000 Italians in the field. In the decisive battle of Bilbao, in June 1937, Italian troops played an important part; it is not true that the Italians generally fought badly. On the other side, though Stalin gave substantial military supplies (over a thousand aircraft), he committed only a handful of men, chiefly military advisers. In return, he insisted on controlling the republic's policies, which led to fierce in-fighting between Communists and other Loyalist factions.

The fall of the French Popular Front government in June 1938 led to the closing of the route through which Russian aid had passed. Even before that, Stalin had begun to withdraw Soviet support from Spain. His intervention had been largely dictated by the desire to forge an alliance with the Western democracies; giving up on that, he lost interest in Spain. Franco soon launched his final offensive in northeast Spain against the last Loyalist stronghold, and the greatly outnumbered Loyalists could not hold him back. Hundreds of thousands of people fled from Catalonia across the border into France. The end came on April 1, 1939, with the unconditional surrender of the last Loyalist forces. France and Great Britain, capping their basically pro-Franco "neutrality," had already recognized the Nationalist government on February 27.

It took Spain a generation to recover from the trauma. For her, World War II had started early. (She stayed out of the 1939–1945 war.) For the rest of the world, Spain was a battle in the war between fascism and communism for the minds of men, with democracy a bewildered onlooker. In the context of 1930s diplomacy, the civil war was a chapter in the history of appeasement, for Britain and France (along with the United States), hoping to avoid war, let Hitler and Mussolini have their way. But in fact Franco's Spain was to be of no value to the Germans in World War II.

HITLER PREPARES FOR WAR

Those in the West who thought that Hitler's goal was simply to restore Germany to her 1914 borders or reclaim only those peoples who were ethnically German failed to judge the true dimensions of his "world view." He intended to conquer and enslave the Slavic East, whose "sub-men" were destined, he thought, to be ruled by the superior Aryans. This *Weltanschauung* was so bizarre that the aristocratic gentlemen at Whitehall and the rational bureaucrats at the Quai d'Orsay may perhaps not be blamed for refusing to believe it, even if Hitler had set much of it down in his autobiography, *Mein Kampf,* some years before. But in fact he was serious.

One element in the National Socialist outlook was a crude social Darwinism. "Nature is cruel, therefore we too may be cruel. . . . I have a right to remove millions of an inferior race that breeds like vermin." Thus spake *der Führer* in 1934. He was to practice euthanasia on sick and old people in Germany, until public opinion forced a halt, and later he would try to exterminate the Jews of eastern Europe. It may be noted that this viewpoint cut right across German nationalism, for Hitler was as prepared to sacrifice the weak to the strong in Germany as anywhere else, and indeed he was prepared to see the whole German nation perish if it could not meet the challenge of struggle. When Germany was losing the war in 1944–1945, Hitler thought the German people should rightly perish, for it "has proved itself weak." Those who remain after the battle are of little value, he reflected, for "the good have fallen." This frighteningly literal and utterly consistent application of the law of the jungle to human affairs was close to the heart of Adolf Hitler's philosophy.

The German frontiers of 1914 obviously had not been good enough, for had not Germany lost that war despite valiant efforts? She must expand or die. "Every people strives for world domination," said Hitler. The key to success in diplomacy and war is "an iron will," an ability to be "fanatical," to stop at nothing. His foes, Hitler thought, did not have this quality. France was degenerate, the United States Judaized (Hitler seems to have thought Roosevelt was a Semitic name), Britain decadent, Russia racially inferior and led by Jewish Marxists. Anti-Semitism was for Hitler "so intensive a mania that it completely shattered the faculty of reason," as one who knew him testified and as is obvious from all he did. Purged of the Jewish poison that infected other states, Germany was bound to be stronger than they. Strength relies basically on the will, on moral factors; Hitler scorned economics and even technology in favor of racial purity, strength of will, "fanaticism" as the most important survival qualities. In this regard, he was a disciple of Machiavelli: "In politics there are no sentiments, only toughness."

The national will-to power must be expressed through its one leader, a principle the Nazis had insisted on from the beginning: *Führerprinzip*, the leadership principle. The democracies' clumsy system of divided counsels and fluctuating government prevented them from acting with firmness and dispatch, as Germany could under Hitler. With this great advantage, Hitler thought he was certain to be an easy winner in any game of power with the democracies. The Nazi dictator was capable of skillful acting. At times a raging madman, he could be charming, relaxed, or totally calm and composed as the situation demanded. He accompanied each of his daring thrusts with soothing words, promising that this would be Germany's final demand.

The end justifies any means. The end, for Hitler, was the power of the German nation and state, driving for world power in an international jungle where the rule was eat or be eaten; do unto others before they do it unto you. In particular, Hitler believed, Germany must have land and food for her growing population. This could be found in Russia, where the Slavs would be conquered and enslaved or exterminated to make way for the Aryans. Since the Jewish Bolsheviks were unable to organize and govern a state, Russia was ripe for the taking. (Hitler seemed unaware that Stalin represented, in part, a Russian anti-Semitic rejection of the Jewish element in the Marxist party.) Reinforcing Hitler's instinctive anticommunism and anti-Slavism, which he had acquired in Austria in his youth, was his attachment to the geopolitical ideas of Professor Karl Haushofer, whose pupil Rudolf Hess was an early Nazi and close friend of Hitler. Haushofer, building on theories of Sir Halford Mackinder, taught that the key to world power lay in control of the Eurasian heartland. "At long last we break off the colonial and commercial policy of the pre-War period and shift to the soil policy of the future," Hitler put it in *Mein Kampf.* Such a formula had the advantage of being consistent with the Nazi yearning for a rural folk community.

Whether Hitler in power would stick to these earlier theorizings was not certain. He had also talked of the need to deal with the implacable enemy, France. Toward the English he was usually more favorably disposed. A tough and tenacious people, racially akin to the Germans, they had much to teach him; he admired their imperialism and seemed willing to let them keep the seas if he could have the land! Hitler's susceptibility to *mal de mer* has been suggested as a reason for his lack of interest in sea-power, a trait he shared with Napoleon; in any case the *Weltanschauung* led him toward a kind of agrarian imperialism. The drive to the East stayed with him, and in 1941, apparently against all reason, he returned to it, feeling then "spiritually free." Meanwhile, the ever-growing might of his Germany, and the weakness of any force that could oppose it, tempted the Nazi dictator to push whatever gates offered themselves for the opening.

November 5, 1937, has been selected by some as the day Hitler definitely opted for war. At least it brought a rather sensational revelation of his grand designs, which he presented to his foreign minister, war minister, and commanders of the army, navy, and air force at a secret conference. Germany must secure space, and this *Lebensraum* would have to be obtained by "the way of force." The time was ripe, for all Germany's rivals were in trouble. It is hard not to agree with Hitler here. The Soviet Union, remember, was in the middle of the purge; a new recession had hit the West. A few more years and it might be too late. Austria and Czechoslovakia would be the first victims; England and France would not defend them. Stunned by the shameless belligerence of Hitler's speech, Neurath, Blomberg, and Fritsch warned of the risks involved. Within a few months, they were all out of office. Not only was Fritsch framed on charges of homosexuality, but the obliging Heinrich Himmler was also able to discover that Werner von Blomberg had recently taken as his second wife an ex-prostitute.

With himself as head of the war office and the subservient Joachim von Ribbentrop, former champagne salesman, as his foreign minister, Hitler was ready to unleash the dogs of war with little to restrain him. Schacht's resignation and the cessation of cabinet meetings mark this as the moment Hitler became absolute master of the Third Reich and embarked on a policy of territorial expansion.

THE DIPLOMACY OF ALLIANCES

What was to stop him from becoming master of all Europe? "For every Frenchman between the ages of 20 and 30 there are two Germans," a French army officer named Charles de Gaulle wrote in 1934. Germany produced twice as much steel as France, and greater quantities of most of the other industrial products that are the sinews of war. Ardent patriot that he was, de Gaulle was forced to concede that alone, France had no chance against Germany. The French at this time overestimated German military strength. They probably held an edge in 1936, we now know, but they did not think so. The French generals were depressed at the low state of French military power, which General Weygand lamented in 1934 had "sunk to the lowest level that the security of France can allow."

The only answer lay in finding allies. Great Britain was a highly unreliable one. She had shrunk back into her old isolation and was not committed to the Continent. The Anglo-German Naval Treaty of 1935 showed that she would make her own terms with Germany without so much as consulting France. France's habit of looking to London for a lead was fatal in 1935, 1936, and 1937, for the British had no intention of "pulling French chestnuts out of the fire." Acceptance of German rearmament and a friendly policy toward Germany were the deliberate policies of the British government, approved in 1935 by Tories and Labourites alike. Britain's strength was simply not great enough to police both Europe and the now unstable Far East.

Given the weakness and the divisions of the smaller countries of eastern Europe, there remained only Italy–and Russia. France tried each in 1935, with little success. The Franco-Italian détente was nourished on hopes that Mussolini did not want Germany to take over Austria, and in 1934 this seemed true. Civil war broke out in Vienna in February 1934, after the failure of a socialist general strike. The army shelled a working-class housing project, the Karl Marx Hof, that was defended by socialist militia. Torn by civil strife, Austria then experienced an attempted Nazi coup after the Christian Socialist head of government, Engelbert Dollfuss, was assassinated. Mussolini sent Italian troops to the Brenner Pass in a show of force that caused Hitler to back away from the Austrian Nazis for the time being. At this time, there was scarcely any love lost between the two Fascist dictators; *il duce*, at least, both feared and disliked Hitler. Not only was the little Austrian a rival in the field of international fascism, stealing Mussolini's thunder in an uncouth way, but he opposed Italian interests in Austria. We must remember that Italy had fought against Germany in World War I.

In April 1935, British Prime Minister Ramsay MacDonald, nearing the end of his career, journeyed with his foreign secretary, John Simon, to join France's Pierre Flandin and Pierre Laval to meet with Benito Mussolini at Stresa in northern Italy. Hitler had just torn up the Treaty of Versailles. The British were even then engaged in negotiating the naval treaty with him that so enraged the French. In retrospect, the "Stresa front" was an abortion, but for the moment hopes were raised of a Franco-Italian-British union, which might deal firmly with the German threat. But not only did it quickly become evident that the British wanted no part of any continental involvement carrying the risk of war, it also became clear that the Italian leader was now on a course that would bring him into collision with the British. The French were caught hopelessly in the middle between their two dubious allies. The Ethiopian crisis was about to distract everybody's attention, allowing Hitler to pick up the Rhineland.

Italians had long smarted from the defeat they had suffered at the hands of Ethiopian warriors in 1896, and Italy had long harbored African ambitions. In a 1934 speech, Mussolini proclaimed that Italy's "historical objectives" lay in Asia and Africa: "Of all the large Western powers of Europe, Italy is the nearest to Africa and Asia." This was the focus of the ancient Roman Empire, which Mussolini yearned to revive.

The Italians had been trying to penetrate Ethiopia for some time. Laval, the French foreign minister, had led Mussolini to believe that France would approve his Ethiopian project in return for opposing Hitler in Europe. But the British did not approve. They had their own interests in this part of the world, so near the Suez Canal, and they reacted by attempting to keep Italy out of all but an insignificant portion of this area.

An incident at Wal Wal led to fighting between Italians and Ethiopians; Ethiopian Emperor Haile Selassie eloquently appealed to the League of Nations for help against Italian aggression; and the British took up the cause of Ethiopia at Geneva. Rome's reaction was an angry one: Perfidious Albion sought selfishly to hog colonial spoils while sanctimoniously condemning anyone else who played the imperialist game. In the autumn of 1935, the issue caught the attention of the world as a test case of "collective security." A general election was impending in Britain, and the League was a popular symbol.

As the small states rallied to the cause of collective security, the League branded Italy an aggressor and voted economic sanctions against her. The British mounted a show of naval strength in the Mediterranean. Italy was almost isolated, and Mussolini's political career seemed threatened. Laval, however, still trying to keep Italy as an ally against Germany, desperately sought a compromise. Hitler offered to help the British against Italy. In return, he wanted British support for his annexation of Austria. The outcome of this almost classic muddle was about as bad as it could be. Economic sanctions, never applied more than halfheartedly, did not prevent Italy from conquering Ethiopia, in an unexpected display of military efficiency. Ill and suffering from exhaustion, the inexperienced Samuel Hoare replaced John Simon as British foreign secretary in June 1935. Adding to the confusion in British affairs was the death of King George V, followed by the dramatic crisis of Edward VIII's abdication, the result of his proposed marriage to an American divorcee. This absorbed British attention throughout the year 1936.

Halfway into the Ethiopian crisis, the British retreated and joined with France in a compromise, the Hoare-Laval plan, which managed to undercut the idealism of the collective security crusade. Having condemned Italy in righteous terms as a criminal, the "police" now offered to give her half of the loot. A public outcry forced withdrawal of this "deal," but the Italians pressed on to capture the Ethiopian capital in May 1936.

Perhaps more important, Mussolini was bitterly estranged from Britain and turned toward Hitler, soon beginning the "brutal friendship" by collaboration in Spain. Hitler, who took advantage of the confusion to occupy the Rhineland (March 1936) was the only clear winner in this comedy of errors, which reinforced his contempt for the democratic leaders.

Laval, an able politician with a reputation for slipperiness that followed him to his tragic end a decade later, also explored the Soviet alliance. Pushed by Louis Barthou during his foreign ministry in 1934, the project suffered a setback when Barthou was assassinated along with King Alexander of Yugoslavia in October 1934 at Marseille. Alexander had been working to form a Balkan alliance aimed at Germany, so that the assassination, the work of Croatian and Macedonian terrorists headquartered in Hungary, perhaps with Italian connivance, was a double blow at the policy of shaping an alliance against Hitler. Laval continued the approach to Russia, and in 1935 a treaty was concluded, in which France and the USSR promised each other aid in the event of "unprovoked aggression."

The Franco-Soviet treaty was anathema to the French right and not very appealing to much of the left either. Events in Russia soon intensified skepticism about the value or the morality of having Stalin's regime as an ally. London was cool to the treaty, which clashed also with the concurrent attempt to woo Italy. Despite the valiant efforts of Soviet Minister Maxim Litvinov, a real "collective security" front against Germany never got off the ground—the main diplomatic tragedy of these years, many think. If leading French and British circles were hysterically anti-Soviet, Stalin was remote and suspicious. He decided early that the rulers of the Western democracies were plotting to appease Hitler at Russia's expense. Their actions in 1937 and 1938 gave all too much support to this paranoid view.

THE DIPLOMACY OF APPEASEMENT

A huge majority of Austrians wanted to join their fellow nationals in Germany after the breakup of the Hapsburg monarchy in 1919, but the World War I victors would not let them. The World Court frustrated an attempt at peaceful *Anschluss,* or union, with Germany again in 1931. It is not surprising that Austrian-born Hitler, who had mentioned the matter on the first page of *Mein Kampf,* raised the *Anschluss* issue early in his career of expansion. He found the way open after he made friends with Mussolini.

Early in February 1938, Hitler invited Kurt von Schuschnigg to his mountain retreat at Berchtesgaden and there browbeat the unfortunate Austrian chancellor into appointing a Nazi as minister of interior and legalizing the Austrian Nazi party. Returning to Vienna, Schuschnigg recovered his courage and proposed a plebiscite on the issue of *Anschluss.* It is not clear whether a majority of Austrians would have supported it now that it meant Nazism. Hitler hastily mounted an invasion of Austria; Schuschnigg called off the plebiscite, but the German troops continued on, unopposed, and Hitler proclaimed the outright annexation of Austria, not just a federal union. Scenes of terror occurred as the Nazis took revenge on political enemies, Jews, leftists. The flight of old Sigmund Freud to London symbolized the end of Austrian freedom on March 11–13.

All this drew no response from the world except perfunctory protests. Hitler was most worried by Italy, in view of the 1934 action, and when Mussolini smiled this time Hitler effusively thanked him. France, as so often, was without a government on this weekend. Neville Chamberlain thought it "an unpleasant affair" but looked past it to better relations with a happier Germany. It is true that serious British rearmament dates from this revelation of Hitler's brutality. But a plebiscite, arranged by the Nazis, soon produced a predictably overwhelming mandate for them in Austria, endowing the seizure with a facade of legitimacy.

The next victim on Hitler's schedule was Czechoslovakia. This was a very different situation. True, a minority of Germans lived along the northern fringe of the land of the Czechs and Slovaks. They had been left there, perhaps unwisely, in 1919. Toward this minority (some three and a quarter million of fifteen million) Hitler directed his propaganda, aided by a vociferous Sudetenland Nazi party. But they were not capable of threatening the Czech state. Czechoslovakia had a substantial and efficient army, a well fortified frontier, a notable arms industry (the Skoda works at Pilsen and Brno were world-famous), and a generally loyal public opinion. She also had an alliance with France. Whether all this could defend her against Nazi Germany remained to be seen. There was hardly any way of "blitzing" Czechoslovakia or of intimidating Prague, as Vienna had been.

"Who is master of Bohemia is master of Europe," Bismarck once said in words that keen student of history, Adolf Hitler, doubtless remembered. After the annexation of Austria, the more populous and prosperous end of Czechoslovakia intruded itself into Germany like a large thumb pressed against her midsection, an obvious target for engulfment. More to the point, Prague was closer to Berlin than was Paris or London; Czechoslovakia was an "aircraft carrier" in the heart of Europe, Hitler said. Still more to the point, Czechoslovakia was vulnerable. Her alliance with France was useless unless France attacked Germany, for neither the French nor the British could get troops to Czechoslovakia by any feasible land route. Having constructed his Siegfried Line of fortifications on the French border, Hitler could be sure the French would hesitate to attack. In any case, the French seemed politically in chaos and quite demoralized. For the future, Russia might be a threat, but hardly now, just after the shattering purges of military and party. Reason enough not to delay; Hitler did not think time was on his side.

He asked for the return of ethnic Germans, oppressed, he claimed, by Prague. The Sudetenlanders had some legitimate grievances but were far from an oppressed people. Yet the German case was plausible enough to win over the British ambassador at Berlin, Nevile Henderson, who asserted that, "It is morally unjust to compel this solid Teuton minority to remain subjected to a Slav central government at Prague." The British, unlike the French, had no treaty commitment to defend the Czechs and made it clear from the start that they did not intend to go to war for them. It is often supposed that Prime Minister Neville Chamberlain gave in at the Munich conference only after long

Munich Conference. Chamberlain and Hitler with Mussolini and Daladier in October, 1938. The climax of "appeasement." (*National Archives.*)

pressure from Germany, but in fact he had never intended to resist. The series of conferences at Berchtesgaden, Godesberg, and Munich in September of 1938, in which Chamberlain and French Premier Edouard Daladier dealt with Hitler, concerned the means by which Czechoslovakia was to be dismembered; the principle was never in doubt.

The disgraceful part, as it later seemed, was that Britain and France actually joined in browbeating the little country into giving up territory without a fight. Their object was to avoid war by granting to the Nazi dictator what he was threatening to seize by force. At Berchtesgaden, Chamberlain agreed to "self-determination" for the Sudeten Germans, and he got Prague to accept this. But when he brought this agreement back to Hitler at Godesberg on September 22, the Germans made new demands: The transfer must take place within eight days, a haste that ensured disorder and humiliation for the Czechs. Angered, Chamberlain returned to London; but on September 29 he came back to Germany and, at Munich, secured only small modifications of this timetable. It was not unlike offering to pay $1,000,000 blackmail, being asked then to pay $2,000,000, and settling for $1,500,000.

Had the Czechs chosen to fight, their excellent defenses and strong army surely could have put up much more than token resistance. The *Wehrmacht* was hardly yet the formidable machine it subsequently became; some of Hitler's generals were restive, and a center of opposition to him appeared in the army at this time. Perhaps this was one of history's great missed opportunities. Such was the legend that later grew: But for cowardice and narrow vision, Hitler might have been stopped in his tracks and World War II avoided. But public opinion in the democracies overwhelmingly supported Chamberlain and Daladier. Cheering crowds greeted them on their return. ("The fools, why are they cheering?" the French premier wondered; Chamberlain seems to have had no such doubts.) Poet laureate John Masefield hailed Chamberlain as a modern hero, going into the night

> To ask that young men's bodies, not yet dead,
> Be given from the battle not begun.

He had snatched safety from danger, saved the world from a horrible war. Very few wanted it otherwise. War was too terrible to contemplate. Simone Weil's view that the Munich *amoindrissement* (or "calming of tensions") was "a thousand times right" was typical of the intellectuals, the Communists apart. President Roosevelt sent Chamberlain a telegram of congratulations.

More realistically, Chamberlain knew that British rearmament was just getting under way and that both Britain and France would be stronger later. No fool, Chamberlain was buying time, aware that the gamble of appeasing Hitler's appetite with Austria and part of Czechoslovakia might fail. "They had to choose between war and dishonor. They chose dishonor; they will have war." Churchill's thrust struck home. But war later may have been preferable to war earlier. By 1940, Great Britain was to have Spitfire fighters and radar, plus something far more valuable: a will to fight that was simply not there in 1938. The gamble of appeasement probably had to be made. Of course, Germany grew stronger too. And Czechoslovakia was far more defensible than Poland was to be. Information was inadequate and erratic; at the time of Munich, the British judged the Germans to be formidable, then prior to the Polish guarantee a year later, intelligence reports swung to optimism.

In the Munich calculus, so often discussed and reassessed, one problematical factor was the USSR. She too had a commitment to defend Czechoslovakia, but only if France did so first. This mutual assistance pact had been negotiated at the same time as the Franco-Soviet pact of 1935, which had proved abortive. No military agreements or consultations ever followed it up. Preoccupied with his own grisly business at home, Stalin watched in sullen silence as Hitler took Austria without consulting him; he was now to see the Czechoslovakian matter also carried out with the deliberate exclusion of the USSR. Stalin was not invited to the Munich party, though even Mussolini was. Eduard Benes, the Czech president, seemed not to wish for Soviet help, despite his desperate straits. On September 20, he asked the Soviet ambassador if Russia would carry out her commitment to help Czechoslovakia and received an affirmative reply. We do not know whether Stalin was bluffing here or not, but in later times the Soviet leaders made much of the West's betrayal of Czechoslovakia when the Soviet Union stood ready to do her duty.

In order to aid the Czechs, Stalin would have had to march troops through Poland or Romania, both of which at this time would have refused this request and fought to prevent it. (Czechoslovakia then had no border with the USSR.) These Eastern European countries feared and mistrusted the Soviet

Union even more than they did Nazi Germany; "better Hitler than Stalin" was the motto of their rulers, too. Poland and Hungary were indeed to take their pound of flesh from Czechoslovakia after Munich, acquiring small amounts of territory in disputed frontier areas. In the end, Benes chose not to ask for unilateral Soviet aid; he preferred the dismemberment of his country to a war in which the Soviet Union would be his only ally, with the West neutral or even hostile. All that he got by way of consolation was a guarantee of the independence of the remainder of his country, in which Britain now joined France. This proved to be worthless. And there was, of course, peace. "We would not be understood by Europe and the world if we provoked the war now," Benes told his generals, who wanted to fight. "The nation must endure. Do not give way, whatever happens, and wait for the right moment. Then we shall enter the struggle again, as we did in 1914. And we shall win again."

It did not quite happen that way.

THE APPROACH OF WAR, 1939

For all the joy with which it was received, Munich left a nasty taste in the West, which grew ever more uncomfortable in the next months. For Neville Chamberlain and British public opinion, the turning point came in March 1939, when Hitler ignored his promise to respect the independence of the remainder of Czechoslovakia. At that time, Germany completed the destruction of Czechoslovakia, conferring nominal independence on a now separate state of Slovakia and incorporating the Czech area into the Reich as the "Protectorate of Bohemia and Moravia." Hitler fomented discontent among the Slovaks as he had the Sudetenland Germans, as a weapon to break up Czechoslovakia. He certainly had not intended to stop with annexation of merely the Sudetenland, and he waited only a few months before fulfilling his vow to smash the hated symbol of the World War I peace settlement. This cannot have surprised Chamberlain, one would think; and yet it seems clear that for him and for British opinion in general, the occupation of Prague was the straw that broke the back of appeasement.

For Hitler had thrown off all pretense of seeking only self-determination and the restoration of German rights. "Is this not, in fact, a step in the direction of an attempt to dominate the world by force?" Chamberlain asked. When Hitler followed with annexation of the city of Memel, extorted from Lithuania, and began to make demands on Poland regarding Danzig[2] and the Polish Corridor, the British government (March 31) joined France in a guarantee of Poland's independence, extending this two weeks later to Romania and Greece. Whether this meant a firm intention to draw the line was not yet clear.

Hitler did not intend to let up while he had the opposition on the run, and he proceeded full steam ahead with his expansionist campaign. Some Germans worried about his recklessness, but no internal force was capable of overthrowing him. Munich was a blow to the anti-Hitler plotters who had begun to appear in Germany. "Bring me certain proof that England will fight if Czechoslovakia is attacked, and I will put an end to this regime," Chief of Staff Ludwig Beck told General Ewald von Kleist on the latter's visit to London in the summer of 1938. Such approaches to the British got nowhere. Beck then tried to organize a kind of strike of the generals against Hitler's war plans but soon resigned in disgust. Beck's successor, General Franz Halder, also disliked Hitler, as did many of the old Prussian officer caste. Halder, together with Schacht, Dr. Karl Bonhoeffer, and others planned a coup d'état to coincide with the outbreak of war against Czechoslovakia. The Munich capitulation cut the ground from under them, and they sank back in despair. It is possible that they could have succeeded in overthrowing Hitler had England and France stood up to him at

[2]Since 1919, Danzig had been a free city under League of Nations supervision. In this chiefly German city, Nazis had won control of the administration and demanded annexation to the Reich. This Baltic Sea port was vital to Poland as an outlet to the sea.

the time of Munich. German resistance to Hitler did not seriously revive again until 1944.

Hitler's popularity had never been greater, by all signs; his fiftieth birthday, April 20, 1939, was the occasion for enormous pageantry and effulgent idolatry, with pictures of *der Führer* in every window. Goebbels's propaganda machine hammered in the image of Germany miraculously reborn under the leadership of the simple soldier who had brought salvation to a troubled people.

Poland was a more popular target within Germany than Czechoslovakia was. Few Germans failed to resent the Versailles boundaries in the east, which forced several million former German citizens to live under Polish rule. Hitler spoke of "frightful mistreatment" of Germans there, and the newspapers blazed with such stories, which in the main were manufactured or grossly exaggerated. But most Germans, with Munich in mind, believed that the Polish "problem" would be "solved" without war. They did not want or expect war, and they were shocked when it came. The same probably can be said for Adolf Hitler. There is, at least, much evidence that Hitler thought the British and French would back down again. Why should they fight for Poland when they had almost fallen over themselves to give him Czechoslovakia? The former country was far less defensible and far more susceptible to the arguments about self-determination for Germans. "I have seen these little worms at Munich," he told his officers on August 22.

Public opinion in the West does seem to have behaved irrationally and thus must bear some responsibility for World War II, the main cause of which was Nazi Germany's brutal campaign of expansion. The United States, like Great Britain, began to rouse herself from her isolationist slumbers after Munich. There, too, the Munich agreement had been hailed for saving the peace, but its delivery of Europe into the hands of Hitler almost immediately produced second thoughts. Western public opinion switched from emotional pacifism to intense indignation at Hitler and his shrill propaganda, bad manners, and constant aggression.

The Poles, bolstered by the British guarantee and perhaps by a national temperament less cautious than the Czechs', now refused to be intimidated as Benes had been. "You have only to show a Pole a precipice and he will throw himself over it," Balzac said in the nineteenth century. Perhaps the romantic Polish temperament was less relevant now than the fact that military officers, headed by Colonel Josef Beck, governed Poland. The military would have fought in Czechoslovakia; it was the influence of the civilian chief, Eduard Benes, that restrained them. The Polish Army did not propose to repeat the disastrous Czech surrender. And thus the stage was set for World War II.

The other ingredient was Russia. Stung by his exclusion from Munich, when Mussolini had joined Hitler, Chamberlain, and Daladier in a pact that seemed based on Fascist dominance of Eastern Europe, Stalin soon came to feel certain that there was a conspiracy to turn Germany against the Soviet Union. Both Hitler and Stalin, those ideological zealots, prided themselves on an ice-cold realism in regard to tactics. This was an aspect, in fact, of their fanaticism: Absolutely sure of their goals, they were prepared to violate any code of ethics to achieve these ends. Neither would hesitate at a marriage of convenience. Sentiments, as Hitler was fond of proclaiming, have nothing to do with the hard-boiled realm of foreign policy. Stalin inherited from Lenin the belief that "morality is what serves to advance the Revolution." There is therefore no real reason to be surprised by the Nazi-Soviet pact that astonished the world in August 1939 and set the stage for the war. The two ruthless dictators needed each other, ironically in order later to fight each other: "Hitler needed food and raw materials from the Soviet Union in order to attack her, while Stalin needed machinery, arms and weapons from Germany in order to be able to fight her off," as Professors Read and Fisher put it.[3]

The victim of this strange alliance was Poland. This was the fourth partition of that unhappy people situated between powerful and expansionist neighbors. In three bites, between 1772 and 1795, the ancient Polish kingdom had been swallowed up by Prussia, Russia, and Austria. Partially restored by Napoleon, it again fell under the dominance of others after 1815. (Congress Poland survived for fifteen years as a ward of Russia, being annexed outright by Russia after the revolution of 1830.) World War I restored the Polish state, which profited from the temporary ruin of all three of her oppressors in that war. Poland went too far in her intoxication of victory after long defeat; she took land in abundance from Russia and Germany, pushing her frontiers out in both directions. She then became the target of territorial claims from both her neighbors as soon as they regained their strength. The two totalitarian states could make a deal in which each satisfied its greed for expansion, at the expense of the smaller states of eastern Europe. Each reserved its action for the future.

For the moment, the Nazi-Soviet pact was an astonishing coup. Hitler and Stalin were soon hailing each other as "good fellows," while mystified Communists in the Western world, who had been denouncing fascism and pleading for a popular front against it, had to tear down the type and substitute stories that attacked the democracies and were silent on the topic of fascism. Excessive antifascism could now land you in a prison camp in the Soviet Union. Western communism never quite recovered from this blow to its credibility. Hitler's old ideological associates were equally dismayed at this sudden friendship with the archenemy and could only take comfort in the reflection that politics makes strange bedfellows.

Qualms on each side were eased by the solid territorial gains and by the discomfiture of the democracies, which had again missed the boat. In the spring and summer of 1939, halfhearted approaches to Stalin from France and Britain failed to achieve anything. One reason was the attitude of the states to which Britain had given guarantees—Poland and Romania. They would still not

---

[3]Anthony Read and David Fisher, *The Deadly Embrace: Hitler, Stalin, and the Nazi-Soviet Pact 1939–41* (London: Michael Joseph, 1988).

consent to the passage of Russian troops across their territory, which was essential in any military alliance aimed at Germany. In all good faith, the British and French could not compel their allies to do so.

What could the western European democracies offer Stalin? Not annexations of territory, as Hitler did. They could only offer to help defend eastern Europe against Germany. But in the first place, they had already given their guarantees to Poland and Romania and did not have this as a bargaining counter; beyond this, the Communist dictator did not trust them. Further, what effective aid could they bring to this region? Buying time for the restoration of his military machine, which had been badly disorganized by the purge of a high percentage of its senior officers, Stalin evidently saw no alternative to a deal with Hitler. The Nazi-Soviet pact was pushed hard from the German side; Hitler was burning for his campaign against Poland. He gave orders to prepare for the campaign on the same day that the pact was signed, August 23. The secret articles of this nonaggression pact divided Poland into Russian and German spheres of influence, and within a month the country had been partitioned. While Germany got the lion's share of Poland, the Baltic states fell to Russia.

Though Mussolini attempted to mediate, there was to be no salvation from war via a Munich agreement this time. Other last-minute peace efforts begun on August 23 through the mediation of a Swede, Birger Dahlerus, led to pleas from London that the Poles negotiate, that is, give up territory to Germany. The Poles refused, or at any rate they delayed too long for Hitler, who ordered German troops to cross the Polish frontier on September 1. When a still hesitant Neville Chamberlain reported to a restive British House of Commons on that day, a member of his own party rose to ask the Labour spokesman, Arthur Greenwood, to "speak for England," and the Tories as well as the Labourites cheered when Greenwood pressed for war. The British ultimatum came on September 3, ordering Hitler to call back his troops or stand in a state of war with Britain. France followed suit later the same day. Except for Russia, the major states of Europe were at war. Stalin momentarily rejoiced.

In 1914, Germany had faced war on two fronts against the powerful encirclement of Russia, France, and Great Britain. In 1939, she had divided her foes—or they had divided themselves—and Russia was neutralized. In 1914, Germany struck first at France. She was to attack France again this time, eight months later, but the war began in 1939 with an attack on a country that had not existed in 1914.

It is also interesting that at the beginning of both World War I and World War II, Germany misjudged the British. On each occasion, the Germans were confident that they would stay neutral. Both times, after some hesitation London decided that she could not resign the Continent to a powerful Germany. The balance of power again was decisive; but in 1939, the ideological currents were stronger. German Nazism and its leader had become a hateful symbol to the British, more so even than the kaiser and the Prussian militarists had been at the start of World War I. In 1939, Germany was more clearly the brazen aggressor; but Hitler had not intended to start a general war. Germany was not prepared for that. Both times, statesmen expected a short war instead of the protracted agony they got.

These are some of the comparisons that may be made between the origins of the two world wars of the twentieth century. The astute student will think of others; but the fact of war was the same. This one would last even longer, prove even more destructive, spread even farther throughout the world. It would end once again in the ruin of Germany, but the path to the destination would not be the same. It would again entail the intervention, somewhat belatedly, of the United States of America. It would include a smashing German victory in France, unlike 1914; but it would also involve what the German leaders of 1914–1918 steadily refused to undertake, a massive invasion of Russia.

8

The Second World War,
1939–1945

THE WEHRMACHT TRIUMPHANT, 1939–1940

World War II engulfed the entire globe, affecting the lives of nearly every one of its more than two billion inhabitants. It took a ghastly toll of lives and caused suffering too immense to be told. When he began it with what appeared to be a short and simple annihilation of hapless Poland, Hitler cannot have had any idea of how the war would spread. Out of this titanic upheaval came incalculable changes in governments, economies, societies, ideas. The imagination can hardly encircle it, and the documents of history can only suggest its magnitude, even though it has become the most written-about historical subject of all time.

The war began with Germany quickly overrunning Poland in September 1939. A curiously unreal optimism prevailed among the Western allies at the beginning of the war. The French Commander-in-Chief, General Gamelin, believed that "Hitler will collapse the day we declare war on Germany." The British thought a bloodless application of economic warfare would soon bring Germany to her knees. But the armored panzer divisions knifed through Poland's plain, which provided excellent terrain for tanks. The weather smiled on Germany–no rain. The Poles had an army not much inferior to Germany's in number but far less well equipped, with scarcely any tanks and a much smaller air force. The blitzkrieg was all over in a few weeks, and the Russians moved into the eastern portion in accordance with the secret agreement. The Polish government escaped to London. France and Britain honored their commitment to Poland by declaring war on Germany, but they did nothing else except drop propaganda leaflets. Gamelin promised a French land offensive within sixteen days, but by that time it was too late. The Chamberlain government in London was firmly opposed to any military action. Hitler had not misread his adversaries.

It has been argued that any sort of attack on the western front, where the French and British much outnumbered the Germans, would have done Hitler in. But the democracies were still morally if not physically unprepared for an offensive war. And so the travail of Poland began. In this the Germans were assisted by the Russians, who shipped several hundred thousand Poles to prison camps and shot thousands of Polish officers at Katyn.[1] The Nazis, of course, saw the Poles as a sub-race to be eliminated in favor of German settlers. The Pole's own holocaust at the hands of the Germans was almost as horrible as the better publicized one inflicted on the Jews, Poles have pointed out: Historians count a toll of three million.

Hitler, who always thought in terms of a *blitzkrieg*–a war won in a lightning thrust–paused after the conquest of Poland. He put out some feelers to the Allies, who refused to listen. Western opinion had completely hardened against the Nazi. The winter of 1939–1940 witnessed what the French called the *drôle de guerre* and the Americans called the "phony war." The war was said to be a joke or a fraud. The British opposed any plans for opening an offensive, at least for the moment; they had convinced themselves that an economic blockade and boycott could win the war, and if any British statesman had the will to send troops back to another continental holocaust, his name was not Neville Chamberlain. The British did use this time to good advantage, however, in building planes. The French government and probably the French people were also without a will to war. Observers reported soldiers' morale low in many of the Maginot Line forts. The Communists in France now devoted their talents to ridiculing the war and fomenting strikes in munitions factories.

At the same time, in this strange interlude of deceptive calm before the storm, the note of Allied overconfidence continued, too. In November, early events in the war that the Soviet Union had suddenly launched against Finland enhanced Allied illusions. This brazenly aggressive assault by a large power on its tiny neighbor strained Soviet-Western relations even more, blighting whatever chance remained for friendship after the Nazi-Soviet pact. A wave of sympathy for Finland swept the democracies; Hitler was almost forgotten for the moment in anger at Stalin. Both totalitarian regimes seemed alike. The defeats that the Finns at first inflicted on the Russians in this winter war convinced Western leaders that Russia was a "colossus with feet of clay." Perhaps both dictatorial states were. Would not the German as well as Russian regimes, lacking

---

[1] In April, 1990, the post-Communist Russian government admitted and apologized for the Katyn murders of 15,000 Polish officers, after having long denied it and attributed the massacre to the Germans.

popular support, collapse at the first serious test? Hitler hesitated to attack because he was afraid, people convinced themselves. There was talk in France and Britain of going to war against *both* Germany and Russia—inconceivable later, but possible in the garish light of the *drôle de guerre* months. Some military men and politicians in Paris and London half-seriously discussed striking at the Baku oil fields in the Caucusus from Syria and Turkey. Moscow, picking up the scent of such stories, confirmed its already deep suspicions of the British and French. Never was illusion more rampant, policy makers more at sea.

As Russia finally overcame valiant Finnish resistance to win the winter war and annex strategically valuable territory near Leningrad, Germany was preparing for the classic blitzkrieg against France and Belgium in the spring of 1940. In fact, Hitler canceled orders to attack or prepare to attack no fewer than eleven times between November and April, either because of the weather or because of foot-dragging by the generals, who argued Germany was not ready. During a confrontation on November 5, Hitler shouted at General von Brauchitsch to shut up. There was an assassination attempt on Hitler on November 8 in Munich, but the generals did not act against him. Hitler continued during this period to build a separate high command (the OKW) with his own men in control, over the head of the OKH—an armed forces high command over the army high command.

The first major clash between Germany and Britain took place at sea, far from Europe. After being chased into the River Plate in South America by British cruisers, the German small battleship *Graf Spee* finally destroyed itself (December 13–17). In February, a British destroyer attacked a German ship in Norwegian waters, and the British and French soon mined the Skagerrak area. German sea and airborne forces then invaded Norway, also occupying Denmark. Norwegian resistance, although aided by British naval power, could not prevent a rapid German conquest during the month of April. The seizure of Norway was cleverly planned and showed the superiority of German air power to British sea power in such narrow waters.

This was but the warm-up for the next month's spectacular campaign, when the western front burst into flames. But this time, unlike 1914, the campaign exploded in a fantastic war of movement. It is often said that the French and British thought in terms of defensive war, mesmerized by a Maginot Line psychology that went back to the lessons of the last war. But in fact the French did attack, and by doing so they committed a fatal error. While the Maginot defenses would surely hold in the south, Belgium was not fortified, and it was here that the Germans were expected to strike. When on May 10 they did attack Belgium, along with Luxemburg and the Netherlands, French and British forces went into Belgium to aid King Leopold III's army. Unfortunately, in doing so they left their right flank exposed. The hilly, forested area of the Ardennes in southeastern Belgium was terrain not thought suitable for tanks and motorized vehicles. It was here that the Germans showed their mastery of a new art of warfare.

The fall of France and the low countries within six weeks was one of the most stunning events in all history. In the bitter post mortems among the French, all kinds of allegations were made. Paul Reynaud said that the French had not allied themselves nor fortified themselves nor armed themselves. But the French, who had spent vast sums on the Maginot fortifications, actually had more tanks than the Germans and probably had better ones. Since 1936 they had not been idle. It was neither in the quantity nor the quality of their armoured vehicles that the Germans excelled, but in knowing how to use them. Rather than dispersing them among infantry divisions as auxiliary forces, young German officers massed the tanks in divisions and used them in combination with motorized infantry, tactical air power, and parachute troops. They were able to knife through in a "scythe cut," as Winston Churchill termed it, and then fan out in a war of mobility, spreading confusion among the defenders. The irony was that a French officer, Charles de Gaulle, early had developed such ideas (1934).

The success of these tactics astonished even Hitler. From the Ardennes breakthrough the panzer forces fanned out to attack the rear of both the Maginot defenses and the Allied troops advancing into Belgium. At the same time, another scythe cut to the south, in Alsace, slashed down the northwest slopes of the Jura Mountains and then turned northeast to take the French in the rear. Through these apertures opened by the panzer divisions sped motor-borne troops to cut communications and disrupt supply lines. They raced to the English Channel at Abbeville, thus cutting the Allied armies in two. Rotterdam and Brussels fell; the Germans were soon at Boulogne, and after long debate, King Leopold III's government decided to surrender. This was on May 28, only eighteen days after the start of the offensive. The British forces, some 250,000 strong, which had rushed to the defense of their allies, were forced back against the sea at Ostend and Dunkirk, along with many French troops.

By June 5, the British had managed to evacuate over 300,000 soldiers across the English Channel from Dunkirk (Dunkerque), a seeming miracle that lifted British spirits. It was not known at the time that Hitler deliberately refrained from preventing the British escape; he hoped for an agreement with the British. In pursuit of other prey, the Germans turned southward to complete the conquest of France. On June 10, Italy declared war on France and tried to invade southern France. On June 13, Germans entered Paris. On June 15, the World War I fortress of Verdun fell. On June 16–17, World War I hero Pétain became head of the French government and immediately asked for an armistice!

This blitzkrieg was at least relatively humane, in terms of casualties. Total lives lost were no more than 30,000 Germans and 100,000 Allies. The French and the Belgians had preferred surrender to hopeless struggle. In later years, the French engaged in lengthy self-scrutiny about the shattering defeat. The right blamed the left, the left blamed the right, and everybody blamed the politicians, who blamed the generals. More objectively, many felt it was inhuman to expect France to fight a second war twenty years after she had lost the prime of an entire generation in the first one. It was not a pretty scene; defeat seldom is. The British almost all thought that the French refused to fight. "F- - - ing French scamper as soon as they see a jerry tank or plane," was a typical British comment, "officers first." But the French believed that the "dirty English" arrived too late and then saved themselves by evacuation, leaving the French and Belgians behind.

According to the armistice that was signed on June 22, France was disarmed and three-fifths of her land given to Germany. In early July, the British sank or captured a portion of the French fleet at Oran in Algeria and seized other French ships in British ports, because they regarded Marshal Pétain's government as a German satellite. Meanwhile, General Charles de Gaulle set up a Free French government in London, rallying a few Frenchmen to continue somehow the resistance against Germany.[2]

Winston Churchill replaced Neville Chamberlain as British Prime Minister and with what seemed foolhardy courage declared, "We shall go on to the end. . . . We shall never surrender." This indomitable spirit amazed and heartened much of the world. As we now know, it was based on some misconceptions. The British still thought the Germans at bottom weak, their economy precariously unable to sustain a long war; and Churchill believed his friend the American President Franklin Roosevelt was about to bring the vast resources of the United States into the war against Hitler. On both counts, Churchill was wrong. It is true that the fall of France awakened the United States from her isolationist slumbers, but America was far from ready to embark on war and would not be for another year or more, during which a furious national debate raged. Roosevelt was no leader to plunge ahead without a mandate from the public. If Winston Churchill had known the real state of affairs he might well have responded to Hitler's overtures and made peace. As it was, encouraged by his illusions, he gave memorable expression to the will of the British people to fight on alone against overwhelming odds and a ruthless foe.

Some historians still argue that Churchill should have listened to Hitler's offers. War between Germany and Russia was inevitable; why not wait until that happened? Harry Truman in 1941 suggested helping Germany if the Russians were winning, and Russia if Germany were winning, which probably reflected the outlook of most Americans then. There was little to be lost, save perhaps honor, by a temporary truce with Germany. The costly aerial bombardments to which the British were subjected in 1940–1941 would have been avoided. But the valiant Churchill had preached the folly of "appeasing" Hitler ever since Munich, and was not about to imitate the leader he replaced as British prime minister.

---

[2]"Why have you brought me this gloomy brigadier?" Churchill asked Major-General Spears when the latter returned from France with de Gaulle. "Because no one else would come," was the reply.

THE WIDENING WAR, 1940–1941

In the summer and fall of 1940, chief attention focused on "the Battle of Britain." With Russia still an ally of Germany and the United States just beginning to think about getting involved, only Great Britain stood against Germany and her allies. These now included Japan as well as Italy, the three countries having signed a pact on September 27, 1940. Hitler's spectacular success withered the faint traces of opposition to him in Germany and made him seem even more of a superman. He had in fact overridden caution among the establishment generals to back the panzer advocates, Manstein and Guderian, whose ideas had proved so successful.

The man who now assumed leadership of the meager forces standing in Hitler's path was no ordinary mortal, either. At sixty-five, Winston Churchill could look back on a remarkable career as writer, soldier, politician, historian— he also painted. He was the British prodigy of the century and had been recognized as such from his early years, when he bulldozed his way to prominence by sheer exuberance. He had fought in wars and written about them later, from his early accounts of expeditions in India and *The River War* in the Sudan (Kitchener's 1898 campaign) through World War I, where we recall his misfortunes with the Dardanelles plan. Churchill had always inspired mistrust in direct proportion to his genius, audacity, and gargantuan energy. He had been in and out of both major political parties until neither one was sure of him. He was often out of step with party and with public. (An example is the abdication crisis of 1936, when he sided passionately with Edward VIII.) He was the bad boy of politics, thought to have, amid all his scintillating gifts, one fatal flaw: lack of judgment. But he possessed one gift that, above all others, guaranteed his political fame, the gift of a matchless eloquence. And, he was thoroughly at home in war. "His high and turbulent spirit is entirely happy when politics and war are merged in one theme," A. G. Gardiner wrote.

Many weaknesses, in fact, Churchill had. His record of having steadfastly opposed Nazism since the beginning was not perfect. He had praised Hitler's restoration of the German people's spirit in 1936–a generous appreciation of other nations' achievements was one of Churchill's many attractive qualities–and in 1937 he had said that if forced to choose between Nazism and communism he would take the former. A Liberal in his youth, Churchill was now a *bête-noire* to the left because of his fierce anticommunism and imperialism. But Austria opened his eyes to the danger of Hitler's domination, and he fought the Munich appeasement, with very few allies. Now his hour came, and he was to make the most of it. He immediately transformed both the spirit and the tempo of the government. Whitehall would never again be the same. Sleeping only a few hours a night, Churchill seemed to be everywhere, bombarding everyone with memos ("Action This Day," the famous stamp demanded). He cut through red tape and galvanized Britons into action by the sheer force of his will, spreading a spirit of confidence throughout the government even as his eloquent speeches heartened the people.

By his own admission, Churchill had not foreseen the new developments in warfare that the Germans exploded on the world. He had not "comprehended the violence of the revolution effected since the last war by the incursion of a mass of fast-moving armour," he said in the history of the Second World War that he lived to write, as he had written the history of the first. Only a few had foreseen it. Churchill failed to learn from two British military writers, General J.F.C. Fuller and General Basil Liddell Hart, who were among the first to argue, totally without effect, that armored and motorized vehicles could revolutionize warfare. But in 1939, the British had foreseen the importance of building "fighter" airplanes for the defense of their island, a decision for which the chief credit seems best given to Thomas Inskip. And, the British were leaders in operational applications of radar.

From 1935 on, the British worked to develop this idea of using radio waves to track the movements of aircraft (not an original idea; the Germans and Russians were working on it too). The system was far from perfected when the war began in 1939, but by July 1940 it was good enough to allow the outnumbered British Spitfire and Hurricane fighters to inflict unacceptable losses on the *Luftwaffe*. Hermann Goering never seems to have understood quite how the system worked and did not effectively bomb the radar signaling stations strewn around the British coast. The Spitfires and radar saved Britain and the world from Hitler's power in the fall of 1940. German control of the air would have been followed by an invasion of Britain or by uncontested bombings of British cities, which would surely force England to sue for peace. It was up to Fighter Command to make the Germans pay an unacceptable price for their bombing of Britain. We know now that the British had another weapon in this battle: knowledge of the German secret code used to transmit *Luftwaffe* messages. (See more later in this chapter on the ULTRA advantage.)

Early German raids, in August, aimed primarily at British air fields, were designed to weaken the enemy's air power. On September 7, raids on London began, continuing to a climax on September 15, when 1,000 planes came at London. Each night brought more terror from the skies. Hitler had been infuriated by a British raid on Berlin and vowed to "wipe their cities off the map." While the *Luftwaffe* suffered heavy losses, so did the British Fighter Command, which was losing both planes and pilots faster than it could replace them. "Never was so much owed by so many to so few," Churchill said in his tribute to the fighter pilots. Hitler set September 22 as the date for the invasion of England, then on September 17 he called it off because British bombers struck hard at the invasion ports on the French and Belgian side of the Channel. Temporarily at least, Britain was saved.

The world watched her heroic resistance, and American opinion was deeply affected. Following the shock of France's fall, the United States moved away from the stringent neutrality she had heretofore adopted, toward aid to the foes of Nazi Germany; but noninterventionists had argued that it was futile to enter a war Hitler had already won. Even a hesitant Roosevelt thought at times that Britain was done for. Now it seemed that Britain was going to hold out. "Give us the tools and we will finish the job," the unquenchable Churchill cried. His inspiring speeches struck the American imagination. American aid now began to flow into Britain.

But Atlantic shipping absorbed punishing blows from German U-boats. German Admiral Doenitz believed that if German subs could sink more of England's merchant ships than she could build, she would have to surrender. It was a "tonnage war." Using "wolfpack" tactics of groups of surfaced U-boats attacking convoys at night, the Germans threatened to win this war. But decoding helped defeat the subs, also. Entry of the United States into this war of the seas was critical, however. Tied by his own antiwar rhetoric and concerned about a still potent "isolationist" force in American opinion, Roosevelt edged obliquely toward an out-and-out military alliance with Churchill; in September he dealt Britain some destroyers in exchange for naval bases.

Although German air attacks did not end after September, they tailed off sharply. Both winter weather and losses reduced them; and the Germans largely abandoned mass bombing of cities in favor of again concentrating on ports and shipping. Antiaircraft guns and balloon cables helped cause the loss of ninety German bombers in the first three months of 1941. By April, Hitler was looking to the East. He had forgotten operation "Sea Lion," the invasion of England, in favor of "Barbarossa," the Russian campaign. It is remarkable that the British, having shown that terror bombings could not break a people's will to fight, soon adopted the same "victory through air power" formula themselves. They sought to destroy Germany with their own bombers, supplemented by American ones from 1942 on.

In March 1941, the United States Congress passed the Lend-Lease Act, granting all possible aid to Britain without counting the cost, after having granted credits earlier. German submarines could not prevent the shipment of millions of tons of convoyed supplies across the Atlantic. Though the United States hesitated to enter the war as a belligerent, "all aid short of war" had become the American policy.

War in North Africa began to attract attention in 1940. In September, the Italians undertook an offensive against Egypt from Libya. But British forces under General Wavell counterattacked in December and routed the Italians, whose military ineptness now became the subject of bitter jokes among the Germans. (In 1939, Churchill is supposed to have responded to a German who had boasted of having Italy as an ally by saying, "It's only fair, we had them last time.") It was in the wake of Wavell's successes that the German commander, Erwin Rommel, landed in Tripoli on February 12 to begin one of the war's legendary stories. The "desert fox" was to bring panzer tactics to the sands of North Africa with brilliant success in 1941, spreading panic among Germany's foes.

Hitler also won 1941 victories in Greece and Crete. Italian ineptitude helped precipitate these victories; in October 1940, Mussolini attacked Greece from Albania, which he had managed to conquer in 1939. He was defeated, however, as the British helped Greece by bombing the Italian fleet. German troops entered Greece after the Yugoslavian campaign of April 1941, capturing British supplies. Then Germany invaded Crete with air power and parachute troops and brilliantly defeated the British navy there, forcing evacuation of a small British army to Cyprus and Egypt. Bad Allied planning and poor coordination with the Greeks have been blamed for this British setback, which failed even though they used ULTRA intercepts. But Cretan resistance continued underground.

The Greek king fled as the Germans took command of Greece. But Hitler did not pursue a Mediterranean strategy. Had he done so, he might have cut the British "lifeline" of Suez and Gibraltar (though in fact traffic was successfully taking the long route around South Africa). He might even had been able to link up with the Japanese after their entry into the war in late 1941. But Hitler was not in search of colonies and preferred partnership with the British Empire to war with it. He had already decided on war against Russia to win a "heartland" empire for Germany.

Spain's Franco helped frustrate Hitler's Mediterranean plans by stubbornly refusing to be drawn into the war. After a meeting with the Spanish dictator on the Spanish border in the autumn of 1940, Hitler said he would rather have several teeth extracted than go through another one. Franco formally acceded to the Axis pact but refused to permit German troops to cross the Pyrenees and march on Gibraltar. According to Albert Speer, Hitler once suggested renewing the Spanish Civil War *against* Franco! But Hitler, as Franco probably knew, "was not in a position to force his hand, having already become a prisoner of his own timetable of aggression in the East," according to historian Donald Detwiler.

After the French debacle, Churchill tried to restore contacts with Moscow, but he had no luck. Stalin was seemingly committed to his pact with Hitler. The latter's victory in the West, however, encouraged the Russians to a bold policy in eastern Europe. Stalin seized the Baltic states and annexed territory from Romania; in Romania he went beyond what the Nazi-Soviet pact had assigned to the Russian sphere of influence, trying to get Bukovina as well as Bessarabia. Stalin must have thought that Nazi Germany had the feet of clay, not his Soviet Russia. These were tough tactics, and they deeply annoyed Hitler. Soviet Foreign Minister Molotov's visit to Berlin in November 1940 was the last straw. The Russians staked out claims to dominance in eastern Europe, which Hitler had long marked for his own. Despite the agreement, he never intended to allow Russia a place in Europe. Stalin might have found a place in Hitler's world had he looked eastward rather than westward–to India or the Middle East. Hitler encouraged this, but when the Soviets stubbornly insisted on a role in Europe, he determined to wage war against them. A directive to seek a military showdown with the USSR by May 15 was issued on December 18.

The greatest mystery about the German attack on Russia, which began on June 22, 1941, is why the Russians were caught by surprise. German policies in southeast Europe from early 1941 on should have alarmed Stalin. Most of the small states in this area jumped onto the Berlin-Rome-Tokyo bandwagon: Hungary on November 20, 1940, Romania three days later, Bulgaria on March 1. Only Yugoslavia balked; the leaders who signed the Tripartite Pact on March 25 were overthrown in a coup at Belgrade the next day, and the ensuing government, while it was careful not to appear anti-German, angered Hitler by seeking Russian support. German troops, already massing in the east, overran Yugoslavia in the first weeks of April. They went on to finish off the Greeks and tangle with the Royal Navy in Grecian waters. This Balkan excursion, caused by Yugoslavia's reluctance to join Hitler's New Order and by Italian problems in Greece, may have delayed the beginning of Operation Barbarossa by a month.

Everybody except Stalin seems to have known about the coming attack on Russia. The British, of course, were reading the German code. In May, Hitler's old comrade Rudolf Hess parachuted into England, without Hitler's permission, to tell the British of the impending Russian campaign and seek to bring about a negotiated peace between Germany and Britain. But Churchill already knew about Barbarossa and had decided he would continue the war against Germany even with the Soviet Union as an ally. Both Churchill and Roosevelt tried to warn Stalin. But the suspicious Russian leader thought they were trying to trick him. Watching the Germans move into Yugoslavia, Bulgaria, Romania, and even Finland, Stalin unaccountably refused to believe they would attack Russia without warning, and he was caught totally unprepared on June 22. Russian troops guarding the border fell into confusion because they received no coherent orders; Stalin did not credit news of the massive attack for hours and then sank into bewildered inaction for more than a week.

Three million attacking troops had achieved virtually total surprise. Hundreds of Soviet planes were destroyed on the ground; hundreds of thousands of Soviet troops were surrounded and killed or captured as the now familiar panzer scythe strokes cut deeply into the Russian plains. The Russians had learned nothing from the western campaign of a year ago; the purged army was commanded by incompetents. Among Hitler's reasons for taking the enormous risk of waging war against Russia, a major one was his conviction that victory would be easy—another blitzkrieg would repeat the lightning successes in Poland and France. In the first few months of the war, nothing seemed to contradict this view.

HIGH TIDE OF THE AXIS, 1941–1942

"No battle in history compares to it," exclaimed Alan Clark, historian of the German-Russian war. This was "the head-on crash of the two greatest armies, the two most absolute systems in the world." Not even the first days of August 1914 could rival this onslaught. More than three million Axis troops, with 3,500 tanks and thousands of planes, opposed an even huger Russian army, not badly equipped—its tanks were probably superior in quality as well as quantity to the Germans'. But the open plain was made for the German tactics, and as the Russian giant stood stunned and bewildered, the invaders drove forward on three fronts to wheel around and encircle vast numbers of Russian troops. In the south, the incompetence of Marshal Budyenny, an old political Communist, lost a great army at Kiev. At the peak of his genius, Heinz Guderian led a breakthrough in the center, annihilating Timoshenko's army. By July 3, General Halder was saying "the war has virtually been won," and in October Goebbels announced "the war is over." No wonder: By then, it is estimated, Russia had lost 2.5 million soldiers, 18,000 tanks, 14,000 aircraft, and more than 300,000 square miles of land, including the richest part of that immense country.

Even as Goebbels spoke, however, there were signs that things were going to get difficult for the attackers. The vast distances engendered supply and communications problems which worsened as the German armies got farther and farther from home; roads were scarce, and the fall rains slowed tanks and trucks. The Soviets rallied after absorbing the first shock. By this time, too, materiel was flowing into Russia from the United States. Gradually, the Russians found able commanders, learned how to fight this kind of war, and brought new armies in from the east. The gaping wounds Germany administered with the first terrible blow would undoubtedly have destroyed a more advanced society. Russia was saved by her backwardness; it was said that the Germans were defeated by their successes. These were the paradoxes of a war unlike any other ever fought.

Among the many factors that combined to determine success or failure in history's greatest battle, two stand out: the question of German military grand strategy and German policy toward the conquered Russian people. In the German High Command, a great debate pitted Hitler against some of his chief generals. Those who were not his creatures—men like Halder and Brauchitsch—basically favored a single-pronged drive on Moscow. Hitler, who had learned to scorn the professional military mind during his experience in the French campaign, stuck to a three-pronged plan. Under Hitler's strategy, a northern finger would reach for the second-largest Russian city, Leningrad, and a southern one would push deep into the Ukraine and beyond, toward the Black Sea, the Donetz basin, and then the oil rich Caucasus. This was to risk straining German resources beyond the breaking point. The southern front, particularly, became too large to be manageable.

What was to be done with all the captured land and all these captured people? Here the Nazis' racial arrogance proved to be their own worst enemy. Millions of Russians felt little or no loyalty to the Communists; the Ukraine was a potential mass of unrest. A German policy based on treating the conquered people sympathetically could certainly have offered prospects of success. Instead, brutal German treatment aimed at enslaving or exterminating the Slavs brought bitter hatred of the invader, and partisan bands arose to harass him.

If Germany's goal had been to destroy Russia's armed strength, she had failed to reach it. Despite the enormous losses inflicted, a land with three times the population of Germany could raise fresh armies and, with Allied aid, equip them. If the goal was to seize and exploit the Ukraine and other western Russian lands, the task was rendered all but impossible by German failure to win the cooperation of the inhabitants. The Nazis had a bear by the tail, a terribly wounded but nevertheless formidable giant. Their woes were compounded by the weather, which now compensated for having smiled on them earlier. The worst winter in 140 years was about to bring acute suffering to soldiers who had not even been equipped with winter clothing. On December 10, the thermometer plunged to an unbelievable –60°F, and men froze to death in their tracks. Shades of 1812! In early December, just as the Japanese were steaming toward Pearl Harbor on the assumption that Germany had won the war, Marshal Zhukov launched a counteroffensive that drove the freezing Germans back a few miles–enough to save Moscow. The Russian offensive soon petered out, but the German force was spent for the time being; the blitzkrieg had failed. After relieving Brauchitsch and assuming personal command of the armies as well as the combined *Wehrmacht,* Hitler ordered a new offensive in the spring of 1942 and again achieved temporary successes. But he was headed for the fateful rendezvous at Stalingrad.

Meanwhile the United States had entered the war, or rather her entrance had been assured by the actions of others. Until December 7, 1941, the Americans still had not officially entered the war against Hitler, but confined themselves to sending war supplies to Britain and Russia, and protecting those supplies by escorting naval convoys. Japan had taken advantage of the collapse of France in 1940 and occupied Indochina (Vietnam, Laos, Cambodia). She had

Pearl Harbor, December 7, 1941. The *USS Shaw* is seen exploding after the surprise Japanese air attack on the American naval base in Hawaii, which brought the U.S. fully into World War II. (*U.S. Navy photo.*)

evident designs on the oil-rich Dutch East Indies (today Indonesia). In September, she signed the Tripartite Pact with Italy and Germany. The United States protested these Japanese advances in Asia and began to impose embargoes on the shipment of products to Japan. In the summer of 1941, Churchill and Roosevelt met and agreed to put pressure on Japan to call off her expansionist ambitions, which might threaten the British possessions of Malaya, Burma, and India, as well as the American-held Philippine Islands. The United States then froze all Japanese credits and assets and added oil to the embargo list. Negotiations between the United States and Japan went on for several months in the late summer and fall of 1941, but they got nowhere. The Americans demanded that Japan withdraw from China as well as Indo-China. Japanese leaders decided that they had no choice but war with the United States or surrender of vital national interests.

Reading the Japanese code, Roosevelt's government knew that Japan was about to strike, but thought the blow would come in southeast Asia. They did not expect the air attack on the Pacific fleet in Hawaii and the Japanese achieved total surprise. On December 7, the Japanese astonished the world by bombing the American naval base in Pearl Harbor. It was startlingly successful, but it aroused the angry Americans to an all-out war effort. Hitler declared war

Winston Churchill with Generals Montgomery and Alexander at the African front. (*Imperial War Museum.*)

against the United States in accordance with his role as Japan's ally, believing that Japan would now divert all the Americans' attention to the Pacific, away from Europe. But the United States was now officially at war with Germany.

The United States had been a de facto ally of Great Britain against Nazi Germany and Italy since at least the Lend-Lease Act of early 1941. She had even been a military ally insofar as she convoyed supply ships and fought German submarines in the Atlantic. She had promptly extended the benefits of Lend-Lease to the Soviet Union on June 22, 1941. Some American critics of the Roosevelt foreign policy could not understand FDR's hostility toward Japan, which formed the background of the Pearl Harbor attack, and a few charged him with conniving to achieve American entrance into the war by provoking an attack, his real goal being the defeat of Hitler. But whatever the explanation, once aroused to fighting fury by the Japanese "infamy," the United States, with its tremendous industrial power, proved able to sustain both wars, unloosing an awesome flow of tanks, planes, ships, and other materials of war while mobilizing millions of men and women in the armed forces.

In the American wartime mind, the European fascist dictators merged with the Japanese warlords in an image of a single plot to conquer and enslave the world. In actuality, Japan and Germany fought separate wars for separate purposes and engaged in no joint military planning. But Japan's ambitions to create an East Asian "co-prosperity sphere" under her control was somewhat analogous to Hitlerite Germany's drive for a National Socialist Europe headquartered at Berlin. The United States now stood fully committed to war against both German and Japanese imperialism, with the almost unanimous backing of a thoroughly bellicose public opinion. It was hardly a good omen for the Germans, who were rapidly becoming bogged down in the vast spaces of Russia.

The Japanese followed up their stunning strike against the American Pacific fleet in Pearl Harbor with a series of additional victories, soon taking the Philippines and the great British base at Singapore, which fell swiftly to the determined Nipponese in a defeat that shocked England. Within a few months, Japan ruled all of East Asia and the Pacific, including Indochina, Thailand, Burma, Hong Kong, Malaya, the Dutch East Indies, and the Philippines. The Chinese government retreated to Chungking, deep in the interior, as Japan took control of the coastal regions and major cities of China. The Japanese mastery of a new mode of warfare combining land and sea operations paralleled the German leadership in mechanized land warfare. About midway into 1942, with the Germans again smashing deep into Russia and the Japanese on the borders of India, the so-called Axis came closest to winning the battle for the world. But the tide was about to turn.

This was also Rommel's year in Africa. The glamorous and capable commander of the Afrika Korps used concentrated armored divisions, joined to artillery and motorized infantry, with spectacular success in the desert war. Initially handicapped by lack of support from Berlin, since all forces had been thrown into the Russian campaign, Rommel received reinforcements in 1942 and drove on Egypt, capturing the port of Tobruk before finally being checked at El Alamein, only 70 miles from Alexandria.

It was in October that the tide really turned in Africa. A British counteroffensive was now led by another of the great World War II commanders, Bernard Montgomery, who abandoned the old tactics to imitate Rommel's massed tanks and artillery. The North African war became an epic of World War II, curiously beloved to all who fought in it and marked by a kind of chivalric grandeur that contrasts with its real importance. It certainly produced two of the most fascinating military mystiques, those of Rommel and Montgomery. But it was less the main arena of world struggle than a colorful sideshow.

El Alamein stands with Stalingrad and, in the Pacific, the naval battles of Midway and Coral Sea as the moment when the Axis was checked at its zenith, thereafter to sink. But of these crucial battles, the mammoth encounter on the Volga was the greatest.

GERMAN DEFEATS

Germany was hardly prepared for a war of attrition. Committed to a lightning war intended to last only a few weeks, Germany's conversion to "total war," with the entire economy geared to war production under emergency government dictatorship, came later than it did to the Allies. Only in 1942, with the dismaying fact of his failure to blitz Russia staring at him, did Hitler move toward a war economy. Fritz Todt and then Albert Speer became powerful national economic administrators. A 55 percent increase in arms production took place in Germany in the first half of 1942. As in other warring countries, women assumed a greatly increased role in both industrial employment and in the nonfighting part of the *Wehrmacht*. Foreign workers and prisoners of war provided a slave-labor force numbering as many as six or seven million. Germany exploited France and other occupied countries effectively by levying vast sums for "occupation costs" and by unequal bilateral trade agreements. In fairness, it should be noted that the Allies also used prisoners of war as a labor supply; at the end of the war some 225,000 prisoners were working in Britain, most of them Italians.

In Poland and Russia, "the savagery of the German administration produced an economic chaos which both prevented any rational economic exploitation of these territories for war purposes and any rational planning for the economic future there," says historian Alan Milward. And, the National Socialist administration in general continued to be chaotic, mixing bureaucratic expertise with party fanaticism and the private empires of various high Nazis. Goering, one of those in charge of economic policy in occupied lands, declared, "I intend to plunder and plunder heavily." "We will take everything we can use," Hitler affirmed. Plunder in Russia was simple and direct. In France, Norway, and the Low Countries, it was indirect but almost equally exploitative. To replace expelled natives, nearly a million Germans were recruited to settle in western Poland. This was the beginning of a projected long-term policy, managed by Himmler, of colonizing the Slavic East with Nordic "pioneers." But in the main, any orderly planning was postponed until after the war.

In 1942, the Allies began pounding German cities from the air. Nevertheless, that same year Hitler was able to mount another great offensive in Russia with even more tanks, planes, and guns than he had the previous year. Hitler again debated with his generals whether to resume the offensive, for the always conservative military establishment feared disaster. But Hitler was now totally in charge, and he was not a man to refuse a gamble. With the United States now in the war, Germany faced a growingly powerful world coalition and needed a quick victory. Russia had surely received mortal wounds and needed only to be finished off. The drive toward Stalingrad was a compromise between the old one-pronged versus many-pronged strategies, for from this center of industry and communications on the Volga (today it is called Volgograd), armies might wheel north to take Moscow from the rear or move south toward the Caucasus.

But Stalingrad was more than a thousand miles from Berlin. Exposure to a Russian counteroffensive increased as the front lengthened. One premature Soviet counterattack came to grief because the Russian central command continued to show incompetence. It was on this occasion that General Vlasov became so disgusted that he let himself be captured by the Germans and later led an anti-Soviet "Free Russian" army. His position was, of course, weakened by the bestiality of Nazi rule in occupied Russia.

Beginning on June 28, almost exactly one year after the start of the war, the German offensive broke through on either side of Kursk and below Kharkov, crossed the Don, and swept through the plains toward its goal. Again, the panzers seemed irresistible, again the Germans were jubilant; "the Russian is finished," Hitler exulted. But at the city of Stalingrad, named after the Communist chieftain, the most terrible battle in history was shaping up. It was the Verdun of World War II: First a magnet, it became a symbol. The Russians pulled troops from the Moscow area to defend it; the Germans insisted on taking it. A million men struggled for possession of a few square miles. They fought street to street and literally room to room until the city was rubble; then they went on fighting in the rubble. The battle dragged on for months, beginning in late August. In November, a Russian offensive from behind Stalingrad began to encircle and trap the exhausted German army. Finally, on February 2, what remained of a German army of half a million, now reduced to some 80,000, surrendered despite Hitler's orders to hold out to the last man, and their general was soon fronting a pro-Soviet movement.

It was the first real German defeat, apart from El Alamein, and others were to follow. In Russia, a Russian winter offensive recaptured Kursk, Rostov, and Kharkov, and in the north it broke the long siege of Leningrad, which had reduced that great city to a state of starvation.

By this time, Montgomery had driven Rommel out of Egypt, toward a

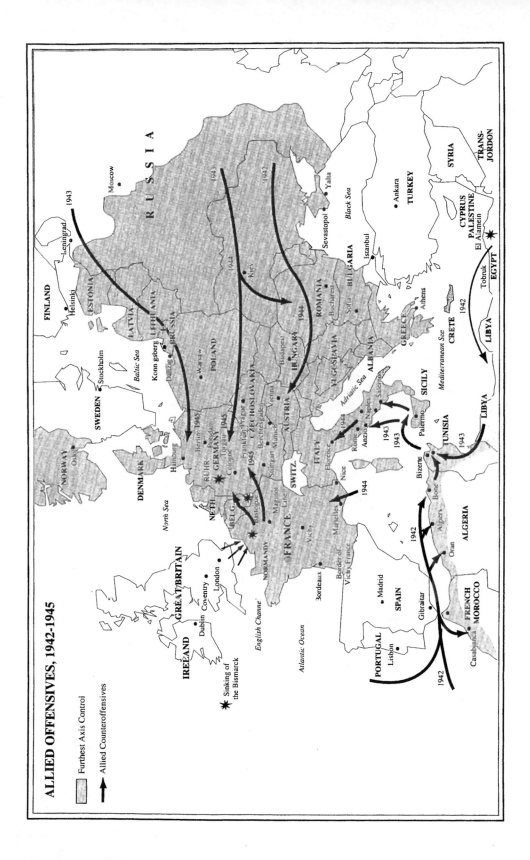

ALLIED OFFENSIVES, 1942-1945

Furthest Axis Control

Allied Counteroffensives

* Sinking of
  the Bismarck

RUSSIA

FINLAND

Leningrad

Moscow

ESTONIA

LATVIA

LITHUANIA

PRUSSIA

Königsberg

Danzig

Warsaw

POLAND

Kiev

1944

1944

HUNGARY

Budapest

ROMANIA

Bucharest

BULGARIA

Sofia

Sevastopol

Yalta

Black Sea

Ankara

TURKEY

SYRIA

TRANS-
JORDAN

CYPRUS

PALESTINE

El Alamein

EGYPT

Tobruk

1942

LIBYA

CRETE

Athens

GREECE

ALBANIA

YUGOSLAVIA

Adriatic Sea

SICILY

Palermo

Mediterranean Sea

LIBYA

1943

TUNISIA

Bizerte

Bône

1943

ALGERIA

Algiers

Oran

FRENCH
MOROCCO

Casablanca

1942

SWEDEN

Stockholm

Baltic Sea

NORWAY

Oslo

DENMARK

North Sea

Hamburg

Berlin

Potsdam

1945

RUHR

Cologne

GERMANY

1945

Frankfurt

Prague

CZECHOSLOVAKIA

Vienna

Munich

Stuttgart

AUSTRIA

SWITZ.

Florence

ITALY

Rome

Anzio

Naples

Salerno

1943

1944

1944

1945

Maginot
Line

Nice

FRANCE

Vichy

Bordeaux

Vichy France

Border of

Marseilles

1944

NETH.

BELG.

Bastogne

NORMANDY

GREAT BRITAIN

London

Coventry

Dublin

IRELAND

English Channel

Atlantic Ocean

Madrid

SPAIN

Gibraltar

PORTUGAL

Lisbon

1943

1942

1943

1943

1942

Istanbul

final doom in Tunis, where 150,000 survivors of the Afrika Korps surrendered in April 1943. An Anglo-American force had landed in French North Africa in November 1942 and advanced on the German forces from the west to spring the trap on Rommel. Operation TORCH did not come off without some hitches. Under General Eisenhower's command, the American landings at Moroccan and Algerian ports were supposed to achieve surprise and coincide with Montgomery's advance westward from Egypt while another British army took Tripoli and Bizerta, before the Germans and Italians had time to react. But French armed forces in North Africa were not wholly neutralized. Some Frenchmen remembered Churchill's destruction of their fleet in 1940 with bitterness. Smuggled out of France in the hope that he could persuade the North African French not to resist, General Henri Giraud proved a grievous disappointment. The Americans then installed Admiral Jean Darlan in Algiers as would-be commander of the French forces; Darlan promised to bring the French around to the Allied side, but this move outraged the entire French resistance movement because Darlan was a notorious pro-fascist. British intelligence then helped get Darlan assassinated! Considerable Anglo-American bickering accompanied this botched political operation. French forces put up more than token resistance. The Germans were able to reoccupy Tunis. The operation cost many thousands of lives, perhaps 10,000 Americans and 13,000 British in all. Hitler occupied the rest of France after the North African invasion, putting to an end Vichy's precarious semi-independence.

Nevertheless, in the end the strategy worked. Like Russia in a smaller way, North Africa had proved to be a drain down which the Germans poured men and supplies, in the end to no avail. The destruction of German power there opened the way for an Allied invasion of first Sicily and then Italy in the summer of 1943. Meanwhile, however, it was from the air chiefly that the Allies attacked Germany itself, and it was on air power that they pinned their chief hopes for victory.

Terror from the skies on a far larger scale than in the earlier war was a ghastly feature of World War II. The Germans, who had wiped out the center of Rotterdam during the 1940 assault on France and the Low Countries, plastered England in 1940 and 1941 in an attempt to break the will of the British. Then it was Germany's turn to suffer from incessant aerial pounding. Huge bombs were carried in planes larger than any known before. World War I spared most civilians outside the immediate zone of battle; the second made them its chief victims. It was entirely appropriate that the war's end came when the invention of the atomic bomb forced the surrender of Japan after two cities had been virtually wiped out, each by a single awful explosion.

Yet, the war in the air also revealed surprising limitations of this horrible form of warfare. If the Germans failed to break the will of Britain and finally had to call off their attacks because of heavy losses, the Allies subsequently failed to break Germany, even though they rained hundreds of times more bombs on her cities. In 1942, the British, joined now by the Americans, thought that aerial bombardment could win the war by paralyzing German communications and destroying key industries. But this "strategic bombing" failed for lack of precision. Radar and fast fighter planes rendered daytime bombing too costly until quite late in the war, when better navigational systems and long-range fighter escort planes were developed. At night, it proved impossible to pinpoint targets as small as a particular factory. And so "strategic bombing" evolved into "area bombing," the idea being to saturate highly industrialized areas on the assumption that something valuable was pretty certain to be hit; or, if not, at least the enemy would have to divert resources of labor and machinery to cleaning up. Quite often, this strategy seemed to degenerate into rather indiscriminate bombing of cities without much attempt to distinguish between industrial and residential sections—often not far apart.

Since few believed that bombing could destroy a people's will to fight, after the first experiences, it is probably erroneous to speak of "terror bombing." Yet this appallingly inhumane policy eventually reduced most German cities nearly to rubble, killing or maiming hundreds of thousands of civilians as well as wiping out priceless historic buildings. Particularly infamous was the raid on refugee-crowded Dresden in February 1945, which killed as many as 50,000 helpless people. Such opposition to the war as existed in the Western democracies (there was in fact very little, though more Conscientious Objection than in World War I) focused on the bombings. Initially patriotic, the leading young American poet, Robert Lowell, wrote to President Roosevelt in August 1943 politely declining an invitation to join the Armed Forces, for which—FDR proving unsympathetic—he spent several months in jail. His reasons included the policy of unconditional surrender as well as the indiscriminate terroristic bombing of German cities.

Some of the bombs weighed as much as 10 tons. Totals rose to a peak of 60,000 to 65,000 tons a month in 1944–1945, when round-the-clock bombing became the rule. German losses from the bombings can only be estimated, but a fair guess is 300,000 killed and 750,000 seriously injured. The amazing fact is that the 1.7 million tons of high explosives and incendiary bombs dropped on Germany did not seem to seriously impair German war production. At least, it did not prevent a steady increase in the manufacture of tanks, planes, guns, ammunition, and other war supplies, which more than doubled in 1942 and continued to climb until about the middle of 1944. After that, the decline could plausibly be attributed to the defeats and invasion on land. By mid-1944, German armaments production as a whole was about three and one-quarter times as much as it had been in 1941.

In return for what damage was done, the Allies paid a high price. No fewer than 57,000 British airmen died in these attacks. Much very expensive materiel was lost, too. The British were losing 170 big Lancaster bombers every month in 1943–1944. They once lost more than 100 bombers in a single raid (March 30, 1944, on Nuremberg). Altogether, 18,000 U.S. and 22,000 British planes were lost or damaged beyond repair. The total cost of the bombing has been estimated at $85 billion.

In the end, the Allies had to do what the "victory through air power" school claimed they wouldn't, that is, mount a huge invasion of the Continent to defeat Germany. Those who called the bombing strategy a crime against civilization were less numerous than those who argued that it was a mistake simply in terms of efficiency: Applying the same resources in other directions would have finished the war sooner. Yet, this debate has never been decisively settled. Some military experts still argue that only this command of the skies and the continual burden it placed on Germany assured Allied victory.

The Allies were able to afford this expenditure of planes for incessant bombing because of the immense productivity of the American war industry. Nearly 100,000 bombers and 200,000 other planes came off assembly lines in the United States during the war, along with 86,000 tanks, 60 million tons of shipping, and vast quantities of other miscellaneous materials of war. No other country came close to matching this record as a whole, though the Russians made more tanks and the Germans built 30,000 bombers, mostly smaller ones. British aircraft production also did extremely well, alone outproducing Germany.

The United States was able to supply the Soviet Union with motorized vehicles, tanks, and planes, and also with great amounts of food and other supplies, in quantities that certainly played a crucial role in keeping the Soviets afloat, however reluctant they were to admit this. Already being shipped in significant amounts by 1942, total aid to Russia during the war amounted to around 17,500 aircraft, mostly pursuit planes or light bombers, 20,000 tanks, 140,000 jeeps, more than a million trucks, 400,000 submachine guns, over 4 million tons of food, and other supplies to a total value of at least $10 billion and a total weight of 16.5 million tons. This stream of supplies traveled via three routes: to eastern Siberia from Alaska, over the oceans to Abadan on the Persian Gulf and thence across Iran, and–the shortest but most dangerous–the Arctic route to the northern Russian ports of Murmansk and Archangel. Nazi subs, planes, and battleships often made the last route a nightmare, but overall losses at sea were no more than 6 percent, or 1 million tons out of 17.5 million shipped. Courageous as they were, the Russians probably could not have prevailed against the Nazis without this freely given American aid, which was conveyed in American and British ships protected by American and British naval and air power. The communist state owed its survival to capitalist America. All this the Americans contrived to do while also fighting the war against Japan; but grand strategy decided that the defeat of Germany was the first priority.

Bombing Germany and sending materiel aid did not suffice to please Stalin, who pressured the Allies to invade Europe, even to the point of threatening to make a separate peace with Hitler in 1943. The Stalingrad victory did not quite end the German threat. Indeed, Hitler, against the advice of his generals, managed another offensive in the summer of 1943. If they could shorten the front, hold key points, and build an elastic defense, the German generals thought, they could hold the Russians off indefinitely. At this point, Hitler began to lose his grip on reality, preparing already for that *Götterdämmerung* of destruction he arrived at two years later in the Berlin bunker. Refusing to retreat and forcing new offensives, he gave the Russians a chance to mount devastating counterassaults. Another mighty battle around Kursk staggered the Germans in July, after which the Russians pushed them steadily back, retaking Kharkov and then Kiev by the end of the year. The Kursk battle, though less famous, may have been even more decisive than Stalingrad.

THE ASSAULT ON "FORTRESS EUROPE"

The British were much more reluctant to launch an invasion of the Continent across the Channel from England than were the Americans, to whom it seemed obvious from the start that this was the shortest, most direct, most effective way of defeating Germany. "The fearful price we had to pay in human life and blood for the great offensives of the First World War was graven in my mind," Churchill conceded. In 1942, the Americans were forced to admit that the difficulties of such an operation were greater than they had thought, though American military leaders did not much like the decision made by President Roosevelt to appease Stalin (and their own itch for action) with the North African operation. Operation "Torch" (Africa) took the place of "Overlord" (invasion of Europe) for the time being, along with a stepping up of the bombing attacks on Germany. North Africa then led to the Italian invasion in the summer of 1943. This did not placate Stalin, and in the end it proved something of a sideshow.

The invasion did knock Italy out of the war, only to expose her to the horror of a Nazi occupation. The war had been a series of disasters for the Italians. They had no military victory to compensate for their steadily falling incomes, and Mussolini had lost all support. A wave of strikes crested in March 1943, even before the Allied invasion of Sicily from North Africa on July 10 and the bombing of Rome a few days later. Fortunately, the Allied bombers managed enough precision to avoid hitting St. Peter's or the Forum. There was a popular movement against fascism, uniting Communists, Socialists, and the more moderate parties, including the newly born Christian Democrats. But the almost bloodless revolution that overthrew Mussolini on July 25 was a revolution from above, managed by army, clergy, and crown. The Fascist Grand Council, rescued from oblivion, voted against the now thoroughly deflated *Duce,* and King Victor Emmanuel III told him he was through. Too dispirited to resist, Mussolini allowed himself to be arrested, amid public rejoicing. The notables who overthrew Mussolini settled on old Marshal Pietro Badoglio, hero of the Ethiopian war, as his successor.

While publicly declaring that "the war continues," Badoglio looked despairingly for a way out of it, hoping for terms from the Allies. But the Americans and British, planning to invade the Italian mainland from Sicily on September 9, refused to grant any terms except those recently agreed upon among the Big Three (Roosevelt, Stalin, and Churchill): unconditional surrender. This formula was destined for much controversy. While the Italian government hesitated before capitulating in so abject a manner, the Germans were able to move additional troops into Italy. Amid a fog of confusion and misunderstanding that has generated debate to this day, the Italians finally signed an armistice on September 2, just as Anglo-American troops landed in the south of Italy. There they discovered that German forces had seized control of Italy and were prepared to offer fierce resistance. To make matters worse, an Italian resistance movement, born at this time, was exposed to German revenge.

Some have thought that better timing might have forestalled the German takeover, and they have blamed either the Badoglio government or the Allies or both. It is certain that the delay of six weeks between July 25 and September 2 helped the Germans. Mussolini, rescued or kidnapped by German paratroopers, again headed a pro-Nazi regime with headquarters in northern Italy near Verona. Enduring a bitter ten-day battle at Salerno before establishing a beachhead, Allied troops encountered further hard fighting in the rough country and narrow defiles of Italy. An attempt to outflank the German line by landing from the sea at Anzio, near Rome, early in 1944 incurred heavy casualties and failed to achieve its goal.

The Italian campaign came in for much criticism later. After invading Italy, the Allies lost some of their interest in this front, as they decided to make their major effort in the cross-Channel invasion—a decision they had really made long before. The Allies were content to advance slowly or not at all in Italy. Always something of a stop-gap, the Mediterranean campaign suffered from the defect that one could not really get at Germany from this direction. The Alps lie between Italy and Germany, and no one thought possible an invasion through them. The justification for the Italian campaign was that it pinned down sizeable numbers of German troops, but this rationale was obviously something of an afterthought. The Italian campaign diverted strength from a possible invasion of France from the south that was to be coordinated with the cross-Channel attack. All in all, the Italian front was frustrating and may have been wasted effort, except for two things: It satisfied the demand for action while preparations for the main event were going on, and it was a training ground.[3]

Meanwhile, D-Day, the much-postponed "Operation Overlord," crept closer through the vast preparations of 1942 and 1943. A costly raid at Dieppe in 1942, carried out by Canadian troops, showed how formidable the task would be against heavy German coastal fortifications. That the invasion was delayed until June 1944 was not, as many Americans believed, the result of British foot-dragging. Churchill did indeed stoutly contend for a strong secondary effort in southeastern Europe, crossing swords with the Americans on this ques-

---

[3]Another unpleasant aspect of the Italian campaign, revealed by Norman Lewis in his book *The Honored Society,* was that the Allied Command had dealings in Sicily with the corrupt and vicious Mafia.

D-Day: Materiel pouring on shore after the June 8, 1944 Allied landing in Normandy. (*U.S. Army Photo.*)

tion; he did not question the need of a cross-Channel attack. It is now generally agreed that any earlier date was not feasible. By 1944, air superiority against the fading *Luftwaffe* was secure. Stalin, of course, believed that his Western allies procrastinated until his armies had bled the Germans white; and it must be admitted that the Allies showed little disposition to risk a major assault until it was clear that the Germans could not win in Russia.

But the huge operation was finally launched on June 6, 1944. The first assault wave on the Normandy beaches used 5,000 ships, artificial harbors ("mulberries"), artificial breakwaters made up of sunken ships ("gooseberries"), an air cover of 10,000 planes, landing 3,000 guns, 1,500 tanks, 13,000 vehicles, and more than 50,000 men including airborne paratroopers. The invasion force included Poles, Belgians, Canadians, Norwegians, Dutch, and French (though Free French leader de Gaulle had not been invited to the strategic planning sessions). There were by this time over a million American soldiers in southeastern England. Within two months, two million men and two million tons of materiel were transported to France.

In planning "Overlord," the Allies also made good use of their secret intelligence weapons, for the Germans were deceived into thinking the attack would come at Calais, just as they had been tricked into expecting a Sicilian invasion in Greece. The choice of Normandy was actually dictated by the need of air coverage from English airports; Brittany was too far away. Calais was well defended and lacked deep beaches.

Even Stalin was impressed: "My colleagues and I cannot but admit that the history of warfare knows no other similar undertaking from the point of view of its scale, its vast conception, and its masterly execution," he wrote to Churchill.

Chilled, cramped, and seasick from crossing the Channel in tightly packed craft in bad weather, the first to land encountered deadly machine gun fire. One of the two American landings almost failed; but the British succeeded in putting three divisions ashore, and the Normandy beachhead was finally secured. Then the American, British, Canadian, and Free French troops fought to break out from the beaches to begin the sweep through France. Aiding them were Frenchmen organized (with British help) in the Resistance, who supplied them with information. German troops under able commanders stoutly resisted, but they could not prevent the troops' landing and subsequent breakout into the plains of France. The Germans clung to the Channel ports and then wrecked them before surrendering, making the Allied logistics problem formidable.

The advance was slow. A bold plan to drop airborne divisions behind the German lines, conceived by General Montgomery, failed at Arnhem. In another long-debated decision, Eisenhower decided against Montgomery's idea of a rapid but risky single-pronged thrust toward Berlin, in favor of a slower but methodical advance on a broad front. American General George Patton, commanding the southern wing, agreed with "Monty" in favoring a single thrust, except that he wanted to be the one to make it.

On August 15, there was a landing in southern France, delayed because of Allied arguments, Churchill having clung to the idea of a Balkan front to link with the Yugoslav partisan fighters. Almost a year of hard fighting remained after D-Day, and as late as the last weeks of 1944 the Germans were capable of a dangerous counterattack at Ardennes, the scene of their first great success four and a half years earlier. (On this occasion, Hitler beat "ULTRA" by ordering radio silence.)

But with the success of the cross-Channel invasion, combined with steady German retreat on the eastern front, the Reich's cause became hopeless. On July 15, 1944, General Rommell wrote as much to Hitler: Germany should seek peace. On July 17, Rommell was seriously wounded by a British plane that strafed his car as he was returning from a trip to the front. He had been prepared to act on his own, as German commander in the West, to negotiate a surrender, a part that he alone perhaps was equipped to play. Three days later, Colonel Claus von Stauffenherg brought a bomb in his briefcase into Hitler's headquarters at Wolfssschanze in East Prussia. The bomb exploded, killing several people but doing little damage to *der Führer*. (In March 1943, a bomb placed on Hitler's plane by Fabian von Schlabrendorff failed to explode. Another bomb plot fizzled when the dictator suddenly cut short a tour of the Berlin arsenal. Another bomb exploded prematurely. Hitler's enemies got the feeling he really was destiny's favorite.) A factor in the July 20 miscarriage was a last-minute shifting of the conference to a building with walls too thin to contain the force of the explosion.

Having learned from Stauffenberg that Hitler was dead (as the courageous colonel thought), the German army in Paris arrested the local SS and SAD preparatory to contacting the Allies for the purpose of ending the war. But news of Hitler's miraculous survival unnerved most of the conspirators. General Karl Stülpnagel, who wanted to continue the coup, shot himself; and Kluge, caught hopelessly in a conflict of loyalties, took poison. Rommel was later to be forced to kill himself, in the course of a terrible vengeance Hitler took on the military rebels. Hitler himself was prepared to say, *Weltmacht oder Niedergang:* rule or ruin. Having proved unworthy of the world role he had marked for her, Germany could perish along with him, in a Wagnerian twilight of the gods.

Thus Germany was not able to do what Italy had done, depose its dictator to shorten a hopeless war. She and the rest of the world were condemned to months more of horror, as the bombs rained on defenseless cities, as European Jews were fed into Nazi gas ovens, and the Russians advanced into Poland, Hungary, Czechoslovakia, and finally into Berlin itself. Why was this so? Hitler's more demonic will and his more total control of Germany were clearly factors. There was no king or other head of state to appeal to; Hitler had taken over all offices. More important, leading Germans in the army, the government, and industry failed to act with sufficient boldness. True, there was a dedicated band of oppositionists, but they were relatively few. Even those Germans who bore no love for Hitler hesitated to turn traitor with the Russian on the doorstep.

The advancing Americans pause amid the ruins of a German town, early 1945. (*U.S. Army Photo.*)

As for the Allies, they continued to demand unconditional surrender and to refuse to bargain with any German. The fiasco of the July 20 attempt had exposed Hitler's enemies, and his revenge was savage. The leading conspirators were killed by slow strangulation, of which Hitler had films taken and shown. The Nazis borrowed from the Bolsheviks the practice of visiting revenge on relatives of the "criminals"; "the family of Count Stauffenberg will be wiped out down to the last member," Heinrich Himmler declared. All the circles of the secret opposition, from Carl Goederler's to von Moltke's Kreisau Circle, were broken. After this, no opposition was possible; links that had been forged over a matter of years were destroyed. Germany could only suffer under the rule of a dying madman.

THE DIPLOMACY OF COALITION WARFARE

By the time Hitler and Himmler vented their rage on the men who had tried to kill them on July 20, not only were the Anglo-American forces bearing down on Paris, but the Russians, having expelled the Germans from Russia, were pushing toward Warsaw. On August 10, anticipating Russian victory, the Polish underground in Warsaw rose up and seized control of portions of the city from the Nazis. The underground looked to the government-in-exile in London for leadership. But Stalin had created his own Polish National Liberation committee and had begun to denounce the London Poles as fascists. The Russians halted their advance toward the Polish capital and waited while the exposed Polish freedom fighters were slaughtered by the Germans. Three hundred thousand Poles were killed in one of the war's most appalling tragedies. On August 12, Churchill ordered a desperate airlift, but the Russians refused landing facilities.

This was hardly an isolated example. Italian partisans failed to receive enough Allied help, as we know; and in the battle for France some premature rebellions were bloodily suppressed when the Germans were able to hold on for a while. The SS wiped out the French village of Oradour-sur-Glane and killed all 600 of its inhabitants. Earlier, in 1942, the Czech village of Lidice had been exterminated in retaliation for the assassination (by British agents) of the able Reinhard Heydrich, chief of the SD (Security Services, of which the Gestapo was a branch). During the drive on Germany through France (November 1944), de Gaulle once flatly defied an order from Eisenhower to pull back out of the city of Strasbourg, which had just been taken, to lend aid in the other crucial sector. He feared Nazi reprisals against French patriots if the Germans returned.

The often acrimonious disputes between Americans and British about military strategy has been mentioned. Churchill's insistence on diverting some Allied forces to a Balkan front failed to impress American leaders and was finally shelved, with Stalin's warm approval. Churchill warned about Russian dominance of the Balkans and wished to link up with the Yugoslav guerrilla movement or movements. This possibility was complicated by the rivalry between Colonel Draza Mihajlovic's resistance group and the Partisans, who were led by the radical Croatian Marshal Tito (Josip Broz). Churchill was willing to support a "stab in the Adriatic armpit" of Fortress Europe by Allied forces.

Of all the resistance movements of occupied Europe, Tito's was by far the most successful. At first, the Serbian Chetniks, followers of Mihajlovic, seemed to most of the world to be the most effective Yugoslav resistance. But the obscure Communist Tito proved to be abler, more energetic, more ruthless in a brutal game. The Chetniks as Serbian nationalists offended the other nationalities (chiefly Croatian and Slovenian) in the multiethnic Yugoslav state. The Partisans were able to forge a unity of all Yugoslav elements, though most Serbian peasants evidently continued to prefer Mihajlovic. The latter allegedly was less interested in fighting the Germans or Italians than in preventing a social revolution. (Tito himself dickered with the Germans on at least one occasion.) Stalin at first supported Mihajlovic but switched to Tito. The British support for the latter was greater. The Chetniks believed that they were betrayed by pro-Communist British advisers, including the notorious Douglas MacLean, who defected to the Soviets after the war. But the real reason for the switch to Tito in 1943 was simply that he had proved far more effective against the Nazis. That he was also a Communist did not disturb Churchill, who remarked that he did not expect to live in Yugoslavia after the war. Indeed, Tito was a remarkable leader and the Partisan movement a most extraordinary one.

But the Americans scarcely understood and were suspicious of the British interest in something other than a direct attack by the shortest route on Nazi-held Europe. And in the end, through superior strength they prevailed. Montgomery's battles with Eisenhower after the Normandy invasion have been mentioned. His chief objection to the slow-paced Anglo-American advance was that it permitted the Russians time to move into all the countries of eastern Europe and a good part of Germany, with no likelihood of soon moving out. Notorious were the feuds of the Allied generals, not only between British and Americans but within the American camp (Bradley and Patton, for example); and between the branches, the haughty air lords often refusing to accept collaboration with ground forces in a tactical plan, as they preferred to pursue general air superiority or even victory by air power alone. This side of the war does little credit, on the whole, to the maturity of these soldiers. The undoubted genius of Montgomery was camouflaged by an outrageous personality, matched on the American side by the colorful and ambitious Patton, "Old Blood and Guts." Over this set of prima donnas, commander Eisenhower presided uneasily, often not very effectively.

The diplomacy of coalition warfare and the planning for postwar politics is crucial in the history of World War II. Dramatically, the high leaders of state met in summit conferences to try to resolve the great issues. Roosevelt and Churchill's meeting at sea off the coast of Newfoundland in August 1941 had produced the Atlantic Charter, a rhetorical proclamation setting forth ideal peace aims. The Allied goal was a world without want or fear, armaments or conflicts. They wanted no annexations of territory contrary to the wishes of the inhabitants, a principle hard to square with Soviet actions in the Baltic states. In his "Four Freedoms" and other pronouncements, President Roosevelt sought to play a Wilsonian role in this war. Once again, high ideals and grim reality clashed. In practice, the Allies had to arrive at a division of power. They agreed that the Axis enemy must be totally defeated and disarmed. It proved harder to agree on the disposition of vast areas of the globe that would be left as a vacuum of power once Germany and Japan fell.

Stalin having refused to come, Roosevelt and Churchill met in January 1943 at Casablanca in Morocco. This meeting took place in the immediate aftermath of the North African invasion, which had raised the problem of the Free French. Roosevelt did not like de Gaulle and tried to bypass him in Africa. The United States recognized the Vichy government. Angered by a Free French effort to seize some French islands off the Newfoundland coast from their Vichy governors, American leaders believed that de Gaulle had little support in France, and while the State Department pursued a pro-Vichy and anti-Free French policy with strange tenacity, Roosevelt found the Free French leader a prima donna and a nuisance.

At Casablanca, the American and British military chiefs also continued to bicker about the cross-Channel invasion. Their discussion of peace terms produced the controversial dictate of unconditional surrender. No terms of any sort would be made with any enemy governments; they must surrender completely. In thus proclaiming total victory as the war's goal, the Allied leaders meant to reassure Stalin and everyone else that they would make no deals with Hitler. They also expressed the unique ideology of this war: total war, total victory, total reconstruction of the enemy countries after victory. The formula ensured war to the end, the invasion and occupation of Germany, and the complete destruction of the enemy's state apparatus, rather than some sort of negotiated peace.

The first meeting between the Big Three—Churchill, Roosevelt, and Stalin—took place late in 1943. The Soviet leader played hard to get, pleading the urgent pressures of the war, and finally forced the others to come to Tehran (Teheran), Iran, near the borders of the Soviet Union. At the conference, Churchill and Roosevelt sparred warily with the legendary Communist dictator. They found him blunt but intelligent and even likeable, and they seemed to reach certain agreements with him. Assured that the long-awaited invasion of western Europe would take place the following spring, Stalin promised to launch a Soviet offensive to coordinate with it. Roosevelt told Stalin that he privately sympathized with Russian plans for Poland's borders but could not say so because there were many Polish American voters—an ominous foreshadowing of the Yalta "betrayal" of eastern Europe to Russia, according to one school of thought. The three leaders issued a very general statement pledging themselves to remain united in their resolve to smash Germany completely—by land, sea, and air—and then to build "an enduring peace" through the United Nations, an international organization that would replace the defunct League of Nations. It was at Tehran that Roosevelt introduced the conception of the "four policemen" who would each patrol a beat in the postwar world–the Soviet Union, the United States, Great Britain, and China. Stalin and Roosevelt, and Churchill more reluctantly, agreed that France should not play the role of a major power after the war.

In regard to Germany, Stalin was inclined to question the demand for unconditional surrender on the grounds that it would intensify German resistance. But he agreed with Roosevelt, who was enthusiastic, and Churchill, who was less so, on the desirability of dismembering Germany. Roosevelt had a plan to divide Germany into five parts. Churchill assumed that Germany would be partitioned, with the south German states perhaps being placed in a federation with Austria. The Big Three decided to turn over the planning of the occupation of Germany to a European Advisory Committee on which the three powers would be represented. When it met in London, it encountered considerable frustration but finally worked out the zones of occupation; Roosevelt and Churchill confirmed these at the Quebec Conference of September 1944.

Many people throughout the world optimistically interpreted Tehran to mean that the Soviet Union and the Western democracies had learned to work together in war and in peace, overcoming their past hostilities and ideological differences. A year later, with victory approaching, public opinion remained optimistic; but with the entrance of Soviet troops into Europe, critical questions arose. As the Americans somewhat sanctimoniously washed their hands of such sordid politics, the harried Churchill had to deal with the Polish government-in-exile in London, whose leaders watched Stalin set up his own pro-Russian, Communist-dominated Polish government. In October, Churchill went to Moscow and initialed a territorial deal with Stalin. The Americans were kept informed of this agreement, which outlined a curious mathematical distribution. The Russians were to have 90 percent influence in Romania, 75 percent in Bulgaria, and 50 percent in Yugoslavia and Hungary. The Western powers were to have 90 percent influence in Greece. The omission of Poland and Czechoslovakia implied that the Russians would have complete sway there, as had been intimated at Tehran. Churchill brushed off the outraged cries of the pro-Allied Poles: "If you want to conquer Russia we shall leave you to do it. . . . You are absolutely incapable of facing facts." The fact the Poles were being asked to face was the loss of their national liberty to Russia. The Russians were there with the Red Army, and nothing could be done about it.

Against this ominous background, the Yalta Conference of February 1945 marked the climax of wartime consultation among the Big Three, but it was also the beginning of the subsequent quarrels between Russia and the West. The ambiguous agreements reached on this occasion were to be bitterly controversial in later years. Had the Anglo-American leaders, in their eagerness to win the war against the Axis as quickly and fully as possible, failed to consider

Churchill, Roosevelt, and Stalin, the Big Three of the wartime alliance, meet at Yalta (Crimea), February, 1945. (*U.S. Army Photo.*)

the postwar balance of power and allowed Soviet Russia to control all of eastern Europe? Could they, even if they had wanted to, have done anything at all to prevent Russia from dominating postwar eastern Europe?

Key decisions reached in the Yalta protocols and agreements concerned such important matters as the organization of the United Nations; policies toward Germany; the fate of liberated Europe, especially Poland; the trial of war criminals; and Russian entrance into the Far Eastern war against Japan. Of these, Poland and the Far East were the most critical and controversial. In regard to Poland, the Western leaders formally gave in and agreed that the pro-Soviet Polish government, organized by the Russians and obviously their puppet, should form the basis of the postwar Polish government. The Polish government-in-exile in London, which had been the legitimate 1939 government and had fled to London after the Nazi conquest, was thus rejected; it was the government on whose behalf the British had declared war against Germany in 1939. These Poles considered themselves betrayed and the war itself a mockery, since Poland had been rescued from Hitler only to be given to Stalin. Stalin did agree to bring a few of the London Poles into his Communist Polish regime and also to hold democratic elections in the near future, but he never did so.

Poland's frontiers were also changed; Russia received territory from 1939 Poland, and in return Poland was allowed to occupy former German soil up to the Oder-Neisse rivers. Britain and the U.S. did not formally agree to this boundary, although they accepted it in effect.

The Yalta decision was in fact a surrender to the Russians in eastern Europe, allowing them to install puppet Communist governments in Poland and subsequently in Romania, Bulgaria, Czechoslovakia, and Hungary without opposition from Britain and the United States. Since Soviet troops were already there, the Western powers could scarcely have done anything different without breaking the alliance and risking a war among the Allies. Perhaps by extracting some concessions toward democracy from Stalin they did the best they could, even though the Soviet leader chose to dishonor these pledges later. But there were unsavory features. Nicholas Kallay, the Hungarian premier, tried to arrange a surrender to the Western Allies, but the latter refused to deal with him. The Allies also delivered hundreds of thousands of refugees, against their will, back to Stalin to be imprisoned or shot.

In regard to the Far East, the Allies agreed that the Soviet Union would enter the war against Japan within three months after the surrender of Germany. In return, she would receive "the former rights of Russia violated by the treacherous attack of Japan in 1904"; that is, the southern half of Sakhalin, the lease of Port Arthur as a naval base, "preeminent interests" in an internationalized commercial port of Dairen, the Kurile Islands, and a share (along with China) in operating the Manchurian railroads. This meant that the Soviet Union would be powerfully established in the Far East. It was also an imperialistic agreement at the expense of China, made without consulting the Chinese government. Some argued later that this decision made possible the victory of the Chinese Communists over Chiang Kai-shek's government in the years after the war. They asked why such concessions had to be made to bring Russia into the war against Japan when Japan was already tottering and would soon be finished off by the atomic bomb. But at this time, the bomb had not been completed, and American military intelligence believed (wrongly) that Japan was strongly entrenched in Manchuria and might be able to hold out there a long time unless Soviet forces helped attack them. Here, again, the Western leaders evidently wanted to secure Russian goodwill by giving them a share in an area that had long been of great interest to the Russians. They hoped for postwar partnership.

At Yalta, the zones of occupation for Germany were confirmed also, and agreement was reached in principle on German reparations. The sum of $20 billion, of which half would go to the USSR, was mentioned "as a basis for discussion." Russia later claimed that she had received a firm pledge of $10 billion worth of booty from Germany. The United Nations, which Roosevelt regarded as a vital part of the new international order, obviously appealed to Stalin only insofar as it might further the interests of the USSR. Details of the United Nations were to be worked out at the San Francisco conference a few months later.

THE HOLOCAUST

Hitler was never the same after Stalingrad. Increasingly an ill and shattered man, he was kept going by the bizarre ministrations of the quack he kept as a physician and was rapidly approaching the certifiably insane—had there been anyone in Germany with the power to so certify. Yet the horrible progress of the Holocaust, or what Nazi jargon had named the "final solution"—the extermination of European Jewry—can hardly be blamed on Hitler's late insanity. In 1939, he had publicly threatened that if the war came it would bring "the annihilation of the Jewish race in Europe," and he continued to harp on this theme at every opportunity. But there were some moments, at least, when he wavered from the terrible goal of annihilation. German and Austrian Jews were allowed to emigrate, at a price; and Hitler played with the idea of settling all Europe's Jews in Madagascar.

Yet the concept of the final solution was well developed even before the war. The decision to carry it out coincided with the drive to the East, for here, in Poland and Russia, was the dwelling place of the great mass of European Jewry. There is no agreement on whether Hitler plunged into the fatal idea out of a sense of euphoria when the invasion of Russia seemed to be going well, or in a gloomy spirit of revenge when it had bogged down. Both views may be found in recent scholarship. Though some have argued for a slightly later date for its genesis, a directive from Goering to SD head Heydrich on July 31, 1941, is the evident origin of the project that led to the organization of human murder as a mass production industry. A conference on January 20, 1942, began the planning; in the summer of 1942 the Warsaw ghetto was cruelly cleared out. The SS was put in charge.

Nor is it clear how the final solution was related to the earlier experiments in euthanasia, killing not Jews but the old, ill, and demented. This program, which was not kept secret, incurred so much criticism that it was abandoned; this was perhaps why Hitler decided to keep the Final Solution secret. How deep the secrecy was is another matter of debate; many Germans surely had to know about a project so large. But Sarah Gordon, in a scholarly study of *Hitler, Germany, and the "Jewish Question,"* has found that most Germans and even most Nazis at the lower level were not anti-Semitic.

It has even been argued that Himmler and Heydrich planned the final solution without Hitler's knowledge, since no such order from Hitler has survived and since he apparently never discussed the extermination plan in his conversations, of which a very substantial amount was preserved. Strange though this is—for Hitler was addicted to interminable monologues in which he bored his involuntary auditors with every last detail of his thoughts—it is incredible to suppose that the Nazi faithful would have mounted such an immense operation without the Leader's knowledge. The project is something Hitler was certainly capable of undertaking. We are left with the hypothesis that Hitler could not psychologically face the concrete results of his theories, and this we

The Holocaust. (a) Germans clearing out the Warsaw ghetto in 1942. This famous picture was used at the Nuremberg trial. (*National Archives.*) (b) Mass grave at Belsen concentration camp, found April, 1945. (*U.S. Army Photo.*)

know to be true: He shrank from scenes of death on many occasions. So indeed did Himmler, who suffered an hysterical attack after once attending a mass execution.

Some responsible historians have argued that the process of mass extermination was not exactly willed or intended by any one person or group, but developed its own uncontrollable dynamic: a bureaucratic nightmare in the context of ideological fanaticism. "Hitler was only one part of a complex, polycentric, governmental system which allowed policy impulses to start from many different origins and meant that Nazi policy and the Nazi government were far from being Hitler's personal creation," Alan Milward has argued. It now seems fairly certain that we must revise as too simplistic the once canonical opinion that the Holocaust sprang directly and solely from Hitler's evil personality. "Extermination will become a human science," Shaw had predicted in 1934. This happened in the most scientific and best organized of countries.

The major murder camps were Majdanek, Treblinka, Belzek, Sobibor, as well as Auschwitz. Belsen, Dachau, Buchenwald, liberated by the West, were not extermination camps, but thousands died there from neglect and starvation in the last months of the war, many of them marched from the eastern camps as the Russians approached. Himmler ordered destruction of the gas chambers in November 1944. Official records and eyewitness accounts eventually convinced the world that this hideous process had really gone on; during most of the war, the Allies refused to believe such stories. The SS officer Kurt Gerstein, who had witnessed mass murders and accumulated hard evidence of them, tried in 1942 to convince the Catholic church and the Swedish government of these stories' accuracy, but they refused to believe him. (The final irony was that the Nuremberg Tribunal selected him for prosecution after the war; he committed suicide on July 25, 1945.) Those who claim that most Germans must have known about the extermination camps have to contend with the fact that non-Germans refused to credit these stories. This curious failure to believe a number of witnesses to the Holocaust attracted much subsequent interest. It seems clear that as early as November 1941, and increasingly after that, certainly by late 1942, Allied leaders were in possession of testimony about the extermination of the Jews that should have convinced them, yet for many months they refused to accept this evidence. The skeptics included President Roosevelt and the American Jewish leader Stephen Wise. The editor of a prominent American Jewish magazine acknowledged that she and other Jewish leaders "did not believe" one who told them in August 1942 that Jews were being massacred in Europe. The reasons for this were partly the legacy of World War I, when similar stories had turned out to be merely propaganda, and partly an inability to comprehend that such acts could take place in the twentieth century.

The Allied leaders seem to have convinced themselves that publicity about the mass-murder of the Jews would be harmful to the war effort, as well as counterproductive in its effect on the Germans. There was also a disinclination to think about where Jewish refugees might be sent: The British as the mandate power in Palestine did not want them there, and the Americans held to their severe immigration restrictions. Herbert Morrison, Churchill's Labourite Home Secretary, said that bringing numbers of Jewish refugees into Great Britain would stir up anti-Semitism.[4] The top Allied leadership adopted the position "Win the war first," then address this issue. "Meanwhile, people perish," as Chaim Weizmann said. But what in fact could be done until Hitler's regime was wiped out? Why were the gas chambers not bombed, it was later asked. They seemed to be one of the few things spared. The Allies did not know the truth about the biggest of the extermination camps until the summer of 1944. Jewish organizations then appealed for bombing of the gas chambers. But the British Air Ministry claimed that bombing the Auschwitz gas chambers was not practicable; bombs were not that accurate. One would have had to destroy the entire camp, killing the inmates.

Some governments of Europe collaborated with the Nazis in turning Jewish people over to the death camps. Romanian Jews mostly survived, while Hungarian ones perished; this was primarily because Romania, closer to Russia, was able to wriggle out of the Nazi embrace by 1944 while the Germans still occupied Hungary. Horthy saved Jews in Hungary until the spring of 1944 when Germans occupied the country, after which in a short period an estimated 470,000 of 750,000 Hungarian Jews perished. In Serbia under German control virtually all Jews were destroyed, but this was not so in Bulgaria. Singularly, the best record may have been that of Hitler's ally, fascist Italy. The Italian government did not turn a single Jew over to the Germans despite great pressure, and 85 percent of Italian Jews survived even though the Nazis took control of northern Italy in 1943. Italian armies helped Jewish refugees; Goebbels noted disgustedly in his diary that Italian troops protected Jews in southern France and Croatia. (In 1938, bowing to German pressure, Italy enacted a version of the infamous Nuremberg laws, but Fascist ideology was originally free of anti-Semitism, with Party membership open to Jews.) By contrast, the Vichy regime in unoccupied France was totally compliant in handing over Jews to the Germans, the darkest mark on its record. Three-fourths of the 325,000 French Jews survived, often with the aid of courageous French people. But the Vichy police rounded up and sent 75,000 to extermination camps; later the police claimed they did not realize, at first, that the Jews were being sent to death camps. (In 1993, after fifty years, the Vichy chief of police, René Bousquet, was assassinated as he faced belated prosecution; in the interim he had become one of France's leading financiers.)

Switzerland kept Jews from entering the country by asking the Germans to identify Jewish descent on passports. Hardly any country could claim

---

[4]In November 1944, the American Army newspaper *Yank* refused to print a document produced by two escaped prisoners from Auschwitz, which has become famous as an accurate eyewitness account of the exterminations; the editors said it was "too Semitic" and would stir up "latent anti-Semitism" in the army.

an honorable record. Grisliest of all, in Poland the Jews themselves via their community councils were forced to do the Germans' dirty work by procuring victims for the death camps. Poland and Hungary suffered the most, containing large Jewish ghettos easily marked for the slaughter. But with obsessive fury, the German Gestapo and SS—sometimes without the knowledge of other German authorities—pursued Jews all over Europe, hunting them down, for example, in Norway and Holland where there were few, often doing so at a cost to the war effort. It was an astonishing chapter in the long story of man's inhumanity to man.

The total number of Jewish deaths, mainly in the gas chambers of the Polish camps, has been variously estimated at anywhere from just over five million to above six million; Auschwitz-Birkenau alone may have slaughtered as many as two million. The camp records were destroyed and the grim arithmetic had to be calculated from many other sources on the basis of painstaking research that is still going on.

THE WEAPONS OF SCIENCE

British and American forces crossed the Rhine in March 1945, as a powerful Russian army was nearing Berlin. Long-range rockets were Germany's last hope in the last year of the war. The V-1s and V-2s on which Hitler had counted to rescue his fading cause fell far short of this goal. From September 1944, the V-2s were a menace; these "first long-range military rockets ever used in warfare" harassed southeast England and the important Allied invasion port of Antwerp. But by February, the Germans had been driven back out of range of vital Allied targets; the V-2s were capable of only a little more than a hundred miles. It is possible that they might have affected the course of the war had there been more time to develop them. Here, again, British manipulation of German intelligence, causing rockets to be mistargeted, was effective in frustrating the Nazis.

Previously mentioned, this spectacular British triumph in the intelligence war played its part in most of the Allied victories. Polish cryptologists accidentally came into possession of a German cipher machine in 1929; a brilliant Polish mathematician named Rejewski, with help from other Polish cryptoanalysts, invented a machine to scan the Enigma machine. (As luck would have it, a German alteration threw the Poles off for a time just at the moment of the German invasion of Poland in 1939.) A German gave information to a French Intelligence officer, and in 1939 the British, French, and Poles began working together. During the war, thousands of people worked at Bletchley Park near London, deciphering a great mass of intercepted German radio material and trying to find the important messages as quickly as possible (no computers were available to help them until, near the end of the war, a primitive one was invented by Alan Turing.)

The British also succeeded in virtually taking over the German spy network in England, the famous "double cross" operation that ranks as one of the greatest *tours de force* in intelligence history. Together, ULTRA and Double Cross allowed the Allies to mislead the Germans about invasion sites, disrupt their atomic weapons program, and in other ways achieve military success. It is estimated that ULTRA and other intelligence feats shortened the war by as much as three years. But for ULTRA, Rommel would have got through to Cairo in June 1942. It made possible the Allied landings in North Africa without losses from German submarines. In the Battle of the Atlantic, the Germans lost so many U-boats they finally withdrew, baffled; Admiral Doenitz never did understand how the enemy could read his movements so well. ULTRA has also been called the best-kept secret in history. It was kept closely guarded until as late as 1976. Despite a few close calls, the British managed to keep the Germans from learning that their code was not safe. The British also broke into another German code, Secret Writer, used by the German supreme command.

Similarly, the Americans had intercepted Japanese messages in July 1941, learning that Tokyo had decided to attack southeast Asia rather than the USSR in the aftermath of the German invasion of June 22; this knowledge led to American steps, including an oil embargo of Japan, that began the road to Pearl Harbor. Carl Boyd, in *Hitler's Japanese Confidant: General Oshima Hiroshi and MAGIC Intelligence, 1941–45* (1993) describes how Japan's ambassador to Berlin had all his despatches to Tokyo decoded, and died in 1975 never the wiser.

It is true that information might prove of no value, as with Stalin in June 1941, or even backfire: When the Allies invaded Italy in September 1943, they knew that Hitler had decided not to defend the peninsula below about Florence; but then *Der Führer* changed his mind after the troops had landed, a fact not picked up in the decrypts until too late. But in general, this battle of wits in the "wizard war" definitely was an Allied, chiefly British, triumph. Intelligence work was one of the Third Reich's numerous inefficient operations. The *Abwehr,* the German intelligence service headed by Admiral Canaris, was demoralized, permeated by anti-Hitler intrigue, and totally incapable of providing effective information about the enemy.

Stories about World War II espionage are too numerous to cite and are still coming out. Paul Rosbaud was a German anti-Nazi who supplied the British with valuable information about the German nuclear and rocket projects, enabling the British to sink a crucial boatload of heavy water in 1944. A high-ranking German embassy officer aided the chief British spy headquarters in France in 1942. Juan Pujol and Nigel West, in *Garbo,* relate the story of how the Spanish antifascist Pujol helped British intelligence deceive the Germans about the site of Operation Overlord. Though the Germans were not without their espionage triumphs, on the whole it seems that far more enemies of Nazism were prepared to risk their lives sending information to the Allies than vice versa. A story came out in 1994, during the fiftieth-anniversary celebration of the liberation of Paris, about a German decoding officer who delayed Hitler's order to destroy Paris before retreating.

In applying advanced science to warfare, the Germans were strangely inferior to the Americans and British in this war. In view of the earlier history of the scientific knowledge necessary for the atomic bomb, one would have expected Germany to be in the lead. German and German-Jewish scientists– Albert Einstein, Max Planck, Werner Heisenberg–had pioneered the new physics on which atomic energy rested. The Hungarian-born Leo Szilard and the Dane Niels Bohr had worked on uranium fission in Germany along with Otto Hahn and Lise Meitner. Berlin and Göttingen were leading world centers of scientific research. Germany had long excelled in the close connection between theoretical and applied science.

But it was exactly these great scientists whom Nazi intolerance drove away. In August 1939, Albert Einstein, who had left Nazi Germany to settle in the United States, wrote a letter to President Roosevelt urging the necessity to begin work on the superweapon, lest Germany win the race to this mighty source of energy. The scientists whose brains made possible the bomb, among them the Italian Enrico Fermi in addition to Szilard, Meitner, and others, were mainly exiles from Hitler and Mussolini. Thus did Nazi racism accomplish its own doom. In October 1943, Niels Bohr escaped from Denmark to Sweden and thence to London concealed in the bomb compartment of a Mosquito airplane.

British, French, and Americans contributed to the vast scientific enterprise. The Cavendish Laboratory in Cambridge, England, where Ernest Rutherford had first achieved atomic disintegration in 1919 and where James Chadwick identified the neutron in 1932, was an important research center; but the multibillion dollar project for building the atom bomb was headquartered in the United States. In 1943, the British were forced to accept a junior partnership in the project. Such brilliant Americans as Arthur Compton and Harold Urey contributed along with the Europeans. The first chain reaction uranium fission was achieved at the University of Chicago in 1942. A huge plant established at Oak Ridge, Tennessee, produced fissionable material in large quantity. Under the direction of American physicist J. Robert Oppenheimer, the actual weapon development took place at Los Alamos, New Mexico.

Before Yalta, Roosevelt had known that a bomb of vastly greater destructive power might be available within six months, but no one knew for sure that this amazing device would actually work until July 16, 1945, when it was successfully tested.

By that time, Germany was already finished, and it was on Japan that the terrible weapon was to be used. It forced her speedy surrender on August 15. In Germany, the "absolute weapon" that might have rescued her from defeat was not in sight of attainment. By 1945, Cherwell thought Germany was three years behind the West. The Germans lagged less in pure theory, about which German scientists knew as much as did Western scientists, than in uranium reactor technology. Hitler took little interest in and hardly seemed to know about the fission bomb prospects. Heisenberg claimed after the war that German scientists deliberately withheld the atomic bomb from Hitler. (Heisenberg was in charge of the project launched in April 1939, well before the American one.) From France, top physicist Joliot-Curie and other scientists smuggled out information about the Germans' interests to England. A pioneer in "heavy water," the kind containing a rare isotope of hydrogen needed for a successful atomic explosion, the French helped to keep a supply of this from the Germans. But the German decision not to go for nuclear weapons has been viewed as economically rational, in the light of limited resources.

Hitler could only hope for a miracle such as had saved Frederick the Great in 1762. That miracle had come about because Prussia's enemies, the Russians and the French, had a falling out. As we know, a similar disagreement was far from an impossibility this time; but at Yalta the Allies managed to pull together their threatened unity and work out an arrangement for the partition of Europe. After the February conference, Stalin furiously complained that the Americans and British made peace with Italy "behind the back of the Soviet government." The surrender of the German armies in Italy in April 1945 was worked out between American diplomats and the SS commander in northern Italy, Kurt Wolff. But the Western armies allowed the Red Army to liberate Prague, Vienna, and Berlin, to the dismay of Churchill and subsequent critics of Anglo-American policy.

Mussolini met his end on April 28, murdered by Italian partisans as he sought to escape. His body was hung up by the heels for public display in Milan. President Roosevelt had died of a massive cerebral hemorrhage two weeks before. Three days after Mussolini's death, with the Russians already in Berlin and the Americans and British smashing through to the south, Hitler and some of his cohorts (Eva Braun, Goebbels, and Goebbels' entire family) committed suicide in the underground bunker beneath the Reich Chancellery in Berlin. There Hitler had spent the last weeks of the war, as Albert Speer was trying to save something from the wreckage. "If the war is to be lost, the nation also will perish," was Hitler's view. On May 7, 1945, German General Jodl surrendered the German armies in the West to General Eisenhower at Rheims, and the next day the Russians received a similar submission. With a ruined, governmentless Germany in their hands, the victorious powers assumed charge of separate zones of occupation, as previously agreed upon by the Allied Control Commission in London.

THE WAR IN RETROSPECT

Hysterically exultant crowds cheered the victorious end of the war in London and Paris; the most exuberant American scenes were reserved for three months later when Japan surrendered. The war, with all its horrors and immense loss of life, had not been a totally bad experience for some of the victor powers. In the United States, which was spared military damage to its own land, the depression had vanished as the government ordered billions of dollars' worth of planes, tanks, ships, guns, construction of military bases, supplies for the armed forces, and supplies for Britain and Russia. In place of the unemployment that had blighted the 1930s, during the war there was overemployment. War industry required millions of new workers, while at the same time the armed forces were expanding from virtually nothing (a few hundred thousand) to twelve million men and women at war's end. Women took jobs in unprecedented numbers. Although inflation obviously threatened under such conditions, consumer prices rose only 30 percent during the war, and national income more than doubled. Wages increased 76 percent. Home-front Americans were better off in material terms by some 25 percent during the war, though with shortages of consumer goods they mostly saved this money, responding to patriotic appeals to invest in war bonds.

Europe was, of course, less fortunate than America, but Great Britain also paid for military production in some measure out of a 64 percent rise in national income. Only in the last period of the war did the economy fail in Germany; and the USSR performed miracles by moving industries from the war areas to the Urals and western Siberia, managing to keep war production up even though consumer goods fell drastically from an already low level. Italy's economy was a disaster. France, first ruthlessly exploited and then a battleground in 1944, also touched bottom. In general, though, the war's experiences contributed to a consciousness of power in dealing actively with economic problems. If such miracles of production had been possible in war, why not in peace? Such documents as the wartime report issued in Britain by Sir William Beveridge's commission, *Full Employment in a Free Society,* were much discussed; they reflected a belief that government regulation of the economy might eliminate poverty and want. President Roosevelt's wartime utterances stressed practical economic goals–freedom from hunger, ignorance, inadequate housing, and poor health.

Much technological innovation had emerged from the war. This included not only atomic energy, which everyone hoped would find a more constructive use than the terrible destruction it brought to Hiroshima and Nagasaki; but also great advances in aircraft design, for example, huge cargo transports with long-range capability; radar; penicillin; and other inventions that, if not born of the war, had been powerfully stimulated by its urgent needs. A pioneer computer emerged from the urgent needs of the Bletchley Park decipherers toward the end of the war. What has been called the first large-scale electronic digital computer was completed in 1945, at the University of Pennsylvania, based on prewar beginnings but encouraged by the government for military reasons. The transistor revolution, which led to the microchip revolution, was an outgrowth of radar technology.

Quite beyond the bounds of calculation were the experiences of millions upon millions of men and women whom the war dislodged from their routine to send to far places, often to their death but sometimes to the expansion of their consciousness and intellect. While World War II's crop of novels and poetry and memoirs did not come close to matching that of World War I, it had value. For decades, both professional and amateur historians would research the war's amazing events as none other in world history had ever been explored.

The war drastically interrupted the affairs of nations in ways that might lead to creative new responses; at least the cake of custom was broken. Obviously, for most of Europe, 1940–1945 was an absolute boundary after which almost everything had to be different, perhaps better. Shattered industries would be rebuilt and modernized. The bombs had leveled slums as well as palaces, and new city planning was necessary in much of the world.

Politically, a battered and enslaved France would have to reevaluate its entire system, its loyalties, its values; the trauma of defeat and Vichyism brought about a renewal of French political life from want of any other choice. Liberation in France found the Free French taking their revenge on the collaborators, those French people who had most brazenly upheld the Vichy regime and worked with the Germans. About twelve thousand were killed and more than 100,000 arrested, their property often confiscated. But this was not a massive wound; in the main, Vichy's repulsive policies, such as delivering up Jews for the Nazi death camps, had united French people of all political persuasions against it, and the Liberation stirred the country greatly—even though, it is estimated, not more than 2 percent of French adults had participated actively in the Resistance. Its greatest literary spokesman, Jean-Paul Sartre, described how the necessity to choose for or against collaboration brought a new sense of purpose, and forged friendships reaching from Catholic priests to Communists.

In other warring countries, war had brought a feeling of national solidarity that at least temporarily broke through class barriers and aided minorities: women, the lower classes, and blacks in the United States. People unanimously testified to the surge of human brotherhood in London that began during the 1940–1941 air attacks and continued all through the war. In the Soviet Union, war patriotism caused even Stalin's regime to make gestures of concession toward national unity. A Patriarch of the Orthodox Church was crowned for the first time since Peter the Great! Party membership was opened up, the peasant glorified, the old tsars allowed to appear as heroic defenders of Mother Russia. The war completed a reversion to almost "bourgeois" values always evident in Stalinism: Marriage, the home, and conjugal fidelity accompanied generally conservative tastes in the arts and architecture. A similar effect of the war in Western countries, which does not please recent feminists, produced more of a marriage-and-family mood in the immediate postwar years than a "liberationist" one.

Despite these possible uses of adversity, the war might be seen in review as a steady flow of unparalleled blunders, affording twentieth-century humanity small grounds for its characteristic pride in achievements. The Western democracies had allowed the swaggering Hitler to take what they had denied the peace-loving Weimar Republic. They had surrendered control of central Europe to Hitler out of weakness, cravenly sacrificing Czechoslovakia and Austria before drawing the line at Poland, which they neither could nor did defend either. They stood inactive while Hitler overran Poland, and then in 1940 they proved they had learned nothing of the new arts of warfare the Germans had almost perfected. For his part, Hitler, having won his war, could not stop. He attacked Russia without any real provocation and without adequate preparations. He compounded this mistake, which cost millions of lives, by refusing to fall back. The Germans mistreated the Russian peoples in so brutal a manner that they could not gain their support. The Nazis allowed the British to outwit them on the intelligence front. Having been beaten in war, Hitler refused to accept defeat. He preferred to sacrifice his country, which had done little to try to overthrow the mad tyrant.

Stalin refused to believe a thousand warnings and allowed the Germans to catch him by surprise, thus losing masses of supplies, soldiers, and territory. His mistreated subjects rallied to the support of his regime only because the Nazis gave them no choice. The immense suffering that Russia endured during the war would not have been necessary had the USSR and the Western democracies cooperated against Hitler in 1939–1941 when Stalin joined Hitler in his greed for Polish territory. For their part, the Allies left no loophole for negotiations, insisting on unconditional surrender while they plastered Europe's cities with high explosives. Advancing slowly across France in 1944 and 1945, after a belated invasion, they let the Russians take Berlin, Prague, Budapest, and Vienna and establish themselves throughout eastern Europe.

This catalogue of ghastly errors might be extended. Manifestly, there is something unfair in so much wisdom after the event. Yet, arguably, all these mistakes were foreseeable and indeed foreseen. The erratic if imaginative Churchill, the naive and sloganizing Roosevelt were not much wiser than the narrow-minded bigots who ruled over Germany, Italy, and Russia. Hitler's occasional lapses into shrieking rages are well known. Churchill was capable of lachrymose sentimentality. Scholars have generally given Roosevelt much lower marks as president than his great public popularity then indicated.

We have referred to the outsize egos and childish personalities of major military commanders. Citizens of every country were blinded by hysterical hatreds. The horrible crimes of the Nazis, in both the extermination of the Jews and the savage mistreatment of Poles and Russians, could be rivaled—if not matched—by the Allies, whose actions included indiscriminate bombing of European cities, the extinction of Hiroshima by an atomic bomb (used despite the pleas of the scientists who had created it, and arguably not necessary for the defeat of Japan), the killing of 100,000 Japanese survivors of torpedoed ships, and the imprisonment in camps of innocent Japanese-Americans—to mention only a few notable cases. Stalin's government uprooted whole nations, such as the Tar-

tars of the Crimea, and sent returning war prisoners and refugees to prison camps, with Anglo-American aid. (Over two million refugees who were outside Russia at the war's end were forcibly deported back. The majority of these people were not Nazi collaborators but simply expellees from war-devastated regions; many were not even Russian citizens but Poles, Balts, South Slavs, or Germans. They were delivered to almost certain death or imprisonment at Stalin's hands.[5])

From this incredible farrago of achievement and stupidity, destruction and construction, the world had somehow to recover after the summer of 1945.

[5]On the forcible return of people to be shot by Stalin or Tito, we have the impressive testimony of Milovan Djilas, at that time pro-Stalinist, that the British knew perfectly well the 20,000 sent back to Yugoslavia would be liquidated.

9

Europe and the Cold War, 1945–1956

EUROPE AT THE END OF THE WAR

"An outraged and quivering world," as Winston Churchill called it, had suffered a total loss of life estimated as high as seventy-five million as a result of global war from 1936 to 1945. Such figures, together with estimates of property damage, loss of wealth, and all the rest, can only be guesses. For Europe, a war death toll of thirty-eight million seems a fairly accurate estimate, of which twenty million were military casualties. Russian losses alone may have reached twenty million, at least half of whom were civilians. A million starved to death in Leningrad; two million Russians died in German prisoner camps. A vast area of Russia had been ravaged by the Germans, so much so that years after the war people were still living in caves or dugouts in White Russia and the Ukraine.

In revenge, German cities had been pulverized by air bombardment into "landscapes of the moon," their main districts reduced to rubble in percentages ranging up to 95 percent for Berlin, and from 60 to 70 percent for the cities of Hamburg, Dresden, Munich, and Frankfurt. Seven and a half million Germans were homeless. But these wagers of the War for the World did not suffer so much, proportionately, as one of their innocent victims, Poland, whose population fell from 23.2 million to 18.8 million. The city of Warsaw lost more people in World War II than the combined casualties of Great Britain and the United States. Sixty percent of Europe's 9.6 million Jews had been killed. Yugoslavia, with one and a half million dead, sustained heavier losses proportionate to her population than did Germany, with her four and a half million casualties.

In addition to those who died—in battle, perhaps frozen to death in Russia, under a hail of bombs rained on their homes, in the Nazi death factories at such places of infamy as Auschwitz and Maidanek, worked to death as slave labor—there was immense suffering through the forced displacement of peoples. The Germans had brought in at least six and a half million forced laborers, mostly Slavic but also some French and Dutch. As the war ended, many of these former prisoners rioted, creating havoc in some German cities. Just after the war, with the sanction of Allied agreements at the Potsdam Conference, some fourteen million Germans were driven away from eastern Germany, Czechoslovakia, Poland, and other eastern European countries under conditions that caused the death of perhaps 15 percent of them. Poles were also moved out of territory now assigned to Russia and into East Prussia or Silesia to replace the uprooted Germans; the entire nation of Poland was "pushed westward" about a hundred miles.

This vast migration of people who had been displaced by the war or the vengeance of the victors added to the extreme chaos in Europe at the end of the war. Invading Russian, French, British, and American soldiers occupied the defeated countries and, not only in Germany, often took the liberties traditional for conquering marauders. Soviet soldiers became notorious for plunder and rape; Tito was to complain about it on behalf of the Yugoslavs, allegedly receiving the reply from Stalin that soldiers deserved a little fun. Gangs of drunken Russian soldiers terrorized portions of east Germany in 1945 and 1946; many German police lost their lives trying to protect Germans from the depredations of Russian soldiers. But in Germany, the French were almost as guilty as the Russians.

Germany, enduring the hatred naturally felt by those who had suffered at her hands, felt hunger and cruel degradation. One scholar maintains that 800,000 German prisoners of war died of starvation and neglect in Allied prison camps in 1945. This has been questioned; but General Eisenhower declared that Germans were beasts. For nearly two years, the object of the occupying powers was to seize their wealth as reparations while deliberately keeping Germans at a bare sustenance level. The death rate in Berlin in 1945 is said to have been unmatched in that country since the Thirty Years War; about half the babies born in August died, chiefly of malnutrition. This was true also in Holland, Poland, and elsewhere. The Hoover Report in 1947 found German nourishment still at the lowest level of any Western nation in modern history. At the end of 1946, German production stood at a level one-third that of 1936. Every newspaper had ceased publication, there was no government save the military fiat of the occupying conquerors, and even the church had trouble delivering a message of consolation. A mission from the Vatican seeking contact with German Catholicism was rejected by the Russians and treated with extreme suspicion by the Americans and British.

War damage in a German city (Münster) during the Allied advance, April 1945. (*National Archives.*)

But except for those few places that had escaped the war–Sweden, Switzerland, and Spain–the rest of Europe was not materially much better off than Germany (large areas of Russia were certainly even worse off). Europe still looked like a vast slum in 1947, when Americans began to give serious thought to assisting in its revival. For the first year or two after the war's end, the victorious Allies, whose armies had met in the middle of Germany, tried to decide what to do with that country besides pillage and humiliate it; they struggled with their own problems of transition from war to peace; and they engaged in exercises designed to purge the world's burden of guilt and sin. Such an exercise was the Nuremberg Trials, which were held in the German city the Nazis had made their moral capital. The object was to discredit Nazism forever by exposing its hideous crimes, and perhaps to exact revenge.

Begun early in 1946 after months of planning, the trials lasted 216 days, led to the printing of ten million words, and accumulated tons of invaluable documents. Four judges from each of the four victor powers, the United States, Great Britain, France, and the Soviet Union, sat in judgment on twenty-one of the leading Nazis who were still alive. The group included Goering, Rosenberg, Streicher, and Ribbentrop, as well as men of industry and prominent generals; the entire General Staff and all the members of the SS and the Gestapo were named in a kind of blanket indictment. Evidence presented at Nuremberg documented the crimes of Hitler's state and made them known to the world in a dramatic way. The death factories of Auschwitz and Maidanek, the extermination of nearly six million Jews, the enslavement of more than six million forced laborers, the barbarities committed against the Russians and the Poles—all this and more emerged from the records. Other books published just after the war, such as Eugen Kogon's *Der SS Staat,* which became a best-seller in Germany, revealed the horrors of the concentration camps.

Called a unique landmark in world jurisprudence, freely compared to the Bill of Rights and the Magna Carta by enthusiastic publicists, the trials nevertheless partly failed in their role as mythic regenerator of the Western soul. Partly this was because of their manifest unfairness. The Germans were allowed one lawyer each, against a battery of some 2,500 attorneys assembled by the prosecuting nations. They did not have access to the documents, and for the most part they were not allowed to raise questions about such Allied crimes as Stalin's mass murders, British and American terror bombing, and the plundering of Germany then going on. While no one doubted Hitler's bestiality, there were nagging questions about how far collective guilt extended; and the attempt to couple the crime of waging "aggressive war" with the Nazi crimes against humanity did not altogether succeed.

One of four counts on which the Nazis were indicted, "crimes against peace" meant planning, preparing, or waging a war of aggression or a war in violation of international treaties. The most practical difficulties lay in the fact that the victor powers had done this too, the Soviets in the Baltic lands, Finland, and Poland, and the British, arguably, in Norway: They had mined Norwegian territorial waters before the Germans invaded Norway. Legally, it was hard to claim that before 1939 any clearly defined and accepted international law barred sovereign states from the right to declare and wage war. In the last analysis, the Nuremberg Trials were unfortunately tainted by more than a faint odor of "victor's justice"; those who won the war wreaked vengeance on the defeated under a thin disguise of legality, while refusing to countenance any discussion of their own crimes. Churchill observed that had Germany won the war, a similar trial would have hanged both FDR and himself.

In the end, perhaps to their credit, although to the great indignation of the American and Russian prosecutors, the International Military Tribunal acquitted three of the twenty-one defendants outright, awarded death sentences to only ten, and let the General Staff as such off with a tongue-lashing. Hermann Goering cheated Nuremberg justice by committing suicide, as scores of high Nazis had done previously—more than a hundred generals died by their own hand in the last weeks of the war. In the ensuing years, the Allies, as well as the German courts, carried out thousands of de-Nazification trials. The Americans, in particular, enthusiastically brought suspected Nazis to trial, amid controversies about who the real Nazis were and how far one should or could go in attempting to punish every German who had signed up as a party member. Gradually, the belief that Nazism lurked just beneath the surface of virtually every German faded, as the climate of opinion changed and Germany moved toward becoming a valued ally as well as a democratic state (in the western half) or a socialist one (in the east). But this process took several years.

The Nuremberg Tribunal had declared the SS a criminal organization, and in ensuing years not only the wartime Allies but Poland, Germany, Czechoslovakia, and other countries tried and sentenced, sometimes to death, the extermination camp personnel—a process that went on for the next three decades. But a historian who studied this chapter of history (Aleksander Lasik) concluded that, in the case of Auschwitz, only about 10 percent of the SS personnel who worked in that most infamous of all death camps ever stood trial. Many of them found refuge in South America where Juan Peron welcomed them to Argentina with open arms as did the Paraguayan dictator.

THE OCCUPATION OF GERMANY

The whole German question, embedded in the larger issue of a postwar peace settlement among the former Allies, scarred the immediate postwar scene. Germany's division was determined at the end of the war, though few then realized it. "This war is different from all earlier ones; the conqueror of a region imposes his own social system on it," Stalin said in 1945, privately. Those parts of Germany and of eastern Europe lying within the zone of Soviet domination were marked for communization. Military occupation, expected to be temporary, turned out to be the basis for the division of Europe into two camps, a division destined to last forty-five years.

But the goal of Russian policy in the immediate postwar period seemed to be to extract as much booty from Germany as possible, to meet the desperate material needs of a Russia exhausted by war, to feed their own starving people and get back into production their own battered industries. At Yalta, the United States and Great Britain had agreed to let the Russians take reparations in kind, both manufactured products and industrial equipment. The Russians had suggested $10 billion, a figure Roosevelt, though not Churchill, had accepted "as a basis for discussion"; Stalin simply assumed the matter settled. At Potsdam just after the war's end, in addition to a license for unlimited confiscation in their own zone of occupation, the Russians won a promise to receive industrial equipment and manufactured goods from the more industrialized American, British, and French zones. Ten percent of industrial plant was to be dismantled and removed to Russia, along with 15 percent of the German surplus of production (beyond what they needed to survive at a low level of existence). The total sum of Russian confiscations has been the subject of various wild estimates; it certainly amounted to many billions of dollars. The value of German industrial plant shipped to Russia between 1945 and 1950 amounted to perhaps $3 billion.

American Secretary of the Treasury Henry Morgenthau, who represented one wing of American German policy and at times had the ear of President Roosevelt, had wished to "wreck every mine, every mill and every factory" in the land that had produced Hitler; if his views did not prevail, they were at least partly represented in 1945 American policy. A people filled with "endemic barbarism," every one a potential Hitler (as the U.S. Army newspaper warned), Germans were not to be talked to, treated kindly, or allowed to convene in public; even children were wicked, and that apparently lovely *Fräulein* smiling at you might be part of a plot for the revival of Nazism. At first, Germans were not even supposed to leave their homes. Anton Webern, one of the century's greatest musical composers, was shot and killed by an American sentry when he went out for a bottle of wine. Such absurdities soon broke down, of course, to be replaced, ironically, by a kind of love affair between American soldiers and the southern Germans who populated the American zone of occupation. (During wartime planning of zones, the Americans had initially wanted the more populous and industrialized northwest as their zone, but the British talked them out of it. The United States did secure an enclave at Bremerhaven for supply purposes.) The children, the young women, and the wine and beer had the last word. But any thought that the United States ought to help German economic recovery scarcely arose until 1946. Meanwhile, the millions of refugees streaming in from the east added to the woe, and the French exploited their zone in the southwest almost as ruthlessly as did the Russians in the east.

In theory, while the four powers each governed its own zone, they were supposed to formulate policies for all of Germany through a Central Control Commission meeting in Berlin and consisting of the four commanders-in-chief. But this never functioned effectively, the French proving even more an obstacle than the Russians. Giving the French an occupation zone, which the British had insisted upon at the Yalta conference and which Stalin had opposed, thus played some part in the ultimate partition of Germany. So economic cooperation tended to break down.

What finally led the United States to break with the policy of ruthless exploitation of Germany was a matter of self-interest, combined with some small measure of humanitarianism. Unwilling to see the Germans starve, the United States began to send them food. The western zones of Germany (occupied by the British, American, and French) had to import food, since they were far from self-sufficient agriculturally. The less industrialized Soviet zone was more self-sufficient in foodstuffs. Stripping West Germany of machinery and manufactures for the benefit of the Russians deprived her of any means of paying for her food needs by exporting other goods. The Americans ended up footing the bill, since neither the economically struggling French nor British could; the bill amounted to some three-quarters of a billion dollars a year.

If it was monstrous to saddle the American taxpayer with the cost of feeding Germany, it was hardly possible to allow mass starvation in Germany, either; wartime hatreds, by 1946, did not reach this far. Another thought began slowly to dawn, too: Total European recovery was linked to German recovery.

You could not make a desert between the Rhine and the Elbe and expect the rest of the Continent to bloom. It was partly to alleviate the financial burden on the United States, Secretary of State James F. Byrnes declared in mid-1946, and partly to pave the way for a general European recovery that the United States decided she must restore the German economy. This was to entail a break with the Potsdam policy and with the Soviet Union. But by this time, other issues had begun to poison Russian-Western relations. The German problem cannot be seen in isolation and was not the only factor in the emerging Cold War. That war had broken out on a number of fronts by 1946.

ORIGINS OF THE COLD WAR

That there were serious differences among the Allies who had defeated the Axis powers, once that job was finished and the war ended, can hardly be regarded as much of a surprise. All previous experience testified to the ease with which friendship can turn to hostility when a common enemy is destroyed and problems of dividing up his inheritance arise. The many old suspicions as well as the obvious ideological gulf between Soviet Russia and the Western capitalist democracies made this rupture of harmony even more likely. A further factor contributing to the breakdown of friendship was the troubled state of the world, with area after area politically vulnerable. Meeting over the body of a nearly lifeless Germany, the recent allies also were inevitable rivals in many other areas, indeed almost all over the "outraged and quivering" world. Power was sharply polarized, and power vacuums existed in Europe and Asia, where the German and Japanese empires had so suddenly and totally collapsed.

Yet this collapse of cooperation between the USSR and the United States dismayed many people. Cooperation seemed so necessary to world survival after the brutal war. And, during the war, hopes had arisen. It later seemed astonishing how much Soviet-American goodwill burgeoned in 1941–1945. Genial, courageous "Uncle Joe" Stalin became almost an American folk hero, and such respectable figures as Ambassador Joseph Davies (a Wisconsin corporation lawyer) and Republican presidential candidate Wendell Willkie assured Americans they had much in common with the peace-loving Russian people. FDR radiated optimism about the postwar future, at least until the very last weeks of his life, and a public opinion poll revealed that Americans expected more problems with Great Britain than with the Soviet Union after the war. Surely, if they had accomplished the titanic job of demolishing the German and Japanese war machines, Russia and the United States, aided by Great Britain, France, and perhaps China, could join together, under the flag of the United Nations, jointly to police and restore to health a world purged of fascism.

What went wrong? The Cold War itself eventually became a battle-ground among historians and pseudo-historians anxious to condemn one side or the other for an avoidable disaster. Still others held to inevitability theories or stressed impersonal forces. Only a few ventured to note that a cold war, after all, is not hot, and that the real disaster of a war between communist and capitalist worlds was mainly avoided. To deplore the Cold War seemed *de rigueur* whether one chose to blame it on Stalinists or McCarthyites. It certainly did seem deplorable at the time, holding as it did the threat of a war even more terrible than the one of 1939–1945.

Eastern Europe more than Germany was a breeding ground for controversy between East and West. The Red Army drove the *Wehrmacht* from Poland, Romania, Hungary, Bulgaria, Czechoslovakia, and Yugoslavia, getting significant help from national forces only in the latter. The Russians thought they had earned a right to exercise dominant power in these places both by the blood they had shed and by the need to prevent a recurrence of the deadly attack launched against them from this area, sometimes with the aid of these countries. Hungary and Romania had joined the war against the USSR; prewar Poland had been anti-Soviet; prewar Czechoslovakia had seemed a tool of the appeasers of Hitler. In the wartime conferences, Stalin had made it clear that he intended to have "friendly" governments in these countries after the war, and the Western allies had agreed. Roosevelt and Churchill had told the Poles they had better accept the need to come to terms with Russia. And, they had given Stalin to believe he had a free hand in Poland.

At the same time, Roosevelt deluded himself into believing that the Polish government could be democratic as well as friendly to the USSR. Stalin knew better. He established his own Polish government, in rivalry with the 1939 government that resided in London during the war. At the Yalta conference, Roosevelt and Churchill got Stalin to agree to accept some of the London Poles into a coalition and to hold elections, as will be recalled. He never honored these promises. Sixteen Polish leaders from the London government were arrested after they had been invited to Poland; they were subjected to the usual mental torture and brought to trial in June 1945. Twelve of the sixteen were convicted and imprisoned. The Soviet security police terrorized anticommunists and censored the press. After protests, the Peasant party leader Mikolajcyzk was allowed in the government where, surrounded by Communists, he was condemned to futility; in 1947, he fled to the West bearing stories of Communist duplicity. Meanwhile, the American ambassador at Warsaw, Arthur Bliss Lane, resigned in disgust and wrote a book called *I Saw Poland Betrayed,* published in 1948. He had tried in vain to insist on democratic processes.

Stalin thought that the West had conceded him Poland, just as he let Britain and the United States have a free hand in Italy and Japan. He was impatient with their meddling in his backyard. The West was shocked at Russia's evident refusal to set up democratic regimes. Stalin thought he had made concessions by allowing a facade of coalition government. (And, at Tehran, indeed, Roosevelt had as much as told him, "Only make it look good.") Government in the "People's Democracies" was nominally in the hands of a bloc, or "front," which included members of some other left-wing political parties but which

Communists dominated. It is perhaps an open question whether Stalin saw this as cynical manipulation or as a genuine concession to the West, but it was bound to look like the former to anyone accustomed to the processes of Western-style parliamentary democracy.

The American and British public resented Stalin's actions as a breach of faith. Public opinion in favor of Russia dropped in late 1945 and into 1946 like the thermometer in a Siberian winter, from 55 percent who thought "we can trust the Russians" in the summer of 1945 to 7 percent in a poll a year later. Only 25 percent of the American people approved Winston Churchill's "iron curtain" speech at Fulton, Missouri, in March 1946; initially, it received a barrage of hostile criticism. But two months later, 83 percent of the American public supported his call for vigilance against Soviet expansion.

President Harry Truman, who admitted that when he was suddenly thrust into the presidency after Roosevelt's death he "didn't know anything about foreign policy," honestly endeavored to carry out what he regarded as Franklin Roosevelt's policy of cooperation with Russia but came reluctantly to an angry belief that the Soviet government was insatiably aggressive and respected only force: "Russia has not kept faith with us," thought the man from Missouri. The same was true of the British Labour government, a party of the moderate Left initially inclined to see itself a bridge between capitalist America and communist Russia. Possessed of enormous goodwill among the British people at the end of the war, Stalin's regime dissipated it by such apparently gratuitous cruelty as forbidding Russian women to leave the USSR with their American or British husbands. In 1950, British Foreign Secretary Ernest Bevin, a veteran trade unionist who became one of the staunchest of the cold warriors, told the Labour Party Conference that he and the government had tried to be friends with the Russians but had got nothing in return except "aggression or threats of aggression."

Eastern Europe was not the only place where Soviet actions seemed menacing. In northern Iran, Soviet troops failed to withdraw as they were supposed to after the war, obviously hoping to detach the Persian province of Azerbaijan. The Kremlin harassed Turkey about naval bases near the Straits and continued to emit a stream of anti-Western propaganda, accusing the United States of wishing to unleash a new war. All this, however, stopped much short of warlike action, for which the USSR was obviously unready.

Those "revisionist" American historians who later wished to show that the Cold War was really the West's fault pointed to certain provocations or unfriendly acts emanating from Washington. The American government ignored Russian requests for a large loan at low interest in 1945 and stopped shipping Lend-Lease supplies at the end of the war. But the British too found themselves summarily cut off from aid after the war's end, which seemed perfectly logical to Washington. They did negotiate a $3.75 billion loan at quite generous terms, but the U.S. Congress approved this loan only under the influence of deteriorating relations with the USSR in the summer of 1946.

Washington also tried to use its atomic monopoly as a bargaining point, though it is absurd to talk of "atomic blackmail." If the West failed to understand how badly the USSR had been hurt by the war and how badly it needed help, this was because of the Russian habit of secrecy and refusal to allow observers in devastated areas. But the West applied a double standard, not wishing the Russians to have any part in peace settlements with Italy and Japan but demanding a voice in Poland and Czechoslovakia. (The Allies never seriously questioned Soviet monopoly of arrangements in Romania, Bulgaria, and Hungary, though Russian high-handedness annoyed them.)

Tempers flared, and rhetoric heated up the Cold War. Truman decided at the beginning of 1946 that he was "tired of babying the Soviets," who understood only "an iron fist and strong language." Stalin responded in February with a speech stressing the incompatibility of communism and capitalism, inaugurating a new hard line. Frustrated, Washington turned for advice at this time to the brilliant chargé in Moscow, George F. Kennan, who explained the Communist mentality: Their hostility to the West is rooted in the need to legitimize their blood-stained dictatorship; they must believe in the inevitable triumph of communism after a final apocalyptic struggle with the beast Capitalism. So they will exploit every opportunity to extend their system and cannot be converted to doctrines of harmony and cooperation. But since they think history is on their side, Communists are in no hurry and will not risk major war; met with firmness, they tend to back off.[1] Therefore, the right strategy is to "contain" them by pushing back. Resist, contain, be firm, negotiate from strength: The Kennan message was eagerly received all over the American diplomatic and military establishment. Kennan was no "cold warrior," in that he believed not in ideological crusades but rather in the realism of power; his authority was perhaps misused by those who welcomed a knockdown fight with the Communists. But it shored up the doctrine of military resistance.

One problem had been that the Americans, innocently convinced that the war was over, had dismissed their vast World War II armies with appalling speed. "In a wide-spread emotional crisis of the American people," General George C. Marshall complained in October 1945, "demobilization has become, in effect, disintegration, not only of the armed forces but apparently of all conception of world responsibility and what it demands of us." It was only gradually that the American people adjusted to the unexpected and dismaying fact that they would have to keep their armaments and armies, play a continuing role in the hard game of world politics, and offer persistent opposition, backed by military power, to the Soviet Communist challenge.

---

[1] In so arguing, Kennan was operating within a long tradition of Russia watchers. Lord Palmerston, the British Foreign Secretary, had written in 1853, "The policy and practice of the Russian government has always been to push forward its encroachments as fast and as far as the apathy or want of firmness of other governments would allow it to go; but always to stop and retire when it was met with decided resistance and then to wait for the next favorable opportunity."

Kennan's analysis (reprinted in the July 1947 issue of *Foreign Affairs*) was not addressed to the masses. In March 1946, Winston Churchill mounted the rostrum in Harry Truman's home state of Missouri to deliver a memorable address:

> From Stettin in the Baltic to Trieste in the Adriatic an iron curtain has descended across the Continent. Behind that line lie all the capitals of ancient states of central and eastern Europe. Warsaw, Berlin, Prague, Vienna, Budapest, Belgrade, Bucharest, and Sofia. . . .

Churchill's message agreed with Kennan's: The Russians despise weakness and will take advantage of it. The Anglo-American alliance of World War II must be restored to counteract this new threat to the freedom of Europe and the world. The embattled orator threw a gauntlet squarely in Stalin's face, as he had done to Hitler seven years earlier.

ESCALATION OF THE COLD WAR, 1947–1949

The result of Churchill's speech was not to tear down the iron curtain (a term not of Churchill's invention) but to strengthen it. Anglo-American policy moved to take the initiative. The United Nations was used to mobilize world opinion against Soviet actions in Iran, forcing them to withdraw their troops. Reparations shipments from the American zone of Germany were terminated in May 1946, an act Soviet Foreign Minister Molotov condemned as unlawful. (It was aimed at the French as well as the Russians.) Washington sent units of the fleet to the eastern Mediterranean in support of the Turks. Secretary of State James Byrnes made a significant speech in Germany in September, suggesting that the economic recovery of Europe depended on German recovery. Truman's secretary of commerce, former Vice-President Henry A. Wallace, resigned from the cabinet at Truman's request after criticizing the new direction of policy for being unkind to the Russians.

Early in 1947, General Marshall replaced Byrnes as secretary of state, and in February came word from the British that they could no longer afford to send military and economic aid to Greece and Turkey. The British decision to pull out of Greece was evidently not deliberately designed to draw in the United States. It resulted from the urgent need to reduce expenses added to a relatively low priority assigned to this theater. An effective memo from "Ernie" Bevin and an eloquent appeal from Undersecretary of State Dean Acheson convinced American congressional leaders of both political parties that the United States must take up this burden, lest the world begin slipping into the swamps of despair and communism. The role of accident in history made an appearance when the weather took a hand in the affairs of man during the terrible winter of 1946–1947. This set in motion a train of events that perpetuated the truly Cold War. Running out of fuel, the beleaguered British found themselves forced to cut their commitments all over the world; they terminated their Palestine mandate at this time, touching off a Middle East war between Jews and Arabs, and they also threw the Greek civil war hastily into Uncle Sam's surprised hands.[2]

Most western European Communist parties were at a peak of their strength just after the war. The French Communist party won 28.6 percent of the vote in November 1946, an all-time high. Even in West Germany, the KPD, which later diminished to almost nothing, could gain close to 6 percent in 1949. In Greece, Communist-led guerrillas, supplied from Yugoslavia, Albania, and Bulgaria, posed a serious threat to the unimpressive government at Athens that the West recognized. The Greek Communists had attempted to seize power in December 1944, when their tactics of mass slaughter turned off a majority of Greeks. But the Communists made a comeback, aided by Tito, not Stalin, who kept to his spheres bargain here. (The United States misunderstood this and thought it was a Russian plot.)

Civil war broke out in Greece in 1946 amid economic chaos and distress. The whole area was strategically crucial. The Truman Doctrine of March 1947 announced aid to Greece and Turkey in the context of a general struggle against communism ("At the present moment in world history nearly every nation must choose between alternative ways of life"). Those who allege American guilt in intensifying the Cold War accuse Truman of an excess of rhetorical anti-communism.

The Soviets gladly accepted the Truman Doctrine's "two rival worlds" idea. Nothing was more congenial to the Marxist notion of a final class struggle to the death, a fight to the finish between irreconcilable systems. The Russians were also to some degree victims of the Munich fixation: Do not "appease" a ruthless foe but resist. Stalin knew well that the USSR was not equal to a war with the United States and her European allies, but one could not give in to them, either. So one waged a war of nerves, a game of chicken, always ready to back off at the last minute if absolutely necessary. Kennan seems to have been right about the Russian psychology.

In May came an American decision to "reconstruct the two great workshops," Germany and Japan, and in June Secretary Marshall's Harvard speech proposed the plan of large-scale American economic aid to all of Europe, in return for their acting in cooperation with each other and liberalizing trade. The year 1947 was crucial for a rallying of "free world" forces to (1) resist Soviet aggressions, (2) shore up the military defenses of the non-Communist world, (3) tackle the problem of European and world economic recovery with massive American assistance, and (4) end the policy of repression of the defeated World War II powers and attempt to secure their recovery. If this was a declaration of

---

[2]The Palestine situation had produced some ill-feeling between the U.S. and Great Britain; the Americans criticized the British for attempting to limit Jewish immigration while, to the great annoyance of the British, refusing to assume any responsibility for the strife that this immigration caused, as native Arabs fought against it.

MARSHALL PLAN AID FROM THE UNITED STATES TO EUROPE, 1948–1952
(in millions of dollars)

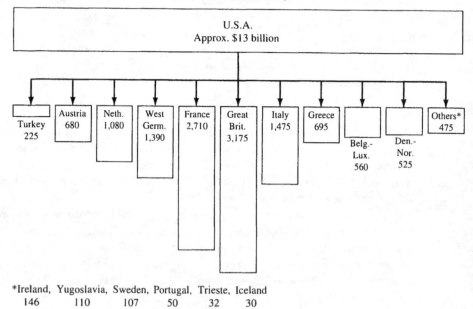

*Ireland, Yugoslavia, Sweden, Portugal, Trieste, Iceland
146 110 107 50 32 30

cold war to some, it was a bracing revival of morale to others. Later it seemed like the greatest of times. Truman's spunk was rewarded by an unexpected electoral victory in 1948, as he overcame isolationist opposition and the secession of the pro-Russian Wallaceites.

As the Marshall Plan pumped American money into Europe, West German economic recovery began to trigger a general European recovery. The cost was a deeper division of Europe. Offered a share in the Marshall Plan aid, the Russians turned down the bait and ordered their satellites to do the same. They denounced it as an American capitalist plot, a scheme to draw east European nations into the American sphere of influence. Initially, they had shown some interest, but only if they could get American money on their own terms, like Lend-Lease during the war.

The division of Germany deepened as the three western zones, soon to be merged, went their own way and indeed began to prepare for the creation of a German government by 1949. When the Russians replied in kind for their zone, there would be two Germanies. Moreover, the Russian reply was to intensify control over the eastern European countries, bringing them even more tightly under the grip of regimes loyal to the Kremlin.

A dramatic example of this process soon appeared in Czechoslovakia.

There, until early in 1948, the Russians had tolerated a coalition government in which several other political parties were represented. They had not proceeded toward full sovietization of the society even though Czech Communists held the dominant position. Outraged by their betrayal at Munich and historically rather pro-Russian, the Czechs greeted the Russian liberators with some enthusiasm. Ejecting more than two million Germans had involved a vast transfer of wealth. In the relatively free elections of May 1946, the Communist party won 38 percent of the vote, far better than it ever did anywhere else. But the popularity of the Communists was waning in 1948. Orders came from Moscow to tighten control and prepare for intensified nationalization and collectivization of property. In February, twelve non-Communist members of the government resigned in protest over communization of the police and tried to force elections.

But on February 25, Prime Minister Klement Gottwald, a faithful pro-Russian Communist, chose a virtually all-Communist government by decree and denied elections. In effect, this was a coup d'état ending the last vestiges of democracy and Czech independence. Then on March 10, the body of Jan Masaryk, son of the founding father and symbol of Czech democracy, was found lying on the street under his apartment window, an apparent suicide. Whether he was dead by his own hand or others', Masaryk's demise shocked the world; it was followed a few weeks later by that of Eduard Benes, the other symbol of a free Czech republic, who had reluctantly and under pressure given his consent to the coup of February 25. The Czech government, which had tried to join the Marshall Plan in July 1947, might have served as a bridge between East and West, some thought, but instead Stalin had forced it to cut all ties to the West.

At this same time, Russia began a general tightening of control over its satellite countries. Previously designated "people's democracies" and allowed some measure of exemption from total Stalinization, they were now to be integrated much more closely into the Soviet system. But in Yugoslavia, this policy backfired. All in all, 1948, the year of the Marshall Plan, the birth of the North Atlantic Treaty (NATO), and the Prague coup, was not a good year for the Russians. The worst disaster was the secession of Marshal Tito's government from the Kremlin orbit.

A loyal Stalinist, Tito had never previously wavered in his faith in Moscow. During the war he had built his own organization and had gained popularity by his courageous resistance to the Nazis, which won him backing from even the Western allies. After the war, he imitated Soviet policies and backed Moscow in its arguments with the West. Quarreling violently with the Anglo-Americans over the city of Trieste, which he wished to wrest from Italy, Tito shot down two American planes in 1946 and was the chief supporter of the Greek Communist guerrillas, against the advice of Stalin. So it is rather ironic that the Yugoslav Communists should have administered to Stalin his most staggering Cold War defeat.

The immediate cause of the Russian-Yugoslav break was Tito's attempts to organize, without Moscow's approval, a Balkan federation with Bulgaria and Albania. This demonstrated an independence to which Stalin was far from accustomed. The creation of the Cominform in October 1947, a sort of successor to the old Comintern, was supposed to herald close cooperation among the communist countries. But Tito was not disposed to take orders. He complained of Russian economic exploitation. Yugoslavia was asking for equality of nations within the Red bloc, not subordination of the others to the Soviet Union. Stalin handled this entire episode badly. Surrounded by adulation, treated as a god, the aging dictator simply had ceased to be able to work with people; he could only issue orders. One of the most damning documents to come out of the affair was written by Tito's lieutenant, Milovan Djilas, after he had been summoned to Moscow for talks. In *Conversations with Stalin,* Djilas later revealed the abysmal degradation of late Stalinism, including its terrible drunkenness and vulgarity. Tito published the resulting exchange of letters with Stalin, in which the Russians looked bullying, insulting, and arrogant.

Yet despite much provocation from the Yugoslavs, Stalin did not unleash the Russian army. He did withdraw Soviet officials and organized an economic boycott of Yugoslavia. He surely could have crushed Tito, but the courageous Yugoslavs would have fought him, as they had fought against Hitler, and fought very well. Stalin always respected strength. Stalin's chief lieutenant, Andrei Zhdanov, an ideologist who specialized in demanding total thought control within the USSR, died in 1948. Some think he was a victim of Stalin; rumors spread that Zhdanov had opposed Stalin's handling of Tito. (Zhdanov's death may well have been natural, but Stalin revenged himself on Zhdanov's followers of the "Leningrad group." Beria and Malenkov replaced the Leningrader as top Stalin aides.) Perhaps there was too much disunity within the normally compliant Politburo on this question, even for Stalin. He took his revenge on other potential Titos; heads rolled among the Communist elite in Poland, Hungary, Bulgaria, and Czechoslovakia in a series of public purge trials reminiscent of the thirties. Bulgaria's Kostov, Hungary's Rajk, and Czechoslovakia's Slansky were executed and Poland's Gomulka imprisoned.

Economic pressures forced Yugoslavia into desperate circumstances, but she did not yield. Eventually she got some help from the West. While retaining her own brand of communism—which eventually developed into a model significantly different from Moscow's, less centralized and bureaucratic— she never really returned to the Soviet camp. In 1948, however, every other Communist party backed Moscow in excommunicating Tito, evidence of the hold that discipline still had over the International. Even the Chinese, who were later to quarrel even more spectacularly with Russia, joined in the condemnation. Yugoslavia was a lone rebel, and Stalin could take comfort in the unity of the rest of the communist world under his leadership, which was enormously prestigious in these years.

The French and Italian Communists, who had been ordered to refrain from rocking the boat too much in 1945–1946, were now unleashed to oppose their governments. This Cold War weapon did not prove very effective, though in 1948 there was lively fear of a Communist victory in the Italian elections. Maurice Thorez, leader of the French Communist Party (PCF), said in 1949 that if the Red Army invaded France, the French people would welcome them as liberators. In the stormy lawsuit brought by Soviet defector Victor Kravchenko against the party for slander as a result of the review in a Communist party journal of his book *I Chose Freedom,* the Communists categorically denied that purges or prison camps existed in the USSR. They of course denounced both NATO and the Marshall Plan as an American plot to dominate the world. From all this, including a party purge that eliminated many of the Resistance fighters, the PCF emerged considerably discredited and weakened though it retained a hard core of loyal support; increasingly Stalinized and subjected for a time to a rather ludicrous Thorez leadership cult, it was isolated from the main body of French opinion. After Thorez suffered a stroke late in 1950, the party went through a leaderless period.

Stalin's largest Cold War thunderbolt also proved something of a dud. This was the Berlin blockade of 1948–1949. Surrounded by the Soviet zone of occupation, the city of Berlin was itself divided into four zones. When the Western powers merged their zones into one and began its economic development in 1947–1948, they technically violated the Potsdam agreement. Therefore, the Russians might well have claimed an end to Berlin's special status. Currency reform, in the form of a new German mark, was a key to the economic revival that now began in West Germany; but it widened the gulf between the two Germanys and added to the Berlin complications. Moreover, the Western allies had no written treaty guaranteeing them access to Berlin. In this city lived 6,500 of their troops, half of whom were Americans, and some two million West Berliners, who were fiercely anticommunist and subject to much Russian harassment. The Russians gradually tightened a blockade on West Berlin, first by delaying shipments, then by a full stoppage (June 24, 1948) of trains, trucks, and barges. Electric power to West Berlin was turned off, the main plant being situated in the largely industrial eastern section controlled by the Russians.

The West had three options: to let themselves be forced out of Berlin, to challenge the Soviet blockade with force, or to find some alternate means of supplying West Berlin. The American military governor in Germany, General Lucius Clay, was determined to resist the Russians and wanted to try to force deliveries through. When he was overruled in Washington, he ordered air supplies, at first merely temporizing. Although the Russians sometimes harassed the planes, they did not try to shoot them down. The airlift program grew, and by the end of September a plane was landing every three minutes. The winter lay ahead, with the need to supply not only food but coal for home heating to the two million Berliners. Fortunately, the winter was mild. With great fortitude, the citizens of West Berlin stuck it out and cheered as new records were set; by April, a plane was arriving every sixty-one seconds. The world saluted the West Berliners' courage and spirit as well as the American achievements in the airlift.

Finally, in May, Stalin agreed to call off the blockade, though reserving a right to renew it. The airlift had lasted more than a year and had cost a lot of money but very few lives; it had flown in over 1.5 million tons of fuel and food. General Clay declared that the people of Berlin had restored Germany's honor and that their courage signaled the rebirth of a democratic people. In this test of wills, perhaps the most remarkable, if somewhat overlooked, factor was the relative restraint shown by both sides. The Russians allowed the planes to land and eventually accepted defeat. The Americans did not try to shoot their way through Russian-held territory but resorted to the expensive alternative of the airlift. Although at one time President Truman considered using the atomic bomb, he had second thoughts: The Soviet Union was about to explode its first A-bomb, in September 1949.

In 1949 and 1950, Stalin decided on a large increase in Soviet armed forces as well as those of the satellite East European countries, whose military would be integrated into the Soviet plan. By 1955, the Soviet armed forces totaled 5.7 million men; those of Poland, Hungary, and Czechoslovakia another million. After the successful test of August 1949, the manufacture of more atomic bombs went forward, and German rocket scientists helped the push to produce long-range carriers. By 1953, Russia had begun to develop an international ballistic missile.

The surprisingly rapid Soviet development of nuclear weapons owed much to the plentiful supply of information they received from devoted European and American communists. The scientist who probably supplied the most important atomic secrets to the Soviets was a German named Klaus Fuchs. Earlier, the Cambridge physicist Alan Nunn May, working in Canada, had passed critical materials to the Russians. Dr. Fuchs was a German communist who emigrated to Britain and then to Canada and so to the Manhattan Project as a British representative from 1944 to 1946, the crucial years; he returned to England to work at the British nuclear weapons site at Harwell in 1949. In 1950, Fuchs confessed to having passed secrets to the Soviets since 1941. It was Fuchs's confession that led to the arrest of Julius and Ethel Rosenberg in the United States; their trial and subsequent execution was one of the Cold War's most startling and controversial episodes.

Soviet achievement of an atomic bomb by 1949 totally shocked the American president Harry Truman, whose intelligence services had told him they would not have one until 1953. Stalin had shown little interest in the bomb until Hiroshima jolted him into action; the Soviet system showed its ability to mobilize resources toward a single big target. The Soviets used western information (publicly provided, as well as from spies and German scientists), but featured a truly heroic as well as cruel crash program such as the centrally planned economy in a dictatorship could organize. They put together a brilliant crew of engineers and scientists. It was an impressive achievement, matching the time of four years that the United States and Great Britain had needed to make a

The mushroom cloud from one of the early A-bomb tests at Bikini Atoll. (*U.S. Navy Photo.*)

bomb (1941–1945). The Russians had started virtually from scratch after the wake-up call of August 8, 1945.

But setting off a plutonium device in August 1949 did not give the Soviets any immediate sense of security; the Americans still had a long lead, bombs had to be manufactured, and means of transporting them found. Moreover, the race to develop the much more powerful H bomb immediately began. Stalin believed a war with the West was inevitable sooner or later, but now was not the time.

The Soviet line in 1948 and 1949 turned toward an exaggerated Russian chauvinism. "Cosmopolitanism" became a crime, stories were made up about how Russians invented everything, and in the biological sciences there was a revival of Lysenkoism; the charlatan who claimed genetics was a bourgeois falsehood returned to high favor and terrorized professors who refused to accept his bizarre theories. Khrushchev would later continue to encourage Lysenko. This hard line, emphasizing the gulf between Western capitalism and Soviet communism, accompanied the heightening of the Cold War in those years.

WORLD CONFLICT, 1949–1953

The Prague coup and the Berlin blockade hastened the creation of the North Atlantic Treaty Organization (NATO). In 1948, British Foreign Secretary Bevin initiated the organization of a "Western Union" alliance among Britain, France, and the Benelux countries (Belgium, the Netherlands, and Luxemburg), which was signed at Brussels. The departure of General de Gaulle and the exclusion of Communists from the government had put France in hands much more agreeable to participation in an alliance of this sort. Twelve countries then signed the NATO pact in April 1949; the United States, Canada, Iceland, Italy, Portugal, Norway, and Denmark joined the Western Union five in an alliance professedly aimed at defense against Soviet aggression: "To safeguard the freedom, common heritage and civilization of their peoples founded on the principles of democracy, individual liberty, and the rule of law." Russians declared NATO to be an "expression of the aggressive strivings of the ruling circles of the United States and Great Britain . . . for effecting the policy of unleashing a new war . . . to establish by force Anglo-American dominion over the world."

It is an error, however, to suppose that the idea of NATO originated with the Americans: credit for it is best given to Ernest Bevin, the British foreign secretary, who found a strong supporter in his French counterpart, Georges Bidault, as well as in Canada's Lester Pearson. President Truman and Secretaries Marshall and Acheson proved receptive (George Kennan was opposed). The Pentagon Proposals of 1948 that formed the basis for NATO emanated from a British-American team, prominent among whom were Nicholas Henderson, secretary at the British Embassy in Washington, and Jack Hickerson of the State Department's European Affairs Desk. American politicians and the American public embraced the NATO idea because it offered a way of participating in world affairs and opposing Soviet power without seeming to descend to the sordid arena of "power politics." Americans no longer believed that world security could come through the United Nations (subject, alas, to Russian vetoes), but they still clung to the idea of some sort of collective security with an ideological base. The "Atlantic" nations were said to be bound together by both common interests and a common democratic commitment.

For western Europe, NATO provided a shield of security behind which economic recovery could take place: It was the political counterpart of the Marshall Plan, which channeled economic aid through the Organization of European Economic Cooperation (OEEC). The United States agreed to consider an attack on its European allies an attack on itself. For the United States, it was a memorable leap out of the traditional politics of "no entangling alliances," an acceptance of the fact that its own security was bound up with Europe's.

Despite its recognized advantages, NATO was subject to problems from the beginning. Neither Great Britain nor France proved capable of providing much military strength for a number of years, partly because each was heavily involved overseas; Indochina and then Algeria preoccupied the French

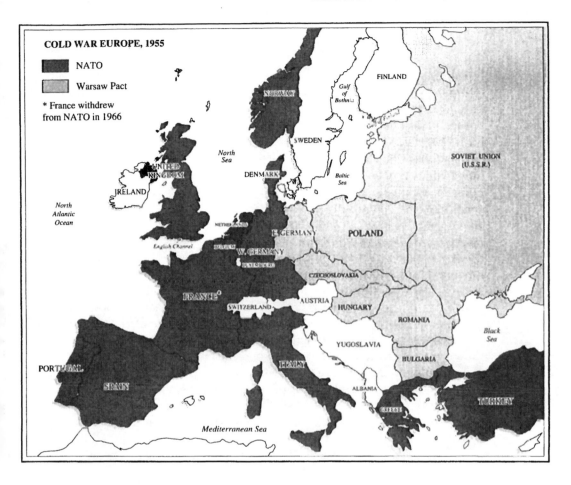

COLD WAR EUROPE, 1955

NATO

Warsaw Pact

* France withdrew
from NATO in 1966

army for the next decade. To raise the question of a German military presence
was premature. The United States alone gave NATO its muscle. It was an unequal partnership and, as such, was sometimes galling to the Europeans and
sometimes annoying to the United States. Increasingly, what counted was not
the ground forces under NATO command in western Europe but the American
"nuclear umbrella" acting as a deterrent against any Soviet temptation to attack.
Nevertheless, General Eisenhower returned to Europe as NATO commander
along with tens of thousands of American GIs for the second time in a decade,
this time to guard the enemy of World War II against one of the former Allies.
While this build-up went on, NATO forces were still outnumbered many times
by the Russian ground forces. What sustained Europe's spirit and perhaps deterred the Russians (who had very little intention of armed attack on Europe)
was the assurance that such an attack would bring the United States, with all its
great resources, into the war.

The bomb the Russians exploded in 1949 was a fission bomb, created by the disintegration of plutonium 239, subsequently mixed with uranium-235. But advances in nuclear technology were about to make this sort of bomb, the one that had horrified the world when it leveled the city of Hiroshima, as obsolete as a six-shooter. The first U.S. explosion of an "H-bomb," as it was popularly known, took place in 1952. The Soviets announced a similar success in August 1953. This fusion bomb, the product of the fusion at extreme temperatures of heavy isotopes of hydrogen, is many times more powerful than the A-bomb. In fact, since it operates by a self-perpetuating chain reaction, there is no limit to the size of an H-bomb except the capacity of the missile or bomber carrying it. A bomber can carry a 100-megaton bomb. The Hiroshima bomb, which killed 80,000 people, was 14 kilotons; that is, about 1/700th as large as a 100-megaton H-bomb. Manufactured from one of the commonest of all elements, the H-bomb could readily he proliferated to a point sufficient to destroy the entire planet. Work then began on the development of rocket-powered missiles capable of carrying nuclear warheads long distances.

This was possibly the most dangerous period for nuclear war. The vast growth in the numbers and kinds of long-range nuclear weapons (on submarines, in underground silos, on moving trains) meant that later neither the United States nor the USSR could hope to escape deadly retaliation, no matter how large its first strike; the deterrent became much more effective than it was when nuclear weapons were few. The world shuddered at the thought of these horrendous weapons deployed by the two great powers which were shouting insults and threats at each other. Yet the logic of the "balance of terror" worked from the beginning. Total war was now too dangerous. It would destroy everybody; there could be no victor in a nuclear war. (This logic engaged the Soviet brains trust in a fervent debate. To suggest that nuclear weapons made war obsolete, or that there could be no victor in such a war, seemed like heresy to dogmatic Communists; there had to be a final victory of the proletariat over the imperialists or the whole Marxist edifice collapsed. But such dogmatists lost ground in the USSR after the death of Stalin in 1953.)

But already, before the appearance of H-bombs and missiles in 1954, war had erupted, not in Europe but in Asia. From one end to the other, that continent had been left as shattered and unstable as had Europe. During their season of power in the Orient, the Japanese had thoroughly upset the old order, and it could not be restored in its earlier form. India had demanded and won independence from Britain, but the subcontinent had to be divided between Hindus and Muslims in 1947. The Dutch in the East Indies and the French in Indochina tried to reassert their authority, only to meet armed opposition. Each waged a losing battle, but the French did not give up until 1954, when a good part of their available armed strength was tied down in futile struggle against Ho Chi Minh's determined guerrilla warriors. All of Asia seemed in revolt against Western domination. The Soviet Union was quick to develop theories that these rebels against imperialism were really on the road to socialism, or they were at any rate allies in the struggle against capitalism and should be treated as such.

Led by Mao Tse-tung, the Chinese Communists won their struggle against Chiang Kai-shek's government in 1948–1949. This seemed to the West like a staggering defeat and to the Russians like a glorious victory. Time was to cast much doubt on this verdict; but in the atmosphere of the Cold War the West, and particularly the Americans, usually did not distinguish among Communists, regarding them as all part of one gigantic conspiracy. The collapse of China into the arms of the Communists caused much criticism of Truman's government in the United States; had it done enough to help the tottering Nationalist regime? Were the new Red leaders of China really Communists, or were they nationalist liberators and reformers essentially different from the Kremlin variety? Such unanswered questions introduced a degree of confusion into American thinking about Asia even before the Korean crisis of 1950.

Her limited ground forces already stretched thin, the United States had seemingly written off the mainland of far eastern Asia. Like Germany, Korea had been divided at the end of the war into Soviet and American zones of occupation, supposedly later to be reunited. The Russians had given much more military aid to the North Koreans than the Americans had given to the South. The USSR saw important stakes in Korea, strategic as well as economic; it feared Japanese resurgence. The initiative for the invasion of South Korea on June 25, 1950, came from North Korea's Kim Il Sung but Stalin approved the attack and even supplied Kim with a plan of war. Stalin did not want to appear less bold than Mao and the Chinese, whose consent Kim had secured. The Soviets did not think the United States would interfere. Stalin's high-placed "moles" in British Intelligence kept him well informed about American as well as British policies all through this period, at least until the flight of Guy Burgess and Douglas Maclean in May 1951. But he hardly needed secret information here, for American Secretary of State Dean Acheson in a public speech had defined Korea as not lying in the zone of American interests; and it seems Stalin would not have approved Kim's invasion but for this statement.

How, after saying this, the Americans could rush to defend South Korea when the attack came is a mystery that must remain locked in the strange processes of the American government. It exasperated the Russians, who found here another reason for mistrusting the Americans. But when some 70,000 North Korean troops attacked across the "thirty-eighth parallel" boundary and quickly drove the South Koreans southward, Truman decided to act to prevent another bastion from falling to communism, and, as he said, to uphold the United Nations and "collective security." Assisting his decision was a United Nations Security Council verdict that this was an act of aggression. (The USSR was boycotting the Security Council at this time and thus could not cast a veto.)

Stationed in Japan since 1945, General Douglas MacArthur's Eighth Army entered South Korea, and in September it launched a counteroffensive that routed the North Koreans. Technically a United Nations army, this was in

Soldiers in the Korean War on the way to a new position, August 1951. (*National Archives.*)

fact overwhelmingly an American one. MacArthur, hearing no clear negative from Washington, decided to pursue the North Koreans beyond the thirty-eighth parallel. He drove them back to the Chinese border at the Yalu River, whereupon Chinese Communist armies struck into Korea, took the U.N. forces by surprise, and almost routed them. By February 1951, the Americans and their allies found themselves again far south of the thirty-eighth parallel, but they rallied and after bloody fighting restored the battle line not far from the original border. After a year of intense warfare, the result was a draw.

This episode brought angry controversy, a dramatic conflict between President Truman and General MacArthur, and much trouble for American policy-makers who had felt so euphoric after NATO. Western Europe was ambivalent: Most people rejoiced that the Americans were willing to fight to resist communist aggression, but they feared the diversion of American strength to Asia, which might leave Europe exposed. In general, the European allies, especially Great Britain, tried to dampen the conflict and thought the Americans too prone to embark on ideological crusades. The Chinese Communists conducted a world propaganda campaign against the Americans, whom they accused of using germ warfare; left-wing European intellectuals, led by Jean-Paul Sartre, accepted these doubtful charges. Their stand was indicative of a significant anti-American wing of West European opinion, which would increase in subsequent years. Sartre himself, along with Bertrand Russell and other European intellectuals who would become almost hysterically anti-American, had generally supported the anti-Soviet side before 1950, out of sympathy with the eastern and central European peoples subject to the Soviet yoke. The switch that tended to take place after that had as its turning point the Korean War, sometimes rather perversely blamed on the Americans and their South Korean clients; especially alienating was the "McCarthyite" anticommunist frenzy that swept portions of the United States at this time.

The Korean War sharpened the split within the British Labour party and thus may have contributed to its defeat in 1951. It caused some economic dislocations in Europe, but it did not seriously blight the economic boom just then getting up a head of steam. It shocked the world with evidence of the destructiveness of modern warfare, though it stopped short of using nuclear weapons. But it also illustrated, like Berlin, a sense of limitations. Despite the wrath of General MacArthur, the Americans refrained from bombing Chinese territory. The fighting largely stopped after June 1951, when the countries began negotiations for a truce. These did not succeed until 1953, after Stalin's death and the election of a new American president provided fresh leadership. But the fighting halted with neither side a victor. Korea remained divided into hostile halves, as it has been ever since, but the great powers restrained their clients from renewing a war that threatened too many dangers. And, the entrance of China into the equation as a third force introduced a new element into world politics.

SEMI-THAW IN THE COLD WAR, 1954–1956

If from 1945 to 1951 lines were drawn and forces consolidated in the two-bloc polarization of world power, the next few years produced tendencies both to intensify and diminish the Cold War, often simultaneously. The Korean War and the anticommunist hysteria that followed it in the United States certainly intensified Cold War passions. The drive to create an effective NATO continued; Greece and Turkey were added to the alliance, at whatever cost to "North Atlantic" logic; and the issue of a German military contribution to NATO was raised. This last caused a commotion. The French in particular, though wishing a strong defense against the Soviets, flinched at the thought of any sort of revived German army. (Someone said that the French wanted a German army that was stronger than the Russian but weaker than the French.) But German opinion itself was, on the whole, opposed to a new *Wehrmacht*. The Americans pushed it hardest. Faced with the need for some German divisions to give NATO credibility, the French countered with a plan for a European, internationalized army. But the British refused to join, and the French Assembly ended by rejecting this European Defence Community (EDC) in 1954, after much debate.

German rearmament soon took place under a different formula. The West German government, in existence since 1949 but not yet fully sovereign (being subject to restrictions of the Allied High Commission), entered the Western Union group. In 1955, West Germany joined NATO and gained full sovereignty, at the same time renouncing atomic weapons and long-range bombers and missiles. The French Assembly was barely persuaded to approve this. The British now promised to keep some troops on the Continent. The Communists bitterly charged the "imperialists" with plotting to use the West German *revanchistes* in aggressive war against the Soviet Union. West Germany had no independent military command; her forces were placed under the integrated NATO command.

This brought a Soviet reaction in the form of creation of the Warsaw Pact, a counter-NATO made up of the eight East European communist-bloc countries: Albania, Bulgaria, Czechoslovakia, Hungary, Poland, Romania, the USSR, and the newly established East German state, the German Democratic Republic (DDR). This creation of separate sovereign East and West German states cemented the division of Germany.

As we have noted, 1954–1955 also brought the H-bomb and the first long-range missiles, hardly encouraging signs for peace unless one fully trusted the "balance of terror." Nevertheless, there were signs of a thaw. The death of Stalin early in 1953 had something to do with this. A Korean truce was achieved. Soviet rhetoric cooled as both Malenkov and Khrushchev, candidates for the post-Stalin leadership, talked of the dangers of nuclear war and the need for a Cold War thaw. (Indeed, the first and short-lived Stalin successor, Lavrenti Beria, pressed for a relaxation of tensions before his career was abruptly terminated.) A 1955 peace treaty ended the occupation of little Austria, which ever since the war had had the great powers as "guests"–"four elephants in a canoe," the Socialist prime minister of Austria once called it. Austria pledged never to unite with Germany or to join a military alliance; in return for this pledge of neutrality and some economic payments, the Russians went home and left the little country its freedom.

Prior to this, the Geneva Conference of 1954 had achieved a settlement in Indochina, ending France's long agony of involvement there. As the French surrendered in the north, the Viet Minh followers of National Communist Ho Chi Minh were supposed to withdraw from the south, thus splitting Vietnam in two and neutralizing Cambodia and Laos. While time proved that this division only set the stage for a new and larger struggle, it seemed a relief at the time.

Early in 1955, the Soviets suggested a settlement with Germany similar to Austria's, that is, unification, neutralization, and withdrawal. After Malenkov's fall, no more was heard of this suggestion. British Foreign Secretary Anthony Eden also proposed unification, but both sides soon decided that two Germanys were more convenient. West German Chancellor Konrad Adenauer visited Moscow in September 1955, a sign of Soviet desire for normalization of relations. The new Soviet leadership paid a visit to Belgrade in May 1955 to offer apologies to Tito, and in general the Soviets seemed to wish to relax Stalinist harshness, both at home and in the bloc countries. Yet clearly the Soviet leaders were not yet prepared to dissolve the entire Stalinist order. Soon after Stalin's death in 1953, there were riots in both Czechoslovakia and East Germany; the latter, beginning in East Berlin, was the more serious. A combination of Soviet tanks and some reforms ended this June 17 *Aufstand,* but stirrings continued in the satellites. There were changes of leadership. Klement Gottwald of Czechoslovakia mysteriously failed to survive his attendance at Stalin's funeral. Then came the spectacular "secret speech" delivered by Nikita Khrushchev to the Twentieth Party Congress in February 1956, denouncing Stalin's crimes. This set the stage for further disturbances. A Polish uprising, centered at Poznan, caused the withdrawal of a Russian general and the appointment of a new Polish Communist leader, Wladyslaw Gomulka, who had been imprisoned. Then in October, Hungary exploded in revolution.

Forced into World War II on Hitler's side, Hungary lost most of her army in Russia, became a battleground at the war's end, and then, failing in an attempt to surrender to the Americans, suffered Russian occupation with severe reparation losses. The only resistance Hungarians could offer to a tough Communist dictatorship was to rally around Roman Catholic Cardinal Mindszenty, who was arrested and condemned to life imprisonment in 1948. Between 1949 and 1953, Matyas Rakosi as the nearly all-powerful Communist tsar pushed a program of sovietization, including collectivization of agriculture. In July 1953, during the thaw after Stalin's death, Imre Nagy replaced Rakosi and brought with him more tolerant policies. But in the spring of 1955, after Malenkov's fall from power in Moscow, Nagy was dismissed from office and expelled from the party. Rakosi was briefly restored, to be replaced in July 1956 by Erno Gero, evidently to appease Tito. But Gero did not please a Hungarian people anxious to bring back the popular Communist professor, Nagy. Nagy stood for what twelve years later would be called "socialism with a human face." A convinced Communist, he believed that real communism should be democratic and free. He had released political prisoners, offered freedom of expression and religion, and slowed down the pace of collectivization and industrialization.

On October 23, 1956, the Hungarian secret police brutally broke up a meeting of students and writers. This led to a spontaneous revolution, during which the Hungarian army and much of its police went over to the side of the young revolutionaries, who destroyed Russian tanks and drove Soviet troops out of Budapest. Even some of the Russians fraternized with the revolutionaries. Nagy was called back, prisoners were released, and Mindszenty was freed and treated as a hero. It was an intoxicating moment, a truly remarkable example of popular revolution.

Deeply embarrassed and perplexed, the Kremlin at first hesitated but then sent in reinforcements. They crushed the revolution and arrested Nagy; he was taken to Romania and later shot. Yugoslavia sided with the Russians here; only much later was it revealed that Tito and Khrushchev reached a secret agreement on November 2. (Tito feared that the rebellion might spread to Croatia.) Two hundred thousand Hungarians fled the country, escaping via the Austrian frontier; thousands of others were killed or deported to Russia. No one who participated in this remarkable event ever forgot its moment of glory. But though they appealed for help to the West and to the United Nations, the valiant Hungarians got none, and alone they could not cope with the might of Russia. They thought that, via Radio Free Europe, the West had encouraged their revolt and then abandoned them.

The event was critical for Western communism, because most of the independent intellectuals, like Sartre, who had swung toward communism now disgustedly repudiated the Party (the French Communist Party attempted to defend the intervention). The spectacle of the country which claimed to represent world revolution acting as the repressor of revolution constituted a moral crisis in the affairs of world communism from which it never really recovered.

In late October and early November of 1956, there was a remarkable coincidence of two major crises. One reason the Hungarians appealed in vain was the West's preoccupation at this moment with the Suez crisis. Suez affected the Kremlin's decision to intervene with strong military force in Hungary, providing them with assurance that there would be no Western reaction. The Russians took the decision to send in troops and crush the rebellion on October 30, after several days of uncertainty. The Israeli attack on Egypt, which began the Suez crisis, occurred on October 29. The Russians could still have called the troops back before November 3. By November 1, the British-French Suez operation had been mounted and dissension within the Western alliance was apparent.

What happened in Budapest was of less moment to statesmen in Washington, London, and Paris than what was happening in Egypt. The background of the war, the intervention, and the international crisis that erupted there went back a number of years. The Arab-Israel feud dated from the creation of the Jewish state and, after a war in 1948, its expulsion of a large population of Arabs. A small number of European Jews, influenced by the ideals of the Zionist movement founded in 1897, had made their way to Palestine after World War I. Committed by the Balfour Declaration of 1917 to help establish a Jewish "homeland" there, the British protected the Jews against frequent Arab hostility. But the trickle of migrants became a flood as the result of Nazi persecution. The British attempted to stem this flow of Jewish immigration, until they gave up in 1947 and abandoned their thankless role as policemen of the Holy Land.

In 1952, humiliated by the weakness of their country and the corruption of its government, a group of young Egyptian army officers overthrew King Farouk and inaugurated a revolutionary regime. They were radical and anti-Western, blaming the establishment of Israel on Europeans. (In fact, in 1948 Stalin had supported the Jews, whose chief enemies then were the British.) The Egyptian revolutionaries were not Communists, but in 1955 they began to buy arms from the Soviet bloc. Rising Arab nationalism focused on the Suez Canal. Though lying within Egyptian territory, the Suez Canal had long been controlled by an international company and protected by British troops. In 1954, the British agreed to withdraw their troops over the next twenty months if freedom of navigation through the canal were maintained. But in July of 1956, Colonel Abdul Nasser, head of the Egyptian government, announced the

seizure of the canal zone and the confiscation of the Suez Company's proper-
ties, alleging a sovereign national right to do so.

The British and the French viewed this as a violation of the Suez treaty
and, more to the point, a threat to their vital interests. Anthony Eden, who became obsessed by hatred for Nasser, said that the Egyptian dictator, whom he
compared to Hitler, had "his thumb on our windpipe." Nasser decided to seize
the canal because the Egyptians wanted to build a huge dam on the upper Nile
to bring economic improvement to their impoverished land. Nasser had hoped
for American aid, but after long negotiations, during which the Soviets entered
the bidding and Nasser raised his price, the United States refused to finance it.
Inept Western diplomacy and Egyptian truculence had led to the worst possible
relations between the Arab world and the West.

The United States did not sympathize with European traditions of imperialism. "We agree in Europe but not in Asia and Africa," American Secretary
of State John Foster Dulles noted. He and Eden simply did not get along, and
communications between them broke down. Eden had recently succeeded the
aged Winston Churchill as prime minister, after long service as foreign secretary (1935–1938, 1940–1945, 1951–1955). Suez was to terminate his distinguished career and sow doubts about his capability as a leader. Impatient with
Dulles and Eisenhower, enraged at Nasser, and convinced that Britain must rise
to meet her challenges or sink into second-rate status, Eden entered into secret
agreements with France and Israel for an attack on Egypt. The Israelis needed
little urging; Egypt and Syria, still technically at war with Israel, had mounted
border raids, or permitted the Palestinian refugees to mount them, and had
closed the Canal to Israeli shipping. The Jews wished to gain more secure frontiers and destroy guerrilla bases. For them, the Arab purchase of Soviet arms,
threatening to upset the military balance, was the last straw. (Only France was
then selling arms to the Israelis.)

As for France, her premier, Guy Mollet, not only joined Eden in fearing economic disaster from Egypt's control of the Suez Canal but resented
Egyptian aid to Algerian rebels, who began to be a problem for France in 1954.
Mollet also was a victim of the "Munich reflex," seeing in Nasser another
aggressor-dictator who must be stopped in his tracks. France was indeed the
driving force behind the plan, eagerly seconded by the Israelis with the British
slightly more reluctant. It was all a bit confusing to the Americans; three of her
best friends, good democratic countries, had conspired to commit aggression,
which was what only Fascists or Communists were supposed to do.

The French, Israelis, and British did indeed plan the attack in advance
at a conference in France, October 22–23, though they long denied this. On October 29, the Israelis struck into the Sinai peninsula and quickly overran it. Two
days later France and Britain delivered an ultimatum to stop the war, a maneuver designed to freeze the Israeli gains. They then began bombing Egypt and, a
short time later, moved troops by air and sea to occupy Port Said, which lies at
the head of the Canal. Their goal was to regain control of the Canal and cause

the fall of Nasser. They had not reckoned on hostile reactions throughout the world, including their own citizens and the United States. President Eisenhower was morally outraged, and the world was treated to a rare case of American-Russian cooperation, as the United Nations condemned the aggression. The United States threatened economic sanctions against the aggressors if they did not withdraw, while the USSR, seeing how badly the West was in disarray, issued veiled threats of trying out "rocket techniques." Egypt blocked the Canal, and oil supplies began to dry up. There was an outcry in the British Parliament against the government, an outcry that extended to some members of Eden's own Conservative party as well as the Labour party.

Faced with such formidable pressures, it is not surprising that the French and British crumbled. Asked about this performance by his erstwhile protégé, Winston Churchill said, "I am not sure I would have dared to start it, but if I had, I'm sure I would not have dared not to finish it." Eden did not dare to finish it. The two countries called off their assault and in early December withdrew their forces, as a United Nations peacekeeping force replaced British and French troops in the canal zone. The Israelis also had to give up their territorial gains, although they had gained military prestige. But Nasser did not fall, and the Western alliance seemingly had cracked open. It was just as well for the West that the Russians were preoccupied with Hungary, though it was a disaster for Hungary that the West was concentrating on Suez.

The first week of November 1956 stands as a kind of climax of the Cold War, the closing scene of its second act. In retrospect, Suez marked the end of the independent world power of Britain and France, which had to accept the fact that they could not make major political moves without the support of the United States. It confirmed the long retreat of the British from their imperial role and opened the era of decolonization. On the other side, it showed that the Soviet sphere in eastern Europe was safe; countries in the Communist zone could not win their freedom by rebellion, for they would get no help from the West. Hungary and Suez underscored the giant role of the two superpowers. It was the apex of bipolarization.

10

The Post-1945 Recovery
of Western Europe

ECONOMIC RECOVERY

Post-1945 international relations seem to have consisted of constant crises, threats of war, divisions of the continent of Europe into hostile blocs, and other near disasters. Nevertheless, war in Europe was avoided, and during this period of Cold War, Europe made spectacular economic progress. This may appear surprising. Stalin's advisers had told him that the capitalist West was finished; uncritical leftists in the West parroted this slogan, claiming (to paraphrase the veteran British socialist G.D.H. Cole) that there were now only two choices for humanity, fascism (Nazism) or communism. Even if he did not think that capitalism was on its death bed, having fallen fatally ill of the Great Depression and been finished off by the war, an observer surveying the physical and moral ruins of 1945 must have thought that recovery was out of the question for many decades. The two years after the war appeared to confirm this diagnosis. Yet the forces of recovery were present, and, boosted by American aid, Europe took off about 1948 on a boom that with only short pauses lasted until well into the 1960s, bringing a higher standard of living than Europeans had ever known. It was an economic miracle.

Western Europe's economic growth rate in the postwar years surpassed that of both the United States and the Soviet Union. In this period, the leading nations of western Europe created instruments of economic cooperation that aided recovery, especially the European Economic Community, or Common

Table 10–1

Year	POPULATION IN MILLIONS (ROUNDED)			
	U.S.	USSR	EEC (6)*	EEC (9)**
1952	160	185	155	
1962	185	220	175	
1972	200	250	190	255
1982	233	276	195	260

	PER CAPITA GROSS NATIONAL PRODUCT			
1972	$5,750	$1,760	$3,475	$3,300
1982	$13,620	$2,600	$10,700	$10,500

*Belgium, France, Germany, Italy, Luxemburg, Netherlands.
**With the addition of Denmark, Ireland, the United Kingdom.

Market, started in 1957; yet the separate countries retained elements of a special national style in social, political, and economic matters. What they shared, at least until the 1960s, was a pattern of steady success. In terms of gross national product per capita, western Europe in 1952 stood at about one-fourth of the United States and lower than the Soviet Union, it appears. By 1962, it had overtaken the USSR and was two-fifths of the U.S. Two decades later, the European Community countries had inched close to the United States[1] and left the now-floundering Soviets far behind.

Germany's economic resurgence was the most amazing of all, a true *Wirtschaftswunder.* Having absorbed at least twelve million refugees, West Germany's population reached sixty million, or about 630 people per square mile (the United States had about 55 people per square mile). With this population, she achieved more than full employment: In 1961, unemployment stood at less than half of one percent, and West Germany began to import labor. By 1969, she had more than a million and a half Italian, Greek, Turkish, and other non-German workers. Real wages rose 139 percent between 1950 and 1966, with a 10 percent shorter work week; although the growth rate was running about 6 percent, inflation was moderate. Unlike Great Britain, which had an unfavorable balance of trade, Germany's was favorable, so that the mark was twice evaluated upward. In 1946, the occupying powers had set an annual limit of 7.5 million tons of steel for all Germany; in 1969, West Germany alone was producing 44 million tons. She became the economic giant of the Continent, with a standard of living surpassed in Europe only by the small states, Switzerland

[1]About $10,600 for the six western European countries, compared to $13,620 for the U.S., according to World Bank figures. The USSR was now far behind, probably $3,000 at a generous estimate.

and Sweden, and rivaling that of the United States. All this occurred in a land that had seemed so shattered, so hated, and so demoralized in 1945 that observers thought it could never rise again.

French recovery was equally spectacular, for France started from a point very nearly as low as had Germany in 1945. She had been occupied and drained during the war and then was a battlefield in 1944. After reaching prewar levels between 1947 and 1950, the French economy more than doubled in gross national product in the 1950s and almost tripled again in the next decade, an advance that just about paralleled Germany's. Since their railroads had been ruined, the French were forced to rebuild them on a modern basis, thus getting perhaps the best transportation system in the world—an example of some of the compensations of disaster, which much of Europe shared: In rebuilding they secured the advantage of getting up-to-date equipment. They were aided by Jean Monnet's genius for pianning; French *planification* was more flexible and subtle than was the centralized planning and state ownership model adopted by the USSR and to some extent by British Labour. There was some nationalization (the Bank of France, railroads, the Renault auto works, airlines, mines, gas, and electricity) but basically France relied on private enterprise; the state used its financial powers to guide investment so that modernization of basic industries occurred first and in the right order. Marshall Plan money from the United States was used wisely for such primary investment.

Though as a victor she did not receive all the advantages of defeat, Great Britain also experienced a very satisfactory rate of economic growth after the war, averaging about 3 percent between 1950 and 1970. Suffering far less war destruction, Britain did not have to modernize industrial plant as Germany and France did, and she paid a price for this in a less efficient economy. Although her advance was slower than that on the Continent, it was not until the 1960s that the English, watching the Common Market countries pulling away from them, were condemned to look a bit threadbare compared to the French, Germans, Swedes, and Swiss. Except for this comparison, the British might have congratulated themselves on raising their average standard of living as they had done in no other era. Wage earners were more than two and a half times as well off in terms of real wages in 1960 than they had been in 1939, not counting benefits from the famous "cradle to grave" social welfare system, which included free medical care. Unemployment was very low, 2 percent or less.

The chief obstacle to even better economic performance was Britain's troublesome balance of international trade, which tended to blight every budding boom by raising imports to an unacceptable level. Britain depended more on imported foodstuffs and raw materials than did any other major European country. Balance of payments problems caused devaluation of the pound in 1949 (from $4.03 to $2.80) and again by another 15 percent in 1967. At least initially, devaluation provided an export boost by making British goods cheaper in terms of foreign currencies, while it also made foreign products dearer for the British buyer, thus discouraging imports. The British hoped devaluation would

not raise the prices of raw materials and foods, which often came from the un-
derdeveloped countries. Balance of payments problems led to a "stop-go" pattern of economic growth that brought headaches to many a British government.

Inflation was the other, and related, aspirin-inducer. Between the end
of the war and 1969, prior to the great inflation of the 1970s, prices more than
tripled. Not until the 1970s, however, did these problems seriously threaten a
basically hopeful economic situation. In 1954, an American magazine reported,
"The British people today enjoy a prosperity unknown in their history," and the
Conservative party won easy electoral victories in 1955 and 1959 on the strength
of this prosperity.

Economic growth was hardly less startling in Italy. After quite impressive rates of annual growth in the 1950s, averaging around 5.5 percent between
1951 and 1955, Italy took off into a real boom following the establishment of the
European Economic Community in 1957. By 1963, Italian production had risen
70 percent over 1958 levels, a rate of growth exceeding that of any other country in the EEC, from which Italy appeared to profit most. Italy, of course, especially southern Italy, had a longer way to go to join the ranks of the modernized
industrial societies. The boom originally even widened the gulf between the "two
Italys," and plans to break up the pattern of stagnancy in the landlord-ridden
south confronted formidable difficulties. But hundreds of thousands of poor
people did leave the land to flock to northern Italian cities, where rapid growth
created a demand for labor; other Italians went to work in Germany or Switzerland or France. These years of her economic breakthrough brought Italy such
unwelcome accompaniments of affluence as the most spectacular traffic jams in
Europe; moneyed Italians rushed to consummate their love affair with the automobile just as tourism reached a peak. (The tourists would migrate to Greece
and Spain later, when Italy grew too expensive.)

Italy struck back at the traffic problem with great superhighway projects, pulling together the once romantically divided peninsula, breaking down
ancient regionalisms, helping to modernize a country long steeped in ancient
habits. Modernization most definitely came to the land of artists, poets, peasants, and long-robed clerics in these years of the 1950s and 1960s, bringing with
it the usual array of problems, some more severe in Italy than elsewhere. A little later, modernization came also to Spain, which had long been considered
hopelessly stagnant, as it had come to France.

Presiding over the postwar capitalist recovery was a system of international money exchange devised at the Bretton Woods conference of 1944, to
which the great John Maynard Keynes lent his genius in the twilight of his career. It established the International Monetary Fund (IMF) and the World Bank,
which still function as pillars of the international economy. We may recall that
the great depression of the 1930s in dealing a death blow to the gold standard
had plunged world trade into chaos. There was no restoring the old order, but
a new order now emerged. The IMF, an agency of the United Nations, used a
fund of money contributed by member nations to buy and sell currencies with

the goal of stabilizing exchange rates. Its board of governors was given powers to vary the exchange rate within limits; the closely affiliated International (World) Bank could grant loans to member nations to stabilize exchange and encourage trade. Headquartered in Washington D.C., the IMF-IBRD system worked spectacularly well in this era because of the economic strength of the United States and of its currency; the dollar became in effect the international monetary standard. (From about 1945 to 1958, the United States had a credit balance with virtually the entire world.) In the 1970s, the Bretton Woods system underwent a crisis as this situation changed, but even after that the IMF maintained its centrality in the economy of the entire world except for most of the communist countries (Yugoslavia and Romania joined it).

All these economic miracles were accomplished with some unevenness. The broad masses did not really begin to reap the fruits of technological modernization and innovation until the 1960s, for investment in basic plant had to come first. Inflation was a recurring problem almost everywhere, bringing special hardship to certain groups, such as pensioners, retirees, and those on relatively fixed incomes. To overtake the rising cost of living, workers frequently went on strike. Complaints that the vaunted national health system actually brought serious deterioration in the quality of medical service enlivened the British and Italian political scenes. Housing was a critical area for many years, since it was both inadequate and too expensive.

It remains a paradox that these years of struggle from 1945 to 1960 were happier ones than the later more opulent times. The spirit was generally optimistic. England, crowning a new queen in 1953, talked of a New Elizabethan Age, later an object of mockery among disillusioned youth. Germans and Italians set to work to rebuild their shattered countries and restore their standing in the world by exemplary behavior. Charles de Gaulle symbolized a resurgence of French national pride. A whole set of new French attitudes toward modernization and technology arose out of the war's trauma. The "work ethic" of this postwar generation—later to get it into trouble with its own children—must be accounted the leading cause of the economic miracle. In the last analysis, whatever the theories of economists or ideologists, what seems to count, so far as economic growth is concerned, is a willingness to work hard, to save, to make sacrifices. Writing in 1949, the Spanish philosopher José Ortega y Gasset thought that the voluntary sacrifices Englishmen made in the years just after the war constituted "one of the most extraordinary examples in history" of "spontaneous and resolute national solidarity." In Germany, the millions of refugees who had lost all when they were ejected from their homelands were willing to work to make a new life; they had no choice. In reaction to the fact of having touched rock-bottom, a crisis or disaster psychology led people to dig in and work hard. It was one of the paradoxical advantages of misfortune.

In taking advantage of an opportunity to start almost all over again western Europeans responded creatively, combining the best features of traditional free-enterprise capitalism with state-directed planning plus state-administered social welfare. Less rigid and authoritarian than the Russian Communist kind, "planning" was a part of the Western model, most notably in France but in some degree throughout the West. The British adopted both a comprehensive social welfare system and a commitment to maintain full employment by using fiscal budgetary devices, reflecting the Keynesian influence. The French plans were designed to direct investment into certain areas and to modernize basic equipment by controlling bond issues and providing tax incentives or disincentives. Even in West Germany, where, amid a reaction against both Nazi and Communist statism, the rhetoric of the dominant Christian Democratic leaders stressed free private enterprise, the slogan was "*social* market economy," and in fact a good deal of direction did come from Bonn in subtle ways. The French word *dirigisme* perhaps best summed it up: a basically free-enterprise, market economy but one directed by a state planning apparatus, thus combining the dynamism of the profit motive with enough central control to keep the engine of private capitalism from running off the track. In Germany, with less state ownership than in France or Britain, experiments in co-management took place: Workers participated in both ownership and management of industrial corporations. But in all countries the basic reliance was on old-fashioned profit incentives. (Faced with a mixture of capitalism and state planning that puzzled them, the European Communists decided to classify this as a variety of "state monopoly capitalism," thus linking it to Lenin's categories.)

French economist Jacques Rueff, a great favorite of de Gaulle, joined the German Wilhelm Röpke, who taught in Geneva but advised Adenauer's government, and the Italian Luigi Einaudi in forming an international coterie of economic experts firmly committed to the virtues of the free market. Such a group, including Austria's Von Hayek, Britain's Lionel Robbins, and America's embattled Milton Friedman, met at Pilgrim Mountain in Switzerland in 1947 to foment a kind of conspiracy to revive that much-maligned entity, capitalism. Perhaps, like Christianity, it ought to be given a real try! At a time when the jargon of the welfare state and planned production was on nearly everyone's lips and Adam Smith was a dirty word, this international elite dared to argue that the private entrepreneur in a competitive society is the best bet to increase wealth and distribute it equitably.

To a considerable extent, the war had wiped out the old possessors and set up a new competition. Thus, the 1948 currency reform in Germany tended to liquidate fortunes and start everyone off anew in a somewhat equal race. "The economic recovery of France," one authority concluded, was "due to the restaffing of the economy with new men and to new French attitudes."

In brief, the post-1945 generation was serious and hard-working. In 1968, its children would rebel against the vulgarity of this preoccupation with work and money. For those who had endured the tragedy of the war, there could be little question of esthetic niceties; they set to work to rebuild their lives because they had no other choice. In so doing, they rebuilt Europe.

POSTWAR POLITICS IN THE WESTERN DEMOCRACIES: FRANCE

There was also encouraging progress in politics, if by "progress" one means stability, less extreme polarization of parties, and a reasonable compromise between democracy and authority. The commitment to a basically pluralistic society, with freedom to dissent and competition among rival political groups, was intensified in western Europe. There was a strong reaction against both Soviet Russian totalitarianism and the defeated, rejected, but still sometimes feared Nazism and fascism of World War II. The 1950s featured a revulsion against political "ideologies," which were considered to be shrill and shallow invitations to hatred. There was little positive attachment either to democracy as an ideology or to any other "system"; people were disgusted with all total political systems that sought to regiment the human spirit in the name of some utopia, and which turned out in practice to mean the terroristic tyranny of a narrow-minded elite. Democracy, as Winston Churchill put it, is the worst form of government except for all the others. Two cheers for it, if not three, British novelist E.M. Forster suggested.

There was a declining interest in politics; up to 51 percent of the people in Fourth Republic France indicated total disinterest. The work-ethic generation was "too busy with their materially-based freedoms to get excited about politics," a letter to a British magazine noted. This end-of-ideology, apolitical, quasi-conservative mood of the 1950s, against which the young people of the late 1960s reacted so sharply, will be discussed later. Here let us briefly discuss the main western European countries, which, for all their apathy, seemed lively and eventful enough.

Between 1945 and 1958, France created a new regime, the Fourth Republic, watched it fail, and changed regimes to the Fifth Republic—all without ruinous civil violence. The Fourth Republic, established in 1946 after an interval during which General Charles de Gaulle served as head of a caretaker government, lived a precarious life. De Gaulle himself disliked the excessively parliamentary nature of this constitution, which he thought would weaken France. It was approved in October 1946 by a very indecisive margin, actually by a minority (31 percent voted against it and 31 percent abstained). The general then "went into the desert," boycotting all politics for the next twelve years. As the Cold War heated up, the French Communist party, which consistently attracted more than 20 percent of the electorate, switched to opposition tactics and by 1947 was voting against every government. With total noncooperation on both left and right, the Fourth Republic repeated the weakness of the Third (and of the Weimar Republic): It was difficult to get a majority in the Assembly, impossible without a coalition of several parties. Adding to this weakness was a system of proportional representation, which magnified the parliamentary representation of the smaller political parties.

In 1951, for example, the Communist party gained 21 percent of the vote; the Socialists (SFIO) 11 percent; while the Popular Republican Movement (MRP), a Christian democratic-socialist party that emerged during World War II, was down to 10 percent. Gaullists of two sorts, some boycotting the whole system, gained 17 percent, the old Radical Socialists 8 percent, various minor Rightists 11 percent; and those who did not care to vote at all made up 21 percent, "the largest party of all" someone said. In Parliament, any government had to muster the support of a miscellany of groups and could expect a short life. There were in fact to be twenty-seven governments in the thirteen years between 1945 and 1958, their life span ranging from one day to sixteen months. (Guy Mollet, who managed, unlike Anthony Eden, to survive Suez, lasted the longest.) By 1958, observers were saying that the Fourth Republic could be pushed over by the first hard wind. The weakness of its government had not prevented France from being administered well by the permanent bureaucracy, and as we know much had been accomplished in the way of economic recovery. But the government was incapable of resolving major problems that called for bold decisions. This was why the Indochina war dragged on for many years and why the Algerian war threatened to do the same.

In fact, it was Algeria that brought down the Fourth and led to a new constitution and the elevation of Charles de Gaulle to the presidency. By 1958, 400,000 French soldiers were trying to put down the revolt of some of the native Algerians against French rule, a struggle marked by atrocities on both sides. It was a second Indochina, the more unsolvable because a million French citizens lived in Algeria and many of the French regarded it as an integral part of their country, lying as it does just across the Mediterranean. They did not consider the activities of the FLN, the National Liberation Front of the Algerian rebels, to be anything other than a mixture of criminal banditry and imported communist subversion. But in fact, the movement established deep roots in Algeria, touching the consciousness of an Islamic populace long despised and subject to discrimination.

The war that grew in Algeria resembled the Spanish Civil War in its fierce and cruel bravery. The French military's use of torture as a weapon against a terroristic insurrection became a scandal in the eyes of many French people themselves. The issue threatened to pull France apart, much as the Vietnam War did in the United States a decade later. Someone tried to assassinate Jean-Paul Sartre, major literary ornament and leading critic of French Algerian policy. (The other major Existentialist, the Algerian-born Albert Camus, was on the other side.) Some blamed the government for not giving up and some for not winning the war, as was also true in the Korean War and later the Vietnam War. On May 13, 1958, the French Army in Algiers revolted, and the Fourth Republic collapsed without defenders; it had ceased to command the allegiance of the French people.

At this desperate moment, almost everybody turned to the sixty-seven-year old de Gaulle as the only hope. The army favored him, but he also had strong socialist support; he was a unique symbol of the France he so passionately loved and had so long served. After negotiations with the general, the Assembly passed its own death sentence, granting de Gaulle a six-month emergency rule during which a new constitution was to be written. When completed, this constitution bore the unmistakable stamp of Gaullism. The Fifth Republic was to be strongly presidential: The president (indirectly elected in 1958, then elected by universal suffrage every seven years) appoints the prime minister, proposes legislation to Parliament (which has limited powers to change it), can appeal to the people against Parliament via a referendum, can dissolve Parliament when he wishes, and in other ways has powers enabling him to dominate the elected Parliament (Chamber of Deputies). Also, proportional representation was replaced by single-member districts, with one run-off by the two top candidates. Minority parties, including the Communists, lost representation under this plan.

Although it was criticized as excessively authoritarian, this long constitution was in some ways democratic, particularly in the provision for referenda. Weary of weak and divided governments, the French people approved the Fifth's constitution by a resounding 79 percent of the popular vote. De Gaulle became president. Further signs of disgust with the old system appeared in a tendency to sweep the old leaders out in the parliamentary elections. Thus given a powerful mandate, the powerful personality of de Gaulle was to dominate the French and try to dominate the international scene for the next eleven years, generally amid a swirl of controversy.

So far as concerns Algeria, contrary to the hopes of the military that had backed him, he moved slowly but steadily toward granting full independence to the Arab state, overcoming enormous obstacles, in what was indisputably his finest achievement. He had decided as early as 1955 that the era of colonialism was over. His own conception of nationalism as the basis of human dignity forced him to this conclusion, he said; how could he deny to other peoples that same right of belonging to a free community that he claimed for his beloved France? At any rate, despite threats of assassination and acts of terror by French Algerians, he granted Algeria independence. The agreements were approved in France by an overwhelming majority in 1962. It had taken four years, much courage, and much patience, but De Gaulle had extricated France from her most tragic postwar dilemma. He followed this by decolonializing the rest of France's old empire in Africa.

He had already shown his independence, and some thought his remarkable stubbornness, when he renewed his quarrel with the British and the Americans that had begun during World War II. He began his term of office by asking for equality within the NATO alliance with the United States and Great Britain—including access to nuclear secrets. He was rebuffed in an episode strangely similar to one going on at about the same time between the USSR and China. (This famous and unexpected quarrel flared when the Russians refused to share nuclear weapons know-how with their supposed ally in 1959.) In the af-

General Charles de Gaulle being cheered in Rennes, France, September 20, 1958. At this time the war hero had been named Premier for a six-month period, while the constitution of the Fifth Republic, of which he would become President, was drafted. (*AP/Wide World Photos.*)

termath of Suez the new British prime minister, Harold Macmillan, had decided to cultivate with the United States a "special relationship," which involved virtually giving up any attempt at an independent role in world affairs for Britain. This was the evident lesson of Suez, but one that de Gaulle saw as insultingly servile.

The French president proceeded to order the removal of NATO fighter bombers from French soil and then to withdraw France from all military collaboration with NATO, though not from the alliance itself. He proceeded at great expense to develop France's own *force de frappe* of nuclear weapons. A tiny one it might be, but a nation must have its pride, the general held; and there can be no pride without independence. He became a thorn in the side of the Americans and was, to Harold Macmillan, "as obstinate as ever." He was to try for good relations with Russia, then with China, then Romania, and then, surprisingly, with Germany, with which he was to heal the ancient quarrel and cement friendly relations in a historic treaty of 1963. Anybody but the Anglo-Saxons, who seemed heartily to reciprocate his dislike.

Charles de Gaulle perceived the movement he led primarily in terms of French nationalism; he aimed at a revival of the country's spirit: "rediscovered élan." But it also involved a conception of democracy. The French leader hated political parties and wanted to embody the general will of his people in a charismatic personality (himself). This caused uneasiness among all those who remembered the recent Fascist horrors; but de Gaulle was committed not only to universal suffrage and free speech but to an elected two-house parliament and an independent judiciary. The man who had led the fight against Hitler certainly did not intend to create a Nazi-like regime. He yearned to heal the rifts in his beloved French nation, end voter alienation, somehow involve the people directly in government, as well as lead it forward to wealth and strength. Surrounded by an able group of people who shared this goal, even if they were not all of one mind about details, President Charles de Gaulle between 1958 and 1970 gave the postwar world its most interesting and impressive political regime.

But, as he realized, he did not succeed. He may have ended the *immobilisme* of the Third and Fourth Republics, too concerned with parliamentary supremacy, but he did not, except perhaps very briefly, unify France or end citizen alienation from government. Many protested this kind of plebiscitary and dictatorial "democracy." And, in the end, de Gaulle could not unite France. "I am like Hemingway's Old Man of the Sea, I have brought back a skeleton," he sighed at the end of his twelve-year reign when the French people repudiated him.

He did bring France back from the low point of frustration and humiliation she had reached in 1940–1944 to something like the dignity befitting the oldest and proudest of Europe's historic states. Many of the Gaullists stressed the tasks of modernization, breaking through the "stalemate society," and leading France into the twentieth century–"getting ready for the twenty-first" by improving productivity, mechanizing agriculture, upgrading roads and airports, and in general reviving the spirit of improvement and enterprise, as against an "old France" that had been content to stick to antique ways. Or they talked about restoring the sense of national community, bringing the working classes out of their profound alienation, and healing the wounds that anomie had inflicted on the people. As with fascism, there was a left and a right wing of Gaullism, one traditionalist and conservative, the other restlessly oriented toward change.

To a great writer like André Malraux, who became the most enthusiastic and the most articulate of Gaullists, the chief appeal was heroism and the grandeur of an authentic historic personality. One-time Communist and Spanish Civil War fighter, later participant in the Resistance, Malraux asserted that Stalin's totalitarian industrial state had betrayed revolutionary ideals. If Trotsky were alive, he would join him, Malraux said. De Gaulle offered a cause with character and dignity after the death of the Communist god. One might, of course, recall the ex-Communists who went over to Mussolini or Hitler or joined the Croix de Feu. At times, the mystique of Gaullism became embarrassingly reminiscent of fascism, with vast rallies, searchlights playing on the Cross of Lorraine, and similar displays. Anticommunism, nationalism, organic community, antiparliamentarianism, stress on heroism and grandeur might remind people of Mussolini and Hitler. But the general preserved freedom of expression, tolerating even the Communists. In his memoirs, Khrushchev records his happy encounter with de Gaulle, with whom he got on famously in the 1960 visit despite their differences over Berlin.

De Gaulle was saved from Nazism or fascism not only by the fact that he had spent the best years of his life fighting Hitler, but by the quality of his civilization. He had a saving component of irony and a sense of tragedy. Too civilized to be a fanatic, he did not hope to rescue mankind or set up a utopia. He knew the inevitable limitations of power, and he shared the disabused, disillusioned spirit of the 1950s. He did not wish to destroy freedom, persecute minorities, or rule without a clear mandate from the people. He did not wish to wage aggressive war but to preserve a balance of power. He was not Hitler but de Gaulle. He was one of the century's greatest men.

POSTWAR POLITICS IN OTHER EUROPEAN COUNTRIES

No other western European political figure rivaled de Gaulle in stature, but Germany's Konrad Adenauer, who became the general's good friend, came closest. He presided over an adjustment to parliamentary democracy that those who remembered the Weimar failure, with its disastrous consequences, found as surprising as it was heartening. While there were to be some criticisms of an authoritarian streak in Adenauer and in the German people, of his commitment to democratic processes there was no real doubt. He had defied Hitler and spent his time in the wilderness during the Nazi period. He did not threaten another such dictatorship.

Germany's achievement of political stability under the representative parliamentary system which began in 1949 can be contrasted with France's unhappier experience with the Fourth Republic. First, the antiparliamentary or antigovernment groups were much less extreme in Germany; Nazism had discredited the radical right, and communism was equally unpopular because of the hatred of Russia. With André Malraux, the Germans might have cried, "Marxism is not something to the left of us but something to the east of us." Neither extreme gained more than infinitesimal support under the Federal Republic. Second, the 1949 German constitution did not adopt proportional representation. This, together with the fact that government funds were given to parties on the basis of their numerical strength, with a party getting less than 5 percent of the vote entitled to no subsidy at all, discouraged wasting votes on small parties. Third, the Germans found in Konrad Adenauer a father figure who did not reject the parliamentary system. Chancellor from 1949 to 1963 (an office roughly similar to that of prime minister but carrying a bit more authority), Adenauer was much beloved. The old man, who was seventy-three when he took office and eighty-seven when he quit, was a salty character, a sort of Teutonic Harry Truman whose folk qualities appealed to the Germans and whose political guile kept his foes at bay.

"*Der Alte*," the Old One, was a member of the Christian Democratic Union, and under his leadership it dominated German elections until 1969. The smaller parties lost strength, and a three-party system emerged. The Social Democrats ran a strong second, and the smaller Free Democrats, a bourgeois liberal group, held the balance of power and normally supported Adenauer. In 1969, the FDP finally swung over to the Social Democrats, by which time the Social Democratic party had abandoned its one-time Marxian stance entirely.

The leading theme in German political life was what might be called wiping out the Nazi past. A certain reluctance to think about the terrible interlude of 1933–1945 and indeed about the whole dreadful experience since 1914 was noticeable in Germany after the war, and it lasted for many years. Albert Grosser tells of a writer who in 1966 addressed a memorial service by saying, "We were the barbarians in the last war, let's face it," and being reprimanded: "We came here to remember our dead sons and not to be told about the Nazis." The average German had much sympathy for the ordinary people who had obeyed orders and who had turned a blind eye to abuses during the Nazi period—"which of us would have done otherwise?" One might compare this feeling with the "I don't want to get involved" attitude of witnesses to crime so often noted in recent years. This unwillingness to face up to the past was frequently criticized, but it should not be confused with real pro-Nazi views. The only neo-Nazi party of any consequence, the Socialist Reich Party, won only 1.8 percent of the votes in 1951, and it was soon declared illegal by the High Court of the Federal Republic.

Books revealing Nazi crimes became best-sellers in West Germany, the leading example being *The Diary of Anne Frank*. So, to be sure, did some memoirs of ex-Nazis such as Albert Speer. Early on, Konrad Adenauer took steps to offer amends to the Jews. He pledged a payment of an indemnity of three billion marks to Israel from 1953 to 1966. "In the German people's name unspeakable crimes have been committed, which demand moral and material reparation," he told the Bundestag in 1951. A German office set up in Ludwigsburg in 1958 sought to track down Nazi criminals who had not yet been caught. Victims of the Nazis received compensation, though there were complaints about the slowness of the procedures and inadequate amounts of money. In 1969, a poll showed that only 44 percent of the German people thought that

Table 10–2   German Elections

	1949	1953	1957	1961	1965	1969
CDU/CSU						
(Christian Democratic/Social)	31	45	50	45	48	46
SPD						
(Social Democratic)	29	29	32	36	38	43
FDP						
(Free Democratic)	12	10	8	13	10	6
Others	18	16	10	6	4	5

Nazi criminals should still be prosecuted. Germans were tolerant about ex-Nazis holding public office, and indeed in 1966 a man who had once been a member of the Nazi party became chancellor. Kurt Kiesinger's election elicited strenuous protest from Germany's leading writers, Günter Grass and Heinrich Böll, who by this time were joining a movement of revolt that accused German society of philistinism and decadence. But German opinion was more decidedly pro-Israel in the 1967 Middle East war than was either French or British.

Adenauer's adroit foreign policy regained a respectable place in the community of nations for the Federal Republic. It became a staunch NATO partner, a member of the EEC, and a friend of France; the signing of a treaty of friendship in 1963 between those old enemies, France and Germany, must surely be accounted one of the leading achievements of the era. Adenauer was even able to keep a line open to Moscow, though in general the Russians always attacked the Federal Republic as a nest of ex-Nazis plotting a war of revenge. (This did not prevent the East German Communist state, the DDR, from using many ex-Nazis in its government and party.) For its part, the Bonn government not only would not recognize the DDR but, in the so-called Hallstein Doctrine, said it would refuse diplomatic relations with any country that did recognize the East German regime. Diplomatic relations with the USSR, which were established in 1955, was the only exception to this policy. For many years, Bonn did not deal with the other countries of eastern Europe.

Locating the capital in the little city of Bonn on the Rhine, which was hardly large enough comfortably to house the growing federal bureaucracy, was intended in 1949 to be a signal that this was a temporary headquarters, to be used until the day when the government returned to Berlin as the capital of a united country. The Berlin Wall was yet to go up; but bitter relations between the two Germanies existed at all times until 1969, when the first Social Democratic chancellor inaugurated a new policy.

Germany's well-known administrative efficiency continued. The staggering task of handling a number of refugees as high as fifteen million (counting those who fled from the DDR) was done with such efficiency that the French used the German model for their resettlement of the three-quarters of a million French Algerians after 1962. The fabulous economic boom guaranteed Adenauer's electoral success, but his party never received more than 50 percent of the vote, and the Social Democrats steadily increased their vote after ineffective leadership early in the Federal Republic's existence. Perhaps West Germany suffered from the lack of an outlet for extreme views. The Communist Party, a tiny minority in any case, was outlawed in 1955; the SPD steadily shed the last remnants of socialism. Political consensus has advantages, but it has the disadvantage of not representing the nonconformists, who may in their frustration turn to other methods. The radical student protest movement of the late 1960s began in Germany.

In the year before Adenauer's retirement, 1962, the government raided the offices of the prominent German weekly *Der Spiegel,* a hard-hitting, brilliantly edited news magazine. It was a kind of German Watergate, which fore-shadowed the scandals and troubles that were to plague the West in this decade. It marked the beginning of a new era, shook the government, and perhaps hastened Adenauer's retirement in 1963 (he was only eighty-seven).

Italian politics stood somewhere between the French and German models. As in Germany, the Christian Democratic party took the lead and held it for a long time, gaining between 35 and 48 percent of the seats in Parliament in the elections between 1946 and 1963. But unlike Germany, and like France, the Italian Communist Party attracted 20 to 25 percent of the voters (under a proportional representation system). The Socialists, at times bitterly at odds with the Communists, at other times exploring a common front for the two Marxist parties, were also strong. A neo-Fascist party gained 5 percent of the vote, and monarchists, who were anxious to restore the House of Savoy (voted out of its long reign by Italian voters just after the war) won from 3 to 7 percent before fading in the 1960s. And, there were a number of other small parties.

Italian politics were thus not as stable as Germany's but not as volatile as Fourth Republic French. The Christian Democrats governed regularly, as in Germany, but they had more trouble putting together a majority in Parliament; they were never close to a majority by themselves except in the Cold War year of 1948, which was dominated by fears of a Red takeover. As they finally came to be outnumbered by Communists and Socialists, they were driven to explore the "opening to the left" by luring at least some Socialists to their side, a strategy encouraged by the liberal papacy of Pope John XXIII during the early 1960s. But this caused rifts in their own camp.

The Italian Communist party (PCI) was the most flexible and in many ways the most moderate of all Communist parties. Forced underground throughout the long Mussolini era, the Italian Communists had to seek collaboration with other antifascists; and they developed habits, quite unusual for Communists, of cooperating with or at least tolerating non-Communists. From their early leaders, especially the remarkable Antonio Gramsci, they inherited a more subtle and flexible Marxism than Stalin's. Palmiro Togliatti, Italian Communist head in this period, was among the most democratic and nationalist of

Table 10–3 Italian Elections, 1946–1963

	1946	1948	1953	1958	1963
Christian Democratic	35	48	40	42	38
Communist	19	31	23	23	25
Socialist	21		13	14	14
Neo-Fascist	—	5	6	5	5
Monarchist	—	3	7	5	2
Others (Liberal, Republican, Social Democratic)	25	13	11	11	16

all Communist leaders; he argued for an "Italian way to socialism" that had to be different from Russia's. Following Gramsci's lead, he construed Marx as teaching not the dictatorship of an elite but a general cultural development as the necessary prerequisite for Communist political power and economic change. The PCI set out in 1945 to build a mass party, not a Leninist elite. The PCI was to enter into a dialogue with the Catholics in the 1960s, and in the next decade it would accept the democratic, pluralistic social order. During the Cold War years, it stopped well short of that; but Togliatti was among the first and strongest Communist voices to welcome Khrushchev's 1956 denunciation of Stalinism and to call for a new Communist path, more humane and democratic. He responded eagerly to Imre Nagy's search for a more popular communism, and relations between the Italian and Russian parties grew strained after the suppression of the Hungarian revolution. On this path of compromise and adaptation, the Italian Communist party led all others. Therefore, it grew more popular in Italy and gradually ceased to be regarded as either a revolutionary threat or a tool of Moscow.

Elected in 1945 in a surprise triumph over Winston Churchill, the Labour party government of Clement Attlee presided in Great Britain over the establishment of Europe's most famous welfare state, and also the nationalization of basic industries. As foreign secretary, sturdy Ernest Bevin was a key figure in the organization of the alliances that shored up western Europe in the face of threatening decay: the Truman Doctrine, the Marshall Plan, NATO. On the other hand, there were disappointments. Expecting to preside over the millennium of plenty, Attlee's cabinet had to face inevitable postwar shortages. It imposed such unpopular measures as rationing, price regulation, and high taxation. The ambitious cradle-to-grave social security system was expensive.

At this stage, the Labourites put their trust almost wholly in nationalization and state controls. But statism is not in itself an answer, as critics were to point out and events in some measure showed. Private, public, or mixed, the important thing is to make the economy go. Productivity must be increased, export markets won, excessive inflation avoided by wise management. Merely

Table 10–4 British Elections, 1945–1966

	1945	1950	1951	1955	1959	1964	1966
Seats in Commons							
Labour	393	315	295	277	258	318	363
Conservative	210	298	321	344	365	303	253
Liberal	12	9	6	6	6	9	12
Other	25	3	3	3	1	0	2
Percent of popular vote							
Labour	48.0	46.1	48.8	46.4	43.8	44.1	48.0
Conservative	39.6	43.4	48.0	49.7	49.4	43.4	41.9
Liberal	9.0	9.2	2.6	2.7	5.9	11.2	8.5

transferring ownership from a private to a public corporation does not automatically ensure this. Such were some of the lessons a Labour party that had never before held sole power, and which lacked experienced and capable leaders, had to learn.

Corelli Barnett (*The Lost Victory*, 1995) has reproached Labour for not recognizing that Britain could no longer afford to be a world power, thus wasting money on arms and diplomacy that might have been invested in economic restructuring. But the Attlee government threw down the burden in Palestine with almost indecent haste, presided over the immense process of withdrawal from India, persuaded the United States to take up most of the European burden, and got a good deal of Marshall Plan money to boot. It is hard to see how the grand tradition of British world power could have been more quickly abandoned, and in fact this cost Labour much popular support, among those millions who felt it as a betrayal of the imperial mission so deeply planted in the national psyche. In 1950, the British sought to retrain the Americans from plunging into a war with China.

Those who were angry with the Attlee government because it had presided over the beginning of the liquidation of the British Empire were destined to some further disillusionment when in the late 1950s a Conservative government responded to the "changing wind" and began to decolonialize all over the map.

The withdrawal from India was the direct result of World War II. The Indian Nationalist movement was already well established in 1939 but took on new force when the British government presumed to declare war on behalf of India, an action that outraged Indian opinion. In order to gain valuable Indian support for the war, the British offered postwar autonomy within the British Commonwealth; the Indian National Congress demanded more. Under the impact of Pearl Harbor and the massive Japanese advance into Southeast Asia, Britain sent the Labour member of the wartime cabinet, Stafford Cripps, to negotiate. In August 1942, the Indian Congress passed a resolution calling on Britain to "quit India" forthwith, to which the British responded by arresting Gandhi, Nehru, and other high Nationalist leaders. With Japan virtually at the gates (Rangoon in Burma fell on March 8) this was a critical moment. The resolution of this crisis and the eventual Allied triumph in the war left India convinced that its contributions to the war entitled it to independence. The dramatic and often tragic circumstances under which Lord Louis Mountbatten presided over the transfer of power to India and to Pakistan amid communal rioting between Hindus and Muslims in 1947 are a part of history that lies outside of Europe. They had immense consequences for England. It was the British Empire's sunset: "On dune and headland sinks the fire."

Perhaps more critical a weakness was that Labour was perennially split between a left wing and a right. The party's left wing was uncomfortable with the Cold War; the fiery Welshman, Aneurin Bevan, resigned from the cabinet in 1951 over rearmament and NATO, taking with him a young man named

Harold Wilson. Bevan was supposed to have cost Labour many votes by referring to the opposing Tories as "vermin."

Also in 1951, an unhappy year for Labour, two left-wing undersecretaries in the foreign office created a tremendous sensation by defecting to Russia, and there were allegations of loose security. The flight of Douglas Maclean and Guy Burgess was a chapter in one of the most famous espionage stories of modern times. It had begun at Cambridge University in the 1930s among a group of bright and alienated students who became Soviet agents and did not end until revelations thirty years later that one of them (Anthony Blunt) was now a distinguished art historian and curator of the Queen's art collection. In 1963, Kim Philby followed Maclean and Burgess to Moscow. The group had all been highly placed in British intelligence and diplomatic service and had passed on valuable information to the Russians, including atomic bomb secrets. Maclean had obligingly kept Moscow thoroughly informed about plans for NATO, as well as for the Korean War. All this, of course, was not primarily Labour's fault–the "moles" had burrowed in under a Conservative government in the 1930s. But in the heightening atmosphere of the Cold War, some left-wing Labourites' sympathies for the Soviet Union became an embarrassment.

After having won so narrow a victory in 1950 that another election was necessary, Labour lost the 1951 election. They would not return to power for thirteen years. The Conservatives increased their majority in the House of Commons from seventeen to forty-six seats in 1955 and won even more comfortably in 1959. They came to their own time of troubles only in 1963. They were fortunate in reaping the rewards of economic recovery. But they had learned something, too. Between 1945 and 1952, the Conservative party had profited from defeat by developing a whole new outlook, organization, and image. According to the historian of the Conservative party, Robert Blake, the party "made a major effort to rethink its political programme, reorganize its internal constitution, and recover its parliamentary morale." It accepted the managed economy and the welfare state but contrasted its own flexible model, which was borrowed in some part from the French, with the straitjacket of Labour statism. The Conservatives worked to present themselves not as hidebound reactionaries but as a more modern, more efficient, and more knowledgeable party than the socialists. They drew on an old tradition of benevolent paternalism in the Tory tradition: the *noblesse oblige* of the upper class toward the lower. Anthony Eden said the Conservatives believed in the strong helping the weak, as opposed to the weak dragging down the strong.

Suez was a blow; but it brought to the prime ministership Harold Macmillan, a man of much culture and charm. Scion of the Anglo-American publishing company, Macmillan was a progressive Tory who favored economic planning, liberating the colonies, and thawing the Cold War. In 1938, he had written a book called *The Middle Way,* which indicated his preference for elements of the welfare state, moderate version. In the end, he was the victim of a rather bizarre scandal in his government. By then, the Conservatives had been in power for an exceptionally long time, and the country was ready for change.

During its long period of exile, Labour did its own soul-searching and underwent an internal struggle between pragmatists and ideologists. The man elected as party leader following Attlee's retirement, Hugh Caitskell, was a moderate who urged his party to turn away from doctrinaire socialism, seek middle-class support, and stop stressing the obviously unpopular nostrum of nationalization. Gaitskell declared in his speech to the fifty-eighth annual Labour Party Conference in 1959 that "Our object must be to broaden our base, to be in touch always with ordinary people, to avoid becoming small cliques of isolated doctrine-ridden fanatics, out of touch with the main stream of social life in our time." To which a leftist, Michael Foot, replied, "In order to win an election we have to change the mood of the people in this country, to open their eyes to what an evil and disgraceful and rotten society it is."

Even more bitter was the continuing debate about foreign and military policies in which "unilateralists" demanded that Britain give up its attempt to be a nuclear power, while the moderate wing rejected this approach as unrealistic. The issue split the left, especially after the militant Campaign for Nuclear Disarmament began to resort to methods of aggressive civil disobedience (obstructions, occupations, sit-ins) in 1960–1961. This movement, featuring the octogenarian philosopher Bertrand Russell, provided a model for further protests in the next decade.

Hugh Gaitskell died prematurely in 1963, on the eve of the long-awaited change of fortune that would have made him prime minister. Harold Wilson, who had moved from the left wing of the party to somewhere near center, inherited the job. He was to encounter grave difficulties during his term, as economic conditions turned downward—bad luck, once more, for Labour. One socialist publicist invented the theory that with diabolical cunning, the Tories managed to arrange things so that they were out of office when economic downswings came, thus contriving to put the onus of bad times on Labour! Oxford political scientists, though, held that the long-term political swing was toward Labour, the more democratic party in an increasingly egalitarian society, and predicted that the Conservatives would never win another election. It took only six years to prove them wrong.

It should be added that the Liberal party often received a significant percentage of the vote in these years, but it never won more than an insignificant representation in Parliament, because there was no proportional representation and the Liberals were almost everywhere a minority. The two major parties could agree on one thing, at least, that they did not want PR. And so the Liberals were condemned to continued frustration. The knowledge that a vote for them was a wasted vote reinforced their low standing in the pools.

We can sum up the politics of western Europe in the generation after 1945 by calling it in the main a politics of growing consensus, corresponding to the economic progress generally characteristic of this era. The extremes tended to become less extreme. The British Labourites and German Social Democrats dropped much of their socialism. On the other hand, conservative parties, accepting the welfare state and some degree of economic planning, heeded the changing winds and adapted to the needs of a new day. The distance between German CDU and SPD, between British Labour and Conservative, or at least between the right wing of Labour and the Tory left wing, narrowed to the point where some observers thought them indistinguishable except for a lingering veneer of rhetoric. Charles de Gaulle's new republic sought to suppress the parties entirely in favor of a politics of national consensus. There was an "integration of the workers into the economic and political life of the nation." Political apathy was the result more of contentment than of disgust. The ominous cloud of nuclear destruction was the chief exception.

If we seek novelty and excitement, that, for the Europe of the 1950s, was more nearly provided by its experiments in internationalism.

THE EUROPEAN COMMUNITY: THE EUROPE OF THE SIX

The origins of the European Economic Community (EEC) lay chiefly in efforts to resolve the role of Germany in western Europe. Ravaged by Germany in World War II, her neighbors hated and feared her yet could not do without her economically. One answer to this dilemma was to contain German strength within an embrace of all western Europe. Just as the European Defense Community and NATO tried to bring German military strength into the Western alliance without setting up a revived *Wehrmacht,* so the various forms of economic integration, beginning with the creation of the Coal and Steel Community, were intended to secure the advantages of Germany's great economic strength without allowing her to regain the ascendancy of Europe.

Then, too, the manifest failure of the old order caused many to look with favor on some wholly new one that would abolish the narrow nationalisms of the past and push Europe toward a fresh frontier. The Marshall Plan gave a boost to the idea of a transnational European economy, for the Americans persistently stressed the formation of a large single market, which should eliminate tariffs and even allow a common currency. The virtues of this became especially evident to such small countries as the Netherlands and Belgium.

The Organization of European Economic Cooperation sought to organize economic cooperation among Marshall aid recipients, but it encountered obstacles. The British in particular were unwilling to abolish tariffs. Had Great Britain been willing to take the lead, western Europe would surely have followed her just after the war. But the British, while reluctantly agreeing to join in military defense through the West European Union and then NATO, hung back when it came to closer integration. Winston Churchill had described the position of England as being at the intersection of three circles, only one of which was Europe. She looked across the Atlantic to her English-speaking brethren in the United States and Canada, and she looked to the other members of the British Commonwealth all over the globe, from Australia to Africa and the Mediterranean. If the traditional British imperial dream was to disintegrate in the next two decades, it was still very much alive in 1945; Churchill had bristled with indignation when he thought Roosevelt was trying to get him to "preside over the liquidation of the British Empire." There were special economic ties between the home country and the Commonwealth lands that interfered with efforts at Britain's economic integration into Europe. Geography and history dictated that the island kingdom would not be quite at one with the Continent.

The lead came instead from two far-sighted Frenchmen, Robert Schuman and Jean Monnet. Schuman was a native of Lorraine, that province that had shuttled back and forth between France and Germany since 1870. It was a region rich in iron ore, which traveled to the steel mills of the Ruhr Valley in Germany. The Ruhr Valley, site of great coal fields, produced more steel than anywhere else in the world between 1900 and 1945. When Lorraine returned to France in 1919, leading industrialists organized a Franco-German cartel; it was a sort of preliminary to the Coal and Steel Community. This international economic cooperation, forced by necessity, transcended the political rivalry of France and Germany between 1933 and 1945. Even during the war, Ruhr industrialists had little enthusiasm for Hitler and maintained contact with their French counterparts. It is no accident that the Coal and Steel Community was to be the nucleus of the economic community.

In the trauma of the immediate postwar years, the French attempted both to seize and to limit German production, while detaching the Saar region (rich in coal also) from Germany. When the economic and political reconstruction of Germany became a necessity, this policy was of course discarded.

The phenomenal technocrat Jean Monnet, who was the genius of French *planification,* also believed that national sovereignty was an anachronism that Europe would have to get rid of if it hoped to keep pace with twentieth-century technology. Robert Schuman, leader of the MRP party and twice French prime minister in the 1948–1950 period, backed a report from Monnet proposing a start on European economic integration via creation of a European Coal and Steel Community. The French proposal was favorably received by Adenauer's government and by Italy, Belgium, Luxemburg, and the Netherlands; negotiations began in June 1950, and what became known as the Schuman Plan soon grew into an organization headquartered in the tiny country of Luxemburg and headed by Monnet. Created in 1952, the Coal and Steel Community proved to be a success.

Along with this internationalization of one important segment of the economy, other European institutions were established, too. These included a Council of Ministers, which represented the governments of each of the six countries involved, a Court of Justice, and a European Parliament. As we already know, the next step toward Europeanization, a European Defense Community, stumbled and fell over the obstacles of French uncertainty, British reluctance to get involved, and fear of German rearmament on any terms. But the indefatigable Monnet continued to enlist support for European programs, and in 1955 the foreign ministers of France, Italy, Germany, and the Benelux countries met at Messina to plan both a full Common Market and joint atomic energy development. The Benelux three were strong supporters at all times, Belgium's Paul Henri Spaak emerging as another dynamic leader of Europeanization.

Still aloof, Britain declined to attend the Messina conference, but a groundswell of popular support for the movement pushed reluctant French and German politicians along. The Suez crisis, coming at this moment, provided an additional impetus, at least as far as France was concerned. Her estrangement from the United States pushed France toward finding friends in Europe; the threat of losing Middle Eastern oil focused attention on atomic energy as a source of power, which helped lead to the pooling of nuclear energy resources (EURATOM). An additional attraction for the French was the hope of finding an expanded market in Germany for their agricultural products.

For about the fourth time, Great Britain now missed the Euro boat. In the aftermath of Suez and Eden's resignation, Harold Macmillan chose to cultivate the "special relationship" with the United States rather than join the Continental states. The treaties of Rome, completed in that city in March 1957, were quickly approved with resounding majorities by the French, German, Italian, and Benelux parliaments. They created the European Economic Community, or the Common Market of the Six.

There ensued a period of spectacular economic success—expanding trade, strengthening of the best industries within each country, economies of scale. It was never entirely clear whether the Common Market was responsible for this boom or whether it would have come anyway; it does appear that the Rome treaties gave a lift to confidence everywhere. The Brussels-headquartered EEC quickly became an important adjunct to the European scene. Its staff was at first small but intensely able and dedicated. The Council of Ministers, which made decisions for it, had to agree unanimously—in other words, each of the member states had a veto—but it developed something of its own momentum and spirit.

De Gaulle's accession to power did not seriously interfere with this pattern. Although the general's nationalism caused him to throw some roadblocks in the way of political unification, he was by no means averse to an economic arrangement that benefited France as much as any country and that coincided with his plans for modernizing the economy. Moreover, his international strategy aimed at improving relations with Germany. Meanwhile, Great Britain had awakened from her insular slumbers and proposed a broader European Free Trade Area (EFTA), to include additional countries—Scandinavia, Austria, Switzerland, Portugal, and Spain. Its purposes would be limited to trade; in brief, a customs union. What England feared was not so much the economic as the political implications of the Common Market; though she was willing to contemplate a business partnership with Europe, she did not wish to commit herself to a marriage. But the vision of Monnet and Spaak aimed at the ultimate pooling of sovereignties in a full political union, creating a United States of Europe.

It was here that de Gaulle became a problem, for his vision was different. Nationalism was not dead, he felt, and no superstate should be attempted. Rather, he wanted a "Europe of the Fatherlands," cooperating with each other but not losing their separate identities, which were so fundamental (he thought) to culture and human dignity. "Europe is no nation," the general said. His most shocking action was the French veto of Britain's belated application for membership in the EEC in 1963. The European Community–the merger of the Coal and Steel Community, EURATOM, and the EEC–was to face a succession of crises on its road to unity. Some of them it surmounted, some it did not; but it remained alive, and interests with a stake in its survival began to grow.

The immediate project was the abolition of all duties on goods among the member countries. In 1962 and 1965, the Common Market passed crucial milestones when it achieved agreements on agricultural policy. Movement of peoples between countries increased, though complete elimination of migration restrictions was a remoter goal, as was a common currency. Still further down the road lay (members hoped) an all-European parliament with real powers and a Council of Ministers not forced to obey the wishes of the individual governments. The hope was that momentum would carry the movement forward from strength to strength, each successive plateau engendering the force to climb to yet a higher one. Pessimists feared that each upward leap would be harder and that the initial impulse might weaken with time. Some argued that political unification would inevitably follow economic partnership, while others said that the task was primarily a matter of building a European spirit or patriotism, something that the most sanguine had to admit was hardly yet much in evidence. Economic integration made more progress than did political cooperation.

De Gaulle's veto of British membership in 1963 (and again in 1967) was widely interpreted as an example of that inscrutable genius's remarkable obstinacy. In fairness to *le grand Charles,* it must be said that many in Europe shared his irritation about Britain's role in the past and his skepticism about whether she really yet accepted all the implications of membership. The Labour party, soon to replace the Conservatives in office, seemed hostile to the whole idea. The British still insisted that exceptions had to be made to allow for their special economic arrangements with commonwealth countries. Nevertheless, most Europeanists were distressed by the French veto and thought it violated the spirit of the European Community. In January 1963, de Gaulle instructed the French delegation in Brussels to break off negotiations, thus putting an end to an agreement that then seemed in sight after long negotiations between Britain and the Six. The general's decision to torpedo Britain's entry, which would have been followed by that of Norway, Denmark, and Ireland, was a reaction to Macmillan's continuing nuclear companionship with the United

States, as reflected in American Polaris missiles being supplied to British submarines.

Despite a 1965 crisis, when France boycotted EEC meetings for seven months, the Common Market reached its goal of abolishing customs duties in 1968, two years ahead of schedule. A complicated Community agricultural plan set uniform prices, protected farmers against cheaper foreign produce by a system of variable subsidies, and financed modernization of equipment. By 1970, General de Gaulle having passed from the scene, negotiations were again underway for British entry, along with other EFTA members. A single currency was scheduled for 1980, a target date that proved much too optimistic. But economically the European Community looked like a success, though it remained to be seen how it would weather an economic depression should one occur.

The political side of unification did not keep pace. The separate nations still held a veto over all major decisions of the Council of Ministers. A directly elected European Parliament, supposed to have come into being according to the Rome treaty of 1957, was delayed time and again until finally the first elections were held in 1979, and then was allowed little more than a ceremonial role. The Council of Ministers insisted on absolute secrecy in its decision-making process. They also resisted suggestions that on some issues at least a majority vote rather than unanimity might prevail. Not notably responsible to the peoples of the different member states was the European Commission, the swelling bureaucracy in Brussels that administered the rules and programs of the Union. Europe's national states hesitated to take the final steps that would convert an instrument of close economic cooperation into a sovereign superstate. De Gaulle's thrust, "Europe is no nation," still struck home.

Should the European Community become a single entity, it would constitute a power equal in population to the United States and even the Soviet Union (depending on how many countries joined it; in 1977 Greece, Spain, and Portugal applied, after the entry of Great Britain, Ireland, and Denmark). It would be equal to or greater than the superpowers in wealth, technological skills, and human resources. But the historic nations of Europe, very old and very deeply rooted, seemed unlikely to merge into a Nation of Europe except over a long period of time. Nevertheless, their attempts to do so, supported by people of genius, was one of the more exciting political ventures of the post-1945 generation.

THE MOOD OF POSTWAR THOUGHT

Few hopes or illusions remained after a war that had been marked by total inhumanity as well as nearly total destruction. Standing amid the ruins of European cities or contemplating the death factories of Auschwitz, one could only feel, with French philosopher Gabriel Marcel, "a more than physical horror and anxiety." Almost before this horror could be absorbed, it seemed that another war was impending. This one would be waged with even more terrible weapons, and Europe would this time be a helpless victim. If mankind had any future, it surely lay outside Europe, in the hands of peoples whom civilized Europeans were much inclined to regard as barbarous. A British historian wrote of *The Passing of the European Age;* a German sociologist–brother of the great Max Weber–bade *Farewell to European History;* and at the end of his long life H. G. Wells, that eternal optimist, for the first time found *Mind at the End of Its Tether.* While a few clung to hope in communism, that hope vanished rapidly in the flood of disenchantment with Soviet Russia. "What have you done with our hope?" André Malraux cried on behalf of a majority of the European intellectual community, addressing Stalin.

It is true that the Communists in France and Italy, even for a moment in Germany, came out of the war with considerable prestige, because of their valiant resistance to Nazism. But their slavish adherence to the Moscow line, along with Moscow's behavior in opposing the Marshall Plan and crushing freedom in Eastern Europe, isolated them and diminished their standing. Growing awareness of the appalling repressive side of Stalinism, the executions and tortures and inhuman prison camps where millions suffered, marked the early 1950s. The party line that decreed hostility to any kind of literature, art, or philosophy except one incredibly naive and obsolete by European standards, was an invincible obstacle for most European intellectuals. Marxism still meant Stalinist "diamat" crudity, literature and art confined to propaganda, and the arts dictated by a narrow-minded set of party officials. European intellectuals had been through that in the thirties and wanted no more of it.

The prevailing mood was a deep mistrust of all ideologies, which–whether Nazi or Communist–had betrayed men into slaughtering each other for abstractions. Both the Algerian-born Frenchman Albert Camus and the British writer George Orwell expressed the feeling that one must destroy the tyranny of concepts and get back to real human beings. Though socialists, they had a strong suspicion of Marxist intellectuals and faceless *apparatchiki;* they were more personalist and more tinged with the tragic view of life than traditional socialism had ever been. That

> The troubles of our proud and angry dust
> Are from eternity and will not fail

needed no demonstrating for those who had seen Nazism and the war.

The handsome, athletic Camus, literary idol of the postwar years, told his audiences that we were all responsible for the war, the gas chambers, the concentration camps, the bombings. Humanity was guilty. Even if one side was somewhat more guilty than the other, "revenge is sour," Orwell said. This neo-Christian sense of original sin and the need for universal forgiveness was an authentic product of the war. The leading political movements to emerge from the war and the Resistance were the Christian parties in Italy, Germany, France, and the Low Countries. They were built on the courage of such martyrs as Martin Niemöller and Dietrich Bonhoeffer and on the reduction of life to the ultimate and simplest values by the "boundary situations" of the war. "Never were we more free than when enslaved" under the Nazis, Jean-Paul Sartre wrote. Humiliated, without rights, people were faced with basic choices and, in the presence of death, made them. The postwar cycle of despair, reduction to human essentials, and revival of hope "on the far side of despair" was identified more with Sartre's radical and atheist existentialism than it was with old-fashioned Christianity, though the latter was strong and was sometimes existentialized. No theologian was more fashionable than Rudolf Bultmann, who brought the post-1919 "crisis theology" of Karl Barth up to date.

But no theologian could compete with the glamorous Sartre. The author of novels and plays as well as philosophical tracts, hero of the Resistance, he was a mordant critic of bourgeois values. In plays like *The Flies* and *No Exit,* he dramatized and popularized the existential analysis of the human condition. He had found this analysis chiefly in the works of German philosopher Martin Heidegger, but other roots of this existentialist philosophy lay in the nineteenth century, chiefly in Nietzsche, Kierkegaard, Dostoyevsky, and Hegel. This mood embraced not only the sense of a powerful crisis, reaching to the very roots of modern humanity's relationship to nature and culture, but also the predicament of the urban dweller's essential loneliness in the crowd, his social anxieties and identity crisis. There was a sense of the total absurdity of existence. Thrown into the world for no reason, we are somehow here, confronting a hostile and meaningless universe, condemned to make sense of it or perish. The human consciousness inside each of us is a radically different kind of being from all other kinds; it has no given structure, no essence. It is a kind of nothingness, a great wind blowing toward objects, a "hole in being." It is wholly free and undetermined, completely unlike physical or objective existence. "I, a stranger and afraid, In a world I never made"—A. E. Housman had caught something of this feeling earlier in the century.

When we realize our predicament, we may be overcome with nausea and contemplate suicide—the only serious philosophical question, Camus claimed. If we decide to live, we must do so in full realization that our arbitrary choices and actions endow the universe with its only meaning. Insisting only on integrity, authenticity, and personal commitment, existentialism was a protean philosophy that might be turned in almost any political direction. In the hands of Camus, who quarreled with Sartre in 1952 on Cold War issues, it was turned in a rather conservative direction, whereas Sartre always remained the embattled and embittered hater of his bourgeois society. Between 1950 and 1956, Sartre was aggressively pro-Soviet, denouncing the United States at every opportunity and visiting the USSR to be lionized and vodka-drenched. But the events in Budapest in 1956 distanced him from the Russian Communists to a degree that was only partly overcome in ensuing years; 1968 in Prague finished the job.

Possibly the best-known and most widely discussed serious book of the 1950s was George Orwell's (Eric Blair) *1984*. The English essayist and novelist finished writing it as a dying man in 1948; it almost immediately became a modern classic. With Hitler and Stalin in mind, Orwell feared the world was heading toward totalitarian slavery. Loss of liberty and individuality, a permanent caste system, perpetual war or the pretense of it marked Orwell's imagined "Big Brother" state run by the Party; so did poverty and a puritanism that withheld love from the masses in order to control them. All this seems very unlike what actually happened in the next generation, with its manifold freedoms, its consumerism, its rejection of authority. But Orwell's pessimism reflected the mood of the 1950s, against the background of the Cold War, the Big Bomb, the persistence of Stalin's state, the morbid fear of Communism in the West.

Popular culture of the 1950s featured men in gray flannel suits, young men with crew cuts, girls who dreamed of marrying the right man and settling down to happy domesticity. It was a conservative decade, the time politically of Eisenhower, de Gaulle, Macmillan. Even in the Soviet Union, one might see Khrushchev's ascendancy as a middle-of-the-road compromise between the extremes of Stalinism and total liberation. This political swing corresponded to the generally successful economic recovery and to the psychology of a generation reacting against the strident ideological battles of the previous decades. There were small currents opposing this main stream—"beat" poets, for example—but even this protest was a quiet one, its adherents fleeing to rural solitudes and cultivating Zen Buddhism. The poetry of the 1950s as represented by Philip Larkin, Donald Davie, and Thom Gunn in England, was a subtle probing of private lives, immensely skillful but wholly nonpolitical. The novels of Graham Greene and François Mauriac and the plays of the Swiss Friedrich Dürrenmatt caught a deeply religious mood, probing the ultimate human corruptions and sins. Movements of strenuous or violent protest, leading to demonstrations and militant movements, largely awaited the 1960s (we have noted the exception of the antinuclearists in England). Untroubled by aggressive radicals, the decade of the 1950s was later to be accused of apathy and resignation in the face of manifest social evils. On its own view, it had moved beyond superficial social theories to discover the existent individual.

Missing too was the aggressive feminism that emerged in the next decade, along with other radical protests. People tended to assume that feminism had won its battles—the vote, legal equality, sexual emancipation, educational rights, professional opportunities—and there was no strong feminist movement until the rather unexpected "second wave" exploded in the 1960s. "Gone are the days of vigorous feminism and anti-feminism," British anthropologist E. E. Evans-Pritchard wrote in 1955. "Surely these are 'issues that are dead and gone.'"

11

Soviet Communism after Stalin

Josef Stalin, born Djugashvili, the virtual dictator of Soviet Russia for twenty-five years, was a political genius who built the huge Communist industrial society out of ruins, led Russia to victory in World War II, and was afterwards venerated as a saint. There are stories of his idealized picture hanging alongside Christ's on Italian walls. In his later years, he permitted an adulation suggested in Nicholas Virta's 1948 play *Stalingrad*, in which the kindly father of his country is painted as ever-vigilant, ever-farsighted (he planned the Stalingrad trap months in advance), yet always ready when time permits for a friendly chat with old comrades. But nothing in Russia could have exceeded the hagiography that emanated from distinguished Western writers. The "myth of Stalin" affected even most Americans, who called him "Uncle Joe" and, like President Harry Truman, attributed difficulties with Russia to evil influences surrounding this essentially amiable person. Millions all over the world mourned his death in 1953 as a blow to world peace and human justice.

There was another Stalin, known to a few earlier but not fully revealed until after 1956, who was a sadistic tyrant and paranoid mass murderer responsible for more deaths than even Adolf Hitler. Along with the industrial cities rose the slave labor camps, concealed from the view of admiring visitors, with a constantly changing population of several million people. It is an amazing tribute to the power of Soviet propaganda and the gullibility of Western intellectuals that so little was known of this ugly side.

"Known" is perhaps not the right word; as in the case of the Holocaust, it was more that people preferred not to see. Russian exiles, especially among the Menshevik group, presented an abundance of evidence early on; but Jean-Paul Sartre expressed a prevalent view among left-wing intellectuals when he observed that even if these things were true they should not be publicized because they damaged the good cause. A recent biography of Walter Duranty, the *New York Times* correspondent in Moscow for many years, paints a damning portrait of a much-honored journalist who did not present an honest picture of the USSR. So also the influential British journalist Alexander Werth.

The "aging god" Stalin apparently grew paranoid again, if he had ever stopped. A professor (Kubanin) who wrote that Russia was lagging behind the United States paid with his life; another (Voznesensky) who proved that Western capitalism was writhing in its death agonies did not escape destruction either. It was dangerous to risk saying anything, and a crowd of toadies desperately tried to read the irritable tyrant's moods in these last years.

Jewish intellectuals were persecuted in 1952–1953 as Stalin discovered the danger of Zionism. Then, in January 1953, nine prominent Russian physicians and medical professors were arrested and accused of causing the death of Zhdanov and plotting to kill other high Soviet officials. They were said to have been agents of "an international Jewish bourgeois nationalist organization" under the direction of American intelligence (January 1953). They were tortured into confessions, two of them dying in the process. Soviet newspapers and journals began to sound the alarm cry of treason and wrecking, an atmosphere sickeningly reminiscent of the mid-1930s. In his 1956 secret speech, Khrushchev charged that Stalin was preparing a purge of leading party members, just as in 1936–1938 he had gotten rid of every one of the old Bolshevik leaders.

Perhaps he was, and perhaps his death came just in time to save Russia from the horrors of another Terror. There was speculation that the top advisers headed by Beria actually murdered Stalin to prevent this and save their own skins. But their complicity in his death evidently extended only to a failure to treat his illness. In late February, the outcry in the press suddenly ceased; a few days later, Stalin was reported to have suffered a stroke, and on March 6 came the news that he had died the previous evening. The eyewitness account published by his daughter Svetlana leaves no doubt that such an attack did take place. The 73-year-old tyrant was left wholly untreated for many hours after the stroke and was never properly cared for; he lay dying on a couch for three days.

The logical heir apparent, at least in his own opinion, was Lavrentia Beria. A fellow Georgian and a man after Stalin's own heart, Beria had been Stalin's most essential assistant, though there were signs of a fall from favor just before Stalin's death. He had been in charge of the vast Gulag prison system as well as of Intelligence; also of the Soviet atomic bomb project. For a few months

Stalin's funeral, March, 1953. Malenkov and Beria are the first two pallbearers, left and right; behind Malenkov is Stalin's son Vasily, followed by Molotov, Bulganin, and Kagonovich. (*Library of Congress.*)

after Stalin's death, Beria did dominate Soviet policy, but there were others among the palace guard who feared and disliked him. They all agreed on the need to relax tensions. Beria even strove to appear the most liberal. The case against the Kremlin doctors was dropped, and Soviet policy moderated in Korea and toward Yugoslavia.

Beria's rivals, who had been among Stalin's top advisers in his last years, included Nikita Khrushchev, Gregory Malenkov, and Nikolai Bulganin. Molotov and General Zhukov were restored to favor. It was the military hero who arrested Beria, but evidently Khrushchev who orchestrated the conspiracy against him. It is still unclear whether Beria was executed spontaneously in June or after his secret "trial" held six months later, on December 23. At the trial, which looks like an attempt to throw a cloak of legality over a *fait accompli,* he was accused of trying to "restore capitalism" and undermine the collective farm system, as well as other miscellaneous crimes reaching back to the civil war era (nothing said, however, about Stalin's terror or the Gulag). He was also said to have tried to keep H-bomb secrets from his colleagues. They all favored pressing ahead with the bomb's development, and the first Soviet thermonuclear test took place on August 12, 1953.

Suddenly Beria was a nonperson. The volume of the Great Soviet Encyclopedia containing Beria's entry had just been published, with a very long article devoted to his career. A letter went out to buyers of this volume requesting them to cut out these pages; replacements would be supplied. When these came they included an exceptionally lengthy treatment of the Bering Straits! "He was a butcher and an assassin," Khrushchev declared later, accusing Beria also of raping numerous young girls. There is much evidence that the latter charge was true. Beria was an example of the total brutalization of late Stalinism.

The widespread impression that Nikita Khrushchev was the first to break with Stalinism, after a struggle with Beria and others of the old guard, does not seem to be correct. Beria's surprising liberalism during his brief season in power was perhaps one reason for his fall. After that, Malenkov emerged for a time as the leading figure. Malenkov was thought to be more "rightist" than Khrushchev. He made suggestions for reform, speaking of the need to put more stress on light industry to help the Soviet consumer, an issue that struck close to the heart of de-Stalinization. Mikoyan observed in a speech in October 1953 that "we have not yet overcome the disproportion between the production of goods and popular consumption, and the saturation of the increasing needs of the masses of the Soviet Union." Orthodox Stalinists still preached the cult of heavy industry's priority.

Agriculture was the other great sore point of the Russian economy. When Malenkov resigned the premiership on February 8, 1955, he mentioned his lack of success in this area. He also preached an extreme version of the "peaceful coexistence" doctrine that Nikita Khrushchev was to stress: War was now unthinkable, because it could only mean the ruin of both sides. By 1955, of course, both the United States and the USSR had succeeded in manufacturing the new and more powerful H-bomb, soon to be carried by long-range missiles. Malenkov was prepared to agree to the unification of Germany under free elections, along with its neutralization, a plan proposed by British Foreign Secretary Anthony Eden in 1954.

Veteran Stalin disciple Vyacheslav Molotov (though a victim of Stalin's disfavor because of his Jewish wife) attacked Malenkov for this heresy. Molotov, familiar in the West as their glowering Cold War enemy of 1945–1947, was an unreconstructed, dogmatic Stalinist. Khrushchev thus emerged as a compromise figure, between Molotov on the right and Malenkov on the left. Malenkov's fall would seem to have been the result of an excess of de-Stalinizing. The old Stalinists, led by Molotov, joined forces with Khrushchev, who may be thought of as occupying the center, to secure Malenkov's downfall.

For some time, the results of this power struggle were unclear, and this uncertainty in the top Soviet leadership is related to the 1956 troubles in Poland and Hungary. Attacks on Molotov broke out in 1955 and 1956, and Khrushchev came to the fore; but he did not have a firm grip on power (a secure majority in the Presidium, as the Politburo was now temporarily renamed) even at the time that he delivered his speech to the Party's Twentieth Congress on February 25, 1956. The materials for the famous speech had clearly been assembled with care, but Khrushchev may have decided to present them on the spur of the moment. He blurted it all out: Stalin had had "a persecution mania of unbelievable proportions"; he had been arbitrary, capricious, and tyrannical. "Thousands of innocent people fell victims to wilfullness and lawlessness" in the Leningrad affair and on many other occasions. Stalin had threatened to "shorten by a head" his minister of state security if he did not obtain confessions in the doctors' plot, and he had ordered the accused put in chains and beaten. ("Beat, beat, and beat again.") The evidence in this case had been "fabricated from beginning to end." At his death, Stalin was planning to "finish off the old members of the Politburo" including Molotov and Mikoyan.

Releasing copies of Lenin's letter of December 1922, which expressed alarm at Stalin's "immense power" and his "crude" nature, Khrushchev accused the long-time Soviet leader of lacking toleration, patience, and ability to cooperate; Stalin simply imposed his views, demanding "absolute submission." Stalin was admitted to have been right in opposing Trotskyists, Bukharinists, and other deviationists; but in 1935–1938 he had passed beyond the bounds of reason and had obtained confessions "through physical duress against the accused." Mass arrests and mass deportations without trial, Khrushchev went on to say, "created conditions of insecurity, fear and desperation." The meeting surged with indignation, according to the report, when the first secretary revealed that of the 139 members of and candidates for the Central Committee elected in 1934, 98, or 70 percent, had been shot, while of 1,966 delegates to the Party Congress of that year, more than half had been arrested. "Diseased with suspicion," Stalin had grown paranoid and used his unlimited power to stifle all free criticism. Khrushchev did not neglect to point out Stalin's virtual collapse at the beginning of World War II and his uncertain leadership during much of the war.

Why didn't the members of the Politburo assert themselves against the cult of the individual? Well, Khrushchev said, at first Stalin had gained great popularity and support through his vigorous leadership; later he ruled by terror and by guile, and finally he bypassed the Politburo altogether. Khrushchev's attempted explanation of why there had been no resistance to Stalin's tyranny during his lifetime and why his tyranny had not even been mentioned until three years after his death was feeble, but at least he thought an explanation necessary. In 1955, when he visited Belgrade, Khrushchev had blamed the mishandling of Russian-Yugoslav relations on the conveniently dead Beria, much to Tito's disgust. Now Stalin himself was accused of all manner of crimes. Not until 1961 would he be removed from Lenin's side in the mausoleum on Red Square and his name removed from place names all over the Soviet Union.

The speech of February 25, 1956, was given in secret session, but it soon became one of the worst-kept secrets in history. The speech was passed on to the Israeli embassy by a Polish journalist who saw it at Polish Communist Party headquarters, in what looks like a deliberate leak. In fact, his colleagues never quite forgave Khrushchev for going public with Stalin's misdeeds; it was a serious breach of Party etiquette. Such matters were supposed to be kept within the small circle of the top leadership.

After 1956, the USSR did not overnight become a liberal or a democratic state, needless to say. It remained guided by an elite leadership of the only party allowed to exist, a leadership that was not elected by the people. This elite still attempted to control or oversee every aspect of society's and every citizen's life. It still arrested and imprisoned or deported dissenters. The controlled press still systematically distorted and suppressed news. There were no free trade unions. The parliament, the Supreme Soviet, met for a few days each year to rubber stamp, invariably by a unanimous vote, what it was allowed to approve, including the budget and a few laws. In 1968, as it did in 1956 only a few months after Khrushchev's speech, the Red Army forcibly repressed rebellions designed to secure (within communism) some measure of intellectual and cultural freedom. In 1971, Tibor Szamuely commented that "everything in the USSR, to the smallest detail, is today essentially as Stalin created it. . . . Khrushchev attempted to tinker with the massive edifice—and failed."

Nevertheless, 1956 was a turning point, perhaps one of history's greatest ones. Torture, summary execution, and imprisonment in slave labor camps ceased to be the means of government. Leaders might be dismissed, but they were no longer shot. The Terror decree of 1934 was annulled. The population of the labor camps declined sharply, though the camps did not vanish altogether. The system did not much change, but the spirit that informed it slowly altered, becoming less grim and brutal, more relaxed and humane. After all, those who claimed to be Marxists could not forget that the end product of revolution was supposed to be not perpetual slavery but the good society, in which human nature realizes its fullest creative possibilities.

The immediate result was shock. "For weeks we talked of nothing else," one who was a student at that time recalls. Bierut, the Polish first secretary, died of a heart attack! There was confusion and sometimes anger at Stalin's traducers; had he not been long presented as the hero-leader? Khrushchev says that he argued that one big shock would be better than years of creeping doubt. The truth about Stalin was certain to be known eventually, and it was better to get it out of the Soviet system in one big purgation than to let the poison go on working. In adopting this plan he showed courage. But it was dangerous to go too far, for this would undermine the very legitimacy of the Soviet order. Stalin had built the system within which Soviet leaders operated. How far could they or should they reform it in basic ways? There were a number of areas in which reform seemed urgent, including the overcentralized and bureaucratic economic planning structure. But the most significant task was providing some freedom and democracy for Soviet citizens.

THE KHRUSHCHEV ERA

"De-Stalinization" was a difficult and dangerous process. All the top Soviet leaders had served Stalin, and some had been all too closely involved with his crimes. The Soviet system as it existed was Stalinist, and the legitimacy of the present leaders' rule rested, in the eyes of millions, on their being Stalin's heirs and successors. The Italian Communist leader, Togliatti, joined the Hungarian intellectual Marxist Gyorgy Lukacs in calling for a clean break with the Stalinist past. But very soon the outbreaks in Poland and Hungary revealed the dangers of too precipitous a break. Imre Nagy's democratic communism quickly led to what looked like democracy without communism. This weakened the position of the de-Stalinizers. There was a brief thaw in the literary and intellectual world, followed almost immediately by a refreeze.

By mid-1957, Nikita Khrushchev had overcome some opposition from the old Stalinists and others to make himself the dominant figure. The launching of the first Soviet Sputnik space satellite in October 1957 reacted in Khrushchev's favor. Molotov, Malenkov, and Kagonavich, his rivals, were dismissed from the Central Committee and branded the "Anti-party" group; assailed with epithets such as "criminal fractionists," "filthy intriguers and splitters," they were not, however, charged with treason and executed. Imre Nagy was executed two years after the suppression of the Hungarian Revolution, and Khrushchev was not above using threats to return to Stalinist methods in arguments with dissident intellectuals; but in general the new style was more humane and introduced a small measure of democracy into the system.

The energetic Khrushchev threw himself into reform efforts including such grandiose projects as the "virgin lands" scheme to open up to cultivation a huge acreage in Kazahkstan: a plan based to some extent on the mystical scientific views of the quack Lysenko, whom Khrushchev supported. (Trofim Denisovich Lysenko claimed that Lamarckian principles of species development were superior to Darwinian because they were more Marxist. Environmental changes could alter heredity; scientists could develop seeds with the ability to grow in the cold and dry climate of the steppes of eastern Russia and Siberia by freezing many generations of them and thus genetically accustoming them to the climate. This, of course, turned out to be untrue, but Lysenko terrorized respectable Russian academic biologists under both Stalin and Khrushchev for many years.) In 1959 and 1963, the expensive virgin lands project got into serious trouble, as disaster struck the crops. Other Khrushchev plans, including the consolidation and increasing proletarianization of the collective farms, did not do much to improve a nagging Soviet problem, the inefficiency of its agriculture.

Khrushchev also attempted to address a critical weakness, as it was increasingly recognized, in the administratively planned economy. He anticipated Mikhail Gorbachev's famed "restructuring" of thirty years later but his substitution of regional planners for central ones did not prove effective and had petered out almost totally by 1966. In 1955, Evsei Liberman first advocated use of markets rather than central allocation of goods, but this bold idea was not pursued. Khrushchev's successor Kosygin sought to install some Liberman-type reforms by devolving many "indicators" from central plan to factory managers, together with some use of profits as a measure. But the most important indicators remained with central planners, and in the end this reform also amounted to little. A decline in Soviet economic growth dates from about 1958, although it became alarming only in the 1970s. Neither Khrushchev's efforts nor those of his immediate successors addressed the problem effectively.

Khrushchev's most visible activities were on the international scene. He traveled almost incessantly, visiting virtually every country in the world. In 1959, he came to the United States, accompanied by a huge entourage, for a long, much-publicized tour—the first visit to the land of capitalism by the ranking leader of the first communist state. During his visit he conferred at length with President Eisenhower. Enthusiastic, ebullient, and good-natured, the earthy Khrushchev and his wife made a hit. He seemed to want to open a dialogue between the West and Russia, ending its suspicious isolation. He was capable of acknowledging that Communists had much to learn from the enemy—these slaves of capitalism live pretty well, he was heard to murmur in Iowa. And, he proclaimed that "the ice of the cold war has begun to melt."

At the same time, under pressure from the "hawks" at home, Khru-

In September, 1959, Soviet leader Khrushchev visited the United States to discuss "peaceful coexistence" with President Eisenhower. (*Department of State Photo.*)

shchev could not push his peaceful coexistence plan too far. While pressing for détente, he could not afford to seem to be doing so from weakness. Sputnik I and Sputnik II had exhibited Russian missile power, which ought to be exploited. So Khrushchev issued threats as well as smiles. In late 1958, he threatened to make a peace treaty with East Germany (DDR) that would end the occupation status of Berlin and invite the DDR to take over the western zone of that city, thus reviving once again the Berlin crisis that had erupted in 1948–1949. West Berlin was "a bone in his throat," Khrushchev declared. It was indeed an anomalous leftover from the Cold War, a Western outpost deep in Communist territory. Bonn claimed it as a part of the Federal Republic. The flow of emigrants to the economically booming West increasingly embarrassed and damaged East Germany. It is not surprising that Khrushchev wanted to resolve the problem.

He blustered and threatened, but allowed the six-month time limit he had placed on securing a German peace treaty to expire, denying that he had delivered an ultimatum. By that time the Soviet leader had other worries, for the quarrel between the USSR and Red China was about to erupt into a public shouting match. It did so openly at the international Communist meeting in Bucharest in June 1960. Khrushchev wished to settle matters in Europe before dealing with potentially greater trouble in Asia.

A summit conference was scheduled in Paris in May 1960 to decide the Berlin question at last. Having laid down what amounted to an ultimatum, Khrushchev was in a tight spot. If he backed down, the Chinese would accuse him of cowardly compromises with the imperialists. Yet he faced a firm front against him from the United States and Europe. On this issue, de Gaulle stood firm, treating Khrushchev's threats with contempt and telling General Eisenhower "We will stand by you on this."

Fortunately for him, an incident provided him with an excuse to call off the impending conference. On May 1, an American reconnaissânce plane (unarmed) was shot down by a Russian rocket over Soviet territory, near the Urals. Its pilot parachuted to safety, was captured, and confessed that he was on a mission to photograph Russian military installations. Such espionage flights had been going on for some time, but this was the first time a pilot had been taken alive. Khrushchev reported the incident in a speech but omitted to say that the pilot had been captured. The United States government quickly responded with a "cover" story, claiming that the plane was on a scientific expedition and had strayed into Soviet territory by mistake. Khrushchev then disclosed the full details; he had trapped the Americans in a lie. Thus exposed, Washington made a full confession, urging the necessity of such "distasteful" espionage to guard against nuclear attack. Upon his arrival in Paris for the conference on May 16, the Soviet leader demanded an apology and punishment of those responsible for the espionage. Eisenhower said that the flights were being suspended but went no further. Khrushchev then stormed out of the conference. He nevertheless took care to announce another postponement in the signing of a separate peace treaty with East Germany.

The U-2 incident thus helped Khrushchev escape a dilemma, and there was even a suspicion that he contrived it. After all, he could have shot down an American plane at any time earlier if he had wanted to. He says nothing about this event in his memoirs. He soon went over to Bucharest to argue with the Chinese, while the United States changed leaders when Democratic candidate John F. Kennedy won a narrow victory in the fall presidential election. Kennedy and Khrushchev met in Vienna in June 1961, and Khrushchev evidently got the idea that the young American could be bullied; he was both inexperienced and liberal-weak. Khrushchev again issued threats about West Berlin and soon set about erecting the most famous of Walls (after the Great Wall of China): the one that barred movement between East and West Germany.

THE CUBAN MISSILE CRISIS

Kennedy did badly mishandle the Cuban situation early in his term of office. When he assumed the presidency early in 1961, he faced the question of what to do about the revolutionary regime of Fidel Castro, which had taken over the sugar island in a revolution against its corrupt rulers in 1959. No Marxist, Castro was no proletarian or peasant either, but the young lawyer came out of obscurity to lead a group of freedom fighters, which filled the power vacuum left by the abdication of the confused and discredited Batista regime. He was a revolutionary adventurer, not a Communist; for this reason the rising New Left, marked by a deep mistrust of all ideology, was to make him its hero. But his violent abuse and threats convinced many Americans that Castro was a danger to Caribbean security, and a growing crowd of Cuban refugees who had fled from revolutionary terror were all too ready to return with arms to overthrow him. On April 17, 1961, some 1,500 CIA-trained Cuban refugees landed at the Bay of Pigs, expecting to ignite a national uprising against Castro. The entire operation had been badly bungled, and it failed.

While Kennedy was trying to figure out what had gone wrong in Cuba, the Russians were putting the first man in outer space. Small wonder that Khrushchev felt he had the upper hand when the two leaders met several weeks later. When after this rather unsatisfactory meeting Khrushchev proceeded to build the Berlin Wall, he caught the West totally by surprise. He then set off a series of hydrogen bombs in a resumption of above-ground testing. For still one more time, however, he refrained from dropping the other shoe on Berlin. The Wall had seemingly taken care of the problem of people fleeing from East Germany, at whatever cost in inhumanity and in admission before the bar of world opinion that people would not stay in communist countries if they could help it.

In October, the Twenty-Second Party Congress met, and instead of threats against the West it produced a barely disguised outbreak of the quarrel with China. The Russians assailed Albania as a substitute for China, that little country having broken away from Moscow's control to side with the Chinese. Meanwhile, the Chinese attacked the USSR under cover of assailing Yugoslavia. And, at this same time, Khrushchev persuaded the party to renew the attack on Stalin, while encouraging another "thaw" in the climate of opinion. The dead dictator's crimes were extended to include his whole regime rather than just the final years. This development reflected Khrushchev's fear of renewed criticism of his policies by the old Stalinists. The truth is that his tenure at the top of the Politburo heap was always more or less tenuous; a sizeable segment of the Party, all Stalin's men in the past, never forgave him for his public exposure of Communist dirty linen and entertained doubts about his stability.

The year 1962 was to bring the worst international crisis since 1956. The unpredictable Khrushchev now thought he saw a way out of the Berlin impasse by exerting pressure on the United States through Cuba. Castro and Khrushchev first met in 1960 when the Russian leader visited New York, entertaining the public by banging his shoe on the table at the United Nations and embracing Castro in a Harlem hotel. On December 1, 1961, Castro announced himself a convert to Marxism. In the main, Soviet policy since World War II had adhered to the implicit bargain about spheres of influence by avoiding any significant involvement in Latin America, even though the volatile politics of this region, which was flavored with much anti-Americanism, offered tempting opportunities. But this time, the temptation was too great, and Khrushchev was prepared to gamble.

Hints about shipping arms to Cuba from the Soviet Union appeared in June 1962. A large amount of equipment flowed into Cuban ports during July and August, and construction work began at sites that were intended to be nothing less than nuclear missile installations. The missiles themselves, with their nuclear warheads, began to arrive in September. Did Khrushchev expect this to go unobserved? If not, did he expect the Kennedy government (about whose "liberal" weakness he had spoken to visitors in recent weeks) to do nothing about it? If so, he had badly miscalculated.

On October 22, 1962, U.S. President John F. Kennedy declared a blockade of Cuba, designed to prevent Russian ships carrying long-range missiles and nuclear warheads, along with other supplies for the Soviet forces and installations already stationed there, from reaching Fidel Castro's island. This was rather late; by some time in November, it is calculated, the Russians would have completed the missile bases together with their antiaircraft protection, and, with numerous medium-range and intermediate-range nuclear missiles in place, would have had the major eastern cities of the United States within range. But certain now of the Russians' intentions, which they had tried to conceal by brazen denials, Kennedy no longer hesitated. He called their bluff.

Khrushchev raged that the Americans were headed toward thermonuclear war, warned of "catastrophic consequences," and asserted that "no state concerned with preserving its independence" could accept the American blockade. U.S. forces all over the world were placed on the alert; submarines received radio information on Polaris missile targeting. Would the Soviets defy the blockade, leading to a confrontation? Would the United States bomb the missile sites being installed or already installed in Cuba, or even attempt to invade Cuba? Would the Russians then retaliate with nuclear weapons? Was this the long-feared nuclear armageddon? For a week, the world trembled while statesmen floundered. We now know that Soviet ground forces in Cuba were armed with tactical nuclear weapons, and the local commanders had discretionary authority to use them. (The Soviet air defense commander who shot down an American reconnaissance plane on October 27, refueling the crisis, was on a loose rein.) There were actually more Soviet troops and more missiles already in Cuba than Washington believed, though Bertrand Russell led a chorus of voices who declared that there were none and that the Americans were warmongers. Castro urged the Russians to launch a nuclear attack on the United States if the Americans invaded Cuba.

These were the evident dangers of an outbreak of nuclear war. But in fact Khrushchev was almost pathetically eager to blunder out of a mess he had blundered into, and despite Castro's howls of betrayal, the Russians had absolutely no desire to die in a war for him, a war in which they would be at a severe disadvantage. Had he known how weak the Soviets were, Castro now says, he would never have invited them in. A reason for the Soviet attempt to plant nuclear bases in Cuba was to offset their grave inferiority in long-range nuclear weapons by gaining bases closer to the U.S. Khrushchev agreed to withdraw the missiles, getting in return a promise that the United States would not invade Cuba. He made this without consulting Castro, who felt betrayed.

Khrushchev, after all, was in a weak position. It was Hungary in reverse: Russia could not possibly defend Cuba from so far away except by unleashing suicidal nuclear war. Several days of frantic exchanges worked out an agreement. The threat of thermonuclear war was perhaps not quite as great as a terrified world imagined (subsequent scholarly opinion about this has varied), but this was without a doubt the scariest eyeball-to-eyeball confrontation of the Cold War. Nevertheless, the episode had some beneficial results. Awed by their nearly fatal collision, the superpowers not only installed a special telephone line and soon reached an agreement on nuclear testing, but they proceeded toward a general détente. After marching up to the brink and looking into the depths, one can only march back and think things over. A grave crisis surmounted often leads to an improvement in international relations.

For Khrushchev, however, it was undoubtedly a serious setback. He had precipitated a world crisis by a rash gamble, and had his bluff called. He had sheepishly retreated, bringing home his missiles while the Chinese waxed indignant at this "shameful capitulation to the imperialists." He could claim to have secured a guarantee of Cuban immunity against U.S. attack, but such an attack had clearly not been imminent; and in any event a simple treaty of alliance between Cuba and the USSR could have gained the same end without all the turmoil. Khrushchev's intentions may have been to subject the United States to nuclear blackmail, forcing it at the very least to give up West Berlin. Aware that the USSR was inferior to the United States in missile strength, he hoped to bridge the gap. (A decade later, the United States was prepared to concede that equality between itself and the USSR in nuclear arms was the only realistic basis for a treaty limiting and controlling the arms race.) In this he had totally failed. President Kennedy was soon in Berlin being cheered by ecstatic crowds as he told them "I am a Berliner!" Critics accused Kennedy of heating up the conflict with rhetoric, as Truman had done fifteen years earlier; but the American President had proved his courage as a leader.

Among the consequences of the Cuban crisis, Moscow vowed to strain every nerve to catch up with the United States so as never to suffer another such humiliation, and this strain on the Soviet economy was one factor in the collapse of that economy in the 1980s. The missile crisis condemned U.S.–Cuban relations to many more years of hostility and ensured that Cuba would remain a reluctant ward of the Soviet Union. Castro was safe from overthrow, condemning Cuba to thirty-five more years of his rule. John Kennedy's assassination the next year may have been another consequence of this memorable event, for the young outcast who gunned him down was a Castro partisan.

His bungling also cost Khrushchev his job two years later, or at least was one black mark on his performance sheet. His handling of relations with China may have been another.

THE SINO-SOVIET CLASH

To many people in the West, obsessed by the idea that world communism was a monolithic entity, the clash between communist China and communist Russia came as one of the great surprises of the 1960s. In actuality, nothing should have been less surprising. They were in competition for the leadership of world communism, for one thing. The Russians had long been used to being the unquestioned head, whose ideas the other Communist parties of the world, all much smaller and less significant, were expected to endorse without complaint. But now a land of greater population, with an old and proud history, asked for equality if not primacy. This was even more true after Stalin's death. Though there was little love between them, Mao Tse-tung was prepared to defer to Stalin's seniority while the latter lived; he was not ready to kowtow to the upstart Khrushchev. Mao once declared that whereas Stalin was a fallen eagle, Khrushchev was a backyard hen! The veteran Chinese Communist leader expected to be recognized as the number-one world Marxist.

Relations between the two communist movements had never been really close. Back in 1927, the urban-based Chinese Communists, under Russian guidance, were wiped out by Chiang Kai-shek's Nationalist party. They regrouped in rural areas, based their strength upon the peasants (quite in contrast to Marxist teaching as interpreted in Russia), and developed ideas and strategies attuned to this backwoods situation. Mao Tse-tung and his fellows thought they were following Marxism-Leninism, but they owed little or nothing to the Russians and developed on their own for many years. In fact, leading Chinese Marxists had learned their theory in Paris, not Moscow, back in the 1920s.

During their successful war against Chiang Kai-shek's Kuomintang Nationalists, the Chinese Communists got little help from Moscow, contrary to a widely held belief in the United States; even in 1948, Stalin seems to have negotiated with the KMT for a north-south division of China. In that year of Tito, he was little inclined to trust home-grown Reds. When Mao visited Moscow in 1949, he made the long journey by train and was treated with none of the honors accorded a major visiting head of state. The treaty he made at that time with the Soviet Union was not marked by an overwhelming generosity on Russia's part, to say the least, and during the Korean War there were indications of a lack of perfect coordination between the communist allies. After Stalin's death, in the atmosphere of general relaxation, the Russians made some gestures of friendship toward Red China, as they did toward Yugoslavia. But this proved to be the lull before the storm.

Against a background of personal jealousies and cultural rivalry, the trouble started chiefly over Khrushchev's "peaceful coexistence" line. The Chinese were much more warlike. The doctrine of perpetual revolutionary struggle was Mao's chief gift to humanity's store of ideas, and he thought the Russians should practice it, too. When, looking at the prospect of destruction of all they had so painfully built, the Russians backed away from nuclear war with the United States, Mao was disgusted. He astonished the Russians in November 1957 by pointing out to them that if 200 million Chinese were killed in a nuclear war, along with 200 million Americans (and 200 million Russians?) there still would be plenty of Chinese left. "Hit the aggressors on the head!" he cried during the Lebanese-Jordanian crisis of 1958.[1] The sight of Khrushchev hobnobbing with Eisenhower at Camp David in 1959 was the last straw—or, if not that, the Soviet Union's refusal at this time to share nuclear knowledge with its ally because it thought Mao too reckless. The Chinese chairman expected Russian support against the United States in his campaign to overthrow Chiang Kai-shek's government on the island of Taiwan, where it had settled after being driven out of China, and which still claimed to be the true Chinese government. He was to find that the Russians did not even support him in a boundary dispute with India.

In the late 1950s, the Chinese Communists proclaimed the "Great Leap Forward," which was supposed to carry them toward the state of commu-

---

[1] In the summer of 1958, American and British troops, now in harmony, landed in Lebanon and Jordan after a revolution in Iraq. Iraqi revolutionaries had assassinated the pro-British king of that country and proclaimed a union with Egypt. Egypt, backed by the USSR, threatened retaliation; but the crisis cooled off when both sides showed restraint.

nism by bringing industry, in the form of small-scale manufacturing, to the villages. This notion was wholly at odds with the Russian idea of centralization, abolition of peasant culture, proletarianization, and urbanization of the countryside. The Russians laughed at such ignorant presumption. Khrushchev thought Mao a "lunatic." Each side began to accuse the other of "revisionism" or "petty bourgeois deviationism"–the Chinese pointing to the Kremlin's soft line on capitalism and to Russian elitism and rigidity, the Russians ridiculing Chinese agrarian "populist" ideology. The Soviet Union accused Red China of "adventurism" and "anarchism"; Mao blamed the Kremlin for "shameful compromises with imperialism."

In July 1960, following the row at Bucharest, the Russians withdrew all their experts from China and began to sharply reduce economic aid to that country. The ideological struggle broke out in earnest. It annoyed the Kremlin exceedingly that other Communists seemed to welcome an opportunity to criticize the Soviet Union, obliquely and cautiously at first but with growing boldness. In 1961, only two-thirds of the world Communist parties supported Moscow on the "Albanian," i.e. Chinese, issue. Mao was playing Martin Luther to the Kremlin's Infallible Chair, sowing dissension, schism, and even heresy among the faithful Marxists of the world. The Soviet Union stood to lose its long-held leadership in the world Marxist and revolutionary movement to this young and potentially powerful rival. It was not prepared to accept this defeat without a fight.

There was also the uncomfortable fact that China and Russia shared a tremendously long border, stretching for more than 3,500 miles through ill-defined regions. The Chinese claimed that the border was based on unjust seizures in the past, and in 1963 they asked that the borders be changed. Doubtless this could have been resolved had basic goodwill existed, but once the quarrel began, the boundary dispute, along with the status of such buffer zones as Outer Mongolia and Sinkiang, added fuel to the fire. In fact, there were later to be actual armed conflicts at some localities along the border. In 1964, the polemical battle raged so loudly that throughout the world even the most ill-informed grew aware of it; from being a family quarrel it had become a public scandal. It was to contribute much to Khrushchev's fall. To some extent, Khrushchev's firmness with China pleased conservative, Stalinist elements in his party, for they were marked by a general hawkishness, admiring strength and toughness in foreign policy. They were psychological "hard-liners," who no more favored "appeasement" of the Chinese than of the Americans. Thus the anti-Chinese line united diverse factions within the Soviet Russian ruling group. At the same time, his indiscreet way of conducting the quarrel exposed Khrushchev to criticism.

China went through the turmoil of the Cultural Revolution between 1965 and 1969. During this time, Red Guards blockaded the Soviet embassy in Peking, causing the withdrawal of Russians from China and counter-riots against Chinese students in Moscow. The Cultural Revolution had indeed begun with a campaign to debate the Russian-Chinese quarrel as a means of "raising the cultural consciousness of the masses" by showing how backward the Marxism of Moscow was. In return, Soviet Russia ridiculed Mao's "infantile" attempt to drastically shake up his party and country. The climax to a decade of hostility came with a major battle fought on the Ussuri River in 1969. As massive Soviet troop movements to the east were observed, there was fear of war. The Chinese dug bomb shelters in their cities.

THE GROWTH OF DISSENT IN THE USSR

While the Soviet economy seemed to register impressive rates of growth in the 1950s, the goal of "overtaking and surpassing the United States" receded further into the distance. The Soviet gross national product remained less than half that of the United States, and was now substantially less than western Europe's, which was growing faster than either of them in the 1960s. On a per capita basis, Soviet production (even without allowing for some doubts about the accuracy of Soviet statistics) was no more than a third that of the United States. This apart from qualitative considerations, which were becoming serious; the USSR was failing to keep up with technological innovation. We are familiar with the economic crisis that afflicted the USSR in the 1980s, when it became serious enough to bring down the basic Communist system. The problems were by no means new. The attempt to plan economic production from the center by bureaucratic allocation may have been theoretically unsound from the start—so leading Western economists had long argued. But it worked better at a stage of primitive capital accumulation than it did as the country moved toward a complex consumer-oriented economy—this much at least was clear.

Nevertheless, few students of Soviet society saw disaster at this time. Nagging worries about efficiency and quality controls were thought to be receiving attention and would ultimately be solved. A bias among Western intellectuals in favor of socialism as, in principle, a more rational system than capitalism, one based on "planning" and not the "chaos" of the free market, doubtless affected judgments. A representative evaluation on the fiftieth birthday of the Communist revolution, J. P. Nettl's *The Soviet Achievement* (1967) in paying tribute to "fifty years of concrete achievement" spoke of "the enormous resurgence of Soviet industry," impressive space technology, and growing interest from the Third World in Soviet methods; he added that "The Soviet consumer will undoubtedly continue to be better off.... His rate of betterment will appear ... extremely favorable in comparison with Western countries." Similar opinions were quite common, even if accompanied by an undercurrent of concern.

The areas that received the most criticism were the political and the civil. The scandal of the USSR was its ghastly past when under Stalin the Gulag Archipelago (the title of Alexander Solzhenitsyn's world-famous book about the

Soviet prison camps) symbolized terrorization of the free human intellect. The system still stood in principle, if mollified in practice. Khrushchev engaged in a complex struggle with the ghost of the man he had dared attack three years after his death. The potent remnants of Stalin's spirit still stood in the path of reform.

The attempt to rehabilitate the victims of Stalin's terror is a good example of the ambiguities of de-Stalinization. By 1964, 65 percent of those purged from the Central Committee after 1934 had been quietly rehabilitated—posthumously, alas, in the vast majority of cases—in the sense that their names were restored to encyclopedias and official histories with no attribution of guilt. But there was no public statement about all this. Nor did rehabilitation go so far as to restore Trotsky to respectability. Political prisoners were released. The power of the secret police (MVD, later KGB) was restricted. Yet laws against criticizing the regime or the party remained. The liberalizing trends brought mutterings from remnants of the old Stalinists and made timid people nervous at the prospect of unleashing anarchy.

All paths led to the ultimate question: In a society built on Marxist dogma but committed in some sense to ultimate liberation, what are the limits of criticism and dissent? The Stalinist party's supervision of literature and the arts had reached a peak in the Zhdanov era, right after the war. Freud, Einstein, and all "formalism" in the arts were banned, and Zhdanov did not hesitate to rebuke such great Soviet artists as composers Shostakovich and Prokofiev and cinema director Sergei Eisenstein, who died in a prison camp. "Formalism" was a term the Soviet ideologists used to embrace much of Western "modernism": nonrealistic art, experimental techniques in the novel and poetry, in fact nearly everything that had been esthetically exciting in the West since late nineteenth-century naturalism. Formalism was denounced as "fanciful innovation which divorced art from the people and made it a possession of a narrow circle of epicure aesthetes." For the writer or artist to express only his or her own feelings was decadent bourgeois individualism. Artists must serve the party by praising its policies and damning its enemies. They must, in brief, become propagandists, under orders from often philistine politicians. "Socialist realism" was the watchword, but it was not supposed to be so realistic as to depict anything unpleasant in the Russian scene; this was "bourgeois objectivism," and constituted treason to the workers' state by showing it in an unfavorable light. As Soviet writer Ilya Ehrenburg put it, "our so-called statesmen . . . lay down the law on what kind of books we are to write and what kind of pictures we are to paint."

There was censorship; anything published had to appear, if it appeared legally, in organs run by the state or party, and indeed it had to be approved for publication by high bureaucrats in the Ministry of Culture (Agitation and Propaganda Department) if it was at all significant. To continue to work, writers had to belong to the Writers' Union, expulsion from which guaranteed nonpublication, membership in which entitled one to rewards. This carrot-and-stick plan, particularly when the stick might be a bludgeon driving one to the firing squad or the prison camp, sufficed to keep most writers, intellectuals, and artists in line.

But awkward contradictions appeared in the effort to mark off a separate Marxist science from the "bourgeois" variety. Building the bomb forced the Russian chiefs to abandon their ideological opposition to the theories behind atomic energy and join the enterprises of Western science; thus, as historian David Holloway suggests, it may have helped cause the Soviet order to unravel. The suspicious Stalin, and Beria who was put in charge of the operation, had to listen to and give much independence to an able body of Russian physicists. There was a memorable telephone conversation in which Beria asked Kurchatov, the leading scientist in charge of the bomb project, to repudiate quantum mechanics and relativity, and the latter answered "if they are not true there is no bomb." Whereupon Beria shut up.

The first thaw began only a few weeks after Stalin's death. Ilya Ehrenburg, a veteran Soviet writer and an apparent pillar of the establishment, led the protest. His wartime writings celebrating the heroism of the Red Army made him well known in the West. The theme of his group was that "the author is not a piece of machinery" who can be wound up and turned on to write according to formula; he creates well only when he is inspired to do so. Bureaucratic control of literature leads to insincere, uninspired work, all too much in evidence in the Soviet Union. Somewhat sarcastically, one writer pointed out that Shakespeare had not been a member of a union. Thirty hacks grinding out propaganda do not equal one Tolstoy, whatever the party leaders may think. Even Mikhail Sholokhov, a prize-winning novelist (*And Quiet Flows the Don*[2]) who was generally loyal to the party line, conceded that "a dreary torrent of colorless, mediocre literature" had flooded the market in recent years in Russia. A few novels and plays critical of Soviet life were allowed to appear in 1953–1954. An orthodox counterattack soon came in force, however, and limited this early spring thaw to a mere trickle.

The next relaxation followed the secret speech of 1956, but it was also fated to a rather brief life. Intense while it lasted ("the year 1956 was a year of passion," an observer wrote), stressing the theme of giving socialism a "human face," this phase of the thaw centered on Dudintsev's novel *Not by Bread Alone*. The very title was an inspiration; the content revealed a time-serving, dishonest, on-the-make bureaucrat named Drozdov, a name suggesting servility, "Mr. Toady."

But in May 1957, Khrushchev threatened these "muckraking" critics of the system. During a tirade at a Writers' Union meeting, he said that shooting a dozen Hungarian writers could have prevented the "counterrevolution" in Hungary. In a confession forced on her according to the customary ritual of self abasement, Margarita Aliger apologized for, among other things, having "substituted moral and ethical categories for political ones." This hard line coincided with the partial retreat from de-Stalinization that followed the Hungarian Revo-

---

[2]There were persistent rumors that this unique achievement of Stalinist literature was in fact partly plagiarized from a White cossack officer killed in the Civil War.

lution, but Khrushchev was not basically prepared to revert to Stalinism. The second thaw was stronger than the first, producing a small flood of new writing and even new journals. It never entirely stopped flowing. Despite continuing denunciations of writers who tried to put themselves above the party, Khrushchev permitted some liberal editors to survive.

But when the Pasternak case came up in 1958, a freezing wind blew across the stream. Boris Pasternak was Russia's greatest surviving poet. Aging by this time, he belonged to the brilliant Silver Age generation, most of whose representatives, as we know, had succumbed in one way or another to the difficulties of life under communism. Rather aloof from politics and perhaps too towering a figure to be easily vulnerable even to Stalin, who sometimes showed a curious respect for true genius among his foes, Pasternak had largely refrained from publishing anything for years. He busied himself with translations (including Shakespeare, Goethe, and some Georgian poets, which may have pleased Stalin) and wrote poems only for private circulation. He had long been working on the novel *Dr. Zhivago,* which in 1956 he decided to submit for publication. It was rejected as too risky even in the climate of the second thaw. He then sent it to an Italian Communist publisher, who published it in late 1957. A year later, the novel, which attracted world-wide attention and was later made into an American movie, received the Nobel Prize in literature. Pasternak first accepted the coveted award of the Swedish Academy but then was forced to refuse it amid an officially inspired chorus of abuse in Russia, which described him as a "moral freak," a filthy pig, a base slanderer. Expelled from the Writers' Union and forced to utter the usual abject apologies, Pasternak died two years later; the great pianist Svyatoslav Richter played at his funeral, but not many dared to attend. The storm of protest aroused all over the world by this brutal treatment of an internationally revered book and author must have given Khrushchev pause. He is said to have fired the people who advised him on this issue.

Pasternak had stepped outside the usual bounds of dissidence by having his work published abroad without permission, setting an example many others were to follow in ensuing years. *Dr. Zhivago* is a study in profound disillusionment, undercutting all the official praise for the Revolution by showing how irrelevant to the spiritual needs of modern man that whole exercise in political violence was. No wonder the Kremlin hated the book.

The next wave of de-Stalinization came in 1961. Stalin's body was removed from its position next to Lenin's, and Stalingrad was renamed Volgograd, a tribute to Khrushchev's continuing dedication to erase, so far as feasible, the cruel past. Ilya Ehrenburg continued to exploit his privileged position in the interests of a cautious liberalization; his 1960 memoirs were very important in Thaw III. Yevgeny Yevtushenko made a sensation with his poem "Babi Yar" about Soviet anti-Semitism, a charge that struck Khrushchev himself fairly close to home; Yevtushenko was abused, but he survived. Khrushchev continued to alternate between loud abuse and tacit toleration of intellectual novelty. He harangued coarsely against the tiny amount of abstract art that managed to surface briefly in 1962: "pictures painted by jackasses," "dog shit." He stormed in to close down an exhibit by the great sculptor Ernst Neizvestny, who was thereafter denied materials and facilities. This was perhaps more the bourgeois-peasant philistine than the Communist ideologue; Hitler hated abstract, modernist art too, and we can imagine Harry Truman reacting similarly, and perhaps even Ernie Bevin (not Charles de Gaulle).

This cultural backwardness, as they saw it, was the most serious problem European intellectuals and writers had with the Soviet Union. Sartre, visiting Prague in 1963, declared that those Marxists who threw out Freud, Kafka, Proust, and Joyce as "decadent" in effect outlawed the entire culture of Western intellectuals and precluded a dialogue. (In Moscow earlier that year, Sartre had found Khrushchev sullen, denouncing the visiting Western writers as henchmen of capitalism.) Yet 1962 was the year of Solzhenitsyn, whose first book, *One Day in the Life of Ivan Denisovich,* perhaps because it dealt solely with Stalin's concentration camps, was not only permitted but showered with official praise. This, needless to say, did not last either.

Thaw and refreeze, thaw and refreeze—in the end, after innumerable cycles, was there a significant decrease in the size of the ice block? Despite the relapses of Khrushchev's successors, the answer seems a clear yes. It was to Khrushchev's credit that he allowed the thaw to begin. He did rather consistently believe that communism should be democratized and humanized, and he tried as best he could—always consistent with stability and security—to move in that direction. Things would get worse, not better, after he left. He was to be overthrown in 1964 by people who feared freedom and feared democracy. They accepted de-Stalinization only to the extent that it meant the removal of complete brutality and illegal methods. Dissidents, that is to say, were no longer shot without trial or hurled into hideous prison camps in the USSR. But they were arrested, tried before biased judges, and sent to mental hospitals or regular prisons after 1965.

THE SOVIET UNION AFTER KHRUSHCHEV

Khrushchev was deposed early in October 1964. In a sudden and rather brutal blow, the Presidium (Politburo) compelled him to resign from that body as well as from his posts as first secretary and chairman. Khrushchev attempted to appeal from the Presidium to the full Central Committee, but this time, unlike 1957, he found no support there. The top positions were divided, Alexei Kosygin becoming head of the government and Leonid Brezhnev the party general secretary. The indictment against Khrushchev spoke of "the cult of personality" and of his "subjectivism," meaning his erratic qualities. No charges were filed against him, and there was no purge of his followers, some of whom, indeed, like Brezhnev and Podgorny, were prominent members of the new team. Khrushchev was allowed to live undisturbed in retirement, and seven years later was buried with no ceremony and little publicity. It was a relatively peaceful and legal change, for the USSR.

Most of Khrushchev's policies were continued, the problem obviously having been more with his manner than with his content. It would seem that his colleagues found him too uncertain a quantity, too much a gambler, too drunken and loquacious, as well as too dangerously reform-minded. He had piled up a formidable list of failures, and he had stepped on many toes, from old Stalinists to entrenched bureaucrats. He was conducting a rather intensely personal style of diplomacy just before his downfall in which he was rumored to be working on a deal with West Germany. He may have been anticipating that need for Western technological aid that his successors came around to five or six years later.

In late 1963, Khrushchev's old sparring partner, American President John F. Kennedy, had been assassinated in the first of many blows the United States was to suffer in this decade. Khrushchev's fall followed very soon after the American decision, taken by Kennedy's successor Lyndon Johnson, to "take all necessary measures" in Vietnam. Khrushchev seems to have wished to disengage his country from Vietnam. His successors reversed this course, pledging support for the North Vietnamese if attacked by the United States. Had Kennedy and Khrushchev survived, they might have avoided the subsequent frightful war in Indochina.

After the terrible god Stalin and his flamboyant critic Khrushchev, the next Soviet leaders were to be conservative and rather faceless, but no less dedicated to perpetuating communist principles. It was an aging elite, a virtual gerontocracy, the oldest governing body in Europe. The average age of the Politburo, as the committee of committees was now again called, soon became well over sixty. The Communist Party lost touch with European youth, who turned to a New Left in this decade. In the USSR, the economic reforms introduced in 1965 were implemented gradually and timidly and in the end amounted to little. The old system was too deeply entrenched. The regime also showed its conservatism by increasing military spending. The effort to close the gap between Soviet and American nuclear missiles was a goal they eventually reached, but at a great cost to the Soviet consumer. There was also major stress on building a powerful Soviet navy able to cruise the waters of the world, and a modern fishing fleet. The Soviet air force was enlarged and modernized. This heavy investment in military hardware, as much as 15 percent of the national product, indicates the strong role of the military bureaucracy in the post-Khrushchevian balance of power; it also reflects the desire to gain freedom from American military superiority, such as had forced the 1962 humiliation. The resources committed to the defense sector became a major cause of Soviet economic troubles, some Western experts thought. The Soviets also entered vigorously into the competition to sell arms to less-developed countries; whether to earn hard currency or to gain converts among their customers, this was a game of doubtful success.

The Soviet leadership may have held it against Khrushchev that he allowed the quarrel with China to escalate, but if so they did not succeed in reversing his policies. After celebrating Khrushchev's departure in 1964 by exploding a nuclear bomb, the Chinese were soon bickering with his successors. Though the Vietnam War brought them together in common support of the North Vietnamese Communist state against the Americans, it also was a bone of contention between China and the USSR. There were rivalries and differences of opinion about the war. The Soviet Union charged that the Chinese delayed deliveries of Russian supplies to North Vietnam.

Leonid Brezhnev gradually emerged as the top Soviet leader. He was to remain in power until his death in 1982, a longevity in office surpassed only by Stalin. But the self-effacing Brezhnev was a team man, a consensus-seeker; his era represented both a reaction against the "personality cult" and a desire to institutionalize the Revolution. These were the second-generation disciples, faithful to the principles of the Revolution in an uncritical manner and wanting only to regularize them. There would be no more capricious tyranny, but at the same time there was a sort of "re-Stalinization," for Khrushchev-like attacks on the great dictator now were out and, though handled in a more legalistic and less savage way, dissent was firmly repressed. This policy might be described as the permanent semifreeze, or "hesitant repression." A bureaucracy of 70,000 was keen to uphold the censorship, codified in article 70 of the criminal code which barred "agitation or propaganda carried on for the purpose of subverting or weakening the Soviet regime."

One might regard this as the degeneration or the organization of the Revolution; its bureaucratization and "normalization." It was marked by a weakening of the idealism that had accompanied the simple faith of the old Communists. Even Stalin had been a true believer, not doubting the mission of Marxism-Leninism to redeem the world—it was the source of his persecutory mania. With the decline of this faith came a deep corruption. Cynically, party chieftains would now use their power to enrich themselves, gaining special privileges in the scarce economy. Irony of ironies, the Marxists through their control of the means of production had become a new ruling class. But some saw this disenchantment as a stabilizing force. No longer ideological fanatics, the Russians were becoming just like the rest of us. Theories of "convergence" proposed a gradual drawing together of communist and democratic-capitalist societies to meet at some middle point blending state socialism and capitalism, pluralism and corporativism.

The hesitant repressors were faced with an increasingly bold and determined band of dissenters. A taste of freedom under Khrushchev had whetted an appetite for more and made the retreat from freedom unacceptable. And, the very hesitancy or moderation of the new leadership tended to encourage dissent, which was no longer nearly so dangerous as it was in Stalin's time. One now had a trial, with opportunities for some publicity. Punishment was likely to be relatively mild, perhaps a year or two in jail; before, one would have been shot or condemned to a labor camp. Under such circumstances, of course, the leadership might be tempted to return to just a touch of terror. The sometimes sinister device of commitment to mental institutions was tried out. In 1965–1966, the arrest and trial of Andrei Sinyavsky and Yuli Daniel received worldwide publicity; they were sentenced to seven and five years, respectively, of "strict regime corrective labor" for "anti-Soviet agitation and propaganda." Sinyavsky, a well-known Soviet literary critic, and his friend Daniel, a translator, had published stories in the West under other names. These contained material critical of conditions in Russia, although in fictional form. The Sinyavsky-Daniel case was clearly intended as a warning to Soviet critics, and it was accompanied by the punishment of a number of other overly bold intellectuals. But it aroused a storm of criticism abroad, as the trial transcript, revealing bullying judges as well as prosecutors, circulated in the West. Among those who denounced it as an outrage was veteran French Communist writer Louis Aragon.

The problem of publication abroad by Soviet authors of works banned in the Soviet Union, which had been initiated by Pasternak's *Dr. Zhivago,* grew to monumental proportions, as Moscow became a more cosmopolitan city with many more foreign visitors. The world learned of such bold Soviet dissidents as Vladimir Bukovsky, who at his 1967 trial asked to know why, since we demand the release of Greek political prisoners, can't we ask for the release of our own! And, he outraged the judge by calmly comparing Moscow's attitude toward demonstrations with Madrid's (then under the "fascist" Franco). Despite his long career as gadfly, during which he was sentenced many times to jail terms, Bukovsky escaped long-term incarceration and bobbed up repeatedly between 1961 and 1974, before finally being deported.

At the time of the Soviet invasion of Czechoslovakia in 1968, a handful of intellectuals attempted to demonstrate in Moscow and were roughed up by police and anti-Semitic crowds. They made a literary coup out of the episode. Natalya Gorbanevskaya's *Red Square at Noon* and Pavel Litvinov's *The Demonstration in Pushkin Square* were soon selling at Western bookstores. Litvinov was the son of Stalin's one-time foreign minister. Another dissident, Peter Yakir, was the son of a celebrated hero of the Revolution, later a Stalin victim who was ostentatiously rehabilitated during the first thaw. Such scions of high Soviet gentry presented special difficulties to the harassed rulers, as did courageous women like Gorbanevskaya and Lydia Chukovskaya.

The mid-1960s witnessed the beginning of the *samizdat* (self-published), privately printed magazines, songs, and books that circulated underground. Typewritten, sometimes photocopied, such material passed from hand to hand, and some of it found its way out of the country. Purely literary works were supplemented by political reportage, the most famous of *samizdat* publications being the *Chronicle of Current Events,* which appeared bimonthly from 1968 until 1972, when the KGB managed to break it up and arrest a considerable number of people involved in it. But within eighteen months the Chronicle had revived and survived numerous arrests of its editors to continue in publication. The works of the most famous of the dissidents appeared in *samizdat* editions.

The two leading figures, presenting the most serious challenge to Soviet orthodoxy, were the brilliant physicist Andrei Sakharov, and the great novelist Alexander Solzhenitsyn. Joining these two giants were others of only slightly less distinction; Roy and Zhores Medvedev, one a historian and the other a biologist, cannot be left off even a short list, nor can the crusading jurist, V. L. Chalidze, a leader of the "democratic movement" that wished to bring legal safeguards of free speech to the USSR. A distinguished biochemist, Zhores Medvedev published an account of the Lysenko affair, along with many essays on the need for freedom and reform in Soviet intellectual life. His twin brother Roy's massively documented history of Stalinism, entitled *Let History Judge,* appeared in English in 1971. Together the brothers also wrote a book about Khrushchev, as well as an extraordinary account (*A Question of Madness*) of Zhores's commitment to a mental institution, from which he was finally released in 1970 after an international campaign of protest.

The Medvedevs had long been dedicated Communists and were protected by their scientific prestige. So too, to an even greater degree, was Andrei Sakharov, one of the world's outstanding theoretical physicists. A Lenin and Stalin Prize winner, never (like Solzhenitsyn) in a prison camp, he was a privileged member of the Soviet elite and the youngest man ever to become a full member of the USSR Academy of Sciences. In 1958 and 1961, he protested against the scientifically unnecessary nuclear explosions that were set off for political purposes. He fought Lysenkoism, and in 1968 his *Progress, Co-existence and Intellectual Freedom* followed up his support of the dissidents with a ringing statement to the effect that without progress toward full de-Stalinization, freedom of thought, and democracy the USSR was doomed to failure; these things were not simply desirable in themselves but essential to a modernized society. "The division of mankind threatens it with destruction" and "intellectual freedom is essential to human society," he said. Socialism, moreover, will lose to capitalism unless it practices intellectual freedom.

Committed to "the defense of human rights" as the highest social goal and to a "convergence" theory that Soviet and Western societies would come together at some intermediate point, the Soviet scientist clearly was far out of line with official party orthodoxy. He was asking about the same question that got the young historian Amalrik an involuntary journey to Siberia: Could the USSR last at all without liberalization? For good measure, Sakharov joined in protests against alleged discrimination against the non-Russian peoples of the USSR and against refusal to allow Jewish emigration. "Freedom to leave . . . is a necessary condition for the spiritual freedom of all." In 1972, he told an American interviewer that he would no longer call himself a Marxist-Leninist, but a liberal. And, he spoke out to warn the West that it should not pursue détente with the Soviet Union unless the latter democratized. He did not escape the attentions of the KGB or severe attacks in the Soviet press, but he was unintimidated. During the Arab-Israeli war of 1973, he again criticized his country's position, and in 1974 he protested the arrest of Solzhenitsyn.

Solzhenitsyn had served seven years in a concentration camp for having criticized Stalin during the time that he (Solzhenitsyn) was an officer in World War II. He was released after Stalin's death. In 1962, his remarkable *One Day in the Life of Ivan Denisovich,* about prison camp life, received high praise in the USSR because Khrushchev blessed it, but this was the last time he had any luck publishing in Russia. His most brilliant novel, perhaps, is *The Cancer Ward;* its message, that there is a spiritual cancer at work in the Soviet Union corroding people's souls, was not one likely to appeal to the heads of Soviet society. Another novel, *The First Circle,* displays Solzhenitsyn as the conscious heir of Tolstoy, the chronicler as well as moral critic of an entire society. In it he focuses on a scientific institution that invents devices for helping the KGB trap innocent people—clearly "rabid slander of our social system," the official verdict was. No Soviet writer had ever been so bold. Solzhenitsyn wrote with the fury of a man possessed by a compulsion to tell the whole ghastly truth and by a fearlessness that sprang from his having been through it all himself. If Sakharov carried conviction because he was so obviously from the highest Soviet intellectual elite, Solzhenitsyn did so because he came out of the concentration camps. All his "novels," down to the *Gulag Archipelago,* which earned him deportation in 1974, were accounts of real people and events. They came from the cancer ward, the first circle of hell, the underground realities of Stalinist life. What made them unacceptable to the guardians of Communist virtue was not so much that they dealt with the Stalinist era, though to do so in any detail was now thought to be in very bad taste; his works radiated a belief that the same poison still works, that Stalinism has not been purged from the system, that the same corruption, materialism, and ideological pettifoggery still exist in the minds of the bureaucrats who run things.

Discouraged by the absence of any popular movement in the USSR, which they attributed to the elimination of dissenting populations by two generations of terror, the dissidents were inclined to look for help abroad. They hoped their appeal to world opinion would have an effect on the Soviet leadership. But the dissidents' chief weakness was their own lack of solidarity. If Sakharov became a liberal democrat, the Medvedevs spoke for a more human socialism, while the great Solzhenitsyn became a fierce reactionary, a kind of belated Slavophile who would return to Russia's ancestral Christian traditions against the whole modern world. In the 1970s, most of the dissidents chose emigration, which the authorities were now prepared to accept and encourage.

The common people, who scarcely understood Solzhenitsyn, made a hero of the songwriter and singer Vladimir Vyotsky, who became a cult figure; "probably the most idolized figure in the Soviet Union today," it was said. His songs radiated a sort of "take that job and shove it" attitude, which often boldly expressed hatred of the Red guards imprisoning the Russian people. Such was Vyotsky's popularity that the authorities attempted to co-opt him, issuing some of his milder songs with official sanction. The others circulated underground on homemade records, the *samizdat* of song. In the popular mind, little evidently remained of the Revolution's dream; indices of social pathology such as rising rates of divorce, suicide, crime, and drug addiction suggested that the USSR was being welcomed to the world club of urban industrial societies.

THE PRAGUE SPRING AND ITS AFTERMATH

The Soviet Union's relationship with the smaller states of eastern Europe that lay between it and the West had been ambivalent from the start. At the end of World War II, as we know, Russian troops came as liberators from the Nazis and yet also as conquerors whose rule was imposed more or less by force against the will of a majority of people in these countries. In the Russian view, of course, they had liberated Poland, Yugoslavia, Romania, and other nations from oppressive and backward regimes to make them "people's democracies" and started them on the road to socialism under the benevolent protection of the USSR. The Russian view of them included this Marxist idea of a progressive revolution to be defended against relapse into capitalism, but it also included the somewhat contradictory perception that these countries were potentially hostile to the USSR, or could be used by those who were, just as Hitler had used them to strike his terrible blow. They were a security zone as well as an area of Communist extension and proselytization. The Kremlin attitude toward them was a blend of contempt and comradeship.

The Yugoslav rebellion against Kremlin tutelage deeply colored this outlook. The strongest and most enthusiastically pro-Russian movement, in the beginning, had proved to be the most intractable; independent Communists were not to be trusted. Yugoslavia remained communist; but she broke away from Moscow, was not a member of the Warsaw Pact, and began in the 1950s to develop a mode of "market socialism" that Stalin's heirs regarded as little more than capitalism in disguise. The Yugoslavians regarded it, however, as truer to the spirit of Karl Marx than the despotic "state capitalism" of the USSR. They appealed also to the Lenin who had spoken of the autonomy of the soviets–the rule of the workers themselves, not of an elite party or an omnipotent state. Yugoslav communism came to be best known for its industrial "self-management," by which the workers in the factories or farms jointly owned and participated in the management of their enterprises. Centralized state planning was kept to a minimum. Yet Tito, who imprisoned some of his critics, was far from a political liberal. For some time, the magazine *Praxis* sent brilliant rays of new Marxism–critical, revisionist, anti-Stalinist–from Belgrade, but eventually Tito suppressed it. During his long life, the Partisan hero dominated Yugoslavia and was a major force in the world by virtue of his prestige.

Russian-Yugoslav relations fluctuated. In 1955, Khrushchev led a delegation to Belgrade seeking reconciliation, though he did not handle the apology well. Tito apparently approved the brutal military action against Hungary. He also approved of Khrushchev's intermittent anti-Stalinist campaigns but was annoyed by the equally persistent backtracking. The Yugoslav leader tried to make himself a magnet for the "uncommitted" nations of the Third World. In 1961, he assembled two dozen heads of state at Belgrade, including India's distinguished leader Jawaharlal Nehru, Egypt's Abdul Nasser, Algerian head of state Ben Bella, and "Kwame" Nkrumah of Ghana. But apart from the negative feature of being more or less hostile to both sides in the Cold War and desiring to remain neutral, these states had little in common. Moreover, the young states were unstable. Leaders rose and fell. Six years after 1961, Nehru was dead, Bella deposed, Nkrumah in disgrace, Nasser discredited. Attempts to build a bloc in the turbulent world of the emerging Asian-African nations were condemned to frustration.

So between 1962 and 1968, Tito swung back to building bridges to Russia, only to be disgusted again by the 1968 Czech intervention. Yugoslavia opened lines to the West sooner than did other eastern European countries. Her percentage of trade with the West grew from 50 percent in 1965 to 61 percent in 1969, during which period her trade with Communist countries declined from 35 percent to 27 percent. And, she achieved a rather impressive record of economic growth for a time.

Conditions in the other so-called people's democracies differed somewhat. All of them were forced to submit to one-party rule, suppression of opposition, and censorship of the press; but these varied in intensity. The Catholic church, for example, was able to exist in Poland and East Germany but was severely persecuted in Hungary, where in 1951 Cardinal Mindszenty and other leading Catholics were arrested and church establishments broken up. In the 1956 revolution, Mindszenty was released from prison to become a hero of the people, then forced to flee when the revolution was repressed, taking refuge in the American embassy, where he remained for many years. In later years, he quarreled with the papacy, which preferred accommodations with the communist regimes to severe criticism of them.

Similarly unevenly applied were the other indices of sovietization: collectivization of agriculture, that is, enticing or forcing of farmers into large cooperatives of which they became paid employees; crash programs for heavy industry; abolition of strikes and conversion of trade unions into tools of the state; and centralized economic planning. Polish agriculture was not collectivized; East German was. Hungary, severely repressed in 1956, quietly became the most liberal of the bloc regimes in the ensuing years, as if the Russians were inhibited from further repression by the burden of their 1956 guilt. Romania had a near-Stalinist internal regime, in return for which she became the most outspoken critic of Soviet foreign policies, siding defiantly with the Chinese, the Albanians, and the Jews. Tiny Albania, with the power of weakness, abused everybody equally—the West, the Soviet Union, and eventually China, too.

In general, the Russian model was not suitable for these countries.

They were attracted to the West. The futile rebellions of 1953, 1956, and 1968 showed that they could not escape by open resistance, but they often gained important concessions by stealth and intrigue. Three million East Germans "voted with their feet" by migrating to the Federal Republic, until the Wall put a stop to it. The members of the bloc differed greatly in degree of economic and social development, from fairly backward peasant societies in Bulgaria and Romania to highly advanced industrial ones in Czechoslovakia and Germany. They varied greatly too in ethnic composition, culture, national characteristics. On the whole, the Stalin model was never applied to these countries as ruthlessly as it had been in Russia, and economic reforms came faster and went further there in the 1960s than they did in the USSR.

In this area arose the idea of "human socialism," which, as Edda Werfel wrote, "terrifies not only the capitalists but the Stalinists as well." It was the idea that somehow one might combine the best features of both East and West, the economic security of communism with the personal liberty of capitalist democracy. Tito, Imre Nagy, and then Alexander Dubcek spoke for the hope of a happier socialism. That this was not achieved is indicated by the Wall around East Germany, periodic revolts in Poland, and the spring of 1968 in Prague. Thirty-two divisions of Soviet troops stationed in the countries of Poland, Hungary, Czechoslovakia, and East Germany guaranteed that these revolts could not succeed, if they were overt and violent. But gradually and silently, and with varying degrees of progress, the movement toward liberalization went on in eastern Europe.

In this process, the events in Czechoslovakia in 1968 and 1969 were a striking landmark. The Czechs are said to be not by nature a volatile or a violent people. Their hero is the Good Soldier Schweik, who outwitted the Austrians by cleverness and not by confrontation. (He pretended to be stupid and fouled up every task.) In 1948, Masaryk killed himself, and Benes died of a broken heart; neither thought of leading resistance to Communist rule. As we noted earlier, much goodwill toward Russia historically existed among both the Czechs and the Slovaks, and the Communist party had a by no means negligible following.

Forced collectivization of agriculture and nationalization of private businesses followed the 1948 coup in Czechoslovakia, with the party firmly in control. Beria's man Slansky endured the last of the grand Stalinist purge trials in 1952; Gottwald, who took over as the top leader then, soon died in Moscow after attending Stalin's funeral. The next strong man was Antonin Novotny, a colorless but efficient "little Stalin" who did not de-Stalinize at all until 1961, at which time the Stalin and Gottwald monuments were torn down. All this suggests a substantial degree of submissiveness in the land of Jan Hus, which can partly be explained by the bitter hatred of Germany implanted during World War II, the knowledge of having been betrayed by the West at Munich, and the feeling of having to lean on the Soviet Union for want of alternative.

But economic progress was slow, and public opinion polls showed strong anticommunism. Western influences could not easily be kept out of this country, which has borders with Austria and West Germany. Something called the "big beat," an import from Western popular music, became a symbol of anti-Soviet attitudes. With economic growth continuing to decline, the Czech economist Ota Sik brought forward a Liberman-like plan for market socialism. Tried cautiously in 1965, it did not work because it was not fully applied. Changing just half the economy, Sik noted, was like changing the side of the street on which cars may drive for just half the streets. His was one of the boldest voices calling for economic reforms. The Czechs, a deeply cultured people, also responded to the rising demand for a more humane, democratic, and open type of communism.

The Imre Nagy of the Czech 1968 was Alexander Dubcek. He was a Slovak who had replaced Novotny when the increasingly irritable dictator insulted the Slovaks (whom many Czechs regarded as their cultural inferiors) after a visit to their national museum. Dubcek's credentials looked impeccable to Moscow; he had been a faithful apparatchik for many years, never disobeying orders or questioning a policy. He had spent three years at Moscow attending the Higher Party school (1955–1958). While he was there, the Khrushchev speech threw the school into confusion, and the invasion of Hungary upset him. But in general, Dubcek looked like a party hack if ever there was one. His transformation into the democratic hero of the 1968 freedom movement was a major surprise.

A certain simplicity of mind and character made this genuine proletarian really believe in communism's promises to lead to a free society. "It is not possible for a small minority to introduce and maintain socialism," Dubcek had come to believe. Under his guidance, or perhaps because he simply followed the public lead, rampant democracy broke out in Czechoslovakia, as it had in Hungary twelve years before. But there was no violence, as there had been in the Hungarian Revolution. Press censorship was ended, and the newspapers celebrated their independence by indulging in all kinds of criticism, even of the USSR. This and support of the Sik economic reforms were the chief Czech sins. It seemed possible that opposition parties might be permitted. "Democratic socialism" aimed at curing the economic blight by making party officials responsible to the public. The Prague paper *Red Truth* declared that the party should not rule in the name of the workers but must be held accountable to them.

The wrath of the Kremlin soon turned in Prague's direction. Russians could be quite sure that the Americans, hopelessly mired in Vietnam, would not challenge them in eastern Europe. After the Czechs refused to obey a summons to come to Moscow and were unimpressed by the visits of other Communist luminaries including East German Walter Ulbricht, Brezhnev himself descended on Prague in July, bringing with him almost the entire Presidium. The Czechs were subjected to a tongue-lashing, but they stood fast. Dubcek proved a wily and patient negotiator, not losing his temper under abuse and threats and promising to bring the situation under control if given time. He once confided that his tactic was to smile and agree with Brezhnev and then do nothing—a true Good Soldier Schweik. But the Russians' patience neared exhaustion. Dubcek was becoming all too popular in Czechoslovakia. "Socialism with a human face" threatened to spread. Dubcek's critics allege that he was unrealistic in doing nothing to dampen the euphoria of the Czech and Slovak people but not preparing them for resistance either.

On the night of August 20, he was arrested and dragged off to Russia or Poland, along with several of his colleagues. The next day, a massive invasion of Czechoslovakia by some 200,000 troops from Russia, Poland, Bulgaria, East Germany, and Hungary began. Dubcek agreed to renounce his ideals and submit. There was no fighting; resistance would have been futile. Dubcek was reinstated and remained in office for six months, presiding over a return to censorship, purging Dr. Sik, and telling his people, to their dismay, that progress was possible only by bending to the Russian will. He accepted the presence of Soviet troops on Czechoslovak soil.

It was a costly victory for the Soviet Union, for the world Communist movement was completely sundered; the split that began with the Yugoslav revolt and continued with the Hungarian Revolution of 1956 and then the Sino-Soviet rift was completed in 1968. It could not be argued that the Czechs had threatened Soviet security, as was the case in Hungary; their only crime was wanting democratic socialism. (But one Russian motive was military-strategic, for they could not allow so critical a land to escape from the Warsaw Pact security system.) It was an event that would have shocked the world more had others not been engaged in their own special crimes and insanities: the Americans in Vietnam, the students in Paris, London, and Berlin protesting against their own governments and societies. They had as little time to worry about the Czechs as had been the case thirty years before. But many Communists of western Europe would never again trust the Brezhnev leadership or accept Russian domination of the communist movement. Eighteen Western Communist parties protested, as did Yugoslavia and Romania. The affair brought to a halt a trend toward improvement in Soviet-Yugoslav relations. The Chinese (who claimed that the Americans and Russians were working together against Czechoslovakia) noted with alarm the Russian attack on another communist state.

Manifestations of anti-Soviet sentiment continued in Czechoslovakia for some time. In January 1969, a young man immolated himself; 800,000 people attended his funeral, but no violent incidents occurred. On March 28, the Czechs beat the Russians in a hockey game, an event said to have been viewed with delight by six million Czechs on television; crowds then smashed some windows in Russian offices. Dubcek thereupon resigned, and full censorship was imposed. Gustav Husak, replacing Dubcek as first secretary, said that "cheap gestures and slogans about democracy, freedom and humanism and the so-called will of the people" were only "naivete and political romanticism." On the anniversary of August 21, huge crowds fought with police in Prague's Wenceslas Square. Dubcek was dismissed from the Czech Presidium on September 26. At least, as Husak said, he was not dragged off to be shot; after a short term as ambassador in Turkey he returned to live in the Slovak village where he was born. Party purges and an extreme Stalinist tone in the press marked an abrupt end to socialism with a human face.

Dubcek made no explicit appeal to the West for help, as Nagy had done in 1956. The United States, in any case, was mesmerized by Vietnam and in the throes of a presidential election to boot. Radical "new left" students in Paris and elsewhere were no friends of old-style Communism, but they had their own agenda at home.

Russian leaders attempted to justify the controversial armed intervention in Czechoslovakia by what became known as the "Brezhnev Doctrine," published on September 28, 1968. Admitting that it was "impossible to ignore the allegations being heard in some places that the actions of the five socialist countries contradict the Marxist-Leninist principle of sovereignty and the right of nations to self-determination," the Soviet secretary-general argued that no Communist party can rightly deviate from basic Marxist-Leninist principles and that, if it does, in the broader interests of socialism as a whole the other socialist states have a right to intervene. "The weakening of any link in the world socialist system has a direct effect on all the socialist countries." In brief, once declared a socialist state, a country has no right to change its mind and will be forcibly prevented from doing so. That they were forcibly compelled to submit to Communist rule in the first place was not, of course, mentioned. In the rigid mental categories of Soviet Communist thought, to change from socialism was not conceivable; this would mean reverting to capitalism. That it might mean going forward to "democratic socialism" or "humane socialism" as opposed to the arbitrary rule of an elite was not considered.

12

Western Europe
in the 1960s and 1970s

A TIME OF TROUBLES

It is difficult not to think that during the half-decade from about 1964 to 1970, the gods were angry. Perhaps they resented humanity's penetration of outer space. It was a time of confusion, during which nearly every people seemed to lose its way, fall into holes, and get badly bruised. The troubles came from unexpected quarters and were often caused by good intentions. The United States, seeking to go about its normal business of "containing" communism by showing firmness against aggression, got lost in a dark Indo-chinese tunnel and, after eight agonizing years, emerged demoralized. For it, 1968 was the year of the Tet offensive, a major attack by the Vietcong that, strangely enough, was a military disaster but a psychological victory that virtually won them the war against the discouraged Americans.

Satisfied with its economic success and political stability, western Europe was suddenly shaken by violent demonstrations from students who were supposedly at work happily learning in the many new universities. At this same time, playing no favorites, fate threw the Chinese into a time of disorder and strife called the Cultural Revolution, which had begun with lofty intellectual aspirations. The fall of Khrushchev led to troubles with dissidents in the USSR. After receiving a setback in the Six Day War of 1967 when its clients, the Arab states, lost to the Israelis, the Soviet Union intervened in Czechoslovakia in 1968, amid protests from all over the communist as well as from the non-communist world. The 1969 world Communist meeting in Moscow was a disaster.

To the long list of unpredictable misfortunes others could be added, such as the eruption of Northern Ireland in 1968 (a problem the British had thought long settled). In that perverse year, the sizable minority of Catholics living in Northern Ireland began a militant protest against alleged discrimination. The Protestant majority replied with attacks on the Catholic demonstrators. At the same time, the extremist Irish Republican Army returned to life in the South, demanding absorption of the North into a united Ireland, with one of its wings advocating armed violence. The British were forced to send in troops, and in 1972 they assumed direct rule in Northern Ireland.

A Labour government returned to power in Britain but lost its way. Leaders fell. A New Left arose to challenge the Old Left as well as the Right. Economic growth slowed at the end of the decade. Man reached the moon and found the thrill oddly disappointing. By no means all was gloom, and one might indeed make out a case for this being a successful era. The disaffected young people of the New Left accused the capitalist order of doing them the cruel injustice of removing all rational grounds for complaint. Turbulence is not failure, and the various uprisings of students could be seen, as their instigators usually wished them to be, as efforts to "raise consciousness." Rising demands for cultural and intellectual freedom in the Soviet Union was an index of its progress. The superpowers continued to avoid a direct clash, and after 1968 there was a significant move toward closer cooperation (détente) between the United States and the USSR.

In 1964, the thirteen-year Tory rule in Britain ended in an electoral victory for Labour. Harold Macmillan had resigned the premiership in 1963 amid the odor of scandal. A member of his government had visited a lady of no great virtue, who kissed and told; he denied this, Macmillan believed him, and when the lie was exposed, the prime minister was accused of poor judgment. The outcry over the whole Profumo-Keeler affair, which included the suicide of a doctor who had been a familiar figure in high circles, marked the beginning of a "satire craze," an appetite among the alienated for discrediting all established authority. Macmillan's government had already run into serious difficulties, including de Gaulle's rejection of its application for Common Market membership. In 1963, Kim Philby fled to Moscow, reviving the Burgess-Maclean affair, and a senior member of Parliament committed suicide in connection with this spy scandal.

The death of Hugh Gaitskell came in 1963–a terrible year for world figures. (In addition to the Kennedy assassination, the remarkable Pope John XXIII died, and Konrad Adenauer retired.) Gaitskell's death gave the brilliant Harold Wilson a chance to head the new Labour government, but Wilson was to suffer severe deflation in the next six years. He ran into a series of economic disasters, fought with his own trade union supporters, devalued the pound, was again rebuffed by de Gaulle, and came under attack first from the hawks for deserting the empire (the 1968 "east of Suez" pullout) and then from the doves for hanging on to nuclear weapons and for publicly giving loyal support to the American ally in Vietnam. (Washington insisted on this as a condition for continued financial support that Wilson desperately needed.) On top of this, the Scots demanded independence, and Northern Ireland blew up. Nothing contributed more to the alienation of radical students in the British Isles than their disenchantment with Wilson, once seen as a Kennedy-like figure of youth and hope, now a fallen idol.

General de Gaulle still reigned in Paris; when he was not disrupting the Atlantic alliance and snubbing the British, he was quarreling with the EEC. He was losing popularity prior to 1968, as the presidential election of 1965 and the parliamentary elections of 1967 showed. De Gaulle clearly had failed to achieve that national consensus he so desired. His charisma was fading. Great and unsettling changes had come to France, as it rapidly modernized, urbanized, mechanized. There was a remarkable rise in the standard of living during these years all over Europe and not the least in France, which had one of the highest growth rates in Europe. At the same time came social dislocations and consequent discontents; a massive movement from country to city converted France from a land still about one-third rural in 1945 to less than one-seventh agricultural by 1970. Technological modernization changed the character of farming as well as manufacturing. Ways of life altered, not always for the better. No one regretted the passing of traditional France more than the man under whose presidency much of this had occurred.

Education was one area of rapid change. Third Republic France had given everyone a free education up to the age of fourteen; beyond that, only a small minority, determined by competitive examination, went on to the luxury of higher education, first in the *lycée* and then in the university. The system was not much different elsewhere in Europe, though France could claim a greater degree of democracy and statism than in England, where far fewer children of working-class origin got to the elite public schools and universities. The total pre–World War II French university population was around 60,000; by 1968 the number had increased tenfold. This student explosion occurred all over the Western world.

Charles de Gaulle, writing later about the events of 1968, blamed them on these startling structural changes in French society; France, he said, long content with her ancient ways, had suddenly plunged into the icy waters of modernization, an unavoidable but traumatic experience. "Forced into a mechanized mass existence," living in nondescript houses, herded and regimented, even their leisure now "collective and prescribed," the French people, he thought, took this change less easily than others. (See his *Memoirs of Hope, Renewal and Endeavor,* 1971). Perhaps so, but the deep unrest that afflicted young people in the 1960s was a worldwide phenomenon evidently with supranational sources. It spread from California and China to Berlin, Bologna, and London even before lighting on Paris.

The student unrest, the Czechoslovakian 1968 movement, and the out-of-control war in Vietnam were only some signs of world cataclysm. In 1967, the Middle East erupted in the Six Day War, which reflected an absence of leadership everywhere. The new Soviet leaders, harassed by domestic problems, allowed themselves to be towed in Nasser's wake. They gave rather passive approval to the Egyptian leader's blockade of the Gulf of Aqaba and encouraged the fanatical Syrian regime. With the United States wholly absorbed in Southeast Asia and the British officially resigning from any world role, the Egyptian leader thought he saw his chance to fulfill his goal of uniting the Arab world in order to crush Israel and gain revenge for 1948 and 1956. Egypt and Syria were clearly the aggressors in this third round of the Arab-Israeli war, which took place in the first days of June 1967. By their blockade and their demand that United Nations forces be removed, they precipitated the blow that Israel struck. Losing enormous amounts of war materiel and the territories of the Sinai, the Golan Heights, and the west bank of the Jordan, the Arab countries (Egypt, Syria, and Jordan) sustained a staggering defeat. The Arabs blamed the Soviet Union for not intervening to save them, but the Russians once again showed restraint when the prospects of an escalation loomed. The Soviet leaders blamed the Arabs for recklessness and incompetence, and in fact had belatedly and ineffectively tried to hold them back. They reequipped the Arab forces but sponsored a U.N. ceasefire while Kosygin visited the United States to confer with President Lyndon Johnson. Since the United States armed Israel to match Soviet weapons in Egypt and Syria, the war did not really end but only diminished for a few years. But the Arabs were disenchanted with their reliance on the Russians, and Nasser, though given a vote of confidence by his people, lived only three years after this defeat.

Two years earlier, the danger of trying to use non-European states as pawns in the power struggle must have forcibly struck the Russians in Indonesia, where they had backed the corrupt dictator Sukarno with massive amounts of aid. A revolution against Sukarno also discharged its strength against the Indonesian Communists, as many as 100,000 of whom were slaughtered in one of the biggest blood baths of the decade. Huge debts to the USSR were repudiated, as both Russian and Chinese Communist influence in this populous land came to an abrupt end. It was a defeat almost comparable to that which the Americans were about to suffer in Indochina. Both drove home the lesson that Asia would not be the vassal or the protegé of any Western power.

Less than two years after the immense Kennedy funeral in Washington in November 1963, the world paused in 1965 to mourn the passing of Winston Churchill. Adenauer, having retired in 1963, died in 1967. De Gaulle by then had only a few years left, expiring in the same year as Nasser and a year before Khrushchev. The old figures were passing. A sense of insecurity, of lack of confidence in government, went along with the pronounced generation revolt that burst forth in these years. The year 1968 coincided with the arrival of a generation born after World War II, knowing none of its experiences and sharing few of its values. "The old faiths loosen and fall, the new years ruin and rend."

STUDENT DISCONTENT AND THE PARIS SPRING

The rebellion of the French students cannot be placed in isolation, for it was part of an international youth revolt that left few parts of the world untouched in the late 1960s and early 1970s. As far as concerns Paris, the most identifiable leader of the uprising was one Daniel Cohn-Bendit, a German born in France of parents who had fled from Hitler and then returned to Germany after the war. Another of its heroes was the main personality in an earlier Berlin student riot, Rudi Dutschke. The uniqueness of the Paris events lay in their magnitude and extent; nowhere else did the "student stirs," as an Oxford professor called them, achieve much more than nuisance value. The French ones spread to the workers and threatened general revolution, and in the long run they caused the fall of de Gaulle's government. Occupation of university buildings, followed perhaps by a pitched battle with police or military, became an all-too-familiar sequence of events in the universities of the world. But they were nothing like the full-scale war night after night that left portions of Paris looking as it had in World War II. The French seemed to have decided to continue their long revolutionary tradition by having one more immense *émeute*.

To some extent the causes of the Paris spring uprising of 1968 were the same as those of the student movement everywhere: boredom with too much pallid conformity, dislike of the technological society, a generation effect among those born after World War II whose world was a wholly different one from their parents'. The drift away from orthodox communism opened the way for a New Left, which celebrated its independence of Marxist orthodoxies by discovering more exciting revolutionary heroes than the old men in the Kremlin: Cuba's Fidel Castro and Che Guevara, China's Mao Tse-tung, Algerian, African, and Vietnamese guerrilla fighters against imperialism. The mixture was complex, but at bottom one found a generation of young people eager for excitement and even violence after a quarter-century of preoccupation with economic growth. They were also bewildered by a society too large to comprehend and usually disgusted with an education that seemed untuned to their needs.

The universities had swollen to enormous size. There were no fewer than 160,000 students in and around Paris. Some thought them spoiled or immature: They had grown up in the affluence of the consumer society and were, in fact, profiting from its prosperity. In any previous generation, most of them would not have been at the university but at work in fields or factories. Typically, the leaders of the revolt were moderately well-off children of professional people. There was at times a levity about the revolt, which disgusted real revolutionaries (including the Communists, who were notably cool to it, calling the student rebels "hare-brained") and justified the joke about Marxism à la

Groucho, not Karl; it seemed to be a gigantic schoolyard prank. Among the chief complaints at Nanterre, a Paris suburb where it all started, was that there were not enough telephones and TVs. Yet the huge new education mills of which the Fifth Republic was so proud were bleak, isolated, and overcrowded. Students felt processed, computerized, treated as consumers of data that were produced by others in the "knowledge factory." Not for nothing were they reading the young Marx on "alienation," that is, the conversion of human needs into marketable commodities.

Many ideological currents worked to excite the students. A Soviet article in 1973 named all the following as false prophets and "revisionists": Scheler, Husserl, Unamuno, Heidegger, Jaspers, Camus (all existentialists), Adorno, Horkheimer, Marcuse (Frankfurt School Marxists), Garaudy, Fromm. In China, the Cultural Revolution, begun in 1965, set an example for an educational takeover by students. The purpose of that tumultuous process, encouraged by Chairman Mao, was to raise the cultural consciousness of the masses so that they need not be guided by any elite but could think for themselves. Beginning with popular discussions of the Chinese-Russian quarrel, the movement soon spread to the universities, where grave professors were dispensing learning, most of it still not extracted from the Thoughts of Chairman Mao, to docile pupils much as they had always done in the Celestial Empire. Students demanding an end to this system caused so much turmoil that the universities closed for more than a year.

Mao's Cultural Revolution was probably the main model for student protest in Europe, though students at the University of California might claim priority in educational disruption. In Berlin, incidents were common in the universities from 1965 on. A student was shot to death in June 1967, during a demonstration against the Shah of Iran. It was at this time that "Red Rudi" Dutschke emerged as a student leader; in April 1968, the young sociologist was seriously wounded by a right-wing student. But the widespread fighting that then broke out in a number of German university cities, including Munich, Hamburg, and Frankfurt as well as Berlin, turned the public against the enraged students. Maddened by the generally liberal *and* conservative viewpoint in Germany—anticommunist, law-and-order—radical students increasingly turned to violence but found themselves isolated from the main body of German opinion, including the trade unionists.

The war in Vietnam provided a focus for all the various discontents the young felt, even though no European countries were directly involved in it. De Gaulle did not even verbally support the Americans, though Harold Wilson in Britain and leaders in West Germany did. Even in the United States, student disturbances at Berkeley and elsewhere preceded the time of major American fighting in Vietnam. One might argue that the youthful reaction against this war resulted from a proneness to rebel that was already present. After all, the Korean War of 1950–1953, which was about as bad as Vietnam in terms of damage and casualties, had aroused no such outcry and was generally supported by liberal elements in the United States as containment of communist aggression. So indeed was Vietnam, at first. Needing some great and manifest evil on which to focus their discontent, university youth found it in the ugly kind of war that steadily expanded in the hills and jungles of Indochina.

Radical students at the London School of Economics "sat in" on March 1967, in an atmosphere of general disillusionment with the Labour government that had been elected in 1964 and 1966. "Politics outside the system" in Britain reached back to the massive if relatively sober protest launched in 1959–1961 by the Committee for Nuclear Disarmament (CND), with the objective of getting Britain to withdraw from the arms race and perhaps neutralize herself in the Cold War. The CND mounted huge marches and rallies that were nonviolent and generally orderly, but it also used provocative tactics of blocking entrances and occupying buildings. Nowhere was the youth mood of bitter hostility to the "establishment" stronger than in England. It was encouraged by the nonagenarian philosopher Bertrand Russell, celebrated in the songs of such rock musicians as the Beatles and the Rolling Stones, and approved by a radical wing of the Labour party that spoke of the "new politics" as one of "direct action" and "confrontation."

Radicalized students added these words to their vocabulary, along with some emanating from Titoism, Castroism, and such New Left theorists as Herbert Marcuse, a German neo-Marxist transplanted to the heady climate of Southern California, or the embattled Jean-Paul Sartre. The New Left did not lack ideas and enthusiasm; its prophets were legion and sometimes contradictory. Nevertheless, in England as in Germany, student unrest did not seriously threaten to overthrow the existing society. The London *Times* in late summer 1968 wrote editorially of "a collapse of order in English universities." A mob of Cambridge students disrupted a minister's speech. But as in Germany, the English students at this time could not overcome the barrier between themselves and the trade-unionist workers.

Violence broke out in late 1967 among Italian students also, when about 1,500 of them held the Turin University's administration building for a month. Florence, Pisa, Bologna, and Rome all followed suit, featuring battles between police and students, and many other Italian schools experienced similar difficulties in 1968. As elsewhere, there was a pressing need for educational reform, given bad overcrowding and an obsolete university structure, but the students seemed less interested in such reforms than in "overthrowing society." The university revolution was supposed to set off further explosions throughout the whole "system." Even the "embourgeoisified" working class, drugged by material plenty, would perhaps awaken to realize its true oppression when prodded by the students. The universities were only the weakest link in a chain binding the whole people in exploitation; nor could they be reformed without reforming the entire society.

Thus thought the student militants, who, typically hostile to any structure of authority, wanted not to substitute one system for another but to tear down all systems. If they often quoted Marx, Lenin, and Mao, their real interest was much less in overcoming material poverty than in removing alleged shackles of the mind and spirit. Philosophies of "liberation" flourished. The emphasis on action for action's sake, without thought, led some of their friends as well as their enemies to identify the young militants with "left-wing fascism" or simply with childish willfulness. Some of the intellectual leaders who inspired the student revolutionaries recoiled from their violence and occasional mindlessness; at various times Herbert Marcuse, Theodore Adorno, Jürgen Habermas, and other intellectual neo-Marxists expressed their disapproval of what was being done in their names. (It is nevertheless true that New Left ideologists like Marcuse, Sartre, and Frantz Fanon, author of the widely read *Wretched of the Earth*, had encouraged violence, which is a constant theme in their writings.) But to the blue-collar workers, to whom they wished to appeal, the students appeared as bizarre ideologists, speaking all kinds of incomprehensible words: Their desire to "demystify bourgeois ideology" was itself a mystification.

In Paris, things almost went otherwise. After a series of incidents beginning in March, Nanterre was ordered closed in early May 1968. Students at the Sorbonne, the main Paris university, rallied in support of their fellow students at a great meeting in the ancient courtyard of this famous university, which is situated in Paris's Left Bank Latin Quarter. Police seeking to expel them began clashes between students and *gendarmerie* that were to become a way of life for the next few weeks. Within days, the battle escalated to a point where it filled much of the university area of the city with overturned and burning automobiles, damaged buildings, and broken or shuttered shop windows. The climax came on the night of May 10–11, "the night of the barricades," when as many as 25,000 students battled the *flics* all night. Only a few were killed, but many hundreds suffered wounds. Meanwhile, great crowds of students assembled eagerly for speeches and demonstrations in a consciousness-raising imitation of the Chinese. While orthodox communism repudiated the uprising as "left-wing infantilism," which "objectively" played into the hands of the right, and the students booed Communist spokesmen, the images of Mao, of Cuban guerilla hero Che Guevara, and of Ho Chi Minh were everywhere. Much in evidence, too, were slogans painted on the walls, which became part of the legend of the Paris spring: "Let us be realistic and demand the impossible." Posted over the Odéon theater, which was "liberated" by the students, were the words, "When the National Assembly is a bourgeois theater, bourgeois theaters must become national assemblies." (Or, in halls where students slept, "We fear nothing, we have the Pill.")

On May 13, a one-day general strike signaled the spread of the troubles to the industrial workers. Their motives were not the same as the students, but they joined in, partly out of sympathy with the students and partly because of their own grievances. The much-divided and often weak French trade unions (divided between communist, socialist, and two kinds of Christian organizations, heavily politicized) now exploded in a wave of strikes reminiscent of

1936. The disorders spread while the government stood helpless. President de Gaulle was abroad on a state visit at the start of it all. Baffled by the sudden outbreak of violence in unexpected places, the government first did nothing and then tried repression, turning to reform only belatedly.

By that time, the situation was out of hand. Half of France was on strike, and the students basked in their newly discovered power to change the world. "Happenings" proliferated. Jean-Paul Sartre addressed 10,000 students. But the student objectives were vague; they wanted to change society, they wanted to help teach courses, they wanted to make some kind of a revolution; but they were themselves deeply if rather happily divided into anarchists, Maoists, Trotskyites, situationists, and other "groupuscules." Violence continued into the last week of May. President de Gaulle made a trip to Baden-Baden, Germany, to seek assurance from the French armed forces in Germany. Returning, he showed a determination to restore order. On May 30, he announced that he would hold elections and reform the universities, but he would tolerate no more violence. That evening an awesome turnout of perhaps 750,000 older people staged a monstrous parade through the streets of Paris (on the *right* bank), rallying to the government's support. The backlash against student disruptions carried over into the ensuing elections, which were held on June 23. The left dropped sharply, while the Gaullist UDR gained ninety-four seats. Meanwhile, the striking workers received handsome pay raises (from 13 to 15 percent) and returned to their jobs. The next months saw work on educational reforms, which included student participation in university governance.

The referendum of April 1969 showed that a majority of the French people thought that de Gaulle had outstayed his time. Searching for an answer to the breakdown of consensus and participatory democracy, the president pushed a plan of government decentralization. Naturally, the politicians in the national assembly rejected it; but so, on appeal, did the people.

De Gaulle's longtime prime minister, Georges Pompidou, won a convincing victory in the June presidential election, so that although de Gaulle himself bowed out, Gaullism paradoxically emerged even stronger than it was during his term of office. It has lived on in France as the inspiration of the major political parties. The great man's death the following year brought tributes to him from all over the world. The last of the European giants of the World War II era, with the single exception of Yugoslavia's Marshal Tito, had passed. Few of the students who helped overthrow him had been alive in 1940 or even in 1945.

IDEOLOGICAL CURRENTS OF THE 1960S

The student militants of the 1960s typically, or at least very frequently, claimed to be rejecting "ideology," all "programs" and "positioning," sometimes even all intellectual activity. The editor of a compilation of revolutionary materials from this era, which he called BAMN (By Any Means Necessary), noted that the movement "owes more to Marinetti, Dada, Surrealism, Artaud, the Marx Brothers, than to Lenin or Mao," much less to such quaint Victorian intellectuals as Marx and Engels. With affinities to the television generation, it valued a happening far more than a manifesto. The riots, confrontations, and bombings reflected this itch for action over thought. If he had heard Goethe's "action is so easy, thought is so difficult," the young street politician of the late 1960s would have challenged it: Thought, he would have answered, leads nowhere except to endless further thought; action gets something started that may prove useful. Cohn-Bendit's advice was to heave some tomatoes and start a riot, anywhere, for no particular reason.

Behind this alleged total rejection of ideology, though, did lie ideas; one cannot really act without any, and the ideology lurking often unacknowledged behind the activism of the New Leftists was partly provided by neo-Marxism. There was an image of violent revolutionary storms sweeping away entire societies. Prone to hero worship, the young rebels found in Che Guevara, Castro, and many other instant *führers* of the Third World, or in black American activists, a model for courage and will—defying the odds, battling the whole society, and perhaps, as in a TV cartoon, miraculously winning. Guevara became the object of a religious cult. His friend Regis Débray's book sold a million copies, and so did West Indian psychiatrist-turned-revolutionary Frantz Fanon's.

At the end of the 1950s, many new ideas impatiently demanded an end to apathy and noncommitment. "Angry young men" appeared, determined, as one of the German "angries" said, to be sand rather than oil in the world's machinery. This vague anger directed at all establishments, striking at anything within range with scorn and satire, reflected a profound alienation. Affluence itself came in for attack. There was too much stupid prosperity! The most identifiable targets were power, bureaucracy, structures of authority, the "technological society," the vastness and impersonality of an order that compelled individuals to adjust to its demand for cogs in the machine. The diagnosis of Max Weber, that magic had vanished from a disenchanted world, or of Émile Durkheim, that dissolution of ancestral authority left young people bewildered and valueless, seem closest to the point. Magic was sought in a host of occultisms as well as in mind-altering drugs, while strange religious cults flourished.

But in their prevailing mood, radical youth still preferred Marx. The trouble with Marx was that he had been appropriated by the Stalinists. That was remedied by recourse to other interpretations of him. The new Marx was born not only of disenchantment with Soviet Marxism but from his youthful writings heretofore scarcely known. They were first published in the USSR in the early 1930s, but the director of the Marx-Engels Institute who was responsible for their publication was soon liquidated; it was too dangerous to go about publishing Marx indiscriminately. These writings talked about "alienation" more than "exploitation," the plight of the human person in an intractable social world more than the necessary advance of history toward an ideal society. The discovery and the interpretation of Marx's early writings, impelled by a desire to rescue him from sterility, was a complicated process to which many minds contributed. Some of them congregated at the Institute for Social Research in Frankfurt in the early 1930s and then fled from Hitler to the United States. The best known of these was Herbert Marcuse. The Hungarian Gyorgy Lukacs, who took part in the Hungarian revolution of 1956 at a ripe age and lived to return in 1968 to Budapest University before his death at the age of eighty-five, had attacked "mechanical materialism" as early as 1923. He proposed a more truly dialectical Marxism.

Because Marxism was "dying of boredom," French professors also infused it with new ideas. Such a Marxism should lead to a democratic socialism, seeking first to elevate proletarian class consciousness rather than seize political power; it should escape the bureaucratic state, that cold monster of dehumanization, by relying on the workers organized in soviets to run the factories and farms themselves. Freeing Marxism from a deterministic system freed the critical mind to reject the whole society, rather than making it the prisoner of social forces; it also restored the autonomy of the so-called superstructure of ideas, which are not automatically dependent on the economic system.

In 1960, Sartre attempted a marriage between existentialism and Marxism in his *Critique of Dialectical Reason*. Criticizing "official," or Soviet, Marxism for ossifying into a dead dogma with "total loss of the sense of what man is," he proposed not to reject Marxism but to "recapture man in the heart of Marxism" with the aid of existentialism and perhaps Sigmund Freud. Such attempts to add a psychology and human values to the sociological structure of Marxism may not have been altogether successful, but they greatly interested the leftist mind at this time. The goal was a radical critique of existing society in the name of human liberation. The underlying assumption–a dubious one, conservatives might say, but who was listening to them?–was that human nature, freed from external oppressions, mystifications, and alienations, is basically good.

Chinese communism fitted somewhere into this picture. In many ways, the Marxism of Mao Tse-tung resembled that of the critical western Marxists. Mao stressed the superiority of dialectical over mechanical Marxism; mind can affect material things as well as vice versa. The important goal is to raise mass cultural consciousness. The rule of an elite cut off from the masses and rigidifying into an authoritarian structure is a danger to be struggled against constantly. The entire Cultural Revolution–disastrous as it turned out to be–was intended to extend ideological consciousness and chasten the elite party and intelligentsia. Chinese experiments in industrialism in the village, and subsequent attempts at deurbanization, also relate not only to the peasant basis of the Chinese communist movement but to the fear of a powerful centralized bureaucracy, which in Mao's view had blighted Russian communism. The Russians had erred in assuming that the superstructure of consciousness automatically follows the transformation of the economic foundation. This simple mechanical model had led them into the trap of elitism, bureaucracy, and dictatorship. They should have kept superstructure and substructure in step, paying as much attention to the former as to the latter. Instead, they had built a bureaucratic industrialism at the price of alienating the masses, a situation that led their party elite ever deeper into the morass of oppression and false ideologies of domination—in brief, back to the same horrors from which the revolution was supposed to have escaped.

In the Soviet view, of course, Mao was never a real Marxist but a peasant anarchist, whose effort to build a modern industrial society through backyard blast furnaces was ridiculous and whose so-called dialectical Marxism was really a reversion to "subjective idealism." It was more irritating that Mao and most of the new Marxists appealed to Lenin, whom they thought Stalin had corrupted. But Moscow was out of step in the 1960s, in more ways than one. The Kremlin, condemning rock music and long hair as bourgeois decadence, or "hooliganism," shocked by drug-taking and sexual liberation, looked very old-fashioned indeed to university youth in the decade of the Beatles. The campus New Left trafficked in obscenity, sexual promiscuity, LSD experiments, Rolling Stones concerts. Easily disillusioned when the miracle of total revolution failed to occur overnight, the "new politics" soon passed into the "counterculture"; the revolution became the Age of Aquarius.

Perhaps the most fundamental contradiction of the New Left was this: As a self-defined revolt of the totally alienated, the utterly unassimilated, negating the whole existing society, how could the New Left possibly interact with or make any contact with that society? It was hard to credit claims to represent "the people" or engage the masses in "participatory" democracy when these came from a tiny minority of defiant outsiders. If the proletariat has been engulfed by capitalism, how is a true revolution possible? Such a revolution would have to be the dictatorship of a small elite; yet New Left theorists usually rejected such a thing. The *reductio ad absurdum* of this position was Che Guevara refusing to have anything to do with the peasants his revolutionary band had come to liberate. Despite such manifest inconsistencies, the explosion of radical ideology in the 1960s was clearly most significant. Through its social disguises one could discern an intense personalism, registering a cry of pain from modern consciousness trapped in a bureaucratic and technological society.

The resort was often to art, music, and literature, which were never so plentiful. Electronic equipment brought symphony orchestras as well as rock music and jazz[1] into everyone's home. A variety of popular musical groups provided the modern equivalent of Roman circuses for the masses. World-Cup

---

[1]The golden age of jazz, led by Miles Davis and John Coltrane, extended from the later 1950s into the 1960s; but at the end of the latter decade, this stunning music declined, overtaken by the cruder rhythms of "rock." Here, most of the young long-hairs revealed their esthetic deficiency.

football and the Olympic games reached hundreds of millions via television. The age of the masses is the age of the mass media; but it is also, paradoxically, the era of the most intense privatization, when each emancipated ego creates its own cultural world in its own house or room.

The relentless "neophilia" of contemporary intellectual life–to borrow a term coined by one cultural historian–condemned every fashion in ideas to a short reign and brought forth constantly new criticisms. This was especially true in the visual arts, where even the museum directors and most critics surrendered to a succession of eccentric fads. Leadership of the art world passed from Paris to New York. In sharp reaction against Existential subjectivism and individualism, the later 1960s veered toward a new outlook called structuralism. Put on the map by the Jewish-French anthropologist Claude Lévi-Strauss, structuralism drew on linguistic theory for a mathematical rationalism that declared human consciousness to be the helpless victim of objective structures, chiefly those implicit in the laws of language syntax. Lévi-Strauss tried to prove that all human myths derive by inevitable logical progression from a few primeval ones. Structuralist analysis was applied to literature, to popular culture, to psychoanalysis, everywhere positing objective laws of the mind–linguistic "deep structures" lying behind the surface phenomena–that impose themselves on our consciousness and, in brief, compel us all to think in certain ways. Formally, human culture is an endless repetition of the same configurations.

Combinations of advanced Marxism and structuralism, mixed perhaps with a flavoring of Freudianism, were possible and fashionable. Such sophisticated academic concoctions were light-years away from the simple eschatological faith of the early Marxists. Yet in Paris, thousands of people, at the height of the student fever of the 1960s, attended debates among Jean-Paul Sartre, Jacques Lacan, Louis Althusser, Michel Foucault, and other high priests of the now-arcane science of society on such subjects as the meaning and nature of the Marxian dialectic.

Marxism, after all, could not possibly be what it had been. Capitalism, even if called "state monopoly capitalism," was an economic success. Socialism, in the USSR, was a moral and increasingly a material failure. The world communist movement was a scene of disunity. The bureaucratic structures that frustrated human nature were much the same wherever industrial society existed. There was little left of the traditional working class. Revolution was a futile shibboleth. A new criticism of society was needed. Dissent, like everything else, had to be brought up to date in a changing world. Intellectuals clung to traditional systems of thought while trying to adapt these to an obviously different situation. The result was a bewildering but exciting array of ideological positions and controversies. The 1960s were electrifyingly alive. The gods, perhaps, were not so angry after all.

THE AFTERMATH OF 1968

Both East and West emerged from the scathing events of the late 1960s considerably scarred. In 1968, the newly elected Republican administration in the United States began a long and painful process of extrication from Vietnam, which was not completed until 1973. The war in Vietnam had played havoc with the principles on which the postwar foreign policy of the United States had been based. There was talk of neoisolationist withdrawal from world commitments. President Richard Nixon said the United States would stand by NATO while getting out of African and Asian commitments, but some senators talked of making substantial troop cuts in Europe. The credibility of the American "deterrent" was in question.

The year 1969 in western Europe saw the weakening of the Wilson government in Britain, leading to its defeat in 1970 and the return of a Conservative government; the defeat and retirement of de Gaulle; and a change in

Jupiter IRBM, Cape Canaveral, 1968. (*U.S. Army Photo.*)

Germany to a Social Democratic government, which under Chancellor Willy Brandt's leadership embarked on new foreign policies. There were deeper changes, justifying the statement that 1968 marked the end of the postwar era. While the student movement as such utterly failed to bring about the total social revolution of which its militant leaders dreamed, after 1968 western Europe lost the economic buoyancy it had had and struggled for the next fifteen years with the consequences of a reduced rate of growth. The age of growth, it seemed, the postwar period of rapid expansion that had resulted first from the need to repair the damages of the war and then to modernize technologically, was over. With a mature economy, the problem was to hold on to what had been gained against the threat of stagnation–accompanied, incongruously, by inflation. People began more and more to talk about the "quality of life" rather than material gains. Allowing for a difference in tone and vocabulary, this is what the students had been saying.

For the USSR, 1968 was a critical moment too. The revolt of the Western Communists at the time of the Czech intervention climaxed the disintegration of world communism under Russian leadership and marked the triumph of polycentrism. In 1969, a long-delayed world Communist conference held in Moscow proved embarrassing to the Russians. Among the ruling parties, China, North Korea, North Vietnam, and Yugoslavia refused to attend, and Cuba sent only an observer. There were no representatives at all from East or Southeast Asian countries. Albania formally withdrew from the Warsaw Pact. Italy's Berlinguer and Romania's Ceausescu openly criticized the USSR about Czechoslovakia, and the only statement that was satisfactory to most of the parties attending was watered down to the point of meaninglessness; some refused to sign even this. World communism was on the point of being in total disarray.

The collapse of Russian domination opened the way for experiments in other roads to communism. The Italian party led the way in democratizing the Communist outlook, preparing to play a role in the parliamentary politics of its country. This increasing participation by Communist parties in parliamentary processes was a leading feature of the 1970s. Clearly, it grew from Western Communist estrangement from the Soviet Union. While the traditional unity of international communism collapsed amid the heated rivalry of Peking and Moscow, new philosophic versions of Marxism further shattered the myth of a single doctrine and party. Why should not each Communist party have the freedom to invent the proper response to its own special national conditions? Moscow called this heresy; but the great myth of its Revolution was dying.

More to the point, the European Communists found themselves diminishing in numbers and influence. Just after the war, the French Communist Party got four million votes, and its newspaper, *L'Humanité,* boasted more than a million circulation. The party proceeded to forfeit this advantage by tying its policies to Moscow's. Opposition to the Marshall Plan, NATO, and EEC cost it support, for these were all popular measures. The Communists had to defend the attack on Yugoslavia, the Prague coup of 1948, the suppression of the Hungarian revolt in 1956. Then they had to swallow Moscow's friendship with its enemies, watching the Soviets woo de Gaulle, the Greek colonels, and even Franco. The French party submitted to a number of internal purges, as those who gagged at swallowing all this were excommunicated on orders from Moscow—André Marty, Marcel Servin, Laurent Casanova, finally Roger Garaudy for showing too much interest in dialogue with Christians. The Communists lost support among both youth and women, whose causes they failed to adopt; the 1968 students treated them as old fogies. Their membership and newspaper readership dropped sharply. Though the party retained a hard core of deeply loyal followers, it was an aging clientele.

The chief remnants of Stalinism or Leninism that were obstacles to the democratization of the Western Communist parties were the advocacy of violent revolution, belief in the dictatorship of the Communist party as surrogate for the proletariat, and the demand for total submission of personal views to the policies decided on by the party (which too often meant those decided on by the Russians). The traditional working class was now declining in numbers. To become a party like other parties in a pluralistic democracy had to be a long and painful process for Communists, filled with many twistings and turnings. The Italian Communists (PCI) led the way toward an acceptance of other political parties, including the Socialists and the Christian Democrats, as equals. A Left-Center coalition of Christian Democrats and Socialists governed Italy between 1963 and 1968. In 1976, the PCI agreed not to oppose the government on key issues, thus in effect becoming a member of a governing coalition really for the first time since the onset of the Cold War, except for a brief period just after the war when Communists participated not only in parliaments but in governments in France, Italy, and Belgium. In 1975, the French Communist party also formally repudiated "the dictatorship of the proletariat."

The Italian Communists in fact had long ruled in some regions and cities of Italy, especially in the north-central area of Emilio-Romagna (By 1970, Italy had carried out a plan of regional decentralization, which had passed Parliament in 1960.) In this capacity, they featured honest government, town planning, educational improvements, and other social welfare reforms, rather than anything a Russian Bolshevik might have thought of as "Communist." Curiously, the Italian Communists functioned for many people as a kind of bulwark of old-fashioned virtue and discipline against the tide of modernism!

In France, a widely discussed book of 1976, written by a socialist, claimed that the leopard cannot change its spots; no Communist party can really accept the rules of democracy. What if a Communist government was voted out after being voted in—would it relinquish power? In power, could it be trusted to hold regular elections and to maintain the rules of freedom to oppose and criticize, or would it try to use its power to end "bourgeois democracy"? On the other side, disillusioned extremists thought that the party had been coopted and corrupted. Leading a splinter-group secession from it, a former member of the Norwegian Communist party said that the party "has become bourgeois and is dying." The next few years were to indicate that whether or not he changed his spots the Communist beast was a sick animal. The French Communist Party found itself overtaken on the left by its old rivals the Socialists, whose junior partner the Communists were compelled to become, and to drop under 10 percent in the polls. The Spanish Communist Party, which in 1978 changed its self-description from "Marxist-Leninist" to "Marxist, revolutionary, and democratic" as it broke with Moscow, remained an insignificant minority, totally outdistanced in the new Spanish democracy (see below) by the Socialists, among others. Even in Italy, the PCI declined somewhat from its peak and had some second thoughts about the bet on democracy. The dilemma seemed to be that as the party was absorbed into the pluralistic system it ceased to be identifiably a symbol of revolt, losing its traditional clientele; yet, it was still mistrusted as a political partner because of its past, and could not hope to secure enough votes to govern alone.

In the aftermath of 1968, the Soviets preferred not to undertake another armed intervention in Eastern Europe. In 1970, food shortages and high prices precipitated rioting in Poland. The Russians yielded to the extent of sacrificing veteran W. Gomulka, Polish chief since 1956, replacing him by Edward Gierek, who had an ambitious program of reform including loans from the capitalist world and greater power for the workers' councils, a move in the direction of Yugoslav self-management. At the same time, Hungary gradually achieved what it had failed to gain in the heroic uprising of 1956; there seemed to be an unwritten agreement by which, if they promised not to repeat those embarrassing events, the Hungarians would in return get privileges from the Russians, but under the table. Cynicism and corruption prevailed, according to some of the old freedom fighters, but so did prosperity under an almost capitalistic economy; Budapest struck its many visitors as the most relaxed and affluent of all the Eastern European capitals. Janos Kadar, the Hungarian leader, expressed interest in Italo-communism. So did Yugoslavia and Romania.

The Communists' growing respectability undoubtedly had much to do with the terrorism that broke out in the 1970s, especially in Germany and Italy. The totally alienated, the extremist personality now had no place to turn. Those disillusioned with the outcome of the great 1968 student-New Left movement might withdraw to quietism; the next years saw the emergence of a "counterculture" that experimented in all manner of esoteric religions and eventually produced in Germany an ecologically oriented political organization, the "Greens," hostile to all modern technology. It owed something to the great philosopher Martin Heidegger, indicter of the whole modern age on spiritual grounds–a view hardly unique, to be sure.

Bolder spirits looked back to a left-wing anarchist tradition. "Urban guerrillas," an idea born in South America, appeared in European cities. Disturbed and angry young people like the leaders of the celebrated Baader-Meinhof gang in Germany were usually the children of the upper bourgeoisie. (Ulrike Meinhof was from a family of theologians; she married a pacifist who made a fortune from publishing a pornographic magazine. Turning to terrorism after the marriage broke up, she became the most fanatical and ruthless of the group.) A wave of bombings, assassinations, and kidnappings culminated in the Italian "Red brigades" kidnapping and murdering an ex-Italian prime minister in 1978. The trial of the four leading members of the German terrorist group in 1975 necessitated the building of a special maximum security courthouse. Amid great excitement three were eventually sentenced to life imprisonment; Ulrike Meinhof committed suicide in her prison cell. (Other members were never caught; one was killed by the Israeli rescue force at Entebbe, Uganda, in 1976 after the hijacking of an Air France plane.)

Special security measures finally brought the European terrorists more or less under control (the Irish Republican Army and the Basque separatists apart); perhaps they exhausted themselves. In the next decade, the world became more accustomed to Arab terrorists, almost forgetting the earlier sensations from Europe.

The consequences of 1968 for the world included some relaxing of East-West tensions in Europe. In 1969, the new West German Social Democratic government began discussions about a new relationship with the Soviet bloc. The Czech intervention might be given some credit for this; it made crystal clear that the Soviet Union would not surrender control of its satellites, nor would the West challenge such control. Chancellor Willy Brandt's government entered into negotiations with Poland, then the USSR, and finally with the DDR with the purpose of recognizing the Polish-DDR borders (the Oder-Neisse line), signing nonaggression pacts, and recognizing the sovereignty of the DDR. The blow was softened by a formal fourpower agreement finally securing rights of access to West Berlin (1971). Thus the long-smoldering Berlin problem was settled at the cost of Bonn's virtually giving up its hopes of a united Germany. Critics of Brandt's *Ostpolitik* wondered just what morality or indeed advantage there was in granting recognition to the Soviet empire in the East, and the several treaties were ratified only after stormy debates in the Federal Republic's Bundestag. These treaties constituted as close to a German peace treaty, formally ending World War II, as there has ever been; it had taken twenty-seven years.

These agreements were arranged in an atmosphere of accelerating détente between the United States and the Soviet Union. Détente flourished because the mood on both sides of the perhaps disintegrating iron curtain was somewhat chastened: The Russians were sobered by Prague, the Americans by Vietnam, Europe by the student revolt, all by economic problems. In addition, the Soviets stood in increasing need of American or West European technological aid, while western Europe, the Europe of the growing Economic Community, worried because its security was dependent on an apparently unreliable United States. Depressed by Vietnam, American legislators muttered about lowering the risks in Europe. A Senate resolution calling for a 50 percent reduction of American troops in Europe attracted much support in 1971, though it was eventually defeated. At this time, also, a quarrel between Greece and Turkey over Cyprus weakened the southern flank of NATO. The island, which was shared by hostile communities of Greeks and Turks, exploded in violence in 1964. The violence subsided with the presence of a United Nations peacekeeping force only to re-ignite in 1971. The strife engendered bitterness between Greece and Turkey, supposed NATO allies, and placed their fellow allies in an awkward spot. Both countries threatened noncooperation with NATO. Following the Turkish invasion of Cyprus in 1974, the U.S. Congress placed an embargo on military aid to Turkey. In 1975, Turkey closed her American bases. In partial compensation for this disarray in NATO ranks, de Gaulle's successors quietly resumed a friendlier French attitude toward the Western military alliance.

The USSR grew ever more estranged from China, and an American move toward China, culminating in President Richard Nixon's visit to Peking in 1972, prodded the Russians to seek American friendship. Such trends formed the background for a European Security Conference, along with parallel negotiations toward arms reduction. The strategic arms limitations talks (SALT) between the United States and the Soviet Union began at Helsinki, Finland, in 1969 and proceeded slowly toward a first-stage agreement in 1972. The SALT talks were facilitated because the USSR had approached numerical arms equality with the United States, so that the Russians could negotiate from strength rather than be frozen in arms inferiority. In fact, the Soviets now had more intercontinental ballistic missiles (ICBMs) than the United States, a fact that caused the U.S. Congress to hesitate before approving the Helsinki accords. This Russian advantage was balanced by the United States having bomber bases near the USSR and qualitatively better weapons.

In May 1972, at the time of President Nixon's visit to Moscow, an agreement was announced that declared a freeze on numbers of ICBMs and submarine-launched missiles, as well as the nuclear-powered subs that carried them. There was also a limitation on antimissile defenses, which threatened stabilization of mutual deterrence. The agreement was to last for five years. It certainly left much out of account, but it seemed a hopeful start. Further agreements were to be reached in 1974. Also announced at this time were a grain purchase agreement and an American oil company arrangement to help develop Soviet oil. Brezhnev spoke of Russian aid in bringing the Vietnamese War to its conclusion, which happened early in 1973 in Paris.

Early in 1973 seven NATO countries and five Warsaw Pact countries began discussions on mutual force reductions. The Soviet leadership mentioned the possibility of cooperation between COMECON and EEC, the rival economic unions of Eastern and Western Europe. Nixon was well received at Moscow, as he had been at Peking. The American president, unfortunately soon to become ensnared in the Watergate scandal that eventually destroyed him, joined his brilliant secretary of state, Henry Kissinger, in talking about a multipolar world, balanced between a number of centers of political if not military power: the United States, the Soviet Union, Europe, Japan, China. These regional powers would cooperate as well as compete with the hope of stabilizing a world marked by continuing but ever-converging nationalism. The affluent, "developed" countries would collaborate to aid the developing peoples and to conserve world resources. Such was the vision. The United States in particular would seek friendly understanding with both China and the USSR.

An unstable world threw doubts on such visions. In particular, the highly volatile Middle East exploded again in 1973 with an attack by Egypt and Syria on Israel to gain revenge for the 1967 humiliation. The bitterly fought Yom Kippur War (so-called) of October 6–25, which forced an energy crisis in the West as Arab oil-producing countries applied an oil embargo against the United States and other pro-Israel states, saw the United States putting pressure on the Soviet Union for a settlement, warning it that it was imperiling détente (with possibly "incalculable consequences"). In the United Nations Security Council, the two superpowers joined in calling for a cease-fire. Negotiations between the Arab states and Israel began under U.S.–USSR sponsorship, after a cease-fire and disengagement was painfully achieved. This fourth Arab-Israeli war ended in something like a draw. It had involved huge amounts of war materiel, supplied by the USSR and the United States to their respective clients. On the Sinai peninsula, it was said, more tanks were in combat than in any battle of World War II.

The clients were somewhat disillusioned. The Arab peoples wanted no part of Soviet-style socialism and grew increasingly suspicious of Soviet motives. Did the USSR really want to help Egypt and Syria regain land from Israel, or did she want to dampen the Mideast fires in order to ease U.S.–USSR tensions? Prior to the 1973 war, Egypt's President Anwar Sadat demanded the withdrawal from his country of Soviet military advisers, estimated to be as many as 17,000. Two years later, after the 1973 war stalemate, Sadat decided to adopt a position of neutrality between the superpowers. He had become convinced that Soviet interests did not dictate complete support of the Arab cause. Better opportunities lay in playing off the two powers against each other. To become the client of one was to put oneself in its power and to become helpless.

Détente was to come sadly apart at the end of the decade (a story told in the next chapter). In the early 1970s, it produced a few promising indicators. Faced with declining economic growth and poor agricultural performance, necessitating imports of American grain in the bad harvest years of 1972 and 1973, Soviet leadership put stress on foreign trade. In order "to ensure that the Soviet people live better tomorrow than they do today," in Brezhnev's words, there must be technological cooperation between the Soviet Union and Western peoples. During his call on the German Federal Republic in 1973, the Soviet leader signed agreements involving extensive purchase of West German technological aid; for example, in building steel works at Kursk. Oil and natural gas were the bait for the Germans. Already, the Italian firm Fiat had begun building mass-production automobile factories in the USSR. Even more interesting for the Soviets was American computer and deep oil-drilling technology. Soviet leaders also showed some inclination to agree that the world energy and environmental crisis transcended politics and could be tackled only by joining East-West resources. A June 1974 agreement on economic, industrial, and technological cooperation (accompanying another presidential visit to Moscow) impressed Brezhnev as a "massive landmark in the history of the relations between the United States and the Soviet Union."

This was also the year of Solzhenitsyn's exile. In the previous year, 1973, an American Senate committee torpedoed a trade agreement with the USSR in protest against Soviet restrictions on Jewish emigration and dissidents. The path to cooperation between the superpowers, or between communism and capitalism in general, was not much smoother than were the sad affairs of a disordered world in the rather cheerless years of 1973 and 1974, whose highlights included an energy crisis, world inflation, Watergate, war in the Middle East, and a world food crisis.

THE CHANGING OF THE GUARD

The middle years of the 1970s saw a considerable turnover in world leadership. President Richard Nixon became the first American President in history ever to resign, as a culmination of the Watergate scandal. He was replaced by Gerald Ford in the summer of 1974. In this year of the locust, plagued by the energy crisis, "stagflation" and an Arab oil boycott, Prime Minister Heath was also a political victim, as Harold Wilson returned to power with another Labour government in the United Kingdom. President Georges Pompidou died suddenly, leading to a lively and somewhat confusing presidential election in France. In Germany, Chancellor Brandt resigned, giving way to Helmut Schmidt. An obviously sinking Chairman Mao presided over a China already maneuvering for the succession; both Mao and Chou En-lai were to die in 1976, ending an era in Chinese and world history.

The last remaining grand figure of the World War II era, President Tito, reached the age of eighty-three (he was to die in 1980), and people wondered whether the somewhat precarious Yugoslav confederacy, recently shaken by Serb-Croat clashes, could survive his passing. This was a time, too, in which the death of Portugal's long-time dictator, Salazar, brought political and economic turmoil to a long-quiescent little country. Her larger Iberian neighbor prepared for the death of General Francisco Franco, which came late in 1975, amid fears that this succession too would be marked by strife. As it happened, it was not. The government of the Greek colonels fell, and democracy returned. Among others who passed from the scene in 1975 were Chiang Kai-shek; Haile Selassie, the Ethiopian emperor; and Cardinal Mindszenty, the embattled symbol of Hungarian freedom. Franco, Selassie, Chiang, Mao, Mindszenty—how much of the twentieth-century's stormy history these men had helped make.[2]

---

[2]Eamon de Valera also died in 1975; in 1919–1920, he had led "the first significant guerrilla war of liberation of the 20th century," had then become the respected leader of Free Ireland, and was president of the League of Nations Assembly in the 1930s. He, too, had helped make a bit of history. *(Thomas Hachey)*

The sudden death of French President Pompidou in April 1974 forced an unexpected election. The Gaullists split on the first ballot, on which there were no fewer than twelve presidential candidates. (Anyone can run for president in France if he or she can find 100 notable people to sign a petition and is willing to put up a fairly small sum of money as a deposit, which is lost if the candidate gets less than 5 percent of the vote.) The more orthodox Gaullist and more conservative candidate was Jacques Chaban-Delmas, who had been Pompidou's prime minister (as Pompidou had been de Gaulle's). But he was challenged by Valéry Giscard d'Estaing, an Independent Republican. On the first ballot, Chaban received only 15 percent of the vote, Giscard 35 percent; the Socialist François Mitterand, supported by all the left parties, led the poll with 43 percent. The run-off election of the two highest vote-getters resulted in a narrow victory for Giscard, 50.8 percent to 49.2 percent. The right also won the Assembly elections of 1978. The results suggested that French politics were moderating. Giscard was a man of the center, Mitterand a moderate of the left; between the two there was not a great deal of distance. Mitterand, supported by the Communists, did not repudiate the Atlantic Alliance nor the nuclear *force de frappe*. Giscard, backed by the right, spoke of increasing social services and reducing inequalities of income. Both were loyal Europeanists. Thirty percent of the working class voted for the Gaullist candidates, while a great many middle-class professional people preferred Mitterand. If a movement of the right to the left was discernible, in that both Gaullist candidates talked of change, reform, and worker participation in industrial management, a movement of the left to the right was equally in evidence, for neither Communists nor Socialists used the language of revolution. French politics appeared to have stabilized around a basically two-party (or coalition of parties) structure, a moderate right and a moderate left of almost equal strength. For all the noise they had made in 1968, the parties of the extreme left, themselves split, polled less than 3 percent of the vote. A Trotskyite candidate named Arlette Laguiller, the only woman to run, got most of these. Eighty-four percent of the eligible voters went to the polls, an impressive number. In a year not marked by serenity, this was a performance suggesting Fifth Republic stability and workability.

A similar pattern of political stability seemed to be emerging in post-Franco Spain. Much had changed since 1939. To the surprise of many, Franco followed de Gaulle in choosing the path of modernization for the country he ruled. Long backward by the standards of the industrialized regions, Spain now took off toward economic development; industry grew, agriculture was modernized, and urban life expanded in an echo of the French and Italian experiences. Standing guard against the anarchy that had brought on the civil war, Franco's military-backed regime refused to allow political opposition, trade unions, or free expression of opinion. Many feared that because a lid had held them down so long, these volatile people were bound to explode when the ponderous weight of the generalissimo was removed. That this did not happen was due in good part to the unexpected skill of Franco's designated successor, Juan Carlos, prince of the former royal house, who became king after Franco's death. He guided Spain on a path that led to a democratic constitution. As if to mock all the stereotypes about the violent, uncompromising Spanish character, almost everybody seemed to behave moderately; attempts by both extreme right and extreme left to foment trouble attracted minimal followings in 1976–1977.

DECOLONIZATION

The other great world political event of the 1960s and 1970s was decolonization. Spread over four decades, the process came to a climax at this time. In 1945, a large part of the world was still ruled or controlled by European states. But World War II was a critical moment in this passage of the non-Western peoples toward autonomy; it destroyed the old colonial order in Asia and Africa beyond repair, caused the incursion of the Jews into the Middle East, fatally weakened the British as well as the French empires. The wrenching experience of India's liberation right after the war had begun decolonization, and in the 1960s African liberation came with a rush. The departure of the French and the Dutch from Southeast Asia and of the Americans from the Philippines were other landmarks in this enormous operation. In 1986, Hong Kong became the last major Crown Colony to leave the British Empire.

Until about 1960, some European powers attempted to hang onto their rule in some places, resulting in armed conflict, notably against the French in Southeast Asia and in Algeria, but also against the British in Kenya and in the Middle East (Iraq, Jordan), the Dutch in Indonesia. But the failure of the colonial powers in these struggles, and the obvious disadvantages of being cast in the role of imperialist oppressor, convinced almost everyone that the tide had set in irresistibly against the old colonial order. In the 1960s, two conservative leaders, Macmillan and de Gaulle, competed with each other in decolonizing their respective empires, chiefly in Africa. No fewer than a hundred new states would emerge in the decade or two after 1959 to more than triple the world's total number of sovereignties. The only holdout was little Portugal, refusing to relinquish Angola in southwest Africa for many years.

Though Macmillan might talk of heeding "the winds of change," and de Gaulle speak of nationalism's legitimate claims, their motives in withdrawing more or less gracefully from direct rule over their colonies were not entirely unselfish. Colonies had always been more of a status symbol than a necessity. Now the European powers could no longer claim to be World Powers. Suez had driven home that lesson. They could simply not afford the cost; the French had hard lessons in Indochina and Algeria, the British in the Middle East. Colonies had often served a strategic military purpose, but in the nuclear age this factor counted for less. Bases were no longer so much needed, either, to refuel ships, as in the past.

To this was added the Cold War advantage that the Russians obtained from pinning the epithet of "imperialist" on the western Europeans. This was in fact the favorite word of Soviet propaganda; their enemies in the West, including the Americans, were always called "imperialists." Now there was a bidding war between the rival power blocs for the favor of Third World countries; one wanted to pose as their friends. After liberating their colonies, France and Britain strove to maintain influence on them. African leaders were usually products of a European education. Some were strongly Christian, like the former schoolteacher and admirer of Gandhi and Lincoln, Kenneth Kaunda of Zambia. They all wished to "develop," to urbanize and modernize, to create a state, to educate the masses, usually in the French or English language. Their poets and novelists wrote in the French or English language; a Nigerian novelist who won a Nobel prize (Wole Soyinka) used the latter tongue. However, the effort of France to maintain close contact with the former African colonies in the form of a French-speaking community had minimal success; the elites of the *jeunes états* –sometimes now assigned the doubtful acronym of LDCs, for less developed countries–were intensely nationalistic (another idea borrowed from Europe).

Decolonization occurred with almost indecent haste, sometimes finding the states that received independence unprepared to cope with problems of government. Civil war in Indochina after the French withdrawal caused major international turmoil, as we know. And, in Africa in 1961, the erstwhile Belgian Congo, now Zaire, erupted in civil war with the attempted secession of a province and became for a time an international trouble spot. Conflicts of this sort reflected tribal divisions and uncertain central governmental authority. In the most populous of black African nations, the Biafra war of 1967–1970, later called the war of Nigerian unity, was touched off by an attempt at secession. It was a major conflict, though overshadowed by events in Europe and Middle East at that time and subsequently almost forgotten. It has been called the first television war, i.e. one brought into the living rooms of millions all over the world by the magic of the new media, which did more than anything else to make Europeans and Americans conscious of the outer world as a vivid reality.

Some of the African countries (advised by Western economists) made the mistake of embarking upon overly ambitious programs of economic development that failed to produce benefits while incurring enormous debts. European countries, the United States, and the USSR (as well as China for a time) competed with each other in sending money to LDCs for development and economic support. In the 1970s, loans on easy terms were virtually thrust on African countries. American economic assistance to sub-Saharan Africa, for example, grew despite some congressional grumbling from about $200 million in 1970 to over $1 billion in 1985. European contributions were more than comparable: The EEC countries claimed to have contributed 43 percent of the world aid total in 1976, a matter of some $5.8 billion–considerably more than either the United States or the USSR. But the latter (Warsaw Pact countries) was estimated in 1984 to have provided some $21 billion in economic assistance to the LDCs over the past thirty years. In 1984, the great bulk of the Soviet Union's $2.4 billion in aid was going to a few client countries (Afghanistan,

Ethiopia, Guinea, Iraq, Nicaragua, Syria). She had begun with a strong ideological belief in the solidarity of the ex-colonies and the USSR as common enemies of capitalistic imperialism.

But this conviction had eroded. The ex-colonies, still struggling to establish their identity and confidence, developed an ideology that ranged both European communists and capitalists together as their enemies: the industrialized, urbanized societies against the rural hinterland of the globe. Quite evidently the Russians had soured considerably on the balance sheet of foreign aid, which they had hoped would garner political advantages. Possibly the West had too; both were kept in the game by their rivalry, and the LDCs exploited this rivalry for their own benefit. The end of the Cold War later confronted them with problems. But in the 1970s, their economies suffered severely from the abrupt rise in oil prices that accompanied the Arab-Israeli war.

As modern "nation-states," most African countries were deeply flawed by being made up of older local, "tribal" societies that had been flung together by the accidents of European colonial rule. They were not yet a social unity. "Tribal" massacres took a toll of several hundred thousand lives in Burundi and Rwanda. (These bloody feuds broke out in 1965, 1969, 1972, and 1988 before they caught the world's attention in 1994.) Other African countries ravaged by civil war or suffering from near-anarchy were Angola, Mozambique, Sierra Leone, Ethiopia, the Sudan, Zaire.

In the first flush of liberation, Africa made more of an imprint on Europe, the young radicals sometimes adopting national leaders like Ghana's Nkrumah and Algeria's Ben Bella as heroes. The failure of their grandiose dreams, and Africa's subsequent severe problems, of economic decay and political collapse, caused this attraction to diminish.

The non-European world included more than Africa, of course. It constituted a heterogeneous mixture with little or nothing in common. It was divided into rich and poor, capitalist and socialist, developed and undeveloped and developing, those barely holding together and those successful and aspiring to be great powers, or at least sturdy dwarfs. It included probably the leading industrial power in the world, as well as the oldest civilization in the world, and the most populous country. The world's largest cities are now in Mexico, Japan, China, India, Indonesia, Argentina, South Korea, Egypt, Iran, as well as in the United States, the Soviet Union, France, Spain, and England. Some African cities like Kinshasha and Lagos are far from small. Eighty percent of the world's 5 billion people lie outside of Europe and North America. Most of them are progressing out of the inertness of traditional peasant cultures into the frenetic volatility of early modernization, always a disturbed, dangerous phase. The ability of some of the less mighty lands of the earth–Vietnam, Cambodia, Iran, Syria, Libya, and Nicaragua, to name a few–to create immense headaches for Europe and the superpowers became notorious.

13

The 1980s: Dramatic Decade

A DISCOURAGING BEGINNING

Perhaps the ninth decade of every modern century is fated to be a turning point
of history. The reader will recall such famous events as the Glorious Revolution
of 1688 and the French Revolution of 1789, while also thinking of the case that
can be made for the 1880s as a crucial milestone of technological and social
modernization. The 1980s brought changes that seem as though they will become equally memorable. Of these, the collapse of the Soviet Communist order
ranks as the foremost. Along with this went a basic restructuring of the European international system, the first since the years just after World War II. The
progress of the European Community toward complete economic integration—
in which the newly liberated countries of eastern Europe might even join—could
turn out to be the most significant of all. Others might want to nominate the
crisis of the natural environment, threatened by modern urban technological
society, or the computer-driven communications revolution.

The decade showed a dramatic change of course from its first to its second half. If the success of the international capitalist economy in presiding over
an era of dynamic growth was a leading theme of the decade, it hardly looked
that way from about 1979 to 1983. In the former year, amid persistence of the
disconcerting "stagflation" that had broken out in the 1970s, the International
Monetary Fund predicted a worldwide depression. There were widespread
strikes in 1979, the year of Britain's "winter of discontent," and a major labor

struggle at the huge Fiat plants in Italy. A Socialist government was about to be elected in France, and then fail in its efforts to find a cure for unemployment and inflation: All governments, stuck with a now ineffective Keynesian formula, seemed at a loss to know what to do.

If posterity is likely to remember the 1980s as the time when new Soviet leadership broke with the Bolshevik past and moved toward an era of accommodation with the West, that too was far from evident as the decade began. Relations between the USSR and the Western powers suffered an almost total collapse in 1980, crushing the rather feeble detente of the preceding years. The Soviet Union chose Christmas 1979 to launch an invasion of Afghanistan, the remote land that formed part of the southern border of the USSR's central Asia region. Afghan relations with the USSR had seemed friendly enough. Why the Soviets chose to mount a massive invasion of this mountainous land (some 100,000 troops, 10,000 of them airborne, entered Afghanistan in the first few weeks of 1980) was far from clear then and is hardly more so today. The Soviet explanations bordered on the bizarre. In some respects this act of aggression was unique in Soviet history. The USSR had attacked Finland in 1939, but there were compelling military reasons for doing so. North Korea's invasion of South Korea in 1950 was approved in advance by Moscow, but it was not carried out by Soviet troops. They had entered Hungary and then Czechoslovakia (along with other Warsaw Pact soldiers) to prevent what the Kremlin leaders regarded as secession from socialism, brought on by rebellions against the Communist Party, in areas of obvious strategic sensitivity. But there was no conceivable threat from the area of Afghanistan to Soviet security, unless one was perceived from the fiercely fundamentalist Islamic regime that had just overthrown the Shah of Iran, which though anti-Marxist was violently anti-American. The Afghan government against which the Russians intervened was a Communist one, which the Russians said invited them in, but on arrival the Russians did away with the government and installed other puppets. The most plausible explanation is that the aging Leonid Brezhnev had lost his grip, and/or wanted a last moment of glory to redeem his miserable reign.

The situation turned for the worse when an outraged Afghan people rose up in resistance, initiating a long and brutal war that pitted Soviet forces and a small number of native collaborators against virtually the entire Afghan population, not, however, very well organized or united. A United Nations resolution condemning the Soviet invasion was approved by 104 to 18 (with a large number of abstentions); a large majority of Third World and Islamic nations voted against the USSR. U.S. President Jimmy Carter, who had not gotten on well with Brezhnev at their 1977 meeting, imposed a grain and technology embargo on the Soviets, exhorting others to do the same. The hottest issue was soon the upcoming 1980 Olympic Games, to be hosted by Moscow; in the event, the United States was joined by some but not all its western European allies in boycotting the games (in retaliation for which the Soviets boycotted the Los Angeles Olympics in 1984).

As if this startling evidence of Soviet aggressiveness (or was it nervous defensiveness?) were not enough, at almost exactly the same time a long-brewing situation came to a boil in Poland. As we know, each decade had brought the Russians a major crisis in their relations with the eastern European countries which, lying between the USSR and western Europe, they considered to be part of their security zone. The Yugoslavs in 1948 made a successful escape, the Hungarians in 1956 were less successful in the short run, and the suppression of Czech democracy in 1968 cost the Communist cause dearly. In 1980, it was the turn of Poland.

Strategically the most important to the Soviets, Poland, bearer of an old and highly developed culture, was also historically the most anti-Russian of the eastern European countries. It was easily the most populous of these *Zwischen-europa* peoples, so often condemned to be the victims of their more powerful neighbors on both sides. And, there had been previous tensions in Soviet-Polish relations, in 1953, 1956, and 1970, which had however been resolved without major conflict.

There were factors that pulled the Kremlin both ways on Poland, toward a more lenient policy, yet, in the crunch, a determination not to let go. Since 1947, the yoke of Moscow at times lay less heavy on Poland than on other countries; there was no collectivization of agriculture, and the Roman Catholic church kept its place in Polish life at the cost of "staying out of politics." In 1956, Polish riots led to the dismissal of the Stalinist boss and his replacement by a milder one. Preoccupied with de-Stalinization and the Hungarian revolt, the Soviet leaders at that time had elected to appease the Poles. Again, in 1970, rising food prices and shortages precipitated working class rioting, which led to the resignation of Gomulka. Once more, a USSR shaken by the recent Czech crisis (which the Poles had helped suppress) did not wish to press Poland too hard.

The new head, Edward Gierek, had ambitious plans for economic development financed partly by Western credits, which the Kremlin tolerated in the détente atmosphere of the early 1970s. There were also substantial loans from the Soviet Union. But six years later, the plan was in trouble. With much of the new investment going into heavy industry, consumer goods were in short supply relevant to purchasing power. An attempt to deal with this problem within the framework of a still largely administered economy brought a sudden and steep rise in prices. Again, there were protests and demonstrations. Arrest of workers led to a Committee to Defend the Workers, staffed by intellectuals—a dangerous alliance. Stirrings took place at this time elsewhere in eastern Europe, in Romania's Jiu Valley and in Czechoslovakia as a result of the Helsinki agreements of 1975, product of détente, in which the communist regimes had seemingly promised to respect civil liberties but in fact did not do so; writers and intellectuals organized themselves as the "Charter '77" movement.

These rumblings of discontent were a premonition of the explosion that took place a few years later with the sensational rise of the Solidarity movement in Poland. It was an extraordinary happening. Anyone wanting to understand the Polish revolution of 1980–1982 would need to see some films, such as Wajda's *Man of Marble* and Jerzy Stuhr's *Top Dog*. A great deal of cultural freedom existed in Poland. Disdain for the Party "sultans" who formed the ruling class was indicated in opinion polls revealing that in a free election only 3 percent of the Poles would vote for the Communist Party. And, in 1981, virtually everyone admired most either the Pope, now a Pole (John Paul II's effect on his countrymen was immense) or Lech Walesa, leader of the spontaneously developed free trade union movement known as Solidarity.

Strikes began in July 1980 in Warsaw and spread to other Polish cities. Solidarity was at pains to keep them nonviolent, but Moscow charged that these were "anti-socialist forces." The Soviet Communist ideology rejected the idea of trade unions free to strike and win concessions as inconsistent with socialism. Military maneuvers on the borders of Poland along with ominous references to Czechoslovakia attempted to intimidate the Solidarity workers. Brezhnev reasserted his Doctrine, while seeking privately to stiffen the backbone of the Polish Communist leaders, who were torn between desires to serve their Russian masters and immense pressure from their own countryfolk. It was clear that the Kremlin hoped to avoid armed intervention from Russia if at all possible, but equally clear that they saw a vital issue at stake: Let the Poles get away with their free trade unions and all the other satellites would follow the example.

Tension persisted through the fall and winter, as a wave of sympathy for Solidarity swept through the West and the Kremlin alleged NATO subversion. Soviet verbal attacks on Solidarity reached a crescendo in 1981, and several times armed intervention seemed imminent. In October, the sinister-looking Jaruzelski replaced Kania as Communist Party chief in Poland and began to mobilize force against Solidarity. Unpopular as his role of Soviet stooge was, Jaruzelki doubtless felt that his repression was preferable to what a Russian invasion would have brought. The Polish Communist Party leadership clearly hoped to do only as much as necessary to stave off Soviet intervention. Nevertheless, the world saw imprisonment and murders of Solidarity leaders, and of priests and intellectuals who openly supported the movement. In December 1981, in order to forestall an upcoming Solidarity demonstration, Jaruzelski bowed to Soviet pressure and proclaimed martial law, arresting 6,000 people. Martial law remained in effect for a year. Jaruzelski was given unprecedented powers for a Communist chief, being head of the armed forces as well as party leader and premier. At the same time, the Soviets pumped more money into the sagging Polish economy; the operation cost them dearly.

The frail plant of détente withered and almost died in the atmosphere of 1980–1981, and the rhetoric of the Cold War returned to fashion. Though U.S. President Carter, plagued also by Iranians holding American hostages in Tehran, was thoroughly shocked by the Soviet actions in Afghanistan and Poland, the election of Republican Ronald Reagan in November 1980 brought an even tougher rhetoric. The French Communist Party suffered when the PCF did not forthrightly condemn the Soviet actions; Georges Marchais, it was revealed, went to Moscow to ask Brezhnev how he should explain the Afghan invasion to France! During the next few years, both the Afghan and Polish situations remained unresolved, as a long struggle set in in both places—a savage war against freedom fighters in the hills of Afghanistan, a continuing test of wills in Poland. The death of Brezhnev in 1982 and subsequent changes in Soviet leadership introduced a new dimension, initially hard to evaluate, eventually epoch making.

A casualty of the freeze in American-Soviet relations was the second strategic arms limitation treaty, SALT II; signed by Carter and Brezhnev in June 1979 after seven years of difficult negotiations, it was destined to be stillborn as the U.S. Senate never ratified it. In the atmosphere of a new Cold War, issues such as the development of more accurate and more mobile nuclear missiles became troublesome and controversial. In 1983, the left mounted a major campaign in western Europe against a NATO decision to station Pershing II and cruise missiles in western Europe to counteract Soviet SS-20s capable of hitting targets in western Europe. The other earnestly discussed arms issue was the development, pushed strongly by American President Ronald Reagan, of defense systems using advanced laser and particle-beam technologies—the so-called Star Wars project (the official American title was Strategic Defense Initiative). Such systems if successful threatened or promised to render the entire vast nuclear arsenal as obsolete as the Dreadnought had once made the old-fashioned battleship. Complicated by such new weapons technology, East-West negotiations on arms reduction totally stalled.

Warsaw Pact forces stationed in eastern Europe outnumbered NATO conventional weapons in tanks, antitank weapons, aircraft and antiaircraft missiles by estimated margins of between 2 to 1 and 6 to 1. Western Europe's defense still depended on the nuclear deterrent, which, increasingly, was felt to be a bluff—would the United States really invite total destruction by launching its missiles were the Russians to invade Europe? Tension also rose within NATO. Defense expenditures were intolerably high. The situation wore on everyone's nerves, despite an increasing feeling that these weapons of mass destruction would never be used, so certain was it now that a successful preemptive strike was impossible; the multiplication of destructive power ensured retaliation and so deterred an attack. But if the "balance of terror" was more effective than it had ever been in preventing all-out nuclear war between the superpowers, it was all the more helpless in the face of conventional wars such as now raged in Afghanistan, Iraq, Lebanon, Eritrea, Angola, and many another trouble spot. In 1981, Israeli forces invaded Lebanon, which had dissolved in civil war.

Other sensational events of the year 1980 included Iranian revolutionaries' holding of Americans as hostages; the beginning of another strange war, between Iran and Iraq, which was destined to drag on through much of the decade; the death of Marshal Tito in Yugoslavia, causing a crisis in the affairs of that country; the trial of the so-called Gang of Four in China, a landmark in the new Chinese leadership's repudiation of Maoism; and, for good measure, a famine in the Horn of Africa and an earthquake in Italy. A Republican won the American presidency and, in the aftermath of 1979 economic horrors, the British Conservative party led by Mrs. Margaret Thatcher began an antisocialist restructuring of the British economy as the Labour party split in two. In retrospect, the recession of revolutionary Marxism might be discerned in all of these. The Age of Lenin was drawing to an end, but it was not so clear at that time.

A NEW POLITICAL ERA IN EUROPE

A movement toward the Right, evident at the end of the 1970s in the Western democracies, lasted through most of the decade. The word in Great Britain was Thatcherism. The embattled leader of the revived and renovated Conservative party is the only British Prime Minister, it has been noted, to have an *-ism* named after her. Under her effective leadership a sharp change in social policy encouraged the free market and competitive capitalism in a country evidently fed up with Labour's bumbling attempts to install a "social democracy." The Labour party lost the 1979 election after a less than happy turn in office, during which the erstwhile peerless leader Harold Wilson retired to be replaced by the unimpressive James Callaghan. A wave of strikes including hospital workers in the wintertime alienated the public. Much of the inevitable public anger was discharged against leaders of the trade unions, whose demands for increased wages seemed to fuel inflation. In its latter days, the beleaguered Callaghan government placed faith in an "incomes policy" based on voluntary restraint of wages by the unions. This did not work. Once associated with reform and progress, trade unions now often tried to block technological change, as the new technology threatened to replace workers with computers or robots. An activist elite of trade union officers seemed bent on dominating the Labour Party and dictating terms to the nation. That the economy was in serious trouble many blamed on such inefficiency, on the growing state welfare sector, and the resulting prohibitive taxation, which did not prevent inflation.

The Tories rode in under the command of the first female prime minister, Margaret Thatcher, who rode out a period of continuing economic difficulties to win again in 1983 by an even larger majority (the greatest since 1945), aided by the flush of victory from a mini-war between Britain and Argentina over the Falkland Islands. Meanwhile, Labour moderates left to form a separate Social Democratic party, soon allying itself with the remnants of the old Liberal party. The old Labour dilemma, reflected in former party feuds, of whether to be a doctrinaire socialist and working-class party or to opt for reformism and appeal to other classes, now was resolved in an actual divorce. The more radical types, mistrusted by a majority of the British people, were left in control of the Labour rump; but the Alliance faced the difficulties confronting any new party, of building an organization and an identity, and also the problems of a third party in a system of single-member constituencies, not provided with pro-

To a society fed up with economic statism, Margaret Thatcher brought an invigorating message of salvation through individual enterprise. (*AP/Wide World Photos.*)

portional representation. After 1983, the new Labour leader, Neil Kinnock, was no far-leftist but struggled with "militant" factions of discordant old-fashioned Trotskyists and new-fashioned Punk Rockers.

The Conservatives took advantage of their opponents' disarray. In June 1987, they won an unprecedented third straight victory, by a reduced but still comfortable margin. However, in none of the elections did the Tories win a majority of the popular vote; they received only 42 percent of the votes cast (less than one-third of the total electorate) in gaining their third consecutive triumph. They profited from the confusion and division of the opposition. A considerable majority of the British public thought Labour unfit to govern.

Mrs. Thatcher's *-ism* was an old one, newly recovered after a long interlude of Keynesian or socialist statism; it was the return to private enterprise in a competitive economy. In the view of her admirers, the first female prime minister rescued Britain from economic decline by setting the people free from bureaucracy and the welfare state, thus motivating hard work and enterprise. Her program featured lower taxes (the top rate came down from 83 percent to 40 percent) and privatization of many state-owned enterprises; for example, in communications and transportation, which were sold to the public in share offerings. She could boast in 1987 that real personal disposable income had risen an average of 14 percent in the past five years. The percentage of home owner-ship also rose, to nearly 60 percent by 1990, as the energetic Iron Lady sold off public housing to its renters at bargain prices. Inflation came down for a while, and productivity improved.

The fortunate discovery of oil in the North Sea aided this performance, which tended to wane as the decade wore on. Critics protested that the burden of the reforms was not being spread equally or fairly. They grudgingly conceded the need to restrict inefficient public enterprises, cut the burden on the tax-payer, perhaps even expose British industry to the invigorating winds of inter-national competition—which would probably entail limiting the power of trade unions. A majority felt the unions had too much power.

No peeress but rather a grocer's daughter, Margaret Thatcher repre-sented a new kind of toryism; she disliked, and was disliked by, the old aristoc-racy as much as by the socialists. She quarreled with the intellectual elite too. Oxford University refused to give her an honorary degree. In return, she did not disguise her contempt for that combination of elitism and statism that had nearly ruined England. Among the many areas she burned to reform was edu-cation, in what might be called a "back to basics" spirit, but also trying to diver-sify, to encourage competition, and allow the better schools to flourish while the poorer ones died out. "Open enrollment" allowed popular schools to expand to limit of capacity, not keeping poorer ones artificially full. "Per capita funding" meant that state money followed the child to whatever school he or she chose; schools would gain resources as they gained pupils.

Not without some understanding of economic theory, this wife of a businessman, herself trained as an industrial chemist, based her crusading old-fashioned liberalism not on theory but on her feelings about morality: restoring self-reliance, individual accountability, ending the dependency culture, freeing people from the paternal state. Hard work and frugality, the primeval capitalist virtues, were to be revived from near death. Like Cinderella, the homely bour-geois turned out to be worth more than her gaudy socialist sisters.

The Thatcher policies were never very popular. In the late 1980s, the Thatcher dynasty lost ground, and polls showed Labour reclaiming a lead in popular opinion. Inflation returned, and unemployment ran high in some parts of Britain; a north-south gap developed. A Thatcher initiative that proved espe-cially unpopular, leading to protests and riots, was a poll tax intended to relieve the property tax of some of the costs of local government.

Faced with this situation, the Conservative party rebelled against Mrs. Thatcher; perhaps it was a masculine revolt against a masterful woman as much as anything. She resigned her more than ten-year leadership of her party and country in late November 1990, succeeded by John Major. As the seceding So-cial Democrats failed to make the grade, the old Labour party opted for a more moderate stance on most issues, and fewer issues of substance separated the two major parties. Controversial was Thatcher's reluctance to go as far and as fast toward European Community integration as the continental members (see below); but this was an old story, and the opposition in Britain was hardly united on this issue either.

A NEW ECONOMIC ERA

The determined presence of Mrs. Thatcher etched a sharp impression on the 1980s, and she might well have qualified as statesperson of the decade had a man called Gorbachev not come on fast in the late running. Because she symbolized the decade's spirit, it might be well here to note the new economic era that arrived in Europe in the 1980s. It involved sweeping technological changes. First, assembly-line factories and smokestack industries became almost as obsolete as they had once rendered the hand tools of the artisans. (Indeed, handcrafts were in some ways more "in" than assembly lines now.) The percentage of unskilled and semiskilled workers in the population—the classical "proletariat"—had greatly declined; allowing some margin for error because of problems of definition, it would seem to have sunk from about 70 percent of the population in 1900 to about 30 percent in Great Britain. In 1986, more than half of all workers were in nonmanual jobs.

Microchips produced far different modes of production. Were Karl Marx alive today, he would doubtless perceive the obsolescence of his industrial proletariat. Trade unionism, the wave of the first half of the century, was now in sharp decline. Insofar as factory labor remained, it was increasingly performed by robots, something long foreseen in science fiction but now a reality. The new electronics technicians might have interested Marx as a revolutionary class, for they were often restive, interested in ideas, trendy. But they were too individualistic a group to form a single class and too critical-minded to remain content with any simple dogma.

The basis of the new economy was in new technology, much of it asso-

CHANGING ECONOMIC PATTERNS
Percent of Italian Workers Employed in Agriculture, Manufacturing, and
Service Sectors, 1951-1990

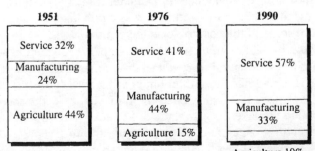

ciated with the electronics and microchip revolutions. Though the first electronic digital computers had appeared just at the end of World War II, no one then foresaw the way they took off in the 1980s.[1] An IBM executive is said to have projected no future for the computer industry in the 1950s since he estimated the total world demand for these monster machines, as they then were, to be no more than fifty. That within thirty years computers would be miniaturized, made far less expensive, and end in the laps of millions of private citizens was beyond anyone's wildest dream. (The sci-fi imagination was hung up on space travel, the very opposite dimension.)

Perhaps the best place to begin this particular voyage into inner space would be at the Bell Telephone laboratory in late 1947 where the transistor was born, as an outgrowth of wartime radar research. No one then recognized the tremendous importance of this smaller and less energy-consuming substitute for the electronic or vacuum tube. The *New York Times* buried a note on it on page 46 of the July 1, 1948, issue, in a "News of the Radio" column. The names of John Bardeen, Walter Brittain, and William Shockley, it would seem, have not even yet been elevated to the level of fame of Edison and Marconi and Curie. Yet the impact on modern life of all that sprang from this development in radio engineering has been as great as any technological innovation in history. The path of this process, some of it carried on by Shockley and his students (among them David Packard and William Hewlett) in California's famed "Silicon Valley," led to transistors of ever-smaller size and greater speed. Computer chips able to store and process information had been created by 1971; a few years later came microcomputers able to perform more than a hundred thousand logical operations per second. These were to become ever more efficient and transform the entire industrial world, spinning off countless new gadgets.

The above breathlessly brief summary, of course, merely touches the surface of this powerful process of scientific and engineering discovery, which spread across the world with amazing speed, so that quite soon the Japanese were doing it better than anyone in the West. It was described as a "communications revolution" because the microcomputer could store, process, and transmit data at speeds and reliability so far outdistancing previous modes as to constitute a multiple quantum leap.

This new technology accommodated itself to a market economy. Production was decentralized and diversified. It rested on brains, on ideas, more than on mighty infusions of capital. A clever electronics engineer with a bright

[1] We have mentioned Turing's pioneer computer developed at Bletchley Park in England during the war (1944–1945). But the German John von Neumann's first work was in 1943. There was a long prehistory of calculating machines, dating back to Pascal in the seventeenth century, and Babbage in the nineteenth. Maurice Wilkes (see his *Memoirs of a Computer Pioneer,* 1986), who had worked with radar during the war, built a computer in 1947–1949 at the Cambridge Mathematical Laboratory. Others appeared in 1949, including Eckert and Mauchly in Philadelphia, where Wilkes went for a time.

idea and a little venture capital might come up with a successful product almost overnight. "Consumerism" meant a huge expansion of all kinds of sales outlets, providing endless opportunities for small as well as large merchants. The growth of private income spawned financial services far beyond the old "bank."

The bureaucratic society required hordes of lawyers, administrative experts, other professional people. (To take off the fat their affluent consumerism produced, people went to diet centers and exercise classes and bought books and video recordings about food and diet.) This society with all its anomie and confusion engendered massive spiritual needs, as we know, so writers, teachers, preachers, prophets, and sages flourished, too. The communications and entertainment industries developed awesomely. All of this added up to something like a paradise of free enterprise, subject to violent economic oscillations.

Meanwhile, government bureaucracy and statism had overextended themselves, if not overstayed their time. Vast deficits were a drag on the economy, entailing either inflation, scarcity of capital, or high, disincentive taxation. Even the welfare state came in for criticism. The ghastly inefficiencies of public health service, especially in Italy, drove anyone who could afford it to private medical care; beset by dirt and corruption, at enormous expense it failed to meet human needs.

The Keynesian program of stimulating the economy by government spending now failed to work. The state sector had grown too large, the debt too great; deficit budgets now produced inflation and currency deterioration without much gain in employment. It was like a stimulant to which the body grows ever more immune, so that ever larger doses have to be administered, until in the end they threaten the patient's life. And, according to some economists (there was a vigorous revival of modified neoclassicism) Keynes's basic analysis had been wrong. Keynes had denied that the economy tends under free-market conditions automatically to adjust itself, and he alleged that aggregate demand might be insufficient to secure full employment and use of resources. This was only true if impediments to the movement of prices existed, in the form of trade unions or monopolies.

The transition to a new kind of economy accompanied a crisis in older industries on which millions had depended—in general, the classic smokestack and assembly-line factories of the older industrial revolution, such as steel, textiles, and shipbuilding. The Rhineland, starved for labor two decades earlier, saw unemployment rates as high as 13 percent in the 1980s. Competition from newer, more efficient producers in Asia—from formerly despised places like Korea, Malaya, Hong Kong—forced Europe's manufacturers to slash costs or go bankrupt. Under such conditions, the trade unions found it difficult to defend existing wages much less improve them. There was certainly no disposition to cast aside the state's welfare funds in dealing with this situation. Generous unemployment benefits and incentives to early retirement helped cushion the shock; immigrant workers were encouraged to go back home, however. But the carrot-and-stick incentives of classical economics now seemed to work best in the adjustment to a new economic order. If "austerity" programs brought un-employment rates like those not seen since the 1930s, the price had to be paid.

The surge toward free enterprise profited from the evident failure of the socialist principle, in the Soviet Union as well as elsewhere. "Socialism," Leszek Kolakowski wrote, if defined as the abolition of private ownership and elimination of the market, "has invariably resulted in abysmal failures . . . and has brought about political tyranny, economic inefficiency and stagnation, poverty and cultural disasters." Attempts to reform it, he added, insofar as they are effective, involve at least partial restoration of the market, that is, of "capi-talism." Suddenly, after decades of disgrace, capitalism was not a nasty word. Adam Smith made a spectacular comeback; his free-enterprise followers, liter-ally driven from the universities in the 1930s and 1940s, now won Nobel prizes (Von Hayek, 1975). Competition is the best way to assure that the consumer gets what he wants at the cheapest price. Efficiency is a result of the free market. Sta-tism equals bureaucratic stagnation and corruption, not equal shares and fair play, much less maximum production; it also entails high taxation.

Policies of privatization, in which governments sold back formerly na-tionalized enterprises to the people, were popular with almost everybody ex-cept the bureaucrats. Led by Mitterand, the French privatized extensively and enthusiastically after mid-decade, even outdoing Mrs. Thatcher. Privatization was the fashion everywhere, not just in Europe but in Africa, South America, Asia. Developing as well as developed countries went in for it. (World Bank case studies included volumes on Chile, Togo, Canada, Sri Lanka, Malaysia, Italy, Spain.) The cause was the need for reducing government budget deficits and se-curing greater efficiency, if less compassion, in all kinds of services. There were various methods: Privatization could take the form of public or private offering of shares; employee or management buyout; sale of assets. The French pre-ferred to sell to big investors, the British to small ones at virtually give-away prices. The Italians sold off huge state monopolies to huge private semimonop-olies, apparently making little difference. They all had in common an urge to take costly and inefficient operations out of the hands of the public bureaucracy and thrust them into the invigorating waters of market competition. Prisons and schools, health services, maybe even the police, certainly the post offices, were targets for "divestment." It might be called the idea of the 1980s.

POLITICS ON THE CONTINENT

The countries of western Europe on the Continent showed a drift to the right ac-companying some disenchantment with statism and a new respect for free en-terprise. In 1980, workers at Fiat, the largest company in Italy, marched in protest against union policies of strikes and class conflict, a landmark in Italian industrial history that led to an era of modernization and efficiency for Italian manufacturing. The murder of one-time prime minister Aldo Moro by terrorists in 1979 shocked Italian opinion and marked the end of an era; Italian terrorism, so prominent in the 1970s, subsided. Privatization was a trend in Italy, too, although in 1990 an Italian economic leader, noting slow progress in divesting the vast and inefficient public sector, said gloomily that East Germany would privatize before Italy did! A huge government deficit, as in the United States, did not much impede economic well-being. Italy moved even with the struggling British in the indices of economic health. As in Britain, a north-south gap remained; despite a huge migration from south to north there was up to 20 percent unemployment in the south (virtually none in the north). The decline of Italy's once successful Communist Party was a sign of the times. Western Europe's most adaptable and least Sovietized CP had moved up sharply in the 1976 elections, when it won about a third of the popular vote. It declined in 1979 and continued to slip back, to under 27 percent in 1987; and in 1988 municipal elections, to 21.9 percent. After 1988, the new party leader, Achille Occhetto, sought to lead the PCI away from "communism" altogether to join social democracy, strengthening ties to Europe's socialist parties and finally dropping the name "communist" altogether—as it had already dropped "Marxist." It joined the Socialist group in the European Parliament at Strasbourg, and Occhetto avoided meeting other communist leaders including France's Marchais.

As in France, the decline of the communists favored the Socialist party, which now held the balance of power; its Leader, Bettino Craxi, became prime minister in alliance with Christian Democrats, still the largest party but by no means a majority and tending moreover to factionalism. In all this, one might see reflected the changing occupational pattern, away from industrial manufacturing of the traditional kind, as well as the retreat from state ownership in the face of its often appalling inefficiencies.

France was an exception to the rightward shift that almost proved the rule; for in 1981 France elected a Socialist as president, but his policies proved conservative. Through the 1970s, the French right had prevailed, though split now into two parties, the more conservative Rally for the Republic (RPR) and the French Democratic Union (UDF). To the latter belonged Valéry Giscard d'Estaing, who won the presidential election of 1974; seven years later, after a brilliant few years, this glamorous personality had fallen under a cloud of scandal marked chiefly by the bizarre episode of his accepting extravagant gifts from the corrupt and cruel dictator of Central Africa, the "emperor" Bokassa. In 1981, the Socialist François Mitterrand defeated Giscard by 3.5 percent; new elections to the National Assembly produced a strong showing for Mitterrand's party, now much larger on the Left than the Communists. In compensation for the Communists' rather grudging support in the presidential race, Mitterrand awarded them four cabinet seats, but the mandate was his own, and he proceeded to use it by embarking on a bold program of wage increases, nationalization, and, to pay for this, higher taxes on the rich plus deficit budgets.

But he soon was forced to beat a dismayed retreat. Inflation and trade deficits with consequent pressure on the franc—which began to sink almost out of sight—were not even given the compensation of any great reduction in unemployment. Mitterand showed courage in reversing himself completely to install an austerity program with reduced government spending and tax cuts, at the cost of much unpopularity. The Communists withdrew from the coalition. Elections to the European Parliament in 1984 saw sharp Socialist losses, and in 1986, elections to the Assembly resulted in a situation often feared, under the Fifth Republic's rules, but never previously encountered: A president of the Left confronted an Assembly controlled by the Right. Mitterand appointed Jacques Chirac, strongest personality of the Right parties, to the office of prime minister. France would have to experiment in government by "cohabitation" of opposing parties, an experiment likely to produce—most thought—weak leadership.

Reelected president in 1988 over Chirac by a margin of 54 to 46 percent and pulling his party with him in the ensuing parliamentary elections, Mitterand was able to end the uncomfortable "cohabitation" period by installing a (moderately) Socialist prime minister. The decline of the Communists continued, to under 10 percent of the vote; some of their erstwhile supporters defected to an ultra-right National Front party whose chief complaint was about Arab immigrants, while their dwindling strength was soon divided between Old Guard stalwarts and those who supported Gorbachev's reforms in the Soviet Union. French socialists, like the British Labourites, appeared to give up on nationalization, accepting "the market economy but with counterweights," and calling rather confusedly for "neither nationalization nor privatization." (British Labour offered "Business where appropriate, government where necessary.")

The conversion even of socialists to capitalism, if by that much-abused term was meant reliance on the competition of private enterprises in a more or less free market as the basic principle of the economic order, could be seen also in Spain. The Spanish Socialist party, led by the personable Felipe Gonzalez Marquez who won reelection in June 1986 and to a third term in October 1989, promoted fiscal restraint to encourage private investment. Now a member of the European Community, Spain boomed with economic growth in the 1980s. Gonzales was the Thatcher of Spain, winning, like her, mostly as a result of the hopeless confusion of his opponents and presiding over a market-oriented economic policy, despite his nominal socialism (and a high unemployment rate).

In Austria, the left-wing chancellor, Bruno Kreisky, left office in 1983, and the little republic gravitated toward the right in the next few years. In the Dutch elections of May 1986, the Christian Democrats increased their majority over Labour as the Communists disappeared from parliament altogether.

Greece, which had swung wildly from left to right and back again ever since the end of the war, having overthrown the government of a military junta and ended the monarchy in 1974, voted in a government of the anti-American Socialist Andreas Papandreou in 1981; he dismissed the veteran centrist Konstantinos Karamanlis in 1985 but in 1989 serious troubles stemming from corruption and economic difficulties compelled the resignation of Papandreou and signaled a turn away from his socialist policies, though Papandreou was to return to office in the 1990s. Greece became a member of the European Community common market.

Even Sweden wavered in its almost institutionalized commitment to the Social Democrats, who as in France, faced with mounting budget and trade deficits, high interest rates, and rising inflation, reversed themselves to work for restraint on government spending. The Social Democrats, who had presided over Sweden's famed "middle way" for several decades before losing narrowly in 1976 to a nonsocialist coalition, returned to power in 1982 and held on in 1985 though now forced to rely on support from the small Communist Party. They won another close victory in 1988, with the environmentalist Green party now holding the balance of power. Deterioration of state-run medical services was an issue in the 1988 election. So was the status of funds transferred from corporate profits and used to buy up industry via the trade unions. The opposition to the SDs however was divided into three parties by no means always agreeing with each other, and, as in the United States, the conservatives when in office had by no means been able to control those deficits any better. In 1988, the percentage of those voting was the lowest since 1964.

In 1988, the Greens for the first time gained enough votes (over 5 percent) to be entitled to representation in the legislature. Strongest in West Germany, the Greens were gaining all over Europe in the 1980s. Their support often came from the far Left, now searching for a new home, but in Sweden at least it seemed to be drawn more from the nonsocialist moderates and liberals. Once dismissed as impossibly archaic in their desire to halt industrial development and urban growth, the environmentalists gained credibility by the obvious urgency of the issues they addressed. The hole in the ozone, the alleged "greenhouse effect" stemming from increasing quantities of carbon dioxide in the atmosphere, concern about nuclear power dangers, which the Soviet disaster at Chernobyl in May of 1986 underscored—such questions attracted far more attention in the 1980s.

The Green viewpoint embraced more than a simple concern about the environmental effects of industrial pollution. It reflected a philosophical rejection of the entire urban-consumerist-production ethos, often confusedly but with a moral earnestness that impressed a generation searching for some new political principles. Hostility to advanced technology, especially nuclear power, rubbed shoulders with feminism, anarchism, and pacifism in a new kind of New Left, hardly coherent but highly significant for the discontents of modernism. The Greens were often unrealistic in their positive policies and were highly fragmented, embracing a vast spectrum of discontents and obsessions. One contradiction was that finding non-nuclear sources of electric power entailed burning more coal, a prime source of the carbon dioxide that threatened global warming. The Greens' increasing numbers nevertheless said something about the state of European politics toward the end of the twentieth century.

In the Federal Republic of Germany, the presence of a minority of embattled Greens, the most numerous and vociferous ones in Europe, did not prevent a rightward trend among the majority. The Social Democrats (SPD), who had held office throughout the 1970s, lost to the Christian Democrats, who held onto a slight lead through the 1980s. In the city of Berlin (West), traditionally a socialist center, the Christian Democrats won by 48 percent to 38 percent in 1981; four years later the SPD fell even lower, as the anti-Establishment Alternative List mostly made up of Greens won over 10 percent of the vote. Observers in the 1980s found a conservative trend among young Germans, as elsewhere in the West. A new generation was reacting against its own sixty-ish parents. Unbearded, success-oriented, nonradical, their hero was not Rudi Dutschke but Boris Becker. The world-changers had disappointed them and in an increasingly affluent society they were prepared to settle for their BMWs, VCRs, and vacations on the Riviera. (In Great Britain, a 1986 survey found that no fewer than 16 million Britons took a holiday abroad.)

The vast majority of European workers were entitled to four weeks or more of paid holiday. In 1986, there were nearly 500 automobiles per 1,000 people in West Germany, around 400 in Britain. One of the chief reasons for the downfall of the East European economy was its failure to produce an acceptable automobile for the mass market, despite an attempt in East Germany that flopped badly. Increasing numbers owned not only autos, TVs, VCRs, but home computers. Those who preferred not to compete in this "yuppie" culture might spend their welfare checks on cocaine.

Increasingly, the great issue in Germany became reunification. This was connected with the sensational changes in the Soviet Union of the late 1980s, and will be described in connection with that stunning development, in the next section.

Western Europe's economic strength expressed itself in a change from economic dependence on the United States to a position of equality or better. In 1967, Jacques Servan-Schreiber's widely read book *Le défi américain* had gloomily forecast the Americanization of France and Europe. Twenty years later, Americans were worried about European capitalists joining the Japanese and Arab oil tycoons in buying up the United States. Most of western Europe had caught up with the United States in per capita income and production; according to World Bank statistics, at least one, Switzerland, had forged well ahead of her. Probably this was true also of the Scandinavian countries, with Germany not far behind.

THE SOVIET UNION IN TRANSITION

Leonid Brezhnev died in 1982, remarkably unlamented by the country he had led for some fifteen years. (A member of his family was subsequently to be arrested and charged with theft.) There were by now unmistakable signs of an impending crisis in the affairs of the vast Union of Soviet Socialist Republics. The crisis was basically an economic one, reaching from this into the moral and political realms. The economic system had proved incapable of meeting the needs of the masses in a consumerist age and seemed to be unreformable. The once-shining vision of a far better life for the toiling masses under socialism-communism had failed to materialize. In a 1979 article titled "The New Soviet Man Turns Pessimist," Sovietologist John Bushnell cited 1976 as the year when hope was abandoned. A popular rock music song (to which genre the Kremlin had finally had to surrender) summed it up: "I don't believe in promises any more." For its failure to live up to its promises, the regime had always before had some sort of excuse: the War, the Cold War. It had kept hope alive by some successes, such as putting the first man in space. Now at last it had run out of alibis.

Yet the abrupt collapse of the Soviet order in 1987–1990 surprised the Sovietologists as much as it did the less expert. Not until about 1983 did most of them begin to predict a serious crisis. They had increasingly noted disturbing areas of weakness; yet most of them also discerned progress. The courageous dissidents–Solzhenitsyn, Sakharov, and others–had apparently failed to shake the stability of the Soviet regime. Most of them had migrated; some had died; Sakharov was under house arrest. Students of the USSR found little worker discontent. In the Brezhnev era for all its cynicism there appeared to be normalization, with the rudiments of a stable civic culture emerging.

Good or bad, the system seemed to have dug in roots. In February 1985, the *Economist* predicted that "Even under new management, the rigid girders of central planning would remain. Even were a new Russian leader prepared to think more radical thoughts about reform, the system that made him would cut him to size again." He would be opposed at every step by a deeply entrenched privileged elite with vested interests in the status quo. Then, suddenly, it all crumbled, like a giant finally worn out by upholding such a heavy load.

Some credit for the startling downfall must be granted to the dynamic nature of capitalism in the 1980s. Marked by a resurgence of economic liberalism, stressing efficiency via competition and featuring a more popular capitalism, the economies of western Europe, the United States, and parts of Asia (the incredible Japanese being joined by Hong Kong, Singapore, South Korea) rebounded from a gloomy situation at the start of the decade–high unemployment with inflation, massive government deficits–to achieve considerable success. Especially did they produce a swarm of new products, fascinating to the man in the street; perhaps it was the electronics revolution that did in the communists. Innovation had long been their Achilles' heel; now, in a period dominated by rapid and sweeping technological change, it proved to be fatal.

The very progress the Soviets had made afforded information to the people about their failings. There were primitive TVs in most Russian households. Hundreds of thousands of soldiers had been stationed in eastern Europe where censorship was less severe. Post-Stalin Russia had gradually relaxed the use of terror. One could no longer conceal the fact that Communist-zone consumer products were far inferior, as well as scarce. The East German automobile became a joke.

Scarcity of goods and decline of morale in the Brezhnev era led to terrible corruption, which it was no longer possible to conceal. Scandals about the *nomenklatura* (the privileged class) surfaced; there was a celebrated exposé in 1976. Perhaps that was why that was the year of final disenchantment. A privileged class existed in the supposed classless society! Privilege was based on the shortage economy: Officials used their position to gain priority access to scarce goods. By a fine irony it was communism, not capitalism, that had produced an egregious class society and was "a fetter on production." Economic inadequacies, political corruption, inequalities of wealth, and privilege were far from unknown elsewhere; they might indeed be said to be of the nature of "capitalism." But in capitalist societies, they coexisted with much personal freedom and might be regarded as the price one had to pay for that freedom. No such freedom existed in the USSR. Stalin's system of one-party dictatorship, secret police power, censorship, and denial of elementary civil liberties might have eroded somewhat, but it still existed. This price was one that supposedly had to be paid for a promised rainbow of wealth and well-being at the end of the storm. When this failed to appear, the oppressive regime became merely disgusting. Political serfdom had led not to material abundance but the opposite; one had slavery *and* poverty.

The economic system of centralized planned allocation of goods, conceived as a substitute for the capitalist order of private property and market competition, had failed. Quite early, capitalist economists had claimed that the planned economy must be inefficient and irrational. A planned economic system has no way to determine real costs of production. The attempt to decide on prices by administrative fiat—the arbitrary decisions of a bureaucracy—can only lead to confusion and breakdown. Likewise, there was a fatal flaw in divorcing managerial performance and managerial reward: The stimulus of the profit system was lost. The Soviet system never worked as well as it claimed. Much of the whole sinister program of terror, propaganda, and isolation from the outer world was forced by the need to conceal this scandal.

Insofar as the system did work, it was not "socialist." Quietly retained was almost as much capitalism as socialism. Apart from the fact that Stalin had abandoned wage equality, so that, for example, factory managers were paid far more than workers, private selling in the market always supplemented the socialist side, and some observers estimated this "second economy" as high as 40 percent of the total. In brief, the system was not socialist, or not entirely so, and insofar as it was, it was a failure. Attempts at reforming it, half-hearted at best, had not succeeded in remedying the flaws.

A new generation of East European economists believed that these flaws, including low worker output, general productive inefficiency, and above all the critical failure to innovate, could only be cured by ending the direct central planning system and going to a market economy; or at the very least, to a "market socialism" with considerable decentralization of planning; preferably, the restoration of private property in the means of production, with prices determined by supply and demand, a real labor market, allowing inefficient firms to go bankrupt, even privatization of some enterprises. In 1986–1987, most Soviet economists became convinced that radical marketization provided the only solution; a total system change rather than just infusions or additions was required. As Mikhail Gorbachev reported, "the rates of economic production had fallen so low as virtually to mean stagnation." Natural resources were being exhausted, plant and machinery were becoming obsolete.

Democratization of party and government and greater freedom of expression were demands that flooded in as the morale of the elite party crumbled. In 1961, during Khrushchev's era, a Russian general named Grigorenko, who had served gallantly in World War II and had been a fervent Stalinist, spoke out in favor of democratizing Soviet elections. He was judged insane and committed to a mental institution where he suffered barbarous treatment, along with others incarcerated for their political beliefs. That he was released after four years and lived to write his memoirs (published in English translation in 1983) indicates some improvement over the preceding era; it was typical of the "hesitant repression" of the Brezhnev years. Each year now saw the dikes of censorship spring more leaks. From about 1987 on this became a flood. Novels dealt openly with Stalin's crimes. Many of these books, including Dudinstev's *White Clothes,* had been written earlier but kept from publication. This pent-up store of books now gushed forth. The will to suppress them had withered away. Perhaps, given modern communication technology, the ability to do so no longer existed.

Mikhail Gorbachev committed himself fully to reform and staked his position on it; he used his attractive personality to mobilize public opinion against the entrenched interests of party bureaucracy. Gorbachev assumed the top office of Party general secretary in March 1985 following two short-lived successors of Brezhnev. Yuri Andropov, who showed some impulses toward reform, and who indeed might claim to be Gorbachev's teacher, suffered from ill health during his entire fifteen months of power, and his successor, Konstantin Chernenko, a reversion to an old line politician, lasted no longer. Gorbachev, a shrewd and practical politician, enlisted support from elements of the Party's middle ranks as well as from the general public, using the new power of the media.

After seven decades of rule by the most formidable agency of minority rule yet devised, the Soviet Union seemed finally to break through toward democracy in the late 1980s. Political opposition became possible. In March 1989, voters were allowed to have a choice of candidates, not just the Communist Party candidate as always before. The law making it a crime to criticize the regime was repealed. In July 1990, Gorbachev officially rescinded the Communist Party's monopoly on access to television and radio, something that in fact had long since gone by the boards. The resignation of popular politician Boris Yeltsin from the Communist Party marked the emergence of a real opposition. Free, open, and often stormy debates now took place in places formerly confined to rubber-stamping Politburo decisions: in the Supreme Soviet, and at the Party Congress of 1990.

Whether this would lead to a full parliamentary multiparty political order was uncertain, but reversion to repressive Stalinist methods was even more unlikely. Gorbachev won a five-year term as president, from a popularly elected Congress of People's Deputies, to be elected by direct popular vote after this every five years. He withstood criticism from both Right and Left at the 1990 Party Congress. He found himself under attack both from those who saw him as too heavily compromised by his party standing and from the Old Guard who yearned for the days when firing squad or prison camp was a remedy for all problems.

Defending himself on June 19, 1990, before the new-found Soviet democracy, Gorbachev boasted of the revolution his leadership had wrought in the largest country in the world: "A profound change accomplished in a huge country during some 1,500 days that is comparable to the greatest and most revolutionary events in world history." The question was whether Gorbachev could survive to finish it.

The difficulty lay in the fact that substituting a market economy for a planned one was likely to make things worse before they (presumably) got better. The old system had in some ways worked. It worked at a low and stagnant level, not, as theory supposed, by outproducing capitalism, but by providing a bare minimum for everyone while not asking too much in the way of hard work. The system epitomized the qualities of a state bureaucracy: No one got fired, firms never went bankrupt, production quotas were low. "Soft budget constraints" and lax management standards in the Brezhnev era represented a reaction against the rigors of Stalinism when the sanctions might well be the firing squad or prison camp. If this genial system, made bearable by plentiful injections of vodka, were suddenly ended many workers might lose their jobs, and many firms would go under. In the short run, inflation as well as unemployment were the results of perestroika, since pent-up demand for goods broke out. Yet nothing less than complete restructuring would suffice to break the vicious circle of backwardness. Here was the dilemma. Meanwhile, the almost total thawing of the great iceberg brought a rush of freedoms including much local autonomy: The city of Moscow went its own way toward a market economy; the Russian Soviet Republic, followed by the Ukrainian Republic, declared that its laws took precedence over those of the Soviet Union.

On September 24, 1990, the Supreme Soviet voted overwhelmingly to go to a free market system, granting President Gorbachev broad powers for an eighteen-month period to carry out the reforms. Many details remained undecided. To pass from communism to capitalism in a few months would be startlingly perilous. No adequate banking and financial system existed in the

USSR, nor was there any experience with a market economy. The temporary result was a fall in production and hyperinflation. Would private production of goods and services respond rapidly enough to the stimulus offered by the reforms? Massive Western aid would be necessary, and it was questionable whether enough was available. Meanwhile, the constituent units of the Soviet Republic continued to declare their autonomy, thus threatening a dissolution of the union.

EASTERN EUROPE IN THE GORBACHEV ERA

In some ways the impulse to *glasnost* (openness, exposure to public opinion) and *perestroika* (rebuilding, restructuring), the words that became symbols of the revolution against communism in Russia, had come originally from the smaller countries of eastern Europe, which had always been reluctant members of the Communist bloc. Hungary early took the lead in producing ideas of a reformed socialism, decentralized and marketized; quietly, under the table so to speak, the Hungarians had created a capitalistic secret economy.

Inspired by its Solidarity movement and its Polish pope, Poland was out of control from the early 1980s on. Under conditions of extreme repression, Czechoslovakia's Vaclav Havel dared to express his utter contempt for a system that was a living lie. After 1986, these peoples took advantage of the new situation in the USSR to escape from communism as they had sought in vain to do in 1956 and 1968. In the summer of 1988, there were smolderings throughout the Soviet bloc: A great strike in Gdansk renewed Solidarity's challenge to the ruling hierarchy in Poland; a huge crowd in Prague commemorated the 1968 movement on its twentieth anniversary; there were demonstrations in the Baltic region as Lithuanians, Latvians, and Estonians clamored for their independence. The quickening pace of reform in the Soviet Union then further emboldened the East European countries to rid themselves of their Communist rulers in a blaze of political action that left the world stunned.

In Hungary, plans for free elections went ahead in the summer of 1989, this time without fear of Russian tanks. On October 23, 1989, after forty-one years under communism, and exactly thirty-three years after the celebrated Budapest uprising, Hungary officially declared itself a democracy (the Republic of Hungary), as opposition parties were legalized, Hungarian flags waved again, and 1956 was officially declared a popular revolution rather than a counterrevolution. Elections on March 25, 1990, brought victory to parties advocating varying degrees of basic economic change toward a free market; despite changing its name from Communist to Socialist, the erstwhile ruling party placed a distant third. Hungary led this race of the Soviet bloc countries toward liberation, which soon became a headlong rush.

Hungary was followed closely by Poland, which might claim to have made the first crack in the Communist monolith with Solidarity's ability to survive as a free trade union movement. While reserving for itself control of the lower house, the Polish Communist Party agreed to permit free elections to an upper house of the Polish parliament, which on June 4, 1989, resulted in a stunning rebuke to the rulers, a landslide for Solidarity. Further elections in September resulted in a Solidarity government; Jaruzelski fell, and by the end of the year, following the lead of the Czechs and East Germans, the Polish parliament deprived the Communist party of its constitutional right to be the leading party. Within a month thereafter, the CP disbanded itself. After forty-four years in power, six months had sufficed to reduce it from omnipotence to nullity. In the presidential election of November 1990, the leading candidates were both from Solidarity.

Meanwhile, East Germany joined the parade of protest against communism. The fateful summer of 1989 began with thousands fleeing the DDR to Hungary whose newly liberalized government allowed them to use it as a corridor to West Germany. Mass rallies for democratic change broke out in Leipzig and Dresden, later in Berlin, as an opposition movement organized. Gorbachev himself visited the DDR, ostensibly for its fortieth anniversary celebration, actually to make clear his support for reform against the Old Guard leaders. Deserted by their master, the puppet rulers of the Eastern bloc were helpless. Hungary's Kadar was gone; Czechoslovakia cheered the fall of Husak and the return in triumph of the old 1968er, Alexander Dubcek, though the new leader was to be its national literary hero, Vaclav Havel. The DDR's Honecker now resigned in disgrace. The wall between East and West Berlin erected in 1961, symbol of the division of Europe, came down on November 9, 1989, amid scenes of indescribable exultation. The Wall's destruction led to a rapid collapse of the Communist Party. Subsequent elections brought victory for Western-style Christian Social and Social Democratic parties preparing the way for reunification with West Germany. June 22, 1990, saw final approval to the unification plan pass the Federal Republic's Bundestag. It had taken just a year to obliterate the forty-year-old division of Germany and Europe.

Amid diplomatic scurryings, West German Chancellor Helmut Kohl, suddenly a much more popular and dynamic figure, gained Gorbachev's approval of united Germany remaining in NATO, in exchange for loans to the beleaguered Soviet economy. East German elections in April 1990 having confirmed the demise of the old Communist leadership by bringing to power a coalition of Christian Democrats and Social Democrats, plans for economic reintegration went through quickly. On June 30, 1990, the two economies were merged as border controls vanished and East Germans prepared for the shock of sudden transformation from planned economy to market economy. Official reunification in October was followed by all-German elections in December.

Soviet Foreign Minister Eduard Shevardnadze declared "The Cold War is over. Our planet, the world, Europe are embarking on a new course." Of

Berlin Wall. This symbol of the Cold War division of Europe, erected in 1961, came down in 1989–1990. (*AP/Wide World Photos.*)

this new course, nothing was more central than the reunification of Germany. Questions about the role of the new Germany in the world remained to be answered. The economic difficulties of reunification would be enormous.

All this in most of the East European countries was accomplished peacefully, a revolution without bloodshed. Virtually the only casualties were the scraped fingers of eager souvenir hunters trying to acquire a piece of stone from the Wall. The Warsaw Pact proved ironically the best friend of reform; the satellite countries did not dispose of their own military power; Moscow's hand was on the trigger and Gorbachev refused to squeeze it in order to suppress the reformers. But one country was different. Romania had long since pulled out of the Warsaw Pact to go its own Communist way. Last to fall, and most bloodily, was the strange and ruinous dictatorship of the Romanian Communist tsar, Nicolas Ceaucescu, who had defied the USSR on foreign policy while maintaining a Stalin-like rule at home. His specially trained elite security forces fired on protesting crowds on December 17 in Timosoala, a city in western Romania. Amid growing outrage as news of the Timosoala massacre spread, Ceaucescu tried to organize a mass rally in support of his government. But the handpicked audience was joined by students and others who booed the chief when he began to harangue them with accounts of how hooligans and fascists—standard smear words from the ancient party vocabulary—had been put down. Ceaucescu seemed stunned and stopped his speech. Millions saw this on TV before coverage abruptly ended.

Further massive demonstrations led to another night of bloodshed all over the country including the capital, Bucharest. In this fighting the army joined Ceaucescu's enemies against the secret police. Ceaucescu fled, was captured, summarily tried by martial law, and executed. As the red star vanished from the Romanian flag, citizens celebrated the end of a hated regime while remnants of the *Securitate* desperately fought on. Perhaps 12,000 people altogether were killed during these ten days that shook the Communist world—a melodramatic finish to perhaps the least appetizing of all the East European regimes, widely reported on and televised throughout the world.

The by-now familiar tactic of abolishing the Communist party's legal claim to a monopoly of power took shape in Romania, then Bulgaria, finally in the Soviet Union itself in February–March 1990. The spring of 1990 saw elections in all the former "satellite" East European countries, everywhere discomfiting the old rulers but turning up a multiparty situation; as in all revolutions, the revolutionaries found it easier to tell what they were against than what they were for. Only in Bulgaria did the Communists, now disguised as Socialists, manage to win the election, but they confronted a formidable opposition Union of Democratic Forces. In these countries, as in Russia, the return of capitalism was not an unrequited blessing. At the cost of stagnation, the communist regimes had provided subsidies of basic commodities. Their termination raised the cost of living. Economic woes remained. Foreign debt, high inflation, archaic industrial plant and infrastructure guaranteed that in the aftermath of their liberation most of these peoples would find themselves caught in between two economic systems, facing the dilemma already alluded to: Complete change was necessary yet painful.

Rather overlooked amid all the commotion elsewhere in eastern Europe, Yugoslavia fell into severe crisis in the 1980s. Her economy also degenerated. Socialist self-management was no guarantee against the defects of planned economies. Yugoslavia, one might say, got the worst of both capitalist and socialist worlds—low productivity and unemployment to boot. And, following the death of Tito, the old nationalities' problem reemerged, threatening to pull the country apart, as each of the six constituent republics of the federation went its own way, even issuing separate currencies. Albanian rebellion, Serb chauvinist reaction, a Slovene-Serb trade war were some of the symptoms of the South Slav illness. As in the other countries, the Yugoslav Communist Party broke up, renouncing its monopoly of power; here, it was one of the last cements holding together the ill-knit union of six states, which began to come apart altogether. Slovenia and Croatia seceded in 1991. The next decade would bring fearful conflict.

Amid the chaos and uncertainty following on the liquidation of the entire post–World War II order, eastern and southeastern Europe looked westward for aid. Western Europe itself was undergoing change. It was engaged in liquidating its sovereign states for a union that might evolve from the economic to the political. Might the East European nations somehow join this to create a united Europe?

THE EUROPEAN COMMUNITY

Through numerous vicissitudes of fortune the European Community (EC) went forward in the 1980s. It continued to grow in terms of member states. In 1981, Greece became the tenth member; five years later, after long negotiations, Spain and Portugal were admitted. The Scandinavian countries (Denmark was already in) were likely prospects in the near future. East Germany would become a member as a result of its union with the Federal Republic once reunification was completed. Austria applied. Would Hungary, Czechoslovakia, Poland follow? Gorbachev seemed at times to suggest even the USSR. Relations with the European Free Trade Area (EFTA) countries (Scandinavia, Switzerland, Austria) became so close that these nations were virtually de facto members of the EC. Meanwhile, the erstwhile communist regimes of eastern Europe looked to the European Community for aid and advice in their difficult conversion to a market economy.

All this happened while the EC was busy preparing for the target date of 1992, when full economic integration was scheduled for completion. In 1984, the European Parliament adopted a blueprint for the establishment of a European Union. Subsequently, the Single Europe Act defined this goal, and the Delors Committee (named after the energetic French Socialist president of the European Commission) pursued it. Heads of government pledged that by 1992 all barriers to "the free movement of goods, persons, services and capital" within the European Community would cease. By the end of 1992, all cross-border excise taxes would be abolished. Already (except for Great Britain) associated in a European monetary system that adjusted exchange rates, the EC expected to move toward a common currency in the near future, despite Mrs. Thatcher's opposition.

Other signs of progress included direct elections to the European Parliament at Strasbourg, the first of which was held in 1981. That body still had no substantial powers but was gaining prestige and experience. On the table was a proposal that the Parliament elect the European Commission's president, presently appointed by the Council of Ministers, whose members were appointed by the various member nations, each of whom in effect thus exercised a veto power.

The European Community's life was never easy. Acrimonious disputes had occurred: The British complained about footing an unfair amount of the funds that subsidized European farmers. Mrs. Thatcher's doubts about the wisdom of full integration rested on an ideological difference between her free-market credo and the greater socialism of the continental members: "We have not successfully rolled back the frontiers of the State in Britain, only to see them reimposed at a European level, with a European super-State exercising a new dominance in Brussels," the first lady of Europe had declared. The European Commission, with its 10,000 employees, was another layer of government on top of the others; it had to bear some of the brunt of the antibureaucracy rebellion. Facing the need to translate official documents into numerous languages, it was estimated in 1986 to use 1,000 tons of paper a year; how much energy and money was expended in running back and forth between the three hubs—Brussels, Luxemburg, and Strasbourg—was anyone's guess.

Nevertheless, there was much excitement preparing to create "by far the largest consumer market in the world." This was expected to increase Europe's rate of economic growth, strengthen her position in research, and establish her as a true rival of both the United States and Japan. Perhaps the final result would be a Europe totally integrated, politically as well as economically. Then again, perhaps not. Many thought that economic unity would inevitably entail political unity; the powers eventually vested in a European central bank would have to be made accountable to a European Parliament. (Not Mrs. Thatcher, to whom "true democratic accountability is through national parliaments.") Could the European Union really stay clear of foreign policy and military affairs, confining itself to the economic, technological, and cultural realms? The Community was a curiously headless superpower. It has no armed forces, no foreign-policy administration. The Persian Gulf crisis of 1990–1991 exposed the Community's foreign policy inadequacies.

Perhaps just because it is so nonpolitical, the EC might expand to include all of Europe. A superpower armed to the teeth trying to absorb still more territory might be feared. One that is armed only with programs for economic cooperation—perhaps not. More troubles, however, lay just ahead.

At any rate, in 1990, all the member nations except perhaps Great Britain seemed determined to drive on toward the goal of a single Europe. France's Mitterand had decided that since Europe held him in thrall he had better try to control it; France stood to gain from going all the way toward a full European Community. The French economy was inevitably part of the larger market. For his part, Chancellor Kohl was equally eager, partly because commitment to the EC made German unification more acceptable; West German Foreign Minister Genscher declared that a unified Germany must be part of a federal Europe. Mrs. Thatcher was depicted as trying to put brakes on a runaway carriage pulled by the continental powers. Her removal from the scene, it was thought, might advance the prospects of a stronger Community. Italy remained the most enthusiastic of all pro-Unionists; it was an Italian, the exuberant Altiero Spinelli, who had formulated the vision of a Single Europe.

INTERNATIONAL RELATIONS IN THE ERA OF PERESTROIKA

The European Community is not the only pathway to European unification or cooperation. The sudden demise of the Cold War, making both NATO and the Warsaw Pact suddenly obsolete, triggered a brief upsurge in the fortunes of the thirty-five-nation Conference on Security and Cooperation in Europe, which had long been in hibernation (it was an abortive project of the détente of the early 1970s). The USSR indicated preference for this organization, not tainted by the Cold War image of NATO, as the basis for European security. The USSR preferred to negotiate an end to both NATO and the Warsaw Pact: "dissolution of military political blocs in Europe." Some in the West, however, clung to hopes that an expanded NATO might evolve into something like the original utopian dream of collective security. In any case, NATO was not likely to be jettisoned soon; prudence suggested it would be wise to wait and see how durable and stable the new European order proved to be.

Yet the abrupt change in Soviet policy encouraged the world to think that its main security fears might be over. The USSR began to withdraw from Afghanistan in early 1989, and Foreign Minister Eduard Shevardnadze in a speech to the Supreme Soviet said that the invasion had been wrong. The USSR also underscored its respect for the freedom of East European countries by promising to withdraw its troops and liquidate its military bases stationed there and in other places abroad (including support for Cuban surrogates in Angola, who decamped in 1989). Soviet troops began leaving eastern Europe in the summer of 1991; the last of them left Berlin in June 1994, along with U.S., British, and French forces, thus ending the long saga of the divided city.

In early 1989, the Soviet government announced a substantial military cutback of troops, tanks, artillery, and military aircraft over the next two years. Part of the arms industry was to be retooled for civilian production. Gorbachev and his advisers made no secret of their view that the Soviet Union had paid far too high a price, which it could no longer afford, for its military standing as a superpower with parity to the United States. The Russian leader opened a new dialogue with the United States when he met President Ronald Reagan at Geneva in 1985. The negotiations continued and culminated in an agreement to reduce both nations' nuclear arsenals: Moscow and Washington promised to scrap their short- and medium-range missiles. Ground-launched cruise and Pershing II missiles, stationed in West Germany and capable of striking Soviet territory in retaliation for a Warsaw Pact ground attack, were to be dismantled in return for Soviet reduction of their conventional forces. American troops in Europe would also be reduced. The zero-zero principle, to abolish whole categories of tactical and intermediate nuclear weapons one by one, became a standard. A Bush-Gorbachev summit in the spring of 1990 continued the long and arduous process of arms reduction. There seemed no doubt it would be substantial, falling well short, however, of total nuclear disarmament. The immediate goal of U.S.–Soviet talks was a one-third reduction in long-range strategic missiles. On November 19, 1990, on the fifth anniversary of the first Reagan-Gorbachev summit, thirty-four nations from both western and eastern Europe signed a non-nuclear arms reduction treaty in Paris, agreeing to destroy more than 100,000 tanks, military vehicles, artillery, and combat aircraft.

Gorbachev spoke of the USSR joining "a common European house," of the world having a new security system. He called for "de-ideologization" of international relations. He backed up this rhetoric by substantially moderating Soviet policies all over the globe, often virtually repudiating long standing positions. This paved the way for possible settlements in Angola, Nicaragua, Cambodia; Americans and Russians began to work together in Afghanistan. In the Middle East, growing Soviet-Western collaboration was evident during the Persian Gulf crisis of later 1991 brought on by Iraq's invasion and conquest of Kuwait in August. In time, however, this abject retreat would breed a certain nationalist reaction in Russia, which increased as the USSR began to break up.

The Soviet Union's role in world affairs seemed certain to be a more modest one for many years to come; she would have to join that world rather than wage war on it in the name of an alternative society. For nearly half a century, the rivalry of Soviet and Western power and ideologies had dominated the international political scene. People had learned to live with this polarity; some had even found it not unsatisfactory. Now that it had ended, some difficulties vanished, but others arose. In any event, the landmark was memorable; an era had come to an end, another had begun.

DEVELOPING AND UNDEVELOPING NATIONS

Contributing to the Communist downfall in the Soviet Union had been a continuing loss of Soviet prestige in the developing nations. Originally, numbers of young states in Africa and Asia had been seduced by the vision of a planned path of industrial development, substituting for a capitalism that they associated with the European imperialism that they abhorred. Almost uniformly, this road had proven disastrous. "African leaders have adopted unrealistic goals," as A. R. Zolberg remarked in his 1966 study of political order in West Africa. They listened only to advisors who promised them a quick and easy path to affluent economies, but soon they suffered cruel disenchantment. Their glum rulers, once hopeful ideologues, now bewildered oppressors, might well have complained that they had been misled by Western intellectuals, who told them that socialism was the hope of mankind and the wave of the future—only now, when it was too late, admitting error. ("Sorry, a trifling mistake, we meant Adam Smith, not Karl Marx.") Now Third World countries began to switch, lining up for advice and loans from the International Monetary Fund, not the Communist International. India, a Soviet ally, found her economic interests better served by Western technology and chose the economic route of free enterprise on which other Asian countries had done so well—Singapore, South Korea, Hong Kong as well as the mighty Japanese.

The success stories were less numerous than the failures. In general, the gap between the high-income and the low-income economies widened: "The average per capita income of the industrial countries has grown from 20 times greater than that of the developing countries in the early 1960s to 40 times greater in the 1980s," according to the World Bank. The difference between the highest and lowest—for example, between the United States, Switzerland, Japan, as compared to Ethiopia, Zaire, Bangladesh—was more nearly sixty to seventy times.

But among the poorer countries of the world were also the vast Asian states of China and India, containing together nearly 40 percent of the world's 5 billion people. Retreating from Maoism after the Great Helmsman's death in 1976 (he was now said to have been hardly sane in his later years), China turned toward a program of economic liberalization in 1978 that included returning private property to the peasants and allowing them to sell on the market—the largest single reversion to "capitalism" of a communist country by far. But political liberalization lagged. The course Gorbachev had chosen, of democratizing first as a means to economic reform, the Chinese Politburo had chosen to reverse; economic reform decreed from above entailed no sort of plans for popular participation in government. In China no really organized counterparty existed. When students rallied in a protest demonstration at Beijing in 1988, the Communist Party reacted with ferocious repression that caused massively hostile reactions throughout the world, capitalist and socialist alike. This ugly estrangement from its own people as well as from much of the outer world on the part of the aging Chinese Communist leadership (something repeated on a smaller scale in Burma) cast a dark shadow over the generally sunny year of Soviet-Western reconciliation.

Vietnam, too, remained committed to the iron rule of a dictatorial elite, even if prepared to echo Soviet reformism in some slight measure. North Korea, said to be building a nuclear bomb, remained defiantly hostile. Despite an end to the war (though not a formal peace) between Iraq and Iran, the Middle East with its unresolved Arab-Israeli conflict was not much less turbulent. Throughout the Islamic world, the rise of a fanatical religious fundamentalism—varying somewhat in details from country to country but widespread from Iran to Algeria–threatened to bring civil war within Islamic societies between modernizers and antimodernizers, rich and poor. Religious conflict was also a serious problem in India and Pakistan, still quarreling over Kashmir. There was longstanding civil war in such a once peaceful spot as Sri Lanka. Africa remained a scandal: civil war, or a state of anarchy, prevailed in large portions of it. The subtitle of a book about the Sudan between 1950 and 1985, *Death of a Dream,* might almost stand for Africa as a whole. The economic problems of the "less developed countries," involving enormous debts, created headaches for the developed ones.

The spread of nuclear weapons and other modern means of dealing death, via biological or chemical warfare, made for unease. The twenty-year-old antiproliferation treaty was hardly effective, and there was opposition to its renewal from the nuclear have-nots, who wondered why only an exclusive few had the right to nuclear arms. Israel, nominally not a nuclear power, actually was known to have nuclear weapons. Iran was headed toward it. The United States protested Russians selling nuclear components to Iran. She kept an anxious watch on Iraq and North Korea, two hostile states hopeful of sneaking in a nuclear capability. India was thought to have the bomb, so Pakistan was straining to get one too. What would the situation be in another twenty years if dozens of nations were making nuclear bombs, in a world torn by hatreds?

Regions such as Cambodia and Afghanistan were sown with land mines, likely to take a human toll for years to come. Miniaturization was applied to nuclear weapons as well as computers; they became smaller and more sophisticated, so that the spectacle of some terrorist carrying the end of the world around in his (or her) briefcase looked to be in view. (A terrorist bomb planted aboard a Pan-Am jetliner exploded over Lockerbie, Scotland, in December 1988 with the loss of 270 lives.)

Adding to the feeling that a fatal curse might lie over late modern man was the AIDS epidemic. This new disease of the 1980s (acronym for acquired immune deficiency syndrome) was described as "the most frightening disease of this century" and was even nominated to take rank with the great scourges and plagues of all time. The appearance of AIDS cases in significant numbers in the West dates precisely from 1980 or possibly a year earlier. By 1981, the apparently new infection had been given a name. Under another name, AIDS was rife in Central Africa as early as 1970, and indeed retrospective diagnosis has located some cases possibly in the 1930s. But for most of the world, the disease seemed to swoop down suddenly like a modern plague. Within a few years, it was the center of a swirl of controversy about its origin, causes, significance, treatment, and especially about its potential to decimate the human race. The cause of AIDS was determined to be a virus, transmitted chiefly by sexual contact, which attacks the body's immune system. Throughout the 1980s it was both incurable and unstoppable; an antidote against the HIV virus was not in sight. Within a few years, the disease had spread outside its apparent original clientele of homosexual men and intravenous drug users to attack increasing numbers of others—women, children, heterosexuals. In parts of eastern and central Africa, where AIDS perhaps originated, it had killed as many as 5 percent of the population—the most vigorous and productive segment—virtually disabling a country like Uganda. In the 1990s, the epidemic spread most alarmingly into southeast Asia, especially afflicting Thailand; this seemed to be the next danger zone of a plague that showed no sign of relenting. AIDS was thought likely to continue its steady increase. In 1987, the British government spent $33 million on an AIDS advertising campaign, which evidently had little effect on sexual behavior. In 1990, the number of deaths from AIDS in France exceeded the number from motor car accidents—far less than the 11,000 who had died from the disease in New York City but still an alarming rate of increase. The number of AIDS cases in Europe was estimated at about 20,000 in 1988, up from a few hundred in 1984—doubling every nine months or so. At the end of the decade, there seemed little prospect of stopping the progress of a deadly contagion which, some doomsayers thought, might be tied to growing sexual promiscuity.

14

The Twentieth Century Winds Down; Europe and the World in the 1990s

THE TRAVAIL OF THE SOVIETS

Along with an economic recession in western Europe described as the worst since World War II, the continuing crisis of the erstwhile Union of Soviet Socialist Republics dominated the early 1990s. Momentarily, it became a Union of *Sovereign* Socialist Republics, then a Commonwealth of Independent States before seeming to vanish altogether, replaced by Russia, a shadowy Russian Confederation, and a dozen independent states.

Behind the dissolution lay, of course, the collapse of the centralized state-planned economy. In July 1991, the Communist Party Central Committee in Moscow listened to Mikhail Gorbachev recommend installing a market economy, privatization, and democratic freedoms. "The model that has been imposed on the party and society for decades has suffered a strategic defeat," the Party leader told his cohorts. "We have to face the necessity for a drastic change of our entire viewpoint on socialism. We will not find an answer in the framework of the old model." Meanwhile, Boris Yeltsin as president of Russia banned Communist Party cells in workplaces. The new constitution had just provided for decentralization of power.

This triggered a last desperate revolt by the old guard. An attempted coup by Communist hardliners on August 19–22 failed; encountering resistance from masses of people in Moscow and Leningrad, the plotters quarreled among themselves, backed down, and in the end lacked the will and the skill to take over all the centers of resistance. After detaining Gorbachev as a prisoner in the Crimea, they let him return to Moscow in triumph. But he was embarrassed by the fact that the leaders of the coup were men he had appointed, including the Defense minister and the KGB chief. Yeltsin emerged as the hero. Gorbachev resigned as General Secretary, and resistance to full liberalization of the USSR crumbled, at least for the moment. A remarkable surge of opinion against the Party caused the *New York Times* to headline "End of Communism's 74-Year Reign."

A few days later (September 4, 1991), the USSR itself was declared dissolved. While the three Baltic states were conceded outright independence, eight of the twelve former republics of the union, including the Ukraine, White Russia, and the Central Asian lands, formed a Commonwealth of Independent States, delegating only certain powers to central coordinating bodies. But a plebiscite in Ukraine voted overwhelmingly for independence. Georgia, Armenia, Azerbaijan, Moldavia also opted for their freedom. The hammer and sickle flag came down from the Kremlin on January 1, 1992, thus officially ending the great socialist experiment of Lenin and Stalin, born three quarters of a century before.

To the question, whether the former Soviet Union could change from one economic system to another without chaos and intense suffering, was thus added the question of whether it could avoid the ethnic violence that accompanied dissolution. In Georgia, Armenia and Azerbaijan, as well as Tajikistan, conflicts would soon break out over ethnic boundaries. A struggle for power and property after the resounding collapse of Soviet Communism was everywhere in evidence.

Boris Yeltsin replaced Mikhail Gorbachev as head of Russia. Gorbachev represented a position halfway between the old and the new which proved to be untenable. No one doubted his courage and his decency; he was the real hero of the revolution against the Stalin system, but he was not the person to carry it through. The man who had presided over the first phase of the liquidation of the communist state was basically not an anticommunist, or at any rate he was a hesitant one; he did not wish to embrace "bourgeois democracy" and give up the privileged position of the Communist Party along with its elite rule ("democratic centralism"). He appealed to Lenin (the Lenin of the NEP) against Stalin, and preferred "market socialism" to privatization. He was doubtful about the separatist claims of the various ethnic minorities. He had wished reform of the system but not, until he was driven to it, its abandonment. The next man of the hour was Yeltsin, who as head of the Russian republic became the leading force in a drastic restructuring.

It was a terribly difficult task to convert the entire economic and political system in the erstwhile Soviet Union. In 1992, the collective farms still existed, a large majority of industry was still state-owned, a large bureaucracy was involved in the now-discredited central planning process. This represented a tremendous vested interest. Curbing deficits, to bring down inflation, involved ending subsidies to inefficient state-owned industries, sometimes at the cost of laying off their workers. Yeltsin had to make such concessions to the old guard that at times it looked like the entire reform drive might be derailed. He issued decrees by the score, dissolving state monopolies and collective farms, privatizing, establishing a free market, but in many areas these were simply ignored; he had neither the funds nor the cadres to make them a reality. Dissolution of the old party-led unitary state left vacuums of power, filled in various ways, often with the old rulers under a new name. Many a Communist functionary emerged with his old powers but a new title.

Yet there was no alternative except to press forward. In 1993–1994, the progress of reform notably increased despite all kinds of headaches, crises, and obstacles. A parliament filled with representatives of the old guard almost impeached Yeltsin; but elections in the spring of 1993 gave him a victory, with a new constitution to be drawn up. He appealed to the people in a referendum and won a vote of confidence. The major world economic powers met in July 1991 to consider what aid they could give the struggling behemoth; in 1993, the International Monetary Fund and a summit conference of the rich nations did approve several billion dollars of loans. All kinds of overseas investors had a potential interest in Soviet economic development, or in tapping into a new consumers' market.

But political turmoil in Moscow in the summer of 1993 brought foreign investment to a temporary halt. In July, the great Paris newspaper *Le Monde* headlined "Russia in Convulsion." In September, Yeltsin dissolved Parliament calling for new elections; the parliament (Duma) replied by declaring itself the legitimate government. Shades of England in 1640! Filled with ex-communists, the parliament had resisted free-market reforms. But Yeltsin had the support of the army and, to a considerable degree, of public opinion. The parliamentary rebellion fizzled out, not without some bloodshed. The spectacle of the president shelling the Congress, to use American terms, became a daily one in Moscow in 1993. Could democratic government possibly survive this?

Crucial Army support for Yeltsin was an inheritance from the Communist era, which had established the principle of military independence of politics. Still, popular generals loomed on the horizon, perhaps a Bonaparte among them. Elections in December approved a new constitution, which gave considerable powers to the president, but the voters elected a legislature dominated more by reactionary than reform members, foreshadowing more trouble. The chief proponent of market reforms and privatization resigned from Yeltsin's cabinet. Extreme right-wing nationalist Vladimir Zhirinovsky, whose party called itself perhaps ironically the "Liberal Democrats," and on the other wing the ex-Communists, seemed the best organized of the political parties, though economic reformer Gregory Yavlinsky was personally popular. Russian politics was in fact a shambles: A dozen parties ranged in size from the tiny to the small, with all kinds of objectives. Several of them were led by now-unemployed military generals. The largest as of 1993 wanted, according to one summary, the conquest of Alaska, free vodka, and shooting criminals on sight. Reform parties combined had probably no more than 25 percent of the total.

In February 1994, the seven leading economic powers told Moscow that aid would continue only if there was a more sincere attempt to control inflation and budget deficits. (This hardly seemed very sporting during a week in which the United States Congress rejected a constitutional amendment to forbid budget deficits.) In ensuing months, inflation was brought under control in Russia and even in the Ukraine. By mid-1995, it was down to 8.5 percent a month, exorbitant by standards of the developed countries but an enormous improvement for Russia. Yeltsin seemed firmly in control, though plagued by stories of his drunkenness. (It was easy to sympathize with the man.) Russia seemed to be turning the corner; a market had been created, goods appeared on the shelves. Even the old Communists did not propose returning to the old state economy. Most of those opposing the reforms tended in a muddled way to want to slow down, mitigate, or compromise the course of market reform (a mistake, in the eyes of economists) but not to stop them.

It was hard to appraise the economy, because much of it did not get recorded. Critics of the turn to capitalism claimed that while a few were getting very rich, the great majority were worse off. On any showing, there was much crime. Mafia-like gangs seized control of much of the economy. Such criminal gangs had long existed in Russia; in their revolutionary days, the Bolsheviks cooperated with them, later they appeared in the prison camps. Now they seemed to be stealing the revolution against communism.[1] There were more murders in Russia than even in the United States, where the 25,000 or so a year had become a national scandal. Murders, including those of prominent people, were said to be running at two a day in the far eastern port city of Vladivostok in 1995, in spite of which, or perhaps because of which, the economy was flourishing. The assassination in March 1995 of a popular TV news personality was blamed on the mafia. Huge revenues were at stake in the process of privatizing the state-owned industries.

Yet inflation was seemingly under control, unemployment low by western European standards, and a great deal of enterprise small as well as large was in evidence. The World Bank in 1994 judged privatization a success. Over 50 percent of total production was of private origin; forty million Russians held shares in companies, 650 investment funds existed. Foreign investors, frightened off by the political uncertainties, were beginning to show real interest in Russia. It was a chaotic but dynamic society. Immense disenchantment amid rapid transformation to a private, market-driven economy somewhat resembled early nineteenth-century Britain. Russia, after all, had never really known private industrial capitalism. The Leninists had hoped to bypass or telescope this phase, while more orthodox Marxists had thought Russia was condemned to pass through capitalism before she could get to socialism. It seemed that they were right. Not many thought it conceivable that Russia would or could return

---

[1]See Stephen Handelman, *Comrade Criminal* (1995).

to the old Communist order; for better or worse, she was launched on a new course.

Yeltsin's popularity sank to a low of 6 percent during a war against the tiny Caucasian republic of Chechnya in 1994–1995, according to public opinion polls. It had stood at one time (1991) at 85 percent. He hoped to get the elections scheduled for 1995 and 1996 postponed. But he survived a no-confidence vote in Parliament on July 1, 1995, using the threat of dissolving the parliament which the constitution gave him—a victory won at the price of dismissing several key ministers involved in the Chechen affair and promising to wind down that unfortunate episode, which was a humiliation as well as a scandal for Yeltsin. Yeltsin suffered a heart attack in the autumn of 1995 and was disabled for several months; he resumed his duties early in 1996 but hardly with his old vigor, and he faced the challenge of a presidential election in the spring. Legislative elections in November dealt the reformers a severe blow. Would a former Communist win over Yeltsin in the presidential race and, if so, would this mean a drastic slowing of reform?

THE OTHER EX-SOVIET REPUBLICS

Twenty-seven countries now make up what had been the USSR, Yugoslavia, and Czechoslovakia. Some of the former soviet republics became totally independent. Other places, such as Tatarstan, were de facto independent though regarded in Moscow as a part of the Russian Federation, created by the constitution of 1993. It was only by refraining from pressing the issue that the pretense of their subjection to Russia could be maintained.

In these lands, power struggles between the old Party stalwarts and democratic forces often led to bloody rioting or civil war, and then usually to some form of dictatorship. In most places, the erstwhile Communist lords hung on to power from lack of any alternative, but they no longer held their old doctrines. Thus in Tajikistan, the boss of the old communist regime headed a government challenged by the Islamic Renaissance Party, while several thousand Russian troops tried to keep the peace. There were said to be 100,000 refugees in the capital city of Dushanbe in 1993. Islamic fundamentalism was a force throughout Central Asia; China's rulers worried about it in Sinkiang, Hindus rioted against it in India. Some feared that neighboring Uzbekistan and Kazakhstan might turn to the Islamic revolutionaries. Headquartered in Iran, which bordered on Tajikistan, radical Islamism was the most dynamic political force in wide areas of northern Africa, western Asia, even Turkey; it appealed to the poorest and most outcast classes.

Few people in the West had even heard of Uzbeks, Tajiks, Kirghs, Turkmen, and Kazakhs before 1990. Now they became part of the world political equilibrium. Some of these Central Asian republics had prospects for economic development and prosperity, now that they no longer had to subsidize Russia and were released from a grossly inefficient economic system, as well as a neg-

New Republics of Central Asia, formerly part of the Soviet Union.

ligent one. (The Aral Sea was an ecological disaster.) Thus, Turkmenistan has large supplies of natural gas, as well as some oil, and is also a major exporter of cotton. Dependent on imports of food, this largely desert country with a backward rural populace had barely entered the market economy and had not begun to democratize.

Uzbekistan, whose capital, Tashkent, was the leading city of Central Asia, also held much potential wealth including oil, gas, gold, cotton. These countries seemed to be stabilizing under some sort of authoritarian government committed to a basically or partly free-market economy. Sometimes they held on to the old command economy and spoke of a slow transition, defying the economists on this issue. Unlike the situation in the Caucasus, they did not fight each other.

The Caucasus was a scene of confusion and sometimes strife as small countries declared their independence and then quarreled with each other over boundaries. Georgia began a state of near anarchy in 1991 as gangs of criminals terrorized the country; a convicted robber and murderer named Yosseliani became one of the most powerful of these warlords. Though a little less anarchical in 1995, Georgia still suffered from mafia gangs, and from separatist rebellions among Ossetes and Abkhazis. Armenia supported the secession of Karabakh from Azerbaijan. Armenians killed or drove into penurious exile hundreds of thousands of Azerbaijanians, whom they called "Turks," thus gaining revenge for the massacres of 1914–1915.

Meanwhile the Ukraine, richest and most industrialized part of the old Soviet Union, after gaining independence was for a while the least reformed of all the ex-Soviet economies. In July 1994, the Ukrainians reelected an ex-Communist as president, over a reform candidate who called for closer ties to the Russian economy. The Ukrainian economy was a total shambles, evidence that failure to reform was even worse than reforming. The country was deeply split between its eastern and western parts; in the west the elected president, Leonid Kutchma, got 4 percent of the vote in some provinces, while in the Crimea he won 90 percent. Kutchma was once a high official in the Soviet arms industry, but he now preached free-market reforms. Dominated by old-line communists, the parliament opposed and obstructed that. So did the huge bureaucratic administrative apparatus inherited from former times.

In 1995, the energetic Kutchma was trying to get a constitutional amendment granting him greater power, and parliament less, in order to put through a privatization program resisted by the people's representatives. It was a pattern familiar all over the ex-Communist world. Privatization had barely begun. The Kiev stock market listed just four companies, and in this rich agricultural region, farming was still collectivized—and backward. Foreign investment had yet to be attracted in any quantity despite the vast potential of the Ukraine. Hope seemed to lie in the president's popularity and in the fact that the voyage down the rough but promising road of free-market reform had at least started.

OTHER EX-COMMUNIST COUNTRIES

Among the ex-communist countries of eastern Europe, Hungary, Poland, and the Czech Republic reformed their economies more rapidly and successfully than Russia. The Baltic states also did better, especially Estonia, which tied its currency to the *Deutschmark*. In general, it appeared that the more Westernized of the ex-communist countries were making the transition to a market, free-enterprise economy successfully. There was often enthusiastic privatization, though also hardships inflicted on many who had lost the protection of the old statism without sharing yet in the rewards of the new capitalism. Sometimes there was a backlash as disappointment with the results of the new order set in. Crime rose, so sometimes did an ugly xenophobia not previously evident.

In June 1992, the Czechs and Slovaks agreed peacefully to separate, forming separate republics—an example that regions of the Balkans and Caucasus regrettably did not follow. The less modernized Slovaks were the more reluctant of the two to abandon central planning. Free-market reforms worked better in the Czech Republic than in any other ex-communist country. Sweeping privatization occurred, but considerable government intervention remained too.

In Slovakia, after victory in legislative elections in October, 1994, Prime Minister Vladimir Meciar muzzled the press and radio and replaced officials of the privatization agency, with evident intent to halt privatization. He named a former Communist police official as procurer-general; President Kovoc refused to invest him.

In elections of May 1994, Hungarians returned to power ex-communists, now calling themselves Socialists, but prepared to continue free-market reforms. Rising unemployment, crime, inflation had soured Hungarians on the liberal Free Democrats elected in 1990. But the results promised to be little different.

Polish parliamentary elections of September 1993 also resulted in a re-buff for the free-market and conservative parties, victory going to the Democratic Left alliance, embracing old Communists and the Polish Peasant party. But even the old Communists declared themselves now to be pro-western social democrats. Their support came from people hurt by the economic reforms, such as workers fired from inefficient industries, also old bureaucrats. Poland had done well at converting to a market economy and had the fastest growing economy in Europe; still, the dislocation cost was so great as to negate this fact. Unemployment was high. Peasants wanted protection and subsidies. Fixed income people demanded price controls. In the Polish presidential election of December, 1995, a former communist, now professing conversion to democracy and the market economy, defeated Walesa.

Romania, Bulgaria, and Albania largely reverted to the old ruling class, no longer calling itself communist but not much different; sometimes converted to economic reform, just as often trying to avoid or postpone it. These peoples remained among the poorest in Europe. Their fate was nowhere near as harsh as that of the former Yugoslavia, which continued to play the tragic role in European and world politics that dated back to 1914.

THE DISINTEGRATION OF YUGOSLAVIA

Milovan Djilas died in April 1995, aged eighty-three, in Belgrade. The Montenegrin-born intellectual and activist had participated in the strange story of his own tormented Yugoslavia, as well as in the drama of world Communism, for

fifty years; in his own words, he had "traveled the entire road of communism."
As a twenty-one-year-old student in Belgrade, he had been arrested for radical politics; he became a Communist at a time when it was fashionable for
intellectual youth to do so. In 1940, he watched the spontaneous uprising of
the people against the Yugoslav monarchy's decision (under severe pressure)
to join Hitler's side. Djilas fought with the Partisan guerrillas against the German and Italian occupiers and became Marshal Tito's chief lieutenant. After the
war when the Partisans formed a Communist government in Yugoslavia, Djilas
was as loyal a Stalinist as he was a Titoist, the two things originally being the
same.

When Yugoslavia quarreled with the USSR in 1948, it was Djilas
whom Tito sent to Moscow to explain why he would not accept Stalin's domination. This was the beginning of Djilas's disenchantment with Russian communism, as he saw firsthand the cynicism and corruption into which its "terrible
dogmatists" had fallen. He wrote about this later in *Conversations with Stalin*. But
Djilas would soon break with Tito's communism as well. Expelled from the Yugoslav government and Communist Party in 1954 for his heresies, he was imprisoned in 1956 as his western-published *The New Class* gained world fame.
The book has a leading place in the story of Western intellectuals' gradual disenchantment with Soviet communism. "The Communist revolution," he wrote,
"conducted in the name of doing away with class" had ended in the creation of
a new ruling class, politically based, whose misrule was worse than any previous
one. By implication, at least, Yugoslavia's communist elite was about to become
an example of the same perverse law of revolutionary failure: In overthrowing
the old tyranny, the revolutionaries forge a new one.

Djilas spent nine years in the same prison he had once briefly occupied
as a youth for opposing the monarchy. But after his release, he visited western
countries and continued writing. Prison, he said, had transformed him from an
ideologist into a humanist. When after Tito's death the dictatorship began to
crumble, Djilas rejoiced at the anticommunist demonstrations in Belgrade in
1991. He opposed the Serbian war against Croatia that ensued, again falling out
of step with the regime; most of the former Serbian communists were now fervent Serb nationalists. He must have pondered the ironies as well as the tragedy
of Serbia's odyssey from 1914 to 1994 through three wars, immense suffering
and loss of life, and much disappointed idealism, ending in a situation worse
than that of 1914.

The disintegration of Yugoslavia perhaps began with its creation, as
Gibbon said of the Roman Empire. The hoped-for unity of all the "South
Slavs," born of the Dual Monarchy's disintegration in 1918, obscured a host of
old differences and animosities, religious, ethnic, economic, cultural. Yugoslavia
was always a Greater Serbia to the intensely nationalistic Serbs, but Croats,
Slovenes and others resented Belgrade's dominance. An assassination on the
floor of the parliament in the 1920s and of King Alexander in 1934 punctuated
this ill feeling. Even the common struggle against Hitler's Germany did not

draw Croats and Serbs together; there were rival resistance movements, and Croats took advantage of the situation to revenge themselves on Serbs.

The death of Tito in 1985 removed the last force holding the ill-matched union together, but it continued for a while as a decentralized federation. The demise of world communism gave a further push to its disintegration. Croatia (along with Slovenia) declared its independence in June 1991 and attempted to secede; the Yugoslav army, now really a Serbian army, then attacked the neighboring republic in September, also blockading Croatia's Adriatic ports. The Croats at first could do little to defend themselves, possessing only a militia force while Belgrade disposed of the Federal army. Fighting intensified in the fall of 1991, when the shelling of the beautiful and historic city of Dubrovnik shocked the world. The European Community and the United States declared an embargo on Yugoslavia, to what useful purpose it was not apparent. From the beginning, it was painfully clear that the outside world had no desire to get pulled into the Balkan quagmire; memories of Vietnam haunted the American imagination, Europe remembered 1914, everybody knew how valiantly the Serbs had fought a guerrilla war in 1941–1945. There was an echo of 1914 here in that Russia, much reduced in power though she was, tended to favor her old ally Serbia.

The European Community countries recognized the independence of Croatia and Slovenia in December 1991, to the indignation of the Serbs. Complicating the picture, of course, was the presence of a sizeable Serb population within the borders of Croatia. Not only were there Serbs in Croatia, and a few Croatians in Serbia, but Serbs, Croats, and Muslims (a Europeanized group, not ethnically different from the other Slavs of the region) all lived in Bosnia, the province that borders Croatia to the south and Serbia to the west. This soon became a battlefield; it was up for grabs between Serbia, Croatia, and those who wanted a separate Bosnian state. The latter were chiefly the Muslims, a group most people had never heard of until Bosnia erupted in flames in 1992. Bosnia provided a new term for mass murder, "ethnic cleansing," euphemism for the slaughter of Bosnian Muslims. A U.S.–NATO security system that had just blasted Iraq with all the arsenal of high-tech weaponry for invading a neighbor ignored the similar aggression of Serbia, followed by something like genocide. At a time when the Bosnian war had claimed more than 100,000 victims, devastated many villages, and made countless refugees homeless, the American secretary of state announced that this part of the world was not "a vital interest" for the United States. The response of the European Union was little better. Both powers hoped the United Nations might do something—reminiscent of the initial response to Hitler in the 1930s.

The shelling of Sarajevo in June 1992 resulted in the first attempted United Nations intervention, by a token group of so-called peacekeeping forces. The upshot showed that the U.N. presence only angered the Serbs while proving wholly inadequate to protect anybody, even the peacekeepers themselves. Sarajevo, where the famous assassination of June 1914 had touched off World War I, was a beautiful city of several hundred thousand population, which the

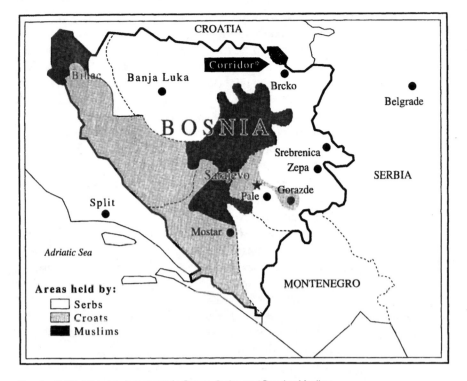

Bosnia, divided between incompatible Croats, Serbs, and Bosnian Muslims,
became a bloody battleground after the disintegration of Yugoslavia in 1992.
In November 1995, a precarious peace created a federal government with
separate Serb and Croat-Muslim subunits.

world had admired only a few years before when it hosted the winter Olympics.
It now began an ordeal unequaled by any European city since 1945. In 1993, it
was a scene of devastation, facing starvation.

A French writer, Ignacio Ramonet, wrote in 1993 that "In the former
Yugoslavia, the unleashing of sadisms and barbarities poses anew, for the
philosophers of our time, the question of the human condition." The next few
years brought little improvement. Desperate truces were arranged, only to be
broken. More United Nations troops came in, to little avail; the Serbs killed
them and took them prisoner to use as hostages. The agony of Sarajevo continued, though some supplies were brought in. Croatia improved its army and in
May 1995 unleashed an offensive to win back that part of its own territory that
Croatian Serbs had seized. The embargo had some effect on the Belgrade Serbs,
who tended to back away from their support of the Croatian and Bosnian Serbs.
The latter, by bombing helpless towns, continuing to harass Sarajevo, and kidnapping U.N. soldiers, forfeited whatever sympathy they had had in world
opinion, and NATO planes bombed their military positions in May 1995—only
to see the enraged Serbs use kidnapped U.N. soldiers as human shields. The
chief concern of European and American policy in 1995 seemed to be how to

withdraw the United Nations soldiers, now some 40,000 spread around Croatia and Bosnia, without unleashing more misery on the region, if that were possible, which perhaps included all-out Serbo-Croatian war. There was also fear that war might spread to Macedonia, where a few of the discredited U.N. forces stood token guard over a potential powderkeg. Kosovo, inhabited by a majority of Albanians but under Serbian rule, might rebel. Macedonia was now independent but Greece as well as Serbia, and perhaps Bulgaria, bore it no love. The Greeks emotionally resented the creation of a sovereign state bearing the name of the Greek province that, as the homeland of Alexander the Great, was an integral part of Greek historic consciousness.

Bosnian Muslims obtained arms, with the aid of Middle Eastern co-religionists, and counterattacked in an effort to break the siege of Sarajevo. As the Bosnian Serbs continued to kill civilians in Sarajevo and other places inhabited by Bosnian Muslims, NATO finally decided to act, in September 1995, with full-scale bombing of Bosnian Serb positions around Sarajevo. A United Nations International Tribunal formally indicted the Bosnian Serb leaders for the crime of genocide in Srebenica where, between July 11 and July 20, 1995, Serbian troops massacred some 6,000 residents of that city, an event to which there were scores of witnesses. In late 1995, under pressure from the United States and NATO the Bosnian belligerents agreed to suspend hostilities, divide the land between Serbs, Muslims, and Croats, and create a federal government. Whether a government based on such hostile elements could possibly work was an unanswered question. Meanwhile, 60,000 United Nations troops including 20,000 Americans were to try to keep the peace.

Meanwhile, both Serbia and Croatia were much worse off than they were before 1990. The Croats had undergone both the breakup of Yugoslavia and the switch from socialism to capitalism. There were floods of refugees from war-torn Bosnia, plus the cost of intermittent war with Serbia and the loss of territory to the Serbs who lived in Croatia (Slavonia). Living standards fell by at least half, and runaway inflation threatened in 1993. But Croatia had been the most prosperous part of Yugoslavia, and the enterprising Croats were taking measures to restore the economy, via a new currency, sharp reductions in government budget, and tying the currency to the Deutschmark. Defense cuts were evidently no part of the package. By August 1995, the Croats had created a thoroughly modern army and began a successful offensive to recapture territory lost to the Serbs a few years earlier.

GERMAN REUNIFICATION

"The most peaceful change of this magnitude in European history," Elizabeth Pond calls the German reunification. It was not entirely untroubled. Huge as they were known to be, Germany found the costs of reunification even greater than expected; the enormous expense of restructuring an economy that lay virtually in ruins strained the resources even of perhaps the richest country in the world, threatening inflation. The *Bundesbank* was forced to tighten interest rates. Germany faced possible budget deficits, something previously regarded as incredible. In 1993, it was estimated that it would take ten years for the richest part of the east to reach the level of the poorest part of west. Two years later, purchasing power in the east was estimated at 78 percent of that disposed of in the west–this despite enormous subsidies. Bonn worked out a plan by which everybody in the west made sacrifices; trade unions, for example, accepted lower wage increases. This was during the recession that struck the world economy at this time. The Dutch guilder replaced the German mark as the strongest European currency.

Discovery of how run-down and unclean the DDR had become during the long Communist reign were matched by even more sensational revelations about the attempts at thought control by the Democratic Republic's secret police (Stasi). The resources that might have been used to save the environment from incredible pollution were spent on a vast system of internal espionage. Eighty-five thousand agents and an army of 300,000 paid informers had turned East Germany into the most bizarre police state of all times. Incredibly, after its collapse and reunification with West Germany, virtually no criminal proceedings were brought against the Stasi directors who had caused thousands of people to be imprisoned for political reasons or shot trying to flee the country. Better to let sleeping dogs lie. Most of the high officials were now very old. The old Communist Party leader, Erich Honecker, was found too ill to stand trial and died in Chilean exile in 1994.

Like most incumbents in the early 1990s, Chancellor Kohl's ratings sank as unemployment rose and the economic miracle seemed over. The Social Democrats, who had suffered successive defeats in general elections in 1983, 1987, and 1990, hoped to break their string in October 1994. Their leader was now a young Rhinelander, Rudolf Scharping, who seemed to move the party back toward the center. Leftists grumbled and called Scharping a Red Cabbage (*rotkohl*). But Kohl won reelection to an unprecedented fourth term by a narrow margin, in an election that saw the Free Democrats virtually wiped out. The CDU along with its allies the Bavarian CSU and the FDP got 48.4 percent of votes; the Social Democrats won 36.4 percent, but were stronger in state elections, enabling them to control the Senate. The Greens continued their strong performance, rising to 7.3 percent–the political environmentalists did better in Germany than in any other country. Surprisingly strong in the east was the old Communist party, reorganized as the Democratic Socialists (PDS): It gained 4.4 percent overall, with almost all of its support in the east. Though neo-Nazis rioting against immigrants caused a scandal, the extreme right failed to qualify for any representation in the parliament.

Considerable disenchantment with the results of reunification appeared in East Germany just as it did in other ex-communist lands. Many people lost their jobs, whether old bureaucrats or workers in inefficient industries. Sudden privatization produced an unseemly scramble in which instant millionaires clawed their way to the top: The ethics of capitalism remained as doubtful as ever. But with German efficiency furiously at work rebuilding the ex-Democratic Republic amid plans to move the capital back to Berlin, Kohl's popularity moved back up. The Social Democrats were again in disarray. In early 1996, the Social Democrats deposed Scharping and replaced him as their leader with a left-winger. Unemployment in 1995 stood at 9 percent in the whole of Germany, much higher in the east than in the west. Predictions were that the Christian Democratic leader, already the longest-serving chancellor in German history, would win again in 1997.

Such prophecies, however, ran up against a prominent fact of late twentieth-century political behavior, extreme voter volatility. Perhaps the politics of the rest of Europe might be approached by identifying several such major themes, found in all countries. Others were the decline of socialism, a tendency toward devolution of power, and widespread corruption.

EUROPEAN POLITICAL THEMES

To the above might be added a tendency toward fragmentation. In German elections since reunification in 1990, one authority noted, the two major parties "have suffered a steady erosion of support to the benefit of fringe parties." These included the environmentalist Greens, as well as neo-nationalist parties of the Right. The same was notably true of Italy, where a veritable revolution in politics diminished or even destroyed the old parties and generated a group of new ones. The revolution grew out of all the themes identified above: Corruption became a national scandal, the centralized state was under attack, economic statism in general lost status.

Both the parties that had dominated Italian politics for a generation, the Communists and the Christian Democrats, disappeared altogether, though tending to reappear under different names. (The Democratic Party of the Left; the Popular Italian Party. There was a small unrepentant PCI). The Communists were caught in the massive wave of rejection of communism at the end of the 1980s, while the CDs were staggered by revelations of fraud (so also the Socialists). A wave of reform swept Italy, exposing corruption that was seemingly endemic in Italian politics. Meanwhile, for the first time, some headway was made in the war against the Mafia. The assassinations of two judges in 1992, the last of many such victims of Mafia vengeance, this time pushed public opinion to a pitch of indignation. An increasing number of former Cosa Nostra underlings repented and testified, leading to the capture (January 1993) of the top Sicilian Cosa Nostra boss, and the arrests of other Sicilian and Calabrian *capos*. Several billions of dollars of Mafia assets were seized. It was hard to say that the great power of this long untouchable organization had been completely broken, but it looked like it might be. No longer was it able to levy tribute and pass death sentences with impunity.

At the same time, corrupt politicians, their ties to this criminal underworld exposed, fell like tenpins. A dozen suicides among Italy's elite in government and business followed the revelations of widespread corruption in high places.

The Mafia struck back; in 1993, bombings of the Uffizi Gallery in Florence, then of Milan's Museum of Modern Art, and two of Rome's most ancient and priceless churches, a veritable assault on civilization, were charged to a desperate Mafia, trying to prevent new elections that would surely sweep the old guard from power. Tens of thousands of Italians paraded in protest against the bombings. A revolution seemed to be underway in Italy, not of one class against another but of all decent people against a deeply corrupt political system that had fastened itself on the Italian state. In 1995, the politician who had dominated Italian public life for decades as the long-time leader of the Christian Democratic party, Giulio Andreotti, went on trial in Palermo charged with having protected and served the Mafia.

New parties sprang up to replace these fallen idols. The Northern League, sweeping through the wealthiest part of Italy and perpetuating an old North-South division, became for a time the leading political party. It threatened a tax strike against Rome. We have mentioned the impulse toward decentralization and localism; Scots were demanding independence from England, just as the Yugoslav federation broke up and nationalities seceded from the Soviet Union. Slovakia removed itself from Czechoslovakia. On the North American continent, Canada seemed on the verge of breaking up into separate provinces.

In Italy, along with the Northern League a neo-Fascist party, the National Alliance, led by Gianfranco Fini, gained strength in the South. Then Silvio Berlusconi, a Milanese billionaire businessman, loomed as the political man of destiny in 1993 with his *Forza Italiana,* Italian Power—only to see the party plummet within a year. He headed a coalition of the center-right, the Freedom Alliance. In 1995, a center-left coalition that embraced both the former communists and some former Christian Democrats displayed the wild improbabilities of Italian politics. The rival Freedom Alliance included Northern League haters of the South and the neo-Fascist party, which demanded government help for the South, as well as Forza Italiana free-marketeers.

The popularity of the League in northern Italy stemmed from rising resentment at the prosperous part of Italy subsidizing the poor part—without any results. Billions had been poured into development of the south but it remained as poor as ever. Northerners believed southerners indolent and corrupt. Southerners believed northerners cold and greedy. The slogan of the Risorgimento, "We have made Italy, now we must make Italians" was still relevant after almost a century and a half; a gulf separated Piedmont or Lombardy from Sicily and the Mezzogiorno. The answer of the National Alliance, the neo-Fascist party, that "an Italian is an Italian wherever he lives" was more an ideal than a reality. But none of these parties seemed more than temporary waves in the turbulent sea of Italian politics, which changed annually.

Berlusconi used his own television channels to project his glamorous personality. Forza Italiana was more of a media event than a political movement, and after spectacular initial success it subsided, showing all the staying power of a soap commercial. Berlusconi became premier but was caught up in charges of corruption and conflict of interest with his vast holdings. Elections in 1994 showed a dispersal of the electorate all over the place, with no party gaining more than about 13 percent. The Berlusconi government fell, and a caretaker government which everybody agreed not to oppose, led by the obscure Dini, governed Italy. Regional elections of April 23, 1995, saw the ex-communist Democratic Party of the Left get the largest vote, about 25 percent. Silvio Berlusconi's Forza Italia had 23 percent. Together with his allies, the Center-Right coalition fell short of a majority; the Center-Left also fell short of a majority in the Chamber of Deputies. Not even bizarre coalitions could muster a majority. The old, unreconstructed Communists got 8.6 percent! The caretaker government of "technicians" headed by Sr. Dini would carry on for the time being. Privatization continued; Italy was in earnest about it by 1993, joining the rest of Europe. With its roots in the South, Fini's National Alliance was not enthusiastic about privatization and the free market, and was thought to be rather hostile to the European monetary union. In the April 1996 general election, the Center-Right coalition of Fini and Berlusconi lost narrowly to an equally incongruous Center-Left coalition; Italy seemed still leaderless and adrift.

Sweden had been the exemplar of the successful welfare state. In a land in which two-thirds of the wage-earners depended on the state, it was hard to slash benefits, but mounting budget deficits and inflation, with unemployment also high by Swedish standards (9 percent) forced this action. Sweden was a prize example of the welfare-state crisis. In all countries, welfare payments had, of course, been growing for many decades; payments from National Insurance and other benefits just about doubled in Britain between 1938 and 1971. France belatedly arrived at a comprehensive social security system in the 1960s, as it urbanized and modernized. Increased government spending on welfare and to decrease unemployment leads to higher taxes and/or (usually both) budget deficits, causing inflation and currency devaluation. Economic stagnation results from high taxation, then higher taxation is needed to counter economic stagnation: a classic spiral. Reform of the system is difficult if not impossible because too many people depend on government outlays for jobs, unemployment benefits, welfare.

The failure of the "Swedish model" was a significant landmark for everybody. Here had been the prize example of using the powers of the state wisely to secure full employment and welfare benefits for everyone without impairing economic progress. Now it had collapsed into huge deficits, high inflation, declining exports. Even Switzerland, generally considered to be the wealthiest country in the world, struggled with mounting budget deficits in the 1990s.

The British Labour Party, prodded by its new and promising leader

Tony Blair, removed from the Party constitution the clause about public owner-ship of "the means of production." This was formally done in March 1995 after long being considered an anachronism but preserved for sentimental reasons. At the same time, the Socialist candidate for president in France in the 1995 election, Lionel Jospin, stressed that he was a social democrat, meaning not op-posed to private property; his success in restoring something like a Socialist presence was based on his projecting a spirit of moderation. The Socialists were now converts to the market economy, otherwise known as capitalism.

Was the welfare state itself ending? Every country was slashing welfare budgets. Welfare might be partly privatized (its services contracted out to pri-vate penologists, doctors, teachers).

France exhibited a similar pattern of volatility, realignment of parties to some extent, retreat from statism, and corruption as an issue. Elected to a sec-ond presidential term in 1988 by a 54-to-46-percent margin over Jacques Chirac, the aging and soon ill Mitterand sank badly in his second term. This was partly because of ineptness in foreign affairs; Mitterand handled both the Iraq war and the attempted coup against Gorbachev badly (hastily recognizing the rebels before they lost). But the tide had turned against the Socialists in the 1990s. French legislative elections of March 1993 resulted in a shattering defeat for the Left. When Pierre Bérégovoy, the ousted Socialist prime minister, com-mitted suicide a few weeks later, it seemed scarcely inappropriate to the disas-ter his party had suffered. (The suicide was evidently connected to a personal scandal as well as the political defeat.) The victorious right-center coalition held some 480 seats to the Left's 90. The Socialist debacle included the failure of many of its leaders to be reelected; the party's number of representatives in the Assembly fell from 258 to 53, an astonishing loss. In some of its regions of tra-ditional strength, the Socialist party was virtually wiped out. The Communists held their little band together better, losing just three seats (from 27 to 24). Nei-ther Le Pen's far-right National Front nor the ecological Greens (themselves di-vided into two factions) succeeded in electing a single representative.

The violent swing clearly registered less a positive choice than a rejec-tion of the status quo. Unemployment, unease at social change, perhaps also at the new Europe without national boundaries, at decay of traditional values, loss of faith in elected representatives—all these played a part. The Right's electoral victory was far out of proportion to its popular vote; as in England in the 1980s, the hopeless fragmentation of the opposition was decisive. In terms of popular vote, at the second turn of the two-stage election, the two parties of the Right gained about 35 percent of the total number of registered voters. Once again, the largest party of all was those who did not vote (a third of the registered voters).

Facing another time of "cohabitation" with an Assembly controlled by the rival party, President Mitterand named Edouard Balladur of the RPR to head the government. For a time, Prime Minister Balladur was almost wildly popular; but a series of financial scandals shook his government in the fall of

1994, forcing resignation of two of his cabinet, and he also plummeted in the polls. An early favorite to replace Mitterand as president in 1995, he failed to survive the first round in the April–May election.

Victor in the 1995 presidential race was Jacques Chirac; defeated in 1988, the veteran Gaullist mayor of Paris prevailed in the run-off over socialist Jospin but not by much. Jospin led a Socialist comeback which saw him beaten only by about 53 percent to 47 percent of the votes cast. Notable was the strong showing of the persistent National Front candidate Le Pen in the first round (15 percent)–a protest vote almost equalled by the combined far-left parties (the renamed Communists got nearly 9 percent). The new president declared that France was "in a state of social emergency." Such a condition, one might reflect, was almost normal for the French. But strikes, an unemployment rate of near 12 percent despite the general economic recovery of 1993–1995, and perhaps Bosnia, where French soldiers serving in the inept United Nations peacekeeping force were killed, fed the sense of malaise.

The electorate's extreme volatility could not be blamed on the proverbial inconstancy of the French temperament, for it was found elsewhere in the western world. The British chose John Major only to turn savagely on him; the Americans turned out George Bush two years after his overwhelming popularity during the war against Iraq; Boris Yeltsin sank from the heights to an abysmal low between 1993 to 1995, while Italian politics went into wild gyration with parties appearing and disappearing almost overnight. In Britain, the huge lead in public opinion polls which Labour held over the incumbent Conservatives owed most to the attractive personality of its youthful leader Tony Blair; the party programs were not very different, and in fact the "New Labour" line, preaching fiscal responsibility and reduced government intervention and accepting most of the Thatcherite restrictions on trade unions–this from the Labour party!–often seemed to outdo the Tories in conservatism. Some observers wondered whether at the next election Labour would not find itself deserted by the voters as in 1992, when it had also seemed to hold a lead in the polls but lost the election.

Corruption affected politics in Spain, where scandal after scandal shook the long-reigning government of Felipe Gonzales, whose 13-year government fell in the election of March, 1996. Even in England, an opinion poll showed that nearly two-thirds of the people thought MPs made money by using their office improperly, and investigations seemed somewhat to bear this out. This new venality seemed a characteristic of the times, the result of mounting *incivisme* among public servants, the vast sums of money being passed about, and the sheer growth of government which made it impossible to maintain controls. "In a disturbing number of democratic countries," Jean-François Revel wrote in his book *Democracy against Itself* (1993), "power transforms itself, as in a dictatorship, into a means not of governing for the common good but of enriching oneself." The perception of political corruption, to be sure, owed something to the TV media, whose throngs of reporters were ever on the alert for some toothsome scandal. Political corruption, to be sure, was no monopoly of the West; it was found everywhere. The Soviet Union before its collapse, as well as after, was filled with it, as is China, and, among other Communist-ruled countries, Vietnam, whose own leader, Du Muoi, inveighed against "debauchery, abuse of power, and embezzlement of public funds" (May 1995). But Europe was supposed to have "clean government," and Europeans often demanded it of the undeveloped world in censorious terms.

Terrorism returned to a degree. We have mentioned the Italian bombings, evidently the work of the Mafia. In the Netherlands, of all places, a group calling themselves Revolutionary Anti-racists, claiming connection to the German Red Army and the Basque ETA, bombed a government building in The Hague in July 1993. There were bombs in the streets and on subways in Paris, in London, in Tokyo, in New York City and a sensational one in Texas, blowing up a government building with great loss of life. Some of these were connected with Arab extremists, others were native-born. Despite affluence, a crisis of authority, or "legitimacy," continued: Modernized Western man and woman had lost faith in public institutions, was completely cynical. To political corruption should be added white-collar crime; that is, fraud, among rich financiers and business people: estimated in *Great Britain* to approach $10 billion a year and to constitute "an increasing threat to the stability of personal investments, savings and pensions" (Brian Widlake, *Serious Fraud Office,* 1995).

Despite all the complaints, which seemed paradoxically to increase with the standard of living, western Europe entered ever more fully into the affluent life. Mrs. Thatcher became a byword for horrors within the ideological Left, paired with Ronald Reagan as a prime example of man's (or woman's) inhumanity to man. But a Labour Party document on "social justice," published in 1994, was honest enough to admit that during the Thatcher years average living standards in the United Kingdom rose, life expectancy continued to advance, infant mortality declined, and the number of jobs increased by two million. In 1995, Britain was reported as drawing more foreign investment in new factories and research enterprises than any other country in Europe (*New York Times,* October 15). Its unemployment rate of 8.2 percent was three points lower than France's.

The new factories that appeared in northern England, replacing now-defunct steel mills and shipbuilding, were manufacturing computer chips and semiconductors, television sets and microwave ovens; they were owned by Koreans, Japanese, Germans, but provided good jobs for a once languishing region. Ever-increasing numbers took for granted ever more sophisticated automobiles, television sets, video recorders, laser discs for recorded music and movies, personal computers equipped now with all kinds of new visual and auditory features. The leading obstacle to "democracy" in the West was public absorption in popular entertainment, including sports, to an extent that precluded any time for serious consideration of public issues.

The advance of technology took place regardless of governments, it seemed. Titanic battles between rival financial tycoons, huge mergers, and hostile takeover wars made the economic news often more exciting than the political. The new empires of telecommunications made fortunes overnight and supplied avenues of rags-to-riches opportunity not known since the days of Samuel Smiles in Victorian times.

Yet for many, it was an insecure economy. Keen competition might wipe out one's company or force it to trim costs drastically. The economy was now global. GATT, the General Agreement on Trade and Tariffs, struggled forward through eight "rounds" of international conferences in a drive to reduce tariffs, quotas, and other obstacles to international trade. Protectionist sentiment delayed the last round for seven years; only, perhaps, the boost to free-market ideas given by the Soviet collapse enabled an agreement to be reached in late 1993, which obviously was far from perfect but represented a significant victory in the long and sometimes lonely fight economists had conducted against all kinds of impediments to the free movement of goods throughout the world–something all economists, and few politicians, regarded as highly desirable. More than 100 countries agreed to cut tariffs. Despite outbreaks of controversy about protectionism such as enlivened U.S.–Japanese relations all through the 1990s, and at times seemed to threaten war between Canada and the European Union over fishing rights, there was on any showing a vigorous international market. In the aftermath of the GATT agreement, regional free trade areas began to proliferate. (It was a nice question whether these conflicted with global free trade, or were steps toward it.) The North American Free Trade Area, perhaps to be expanded to include South America; an Asian-Pacific Economic Cooperation forum, a South Asian Preferential Free Trade Area, a Central European Free Trade Area that would include Hungary, Poland, the Czech Republic, Slovakia, and Slovenia (a relic of the old Yugoslavia)–these in addition to the growing European Union were either in place or being seriously discussed in the mid-1990s. Seventy percent of western Europe's total trade was interregional.

The explosion of productivity in East Asia, from the little "tigers" Singapore, Hong Kong, South Korea, and increasingly too from China and India and Indonesia, joining the fabulously successful Japan, threatened to wrest world economic leadership from the haughty Europeans and Americans. A Singapore leader boasted in 1995 that "East Asia's GDP is already larger than that of either the United States or the European Community," and the fastest growing. The tallest building in the world was being built in Kuala Lumpur; Malaysia was one of the world's most prosperous and progressive countries. Probably the richest country in the world was little Brunei, where everybody seemed to own a Mercedes and the sultan was said to have once left a $170,000 tip.

European and American jobs were migrating to Asia and other foreign lands as a result of the communications revolution, which made possible rapid transmission of all sorts of data to all parts of the world. Swiss bankers might find it cheaper to have their records kept in Singapore. A New York corporation's letters might be typed in Jamaica. Not to mention the fact that lower taxes tempted international companies to settle their headquarters in Hong Kong, Brunei, or Cayman Island.

WHICH WAY EUROPEAN UNION?

The European Union (new name for the old European Community) struggled unevenly forward. An ambitious attempt at takeoff almost crashed in the first years of the 1990s. Riding what seemed a crest of confidence, the Maastrict conference of December 1991 approved a common European currency, to be completed by 1999. Revising the original 1957 Treaty of Rome, it also mandated the creation of common foreign and defense policy machinery, even a European police force to supersede the national ones. The European Parliament was given greater powers. The Parliament, the Brussels bureaucracy and the Luxemburg court were, it seemed, to become in effect a federal government, replacing or superseding the various national governments.

In the economic conditions of 1991, this was to go too far too fast. The Maastrict treaty immediately ran into strong opposition, and faced a rocky road to approval. Great Britain opted out of the currency and social legislation features at the start. Denmark rejected the treaty in a popular referendum of June 1992, sending shock waves through Brussels. France then decided to hold a referendum on the issue too; French voters approved the treaty but by a narrow margin, after President Mitterand, at that time very unpopular, pleaded with French voters not to vote against Maastricht because they hated him. All this uncertainty induced a financial crisis during which Britain left the Exchange Rate Mechanism, created in 1979 as a lead-in to the single European currency. The ERM collapsed entirely in 1992.

But from this low point a rally occurred. The British Parliament eventually ratified the treaty with reservations, and at a second try the Danes reversed themselves (May 1993). Maastricht finally completed its ordeal in November of that year, after two years and many battles. Though all members—with numerous reservations and amendments—finally ratified it, the treaty had lost much of its mystique. Dreams of a true European state had vanished for the time being; no more than a simple confederation was within reach. The common currency was still scheduled for 1999 but few thought this deadline likely to be met. A common foreign policy seemed as remote as a monetary union; the fiasco of Bosnia showed how powerless Europe was to deal with a war on its doorstep.

So as the century neared an end, the European Union suffered from about as many nagging concerns as ever. It still seemed to have irresistible momentum, but there was not a great deal of popular enthusiasm for it. Elections to the Parliament of Europe in June 1994—a parliament soon to have enlarged powers—aroused little interest except, ironically, as a means of registering ap-

The pooled flags of the separate nations at Strasbourg, home of the Council of Europe, which became the European Parliament, symbolized the hopes for European unity. (*European Community Information Service.*)

proval or disapproval, usually the latter, of the governments in power in the separate countries. The Parliament itself impressed few as having much drive. Pro-Europeans almost entirely avoided slogans about a federal Europe, which no one thought possible in the immediate future. Few saw closer union as an answer to the urgent economic and social problems of Europe. While no one on the Continent, at least, was suggesting that the Union be dismantled, little remained of the grand idealism that had inspired the early days of the movement.

Some of the political parties that had identified themselves strongly with Europe, such as the Christian Democrats in Italy, had passed from the scene, and the new parties were not focused on the Union as the old ones had been. In Britain, the Conservative party was badly split between pro- and anti-Europeanists, though Labour, favored to win the next general election in 1996 or 1997, was now pro-Union, and Scottish nationalists dreamed of bringing Scotland into the Union as an independent country (really a nationalist sentiment using internationalism as a crutch). A dissident member of the French UDF ran on an anti-Europe platform in the 1994 Euro-parliament elections and gained 12 percent of the vote. But so did a deviant from the Left who was strongly pro-Europe. The French anti-Europeanist candidate got only 4 percent in the presidential election of May 1995.

In 1994, Norway, Sweden, Finland, and Austria all held referenda on their impending entry into the Union. The latter three approved, the Swedes by a narrow margin, but Norway, the country that had so proudly taken the center of the world stage during the Winter Olympics of 1994, refused to join a greater Europe. Switzerland had already declined to abandon its traditional isolationism. The Swedes looked like joining Britain and Denmark in opting out of the common currency. Greece, recently admitted, was already disillusioned. So also in some degree was Spain, once enthusiastically pro-European. These countries both experienced an economic surge forward right after entry into the common market, but then tended to slide back again after a few years. Other applicants, who had lined up eagerly a few years before, might have second thoughts, though Poland, Hungary, the Czech Republic, and Slovakia still seemed eager to join what was to them a prestigious rich man's club. The EU was hardly ready for the formidable task of breaking in these awkward new applicants. It was generally agreed that Russia, as a prospective member, was simply too big and unmanageable; and if not Russia, then not the Ukraine or other fragments of the former USSR.

Britain, as usual, was the least dedicated to European union. At a European summit meeting in June 1994, her prime minister, John Major, cast the lone vote against a Belgian candidate for president of the European Commission to succeed Jacques Delors, blocking him against the will of eleven other states because Major thought him too interventionist. This seemed to be a gesture aimed at appeasing the Euro-skeptics in Major's own party. This cast a shadow over a meeting at which invitations to four new members were issued and a trade deal with Russia signed. Britain was also the lone dissenter in 1995 on the issue of the powers of the EU criminal intelligence agency (EUROPOL). When border signs came down, marking an end to customs and immigration barriers all over Europe in September 1994, Britain, Ireland, and Denmark were exceptions.

Attaining monetary union by 1999 depends upon members meeting certain criteria indicative of their economies being close enough together; inflation rate, interest rate, budget deficit, national per capita debt would have to be in roughly the same range. Some thought it could be years before the various economies converged enough. Others thought the Deutschmark would become the European currency. (Countries anxious to reform, like Croatia and Latvia, attached their currencies to it.) A controversy broke out in 1995 within the Brussels establishment itself about the wisdom of a single European currency. Yet this had become the test of whether the EU would press on to a Single Europe at last, or would get permanently stuck on a mere plan of economic cooperation among the sovereign states. One suggested reform was that a majority vote rather than unanimity should prevail in the Council of Ministers, at least at some stage of the decision-making process. But even France was opposed to this and it seemed unlikely to happen. The member states would continue to exercise a veto power over EU legislation.

Not helping the cause of European Union was the French government's decision to conduct underwater nuclear tests in the south Pacific in the summer of 1995 (timing this action neatly to coincide with the fiftieth anniversary of the Hiroshima bombing of 1945). Amid protests from Greens all over the world, the European Parliament passed a resolution condemning France. Apart from the emotional environmental issue, the incident showed how far Europe was from a common military direction.

INTERNATIONAL AFFAIRS

Initially, the collapse of the Soviet Union, presumably meaning an end to the Cold War, brought sighs of relief all over the world, even in Russia. Drastic disarmament would follow; the world would no longer have to live under the threat of nuclear destruction. The U.S. and the USSR signed an arms reduction treaty in July 1991, an agreement soon rendered moot by rapid disintegration of Soviet power. The only question became one of control over the Soviet arsenal, distributed now among several largely independent commonwealths.

Both of the superpowers that had loomed large over Europe's affairs for the last half-century had almost disappeared from view. If the Soviet Union was no more and Russia a shambles, the United States of America seemed bewildered by the sudden loss of her great Cold War adversary, like a person who finds the great weight he has been straining to hold back suddenly released and goes staggering into space. It appeared that the United States no longer wished to play a major part in Europe's political affairs. She declined for several years to take any part in the Balkan crisis and showed more interest in the Pacific than in Europe. The Clinton administration was distinctly cold toward the EU, criticizing its trade policies. For Europe, accustomed ever since 1947 to American leadership via NATO and other intercontinental organizations, this caused problems. Bosnia more than anything else revealed that the European Union was far from ready to take charge of foreign policy, and NATO shorn of American leadership was a ship without a helmsman.

The world, it soon became clear, was hardly less peaceful in the new era; in many ways, it was less so. As we know, the breakup of the Soviet Union and of Yugoslavia entailed armed struggles among the successor states for territory. The end of Cold War left vacuums of power throughout the world as one of the superpowers disintegrated and the other largely withdrew. Many countries had received subsidies from one side or another, perhaps both, and now lost this support and an accustomed role. An example is Yemen, where during the Cold War one regime in the north and another in the south had been supported by the Cold War rivals. With their withdrawal, Yemen reverted to traditional tribalism and drifted into a war between north and south that was now not ideologically oriented but simply a feudal power struggle. Cuba and Vietnam, which had been heavily subsidized by the USSR, now lost these subsidies and faced crisis. Afghanistan, deprived of her Russian tormentors (the new Russian leadership apologized for the intervention) did not find peace but a struggle among the rival warlords who had sprung up during the resistance against the Russians.

The responses struck many observers of the international scene as capricious. *Le Monde* (July 1993) commented on the strangely haphazard selectivity of intervention. Some starvations and genocides were ignored, others made occasion for grand rescue operations. The United States unleashed its awesome weaponry on Iraq in a far-off Middle Eastern boundary dispute, but studiously ignored anarchy and mass slaughter in southeastern Europe. Indeed, after forcing the sinister Iraqi dictator Saddam Hussein to give up his designs on tiny Kuwait, the United States and her allies permitted him then not only to continue his rule over Iraq but to exterminate Kurds and Shiite Arabs, and apparently to continue his work on an atomic bomb. Though during the Desert Storm war of 1991–1992 the Americans and their European allies painted the Iraq leader as a sadistic tyrant worse than Hitler, they did not demand his unconditional surrender and occupy his country as they had done to Nazi Germany, but called off the war as soon as Iraqi forces withdrew from Kuwait; as if in World War II they had stopped at the borders of Germany and permitted Hitler to continue in power. (Margaret Thatcher would have liked to emulate Winston Churchill but was overruled.)

It was on Bosnia that the pathetic weakness and indecision of both the European Union and the United States created an embarrassment as well as a near-holocaust in the land divided between Serbs and Muslims; a humiliation not least for the United Nations, pushed into the breach via a few ill-armed peacekeeping forces that were then abandoned to the tender mercies of the Bosnian Serbs. (See above.) The incident discredited the European Union's potential for foreign policy, and probably did in the United Nations too, except as a dumping ground for problems the Powers did not want to face themselves. The belated rally to rescue Bosnia, under American leadership, did something to restore a sense of purpose in early 1996. Some wondered if the hesitancy of U.S.–European policy here might not encourage other of its foes. North Korea stood ready, as did Iran, a revenge-minded Iraq, and others. Boris Yeltsin perhaps mounted his assault on Chechnya because he saw how little he had to fear from any reaction in the West.

An emasculated Russia spent its fury on a tiny land in the Caucasus few had ever heard of before and botched the attack badly; the Russians were seen on world television as brutal bullies who were also inept. But many other portions of what Russians called "the near beyond" remained conflict-ridden and unstable.

Such scenarios throughout eastern Europe constituted a sorry disillusionment for those in the West who had supposed that after the fall of the communist regimes, all would be well. "The hopes born of the fall of the Berlin Wall are dimmed," editorialized the Paris oracle *Le Monde* in May 1993, mentioning especially the two wars that, for the first time in forty years, ravaged the Old Continent. (Georgia-Azerbaijan in the Caucusus, as well as Bosnia. This was before Chechnya). There were even hints of a cold-war renewal. Yeltsin furiously denounced plans to expand NATO by bringing in East European countries, and Russia was at odds with the West in Bosnia, supporting the Bosnian Serbs who figured as the villains in the Western press. The Russian chief was under considerable pressure from Russian nationalists enraged by their country's sudden decline in prestige.

The in-between countries of east-central Europe, Poland, Hungary, and the Czech and Slovak republics were once again in an awkward position. Should they join NATO, as well as the European Union, to create a super-Europe? They wanted to, and NATO at least was interested. But some in the West also wondered whether this was wise. Would it not drive Russia into sullen isolation, or into Asia? Would she regain her strength and try to put her empire back together? Russia must either advance to the Adriatic or retire behind the Urals, the Pan-Slavist Fadayev had declared a century earlier. Was this still true?

In the Far East, the dissolution of communist states seemed to be continuing. China, amid spectacular economic growth under a freer economic plan, saw the provinces gain power at the expense of Beijing. When the aged Deng Xiaoping dies, the center might not hold. China had broken into pieces before; for example, in the 1920s. Virtually alone in the world (except for Cuba, which was in total decay after her loss of Soviet subsidies, and, partly, Vietnam), China's Communist government refused to recant or to crumble. On the other hand, unlike the USSR prior to 1990, the Chinese communist rulers had permitted a great deal of economic liberalization. This led to a spectacular economic boom in the 1980s. The Chinese took to capitalism as they had never taken to communism. But the Communist party dictatorship remained, apparently determined to preside as a ruling mandarin elite over a process of economic liberalization. (But huge, inefficient state-owned industries remained, too, and were a drag on the economy.) Amid the perils and problems, not to say horrors, of economic development and modernization, with bureaucratic corruption, gangsterism, and terrible environmental pollution, the rulers sometimes seemed to have lost control of the situation in the 1990s; local autonomy was increasing, the decrees emitted from Beijing, like those from Moscow, often had little effect, and the party leadership seemed mystified about everything except one point, that it intended to hang on to absolute power.

The decline of Africa, which had begun in the 1970s, continued in the main. There was a bright spot in South Africa, where the white ruling class finally gave up and accepted racial equality; despite a great deal of conflict between rival blacks as well as resistance from die-hard white proponents of *Apartheid,* elections were successfully held, and Nelson Mandela became head of the government to preside over a hopeful new order of things. There was little success elsewhere. Faced with negative growth rates, some African countries undertook major structural reform in the direction of market economies, a task rendered difficult by political instability. A 1994 World Bank study (*Adjustment in Africa: Reforms, Results, and the Road Ahead*) found only six of twenty-nine countries studied had achieved much success in reform.

The list of African countries ravaged by violence was a long one. Ethiopia struggled in the 1990s to restore constitutional order after the flight of the "Marxist" tyrant Mengistu, under whom a Red Terror took an estimated 100,000 lives in 1976–1978. In Zaire, two governments competed for power amid growing anarchy. After the capture and killing of Liberian President Samuel Doe by rebels in 1990, a divided army and contending warlords led to almost total anarchy; other African states intervened attempting to restore constitutional order. Elections held in Chad at the insistence of the old colonial ruler, France, bred violence between the different religions and regions; as in strife-torn Sudan, Muslims in the north opposed animists and some Christians in the south. Genocide was the term used by the human rights organization Amnesty International to describe the persecution of the black peoples of the Nuba Mountains in the Sudan. More than 500,000 people, perhaps as many as a million, have been killed over the last dozen years or so in the Sudanese civil war. A similar civil war in Sierra Leone that broke out in 1991 was so small in comparison that it was almost overlooked, though it claimed 10,000 lives in the ensuing four years.

The United Nations called civil strife in Angola, which had gone on for decades, the worst of all such cases, estimating in 1993 that it cost a thousand lives a day. But Mozambique could claim a similar endless civil war. In 1994, the slaughter of several hundred thousand people in Rwanda and Burundi, in a renewal of clashes between what Westerners called rival "tribes," shocked the world. There had been earlier outbreaks here in the 1960s, 1970s, and 1980s, but the media had not caught up with these; some of the sense of a growingly turbulent world came from the greater effectiveness of international news coverage and television exposure.

While American soldiers brought relief to starving Somalia, some wondered how this particular island of misery was selected for charity over numerous others equally forlorn. In Somalia, the forces which intervened in the name of the United Nations soon got into conflicts with the people they were supposed to be helping and finally withdrew painfully. A year after the U.N. withdrawal in 1994, Somalia was again nearing famine amid fighting between rival warlords, using military equipment left behind or stolen from the U.N. forces. The intervention had been wholly in vain and was not likely to be repeated; nobody talked about Somalia any more. The United States had meanwhile turned its attention to a case much nearer its doorstep, in Haiti, and after restoring a deposed regime to power quickly forgot about this theater too. These operations all seemed more like media events than serious policy.

In north Africa, an Algerian military dictatorship attempted to put down Islamic fundamentalists whose Liberation Army beginning in 1992 practiced assassination and terrorism: Different players were reenacting the scenarios of 1954–1962. This virtual civil war was estimated to have cost 30,000 lives by 1996. The radical Islamicist political movement loomed as a powerful one throughout the African and Asian regions where the faith of Mohammed traditionally held sway. Even in Turkey, the classic example of adaptation to Westernizing patterns, a rebellion against the modernizing, secularizing process, led by radical Islamicists (Refah), made startling gains in the 1990s. This "Fresh Breeze" fundamentalism of the Middle East resembled the Panyat movement of ultra-Orthodoxy in Russia and even the Christian political right in America, in dreaming of some purer, less complicated past while indignantly rejecting a corrupt, materialist present. In their appeal to the poor and outcast, radical Islamic movements to some extent filled a vacuum left by the collapse of world Communism. Their followers looked to Teheran or Khartoum now rather than to Moscow or Peking.

A branch of radical Islam was active in the Gaza strip, not very long after Yasser Arafat, leader of the Palestine Liberation Organization, had finally, after long and painful negotiations, reached agreement with Israel's Yitzhak Rabin in 1993 on Israeli withdrawal from Gaza and Jericho, providing for the PLO's gradual assumption of government in these regions long occupied by Israel. This beginning of a dialogue that might eventually bring real peace between Arabs and Jews in the Middle East was a hopeful process of the 1990s, but a vast gulf remained and violence continued. The radical Palestinians repudiated Arafat and considered him a traitor for dealing with the Jews. Their terrorism was matched by Jewish extremists who regarded any compromise as a betrayal. On February 25, 1994, a Jewish doctor opened fire with an automatic weapon on a congregation of Islamic people at worship in Hebron, killing some thirty of them. The next year, in an event that shocked the world, a Jewish student assassinated Israeli Prime Minister Rabin. Despite all this, the return of places to Palestinian rule went on successfully in 1995–1996.

These were some of the sad spots of a troubled world. There were others. Between 1983 and 1995, more than 30,000 had died in the Sri Lanka civil war, still going on with little hope of settlement. The Indonesian government has been accused of conducting a campaign of genocide in western New Guinea (Irian Jaya); informed estimates of the number of Papuans killed by Indonesian forces in the past twenty-five years or so run as high as 150,000. The United Nations approved Indonesian annexation of this region in 1970, and the massacres have never been officially condemned. For political reasons, the United Nations also refused to condemn atrocities the Indian government has committed against native Muslims in Kashmir.

Closer to the heart of Europe, the Irish Republican Army, with brief respites, engaged in bombings, assassinations, hunger strikes and all the other weaponry of terrorism, tactics that grew out of a fervent desire, such as perhaps only the Irish could generate, to unite all Ireland and rescue their co-religionists in the North from Protestant persecution. The Northern Irish replied with their own death squads and an equally fervent determination never to surrender their land to Catholic Dublin. Neither side saw any possibility of compromise. So this long struggle seemed destined to continue without hope of final settlement. The only hope was that perhaps, in the end, it would simply exhaust itself. As members of the European Union, both Irelands made economic gains, and there was every reason for them to cooperate with each other.

Amid such tales of political and social violence in the world, perhaps it escaped notice that in the United States since 1975 there have been four times as many lives lost through murder as were lost in the Vietnam War. Nearly as many Americans as fell on the battlefields of World War II have been murder victims in the last two decades. In November 1993, an American government survey reported that violent crime is the leading cause of death among young people, surpassing deaths from AIDS or drug abuse or automobile accidents. A Department of Justice National Crime Victimization Survey for 1993 claimed that 36.6 million people have been criminally hurt since 1973. In 1992, there were 1,995 homicides in New York City, compared to 172 in London, even though the British thought they were having a crime wave. But in 1993, an estimated 30,800 people were murdered in Russia, with rates on the upswing, exceeding even the American record.

This suggests a radical sickness in portions of Western society, as well as other portions of the globe, lying beneath the surface of politics. It will be the main theme of our final chapter.

15

Conclusion:
In the Dying Century,
a Dying Civilization?

SCIENCE AND ANTISCIENCE

An observer of the European and world scene (the two were now almost joined)—say, perhaps, some creature from Outer Space, such as the popular imagination liked to invent[1]—might find himself equally amazed by how creative and productive this civilization was, and, on the other hand, by its failures and evident tendency to self-destruct. Science, its most impressive and massive intellectual venture, supplies examples.

The failure of medical science to come up with a remedy, despite frantic efforts, for the AIDS pandemic, itself self-induced by modern sexual practices, suggested a limit to the vaunted skills of health care; the conquest or amelioration of some deadly ailments only left room for others even more dreadful. The germs seemed to have won this latest round in their warfare with humanity. ("It can be argued that the true beneficiaries of the sexual revolution have been the viruses and bacteria that exploit the new vectors created by widespread promiscuity and unusual sexual practices," wrote British author John Ryle.) Yet the speed with which the AIDS virus was identified (whether first at the Institut Pasteur in Paris or in the United States, 1983) and the mobilization of international scientific brains in search of an answer to it was a remarkable

---

[1]It is highly unlikely, to say the least, that any such creature could find his way to this planet, or, if he could, would want to.

achievement, which no previous age could have matched. One had to wonder which was most extraordinary, the ability of modern humanity to dig itself into holes or its energy and skill in climbing out of them.

The medical industry is one of the most rapidly growing ones, now absorbing over 10 percent of the gross national product in the United States, with Europe likely to follow suit. The reasons for this included a population far older on the average than ever before. Fifteen percent of the populace is now over age sixty-five. The very success of public health created a population more susceptible to various ailments. It also brought the possibility of prolonging life at great cost: through organ transplants, for example, made possible by modern advances in surgical techniques. The right to die became, paradoxically, one of the most debated public questions, joining other soul-searing issues of "medical ethics."

Medical historian Roy Porter (in *TLS* 1-14-94) noted the rather discouraged state of mind of the one-time miracle workers, who a generation earlier had mounted a series of great breakthroughs, including penicillin and a vaccine for polio, heart transplants, and laser surgery. A historian of medicine declared that "In the first three-quarters of the twentieth century more specific remedies and preventives were devised for the control of infectious diseases than during the entire history of mankind before that time." Eradication of smallpox was proudly announced in 1977, just in time for the debut of the AIDS scourge. Now, "The atmosphere is one of hollow conquest, as at the end of the Gulf War," Porter thought. No cure for AIDS or for Alzheimer's disease, a curse of the aged, was in sight; there had not really been much progress in either, despite a huge investment of work and money. The mosquitoes had finally won the battle of malaria, it was reported from southern Africa. Once thought conquered, TB, the scourge of the nineteenth century, seemed to be making a comeback. Antibiotics had prodded the bacteria into a creative response. The National Health Service was falling apart in Great Britain, while the major issue in the United States in 1993–1994 was a crisis in health care. Despite all the miracles there seemed to be more unhealthy, or at least unhappy people in the world than ever before.

Doctors got sued more often than honored. Increasingly they were accused of fraud in their research. Rival claims about priority in discovering the AIDS virus gave rise to a controversy in which the Americans (Robert Gallo and the National Institute of Health) were eventually judged to have been guilty of first stealing from the French and then covering this up in classic Watergate manner. There were other well-publicized cases of scientific deception. In 1993, a number of French physicians were prosecuted for having allowed HIV-contaminated blood to be used in transfusions. Doctor Kildare, a TV hero of the 1960s, was not a candidate for reruns. Recent TV medicals are more likely to have committed some awful blunder or perhaps harassed their patients, if not engaged in plotting a genetic monstrosity. Genetic engineering (see below) aroused fears of some terrible catastrophe. There were also fears, not wholly unjustified, of even more deadly germs that might escape and decimate the human race.

Obsession with gene research in the quest for some understanding of ailments like Alzheimer's disease was oddly sterile. Arduous and expensive study turned up an obscure fragment of hereditary protein that might be associated with a disposition to succumb to this blight of (for the most part) the elderly. But what if this was indeed the case? Was everyone to undergo elaborate genetic analysis and engineering to remove or replace something that might predispose him or her to a malady many decades later? Research seemed far removed from therapy.[2]

Perhaps the most persistent criticism of medical treatment, however, concerned its human qualities, relating not to science per se but to social organization. As the price of a perhaps overly elaborate accumulation of medical tests and procedures, and of coverage that was usually low-cost and nearly universal, the patient submitted to an impersonal bureaucracy. The old-fashioned doctor who made house calls was now as quaint an anachronism as the nonemployed mother. The huge health industry with its immense paperwork (which the computers did not seem to simplify) might lose a patient or give him the wrong treatment—such stories, like the man who had the wrong foot amputated, frequently made the news; sometimes the errors were lethal. Or at great cost the process might fail to diagnose a simple problem: to go in with a nosebleed was to risk being X-rayed and punched with needles all day to no particular purpose. Instead of general practitioners exercising common sense, there were hordes of tunnel-visioned specialists. In some places, at least, there was corruption as well as inefficiency. So, at least, it seemed to many recipients of "health care" supplied by the welfare state; they would still appreciate the amazing advances in medications and surgical techniques which might provide, if you could surmount the bureaucratic obstacles, a quick cure for what formerly was a painful ordeal or a death sentence.

Fascinating research conducted with all the formidable facilities of internationally organized science was a multi-billion-dollar industry not only in medicine. The space program—in which Europe played some role though a minor one, in cooperation with the United States—ran up against the dilemmas of whether putting people on Mars or colonizing the moon would be worth the enormous cost. Exploration of outer space, which had been exciting in the 1960s, lost some of its popular appeal after that, perhaps because no intergalactic "star treks" materialized. The United States recovered from the humiliation of the 1950s to put a man on the moon in 1969, but the thrill was short-lived. Beyond this frontier lay the planets, but such horribly expensive projects suffered in the deficit-ridden and budget-conscious atmosphere of the 1980s and

---

[2]The dissociative Alzheimer's disease would seem a good candidate for a psychosocial diagnosis, if this had been in style: related to the bizarre pluralism of contemporary culture. No gene had apparently been found to account for another puzzling ailment, anorexia, in which young women starve themselves to death.

1990s. Unmanned spacecraft visited distant planets in search of data, not always successfully; the Americans thought about sending a man to Mars by 2019. A severe setback came when the Challenger space shuttle blew up shortly after blasting off in 1986, costing lives. And, a $1.5 billion telescope launched into outer space in 1990 to make unprecedented observations of the cosmos turned out to have a defective mirror.

These penetrations of relatively short distances beyond the earth (as cosmic dimensions go) facilitated communications transmission, and turned up data interesting to those who speculated about the age of the universe, whether 8 billion years or 20 billion. Telescopes sent into outer space on a Cosmic Background Explorer satellite revealed new puzzles, apparently telling us, for example, that the universe is younger than its oldest stars. In 1992, the evidence from COBE of irregularities in the cosmic microwave background radiation (discovered in 1965) was said to confirm the still controversial "big bang" theory of an original exploding atom, which grew in a billionth of a billionth of a second to grapefruit-size—the latest version. But riddles remained, even if one swallowed this scenario. It was still not clear whether the universe would continue expanding through all infinity or would eventually fall back into its original tiny state. Or perhaps collapse into one gigantic Black Hole.

In search of the elusive secrets of the universe, countries also vied with each other in building multi-billion-dollar supercolliders to smash subatomic particles. Such immense and doubtful enterprises called out for international collaboration, and there were tentative approaches to it—a Japanese, Russian, European, American consortium to work on fusion, for example—but national pride and state sovereignty still ran high.

The biologists were not to be left out of this competition for funding of mind-boggling projects. Discovery of the hereditary molecules, the DNA, that pass from parents to their children carrying elaborately coded instructions for growth, was one of the most exciting scientific events of the 1950s. Genetic engineering became a growth industry in the 1980s, when synthetic genes began to serve as cures for human ailments and as creators of improved vegetables and livestock. In the next decade, expensive projects were underfoot; the biologists' answer to the particle accelerator, estimated to cost the taxpayer several billions of dollars over the next fifteen years or so, was an undertaking to sequence the human "genome" or DNA set. Each of the two sets of DNA everyone inherits, one from each parent, is said to contain some 3,000,000,000 nucleotide units. A complete record of these would probably turn up many previously unknown genes. As in the case of atom smashing, what this might mean in terms of a fuller understanding of the nature of reality, or a fuller life, was not clear. But the quest went on; a quest the scientists sometimes compared to the old search for the Holy Grail. Was it likely to be found in the intricate chemical language with which nature transmits its information about life? If so, what would it mean?

None of these projects would be possible, of course, without computers, the miracle invention of the last half of the twentieth century. The microcomputer could store, process, and transmit "data" at speeds and reliability so far outdistancing previous modes as to constitute a multiple quantum leap. It could perform mathematical calculations previously out of the question because they would have taken centuries. It could picture or model relationships between vast amounts of data to open up whole new realms of knowledge. Every few years, faster computer chips were produced. The computer screen could display three-dimensional maps of the cosmos, and simulate a completed building for the architect to check.

All this and many other wonders opened up in the age of Turing. Michael Shallis, in *The Silicon Idol* (1984), declared the microchip revolution dehumanizing. But, as he realized, it was only an extension of what the telephone had begun. At that time, he had yet to confront the Fax revolution or electronic mail. This determined flat-earth-society mentality (which had some distinguished precedents in Tolstoy and other antimaterialists) arouses our admiration along with amusement. Mr. Shallis probably wrote his book on a computer, while listening to music on his laser disc, and retrieved his information with the aid of library electronics; interrupted perhaps by visits to dentist and doctor made far more comfortable by the progress of medical technology. Few if any are likely to reject all these modern conveniences. Culturally, they mean the ability to bring movies, plays, concerts, operas as well as sports events into homes in virtually living form via VCRs and television, vastly increasing the audience for high culture as well as low.

Simon Nora and Alain Minc wrote a tract addressed to the President of France in 1980, on *The Computerization of Society,* which identified IBM (the computer company, not the ballistic missile) as one of France's chief enemies. They were right at least in asserting that this technology "will alter the entire nervous system of social organization." For one thing, the world learned almost instantaneously of wars and other disasters by computerized, satellite-transmitted, laser-printed information wonders. Earthquakes, hurricanes, genocides, and famines that in former times would have been known dimly if at all to Americans and Europeans now came up on the TV screen as soon as they happened.

Artificial intelligence was a subject of great interest to the "cognitive scientists." By the year 2000, computers will have entirely replaced theoretical physicists, Stephen Hawking claimed. Would Man become obsolete? Computers could also "simulate reality," so that real people (it was conjectured) might have a future if they made love via computers, among other forms of communication. Computers could beat all but a few humans at chess, quickly calculating the best move from millions of possibilities; but they could not plan a strategy. A world chess champion defeated a supercomputer four games to two in a much-publicized match of February, 1996. Philosophers refuted the naive view that the mind is only a computer and could be replaced by one.[3] The attributing of meanings to linguistic symbols, the whole of humanistic culture, of

---

[3]See John R. Searle, *The Rediscovery of the Mind* (1992); Hubert L. Dreyfus, *What Computers Still Can't Do* (1992).

art and history, lie outside the computer's range. Human consciousness lies behind the computer itself; it is, after all, a human invention. Consciousness cannot be studied scientifically at all.

At the end of the quest mystery remained. "The more we know, the more elaborate and complex living organisms seem to be," microbiologist John Tyler Donner observed. The more we know, the more mystery unfolds. Electron microscopes unveiled a deeper world of the structure of the cell. Living organisms with their incredibly intricate genetic codes became far more complicated and enigmatic than anyone had suspected. "Chaos theory" proposed that some self-propelling tendency causes things to become ever more complicated as they grow, like a Committee.

All this provided glorious entertainment for the skilled players, but passed well over the heads of the rest. One philosophical scientist, David Lindley, (*The End of Physics: The Myth of a Unified Theory*, 1995) foresaw the end of physics in a cloud of speculation ungrounded in any empirical evidence, if indeed this had not already happened. (Those who continued to pursue Einstein's old quest for a "unified theory," tying all the forces together, postulated that physical reality did not consist of particles but of strings or loops.) Sociology and philosophy of science produced a body of thought arguing that science is a mode of discourse without much to do with external reality: See, for example, Alan G. Gross, *The Rhetoric of Science* (1991). Rhetoric, indeed, the quaintest of medieval subjects, became the rage, as modern as nuclear physics; all knowledge turns on how it is linguistically structured.

Shamans and witches and satanists once confined to the counterculture were now not so far removed from advanced science. A reputable physicist, Fred Alan Wolf, author of a book explaining quantum mechanics to the layman, wrote *The Eagle's Quest: a Physicist's Quest for Truth in the Shamanic World* (1992). He went to Santa Fe for instruction in an urbanized Native American shamanism! Medicine now took folk remedies seriously; Druid or ancient Chinese herbal mixtures turned out to contain valuable enzymes.

The "quarks," some called Strange and Magic, identified as the ultimate building blocks of the universe, had been so called by a brilliant and imaginative physicist who picked up the name from *Finnegans Wake*, thus tying together two great realms of the incomprehensible in modern culture. The world of the scientists was as strange as the dream-world of Humphrey Chimpden Earwicker.

ENVIRONMENTAL CONCERNS

Modern humanity seemed terrified by the monsters its technological miracles and awesome power over nature had unleashed. The rise of "environmental" concerns, leading to "Green" political parties, was a feature of the 1980s and 1990s. Fashionable doomsayers turned from nuclear extinction to perils arising from chemical pollution or industrially created atmospheric changes. To be sure, the catastrophe at the Soviet nuclear plant at Chernobyl near Kiev in 1986, sending clouds of radioactive gases around the world, did little to ease nuclear-energy fears. (Chernobyl had something to do, also, with the Soviet collapse, shattering confidence in the political leadership. Published in 1989, Grigori Medvedev's *The Truth about Chernobyl,* by the chief engineer who headed the official investigation, with a foreword by Andrei Sakharov, documented the horrifying incompetence of the disaster's handling.) In famed German novelist Günter Grass's novel *The Rats* (*Die Rättin,* Munich, 1986), *Der grosse Knall* (the big bang) will doubtless get us in the end; but if it doesn't, then ozone depletion or acid rain will. Or, perhaps, we will run out of usable sources of energy. Hopes for a pollution-free, cheap source of energy via nuclear fusion—the same process that powers the stars as well as nuclear warheads—had proved elusive.[4] Existing nuclear plants hold all their outputs bottled up inside them, threatening catastrophe in the event of accident or sabotage.

But other sources of the energy modern urban humanity so greedily consumed were equally dangerous. The chief though by no means the only environmental concerns were ozone depletion and increases in carbon dioxide levels. In 1985, the British Antarctic Survey discovered that vast amounts of ozone had been disappearing from the Antarctic stratosphere. It was subsequently learned that the perpetrators of this hole in the sky were chlorofluorocarbons resulting from industrial chemicals used in refrigeration, air conditioning, computers, foam blowing, and so on. Depletion of the protective ozone layer, which absorbs harmful ultraviolet rays, threatened an increase in skin cancer and also changes in climate.

A dramatic increase in the carbon dioxide content of earth's atmosphere, some scientists thought, would induce a global warming of temperatures. Atmospheric CO_2, which traps the warmth radiated by the earth, had increased by 25 percent since the century began and was continuing to rise about 0.4 percent a year, they claimed. The world's ever-mounting energy consumption relied chiefly on fossil fuels, which create CO_2. Emission of pollutants from gasoline-burning engines was a major factor, and so was the diminishing of forests, which consume CO_2. Projected increases in temperatures at earth's surface of between 5 degrees and 10 degrees within the next half-century would, among other things, melt the ice of polar seas, thus raising sea levels and causing coastal flooding. But some scientists questioned the whole "global warming" argument, finding no persuasive evidence that any such thing was happening, or, if it was, that it would have an adverse effect on life. Nevertheless the "greenhouse effect" leading to disastrous "global warming" remained an article of faith in the Green gospel.

---

[4]Fusion research went on (western European efforts were concentrated in Oxfordshire, England), but whether it would ever pay off, at vast expense, remained uncertain. Perhaps scarce resources would be better applied to wind, tide, solar, or geothermal possibilities. Hard choices of this sort faced scientists and the governments who footed their bills with funds wrung from hard-pressed taxpayers.

Environmental considerations weigh the more heavily when one thinks about the future growth of the world's as yet undeveloped regions. Relatively few people in the world live in "high-income economies," technologically advanced and fully "modernized"; apart from western Europe, the United States, and Canada, these countries numbered Australia, New Zealand, and a smattering of Asian areas, including Japan, Hong Kong, Singapore, plus Israel and some of the oil-rich Arab nations. Their combined population was no more than 15 percent of the world total. They consume extremely disproportionate amounts of energy—the United States, for example, stands at a ratio of about 7,200 to Nigeria's 133 per capita—and excrete disproportionate amounts of waste and pollution. What happens when and if the other 85 percent of the world travels down the road of "development" to reach the same plateau as the presently privileged peoples? Some of the developing countries are already poised on the brink of it; others, including the giant populations of India and China—together more than a third of the world total—are striving toward the goal. Indeed, virtually the entire globe wants to emulate the wealthy Europeans and North Americans, little chance though some of them, as things now stand, appear to have of doing so. To think of 8 billion people (the world's population only a few decades from now) consuming energy and producing waste and pollution and despoiling nature to the same extent as less than 1 billion now do boggles the mind. (Poor countries engaged in economic development cannot afford the cost of technology that protects the environment. The Communist bloc's environmental record was deplorable. The Soviets destroyed one of the world's largest inland waters, the Aral Sea. West Germans were appalled at the industrial pollution found in ex-communist East Germany when they took it over.)

Western Europe's own house was not all that ecologically clean. According to a World Bank study, "The environmental degradation of the Mediterranean is severe and in many areas is worsening by the day. . . . Public health is threatened." The Rhine River's condition, too, had become a scandal. Problems of maintaining a relatively clean environment were monumental in all the advanced industrial countries. Pollution, ironically, was worst in Athens, the pure ancient source of Western Civilization. Almost all major European cities experienced terrible automobile congestion, as deficit-plagued governments struggled to keep up with the demand for more and better roads. Effective public transportation existed in cities such as Vienna and Stockholm, but London's great pioneer underground railway had fallen into decay, while Berlin's streets were blocked by massive construction projects designed to knit the long-separated eastern and western parts back together.

Yet an optimist would find reason to believe that science and technology can find ways of dealing with these problems. In reply to a Green manifesto called *Global 2000,* Julian L. Simon and Herman Kahn assembled optimistic evidence for *The Resourceful Earth* (Blackwell, 1984). The Greens lived more by faith than by science; they saw in modern technology a demonic enemy. The

Green spirit dated from the 1960s, when the young leftists rejected the whole technological society. "Western rationality had made a dreadful mess of a lovely planet" (Mark Vonnegut). Now, they were divided into factions; the more extreme ones were accused by "responsible environmentalists" of a fanaticism that would unintentionally do even worse damage to the environment. Some tried to invent a middle ground of "progressive" environmentalism, having one's cake and eating it too, modern technology without contamination. After all, "The pre-scientific age was far more 'polluted' than ours," with plagues, germs, dirt, squalor, disease, poverty. If one followed the more extreme environmentalists and abolished the whole of modern technology, did you not return to a condition far more dangerous to life than the present one?

Fuller study often found no completely safe path. If you use battery-powered automobiles to avoid carbon dioxide, you risk poisoning the earth with lead. The alternative to atomic energy, which environmentalists detested as an article of faith, was burning coal or oil, and that was now bad because it produces carbon dioxide.

Thus there were numerous critiques of environmentalism, and divisions within the movement itself, with a hard-core left ranged against a moderate, compromising wing just as in other activist crusades, like socialism. One historian in 1995 predicted "The Fading of the Greens" as a political movement. But their drastic pessimism, shared with radical feminists, about the whole course of Western civilization was probably the most pervasive mood of the day among intellectuals. To be sure, there were other scenarios of final extinction than the ecological. A huge meteorite, such as apparently had wiped out whole species and drastically changed the course of evolution some sixty million years ago, might hit the earth again. (A massive one had indeed leveled a remote area of Siberia early in this century.) Earthquakes, volcanoes, and hurricanes did cause immense damage every decade, at various places around the world, in California, Florida, Chile, China, Japan, Turkey; about their causes and control, science appeared to be almost totally ignorant. We have mentioned the fear of some terrible epidemic, launched by the victorious bacteria, a super-AIDS that would indeed wipe out the human race.

In any case, whatever the fate of the whole cosmos, all solar systems eventually exhaust their energy supply and die, in one way or another. Our own sun will go the way of all stars in a few billion years. So the scientists assure us.

SOCIAL PATHOLOGIES

In a passage from his classic *Decline and Fall of the Roman Empire,* Edward Gibbon had observed that "man has much more to fear from the passions of his fellow creatures than from the convulsions of the elements." Noting the "violent and destructive earthquake," followed by huge tidal waves in the Mediterranean, that shook the greatest part of the Roman world on July 21, 322 A.D., causing immense loss of life, the great historian saw this as little compared to the wars just then descending on the Empire: "The invasion of the Huns precipitated on the provinces of the West the Gothic invasions, which advanced in less than forty years from the Danube to the Atlantic and opened a way by the success of their arms to the inroads of so many hostile tribes more savage than themselves."

It might similarly be said of the modern world that wars and massacres, civil strife and murder and suicide, have taken far more lives than natural disasters. Some of these were mentioned in the last chapter. So far as concerns Europe, the orgy of slaughter in the era of the two World Wars, Russian Communism, and German Nazism eased in the last half of the century, at least until the conflicts of the east European Communist succession. But the toll in terms of human unhappiness seems to go on in other ways. Irving Kristol marveled that although since 1945 "the average citizen has achieved a level of economic affluence and economic security that would have been regarded, at the time, as visionary," making this the most remarkable half century in world history, yet "this economic progress has been accompanied by an unforeseen tidal wave of social disintegration and moral disorientation." There were disturbing indices of suicide, mental disorder, drug addiction, crime (rising in Europe even if far short of American standards; apparently rife in the USSR). A German report indicated that 10 percent to 12 percent of all Federal Republic inhabitants at some time needed the services of a psychiatrist. (Psychiatry itself was in as much disarray as economics as far as concerned any agreed-upon body of thought; there were innumerable schools with dominant trends succeeding each other seasonally.) A West Berlin survey of 1985 found that one of every twelve students had attempted suicide. The centers of such cities as London and Zurich featured scenes of grotesquely dressed youths stoned on drugs or alcohol, aiming to live probably short lives in a continual "high."

Once regarded as an American degeneracy (like AIDS), use of "hard" drugs had spread to Europe in the 1960s, and with temporary remissions continued to do so; "all the available figures suggest that drug use is spreading" in Britain, it was reported in 1989. The young revolutionaries, terrorists, and sexually emancipated nihilists such as one met in fashionable movies, plays, and novels used drugs as a matter of course. The "rave" pop culture fashionable in England in the 1990s centered on mood-altering amphetamines and sophisticated sexual orgies. All efforts to enforce anti-drug laws had ended. In the late 1960s and early 1970s, such matters had been confined to the special areas where the counterculture flourished, such as Copenhagen's "free city." Not so a decade later. It was still illegal to possess or sell addictive drugs such as cocaine and heroin, and indeed American policemen seemed to spend most of their time searching for these substances, but efforts to enforce the law encountered a losing battle and voices were raised in favor of legalization. The "rave" drugs were technically illegal but open and public use of them went on in the best circles.

Violence was the pervasive theme of serious literature and art as well as popular television, which displayed little else except (often quite violent) sports. (It was somehow appropriate that the leading public event of 1995 in the United States was the trial of a sports hero for murder.) Violence, death, disorder may be found in the greatest artists of our century. The recently deceased Francis Bacon, for example, often regarded as the greatest British painter of the post-1945 era, filled his canvases with twisted, convulsed, screaming figures, obscenely wounded or crippled—hardly surprising for an artist who was born during World War I, grew up surrounded by civil war in Ireland, and reached maturity in London during World War II.

A study of youth literature in 1976 found that it had changed sharply from the familiar happy ending to preoccupation with "flawed development and psychic catastrophes, violence, injustice, unmerited destruction."[5] Novels written for young adults in the 1980s scorched pages with accounts of rape, parental abuse, drug-peddler boy friends, sexual adventures, and abortions.

A representative German novella of the 1990s, Bodo Kirchhof's *Gegen die Laufrichtung* (Against the Current), in the course of its eighty-six pages, features a tennis-pro hero who stabs his wife's lover and slits the throat of his girlfriend's admirer. Other German novels show a preoccupation with the murderous deeds of the East German Stasi, prior to the final collapse of the Communist secret-police state in 1989. East German theatrical director Peter Zadek (April 1995) charged that "brutal theater is driving east Germans toward fascism." While Zadek accused the Berliner Ensemble of promoting "right-wing nationalism," playwright Heine Müeller as director of the theater was producing a play by a Stalinist author. Nazism or Stalinism, the attractive ingredient seemed to be violence. Müeller, a former socialist with Stasi contacts, praised riot and war in a somewhat Futurist manner.

Suicide rates were among the highest in the world in Sweden, an exemplar of the successful industrial society. For some years, the Swedes with all their comforts had been strangely not all that happy. There was widespread abuse of alcohol and drugs, evidence of stress and dissatisfaction, and a low level of confidence in public institutions. The Swedes held an earnest debate about all this in the 1980s. Now that nearly everyone is materially well off, why aren't they happy? Among the answers given were predictable ones: Society is too big, the individual feels helpless and isolated, the family isn't what it used to be, we are too far away from nature, with all their gadgets people are bored, the bureaucracy is faceless, urban architecture is dismally standardized.

Sweden in fact led all others in the indices of family disintegration as measured by rates of births out of wedlock. Marriage had become less common and divorce much more so. Single-parent families were now commonplace (over 20 percent in Britain). There are more single young women. The percentage of babies born outside wedlock rose from 5 percent in 1960 to 23 percent in

---

[5] *Stimmen der Zeit*, November 1976, p. 767.

THE DISINTEGRATING FAMILY

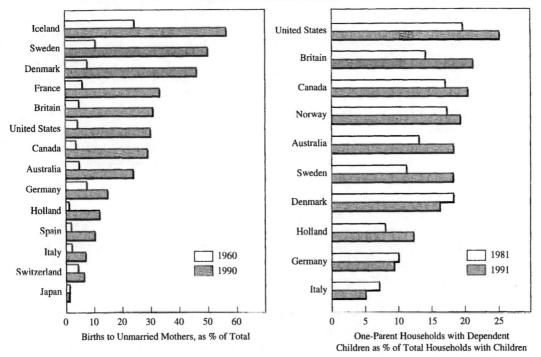

Source: *The Economist*, Sept. 5, 1995.

1987 and then to over 30 percent in 1995. In Sweden it was 50 percent! Sweden has a higher proportion of women in the workforce than any other country and a tax policy that offers no incentive to marriage. Throughout Europe, far more women had received an advanced education (so had men, but women's rate of increase was greater). Women bore one fewer offspring each on average than in 1960. Many more women are in the job market: More than 50 percent of them were employed outside the home in most western Europe countries by 1990, and women constituted 40 percent of the civilian work force.

This disintegration of the family some thought the greatest revolution thus far in history. "We have simply ceased to live in these respects as all previous societies have lived," demographer-historian Peter Laslett observed. French President Pompidou declared that "the very foundations of social life stand in danger," pointing to the dissolution of the family, the church, ancient institutions. Mental illness, suicide, crime, youth gangs; drug addiction, pornography, abortion, nonmarital sex; all of these disquieting features of the modern urban society might, according to some, be connected with family disintegration. Feminists usually applauded rather than deplored the decline of the traditional family and "familial values," which to them meant confining women to child-bearing and dish-washing roles. But did not the new order expose most women to more insecurity and oppression than formerly? The one parent in the family was more likely to be the mother than the father.

There were frequent cases of sex-role reversal in which the wife functioned as the primary breadwinner while the husband kept house. More and more preschool children spent a substantial part of their time not in the home but in public or private child-care establishments that were professionally staffed. The tendency to eat at restaurants rather than at home was one significant aspect of the new service economy. Still, technology tended to privatize entertainment: People watched movies, plays, concerts, sports events at home on their VCRs and TVs far more than in public theaters and arenas; though a rich variety of musical festivals, art exhibits, operas, concerts marked the European season, drawing throngs of tourists and providing for every kind of taste from traditional to pop, jazz to classics.

Demographically, Europe's population has ceased to grow, is even contracting: The population of Italy, Germany, Hungary, Denmark, and Switzerland is projected to decline between 1987 and 2000 and even more by 2025. By the latter year, the population of western Europe as a whole will be almost the same as in 1988 (some 356 million). Its percentage of the world population will have declined from 6.3 to 4 percent.

The breakdown of restrictions on personal behavior and in literature continued in late twentieth-century Europe and America. For the English-speaking world, a landmark in the battle against censorship was the *Lady Chatterley's Lover* case of 1960, in which a British court swept aside long-established taboos on language in literature, at least in the case of one modern masterpiece. In ensuing years, there were several rear guard actions against increasingly scandalous books and magazines, but by 1980 obscenity prosecutions had been given up as hopeless. Julian Symons' estimate of the British situation in 1982 was that "almost anything may be published without risk of prosecution and anything short of closely simulated sex acts is permitted on films or stage." Since then, there has been even more progress, with "hard-core" sex films readily available on VCRs and television.

Needless to say, this unprecedented process did not go unchallenged.

Table 15-1   Population of Europe at End of Century
(in millions)

The European Union (15 countries)	366	
12 potential additional members of Union*	107	
Russia in Europe	116	
Other countries of Europe	104	
Total population of Europe from Atlantic to Urals		693
Asiatic part of ex-USSR	100	
European % of world population 1975:		18.4%
est. 2000:		13.7%

*Includes Poland, Hungary, Czechs, Slovaks, Romania, Bulgaria

Along with much hailing of this wholesome release from repression and hypocrisy, an occasional voice protested that it meant virtually the end of civilization: "a horrible epidemic . . . that threatens our country's psychic health," cried British author and educator David Holbrook, in 1972, well before the peak of the "epidemic." Some feminists thought pornography an instrument of male debasement of women; the "modernization of sex" thus clashed with another mode of modernization. In earlier times, the subjection of ever-increasing portions of the populace to control and regulation of sexual appetites by moral rules and institutions had been regarded as a civilizing process; only outcast intellectuals and antisocial poets took the opposite view. Now such regulation came to be regarded as oppressive, and in practice social controls broke down. In Ireland, a national referendum defeated abortion and divorce, but Italy approved them, and aside from Spain all the major European countries legalized abortion; the French invented a pill to make abortion easier and safer. The numbers of legal abortions during the years 1984 to 1986 ranged from 84,000 in West Germany (where some restrictions existed) to 227,000 in Italy. In eastern Europe, abortion on demand, at least in the first three months of pregnancy, was the rule. Rare in Europe were the militant protests against abortion found in the United States.

The 1980s also saw a steady increase in the visibility of male and female homosexuals and tolerance for them. There was even an organization aimed at protecting the sexual rights of children. Only Islamic fundamentalists, it seemed, wanted to visit punishment on unlicensed and irregular sexual activity. The feminists who attributed the pornographic debasement of women to male compulsion ignored the fact that liberated women freely posed for pictures in *Playboy* and performed in x-rated films. The distinction between "x-rated"–that is, "pornographic"–movies and standard cinema in fact became quite indistinct. In any case, x-rated movies were available for rent in every shopping mall.

If much of this international urban culture came from across the Atlantic, some of it was distinctively European in origin. Youth tribes seemed a specialty of the British whose "punks" and "skinheads" were imitated virtually all over the world; rock music too owed as much to the British as to the Americans. Rock and its various offshoots were now global, listened to in Siberian villages and Japanese parks. The communications revolution ensured the rapid transmission of every cultural novelty. "Russians share in the sickness of the spirit that infects all twentieth century industrial societies," Sovietologist Robert A. Maguire had remarked before *glasnost*. Puritanical Old Guard Bolshevists had tried vainly to stem the influx of rock music, pornography, sexual permissiveness, drugs (holding on to their vodka, however) but in the end had to surrender to these "decadent" modernisms. Rock music, jazz, blue jeans, and "pot" smoking were badges of a youth revolt in the Communist society that had much to do with its eventual collapse.

The above catalog of distress signals could be elaborated on almost endlessly. Government, as we noted in the previous chapter, confronted a crisis of authority or of competency. The parliamentary political systems of Europe were in turmoil in the 1990s, as they tried to run the complicated affairs of a modern state while appeasing the whims of a demanding and often volatile public (the ungovernable in pursuit of the impossible, someone called it). "The key to the twenty-first century," the *Economist* claimed on the two-hundredth birthday of the American republic, is "the art of making sure that people elect their governments." At that moment when the dictatorial Soviet Russian state had finally crumbled, democracy enjoyed a brief euphoria, but it did not last long. The political crisis embraced widespread corruption, the breakdown of the welfare state, a total fragmentation of parties and interests.

Ever more extreme specialization led to loss of contact with other fields and with the general public. "Literature today is fragmented. . . . Scholarship is fragmented too; so is life." Thus lamented a distinguished British scholar in 1968. The situation was to get steadily worse. Charles Martindale, reviewing a batch of Milton books (*TLS* February 5-11-88) found this academic writing "opaque, windy, with frequent neologisms." "It is a worrying thought that few ordinary educated persons interested in Milton would be likely to want to read any of these books."

Religion was in as much trouble as the family or sexual customs. The Christian or Judaic religious orthodoxies, which had served for many centuries as the regulator of life, had been in slow decline for more than a century; ever since Darwin, at least. It is true that the old churches showed a surprising resiliency. The Orthodox faith survived six decades of persecution in the Soviet Union; persecution, after all, is the seed of any church. The Roman Catholic pontiff had emerged as the chief source of resistance to communism in Poland in the 1980s and thus might claim credit for the collapse of the whole Marxian edifice of atheism. Pope John Paul II continued his energetic mission by traveling all over the world, to be greeted by huge crowds whether in New York or Manila or Rio de Janeiro.

But increasingly in the cosmopolitan minglings of the modern urban world, religious impulses escaped entirely from the old Christian or Judaic molds. A host of cults ranging from the Anglo-American Scientology and the Unification Church, one of many Oriental imports, testified eloquently to the need for faith at the popular level. All sorts of mixtures of eastern and western religions flourished. Such a strange variety of spiritual phenomena had not been seen since the age of the Reformation. But this new "religious consciousness" in the end seemed to mean little except that modern humanity is disturbed. The indices of mental illness, suicide, crime, divorce, and drug addiction are symptoms of anomie and anxiety. If the function of religion is to provide a core of values that all can share, uniting and stabilizing the community, then these numerous crazes flitting through the heated urban world do not function as religion, but are rather signs of its absence. The vast process of secularization, so basic a part of modernization, has continued on; the very nature of modern society is nonreligious. The offer of heavenly salvation no longer operated as a vital option for most modernized urban people. A faith of earthly salvation, in the form of various secular religions, had replaced or supplemented the older religion in the nineteenth century: Such above all was the socialist utopia, with its belief in the future good society shaped by human intelligence to allow people to lie down in the green pastures of brotherhood and plenty. That hope too had faded. The "overwhelming experience of the twentieth century," historian Peter Jenkins wrote, is "the moral failure of socialism." "No confident model for the socialist organization of society at any stage of development survives with its credibility intact," conceded the relatively sympathetic political scientist John Dunn. So much for a cause in which nineteenth- and twentieth-century political idealism had invested most of its capital.

A comparable beacon of hope was lacking, despite some evidence of a return to religion: not only the mainline churches and faiths, given new sobriquets such as "Pentecostal," but also scores of exotic cults from the Orient. The radical Islamicist political movement of the Middle East resembled the Panyat movement of ultra-Orthodoxy in Russia and the Christian political right in America, in dreaming of some purer, less complicated past while indignantly rejecting a corrupt, materialist present.

Aside from these, probably the leading "causes" in the last decades of the century that won the allegiance of devoted acolytes were radical feminism and environmentalism. Both were tinged with a deep negativism, at bottom resting on a bitter rejection of the main values by which Western civilization had lived virtually since its beginning. They contemplated some vague total revolution or apocalypse. Visions of apocalypse permeated popular literature (science fiction, notably). Apocalypse meant neither the Judeo-Christian end of the world followed by judgment and redemption, nor the socialist Great Day of final revolutionary triumph, but some absolutely final end: end of the planet, of the solar system, of the universe itself. (Though perhaps there would be a revival on some other star, some other possible world.)

Contact with nature was being lost. In the nineteenth century, the farm, the village, the countryside with its craftsmen still remained close even after considerable urbanization. "A morning's walk from the largest city and you were in the midst of it," Alan Everitt remarks of the late nineteenth century, "it" being a traditional society where one might meet shoemakers, saddlers, millers, and farmers come to market. Today in England, less than 3 percent of the population earn their living by agriculture, and these are largely machine tenders—factory workers on the land, as it were. The urban megalopolis has swallowed up virtually every other kind of social environment.

By the 1970s, there were fifty cities in Europe and the USSR with a population, counting the entire metropolitan area, of over a million people. A collection of Dutch cities with five million inhabitants or so had merged into one continuous megalopolis, something almost true of the German Ruhr. Indeed, the Netherlands virtually consisted of a circle of cities, a *Rondstad,* with park land in the middle, Holland thus becoming in effect one great city with a central park. Despite government efforts to plan decentralization, nearly a fifth of the French populace lives in and around Paris.

These cities were marvels of technology. There was an enormous amount of building; "Europe has never built as much as in the past four and a half decades," Joseph Rykwert wrote in 1990. This began with rebuilding war-ravaged cities, then fed on the booming economic development of the 1980s. But there was "widespread dissatisfaction" with the esthetic quality of public architecture. We may recall the Swedish complaint about this. Not to be left out of the equation of Soviet breakdown was the dismal state of its architecture; a barracks-like style of urban "flats" which laid no claims to beauty but was supposed to be functional, could not even keep up with the demand, so that the shortage of housing became perhaps the most scandalous example of the planned economy's failure. (Avant-garde urban architects and planners had been terrorized and destroyed as a part of the war on Modernism in the name of Socialist Realism.[6])

The mad Romanian dictator Ceaucescu totally destroyed much of beautiful old Bucharest to make way for bleak Stalinesque giganticism. But this practice was not confined to the Communist lands. In Paris, the tearing down of old neighborhoods like Les Halles went on under Gaullist rule; the great art museum named after President Pompidou was a strange and debatable modernism. Between 1965 and 1975, the French government planned and built five new towns and remodeled several older suburbs outside of Paris, supposedly in order to create a rational pattern for urban growth. "A failed world of the future," Ada Louise Huxtable pronounced it, apparently agreeing with most of the inhabitants. Glass walls, futuristic designs, vast bleak towers left "a predominant effect of emptiness," which contrasted with the warm humanity and natural beauty of the old Paris, where visitors still want to go; they would visit these suburban exercises in cold logic only as curiosities. Based on Le Corbusier's towers in the park, they were evidently a travesty of the great pioneer modernist's ideas.

The Modernism of Le Corbusier, Gropius, and others of the classic early twentieth-century revolution in architecture could not last; new architects had to create new, "post-modernist" styles. Fads in architecture became as changeable as clothing styles; "post-modernism" led on to "deconstruction," which Joseph Rykwert says did not much resemble the literary-philosophical movement of that name. Each lasted but a season, it seems. "Eclecticism in style," a "premeditated chaos," was a notable feature of architectural postmodernism: pillage the past in any way you choose, make up arbitrary combinations. So imposing constructions like Paris's new National Library (Bibliothèque Nationale) or London's Canary Wharf produced public controversy.

Probably the most impressive construction project of the 1980s and

---

[6]Hugh D. Hudson, Jr., *Blueprints and Blood* (1994) tells the story of the Stalinization of Russian architecture.

The New urban environment. (top) The Farsta Center, near Stockholm, Sweden; (bottom) The Mirail, suburban Toulouse, France. Planned community developments of this sort where people live, work, and play, are a creative feature of contemporary Europe. Candills, architect of the Mirail, is a disciple of Le Corbusier. Can urban people really make themselves at home here? (*Swedish Information Service and Photo YAN, Toulouse.*)

The new urban architecture. Brussels, Belgium: A litter of the old and new, with European Community buildings prominent among the latter. (*European Community Information Services.*)

1990s was the "chunnel" built underneath the English Channel to link Paris/ Brussels and London by rail, a three or three-and-a-half hour journey for those who could afford it, a group somewhat more numerous than those who were able to fly on the celebrated Concorde airplane from Paris to New York in four hours. These were modern wonders of the world, as were the Disney World amusement parks, the space shuttles, and other shrines to the modern religion of technology. But the Chunnel project lost incredible amounts of money, as did the attempt to export Disney to Paris, London's Canary Wharf superdevelopment, and, indeed, most of the major airlines. Los Angeles was facing bankruptcy, joining the Italian government among others in this category, while national politicians struggled in vain to reduce mounting deficits. One had to wonder whether twenty-first century society would be able to afford its ambitious entertainments.

The instinct for lost communal solidarity came out in sports and mass entertainment. The football stadium was the largest structure in any European city, the World Cup quadrennial rites the biggest event. Latin American and African countries challenged European ones–both East and West–for supremacy, and even the United States appeared interested in "soccer." But commercialization brought grotesque salaries for athletes who no longer represented their native cities but were bought up in an international auction—an Italian team might feature Scottish, German, African, Brazilian players. Corruption scandals appeared here also. The Marseille football team had to be suspended.

Such phenomena, including the decadent tastes as well as the declining population, the violent youth gangs[7] as well as the wars and massacres, had also marked the last days of the Roman Empire. Out of that experience had been distilled the Christian religion, besting a host of competitors that appeared in the polyglot urban society of late antiquity. So today, there appear a strange melange of cults, crazes, obsessions, addictions. In England, excited believers in etas and ufos claimed to discover "crop circles," mysterious markings in farm fields, and wrote best-selling books about them. Cropwatchers joined shamanists and satanists in the lunatic fringe of pop culture that seems to include honest loonies, far-out religious seekers, and cynical entrepreneurs in the occult market, or just practical jokers. Satanic cults arose among the supposedly placid Norwegians.

All the problems identified by a series of twentieth-century social and cultural theorists remain without assured solution: the bureaucratization and disenchantment of modern life; dehumanization in a technological and commodity-market economy; the fragmentation of culture and thought via hyperspecialization, professionalization, and "reification"; gaps between high and low culture, between generations, between classes, between sexes; loss of contact with nature in a heavily urbanized world; destruction of traditional values by pervasive skepticism and overly rapid change; collapse of organic relationships and primary social institutions into anomie and the "lonely crowd"; psychic individualism on a collision course with social regimentation; and others, all connected with the question of the individual in a mass, urban, technological culture.

EUROPEAN SUCCESS

Truly one might agree with the title of a novel, *The Age of Death,* applied to the present. Like Macbeth, this century has "supped full of horrors"; no direness can any longer startle it

And yet the twentieth century has kept far more people alive than ever

---

[7]"No place was safe or sacred from their depredations," Gibbon wrote of the rival Blue and Green gangs of the late Roman Empire, associated with sports fans. "To gratify either avarice or revenge they profusely spilled the blood of the innocent; churches and altars were polluted by atrocious murders. . . . The dissolute youth of Constantinople adopted the blue livery of disorder; the laws were silent, and the bonds of society were relaxed; creditors were compelled to resign their obligations; judges to reverse their sentence; masters to enfranchise their slaves; fathers to supply the extravagance of their children; noble matrons were prostituted to the lust of their servants; beautiful boys were torn from the arms of their parents; and wives, unless they preferred a voluntary death, were ravished in the presence of their husbands" (*Decline and Fall*).

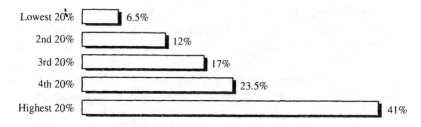

Average Income Distribution in 14 Western Europe Countries, ca.
1980. Percent (in round numbers) of income received by each quintile of the population.

before. In sheer quantitative terms, it outweighs all the rest of human history.
We might as aptly describe it as the Age of Life. One of the critics' prime complaints is about the world's overpopulation. One of its greatest problems is a su-
perabundance of everything, knowledge and manufactured products as well as
human beings. So far as Europe is concerned, the rise in average life expectancy
from around fifty to over seventy years has obviously added the equivalent of
more than a third to the total of human life-years, in effect further increasing
population by about 200 million. People not only live longer but live more actively in their later years, a change that Laslett has described as a "Third Age"
added on to human life. These people have been kept alive at a higher standard
of living as well as a richer content of consciousness.

Since 1900, and particularly since 1945, Europe has made extraordinary material progress. Seebohm Rowntree, who in 1900 had estimated that 28
percent of the British population lived in poverty, found that by the same criteria this number had sunk to 2 percent in the 1950s, and today it is virtually
nonexistent; poverty as the Edwardians defined it has been eliminated. Hours
of work, which averaged sixty-seven per week in the nineteenth century and
fifty-three in 1910, have gone down to around forty. In Sweden, the weekly average hours of work in nonagricultural jobs was thirty-six. Stress on "quality of
life" (the French created a government department with this name!) brought
more concern with longer holidays and pleasanter conditions of work than with
shorter hours on the job.

Needless to say, many such products as electric refrigerators, automobiles, and TVs, which had been nonexistent or owned by a very few before
1914, have become commonplace. Critics of the economics of capitalism often
claim that this wealth is distributed too unequally. However, the kind of economic society typical of late capitalism, with a market-ordered system mediated
by the welfare state, seems to produce as much egalitarianism as is consistent
with a dynamic economic order; certainly more than in premodern societies.
The gap between rich and poor typically diminishes as a country modernizes.
The Marxist claim of a widening social gap as capitalism progresses is a myth,
or was true only for a short time in the first stages of industrialization. Today,

"The southeast of England is one of the most classless places in Europe," the London *Economist* noted. There was even concern in a country like Sweden that nearly total equality would destroy incentive, since there was no longer much of a top to rise to nor a bottom to sink to. Some, of course, still suffer from an unequal share; for example, ethnic minorities such as Algerians in France and Pakistanis or blacks in England. But it seems reasonable to conclude that such disparities are diminishing.

The vigorous feminist movement pointed out that the gap between women and men's earnings was still large, and that women were still rare at top levels in business and many professions. The computer-engineer technocratic elite remains strongly masculine, a fact working against the progress of gender equality. But a third of the doctors in Britain and Portugal were women; there were female prime ministers of Britain and Norway in the 1980s and 1990s, also of Turkey and perhaps soon of Sweden. Women made up 31 percent of Denmark's parliament.

In 1900, only a fraction of 1 percent could expect to receive a higher education, a number that was over 25 percent by 1985. In 1900, indeed, only about 1 percent of the working class even reached secondary school. Now a secondary education is universal, and university grants on a merit basis are widely available. In the 1980s in any school year, more than two million people in the United Kingdom were taking some kind of advanced educational courses, either full-time or part-time (685,000 full-time; 295,000 of these full-time university students). In the 1960s and 1970s, secondary comprehensive schools replaced selective ones in most of Europe, ending the old system that kept the great majority from going on to the universities.

Such statistics, indicative of a startlingly improved standard of life, could be cited almost endlessly. Were there an objection, especially by members of the recent generation, that such affluence has come at the cost of the environment, the reply might be that London's air is immeasurably cleaner today than it was in 1900, that sanitation is better, that diet has improved.

The twentieth century cannot be denied a rich contribution to humanity's store of ideas, its art and literature, its knowledge and practical skills. Advances in those technical arts that make our lives more comfortable, from ways of having a tooth filled or an operation performed to writing a letter or book, listening to music on the stereo, looking up something in the library or on a computer network, or taking an airplane trip. "Progress" is least deniable in this area, and even those who complain of too many gadgets and the tyranny of technology are hardly ever found denying themselves the benefits of such facilities. The quality of the music people listen to or the books they read, the reasons for the trips they take, may form an incongruous contrast to the means they employ, but at least they have the opportunity; and technology cannot reasonably be blamed for the misuse of its services. The twentieth century has provided us with cultural opportunities never before matched.

It has also provided us with cultural instruments, in the form of literature, art, music, philosophy. A reviewer of an edition of the poems of Osip Mandelstam, the martyred Russian literary giant, observed in 1978 that, "It is a miracle that the worst of times produced the best of poets." This might be said of the whole century. If we agree that the twentieth century has brought forth some of humanity's worst times, it has also produced great quantities of excellent poetry, music, and all other forms of art and thought. It is our prerogative, if we choose to exercise it, to reject the century's dismal side and build on its proud achievements.

So we may end where we began, with the spectacle of a century in which for the first time the masses of men and women cease to be passive objects of natural forces and increasingly act to try to determine their own destinies. They have partly succeeded and partly failed. The dissolving of traditional social structures and bonds has led to a society that is richer, freer, in many ways far more in control of natural forces via its science and technology; one which keeps alive longer people who have much more mobility and choice. At the same time, these people are psychically less secure and the society in other ways far less in control—of its economy, its political equilibrium and social stability. The West may have built a society that provides a relative abundance of material goods at the cost of an intolerable organization of life and labor. Such an analysis is plainly an oversimplification, as any brief statement must be. The world sits on the edge of many a volcano that might erupt into devastating destruction, whether nuclear war or technological disaster or political breakdown. It also glimpses possibilities of new scientific and technological breakthroughs; perhaps there will be a cultural renaissance. Nothing is excluded from the range of contemporary possibility. "A world at once fragile and boiling . . . as full of promises as of dangers," French commentator Claude Julien observed (1988). It is indeed the best of times and the worst of times.

The twentieth century has thus far defied all the prophets, so there is no reason to think it will not continue to do so. At its beginning, people forecast perpetual peace and got the worst wars of all time. Socialists predicted the doom of capitalism, but it has survived wars and depressions. Virtually no one foresaw World War I, the Russian Revolution, the Nazi dictatorship, atomic energy, microcomputers. In 1945, predicting the past, most experts expected a gloomy time for the war-shattered Continent, only to see it make a miraculous recovery. And the catalog of surprises continued, in small matters as well as great: The student revolt of 1967–1968 was as unexpected as Khrushchev's "secret speech" had been or Watergate would be. Most observers thought Charles de Gaulle securely on his perch in 1968. In 1972, veteran international commentators thought nothing less likely than another Arab-Israeli war.

Eugene Lyons once reflected that everything in history seems astonishing when it happens and inevitable after it has happened. Few Sovietologists saw the collapse of the Soviet economic system coming; more economists in the early 1980s were predicting such a crisis for Western capitalism, only to reverse themselves later (some of them, anyway; economic science was in considerable disarray). In 1987, historian John Ardagh published a book on Germany (*Germany and the Germans,* Penguin) in which he declared German reunification inconceivable and the GDR here to stay. Nothing daunted, he got out a second edition in 1991; one hopes that his prediction that the enlarged greater Germany will be stable and democratic proves more accurate.[8]

This catalog could go on. Thus, we may probably expect more surprises, and only hope that most of them are pleasant.

Some things appear not to change much. According to the British *Annual Register,* the year opened "amid political lassitude, and with gloomy prospects alike in foreign politics and in finance." The Middle Eastern outlook was alarming, and an earthquake in Italy had been terrible. Claims for old age pensions (social security), having exceeded estimates, were threatening the solvency of the fund. Ireland was becoming more and more disorderly, and the women were continuing their agitation. There was rising unemployment. There had just been a Bosnian crisis, and there was concern about what the Russians might do next. An arms race was on, despite a recent disarmament conference.

The year was actually 1909, but for how many other years in the twentieth century might much the same summation have served reasonably well? We see here some perennial trouble spots, which simmered and festered pretty much throughout the century. The debate between private and public, capitalist and socialist economic ideas had just then erupted with Beatrice Webb's famous report on the Poor Laws; at the end of the century another woman, Margaret Thatcher, had thrown down a gauntlet in the other direction. The same debate was still going on, without much hope of a resolution.

In concluding our survey of this century, we might reflect that "modernization" has been going on for just about a century. The 1880s, we recall, was the decade of the first automobiles, electric lights, electrodes, radio waves, movies, democracy (the first mass political parties, mass-circulation newspapers), intellectuals, sociologists, psychologists, professionally organized scientists, socialism (the historian of British socialism begins his account with the year 1884)—and how many other indices of the modern. Around the beginning of the twentieth century arrived the first airplane, radio, the beginnings of nuclear physics with Curie and Einstein, professional sports, modern art and music and literature. So modernized humanity is a century old. It has already become "postmodern," some pundits claimed—this was an intellectual buzzword of the 1980s. Has it been a success? Readers must answer this value-laden question for themselves.

---

[8]Another clouded crystal ball: From advertised synopsis of Penny Junor, *Charles and Diana: Portrait of a Marriage* (Headline Books, 1991): "This frank yet sympathetic account, based on years of research, shows how Charles and Diana have emerged triumphantly, with a strong and successful partnership."

Many saw in the breakup of the British royal marriage, amid sexual scandal and journalistic sensations, a significant sign of the times.

Bibliography

The enormous number of books about the various facets of twentieth-century Europe renders absurd any attempt at a complete listing, even of just the truly noteworthy ones, in the short space we have. But the student curious enough to want to read further on some topic deserves some guidance. The following is a highly selective and no doubt inevitably somewhat subjective choice. In the main, its stress is on recent scholarly publications. Listed at the end are some guides that enable one to locate a fuller bibliography.

Chapter 1

Listed here are some general histories of the several lands of Europe, as well as a selection of studies of the 1900–1914 era.

Alfred G. Havighurst, *Britain in Transition: The Twentieth Century,* (1985); Keith Robbins, *The Eclipse of a Great Power: Modern Britain, 1870–1975* (1983); José Harris, *The Penguin Social History of Britain 1870–1914;* Paul R. Thompson, *The Edwardians: The Remaking of English Society* (1975); Standish Meacham, *A Life Apart: The English Working Class, 1870–1914* (1977); Andrew Rosen, *Rise Up Women: The Militant Campaign of the Women's Social and Political Union, 1903–1914* (1974); Samuel Hynes, *The Edwardian Turn of Mind* (1968); Wray Vamplew, *Pay Up and Play the Game: Professional Sport in Britain 1875–1914* (1989). Thomas E. Hachey and Lawrence J. McCaffrey, eds., *Perspectives on Irish Nationalism* (1989); John Grigg, *David Lloyd George* (1985).

Wolfgang J. Mommsen, *Imperial Germany, 1867–1918* (1995); Hans Ulrich Wehler, *The German Empire 1871–1918,* trans. Kim Traynor (1985); V. R. Bergbahn, *Modern Germany: Society, Economy and Politics in the Twentieth Century* (1982); Dietrich Orlow, *A History of Modern Germany: 1871 to the Present* (1986); Vernon Lidtke, *The Alternative Culture: Social-*

ist Labor in Imperial Germany (1985); W. J. Mommsen and H. G. Husung, eds., *The Development of Trade Unionism in Great Britain and Germany, 1880–1914* (1985).

Eugen Weber, *France, Fin de Siècle* (1988); Theodore Zeldin, *France, 1848–1945,* 2 vols. (1973, 1977); James McMillan, *Dreyfus to DeGaulle: Politics and Society in France 1898–1968* (1985); Barnett Singer, *Modern France: Mind, Politics, Society* (1980).

Denis Mack Smith, *Italy: A Modern History* (1969) and *Italy and Its Monarchy* (1990); A. W. Salomone, *Italian Democracy in the Making, 1900–1914* (1960); Ernest H. Kossman, *The Low Countries, 1780–1940* (1978); R.A.H. Robinson, *Contemporary Portugal: A History* (1979); Gerald Brenan, *The Spanish Labyrinth* (1943).

N. V. Riasanovsky, *A History of Russia* (5th ed., 1993); Tibor Szamuely, *The Russian Tradition* (1974); Hans Rogger, *Russia in the Age of Modernization and Revolution, 1881–1917* (1983); Marc Raeff, *Understanding Imperial Russia* (1984); Anna Geifman, *Thou Shalt Kill: Revolutionary Terrorism in Russia 1894–1917* (1993); John D. Klier and Shlomo Lambroza, *Pogroms: Anti-Jewish Violence in Modern Russian History* (1992); Philip Pomper, *The Russian Revolutionary Intelligentsia* (1970); Walter Sablinsky, *The Road to Bloody Sunday* (1977); Andrew M. Verner, *The Crisis of the Russian Autocracy: Nicholas II and the 1905 Revolution* (1990); Abraham Ascher, *The Revolution of 1905: Russia in Disarray* (1988); Ann E. Healy, *The Russian Autocracy in Crisis, 1905–1907* (1976).

F. R. Bridge, *The Habsburg Monarchy among the Great Powers 1815–1918* (1991); M. K. Dziewanowski, *Poland in the Twentieth Century* (1977); Keith Hitchins, *Rumania 1866–1947* (1994); Richard J. Crampton, *A Short History of Modern Bulgaria* (1987) and *Eastern Europe in the Twentieth Century* (1994).

Thomas Pakenham, *The Scramble for Africa* (1991); John M. MacKenzie, *The Partition of Africa 1890–1900* (1983); Anthony Brewer, *British Imperialism in the Nineteenth Century* (1984); David Gillard, *The Struggle for Asia 1828–1914* (1977); Heinz Gollwitzer, *Europe in the Age of Imperialism* (1969); John Gross, ed., *The Age of Kipling* (1972).

Joseph Bradley, *Muzhik and Muscovite: Urbanization in Late Imperial Russia* (1985); Michael F. Hamm, *Kiev, A Portrait 1800–1917* (1993); John Lukacs, *Budapest 1900* (1989); Carl E. Schorske, *Fin de Siècle Vienna* (1980); Anthony Sutcliffe, *Paris: An Architectural History* (1993); John Richardson, *London and Its People: A Social History* (1995): Warren Wagar, *Good Tidings: The Belief in Progress from Darwin to Marcuse* (1972); Karl Bracher, *The Age of Ideologies: A History of Political Thought in the Twentieth Century* (1984); Roland N. Stromberg, *European Intellectual History Since 1789,* 6th ed. (1994); H. Stuart Hughes, *Consciousness and Society: European Social Thought, 1890–1930* (1958); Richard J. Evans, *The Feminists: Women's Emancipation Movements 1844–1920* (1977); Stephen Brush, *The History of Modern Science: A Guide to the Second Scientific Revolution 1800–1950* (1988); Albert S. Lindemann, *A History of European Socialism* (1983); Malcolm Bradbury and James McFarlane, eds., *Modernism, 1890–1913* (1976); Christopher Butler, *Early Modernism: Literature, Music and Painting in Europe 1900–1916* (1994); Mikulas Teich and Roy Porter, eds., *Fin de Siècle and Its Legacy* (1990); Mogali S. Larson, *The Rise of Professionalism* (1977); Harold Perkin, *The Rise of Professional Society: England Since 1880* (1989).

Chapter 2
The Background of the First World War:

R.J.W. Evans and Hartmut Pogge von Strandmann, eds., *The Coming of the First World War* (1990); H. W. Koch, ed., *The Origins of the First World War* (1972); Christopher Andrew,

Théophile Delcassé and the Making of the Entente Cordiale (1968); William L. Langer, *The Diplomacy of Imperialism* (1951); Zara S. Steiner, *Britain and the Origins of the First World War* (1977); F. H. Hinsley, ed., *British Foreign Policy under Sir Edward Grey* (1977); Samuel Williamson, *The Politics of Grand Strategy: Britain and France Prepare for War, 1904–1914* (1969); Paul Kennedy, ed., *The War Plans of the Great Powers 1880–1914* (1985); V. L. Bergbahn, *Germany and the Approach of War in 1914* (1973); Holger H. Herwig, *Luxury Fleet: The Imperial German Navy, 1888–1918* (1980); Peter Padfield, *The Great Naval Race: The Anglo-German Naval Rivalry, 1900–1914* (1974); Fritz Fischer, *War of Illusions: German Policies from 1911 to 1914* (1975); Gerhart Ritter, *The Schlieffen Plan* (1958); Vladimir Dedijer, *The Road to Sarajevo* (1966); Wayne Vucinich, *Serbia Between East and West, 1903–1980* (1954); D.C.B. Lieven, *Russia and the Origins of the First World War* (1983).

Keith Eubank, *Paul Cambon, Master Diplomatist* (1960); Norman Rich, *Holstein* (1965); Judith Hughes, *Emotion and High Politics: Personal Relations at the Summit in Late Nineteenth Century Britain and Germany* (1983).

Roland N. Stromberg, *Redemption by War: The Intellectuals and 1914* (1982); Georges Haupt, *Socialism and the Great War: The Collapse of the Second International* (1972); Anthony A. J. Morris, *Radicalism against War, 1906-1914* (1974).

Chapter 3
The First World War:

Martin Gilbert, *Atlas of World War I* (1994); Keith Robbins, *The First World War* (1985); Denis Winter, *Death's Men: Soldiers of the Great War* (1978); Guy Chapman, ed., *Vain Glory* (1968); John Buchan, *A History of the First World War* (republished 1993); Trevor Wilson, *The Myriad Faces of War: Britain and the Great War 1914–1918* (1987); Paul Guinn, *British Strategy and Tactics 1914–1918* (1965); Corelli Barnett, *The Swordbearers* (1964); Richard Hough, *The Great War at Sea 1914–1918* (1986); N. Sombart and J.C.G. Röhl, eds., *New Interpretations of World War I* (1982).

Brian Gardner, *The Big Push* (1963); Alistair Horne, *The Price of Glory: Verdun 1916* (1963); Robert Rhodes James, *Gallipoli* (1965); Philip Warner, *Passchendaele: The Tragic Victory of 1917* (1987); John Terraine, *To Win a War: 1918, the Year of Victory* (1978); Donald Richter, *Chemical Soldiers: British Gas Warfare in World War I* (1993); Paddy Griffith, *Battle Tactics on the Western Front: The British Army's Plan of Attack 1916–1918* (1994).

R.J.Q. Adams, *Arms and the Wizard: Lloyd George and the Ministry of Munitions, 1915–1916* (1978); Martin Kitchen, *The Silent Dictatorship: Politics of the German High Command under Hindenburg and Ludendorff 1916–1918* (1976); Jere C. King, *Foch Versus Clemenceau* (1960); Fritz Fischer, *Germany's Aims in the First World War* (1967); Z.A.B. Zeman, *Diplomatic History of the First World War* (1971); David F. Trask, *The AEF and Coalition Warmaking, 1917–1918* (1993); Leonard Stein, *The Balfour Declaration* (1961); Victor H. Rothwell, *British War Aims and Peace Diplomacy, 1914–1918* (1971); Kenneth J. Calder, *Britain and the Origins of the New Europe 1914–1918* (1976); Daniel Horn, *The German Naval Mutinies of World War I* (1969); Richard M. Watt, *Dare Call It Treason* (1963); F. L. Carsten, *War Against War: British and German Radical Movements in the First World War* (1982); C. Paul Vincent, *The Politics of Hunger: The Allied Blockade of Germany, 1915–1919* (1985). Gerd Hardach, *The First World War, 1914–1918* (1977) is part of a series on the history of the world economy in the twentieth century.

J. M. Winter, *The Great War and the British People* (1987); Arthur Marwick, *The Deluge: British Society and the First World War* (1965), and *Women at War 1914–1918* (1977); John N.

Horne, *Labour at War: France and Britain 1914–1918* (1991); Jurgen Kocha, *Facing Total War: German Society 1914–18* (1984); I.F.W. Beckett and Keith Simpson, eds., *A Nation in Arms: A Social Study of the British Army in the First World War* (1987); Richard Wall and Jay Winter, ed., *The Upheaval of War: Family, Work and Welfare in Europe 1914–18* (1989).

Paul Fussell, *The Great War and Modern Memory* (1985); Bernard Bergonzi, *Heroes' Twilight: A Study of the Literature of the Great War* (1965); Brian Gardner, ed., *Up the Line to Death* (1964).

The Russian Revolution:

W. Bruce Lincoln, *Passage through Armageddon: The Russians in War and Revolution, 1914–1918* (1994); Leonard Schapiro, *The Russian Revolution of 1917: The Origins of Modern Communism* (1984); Sheila Fitzpatrick, *The Russian Revolution* (2nd ed., 1994); John H. L. Keep, *The Russian Revolution: A Study in Mass Mobilization* (1977); Max Weber, *The Russian Revolutions* (trans. and ed. 1995); Evan Mawdsley, *The Russian Civil War* (1987); Robert M. Slusser, *Stalin in October: The Man Who Missed the Revolution* (1987); Richard Pipes, *The Formation of the Soviet Union* (1964); Oskar Anweiler, *The Soviets* (1975); Peter Avrich, *Kronstadt 1921* (1970); Robert Service, *The Bolshevik Party in Revolution, 1917–1923* (1979), and *Lenin: A Political Life* (1985); Dmitri Volkogonov, *Lenin* (1994); Richard Abraham, *Alexander Kerensky* (1987); Baruch Knei-Paz, *The Social and Political Thought of Leon Trotsky* (1978); Dmitri Volkogonov, *Trotsky, The Eternal Revolutionary* (1995); Philip Pomper, *Lenin, Trotsky, and Stalin* (1990); J. Frankel, R. Frankel, and Knei-Paz, eds., *Revolution in Russia: Reassessments of 1917* (1992).

Chapter 4
The Peace Conference:

Harold Nicolson, *Peacemaking 1919* (1933); Stephen Bonsal, *Suitors and Suppliants: The Little Nations at Versailles* (1946); Arno W. Mayer, *The Politics and Diplomacy of Peacemaking* (1967); Charles L. Mee, *The End of Order: Versailles 1919* (1980); John M. Thompson, *Russia, Bolshevism, and the Versailles Peace* (1966); Bela K. Kiraly, Peter Pastor, and Ivan Sanders, eds., *Total War and Peacemaking: A Case Study on Trianon* (1982); Sally Marks, *The Illusion of Peace: International Relations in Europe, 1918–1923* (1976); John Maynard Keynes, *The Economic Consequences of the Peace* (1919).·

Roland N. Stromberg, *Collective Security and American Foreign Policy* (1963); George W. Egerton, *Great Britain and the Creation of the League of Nations* (1978); Robert H. Ferrell, *Peace in Their Time: The Origins of the Kellogg-Briand Pact* (1957).

Europe in the 1920s:

Charles S. Meier, *Recasting Bourgeois Europe: Stabilization in France, Germany and Italy in the Decade after World War I* (1975); Derek H. Aldcroft, *From Versailles to Wall Street: The International Economy in the 1920's* (1977); F. L. Carsten, *Revolution in Central Europe, 1918–1919* (1972) and *The Reichswehr and Politics, 1918–1933* (1966); Ivan Volgyes, *Hungary in Revolution, 1918–1919* (1971); Rudolf L. Tokes, *Bela Kun and the Hungarian Soviet Republic* (1967); David M. Morgan, *The Socialist Left and the German Revolution, 1917–1922* (1975); R.G.L. Waite, *Vanguard of Nazism: The Free Corps Movement, 1918–1923* (1951); Werner T. Angress, *The Stillborn Revolution: The Communist Bid for Power in Germany,*

1918–1923 (1963); Albert S. Lindemann, *The Red Years: European Socialism versus Bolshevism, 1918–1920* (1974).

Andreas Dorpalen, *Hindenburg and the Weimar Republic* (1964); Gerald D. Feldman, *The Great Disorder: Politics, Economics, and Society in the German Inflation, 1914–1924* (1993); Henry Ashby Turner, Jr., *Stresemann and the Politics of the Weimar Republic* (1963); Walter A. McDougall, *France's Rhineland Diplomacy: 1914–1924* (1978); Stephen A. Schuker, *The End of French Predominance in Europe: The Financial Crisis of 1924 and the Adoption of the Dawes Plan* (1977).

Trevor Wilson, *Downfall of the Liberal Party, 1914–1935* (1966); Brian Harrison, *Prudent Revolutionaries: Portraits of British Feminists between the Wars* (1987); Sheila Lawlor, *Britain and Ireland, 1914–1923* (1983); Sean Glynn, *Interwar Britain: Social and Economic History* (1976).

Jan Karski, *The Great Powers and Poland, 1919–1945* (1985); Richard M. Watt, *Bitter Glory: Poland and Its Fate, 1918–1939* (1979); Norman Davies, *White Eagle, Red Star: The Polish-Soviet War, 1918–1920* (1972); Neal Pease, *Poland, the United States, and the Stabilization of Europe, 1919–1933* (1986); Jon Jacobsen, *Locarno Diplomacy: Germany and the West, 1925–1929* (1972).

Alexander De Grand, *Italian Fascism: Its Origins and Development* (1982); Adrian Lyttelton, *The Seizure of Power: Fascism in Italy, 1919–1929* (1973); Alan Cassels, *Fascist Italy* (1984); Denis Mack Smith, *Mussolini* (1981) and *Mussolini's Roman Empire* (1976); Tracy H. Koon, *Believe, Obey, Fight: Political Socialization of Youth in Fascist Italy, 1922–1943* (1987).

Chapter 5

Walter Laqueur, *Weimar: A Cultural History* (1974); Keith Bullivant, ed., *Culture and Society in the Weimar Republic* (1978); Anthony Phelan, ed., *The Weimar Dilemma: Intellectuals in the Weimar Republic* (1985); Alan Bance, ed., *Weimar Germany; Writers and Politics* (1982).

Uwe Westphal, *The Bauhaus* (1991); Reginald Isaacs, *Gropius* (1991); Peter Blake, *The Master Builders* (1976); H. Allen Brooks, ed., *Le Corbusier* (1987); Peter Gay, *Freud: A Life for Our Time* (1988); Robert S. Steele, *Freud and Jung* (1982); Harry Trossman, *Freud and the Imaginative World* (1985); Steven Marcus, *Freud and the Culture of Psychoanalysis* (1984).

Leon Edel, *Bloomsbury: A House of Lions* (1979); C. K. Stead, *Pound, Yeats, Eliot and the Modernist Movement* (1986); Stanley Sultan, *Eliot, Joyce and Company* (1987); Richard Ellmann, *James Joyce* (rev. ed., 1982); Graham Hough, *Image and Experience: Studies in a Literary Revolution* (1960); Quentin Bell, *Virginia Woolf* (1972); Anthony Burgess, *Flame into Being: The Life and Work of D. H. Lawrence* (1985); Gamini Salgado and G. K. Das, eds., *The Spirit of D. H. Lawrence* (1988); Ritchie Robertson, *Kafka: Judaism, Politics, and Literature* (1985); Robert A. Maguire, *Red Virgin Soil: Soviet Literature in the 1920s* (1968).

Valerie Steele, *Fashion and Eroticism: Ideals of Feminine Beauty from the Victorian Era to the Jazz Age* (1985); John Stevenson, *British Society, 1914–1945* (1982); John Stevenson and Chris Cook, *Social Conditions in Europe Between the Wars* (1977).

Arthur Miller, *Einstein's Special Theory of Relativity: Emergence and Early Interpretation* (1981); also his *Frontiers of Physics 1900–1911* (1986); Cornelius Lanczos, *The Einstein Decade* (1974); George Gamow, *Thirty Years That Shook Physics* (1966).

Chapter 6
The Great Depression:

Charles P. Kindleberger, *The World in Depression, 1925–1939* (1973); Philippe Bernard, *The Decline of the Third Republic 1914–1938* (1985); Eugen Weber, *The Hollow Years: France in the 1930s* (1987); Julian Jackson, *The Politics of Depression in France, 1932–1936* (1985); David Marquand, *Ramsay McDonald* (1977); Joel Colton, *Leon Blum* (1966).

Ronald Tiersky, *French Communism, 1920–1972* (1974); Ben Pimlott, *Labour and the Left in the 1930s* (1978); Nathaniel Greene, *Crisis and Decline: The French Socialist Party in the Popular Front Era* (1969); Peter Clarke, *The Keynesian Revolution in the Making, 1924–1936* (1989); G.L.S. Shackle, *The Years of High Theory: Innovation and Tradition in Economic Thought, 1926–1939* (1967); Robert Skidelsky, *John Maynard Keynes: The Economist as Savior, 1920–1937* (1983); Stanley Weintraub, *The Last Great Cause: The Intellectuals and the Spanish Civil War* (1968); David Caute, *The Fellow Travellers* (1988); Valentine Cunningham, *British Writers of the Thirties* (1988); Norman Ingram, *The Politics of Dissent: Pacifism in France 1919–1939* (1991).

Nazi Germany and Adolf Hitler
(see also World War II, Holocaust):

Joachim Fest, *Hitler* (1975); Werner Maser, *Hitler, Legend, Myth, and Reality* (1973); Rudolf Binion, *Hitler among the Germans* (1976); R.G.L. Waite, *The Psychopathic God* (1977); Harold J. Gordon, *Hitler and the Beer Hall Putsch* (1972); A. J. Nicholls, *Weimar and the Rise of Hitler* (1979); Henry Ashby Turner, Jr., *German Big Business and the Rise of Hitler* (1985); Harold James, *The German Slump: Politics and Economics, 1924–36* (1987); Woodruff D. Smith, *The Ideological Origins of Nazi Imperialism* (1986); Thomas Childers, *The Nazi Voter: The Social Foundations of Nazism in Germany, 1919–1933* (1983); Peter H. Merkl, *Political Violence Under the Swastika: 581 Early Nazis* (1975); Peter Pulzer, *The Rise of Political Anti-Semitism in Germany and Austria* (rev. ed., 1988); Eberhard Jäckel, *Hitler's Weltanschauung* (1972) and *Hitler in History* (1984).

Karl D. Bracher, *The German Dictatorship* (1970); Klaus Hildebrand, *The Third Reich* (1984); Sarah Gordon, *Hitler, Germans, and the Jewish Question* (1984); Ian Kershaw, *The Hitler Myth: Image and Reality in the Third Reich* (1987); Michael Burleigh and Wolfgang Wipperman, *The Racial State: Germany 1933–45* (1992); J. E. Farquharson, *The Plough and the Swastika* (1977); Max Kele, *The Nazis and the Workers* (1972); John Gillingham, *Industry and Politics in the Third Reich* (1985); Alan D. Beyerchen, *Scientists under Hitler* (1977); Kristie Mackrakis, *Surviving the Swastika: Scientific Research in Nazi Germany* (1993); Harold C. Deutsch, *Hitler and His Generals* (1974); Oron J. Hale, *The Captive Press in the Third Reich* (1964); Jill Stephenson, *Women in Nazi Society* (1975).

Peter Hoffmann, *The History of German Resistance, 1933–1945* (1977); F. L. Carsten, *The German Resistance to Hitler* (1970); Patricia Meehan, *The Unnecessary War: Whitehall and the German Resistance to Hitler* (1992); Victoria Barnett, *For the Soul of the People: Protestant Protest against Hitler* (1992); Klemens von Klemperer, *German Resistance against Hitler: The Search for Allies Abroad* (1992); Ian Kershaw, *Popular Opinion and Political Dissent in the Third Reich* (1985); D.J.K. Peukert, *Inside Nazi Germany* (1987).

Stephen J. Lee, *The European Dictatorships, 1918–1945* (1987); Stein Ugelvik Larsen, Bernt Hagvet, Peter Myklebust, eds., *Who Were the Fascists?* (1982); Renzo de Felice, *Interpretations of Fascism* (1977); Hannah Arendt, *Origins of Totalitarianism* (1966); Walter Laqueur and George L. Mosse, ed., *International Fascism, 1920–1945* (1966); Stanley G. Payne,

Fascism: A Comparative Approach Toward a Definition (1983) and *A History of Fascism 1914–1945* (1995); Robert Soucy, *French Fascism: The First Wave, 1924–1933* (1986) and *The Second Wave, 1935–39* (1995); Zeev Sternhall, *Neither Right nor Left: Fascist Ideology in France* (1986); Robert Skidelsky, *Oswald Mosley* (1975).

The USSR and Stalinism:

Richard Pipes, *Russia under the Bolshevik Regime* (1994); Alexander Erlich, *The Soviet Industrialization Debate, 1924–1928* (1961); Naum Jasny, *Soviet Economists of the 1920's* (1972); Stephen E. Cohen, *Bukharin and the Bolshevik Revolution* (1973); Adam B. Ulam, *Stalin: The Man and His Era* (1973); Robert H. McNeal, *Stalin: Man and Ruler* (1988); Robert C. Tucker, *Stalin in Power (1928–41)* (1991), the second volume of a projected three; Dmitri Volkogonov, *Stalin: Triumph and Tragedy* (1991); Sheila Fitzpatrick, ed., *Cultural Revolution in Russia, 1928–1931* (1984); Hiroaki Kuromiya, *Stalin's Industrial Revolution: Politics and Workers, 1928–32* (1988); Graeme Gill, *The Origins of the Stalinist Political System* (1990); William L. Blackwell, *The Industrialization of Russia* (1982); G. R. Urban, ed., *Stalinism* (1982); Robert Conquest, *The Harvest of Silence: Soviet Collectivization and the Terror Famine* (1987); Lynne Viola, *Peasant Rebels under Stalin* (1995); Sheila Fitzpatrick, *Stalin's Peasants: Resistance and Survival in the Russian Village after Collectivization* (1994); Edwin Bacon, *The Gulag at War: Stalin's Forced Labour System in the Light of the Archives* (1995); Robert Conquest, *The Great Terror* (rev. ed., 1990); David Jorasky, *The Lysenko Affair* (1970); Valery N. Soyfer, (trans. L. & R. Gruliow), *Lysenko and the Tragedy of Soviet Science* (1994); Lih, Khlevniuk, and Naumov, eds., *Stalin's Letters to Molotov* (1995); Walter Laqueur, *Stalin: The Glasnost Revelations* (1991); Arkoly Vaksberg, *Stalin against the Jews,* trans. A. W. Bouis (1995); David Holloway, *Stalin and the Bomb* (1994); Amy Knight, *Beria: Stalin's First Lieutenant* (1993).

Chapter 7
The Origins of World War II:

Raymond J. Sontag, *A Broken World, 1919–1939* (1971); Hans W. Gatzke, ed., *European Diplomacy Between Two Wars, 1919–1939* (1972); William R. Louis, ed., *The Origins of the Second World War: A.J.P. Taylor and His Critics* (1972); Gordon Martel, *"The Origins of the Second World War" Reconsidered: The A.J.P. Taylor Debate After Twenty-five Years* (1986); Gerhard L. Weinberg, *The Foreign Policy of Hitler's Germany, 1933–1939* (1980); Anthony Adamthwaite, *France and the Coming of the Second World War, 1936–1939* (1977); Robert J. Young, *In Command of France: French Foreign Policy and Military Planning, 1933–1940* (1978); Maurice Cowling, *The Impact of Hitler: British Politics and British Foreign Policy, 1933–1940* (1975); F. W. Deakin, *The Brutal Friendship: Hitler and Mussolini* (1962); J. T. Emmerson, *The Rhineland Crisis* (1977); Keith Robbins, *Munich 1938* (1968); I. W. Bruegel, *Czechoslovakia before Munich* (1973); Anthony Read and David Fisher, *The Deadly Embrace: Hitler, Stalin, and the Nazi-Soviet Pact, 1939–41* (1988); Donald C. Watt, *Too Serious a Business: European Armies and the Approach of the Second World War* (1975); Arnold A. Offner, *The Origins of the Second World War: American Foreign Policy and World Politics 1917–1941* (1975); Robert A. Divine, *The Reluctant Belligerents: American Entry into World War II* (1979); Norman Rose, *Churchill, The Unruly Giant* (1995); Wesley Wark, *The Ultimate Enemy: British Intelligence and Nazi Germany 1933–1939* (1986).

Spain:

Shlomo Ben Ami, *Fascism from Above: The Dictatorship of Primo de Rivera in Spain, 1923–1930* (1983); Stanley Payne, *The Spanish Revolution* (1970); Hugh Thomas, *The Spanish Civil War* (1977); D. A. Puzzo, *Spain and the Great Powers* (1972).

Chapter 8
World War II

Gerhard L. Weinberg, *A World at Arms: A Global History of World War II* (1994); I.C.B. Dear and M.R.D. Foot, eds., *The Oxford Companion to World War II* (1995); Martin Gilbert, *The Second World War* (1990); M. K. Dziewanowski, *War at Any Price: World War II in Europe 1939–1945* (1987); H. P. Willmott, *The Great Crusade: A New Complete History of World War II* (1989); A.J.P. Taylor, *The War Lords* (1977); The British *Official History of the Second World War* was completed in eight volumes in 1988, two more than Winston Churchill himself required in *The Second World War* (1948–1954); Klaus A. Maier, Horst Rhode, Bernd Stegemann, Hans Umbriet, trans. Dean S. McMurry and Ewald Osers, *Germany's Initial Conquests in Europe* (1991), is vol. 2 of a multivolume, multiauthored German series on Germany and the Second World War.

Antony Beevor, *Crete: The Battle and the Resistance* (1991); Nicholas Bethell, *The War Hitler Won: The Battle for Poland, 1939* (1972); Alistair Horne, *To Lose a Battle: France, 1940* (1969); Len Deighton, *Fighter: The True Story of the Battle of Britain* (1977); John Erickson, *The Road to Stalingrad: Stalin's War with Germany* (1975); Carlo D'Este, *Bitter Victory: The Battle for Sicily 1943* (1988); Dominick Graham and Shelford Bidwell, *Tug of War: The Battle for Italy 1943–1945* (1986); Max Hastings, *Overlord: D-Day and the Battle for Normandy* (1984); Stephen E. Ambrose, *D-Day, June 6, 1944;* Theodore A. Wilson, ed., *D-Day 1944* (1995); Ronald J. Drez, ed., *Voices of D-Day* (1994); Ronald Shaffer, *Wings of Judgment: American Bombing in World War II* (1985); Peter Padfield, *War beneath the Sea: Submarine Conflict 1939–1945* (1995); Alan P. Dobson, *U.S. Wartime Aid to Britain, 1940–1945* (1986).

Political and Strategic Decisions:

Norman Rich, *Hitler's War Aims* (1973); Robert M. Hathaway, *Ambiguous Partnership: Britain and America, 1941–1947* (1981); Keith Eubank, *Summit at Teheran* (1985); Walter S. Roberts, *Tito, Mihailovich and the Allies, 1941–1945* (1973); Edward J. Rozek, *Allied Wartime Diplomacy: A Pattern in Poland* (1957); Russell D. Buhite, *Decisions at Yalta: An Appraisal of Summit Diplomacy* (1986); Remi Nadeau, *Stalin, Churchill, and Roosevelt Divide Europe* (1990); Gaddis Smith, *American Diplomacy during the Second World War* (1985); John Charmley, *Churchill's Grand Alliance* (1995); Sheila Lawlor, *Churchill and the Politics of War, 1940–1941* (1994).

The Intelligence War:

F. H. Hinsley et al., *British Intelligence in the Second World War: Its Influence on Strategy and Operations* (4 vols., 1979–1980) is the official British history; Peter Calvocoressi, *Top Secret Ultra* (1981); Richard Langhorne, ed., *Diplomacy and Intelligence during the Second World War* (1985); Ralph Bennett, *Behind the Battle: Intelligence in the War against Germany 1939–45* (1994); Anthony Cave Brown, *"C": The Secret Life of Sir Stewart Menzies, Spymaster to Winston Churchill* (1987), and *Bodyguard of Lies* (1975); Charles Cruickshank, *Deception in World War II* (1980); John C. Masterman, *The Double Cross System in the War of 1939–45* (1972); William Stevenson, *A Man Called Intrepid* (1976); Arnold Kramish, *The Griffin: The Greatest Untold Espionage Story of World War II* (1986).

Margaret Going, *Britain and Atomic Energy, 1939–1945* (1965); Richard Rhodes, *The Making of the Atom Bomb* (1986); Martin J. Sherwin, *A World Destroyed: The Atomic Bomb and the Grand Alliance* (1975); Mark Walker, *German National Socialism and the Quest for Nuclear Power, 1939–49* (1990); David Holloway, *Stalin and the Bomb* (1994).

Henri Michel, *The Shadow War: European Resistance, 1939–1945* (1972); John F. Sweets, *Choices in Vichy France* (1986); Robert O. Paxton, *Vichy France, 1940–1944* (1972); Herbert R. Lottman, *The People's Anger: Justice and Revenge in Post-Liberation France* (1987); Charles F. Delzell, *Mussolini's Enemies: The Italian Anti-Fascist Resistance* (1961); Ian R. Cross, *Polish Society Under German Occupation, 1939–1944* (1979); Matthew Cooper, *The Phantom War: The German Struggle Against Soviet Partisans, 1941–1945* (1979); Milovan Djilas, *Wartime*, trans. Michael Petrovich (1977), and *Tito: The Story from Inside* (1980); Wilfrid Strik Strikfeldt, *Against Stalin and Hitler: Memoirs of the Russian Liberation Movement, 1941–1945* (1970); Nikolai Tolstoy, *Victims of Yalta* (1978); Robert Conquest, *The Nation Killers: Soviet Deportation of Nationalities* (1970); Wolodymyr Kosyk, *The Third Reich and Ukraine* (1993).

Alan S. Milward, *War, Economy, and Society, 1939–1945* (1977); Leila J. Rupp, *Mobilizing Women for War, 1939–1945* (1977); Martin Kitchen, *Nazi Germany at War* (1994); Ilya Ehrenburg, *The War: 1941–1945* (1964); Albert Speer, *Inside the Third Reich: Memoirs* (1970); Marlis G. Steinert, trans. T.F.J. de Witt, *Hitler's War and the Germans: Public Mood and Attitudes During the Second World War* (1977); Earl R. Beck, *Under the Bombs: The German Home Front, 1942–1945* (1986); Harold L. Smith, ed., *War and Social Change: British Society in the Second World War* (1987); Stephen Brooke, *Labour's War: the Labour Party and the Second World War* (1992); Paul Addison, *The Road to 1945: British Politics and the Second World War* (1975); Andrew Shennan, *Rethinking France: Plans for Renewal 1940–1946* (1990); Jean-Pierre Azema, *From Munich to the Liberation, France 1938–1944* (1984).

Holger Klein, John Flower, and Eric Homberger, *The Second World War in Fiction* (1984); Frederick J. Harris, *Encounters with Darkness: French and German Writers on World War II* (1984).

Hugh Trevor-Roper's classic account *The Last Days of Hitler* is still in print (latest edition, 1987).

The Nazi Mass Murders:

Eugene Kogon, et al., eds. *Nazi Mass Murder: A Documentary History* (1994); Philippe Burin, *Hitler and the Jews: The Genesis of the Holocaust* (1994); Christopher R. Browning, *The Path to Genocide: Essays on Launching the Final Solution* (1992); Gerald Fleming, *Hitler and the Final Solution* (1984); Raul Hilberg, *The Destruction of the European Jews* (1985); Michael Burleigh, *Death and Deliverance: Euthanasia in Germany 1900–1945* (1994); Richard Breitman, *Architect of Genocide: Himmler and the Final Solution* (1992); Ysrael Gutman and Michael Berenbaum, ed., *Anatomy of the Auschwitz Death Camp* (1994); Lucy Dawidowicz, *The Holocaust and the Historians* (1981); Yehuda Bauer, *A History of the Holocaust* (1982), and, with Nathan Rotenstreich, eds., *The Holocaust as Historical Experience* (1980); Gerhard Hirschfeld, ed., *The Policies of Genocide* (1986); Michael R. Marrus, *The Holocaust in History* (1987).

Robert O. Paxton, *Vichy France and the Jews* (1983); Susan Zuccotti, *The Italians and the Holocaust* (1987) and *The Holocaust, the French, and the Jews* (1993); L. Dobroscycki and J. S. Gurock, eds., *The Holocaust in the Soviet Union* (1993); Martin Gilbert, *Auschwitz and the Allies* (1981); Michael J. Cohen, *Churchill and the Jews* (1985); Walter Laqueur, *The Terrible Secret* (1981); David S. Wyman, *The Abandonment of the Jews: America and the Holocaust, 1942–45* (1984); Deborah E. Lipstadt, *Beyond Belief: The American Press and the Holocaust* (1993), also *Denying the Holocaust: The Growing Assault on Truth and Memory* (1993).

Richard C. Lukas, *The Forgotten Holocaust: The Poles Under German Occupation* (1986); Shmuel Krakowski, *The War of the Doomed: Jewish Armed Resistance in Poland, 1942–1944*

(1984); Vera Laska, ed., *Women in the Resistance and in the Holocaust* (1983); Lawrence L. Langer, *Versions of Survival: The Holocaust and the Human Spirit* (1982).

Chapter 9
The Cold War; International Relations after 1945:

Peter Calvocoressi, *World Politics Since 1945* (4th ed., 1982); Martin McCauley, *Origins of the Cold War* (1983); David Reynolds, ed., *The Origins of the Cold War in Europe* (1994); Adam Ulam, *The Rivals: America and Russia Since World War II* (1971); John Lewis Gaddis, *Strategies of Containment: A Critical Appraisal of Postwar American National Security Policy* (1982); Victor Rothwell, *Britain and the Cold War, 1941–1947* (1982); Ritchie Ovendale, ed., *The Foreign Policy of the British Labour Government 1945–1951* (1984); Michael Dockrill and John W. Young, eds., *British Foreign Policy 1945–1956* (1989); Corelli Barnett, *The Lost Victory: British Dreams, British Realities 1945–1950* (1995).

Alfred E. Zayes, *The Terrible Revenge: The Ethnic Cleansing of East European Germans 1944–1950* (1994); Norman M. Naimark, *The Russians in Germany: The History of the Soviet Zone of Occupation, 1945–49* (1995); Michael L. Hogan, *The Marshall Plan* (1987); Henry Pelling, *Britain and the Marshall Plan* (1988); Alan Bullock, *Ernest Bevin: Foreign Secretary, 1945–1951* (1983); Nicholas Henderson, *The Birth of NATO* (1983); Lawrence S. Kaplan, *The United States and NATO: The Formative Years* (1984); G. M. Alexander, *The Prelude to the Truman Doctrine: British Policy in Greece, 1944–1947* (1983); J. F. N. Bradley, *Politics in Czechoslovakia, 1945–1971* (1981); Karel Kaplan, *The Short March: The Communist Takeover of Czechoslovakia 1945–1948* (1987); Noel Barber, *Seven Days of Freedom: The Hungarian Uprising, 1956* (1974); David Pryce-Jones, *The Hungarian Revolution* (1969); William Roger Louis and Roger Owen, eds., *Suez 1956: The Crisis and Its Consequences* (1989); Ann and John Tusa, *The Berlin Blockade* (1988); Hristo H. Devedjiev, *Stalinization of the Bulgarian Society, 1949–1953* (1975); Vladimir Dedijer, *The Battle Stalin Lost: Memoirs of Yugoslavia, 1948–1953* (1971); William Stueck, *The Korean War: An International History* (1994).

Chapter 10
European Politics after 1945:

Alan S. Milward, *The Reconstruction of Western Europe, 1945–1951* (1984); Alfred E. Ecks, Jr., *A Search for Solvency: Bretton Woods and the International Monetary System, 1941–1971* (1975); John Williamson, *The Failure of World Monetary Reform, 1971–1974* (1977); Herman Van der Wee, *The World Economy, 1945–1980* (1986); Sima Lieberman, *The Growth of European Mixed Economies, 1945–1970* (1977); Daniel Bell, *The Coming of Post-Industrial Society* (1973).

Arthur Marwick, *British Society Since 1945* (1984); G. C. Fiegehen, P. S. Lansley, and A. D. Smith, *Poverty and Progress in Britain, 1953–1973* (1978); C. J. Bartlett, *A History of Postwar Britain, 1945–1974* (1977); Kenneth Morgan, *Labour in Power 1945–1951* (1984); Henry Pelling, *The Labour Governments 1945–51* (1984); John Campbell, *Aneurin Bevan and the Mirage of British Socialism* (1987); Vernon Bogdanor and Robert Skidelsky, eds., *The Age of Affluence, 1951–1964* (1970); Robert Rhodes James, *Ambitions and Realities: British Politics, 1964–1970* (1972); Anthony Seldon and Stuart Bell, eds., *Conservative Century: The Conservative Party since 1900* (1994); Bernard Elbaum and William Lazonick, eds., *The Decline of the British Economy* (1986); Martin Wiener, *English Culture and the Decline of the Industrial Spirit, 1850–1980* (1981).

Martin McCauley, *The German Democratic Republic Since 1945* (1983); A. J. Nicholls, *Freedom with Responsibility: The Social Market Economy in Germany, 1918–1963* (1994); Peter

Pulzer, *German Politics 1945–1995* (1995); Gordon R. Smith, *Democracy in West Germany: Parties and Politics in the Federal Republic* (1979); Edwina Moreton, *Germany between East and West* (1987).

Bernard Ledwige, *De Gaulle* (1982); Merry and Serge Bromberger, *Jean Monnet and the United States of Europe* (1969); Jean-Pierre Rioux, *The Fourth Republic, 1944–58* (1987); John Ardagh, *The New France* (1973); John C. Cairns, ed., *Contemporary France: Illusion, Conflict, and Regeneration* (1978); David Hanley, A. P. Kerr, and Neville Waites, *Contemporary France: Politics and Society Since 1945* (1984); Michalina Vaughan, Martin Kalinsky, and Peta Sheriff, *Social Change in France* (1980); Irwin Wall, *French Communism in the Era of Stalin, 1946–1962* (1983).

Sidney Tarrow, *Democracy and Disorder: Protest and Politics in Italy, 1965–1975* (1989); Fredric Spotts and Theodor Wieser, *Italy: A Difficult Democracy* (1986); David I. Kertzer, *Comrades and Christians: Religion and Political Struggle in Communist Italy* (1980); Stephen Hellman, *Italian Communism in Transition: The Rise and Fall of the Historic Compromise in Turin, 1975–1980* (1988); Joan Barth Urban, *Moscow and the Italian Communist Party: Togliatti to Berlinguer* (1986).

Stanley G. Payne, *The Franco Regime, 1936–1975* (1987); Raymond Carr and J. P. Fusi, *Spain: Dictatorship to Democracy* (1981); Paul Preston, *The Triumph of Democracy in Spain* (1986); Richard Gunther et al., *Spain after Franco* (1986); Victor M. Pérez-Diaz, *The Return of Civil Society: The Emergence of Democratic Spain* (1993); Marianne Heiberg, *The Making of the Basque Nation* (1988); Kenneth Maxwell, *The Making of Portuguese Democracy* (1995); Stig Hadenius, *Swedish Politics during the 20th Century* (1988); Marquis W. Childs, *Sweden: The Middle Way on Trial* (1980); Henry Milner, *Sweden: Social Democracy in Practice* (1989); Richard Clogg, *Parties and Elections in Greece: The Search for Legitimacy* (1988); Ronan Fenning, *Independent Ireland* (1983).

Neal McInnes, *The Communist Parties of Western Europe* (1975); Rudolf L. Tokes, ed., *European Communism in the Age of Detente* (1978); Adam Przeworski, *Capitalism and Social Democracy* (1986).

Intellectual Currents:

Mark Poster, *Marxism and Existentialism in Postwar France* (1976); Eugene Lunn, *Marxism and Modernism* (1982); Martin Jay, *The Dialectical Imagination: A History of the Frankfurt School, 1923–1950* (1973); J. G. Merquior, *Western Marxism* (1986); Arthur Hirsh, *The French New Left: An Intellectual History from Sartre to Gorz* (1981); Tony Judt, *Past Imperfect* (1992), Sunil Khilnani, *Arguing Revolution: The Intellectual Left in Postwar France* (1993); Ronald Hayman, *Writing Against: A Biography of Sartre* (1986).

Chapter 11
The Soviet Union after Stalin:

John Keep, *Last of the Empires: A History of the Soviet Union 1945–1991* (1995); Abraham Rothberg, *The Heirs of Stalin: Dissidence and the Soviet Regime, 1953–1970* (1972); Nikita Khrushchev, *Khrushchev Remembers* (2 vols., 1970, 1974); Jerrold L. Schechter and V. L. Luchkov, eds., *Khrushchev Remembers: The Glasnost Tapes* (1990); Roy Medvedev, *Khrushchev*, trans. Brian Pearce (1984); Joshua Rubenstein, *Soviet Dissidents: Their Struggle for Human Rights* (1987); Seweryn Bialer, *Stalin's Successors: Leadership, Stability, and Change in the USSR* (1980) and *The Soviet Paradox* (1986); Adam B. Ulam, *Dangerous Relations: The So-*

viet Union in World Politics, 1970–1982 (1983); Raymond L. Garthoff, *Reflections on the Cuban Missile Crisis* (1989); James G. Bright and David A. Welch, *On the Brink: Americans and Soviets Reexamine the Cuban Missile Crisis* (1990); Robert Smith Thompson, *The Missiles of October* (1992); Elizabeth Kridl Valkenier, *The Soviet Union and the Third World* (1983); John B. Dunlop, *The Faces of Contemporary Russian Nationalism* (1984).

Karen Dawisha, *The Kremlin and the Prague Spring* (1984); H. Cordon Skilling, *Czechoslovakia's Interrupted Revolution* (1976); Vladimir Kusin, *The Intellectual Origins of the Prague Spring* (1971) and *From Dubcek to Charter 77: A Study of Normalization in Czechoslovakia, 1968–1978* (1978); Robert L. Hutchings, *Soviet-East European Relations: Consolidation and Conflict, 1968–1980* (1983); John D. Bell, *The Bulgarian Communist Party from Blagoev to Zhivkov* (1986); Charles Gati, *Hungary and the Soviet Bloc* (1986).

Chapter 12

David Caute, *The Year of the Barricades* (1988); Richard Taylor, *Against the Bomb: The British Protest Movement, 1958–1965* (1988); Jillian Becker, *Hitler's Children: The Story of the Baader-Meinhof Gang* (1977).

Max Jansen, *History of European Integration, 1947–1975* (1975); William Wallace, *The Dynamics of European Integration* (1991); A. H. Simonian, *The Privileged Partnership: Franco-German Relations in the European Community, 1969–1984* (1985); Dennis Swann, *Economics of the Common Market* (5th ed., 1984); Stephen George, *Politics and Policy in the European Community* (1985); Dudley Seers and Constance Vaitsos, eds., *The Secondary Enlargement of the EEC* (1982).

Max Beloff, *Imperial Sunset* (2 vols, 1969, 1989); D. A. Low, *Eclipse of Empire* (1991); Franz Ansprenger, *The Dissolution of the Colonial Empires* (1989); J. D. Hargreaves, *Decolonization in Africa* (1989); Raymond F. Betts, *Uncertain Dimensions: Western Overseas Empires in the Twentieth Century* (1985); P. T. Bauer, *Reality and Rhetoric: Studies in the Economics of Development* (1984).

Chapter 13
The Collapse of the Soviet State:

Marshall I. Goldman, *USSR in Crisis: The Failure of an Economic System* (1983); Janos Kornai, *Contradictions and Dilemmas: Studies on the Socialist Economy and Society* (1986); Loren R. Graham, *The Ghost of the Executed Engineer: Technology and the Fall of the Soviet Union* (1993); Gale Stokes, *The Walls Came Tumbling Down: The Collapse of Communism in Eastern Europe* (1993); Anders Aslund, *Gorbachev's Struggle for Economic Reform* (1989); Moshe Lewin, *The Gorbachev Phenomenon: A Historical Interpretation* (1988); Stephen F. Cohen, ed., *An End to Silence: Uncensored Opinion in the Soviet Union* (1982) and *Rethinking the Soviet Experience* (1985); Grigori Medvedev, *The Truth about Chernobyl*, trans. Evelyn Rossinge (1991); Carola Hansson and Karen Linden, *Moscow Women: 13 Interviews* (1984); Suzanne Rosenberg, *A Soviet Odyssey* (1988); Mark Galeotti, *Afghanistan: the Soviet Union's Last War* (1995).

Joseph Rothschild, *Return to Diversity: A Political History of East Central Europe since World War II* (1988); Z.A.B. Zeman, *Pursued by a Bear: The Making of Eastern Europe* (1989); Keith J. Lepak, *Prelude to Solidarity: Poland and the Politics of the Gierek Regime* (1988); Timothy G. Ash, *The Polish Revolution: Solidarity, 1980–1982* (1983); Mary Craig, *The Crystal Spirit: Lech Walesa and His Poland* (1986); Anatol Lieven, *The Baltic Revolution* (1994).

Martin Holmes, *The Labour Government 1974–1979* (1985); R. Emmett Tyrell, ed., *The Future That Doesn't Work: Social Democracy's Failures in Britain* (1983); Patrick Dunleavy and Christopher Husbands, *British Democracy at the Crossroads: Voting and Party Competition in the 1980s* (1985); Peter Jenkins, *Mrs. Thatcher's Revolution: The Ending of the Socialist Era* (1989); Robert Skidelsky, ed., *Thatcherism* (1989); Shirley Robin Letwin, *The Anatomy of Thatcherism* (1992); Ian Gilmour, *Dancing with Dogma: Britain under Thatcherism* (1992); David Willetts, *Modern Conservatism* (1992); Barry Cooper, Allan Karnberg, and William Mishler, *The Resurgence of Conservatism in Anglo-American Democracies* (1988).

S. S. Acquaviva and M. Santuccio, *Social Structure in Italy: Crisis of a System* (1977); John Haycraft, *Italian Labyrinth: Italy in the 1980's* (1986); John Ardagh, *France in the 1980s* (1982); Michel Forsé and others, *Recent Social Trends in France, 1960–1990* (1993); Daniel N. Nelson, ed., *Romania in the 1980's* (1981).

Chapter 14

John B. Dunlop, *The Rise of Russia and the Fall of the Soviet Empire* (1993); Boris Yeltsin, *Against the Grain: An Autobiography* (1990); Walter Laqueur, *The Dream That Failed: Reflections on the Soviet Union* (1994); Karen Dawisha and Bruce Parrott, *Russia and the New States of Eurasia* (1994); Adam Hochschild, *The Unquiet Ghost: Russia Remembers Stalin* (1995); Anders Aslund, *How Russia Became a Market Economy* (1996); Maxim Boycko, Andrei Shleifer and Robert Vishny, *Privatizing Russia* (1996); John Lowenhardt, *The Reincarnation of Russia* (1996).

Peter Cipkowski, *Revolution in Eastern Europe* (1991); Vladimir Tismaneanu, *Reinventing Politics: Eastern Europe from Stalin to Havel* (1993); Vaclav Havel, *Living in Truth* (1990); Victor Nee and David Stark, eds., *Remaking the Economic Institutions of Socialism: China and Eastern Europe* (1989); Elizabeth Pond, *Beyond the Wall: Germany's Road to Unification* (1995); Timothy Garton Ash, *In Europe's Name: Germany and the Divided Continent* (1993); Mario B. Mignone, *Italy Today* (1995); Terry Cox, ed., *Hungary: The Politics of Transition* (1995); Jiri Musil, ed., *The End of Czechoslovakia* (1995).

Harold Lydall, *Yugoslavia in Crisis* (1989); Christopher Bennett, *Yugoslavia's Bloody Collapse* (1995); Susan L. Woodward, *Balkan Tragedy* (1995); James Seroka and V. Pavlovic, eds., *The Tragedy of Yugoslavia: The Failure of Democratic Transformation* (1992); Martin Bell, *In Harm's Way* (1995) (good reportage on the war in Bosnia); Mark Pinson, ed., *The Muslims of Bosnia-Herzegovina* (1994); Mitchell Reiss and Robert Litwak, eds., *Nuclear Proliferation after the Cold War* (1994); Efraim Karsh, ed., *Peace in the Middle East: The Challenge for Israel* (1994); Lawrence Freedman and Ephraim Karsh, *The Gulf Conflict, 1990–1991* (1995).

Chapter 15

Nicholas Timmins, *The Five Giants: A Biography of the Welfare State* (1995); Ross M. Martin, *Trade Unionism* (1989); Walter Eltis and Peter Sinclair, eds., *Keynes and Economic Policy: The Relevance of the General Theory after Fifty Years* (1989); Janos Kornai, *The Road to a Free Economy* (1990); J. R. Shackleton and Gareth Locksley, eds., *Twelve Contemporary Economists* (1981).

Roland N. Stromberg, *After Everything: Western Intellectual History Since 1945* (1975) and *Five Twentieth Century Thinkers* (1991); W. Matei Calinescu, *Five Faces of Modernity* (1987); Robert A. Nisbet, *The Twilight of Authority* (1975); M. Ashley Montague and F. Watson, *The Dehumanization of Man* (1983); Jean Guehenno, *The End of Democracy* (1993).

William Aspray, *John von Neumann and the Origins of Modern Computing* (1990); Herman H. Goldstine, *The Computer from Pascal to von Neumann* (1993).

Jeffrey M. Diffendorf, ed., *Rebuilding Europe's Bombed Cities* (1990), and *In the Wake of War: The Reconstruction of German Cities after World War II* (1993); John Ardagh, *A Tale of Five Cities: Life in Europe Today* (1979); C.W.E. Bigsby, ed., *Superculture: American Popular Culture and Europe* (1975); Stanley Hoffman and Paschalis Kitromilides, eds., *Culture and Society in Contemporary Europe* (1981); J. Mordaunt Crook, *The Dilemma of Style: Architectural Ideas from the Picturesque to the Post-Modern* (1989); Arnold Whittall, *Music Since the First World War* (1995); Beatrice Gottlieb, *The Family in the Western World: from the Black Death to the Industrial Age* (1993).

Anna Bramwell, *The Fading of the Greens: The Decline of Environmental Politics in the West* (1994); Russell J. Dalton, *The Green Rainbow: Environmental Groups in Western Europe* (1994); Andrei S. Markovitz and Philip S. Gorski, *The German Left: Red, Green, and Beyond* (1993); Charles A Kupchan, ed., *Nationalism and Nationalities in the New Europe* (1995).

John Sutherland, *Offensive Literature: Decensorship in Britain, 1960–82* (1982); John Carswell, *Government and the Universities in Britain: Programme and Performance, 1960–1980* (1986); Sheila Rowbotham, *The Past before Us: Feminism in Action since the 1960s* (1989); Harold L. Smith, ed., *British Feminism in the Twentieth Century* (1990); Hester Eisenstein, *Contemporary Feminist Thought* (1983); Mirko D. Grmek, *History of AIDS* (1990).

Reference Works:

B. R. Mitchell, *European Historical Statistics, 1750–1970* (1975); United Nations Educational Scientific and Cultural Organization (UNESCO), *Statistical Yearbook and Demographic Yearbook* (various years); United Nations Department of International Economic and Social Affairs, *Statistical Yearbook;* International Labour Office, *Yearbook of Labour Statistics* (annually since 1935); The World Bank, *World Development Report* (annually since 1978); International Monetary Fund, *World Economic Outlook* (twice yearly); *Annual Register of World Events* (since 1980); *The Longman Guide to World Affairs* (1995). Publications of Her Majesty's Stationery Office, London, include *Annual Abstract of Statistics, Britain at a Glance,* and *Social Trends* (annually). Europa Publications (London) publish *The Europa World Year Book* (annually); *The World of Learning* (1994); and *The Environmental Encyclopedia and Directory.*

Patrick H. Hutton, ed., *Historical Dictionary of the Third French Republic, 1870–1940* (1986); Frank J. Coppa, ed., *Dictionary of Modern Italian History* (1985); Archie Brown, Michael Kaser, and Gerald S. Smith, eds., *The Cambridge Encyclopedia of Russia and the Former Soviet Union* (1995); Elizabeth Devine, Michael Held, James Vinson, and George Walsh, eds., *Thinkers of the Twentieth Century: A Biographical, Bibliographical and Critical Dictionary* (1983).

T. Vogelsang et al., eds., *Bibliographie zur Zeitgeschichte, 1953–1980,* 3 vols. (Munich: Institut zur Zeitgeschichte, 1983), is continued in issues of *Vierteljahrhefte fur Zeitgeschichte* (Quarterly Journal for Contemporary History). Standard guides to the periodical literature are *Historical Abstracts, Philosopher's Index, Index to Economic Articles,* and *RILA (International Repertory of the Literature of Art).*

Today, a student normally has access to a computer terminal through which it is fairly easy to summon up a list of books on a given topic that are in the university or college library; with a little more ingenuity, he or she can enter the catalog of a much larger library. Periodical bibliographies like *Historical Abstracts* are also on-line. This is an improvement on the method of thumbing through drawers of library file cards; but it still provides no critical evaluation of all these writings. An annotated bibliography may help. Susan K. Kinnell, ed., *Communism in the World since 1945, an Annotated Bibliography of Works Published 1974–1985* (1987) is one of several annotated bibliographies published by the ABC-CLIO press in Santa Barbara, California. See also Keith Robbins, *Bibliography of Writings on British History* (1996). Other guides to the literature of a subject often appear in scholarly journals; thus Justus D. Doenecke, "Historiography: U.S. Policy and the European War, 1939–41," *Diplomatic History* 19:4 (Fall 1995). Among the more valuable journals for twentieth-century Europe are *Soviet Studies, West European Politics, Bulletin of the European Economic Community, Radio Free Europe Research, Contemporary European History.* The Woodrow Wilson International Center for Scholars periodically publishes a valuable *Cold War International History Project Bulletin.*

Index